Children and Youth
Psychosocial Development

Children and Youth
Psychosocial Development

Boyd R. McCandless
Emory University

Ellis D. Evans
University of Washington

The Dryden Press   *Hinsdale, Illinois*

To Our Wives and Children
With much love and gratitude

Preface

The two of us who have written this book—exactly on a fifty-fifty basis so that it is difficult to know when one leaves off and the other begins (or vice versa)—are teachers by profession. We are always looking for ways to present our central preoccupation to students. This preoccupation is, of course, to communicate information and a point of view about the complex and fascinating process of human development. We earn our living this way, and we enjoy and believe in what we do.

As both of us have taught (in all settings, ranging from large state universities through relatively small private universities to public schools and foreign universities), we have been impressed with the need for a reference book that combines up-to-date research and practice concerning children and youth with a broad perspective on psychological development. In this book, we have tried our hands at creating such a product. It is up to the reader to judge how successful we have been. The collaboration has been very pleasant for both of us, although arduous. We hope it is rewarding to readers. Certainly, we have thought and discussed a great deal about what we have said here, and we believe that some of it is new and constructive.

In our attempt to provide a fresh account of human development, we have moved away from a cold, hard, factual approach and dealt with generalizations about children and youth that are meaningful to us

and, we hope, to our readers. We have not neglected the hallmark of scientific writing—research data—but we have tried to go a step beyond these data to consider their implications for social action. As parents, teachers, and researchers, we have found ourselves continually faced by dilemmas about human development and interaction that are seldom articulated in our professional literature. Our desire to share with others the variety of dilemmas and points of view about human development has been a major motivation for this book. This sharing, we believe, can lead to useful discussions that are rare in courses of study about the development and behavior of children and youth.

Clearly, human development ranges from conception to the grave. For practical reasons, we begin this book with birth, not conception; and we deal very little with human development after early adulthood. The age range we consider, then, is from infancy to the mid-twenties. We know that most of life is lived *after* the mid-twenties; perhaps someday we will write a book or series of articles about adult development. For the moment, we are content to have written about children and youth with the recognition that this is far from the complete story of human development.

We emphasize again that this collaboration has been an exhilarating intellectual and social experience for us and our families. Our collaboration has gone on for a long time, and we hope that it will continue for a long time. Many others have contributed to this book, and we deeply appreciate their help. Again, our wives and children have made significant suggestions, have (sometimes without their knowing) provided illustrative content, and have been important readers and typists. We have tried out many of our ideas on students, and often modified them as a result of our trials. Roger L. Williams, of the Dryden Press, has been a creative and kindly editor. We appreciate the help that several critic editors have given. Finally, we thank all those who have provided the scholarly thinking and research referenced throughout the book.

Atlanta, Georgia
Seattle, Washington
January 1973

Boyd R. McCandless
Ellis D. Evans

Contents

xi
Contents

Children and Youth

Psychosocial Development

Part I
A View of Human Development and Society

As professional developmental and educational psychologists the authors consider themselves fortunate if for no reason other than that they heartily enjoy their work. Whether the children belong to them or to others, they find children and youth pleasant to be around and interesting — even fun — to watch, talk to, become friends with, think about and study, and, hard work though it is, even to write about. They hope some of the pleasure they take in their work will come through to readers.

This book is about children and young people from the time they are born until they reach maturity. On the average, the authors believe that maturity is reached at about the age of 24 or 25, although they fully realize that many people mature much earlier; and that many remain fixed at a childish or an adolescent level until much later, some for perhaps all their lives.

In Part I of this book, comprising Chapters 1–3, the authors try to give a working definition of human development; discuss how they approach it intellectually and methodologically; present briefly the more common ways of viewing human development; and talk of the dilemmas of development, both for the individual who is developing — the child or the young person — and for the scholar who is studying and

1

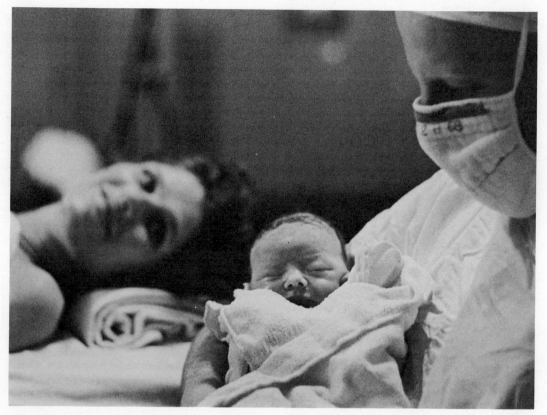

This little fellow has just entered the world. Developmental theorists will apply many different interpretations to the course of his development over the next several years. (Photo by Inger McCabe)

attempting to systematize development. Throughout these and subsequent chapters the authors attempt to provide a discussion that is both helpful and understandable to students of human growth and development, our *Peanuts* friends, Patty and Franklin, notwithstanding.

The authors believe that a book on psychology should be good and understandable.

1
Basic Concepts of Psychosocial Development

INTERACTION AND THE WHOLE PERSON

Anyone who has read or listened much to what educators, philosophers, and psychologists say about human beings has heard the terms "the whole child" and "the whole person" so often that the expressions have likely become clichés to him. Nothing in particular is conveyed by the terms, which often trigger boredom. Clichés do not arise accidentally, however. When first coined, they usually summarized some common aspect of experience cogently enough that they were widely accepted, overused, and eventually fitted the classification *cliché*.

In the authors' minds, "the whole child" or "the whole person" also evokes the notion of a globe — something round, large, undifferentiated, and thus difficult to manipulate, analyze, study, or write about. In thinking about or working with people, one cannot cope with "all of the person," at least at any one time. He has emotional–social, intellectual, or physical dealings with another person, or a mixture of all three. Professionally, it seems sensible, and has been useful to the authors, to conceive of human beings according to certain broad classes of behavior and personal characteristics. With his own children, one has intellectual dealings, social and personal dealings, and physical dealings. With one's college students, the professorial–student relation is by far the most common; interactions are mainly academic and intellectual, but there are prominent and frequent personal–social, and sometimes quite intensely emotional, interactions. Unless a person is a physical education teacher, a doctor, or a nurse, however, he has few dealings with his students in terms of their physical–motor development.

The authors have found it helpful to formulate their thinking about children and youth according to the following model. Each of the three major portions of the model represents for them a concen-

3

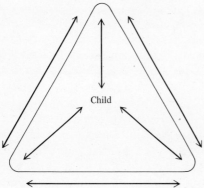

Figure 1.1 *A sketch of how the child and his behavior and characteristics may be usefully viewed. The double-headed arrows indicate interactions.*

tration of certain behavior or developmental characteristics. Each of these three concentrations interacts in important ways with the other two. This model, or schema, is given in Figure 1.1.

From kindergarten or first grade on, teachers are likely to concentrate on corner A, cognitive–intellectual–achievement. Unfortunately, however, because there are children and young people who "present problems," teachers are often forced to concentrate on corner B, the personal–social–emotional behavior of a given child or young person. The regular classroom teacher is seldom concerned much with corner C, the physical–motor, or body-build, time of physical maturity area of behavior. For those who present problems in this area, attention is compelled; extra attention is often received by those who are especially strong, or large, or graceful, or early maturing, or handsome or beautiful. Doctors, nurses, dentists, and physical education teachers are more likely than classroom teachers to concentrate their thought and efforts in

corner C, neglecting A and B. Personnel workers, clinical and school psychologists, psychiatrists, and social workers are typically preoccupied with corner B, all too often neglecting A and C. Parents are usually aware of "the whole child" or "the whole youth," because they must live with him all day long, year in and year out. But bookish parents may concentrate heavily on corner A, the father who is or was an athlete on corner C, and so on.

Examples of Interaction

James was a small, thin, somewhat sickly farm boy, the third in a family of four brothers. The other three brothers were husky, well built, athletic, and able to work usefully with their father in the fields. The youngest brother was a particular thorn in James's side: Although two and one-half years younger than James, he caught up with James in size while both were still of preschool age and, by the time James was 9 and his brother $6\frac{1}{2}$, the brother could outrun, outwrestle, and outwork James. The brother inflicted the final humiliation when he reached puberty earlier than James.

From elementary school years on, the three husky brothers, because they worked with their father, were closer to him than James was. James, sickly, spent much more time with his mother, a bookish woman who had been a school teacher before she married. James became the recipient of her confidences, and was perhaps her favorite. Somewhat aloof from his brothers and his father, James developed into a book-loving, somewhat effeminate boy with strong academic interests supported by a good mind. His brothers, bright enough, were only mildly interested in academics. Eventually, James was the brother who went to college.

When farms were mechanized, there was not enough land for more than one son, and the eldest brother eventually took over the family farm. The second and the fourth brothers moved from the farm, went into construction work, and have led modest lives, the one as a skilled carpenter and the other as a small-business man. James's college education led to a job as teacher in high school, then to graduate school, and finally to a successful university career in the sciences. As a young man, James became aware of his effeminacy, pushed it aside, and, like his brothers, married quite well and is a reasonably good father to his three children.

For James, sickliness, slight stature, and late maturity (corner C of our schema in Figure 1.1) pushed him into a way of life almost by default—he became his mother's boy, rather than his father's, somewhat out of the mainstream of healthy, rural, male life (adaptations within corner B). The entire pattern of his life has been one of interaction of slight, frail body, forcing him into a concentration on academics (corner A) in order to survive in the setting in which he was born.

Judy has inherited the busty, stocky, almost squat body of her peasant ancestors, but she has been born into a world where men's choices of women are dictated more by *Vogue*, television, and Hollywood than by a suitor's estimate of how well a woman can work and how easily she can bear children. Judy's parents had worked themselves up from lower-middle-class origins (both their own parents had been struggling shopkeepers) to high-level, financially comfortable professional status. Judy had as much intelligence as her parents. In the excellent suburban or private schools she attended, she achieved intelligence test scores

ranging from a low of 130 (superior) to 165 (truly exceptional). But she never did well academically after the fourth grade, at which time she became aware of and began to brood about her ungainly body. Her body complicated matters still further for her. She matured early and began to menstruate shortly after her tenth birthday. At the time, she was a head taller than any other girl or boy in her class. From that time, she became more and more socially aloof, and had no close friends through the rest of elementary school and all of high school.

Judy barely made it through high school, refused even to apply to the prestige colleges her parents wanted her to attend, was admitted to a small state college that had previously been a state normal school, and was graduated after five years with a degree in business administration and a scholastic average barely high enough to merit receiving her degree. She had a few girl friends and no boy friends during college, and blamed her entire situation on her "ugliness."

She began to talk of suicide shortly after college graduation. Her parents pushed her firmly into psychotherapy. A year of counseling produced some understanding of her years of conflict and gave her some hope of self-sufficiency. She made determined efforts at weight control and good grooming, and began to date occasionally—young men she met in the business firm where she had found a job (more because of her parents' prestige than her own record). To her surprise, she enjoyed her job and was successful at it. By the time she had reached her mid-twenties, she seemed to have handled the old bad years and looked forward to some better ones.

Again, Judy represents an interaction. Corner C of our rounded triangle (Figure

1.1) was unfortunate for Judy. A stocky, busty, build was not *de rigueur* in Judy's world. Her reaction was self-negation so severe that for many years she failed to use her high-level intelligence (corner A of Figure 1.1) and allowed her personal–social–emotional life (corner B) to be blunted. Depression so deep that suicide seemed imminent finally mobilized her and her parents, and, fortunately for Judy, psychotherapy worked. Of course, she had the background and the basic personal tools to make it work; it was just that they had not been used previously.

Matthew is the third and final example of interaction of body, mind, and social–personal interaction. He is the fourteenth of a family of fourteen children born to a poor black woman who had come north from rural South Carolina, where she had been born and lived until she was 15. As the baby, Matthew received more attention from his mother than she had been able to give most of the older children. By the time he was 14, he was a bright, somewhat delinquent, exceptionally handsome boy with more self-confidence than many poor black male youth seem to have. He was thinking of dropping out of school, and his borderline delinquencies had alerted the police who manned his slum neighborhood to keep a watchful and a usually hostile eye on him. Truant one day, he came to the attention of a young patrolman, who summoned Matthew to him. Instead of subjecting Matthew to a barrage of pointed and unfriendly questions (which he expected), the policeman seemed interested in *why* Matthew was truant. This friendly, big-brother kind of questioning proved the beginning of a friendship, and, after some weeks, Matthew consented to go, as the young patrol-

man's protégé, to a recreation center operated by the police department. Here, his potential as a boxer came to light. By his late teens, Matthew was an outstanding Golden Glover with the prospect of a successful ring career ahead of him. As a result of the friendship of the patrolman and the reception Matthew received in the recreation center, Matthew did not drop out of school, but finished high school and received his diploma.

At this time a woman sponsor of the recreation center, divorced, lonely, wealthy, and much older than Matthew, who frequently came to the center to watch the boxers, took a special interest in Matthew. Her friendship led to a sexual relationship, and Matthew moved into her home. The woman urged him toward college. Matthew went, succeeded, and eventually received a law degree. The sexual relation was finally terminated by mutual consent and with no apparent hurt to either Matthew or his partner. Matthew is a promising civil rights lawyer, and his sponsor and long-time mistress is the godmother of the first child born to Matthew's marriage to a social worker at about the time he finished law school.

The grace and strength of Matthew's body and his good looks (corner C of our schema in Figure 1.1) interacted with his special place as baby in the family (corner B) and his better-than-average mind (corner A) to make life very different from what sociologists would have predicted from the formal circumstances of his birth and upbringing. His present life, although the pathway toward it has not been conventional, seems to him, and probably is, much better than the life of unskilled labor and crime that would logically have been predicted when Matthew was 14. Certainly, he is much happier and more useful within society.

INDIVIDUALS AS FACTORS IN THEIR OWN DEVELOPMENT

Development is a two-way street. James, Judy, and Matthew, just discussed, were each affected by their bodies: James's body pushed him toward his mother and books; Judy's toward isolation, depression, underachievement, and near-despair; Matthew's opened doors that led him from delinquency and the slums to a professional career in which he is of real service to his people.

But in no case was the process quite so simple as described. Even as James was modified by his own physique and learning opportunities, so he modified others. He provided his mother with special satisfaction not afforded her by her straightforward, active, farmer husband and her other sons. As James gave his mother satisfactions, so he deprived his father of satisfactions. As a consequence, his mother drew ever closer to him, and his father and brothers grew ever further away. Because Judy forced her parents to become belatedly more aware of the complexities of human nature and development than they would otherwise have been, they were eventually able to respond to her and back her firmly in her decision to seek professional help for her distress. Matthew became the light of his mother's life, and added much, though unconventionally, to the lonely life of the older woman who took such an important role in his life. As Matthew became more and more aware of the world of learning, it had more and more effect on him. At present, he is himself an exceptionally active and constructive force for social change.

In short, the human being is both molded by and molds his environment through a set of feedback loops. Some-

thing happens to him; then, because he is changed, he makes new things happen in his environment; he must now react to the environmental change, producing still more change; and so on and on throughout life. The feedback loops may be partially constructive, as they were for Matthew from the time he was 14; or nonconstructive, even destructive, as they were for Judy from the time she was in the fourth grade until after she was graduated from college.

In summary, these brief case descriptions can be taken to illustrate at least three important principles. First, it is apparent that all aspects of development interact. This interaction is complex. Some features of this interaction are better understood than others, although hard and fast generalizations about behavior and development do not come easily. Second, implicit in these case descriptions is the notion that experiences have a cumulative effect over time. For example, Judy's life frustrations piled up so that, by the time Judy had left the shelter of college and had to face society without formal institutional protection, she had no strength left to go ahead on her own. Third, the individual is an active force in his own development. An individual's behavior is largely determined by his encounters with his environment, although these encounters are not simply a matter of reacting—they also involve his acting on his environment, thus furthering his personal development.

THE LANGUAGE OF HUMAN DEVELOPMENT

The first, often frustrating, task for a student of human development is learning the vocabulary of developmental psychology. All specialized fields or endeavors have their own unique vocabulary so that those in the field can communicate clearly, efficiently, and precisely. This is as true of medicine, law, football, or farming as it is of developmental psychology. Such special vocabularies ("appendix" or "touchback") also serve to describe phenomena for which the common language is unsuitable or a common language does not exist.

Developmental psychologists, unfortunately, do not always agree about the exact meanings of terms and concepts. Different psychologists may mean very different things when they talk about such concepts as intelligence, cognition, creativity, anxiety, or adjustment. This is why students must be aware that there is rarely universal agreement among psychologists about the language of psychology. In this book, the authors always try to give clear definitions and also to provide readers with conceptual meanings that are generally accepted within the broad discipline of psychology. They can appropriately begin by discussing the various meanings associated with the concept of development itself.

Development as Change through Time

The differences in behavior between a newborn infant (neonate) and a 3-year-old child are obvious even to the most casual observer. An elementary school child is strikingly different from a 15-year-old adolescent. Children and youngsters with several years' age span between them differ enormously in physical–motor, personal–social, and intellectual–academic skills. The neonate, for example, depends completely on others for survival, and he is more a responder to his environment and body tensions than an initiator

or actor-on-them during his first few weeks of life. He cannot roll over or sit up. He cannot distinguish his mother or principal caregiver from other adults or older children in his environment. About the only way he has to communicate the fact that he needs something is to cry. Although his potential is enormous and wonderful, he shows little in the way of organized behavior. However, there is no doubt that he is learning even in the first few days of his life.

In contrast, a normal elementary school child can handle such complex matters as hopscotch and tetherball play; talks much like the adults he knows best; and leads a sophisticated social life both with his family, his peers, and the nonfamily adults in his world, such as teachers and storekeepers. He has learned how to compete and cooperate, how to please and offend, how to lead and follow, for example.

Differences like these that are associated with age may be viewed both as a process and as the result of progressive changes over time. They represent successively higher degrees of differentiation and complexity in behavior. "Differentiation," as used here, means finer and usually more precise gradations of behavior. Increasing differentiation is usually accompanied by increasing complexity. The 14-month-old child may call out, "Water." This may mean any number of things (it is actually used as a one-word sentence), which the child's caregiver must guess from intonation, gesture, and context. Within a year or two, the child's language will have become more differentiated and complex, in that the child will supply a pronoun, an action verb, a modifier, and a predicate — "I want some water," or "(You) see the water." In the first few months of life, although an infant may recognize and attempt to obtain an object within his reach, he can only swipe unsuccessfully at it. By the time he is 6 months old or a bit older, he can oppose his thumb and fingers and grasp what he wants with great efficiency (a case of motor differentiation).

In short, as the human being grows, he constantly reorganizes the ways in which he interacts with the things and people in his environment. His reorganizations, his style, his very ability to interact effectively with his environment, all result from combined effects of *maturation* and *learning*.

Maturation

Maturation refers to developmental changes that are extensively if not totally controlled by genetic or hereditary factors, including species specific behavior. For example, all normal children, if exposed to other human beings who talk, learn to talk; but no other species possesses this elaborate formal language. All normal English hen sparrows build untidy nests of twigs, straw, and feathers, and lay brown speckled eggs in them. Few if any human beings build untidy nests of twigs, straw, and feathers; and no human beings lay brown speckled eggs.

The importance of genetic makeup to the nature of one's life experiences must not be underestimated. On the other hand, neither must the potentials for modifying genetic potential through learning. Physical appearance, motor competence, sensory functioning, and perhaps emotional reactivity and energy supply and release are human characteristics that are strongly shaped by heredity. Genetic factors may also be critical for intellectual and social development, although probably less so than for characteristics of biological structure of function. The point is that many developmental changes are strongly influenced by biological maturation. The timetable for such changes is controlled by genetic givens established at conception. If provided with equally good care for health and nutrition, two male or two female children will reach puberty at widely different times, one sometimes several years earlier than the other. Barring accidents and, again, with equivalent health, physical care, and nutritional treatment, Gallagher may die of natural causes at 65, Shean at 95. Such different timetables are generally agreed to be partially laid down by genes, although they may be drastically modified by environmental variables such as nutrition, health care, disease, accident, and perhaps climate and psychological stress (12, 13).

Biological maturational factors, however, are less responsive to environmental effects than social and psychological factors. A person's happiness, it seems probable, is more a matter of how that person was reared than of what his genes are.

Learning

Learning acts in concert with maturation on the human being's progressive change through time. Learning refers to relatively enduring behavior changes that come about from experience. Thus, behavior changes due to disease, drugs, fatigue, and the like, are excluded from the domain of learned behavior. Experience results in learning in different ways. Arranged experiences, such as school or specific tutoring in skills, are one way to provide learning. Other learning seems to result from unarranged experiences such as those which come from normal adaptation to one's often random and quite unpredictable environment, or from free play and apparently idle verbal interchange among people.

Learning varies (the culture affects and changes people) according to the nature of the tasks involved. Some learning is academic, such as reading a book at grade level; other learning is social, such as resolving a conflict about rule infraction during a game. Still other learning is perceptual–motor, such as learning to draw a triangle, to make a doll dress, or to catch a ball with a mitt. Regardless of the kind of learning, successful responses (those for which the person is in some way rewarded) are more often maintained and perfected than they are eliminated and discarded, whereas unsuccessful responses are more often dropped from, rather than consolidated into, more permanent behavior. However, the information available to the person also plays a part in whether a response is maintained or dropped. Some so-called superstitious behavior (irrelevant for reward and thus inefficient) is often maintained for long periods, even permanently. If the pigeon ruffles his feathers at the same time he pecks and secures food from the food dispenser, he may continue to ruffle his feathers consistently as he pecks. The feather ruffling is irrelevant to his reward, but, because he is consistently rewarded for feather ruffling *and* a certain pattern of pecking and does not possess the information about the irrelevance of feather ruffling, both behaviors persist. Many human superstitions and irrelevant behaviors may be similarly perpetuated, such as rapping on wood after making a hopeful, positive prediction. Body English is another common form of superstition among human beings. For example, after releasing the ball, some bowlers go through real, often bizarre bodily contortions as though they could transmit the movement of their bodies to influence the direction of the ball.

Much learning depends on three things —a person's maturational stage, his opportunity to learn, and his practice. Walking is a good example. Regardless of opportunity and practice, few if any 6-month-old children can learn to walk. Given only a little opportunity and practice, the average 15-month-old learns to walk quickly and well. Few if any 9-year-olds learn to make love, but given opportunity and practice, most 15-year-olds can learn the skills quickly and well. Maturation, opportunity, and practice enter into successful mastery of such things as toilet training, bicycle riding, violin playing, and learning a foreign language. On the other hand, learning to avoid mother when she is angry seems to be less a matter of maturation and more a matter (from a very early age) of learning. Nonetheless, almost all conceivable behavior requires both "raw material that grows and matures" (maturation) and experience of one sort or another, both *readiness* and *opportunity*. Of course, it should be recognized that readiness is essentially nothing more or less than the possession of all the prerequisite skills necessary for the mastery of a task at a new level of difficulty (7).

To summarize the last two topics, development may be thought of as change through time. Interaction of learning and maturation is the master change agent. A little later, we shall consider various genetic and experience factors that seemingly influence both the rate (speed) and the quality of development over time. First, however, let us look at two broad approaches to the description and analysis of developmental change.

An Age Concept of Development

Development can be described in different ways. The traditional and still most com-

The acquisition of a new skill is the outcome of many factors—learning, maturation, opportunity, and practice. (Photo by Lawrence Frank)

mon way is according to chronological age. Human development is ordered by observing and describing the behavior, for example, of 1-year-olds, 2-year-olds (the terrible twos), 3-year-olds, and so on. For each age level chosen, descriptions and averages are developed according to complexity, variety, frequency, strength, differentiation, and organization (3). Such a way of ordering behavior development is sensible if for no reason other than that children *do* appear and behave differently at successive ages. As they grow older, children learn new and more complex tasks. The skills required for the different tasks at the different ages can be analyzed. As we learn more about human development, prediction about what behaviors are likely to appear at what time becomes more accurate, and, with fair confidence, it can be specified what the average child can do at any given point in his development.

Table 1.1 contains generalized age-based descriptions (norms) of behavior, with emphasis on the first five years of life. As can be seen, such norms refer to the average, or typical, case and do not explain developmental changes in behavior. Nevertheless, norms can be useful in the

Table 1.1 *Normative Stages of Development**

Physical and Language Development	Emotional Development	Social Development
BIRTH TO 1 YEAR		
0 to 1 Month		
Birth Size: 7–8 lbs., 20 inches	Generalized tension	Helpless
Feedings: 5–8 per day		Asocial
Sleep: 20 hours per day		Fed by mother
Sensory capacities: makes basic distinctions in vision, hearing, smelling, tasting, touch, temperature, and perception of pain		
Reflexes: sucking, swallowing, crying, hiccoughing, grasping, pupillary contraction		
2 to 3 Months		
Sensory capacities: color perception, visual exploration, oral exploration	Delight	Visually fixates a face
Sounds: cries, coos, grunts	Distress	Smiles at a face
Motor ability: control of eye muscles, lifts head when on stomach	Smiles at a face	May be soothed by rocking
4 to 6 Months		
Sensory capacities: localizes sounds	Enjoys being cuddled	Recognizes his mother
Sounds: babbling, makes most vowels and about half of the consonants		Distinguishes between familiar persons and strangers
Feedings: 3–5 per day		No longer smiles indiscriminately
Motor ability: control of head and arm movements, purposive grasping; rolls over		Expects feeding, dressing, bathing
7 to 9 Months		
Motor ability: control of trunk and hands, sits without support, crawls (abdomen touching floor)	Specific emotional attachment to mother	Enjoys "peek-a-boo"
	Protests separation from mother	
10 to 12 Months		
Motor ability: control of legs and feet, stands, creeps, apposition of thumb and forefinger	Anger	Responsive to own name
	Affection	Waves bye-bye
	Fear of strangers	Plays pat-a-cake
Language: says one or two words, imitates sounds, responds to simple commands	Curiosity, exploration	Understands "no no!"
		Gives and takes objects
Feedings: 3 meals, 2 snacks		
Sleep: 12 hours, 2 naps		
Size at one year: 20 lbs., 28–29 inches		

* See page 14 for source.

Table 1.1 *(continued)*

Physical and Language Development	Emotional Development	Social Development
1 TO 1½ YEARS Motor ability: creeps up stairs, walks (10–20 months), throws a ball, feeds himself, builds a 2–3 cube tower (18 months), makes lines on paper with crayon	Dependent behavior Very upset when separated from mother Fear of bath	Obeys limited commands Repeats a few words Interested in his mirror image Feeds himself
1½ TO 2 YEARS Motor ability: runs, kicks a ball, builds 6 cube tower (2 yrs.) Capable of bowel and bladder control Language: vocabulary of more than 200 words Sleep: 12 hours at night, 1–2 hour nap Size at 2 years: 23–30 lbs., 32–35 inches	Temper tantrums (1–3 yrs.) Resentment of new baby Negativism (18 months)	Does opposite of what he is told (18 months)
2 TO 3 YEARS Motor ability: jumps off a step, rides a tricycle, uses crayons, builds a 9–10 cube tower Language: starts to use short sentences, controls and explores world with language, stuttering may appear briefly Size at 3 years: 32–33 lbs., 37–38 inches	Fear of separation Negativistic (2½ yrs) Violent emotions, anger Differentiates facial expressions of anger, sorrow, and joy Sense of humor (plays tricks)	Talks, uses "I," "me," "you" Copies parents' actions Dependent, clinging Possessive about toys Enjoys playing alongside another child Negativism (2½ yrs.), resists parental demands Gives orders Rigid insistence on sameness of routine Inability to make decisions
3 TO 4 YEARS Motor ability: stands on one leg, jumps up and down, draws a circle and a cross (4 yrs.) Language: asks questions, actively conceptualizes, complete sentences of 6–8 words (4 yrs.) Self-sufficient in many routines of home life Size at 4 years: 38–40 lbs., 40–41 inches	Affectionate toward parents Pleasure in genital manipulation Romantic attachment to parent of opposite sex (3 to 5 yrs.) Jealousy of same-sex parent Imaginary fears of dark, injury, etc. (3–5 yrs.)	Likes to share, uses "we" Cooperative play with other children Nursery school Imitates parents—beginning of identification with same-sex parent Practices sex-role activities Intense curiosity, asks questions Interest in other children's bodies (3 to 5 yrs.) Imaginary friends (3 to 5 yrs.)

Table 1.1 (*concluded*)

Physical and Language Development	Emotional Development	Social Development
4 TO 5 YEARS		
Motor ability: mature motor control, skips, broad jumps, dresses himself, copies a square and a triangle (5 yrs.)	Responsibility and guilt Feels pride in accomplishment	Prefers to play with other children Becomes competitive Prefers sex-appropriate activities
Language: talks clearly, uses adult speech sounds, has mastered basic grammar, relates a story, knows over 2,000 words (5 yrs.)		
Size at 5 years: 42–43 lbs., 43–44 inches		
5 YEARS TO PUBERTY		
Gets first permanent teeth (6 yrs.)	Basic emotions all established	Independence of parents (5–6 yrs.)
Major increase in growth (10 to 11 yrs.)	Emotions continue to develop in subtlety and connotative richness	Clubs, comic books, TV (7 to 11 yrs.)
Puberty: girls 11–13, boys 13–15 yrs.		Dating (12 yrs. on)
Growth tapers off (17 to 20 yrs.)		

* The contents of this table have been abstracted from a variety of sources including Gesell and Ilg (1943), Mc-Candless (1961), and Mussen, Conger and Kagan (1963). Adapted from Charles P. Smith *Child Development* (1966), pp. 8–9. Reprinted by permission of the William C. Brown Company.

ways discussed in the accompanying text. (See the section on Expectancies in Chapter 6 for comment on normative data.)

Plans for children and adolescents, such as schooling, can be made with some but only partial accuracy according to the person's age, because factors of emotional and intellectual maturity (to name only two) are responsible for wide variations in behavior of children of the same age. Age alone provides only a general but convenient index for cataloguing developmental change. Some limitations in using age as a developmental index should be noted.

First, age is only a shorthand method of charting developmental change over time. Giving a person's age does not specify the exact biological and cultural factors that contribute to development. The intellectual, problem-solving superi-

ority of an adolescent over a preschool-aged child is by no means explained by saying, "The adolescent is older." A specification of the precise characteristics of intellectual behavior at these two periods of development and a charting of the forces that produce these characteristics are much more helpful than a simple statement of age. What have been the different learning experiences? What have been the effects of pubescence and the changes in self concept and social expectations that accompany sexual maturity? What is the effect of the adolescent's increased strength and mobility within his environment?

A second limitation of age as a developmental index is the great variation in developmental status that exists even among children of the same age. We usually describe a 4-year-old or a 14-year-old according to characteristics of "average" 4-year-olds or "normal" 14-year-olds. But there are very wide variations around these averages. Some 14-year-olds, for example, are 5 feet tall; others are 6 feet 1 inch tall. Some 14-year-olds are fully mature sexually; others are not yet even pubescent. Some 14-year-olds are still in the fifth or sixth grade, others are in the tenth and eleventh grades. In other words, for an accurate picture of development, one must move beyond the *average* (or mean) and consider the range in developmental variation at different ages. Such a compilation of data around the average, and the range of children and youth around this average, is known as a norm. For most human characteristics, the bell-shaped curve charts the norm.

In Figure 1.2, the curve for the distribution of intelligence quotients for physically and neurologically normal children is given. As can be seen, the high point of the curve (the largest single number of children or youth) defines the average, which is an IQ of 100. But as can be seen

from pegging the altitude (height) of the curve, there are almost as many children and youth of 99 or 101 IQ; fewer of 95 or 105 IQ; and very few of 50 IQ or lower or 150 IQ or higher. "Normality" is often considered to lie within one standard deviation above and below the mean or average for intelligence; and the standard deviation for intelligence quotients is usually set by test makers at 15 or 16 points. This means that about two thirds of all children who are represented by the curve in Figure 1.2 have IQs between about 84 or 85 and 115 or 116 (the range from one standard deviation below to one standard deviation above the average).

A third limitation of age as a means of organizing development is that most of our information about behavior of children and youth comes from studying them where we find them. In other words, we do not look for ideal environments or special enriching or debilitating environments, but try to take average children in normal conditions. The descriptions that result indicate only what children are like under those conditions, not what they could be like or are like if the conditions are altered sharply for better or for worse.

Limitations aside, the universality of an age-dependent concept of development cannot be denied. In fact, the way in which American society is organized (educationally, economically, legally), it is tempting to suggest that developmental changes and expectancies for children's behavior are "programed in" by virtue of a priori chronological-age-based standards. For example, important life events such as school entrance, acceptance for gainful employment, marriage (without parental permission), and legal suffrage usually are determined solely on the basis of chronological age. The complete rationale for adhering to this criterion for such

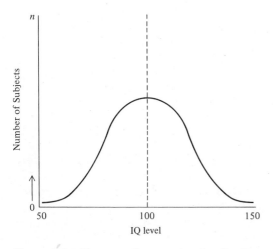

Figure 1.2 *The normal curve for the distribution of intelligence quotients.*

wide-ranging privileges is not easily clarified. Within our society (and most others), however, chronological age seemingly represents the best *single* indicator of successive levels of maturity. This age-consciousness is also reflected in the work of psychologists who study and chart the psychological development of children and youth. Chronological age, for example, is commonly viewed by psychologists as an index of relative homogeneity or commonality in behavior among children and youth; hence, the "shorthand" or "summarizing" function of age as mentioned earlier.

An orientation to development based on chronological age has led many authors to organize their writings about children and youth according to age level. That is, it is common for a textbook in developmental psychology to consist of generalized descriptions of children and youth in terms of basic age categories: infancy (the first two years of life), the preschool years, the early school years, middle childhood, preadolescence, early adolescence, middle adolescence, late adolescence, and the like. As the table of contents for this book indicates, an alternative framework for discussion has been selected in an effort better to preserve the *stream* of development in critical areas such as language and cognition, psychosexual development, moral–political development, self-development, and the like. Moreover, since individual children differ in their rates of development, the *range* of individual differences in behavior increases markedly with time. This, the authors believe, makes it increasingly difficult to paint meaningful portraits of behaviors based only on an age-relevant concept of development. They do retain, however, a strong emphasis on *age-related trends* in the basic areas of psychological develop-

ment, as will become increasingly clear throughout Part II of this book.

The authors have always believed that a treatment of developmental psychology in terms of only chronological age lends itself to a simplistic approach—a "how to do it" set of techniques for "the terrible 2s," "the moody 13s," "the senile 70s," and so on. In other words the uniqueness of children, youth, and adults gets lost, the authors think, when they are rigidly categorized by age. To put it another way, the authors believe that people are more interesting when thought of in terms of more complex characteristics than of chronological age alone.

Chronological age, then, is a popular, convenient, and useful way of describing developmental change. However, the authors believe that developmental change can be described and analyzed without necessarily depending on the age variable, and find a "sequence-relevant" approach particularly useful.

A Sequence-Relevant Concept of Development

If we observe three groups of infants 3 months old, 6 months old, and 12 months old, and see that the first group is able to roll over, but not to sit up or walk with support, that the second group can all roll over and most of them can sit up with little or no support, and the third group can almost all walk a little bit with support, we believe we have exposed a sequence of motor development: rolling over precedes sitting up, and sitting up precedes walking. If no infant deviates from this sequence, we say it is invariant and applies to most and perhaps all normal children.

This order, however, indicates only the outcome, or the typical timing of this kind of motor development (which some call antigravity postures) (50). The processes or forces that have produced the motor changes cannot be determined from descriptive or normative information. Even less can the specific points in time at which a given force or set of forces operates to produce change be selected. One may assume that biological maturation is the major factor involved in developing antigravity behavior. However, development of motor behavior can be greatly retarded and even prevented under conditions of severe malnutrition or total isolation of an infant or a young child. We might say, then, that norms, whether age norms or sequence-relevant norms, only describe. *Norms do not explain.*

Another example of a sequence-relevant aspect of development is discriminating left from right in a useful way in one's dealings with his environment (3). According to age norms, it is not until about age 7 that most children can manage this conceptual task. Few 4-year-olds have a clear generalized grasp of left and right. The important question is, "What occurs between ages 4 and 7 that enables the older child to reach or surpass this developmental landmark?" If a sequence of learning experiences could be isolated so that we could bring a 4-year-old rapidly into mastery of left and right (say, in thirty minutes), we can certainly state that change through time has occurred. But we cannot really say that the 4-year-old was older (in the usual sense of age) at the end of one-half hour than he was at the beginning. Age, in other words, does not explain the mastery of the left–right idea. We should have to say that change has resulted from training. Such condensing of what usually takes three years into a thirty-minute training period is striking and leads us to state that in many cases

specific training can shortcut the inefficient learning that would ordinarily have taken place in the child's natural environment.

Developmental change involving left–right learning has actually been produced much as described above (3). The sequence-dependent or sequence-relevant approach is based on the idea that changes that ordinarily occur with extended time periods can perhaps be accomplished in a far shorter time through efficient training. If this is so, many developments within the natural environment may reflect comparatively inefficient or confusing programs of learning for most children and youth. Where speeding up is desirable, the assumption of sequence dependency may lead to a concentration on intervention and training with real advantages to a child or a youth. This idea is related to what was said above about readiness: Readiness is essentially the possession of the skills necessary to move on to the next level of behavior.

No one has yet demonstrated that all kinds of developmental change either can or should be achieved through precise learning technology, nor do psychologists and educators necessarily view the human being's natural environment as an enormous, imperfect program of learning (49).

Many psychologists actually maintain that there is no substitute for age-related natural experience, particularly for intellectual development. If the child (or the adolescent) is not ready, such psychologists, educators, and epistemologists (students of the basis of knowledge) state, no possible training procedure will produce change. Only when readiness exists (when the appropriate, usually age-related developmental stage has been reached) will there be a match between organism and environment so that the desired behavioral sequence will occur.

The authors believe, however, that an approach to development less closely bound to chronological age has merit for at least three reasons. First, it suggests the possibility that some aspects of development are less dependent on the passage of time (increase in age) than on the timing of the particular learning experience. In other words, a child does not necessarily have to be 6 before he can learn to read. Imaginatively viewed, many 4-year-olds (or even younger children) are ready to read, will enjoy learning to read, and will profit from this new skill acquired at an early age. Of course, the methods and materials for learning to read used with 4-year-olds may be different from those typically used with 6-year-olds in the schools.

Second, an age-irrelevant approach to development more clearly opens up the possibility that more than one effective environmental sequence or program can facilitate a specific developmental outcome. Just as "many roads lead to Rome," so may many different but equally sound sequential programs of learning accomplish the same developmental task.

Third, it is quite possible that viewing development as sequence dependent or sequence relevant and studying it scientifically and sophisticatedly from that point of view can lead to devising programs or training plans that will speed up a specific developmental process, if such speeding up is useful; or that will remedy one that has lagged, as in compensatory education (for example, some Head Start programs and tentative results from Sesame Street). These ideas are further treated in Chapter 3, in which issues related to stages and critical periods in human development are discussed.

MEDIATORS OF THE PATTERN OF CHANGE

Patterns of change through which an individual goes from infancy to young adulthood are complexly determined. The various factors that facilitate, condition, or modify these patterns—the *mediators* of change—interact with one another in equally complex ways. Many of these mediators, or change factors, are not yet well understood, some not at all. For example, the brief life summaries of James, Judy, and Matthew presented at the beginning of this chapter, crude as they are, suggest that a host of forces is at work to produce individual differences in development and behavior. Even if the details of these three persons' lives are known, a clear analysis of the causes of their behavior would be incredibly difficult or impossible.

The difficulties faced in understanding human development should not, however, discourage us from working toward this goal. Obviously some progress has been made. Otherwise a book such as this one would be impossible. This progress can be measured in relation to at least two major goals of developmental psychology. The first concerns man's quest to know and to understand himself and his development through the entire life span. The second concerns a search for conditions that promote maximum, positive human development. As these conditions are identified, it is to be hoped that they can be translated into programs for improving the human condition.

In the pages to follow, the authors have chosen to discuss eight mediators of the pattern of developmental change about which at least something is known. Other authors might select a different set of mediators, but thinking in terms of the following eight has proved useful and convenient to the present authors. A further advantage of these mediators is that they introduce important ideas that are pursued in more detail in subsequent chapters.

The eight mediators are discussed in this order: Effective culture as it impinges on the individual; the influence of socioeconomic status (one more specific face of the effective culture); the sex of the individual; intelligence or problem-solving ability; biological factors, including nutrition; ethnicity; schooling; and religion.

The Effective Culture

Definitions of culture vary from one writer to another, yet most reflect the idea of shared ways of behaving within a given group of people. According to one source, for example, a culture is comprised of "individuals who share a set of values, beliefs, practices, and information, and who pass these views from one generation to the next" (38). Another authority has suggested that culture is a very loose term that indicates "the general methods by which a group of people organizes its life from the cradle to the grave . . . and takes into account the major group methods of dealing with common life problems" (33). A similar idea is expressed by the following inclusive definition of culture:

The culture of a group consists of the modes of acting, knowing, and feeling customary in the group. A culture may be thought of as a descriptive statement of uniformities found in the observation of many particular incidents, as abstractions formulated either by a participant in the culture or by an observer from outside. Alternatively, a culture may be thought of as a set of norms of ideals which in some way regulate or determine what occurs in particular incidents (8, p. 83).

Perhaps the important thing to consider about culture is that it involves both uniformity and the organization of diversity in the behavior of its participants. There is usually considerable uniformity, for example, in valuing achievement in United States culture; but there are also plans for diversity (acceptance of various religious groups in the United States as part of the culture of democracy and the Bill of Rights).

The characteristics of a culture may be *formally* defined. These formal characteristics may not apply to a particular person or group within that culture, although for most there will be some relation between the *formal* and the *effective* aspects of a culture. By *effective*, we mean those aspects that operate as mediators of the patterns of change in development, that actually *impinge* on and affect individuals and groups.

For example, we can think of United States culture formally and say that it is republican (relating to a system in which elected representatives presumably work for and reflect the will of those who have voted for them). Culture can also be described as achievement oriented ("It is good to get ahead, to work, to acquire property and prestige."). United States culture is competitive and materialistic; at the same time it is idealistic and is based on a Bill of Rights that, when observed, provides powerful protection from the tyranny of a majority toward minority individuals and groups. Our culture is also individualistic and technological (industry oriented and science oriented) and is characterized by fairly clear sex-role stereotypes in that females are clearly expected to behave differently from the approved and valued behaviors for males.

These *formal characteristics* are translated quite directly into the effective culture for many groups in the United States. Many of these characteristics are most clearly reflected in the life style and child-rearing practices of middle-class groups who succeed within the culture and who are quite willing to meet its demands for the sake of the benefits they obtain for themselves within the cultural framework. As such, these characteristics define a life often qualitatively different from that experienced in cultures outside the United States. This difference in orientation to life can be observed in the attitudes and behavior of young children as well as in those of older persons. Even children from different *Western* cultures (United States, English, Russian, and Swiss), place differing degrees of importance on standards of honesty, intellectual inquiry, aggressive masculinity, manners, individual indus-try, and achievement. Presumably these differences reflect cultural factors impor-tant for personal–social and intellectual development (44).

Even within the same cultural group, however, formal characteristics of the overriding culture may not be translated into *effective* characteristics. In the United States, for example, the very poor Black, Chicano, or American Indian child or ado-lescent often becomes estranged and may believe that no elected representative really works for his welfare; that little is to be gained by working hard and struggling upward, since because of his poverty, race, language, or religion, he will not suc-ceed anyway. Youngsters in such groups can see the materialism of America repre-sented on television or in the motion pic-ture, but few of its goodies are available to them. Similarly, the Bill of Rights may seem an empty abstraction, because they see themselves and their elders as unpro-tected by its provisions. They may have little opportunity to avail themselves of technology and science because of their poverty and their lack of formal education, and the sex-role stereotypes considered right and proper by the middle class may not hold for their own minority culture groups. For instance, it is often easier for a poor black woman to hold a steady job and obtain her rights within society than it is for a poor black man. Thus the stereo-type of the respected aggressive, domi-nant, male-leadership role that is held and practiced among middle-class people may not apply for many poor Black peo-ple.

Effective culture is transmitted to a child or a youth mainly by the *primary* group: his family, neighbors, close friends, and classmates. Within this primary group, customs and values of the culture are translated into behavior that can be imitated and practiced, into patterns of reward and punishment, and into oppor-tunities for discovery. While these cus-toms and values may not always be con-sistent within the primary group, they generally represent a sustained influence on the developing person. Moreover, sec-ondary groups also have some effect in transmitting the culture to the individual and to other members of the primary group to which he belongs. Examples of secondary groups include all the mem-bers of the individual's precinct, his church congregation, members of scout-ing troops other than his own whom he sees at jamborees but few of whom he knows, and other organizations of people with which he associates infrequently or temporarily. Still other determiners of the effective culture—such as socioeconomic level, religion, and the mass media—are discussed separately.

One way to illustrate the impact of ef-fective culture more concretely is through a representative cross-cultural study of behavior (4). Example 1.1 involves two groups, one a tropical subsistence culture, the Temne, in which life depends on growing and conserving one rice crop a year; the other an Arctic Eskimo group, also a subsistence culture, but one whose survival depends on the individual initiative and skill of the hunter. As this study indicates, pressure toward group conformity among the Temne and toward individualized skill among the Eskimo apparently contributes to marked personality differences (strictly speaking, differences in conformity revealed by the particular measure of personality used in the study).

1.1 Culture and Conformity

Berry (4) carried out a measurement of conformity among carefully selected members of Baffin Island Eskimos and the Temne people of Sierra Leone. He then compared the results from these groups with results obtained from people of an industrialized Western society, the Scots. Berry measured conformity in a way that has often been used: He recruited confederates who agreed to make a false consensual report about their judgment of the length of a line. The innocent subject, who had already made his independent judgment, was asked to judge again after hearing the false but consensual report. The more he shifted his judgment in the direction of the false group judgment, the more conforming he was presumed to be.

It is commonly agreed that the Eskimo must rely to an extreme degree on his own judgment and ingenuity. Berry documented such tendencies from previous anthropological evidence, and predicted that his Eskimo subjects would be ruggedly independent and thus

would resist group pressure to conform to the false consensual report about the lengths of lines.

The Temne live on rice, harvesting only a single crop a year. The rice must be meted out to all members of the group in carefully planned, regular daily units until the time of the next harvest. Hence, the welfare of each individual is directly related to the welfare of the entire group. This is so clearly recognized that nonconformity to the rules of Temne society is severely punished. The only similarity between the Eskimo and the Temne is that both are subsistence cultures—there is never more than just enough food to go around.

Berry's data clearly supported his predictions. The average traditional ("old line, un-Westernized") Temne changed his estimate of length of line 9 units in the direction of the false consensus, while the traditional Eskimo averaged a change in the direction of the false consensus of only 2.8 units. Berry also measured groups of more Westernized Temne and Eskimo and found that much the same conformity pattern occurred for them as had held for the old-line groups. He believes this signifies the strong staying or holding power of cultural norms, even when the old ways are changing.

Berry also secured samples of rural and urban Scots. The Scots were more individualistic than the Temne, but more conforming than the Eskimo. As might be expected from the stereotype of the ruggedly individualistic, proud Scot, the Scots were closer to the Eskimo than to the Temne, but yet significantly more conforming than the Eskimo.

The authors wish to close this brief section on effective culture by stressing two major points. First, patterns of developmental change are perhaps best understood in cultural perspective. Although certain patterns of change may be identical or similar in different cultures, the authors believe that an understanding of change can best emerge if one carefully considers the cultural setting for change. This is particularly important in United States culture, which is itself characterized by rapid change. Second, it is clear that both uniformity and diversity can be found in any given culture. Most cultures are described formally, but the effective culture for a given individual or subgroup in that culture may not coincide with the formal aspects of the broad culture. It

therefore becomes necessary to examine the components of effective culture carefully in the interests of improved understanding of behavior and development. One such component is socioeconomic level.

Socioeconomic Status
In the preceding section socioeconomic status was mentioned as one specific aspect within any given culture, except possibly in the simplest of the nomadic or hunting cultures. Even there, the strongest man, the best hunter, and the woman who bears the most and the healthiest children or who most effectively handles

Oppressive poverty is a dominant component of the effective culture experienced by this fatherless family in southwestern United States. (Wide World Photos)

her responsibilities as wife and mother are given more prestige and status than other members of the group. In complex industrialized societies, people typically associate socially almost entirely with others of their own social class. Upper-middle-income whites and blacks flock to the suburbs, where they associate with others like themselves and send their children to schools filled with other children much like their own. Because they must do so, low-income people more often stay in the inner or decaying marginal areas of cities or in the rural slums that can be seen from any highway. They too associate mainly with others of their income level and most frequently of their own ethnic group or race. They send their children to inner-city or slum or rural schools that are on the whole less well equipped and staffed and less well supported than suburban schools. The similarity of social class to the interaction and feedback system discussed earlier is apparent. One affects and is affected by life and culturally relevant experiences and reactions that perpetuate him in the social class into which he was born. By the same token, the individual contributes to the system reactions and a way of life that support the status quo.

The authors consider the terms socio-economic class, social status, and social class as virtually synonymous (more purist writers often make distinctions). The most usual factors that are included in the socioeconomic equation or index are the level of education of the heads of the family, the father's or the mother's occupation, the characteristics of the part of town and the house in which one lives, and the source (and, when the information can be obtained, the size) of the family income. The higher the level of parents' education, the higher the social class. The more

education required for the occupation, the more prestige the occupation usually possesses in the community. The more power the man or the woman who follows the occupation can exert over others, the higher the socioeconomic status. Physicians and judges, for example, are almost invariably considered very high status or prestige in all American communities. The more affluent the area lived in and the larger and better the condition of the house, the higher the socioeconomic status. Inherited income and income from investments are considered higher status income than earned income (54).

As example, newspaper editors, high-level judges, professors, managers and/or owners of large respectable businesses, ministers within churches where high theological degrees are required—such people are thought of as upper class or upper-middle class.

Semiskilled and unskilled workers with low-level educations are considered lower class (or disadvantaged, perhaps a more acceptable term). White collar workers with high school diplomas and perhaps a year or so of specialized training beyond high school are considered to be middle class, or perhaps lower-middle class, and rank about the same as highly skilled laborers, such as electricians.

It is fashionable today to talk about poverty as opposed to affluent or advantaged cultures, rather than to use terms such as upper-middle, middle, or lower class. However, income alone is only partly a determinant of social prestige and power, even in as materialistic a culture as our own (a pompous 6-year-old friend of the authors once said, more aptly than he knew, "You know, sir, you can't buy money with happiness").

Income is often characterized as respectable and nonrespectable. Respectable income is earned through work at socially accepted occupations. The wages of the poor but honest man are respectable income; the fees of the honest lawyer or the salary of the faithful legislator are respectable income. So is the interest from the investments left to the wealthy man by his rich father. Income deriving from major or minor crime, including bribery and embezzlement, and income from chronic welfare are ordinarily considered nonrespectable income. Nonrespectable income seldom gives one power and prestige, except possibly in narrowly circumscribed groups that are comparatively alienated from the general culture (for example, the numbers man or woman, the heroin pusher, the successful hustler, the bookie).

As a general rule in America, the higher one's respectable income, the more his power and prestige. There is also a commonality among all the cultures of the poor: truly inadequate incomes, whether respectable or nonrespectable, overwhelm families and whole communities such that the joy of life can scarcely be experienced at all.

As has been stated, socioeconomic status is a shorthand expression, such as age or IQ. To categorize a person according to social class explains nothing. However, certain functional correlates of social status have emerged that come closer to explanation than the index alone (40). These correlates include the breadth and quality of early learning experiences, the type of adult models available to children for patterning their behavior, the amount and quality of health care and nutrition, the amount of opportunity for intellectual stimulation, the kind of behavior control that is exerted over the child or the youth, and so on. These are the dynamic forces that bear some relation to socioeconomic

status and which are genuinely useful in shaping and predicting development.

Most of the information concerning socioeconomic status as a mediator of developmental patterns has come from comparisons of middle-class (affluent, advantaged, relatively speaking) and lower-class (poor, not well-educated) parents and their children. Of course, social classes do not break down that cleanly, and there is much overlap, particularly for groups that are upward mobile. Upward mobility is characteristic of many immigrant families, poor when they first arrive in the United States, but moving rapidly up in income, education, prestige, and power; or groups that are downward mobile ("shirtsleeves to shirtsleeves in three generations"). Considerable overlap and similarity in personal values, skills, and characteristics exist from one class to another.

Still, there are important differences from one social class to another, most strikingly when we move from lower-middle class (for example, the white collar worker, the highly skilled tradesman) toward the bottom of the social power ladder: those who are semiskilled or unskilled occupationally speaking, who are on chronic welfare, who live by petty criminal means, and who have less than high school education. Such people usually enjoy little prestige or power within their communities. Many summaries of social class differences exist. For convenience, the authors have drawn from some of their own writing and from consensual literature (24, 58). Between the advantaged and the poor, there are great average differences in family stability, job security, and marital satisfaction among women (in the direction of favoring the advantaged). It seems reasonable that such differences can affect parent–child relations in important ways. As a group, the affluent, more than the poor, bring up their children to be achievement motivated and to work hard, to control their aggression, to conceal their sexuality, and to communicate with their parents. Advantaged parents are more likely than the poor to be liberal in child-rearing practices. This may be mainly because they have the time and the vocabulary that are required to practice liberality and hence democracy. When you are poor, when you are not well educated and not articulate, when you have to work very hard, and when you have many children one after the other, democracy is something of a luxury.

Advantaged parents have been found to use less physical discipline and show more affection toward their children. For better or worse, they seem to influence and control the behavior of their children even when they are grown more than do poor people. In advantaged families, joint activity and togetherness are stressed more than they are in poor families. Attitudes (particularly moral attitudes) of advantaged parents and those of their children are more similar than is true in poor families.

On the whole, children from poor families do not test as high on IQ tests, do not learn as well in school (often because of poorer schools, the authors suspect), may be more impulsive and less self-critical than children from affluent families. Moreover, children from poor families may have lower self-esteem, may tend less to plan ahead, are less likely to believe they are masters of their own destinies, may begin premarital sexual intercourse earlier and indulge in it more often, and may be repeatedly delinquent (or perhaps they only get caught and booked more often).

All told, there are simply too many important behavior correlates with socioeconomic status to do other than take socioeconomic status seriously as a mediator of human development. Documentation of these relationships, however, does not explain *why* socioeconomic factors are apparently so pervasive. Of course, it does not require a trained psychologist or social worker with a case book to see that poverty almost always seriously delimits the positive growth experiences of many children and adolescents (although many of America's finest and most successful people have come from a poverty background. There is, of course, a difference between respectable and nonrespectable poverty, just as there is a difference between respectable and nonrespectable income.) But poverty, particularly nonrespectable poverty, combined with racial discrimination, poor nutrition, segregated and inadequate schools, ghetto neighborhoods, and socially maladjusted models, is most clearly counterproductive. If behavioral development within maturational limits is the product of cumulative learning, it is reasonable to say that developmental rate can be seriously impeded in impoverished conditions. Of course, social–emotional poverty can and does occur in homes that, according to formal socioeconomic criteria, are upper-middle class or upper class. Many children in the "best parts of town" and from the finest homes are neglected, are farmed out to inadequate caretakers, or are openly rejected by compulsive achievement- and status-seeking parents.

On the whole, however, higher socioeconomic status is associated with developmental advantages that are observable as early as the first and second years of life (17, 21).

Sex

The third mediator of the patterns of developmental change chosen for discussion is the sex of the individual. Actually, of all the mediators of pattern, sex is perhaps the single most important one for general psychological and social development. Sex affects how the individual is treated by others, the nature of expectations for behavior that others hold for the individual, the structures of opportunity made available within the individual's culture, and how the individual views and treats himself throughout life (42). For example, an accent on gender is apparent at birth. The physician or the nurse commonly introduces the new baby to its parents by saying, "It's a fine baby girl (or boy)." For many infants a sex role distinction literally begins with the color of swaddling clothes at birth: pink for girls and blue for boys. During the preschool years, boys and girls are usually given different toys, play equipment, and play opportunities, and urged to take advantage of them by their parents. Even casual observation of groups of children as young as 2 years old reveals that most boys are playing differently from most girls. Boys gravitate toward wheeled toys, big blocks, and rougher toys. Girls are usually quieter, and are more likely to be playing with the doll and playhouse facilities that can be found in most nursery school settings. Since there is little, if any, difference in size, strength, or motor skill between preschool boys and girls, such clear play preferences must certainly be strongly influenced by early teaching (however subtle it may be) rather than biology.

Sex differences apparent to the casual observer have been rather precisely documented through psychological research. Such differences are so pervasive that rarely do studies *not* show them, even when a research worker may not be looking for them. In fact, entire volumes are devoted to sex differences and the functions they may serve in personality development (30, 31). During childhood, sex differences have been documented across a wide spectrum of behavior, including problem-solving styles, verbal skills, dependency, aggression, susceptibility to disease, and learning disabilities. Sex-linked differences also continue to appear through puberty and beyond. During adolescence, these differences range from vocational skills and aspirations, social interest, and conformity to specific cognitive abilities, forms of delinquency, and the way sexual feelings are expressed (23, 42).

Although the description of sex differences in behavior and development is a fairly straightforward task, the explanation of these differences is not. Physiology, including sex hormones, and various kinds of learning experiences apparently interact in different ways to produce different sex-related characteristics. As mentioned earlier, differences in culturally determined learning experience for boys and girls begin very early in life. These experiences generally reflect cultural values about what is (or should be) masculine and feminine. Because it is instructive to consider what is valued for masculine and feminine sex roles in United States culture, an account pertinent to this issue (45) is included in Example 1.2. The results suggest at least two things. First, the responses of these college students apparently reflect their own learned values concerning sex role behavior; and second, these values presumably influence their responses to others, including eventually their own children.

1.2 Stereotyped and Valued Behavior for Males and Females in the United States

A group of college students in north-eastern United States was asked to specify and evaluate masculine and feminine characteristics. It is significant that agreement among male and female students both about what is *feminine* and *valued* and about what is *masculine* and *valued* approached 100 percent. (Correlations between the judgments of males and females concerning femininity, masculinity, and value were in mid-90s, which is about as close as one can come to unity in the area of human behavioral research.) The results are listed below.

Traits Valued and Masculine

Aggressive
Unemotional, hides emotions, never cries
Independent, not easily influenced
Adventurous
Objective, logical
Dominant, acts as a leader
Likes mathematics and science
Not excitable in a minor crisis
Active, worldly
Competitive, self-confident
Direct, makes decisions easily
Skilled in business
Able to separate feelings from ideas
Talks freely about sex with men
Not conceited about appearance
Thinks men are superior to women

Traits Valued and Feminine

Talkative
Does not use harsh language
Tactful
Gentle
Aware of others' feelings
Religious
Interested in own appearance
Neat in habits
Quiet
Strong need for security
Appreciates art and literature
Expresses tender feelings

From these two lists it can be seen that at least one group of modern college students sees men as having most of the fun and possessing most of the competence and strength in the culture. In contrast, women are perceived as gentle, mild, aware of social interrelations, and somewhat self-centered. On the whole, the "esteemed woman" as described above seems to the present authors as a bit less than exciting and certainly one who may not represent total self-development and fulfillment. The "esteemed man," on the other hand, emerges as a rather intriguing and active person.

Such stereotypes as represented by these data must be partially learned. Biology alone seems insufficient to account for them. These stereotypes are also clearly demeaning to females and disadvantageous to males. Little if any latitude is given the female for personal competence and appropriate aggressiveness; just as little room or value is given to males for gentleness, self-expression, and sensitivity toward others. This matter of stereotypes raises the important issue of how cultural conditioning may variously facilitate or impede the development of human potential.

Further data from the same group of students who provided the above list of valued male and female traits were obtained in a second study (52). When the college students were divided into groups according to whether or not their mothers had worked during their childhoods, it was found that the students whose mothers had worked made less distinction between male and female valued characteristics than the students whose mothers had always been house-wives. The offspring of working mothers took away nothing of the tenderness and social sensitivity from girls' and women's role, but added attributes of social competence; for valued and typical male roles, none of the independence, competence, and assertiveness of the valued male role was subtracted by the sons and daughters of working mothers. Rather, they added to the valued male role those characteristics of tenderness and aware-ness of social relations that were considered primarily feminine by the children of nonworking mothers.

Within a society, is it not more useful for girls and women to be competent as well as tender, and for boys and men to be loving and understanding as well as competent and assertive? Such results as these reported for the children of working mothers suggest that it is possible for each sex to be assigned the desirable attributes of the other sex without losing the desirable attributes of its own. Such results also suggest that a large portion of sex role stereotype is learned rather than inherent and biologically dependent.

Intelligence

The authors have stressed the point that the individual is a significant factor in his own development. That is, by virtue of the things he says and does, the individual determines much of how he is viewed and treated by others. The treatment he receives from others and the environmental consequences of his actions in turn influence his future behavior. Certainly one important indi-vidual characteristic in this regard is intelligence. The concept of intelligence, its measurement, developmental considerations, and research problems is explored later in the book. For the moment intelligence is defined in terms of the ability to solve problems in ways that help one deal successfully with his environment—whether this environment be the bush country in Australia, the plains of Kansas, or the sidewalks of New York.

If there is any one thing about which psychologists agree it is that people differ among themselves in intelligence. If intelligence is defined as problem-solving ability, then one child, Frank, is considered more intelligent than another child, Roger, to the extent that Frank can solve more varied and more difficult problems faster than Roger. Problem-solving ability has profound implications for the nature of development, including relationships with parents and peers, degree of scholastic success, vocational success, and countless other aspects of human existence.

Differences in intelligence appear as early as infancy and increase in magnitude through childhood and adolescence. Among some of the more pronounced relationships between measured intelligence and other areas of development and behavior are age of talking and general language ability, memory, rate at which new concepts are learned, and general resourcefulness (2). Intelligence is also a determinant or source of individual differences for a broad range of behaviors. These include such varied characteristics as sense of humor, leadership, popularity, and fear (2). A further aspect of intelligent behavior—creativity in children and adolescents—also deserves mention.

Until the last two scientific generations, it was widely believed that intelligence was determined so preponderantly by hereditary factors that experience made little difference. That is, one's intelligence quotient (IQ) was viewed as quite fixed at birth, something that would not change appreciably because of learning. Accordingly, the effects of early experience during infancy and preschool or, for that matter, during adolescence were not considered very important in intellectual development. Most psychologists now believe, however, that experience plays an important role in intellectual development. Thus a complex interaction of heredity and environment provides the basis for most contemporary thinking about intelligence.

Biological Factors and Nutrition

The important part heredity plays in affecting maturational processes in human development has already been discussed. A person's genetic blueprint includes many partial or total determinants of development and behavior as they occur over the life span from birth to death. Among behaviors that are widely thought to be importantly affected by genetics are activity level, crying behavior, and reactions to sensory stimulation. Great individual differences in activity, crying, and sensory response can be observed from the time of birth, although these may later be much affected by learning experiences, including the amount of stress under which an individual is placed. Some recent experiences in working with specific learning-disability children, who are apparently born quite literally with a "different wiring system" than normal children, indicate that many of these children profit greatly from ingenious educational intervention procedures. Whereas formerly such children, even though of

normal and even superior intellectual ability, were usually doomed to school failure, such as inability to read or to handle numbers or spatial factors, some school programs now succeed in returning these children to regular classrooms as normal achievers after a year or two of intervention efforts by a specially trained program staff.

Other human characteristics, such as differential susceptibility to disease, developmental disorders that involve physical and mental retardation, probably some emotional disorders, age of arriving at puberty, and even longevity, all seem to be strongly genetically blueprinted. The summary of Judy's life, given early in this chapter, is an example of how a genetic blueprint (in her case, an unfashionable, stocky, peasant body) can interact disastrously with cultural expectations and interfere with other exceptionally positive developmental mediators (in Judy's case, high socioeconomic level and great intellectual ability).

The study of biochemistry and human development is very new. At least two hormones, androgen (the male hormone) and estrogen (the female hormone) affect the development of biological and, probably, psychological maleness and femaleness. Sex-related behavior of aggression in males and of maternalism in females is also affected by these hormones—high-androgen males apparently being more aggressive, high-estrogen females more maternal. Biological factors, including hormones, also crucially affect the rate of growth in height, weight, and bone ossification (ossification is the process of moving from the cartilage of infancy to the brittle bones of old age).

Striking individual differences in rate of growth can be clearly observed very early in life. For example, there may be a range of as much as eight or more inches in height between the shortest and the tallest child in a group of twenty-five or thirty "normal" 5-year-olds. An early-maturing girl may be half a head taller than her classmates at the time she begins to menstruate, yet be one of the shortest of the girls in her class when all girls have reached mature height (puberty interrupts growth in girls and affects it much less among boys, so that at maturity there is little difference in height between early- and late-maturing boys). Size certainly affects the kind of physical activity a child or a youth can engage in, and results in very different kinds of social recognition. Early-maturing boys, tall, strong, and muscular, seem to gain from the recognition and leadership opportunities that are offered to them; and hold on to these advantages for many years (although they may begin to fall back as their bodies begin to fail them in middle life).

Maturation, a reflection of biological factors, is also important, even crucial, in acquiring various motor skills during childhood. Depending on the maturational level of a child, it may be disastrous (or strikingly advantageous) to introduce a given skill training at a given age. Introducing shoe tying at age 3 is generally an educational mistake; the average 3-year-old is ill-equipped to learn to tie his shoes effectively because of the complex fine motor skills involved. Pressures for children to do these things before they are ready may have negative effects: Severe frustration (depending on how much pressure is applied) may result, and the child may be permanently turned off from the activity. For example, many middle-class parents introduce music lessons before their children are mature enough to profit from them. The authors suspect that many a musical rebel has been pro-

duced by such a premature introduction to formal musical training. It may be equally unfortunate to introduce an activity too late. Although there is little sound evidence concerning the fact, the authors are willing to advance the proposition that in America foreign language training is ordinarily introduced too late to be as effective in developing bilingual or multilingual fluency as it might be if introduced earlier. The authors know many children, both disadvantaged and advantaged, in southeast Asia, for example, who are proficient in three, four, and even five languages without having suffered any apparent conflict or trauma while learning the languages; yet few or none of our young American friends are truly proficient in even one language besides English.

Finally, the significance of nutrition for physical and cognitive growth should be noted. Bad nutrition clearly delays growth (11). Truly deficient nutrition interferes with both physical and mental growth, as well as with general health and energy. The accompanying summary (1.3) of nutritional research documents the effects of grossly inadequate nutrition (6). Briefly, the conclusions from this study are that extreme protein calorie deprivation results in malnourished children who are weak in such problem-solving skills as sorting objects into categories of shape, size, and color (skills that are useful foundations for later reading, among other things).

The study of biological effects on human behavior is even more recent than the study of the psychology of human development. The discussion of this section can be continued on the basis of speculation, anecdote, and personal observation, but the basic outlines have been presented to a sufficient degree for the reader to do some independent thinking of his own and to read further if he wishes (43). Chapter 2 includes more detailed material about the heavily biologically determined variables of physical growth and motor development.

1.3 Nutrition and Cognitive Development

Brockman and Ricciuti (6) studied twenty Peruvian children who were so severely malnourished that they had been hospitalized for nutritional treatment. All were diagnosed as marasmic (their body weight on admission was less than 50 percent of that expected for their ages, they were free from apparent edema—a collection of water in tissues, often accompanied by swelling, and their serum albumen was normal). When the authors tested the children, they ranged in age from 11.8 to 43.5 months. They had emergency hospital treatment, then a longer period of remedial treatment in a nutrition center. These experimental subjects were matched by age and sex with nineteen children who came from slum areas of Lima, Peru, but who were physically normal, and who were in Day Care. Seven other Day Care children suffering from malnutrition, but not as gravely as the experimental children, were also studied.

Comparisons among these groups were made at the beginning and end of the treatment for the experimental subjects. This resulted in a twelve-week interval from the first to the second tests. Under the guise of playing with toys, both the experimental and the control subjects were given ten sorting tasks (put together the things that are alike, when there were two dimensions, such as red and green). Some sorting tasks were according to size, some according to color, and some according to texture. There were eight simple objects in each sorting task, four belonging to one category within each of the dimensions and four to another category. Full records were kept of how each child handled the task, from his initial approach to his final solution.

The experimental control comparison made at the beginning of treatment revealed that the control subjects performed about twice as well as the experimental subjects. The experimental subjects made almost no improvement in performance from the beginning to the end of treatment. Follow-up testing was done for only three controls. Two improved greatly, one did more poorly. The normal control subjects did about as well on these tasks as normal North American children. The experimental subjects showed from six to eight months of retardation.

Brockman and Ricciuti conclude as follows:

Hence, the strikingly lower sorting task scores of the experimental subjects appeared to be due to neither a lack of maintained interest nor to less frequent contacts with the objects. Rather, their performance reflected a relative inability to discriminate the similarities and differences among task objects. . . . and to group or categorize on the basis of the discriminated differences (p. 318).

Ethnicity

The terms *ethnic, ethnic group,* and *ethnicity* are often used in much the same way as the terms *race* and *racial group*. The two groups will be differentiated here, reserving ethnic, ethnic group, and ethnicity in reference to the culture, religion, and language traditions of a people or a culture, such as Italian Americans or Jews.

"Race" will be used in reference to a subdivision of the human race characterized by distinguishable physical characteristics transmitted from one generation to another.

Obviously there are many more ethnic groups than racial groups. Every country with a common language can be called an ethnic group without doing violence to the definition. The authors believe that only three racial groups can be clearly justified: Caucasian, or Caucasoid; Mongolian, or Mongoloid; and Negro, or Negroid.

Most "white"—strictly speaking, pinkish—people are Caucasian, but there are also many, many black or dark-brown Caucasians, as in the subcontinent of India–Pakistan. The Chinese, Japanese, Koreans, most Southeast Asians, and the people of Macronesia and Micronesia are considered Mongolian, as are the Eskimos and the American Indians. Most Negroes (except in formally anthropological references, the term Blacks or black people will be used instead of the white man's term *Negro*) have all or some of their national origin in Africa, but many anthropologists consider the Australian native to be Negroid, as well as some of the original residents of the islands off Australia and southeast Asia, such as Borneo. In the United States, "Negro" or "black" for many persons is a sociological, not a racial, term. For logically indefensible reasons, custom dictates that anyone with a discernible or documented trace of his original African heritage is called Black or Negro, even though he may be 75 percent or 87½ percent or more Caucasian (or white) by heredity.

How much effect on developmental change can be attributed to ethnicity and race? The simple truth is that an exact answer to this question cannot be given. At least for personal–social and intellectual–academic development, the authors are inclined to believe that socioeconomic level and other cultural factors are more important than racial or ethnic characteristics. There are ample data to support this belief (51). For example, when socioeconomic factors are carefully controlled, commonly reported personal–social differences between black and white populations are diminished or disappear completely. These differences include such characteristics as self-esteem, goal-setting behavior, and beliefs about one's ability to control his destiny. Yet sharp differences in these characteristics, usually in favor of white children, typically appear when comparisons involve poor blacks, poor whites, and advantaged whites.

Recent data have indicated that poor Black and Puerto Rican children may actually possess more positive views of themselves than their advantaged white peers (47). Still other authorities report clear self-concept disadvantages and other disabilities as characteristic of poor Black children and youth, especially young males (29). The point is that it is difficult to generalize about racial and ethnic differences apart from knowledge of cultural background. There is nothing definite to suggest inherent differences in personal–social behavior among children and youth of various ethnic and racial groups in the United States. It is possible, of course, that some differences may exist but have not yet been measured.

Differences in physical–motor characteristics may be quite another matter. For example, during the early years of life, black infants are generally more advanced in motor development than whites, although the psychological significance of this difference (if any) has not been recorded (33). Again, casual observation of athletic activities suggests that in America distinct differences exist between blacks and whites. Blacks seem to excel in activities in which success depends most upon agility and bursts of speed—the jumping events and sprints in track, for example. Further, black superstar athletes seem to be disproportionately represented in sports such as professional baseball, basketball, and football. On the other hand, whites seem to dominate in sports that involve buoyancy and endurance—swimming and long distance track events (with some conspicuous exceptions). Just how strongly physiological (versus cultural) factors are implicated in these differences cannot be said. But the issue is currently among the most interesting in the study of human development and behavior. Perhaps most controversial, both scientifically and morally, is the study of racial differences in intellectual–academic behavior. That clear differences in this aspect of development have been documented again and again cannot be denied. The authors cannot comment definitely on how much or what aspects of an individual's intellectual equipment is racially determined. Intellectual and academic development is so inextricably tied in with the language and learning opportunities of one's culture that the answer to this question may never be found. Much more is said about this matter in later chapters.

As suggested, any conclusions about the effects of race and ethnic differences on development represent at best a "mixed bag." Perhaps most critical is that a child or youth belonging to a minority group toward which prejudice is consistently expressed and which has been educationally and economically handicapped must suffer severe problems in his development. But these problems or handicaps seem logically to be due more to prejudice and deprivation than to the fact of race. (See Example 1.4.)

1.4 Advantage and Disadvantage in United States Co-cultures

Working from a classification made by Horowitz and Paden (26), the authors have formulated the following way of considering advantage and disadvantage, including ethnicity and race.

1. Prejudiced-against co-cultures with common ways of behaving that do not equip them to function very well according to the criteria of conventional success (educational, vocational, and economic). Such groups are Blacks (particularly poor Blacks); some of the Hispaño people (particularly the Chicanos—those of Mexican descent, the Puerto Ricans, and the poor Cubans—but *not* middle-class Cuban immigrants); many from the new wave of Chinese immigrants; almost all American Indians; and many who have native Hawaiian and Eskimo heritage. Of course, there are many other prejudiced-against and disadvantaged minorities, but the groups that have been named are the most numerous and/or noticeable.

2. Disadvantaged co-culture groups that are not victims of any sort of ethnic or racial prejudice. The very large number of Appalachian and poor white children and youth belong to this group. This group can be logically called the "indigenous poor."

3. Prejudiced-against co-cultures that cope adequately or well according to United States standards of success (low crime rate, good education, vocational

success, and so on). The Japanese Americans, a large proportion of the older Chinese Americans and their descendants, and the Jews belong to this group. Strictly speaking, *Jew* refers to religion only, but, as suggested above, common usage adds an ethnic association to "Jew" that, whether accurate or not, cannot be ignored.

For group 1—distinctive co-cultures toward which prejudice is directed but which have not learned to surmount it in order to achieve success and security in the culture—certain compensatory procedures seem to be quite effective. The school achievement and morale of Black, Hispano, and American-Indian youth can be almost immediately much improved by sensibly developed programs of Black studies, Chicano studies, and American-Indian studies. A sense of group or ethnic pride is developed, motivation seems to be increased, and self concept may well be improved. All these things together are likely to help children and youth master some of the basic tools they need to obtain their share of success in the "American way," with no loss, but rather an enhancement, of their own pride in themselves and their ethnic or racial group.

For group 2, the Appalachian and poor white, no such easy partial remedy appears. Such children and youth typically come from old-line WASP stock. Their skins and eyes and surnames are considered "right" in United States culture. Yet they are born to great difficulty. It may be confidently predicted that no easy partial remedies can be found for improving the motivation and achievement of white members of the culture of poverty.

Those ethnic and racial minorities that fall into group 3 (prejudiced-against but coping with United States culture adequately or well) seem to possess pride of heritage, religion, and language; strength of family ties; and belief in education. Despite the forces of prejudice aligned against them, such groups not only cope but also succeed on the average at least as well as, and often better than, the core WASP population.

Schooling

It is logical to think that school experience profoundly affects development, probably second only to the influence of family. Academic accomplishment and social experience should be particularly affected by school. Almost no authorities would question such an assumption. Curiously, there are few data to support the assumption, and the available data bear more on high school and college experience than on the lower grade and preschool educational experiences.

Fortunately, some reasonably good data about early school experiences exist. Special education efforts on behalf of children have shown moderately positive results, particularly for children from disadvantaged backgrounds (20). Children in such programs have improved in health and gained greater competence in language and other skills that are important for school success. Elsewhere, differences in school attitudes, problem-solving skills, initiative, and self concept have been registered for children in different kinds of schools. Schools that range from traditional to modern in educational philosophy and methods have apparently produced noticeable differences in pupil behavior (41). English studies reveal that good schools can counteract home deficiencies among children, if these are not extreme; and that severe negative effects come from inferior schools (14, 15). The Coleman report (10) includes data suggesting that poor children are more vulnerable to the effects of schools (for better or worse) than children from more affluent families.

Studies of children and youth at higher educational levels fit with the findings reported in the previous paragraph. High school environments differ in quality, and the differences in quality are associated with differences in student behavior. Depending on the school environment, student bodies differ in amount of aggression, quality of school spirit, involvement in school activities, academic motivation, and scholastic achievement (36, 37). While it is not clear exactly what is involved, it is promising to examine faculty quality, kind of control, and classroom atmosphere (53).

Schools do not operate in isolation from the community, because schools are direct reflections of the community, and in the United States are supposed to be locally (community) controlled. In middle-class (affluent) neighborhoods, the schools seem to be a direct reflection of the consensual middle-class culture. In inner-city slums and poor rural areas, community control is often a myth, and the schools are operated according to the middle-class values of administrators and teachers, often satisfying few of the needs of the clientele. Wrangles over school control in some of the poor, particularly the Black, sections of New York City exemplify this point. Data from Head Start and many other sources also clearly illustrate that schools are usually more effective as parents become more involved in discussions and policy making (20, 22). A further comprehensive examination of the school's role in childhood socialization is presented in Example 1.5.

1.5 The Many Faces of School Influence

One of the most interesting investigations of how schools affect children is a long-term study by Himmelweit and Swift (25). The research workers' main goal was twofold: (1) How do different kinds of school affect children who come from much the same background? (2) How does the same school affect children who differ sharply in ability and/or who come from different social backgrounds? The powerful effects that school apparently can have emerge from this study. One striking finding is that, according to these authorities, more accurate predictions can be made about children's behavior, outlook, values, and achievements by knowing about their schools than can be made from information about socioeconomic status or intelligence.

Such findings led the authors of this study to construct a model of childhood socialization. They believe that school is the most important variable. In their model, they isolate several specific aspects of the school environment. Furthermore, they believe these specific aspects, when combined, may determine the degree to which students are affected by their schools.

First, it is important whether the *values* held by school administrators are actually integrated and consistently put into educational practice. Second, to what degree are these values contradicted or supported by other values to which the students are or have been exposed? For example, if the values are all college preparatory, but the community influences lead most students to think that college is an impossibility, the effectiveness of the school is likely to be impaired.

Third, what is the nature of the long-term and short-term rewards offered by the school in return for the students' cooperation in keeping the school going smoothly? Fourth, how does the school administration deal with students who do not cooperate or who reject the objectives of the school? Finally, fifth, the student's status within the school is important. This includes the degree to which the student is actively engaged in working out or adapting to school-defined roles (school-defined roles, by way of example, are good algebra student, obedient student, good athlete, competent class officer).

As indicated, the effectiveness of school depends on many things—for example, the nature of the school, the nature of the community, parental values, and the degree to which parents participate (9), as well as the student's sex. It has been argued with evidence that schools fit better with the United States stereotype of girls and women than with what the society expects of boys and men (32). Schools seem to reinforce the feminine stereotype of social sensitivity, obedience, and conservatism of the "don't rock the boat" kind. Thus, in a sense, the prevailing United States school atmosphere supports the idea that girls are "sugar and spice and everything nice." Conversely, boys are more often expelled, punished, criticized, and are graded lower for achievement that is about the same as that of girls. The central, competence aspect of the male in this culture, then, seems also to be discouraged by the typical American school of the fifties and sixties. It is hoped that improvement will occur in the seventies, for both boys and girls.

There is also some evidence that current school practices are such that teachers grade advantaged children, whether black

or white, according to an even mix of the student's intelligence and his degree of social conformity. This is particularly true for advantaged white boys. On the other hand, poor students are graded according to a more or less even mix of intelligence and objective achievement of the sort that shows up on standardized achievement tests. This is particularly true for black girls. Thus, the schools seem to be somewhat unfair, at least as far as grading practices are concerned, to all sorts of children. If advantaged children are not "good" (nice socially), they are graded down. If disadvantaged children are "good," they receive little credit for it. It should be noted that these conclusions come from only one study (34), carried out in a metropolitan school district in Atlanta, Georgia.

Even friendly critics of American schools agree that few schools achieve their constructive potential for affecting children's and youths' lives. Many schools are clearly instrumental in producing negative attitudes among students, even to the point of alienating them. It is certain that many of the about one-third of American students who drop out of high school before graduating could have stayed in school and have been graduated creditably if they had been happier in school. Thus, many schools and their students seem to be caught up in a self-defeating cycle.

The human factor is probably the critical one in schools (27). Teacher–student and student–student relationships collectively may be more important than all other aspects of the school experience. This leads to the consideration of teachers as models for behavior and as agents in promoting positive human relations in school settings. This important matter is discussed in detail in Chapter 12.

Religion

The eighth and last mediator of developmental change is religion. Unfortunately, comparatively little is known about how religion affects people. The reasons are fairly obvious: People are sensitive about having their religious feelings probed into by research workers. This is true whether it is an individual consenting to be interviewed or a religious leader opening up his congregation for a research undertaking. It is possible that social scientists are sensitive about investigating religion. It may also be that these scientists are not deeply interested in religion as an important variable affecting human development, because most people spend relatively little time in formal church and church-related activities. Finally, it is extremely difficult to separate the possible effects of religion on development from other related factors such as ethnicity and socioeconomic status.

When religion has been studied, its impact on behavior represents something of a paradox (32, 38). On the whole, those who profess to be religious appear to be less forgiving, more prejudiced, and more rigid than those who are less "religious." However, the matter is not simple: Further study of church going suggests that persons who attend frequently and regularly and those who attend not at all are less prejudiced than those who attend only sporadically, yet who profess nonetheless to be religious. This finding suggests a motivational factor that may be thought of in terms of intrinsic or extrinsic religiosity (1). Extrinsically religious people value the trappings of religion, the social contacts, and the status and security of church membership. Such persons are not necessarily devoted attenders, but they are the church members who are typically most prejudiced. Others go to church for intrinsic reasons: They value the ethics, the spirit, the guiding light of the church. They *live* and have internalized their religion. Such intrinsically religious people are basically tolerant and unprejudiced.

Still a third group of people can be described: the indiscriminately religious — those who ascribe all good things to religion, whether extrinsic or intrinsic. And these persons are often the most prejudiced of all (1).

Additional research has resulted in a somewhat different classification of churchgoers: the orthodox versus the ethicalists (48). On the whole, the orthodox are the power figures and financial supporters of the church. They provide the money and hold the church offices (this finding is most applicable for the Protestant Christian churches). However, the orthodox are also conservative and are among the more prejudiced, unforgiving, and inflexible members of their congregations. The ethicalists, in contrast, may be less influential in the church and are often more questioning of its practices, yet they embody the church spirit to a greater degree than their orthodox counterparts. As one might expect, the ethicalists are comparatively tolerant, flexible, and unprejudiced (and also, according to findings from this research, are becoming less and less active in the church — for many, a depressing state of affairs).

Thus far the discussion has related most specifically to different kinds of religious involvement. Moreover, it has been focused on churchgoing and church membership, neither of which tells the whole story of religion. One could argue that a more relevant concern is the impact of religious experience on the developing child and youth. Clear-cut answers to this question cannot be provided. Yet the im-

Religious beliefs influence the form of socialization experienced by many children. For example, grouping by sex will affect the nature of peer interaction. (Wide World Photos)

portance of religion, as a potentially strong element of effective culture, can be highlighted in at least two ways.

The first concerns the way in which religion affects child-rearing practices (parent–child relationships), educational experiences (for example, parochial versus secular schooling), social activity (for example, Christian Youth groups), intergroup relations (for example, anti-Catholicism), and quasi rites of passage to denote the coming of age (for example, bar mitzvah in the Jewish faith). It does not require much imagination to envision how variations in religiously based human activity can contribute to differences in knowledge, attitudes, and ways of thinking. Marked differences in methods and goals of child training have been observed among families, as well as in societies, with different religious orientations and beliefs (57). These differences range from the degree to which disciplinary practices are employed by parents to the relative emphasis they place on self-reliance. For example, a belief in a malevolent god has been associated with a more punitive approach to child rearing (28). Similarly, differences in motivation for achievement among children and youth have also been linked to variations in the religious affiliation of their parents (18, 19). Children from Jewish homes, for example, frequently rate higher in their achievement motivation than their Catholic peers.

A second, perhaps more indirect way in which religion is implicated in the *effective* culture is its possible relationship to broader political and economic factors. The last two, of course, are extremely potent factors in shaping both the development of a culture and its individual members. One classic treatise concerning the political–economic–religious interaction relates to the Protestant ethic and the rise of capitalism (56). In this treatise, the Protestant personality is characterized as individualistic, thrifty and self-sacrificing, an efficient user of time, strong in personal responsibility, and committed to the supreme value of personal productivity. In turn, the attainment and practice of independence, self-sufficiency, and accumulation of resources through productivity presumably are the means for increasing the probability of personal salvation. The point is that, since the Reformation, religiously grounded beliefs have conceivably influenced the nature of family patterns. In turn, these patterns may have facilitated a strong orientation to personal achievement, competitiveness, and standards of excellence. It is this orientation that is seemingly vital to the successful practice of capitalism (35). Thus the achievement thrust in entire societies may be traced, at least in part, to a religious base.

As our culture becomes more heavily bureaucratic, the classic Protestant ethic may diminish as a source of cues for child-rearing and educational strategies. It seems clear, however, that religious thought, whatever the specifics, has a central role in determining matters related to moral–ethical codes and what constitutes the "good life." Even though the exact influence of religion is not clear, it is a force that deserves careful attention from students of human development. At the very least, the church often provides children and youth a place where they can be accepted for themselves alone. For many young people, church activities have made possible a primary group relationship—a place where youth can shine and be appreciated—not available to them otherwise at home, in school, or in the broader community.

Concluding Remarks

In addition to the eight mediators of developmental change patterns just discussed, many others have been studied and conjectured about. Although a listing of all possible mediators would be an exhausting and perhaps a fruitless task, it is constructive to consider a few examples.

One such mediator concerns various aspects of family structure—for example, birth order in the family. Although our information about family structure is spotty and sometimes contradictory, the indications are that it can make a difference in a person's development if he is a firstborn or an only child, or a later or a last-born child; if the immediately older and younger siblings (his brothers and sisters) are of the same sex or of the opposite sex; if the children in the family are widely or closely spaced; if he comes from a small family of two or three or from a large family of eight or more, and so on. But family patterns are elusive matters for psychological study, and the results from study in this area are therefore not clear cut. One survey of the massive number of studies of birth order, for example, has revealed only three even tentative generalizations: (1) a higher proportion of firstborns (versus later borns) than would be expected are found in United States colleges; (2) firstborns are generally more susceptible to social pressure than their later born siblings; and (3) firstborn women seem especially attracted to the company of others in threatening or disturbing situations (55). These findings are only generalizations, however, and may not apply at all to a particular firstborn person; and a more recent review throws even these conclusions into doubt (46).

Another developmental mediator concerns father-absence or father-presence (or broken versus intact home) (5). The study of this factor has led to one fairly clear generalization, namely, that boys (in particular) suffer when they grow up without fathers. This negative effect is usually greater the earlier the father leaves and the longer he stays away from the home. Of course, in many cases the negative effect of father-absence can likely be offset if a positive father-substitute is available. Father-absence and children's development are discussed in detail in the section on sex typing and identification in Chapter 7.

Rural–urban or big-city–small-town residence is still another possible mediator. There is some indication that in today's society rural children and youth are more alienated and cope less well than their urban counterparts (16). Surprisingly few convincing data are available, however, concerning the impact of rural versus urban life on the total developmental pattern.

Most United States families are nuclear. That is, one or both parents and the children live in their own home, and frequently the grandparents and other relatives live some distance away. However, there are still some extended families in the United States, where father, mother, children, grandparents, and uncles and aunts all live together or in close proximity. More often than not, the psychological ties among the kinship family are also very close. In the extended family, a child may in effect have many parents, and he may live with cousins in much the same way that the average American child lives with his siblings. Thus children from extended families generally experience a stronger built-in primary group than the average child in a nuclear family. The extended family still exists in many parts of the world and has been studied by sociologists, particularly in India and Pakistan. In the United States, however, little is known about the impact of the extended family on development.

The final addition to the list of briefly discussed mediators relates to the implications of parental occupation for family interaction and child rearing (39), with specific reference to bureaucratic versus entrepreneurial occupations (39). It has been argued that this distinction cuts across and transcends traditional social class lines. For example, a bureaucratic occupation is characterized by a direct salary and carries a comparatively high degree of job security; public school teaching, civil service, the military, and many industrial or corporate-based jobs are generally bureaucratic occupations, but the salaries of each group represent a wide range of annual income. Similarly, occupations in which persons are self-employed or work on a direct commission basis — more entrepreneurial in that they involve a higher degree of risk taking and competition — may represent a wide spectrum of personal income. Contrast, for example, the highly successful physician in private practice with a door-to-door broom salesman working on a commission.

Studies have indicated that the goals and methods of child rearing often differ between bureaucratic families and entrepreneurial families. Parents of the former group tend more often to stress equalitarian practices and to emphasize social adjustment, or "getting along." Among entrepreneurial parents, much more emphasis on independence training, mastery, and self-reliance has been observed. The entrepreneurial parents also make ample use of psychological techniques of discipline. It is therefore likely that, in general, growing up in an entrepreneurial home or in a bureaucratic home could represent quite a difference, especially in terms of the values reflected in family interaction.

Human development may be conveniently regarded in terms of a rounded-triangle schema, the first corner devoted to intellectual, cognitive, academic, and other sorts of substantive learning. Personal–social–emotional traits and behavior can be represented by the second corner, and physical and motor skill factors fit into the third corner. Under physical factors, such things as body build, attractiveness, and time of reaching sexual maturity are included.

Human development is viewed as a matter of change through time. Age is a convenient, traditional method of organizing change through time, but it has no explanatory power. Employing it as one's only way of ordering behavior is likely to result in paying too little attention to individual differences and to learning. A sequence-relevant method of ordering developmental phenomena seems more useful, leading closer to explanation and manipulation of developmental sequences and rates than is true when age is the only organizer.

Patterns of developmental change are mediated by factors. Eight major mediators were chosen for discussion. These are the effective culture, socioeconomic level, sex, intelligence or learning aptitude, biological factors including nutrition, ethnicity and race, schooling, and religion. Many more mediators could have been discussed, such as birth order and family size, rural–urban residence, and intact or broken families; but the eight chosen have been found most useful by the authors.

It should be noted that these mediators of the pattern of developmental change range from factors that are primarily genetic–constitutional to factors that appear to be exclusively culturally determined, such as education and the schools, or religion. Even biological factors, however, are subject to environmental modification. The child reared in total isolation is likely to be severely retarded in motor development, as is the child with grossly inadequate nutrition. Matters that on the surface seem entirely cultural–environmental are often modified in their effect on a person by interaction with constitutional factors such as body build, physical appearance, and general health. In other words, the use a person makes of his environment depends on many constitutional factors. An individual's facility in dealing with his environment depends not only on his body and its senses but also on his mind. While no one can say for sure to what degree the keenness, or power, of one's mind is a function of nature (heredity) or nurture (learning opportunity), it is plausible to estimate that both nature and nurture contribute substantially to "brain power," although the authors' emphasis is more on environmental than on genetic or constitutional determinants of intelligence.

REFERENCES

1. Allport, G. W., and J. M. Ross. Personal religious orientation and prejudice. *Journal of Personality and Social Psychology*, 1967, 5, 432–443.
2. Ausubel, D. *Theory and problems in child development.* New York: Grune & Stratton, 1958.
3. Baer, D. M. An age-irrelevant concept of development. *Merrill-Palmer Quarterly*, 1970, 16, 238–245.
4. Berry, J. W. Independence and conformity in subsistence-level societies. *Journal of Personality and Social Psychology*, 1967, 7, 415–418.
5. Blanchard, R. W., and H. B. Biller. Father availability and academic performance among third-grade boys. *Developmental Psychology*, 1971, 4, 301–305.
6. Brockman, L. M., and H. N. Ricciuti. Severe protein-calorie malnutrition and cognitive development in infancy and early childhood. *Developmental Psychology*, 1971, 4, 312–319.
7. Bruner, J. *The process of education.* New York: Random House, Vintage Books, 1960.
8. Child, I. Personality in culture. In E. Borgatta and W. Lambert (eds.) *Handbook of personality theory and research.* Chicago: Rand McNally, 1968, 82–148.
9. Christopher, S. A. Parental relationship and value orientation as factors in academic achievement. *Personnel and Guidance Journal*, May 1967, 921–925.
10. Coleman, J., E. Campbell, C. Hobson, J. McPartland, A. Mood, and R. York. *Equality of educational opportunity.* Washington, D.C.: U. S. Government Printing Office, 1966.
11. Dayton, D. H. Early malnutrition and hu-

man development. *Children*, 1969, 16, 210–217.
12. Dennis, W. Causes of retardation among institutional children. *Journal of General Psychology*, 1960, 96, 47–59.
13. Dennis, W., and Y. Sayegh. The effect of supplementary experiences upon the behavioral development of infants in institutions. *Child Development*, 1965, 36, 81–90.
14. Douglas, J. W. B. *The home and the school.* London: MacGibbon and Kee, 1964.
15. Douglas, J. W. B. *All our future.* London: Peter Davies, 1968.
16. Douvan, E., and J. Adelson. *The adolescent experience.* New York: Wiley, 1966.
17. Edgewood (Atlanta) Parent Child Development Center. Unpublished data, 1968–1971 (personal communication).
18. Elder, G. H., Jr. Adolescent socialization and development. In E. F. Borgatta and W. W. Lambert (eds.) *Handbook of personality theory and research.* Chicago: Rand McNally, 1968, 239–364.
19. Elkind, D. The developmental psychology of religion. In Olive H. Kidd and Jeanne L. Rivoire (eds.) *Perceptual development in children.* New York: International Universities Press, 1966, 193–225.
20. Evans, E. D. *Contemporary influences in early childhood education.* New York: Holt, Rinehart and Winston, 1971.
21. Golden, M., B. Birns, W. Bridger, and A. Moss. Social-class differentiation in cognitive development among black preschool children. *Child Development*, 1971, 42, 37–45.
22. Gordon, I. J. *Parental involvement in compensatory education.* Urbana, Ill.: Research Press, 1971.
23. Hauck, B. B. Differences between the sexes at puberty. In E. D. Evans (ed.) *Adolescence: Readings in behavior and development.* Hinsdale, Ill.: Dryden, 1970, 24–42.
24. Hess, R. D. Social class and ethnic influences on socialization. In P. Mussen (ed.) *Carmichael's manual of child psychology* (3rd ed.) (Vol. II). New York: Wiley, 1970, 457–558.
25. Himmelweit, H. T., and B. Swift. A model

for the understanding of school as a socializing agent. In P. Mussen et al (eds.)
*Trends and issues in developmental psy-
chology*. New York: Holt, Rinehart and
Winston, 1969, 154–181.

26. Horowitz, F. D., and L. Y. Paden. The effectiveness of environmental intervention programs. In B. M. Caldwell and
H. Ricciuti. (eds.) *Review of Child Development Research, Vol. III* (in press).

27. Hoy, W. K., and J. B. Applebury. Teacher-
principal relationships in "humanistic"
and "custodial" elementary schools.
Journal of Experimental Education, 1970,
39, 27–31.

28. Lambert, W. W., L. M. Triandis, and M.
Wolf. Some correlates of beliefs in the
malevolence and benevolence of super-
natural being: A cross-societal study.
*Journal of Abnormal and Social Psychol-
ogy*, 1959, *58*, 162–169.

29. Lang, B. Critique of Soares and Soares.
Self-perceptions of culturally disadvantaged children. *American Educational Research Journal*, 1969, *6*, 710–711.

30. Lynn, D. *Parental and sex role identification*.
Berkeley, Calif.: McCutchan, 1969.

31. Maccoby, E. E. (ed.). *The development of sex
differences*. Stanford, Calif.: Stanford
University Press, 1966.

32. McCandless, B. R. *Adolescents: Behavior
and development*. Hinsdale, Ill.: Dryden,
1970.

33. McCandless, B. R. *Children: Behavior and
development*. New York: Holt, Rinehart
and Winston, 1967.

34. McCandless, B. R., A. Roberts, and T.
Starnes. Aptitude, standard achievement, and teacher marks variation by
sex, race, and social class. *Journal of
Educational Psychology*, 1972, *63*, 153–
159.

35. McClelland, D. *The achieving society*.
Princeton, N. J.: Van Nostrand, 1961.

36. McDill, E. L., E. D. Meyers, Jr., and L. C.
Rigsby. Institutional effects on the academic behavior of high school students.
Sociology of Education, 1967, *40*, 181–
182.

37. McDill, E. L., L. C. Rigsby, and E. D.

Meyers, Jr. Educational climates of high
schools: Their effects and sources.
American Journal of Sociology, 1969, *74*,
567–586.

38. Medinnus, G. R., and R. C. Johnson. *Child
and adolescent psychology*. New York:
Wiley, 1969.

39. Miller, D., and G. Swanson. *The changing
American family*. New York: Wiley, 1958.

40. Miller, G. W. Factors in school achievement
and social class. *Journal of Educational
Psychology*, 1970, *61*, 260–269.

41. Minuchin, P. *The psychological impact of
school experience*. New York: Basic
Books, 1969.

42. Mischel, W., and H. Mischel. The nature
and development of psychological sex
differences. In G. Lesser (ed.) *Psychology
and educational practice*. Glenview, Ill.:
Scott, Foresman, 1971, 357–379.

43. Mussen, P. H. (ed.). *Carmichael's manual of
child psychology*. New York: Wiley,
1970. Part I. *Biological basis of development*, 1–283.

44. Rodgers, R., U. Bronfenbrenner, and E. C.
Devereaux, Jr. Standards of social behavior among school children in four
cultures. *International Journal of Psychology*, 1968, *3*, 31–41.

45. Rosenkrantz, P., S. Vogel, H. Bee, I. Broverman, and D. M. Broverman. Sex-role
stereotypes and self-concepts in college
students. *Journal of Consulting and Clinical Psychology*, 1968, *32*, 287–295.

46. Schooler, C. Birth after effects: Not here,
not now! *Psychological Bulletin*, 1972,
161–175.

47. Soares, A. T., and L. M. Soares. Self perception of culturally disadvantaged children. *American Educational Research
Journal*, 1969, *6*, 31–45.

48. Stark, R., and C. Y. Glock. Will ethics be
the death of Christianity? *Trans-action*,
1968, *5* (No. 7, June), 7–14.

49. Sutton-Smith, B. Developmental laws and
the experimentalist's ontology. *Merrill-
Palmer Quarterly*, 1970, *16*, 253–259.

50. Thompson, G. G. *Child psychology*. Boston:
Houghton-Mifflin, 1962.

51. Tyler, L. E. *The psychology of human differ-*

ences (3rd ed.). New York: Appleton, 1965.

52. Vogel, S. R., I. K. Broverman, D. M. Broverman, F. Clarkson, and P. S. Rosenkrantz. Maternal employment and perception of sex-role stereotypes. *Developmental Psychology,* 1970, *3,* 384–391.

53. Walberg, H. J., and G. J. Anderson. Classroom climate and individual learning. *Journal of Educational Psychology,* 1968, *59,* 414–419.

54. Warner, W. L., M. Meeker, and K. Eells. *Social class in America.* Chicago: Science Research Associates, 1949.

55. Warren, J. Birth order and social behavior. *Psychological Bulletin,* 1966, *65,* 38–49.

56. Weber, M. *The Protestant ethic and the spirit of capitalism.* Trans. by T. Parsons. New York: Scribner, 1958.

57. Whiting, J. M. W., *et al.* The learning of values. In E. Vogt and E. Albert (eds.) *Peoples of Rimrock.* Cambridge, Mass.: Harvard University Press, 1966.

58. Zigler, E. Social class and the socialization process. *Review of Educational Research,* 1970, *40,* 87–110.

2 Ways of Viewing Human Development

In a book such as this, why should a separate chapter be devoted to a topic as abstract and apparently impractical as ways of viewing human development? The authors have at least two reasons. First, to a considerable degree, the way a person looks at things determines what he finds out about them, what conclusions he draws, and how valid and useful his conclusions are. The practical implications that follow can be enormous. For example, consider the implications resulting from different views of metropolitan planning: the view taken by a highway engineer in contrast to that of an ecologist; or, the view of automobile design taken by a style-conscious body designer and that by a safety-oriented Ralph Nader.

So it is with different ways of looking at human development. A person values and looks for different things; he sees children, youth, and adults from different theoretical perspectives; he studies different phenomena, often seeks different goals, and is likely to reach different conclusions depending upon the way he looks at developmental patterns. These different perspectives and conclusions, in turn, often result in different implications for human development and education.

A second reason for exploring different views of development concerns the belief that it is valuable for the student to examine carefully his own perspective on development, or, if he does not have a clear perspective, to strive to establish one. The student can often best examine his perspective or can establish one by carefully considering the perspectives created by professional psychologists whose life work is the study of development and behavior. In the process of establishing or examining one's own view of development and behavior, it usually becomes necessary to make his assumptions and beliefs explicit, consider their validity, and systematize his observations of children and youth. Such actions, the authors believe, can themselves be educational.

45

Certainly they are essential for those who practice the behavioral sciences and the helping professions. This idea is appropriately summarized by the following quote.

Yet, of course, all . . . are theorists. They differ not in whether they use theory, but in the degree to which they are aware of the theory they use. The choice before the man in the street and the research worker alike is not whether to theorize, but whether to articulate this theory, to make it explicit, to get it out in the open where he can examine it. Implicit theories — of personality, of learning (of development), and indeed of teaching — are used by all of us in our everyday affairs. Often such theories take the form of old sayings, proverbs, slogans, the unquestioned wisdom of the race. The scientist on the other hand explicates his theory. (10, pp. 94–95).

The authors do not wish to imply that the readers all become scientists, only that they become more aware of both formal and informal, or personal, psychological theory. Equally important, however, is the recognition that psychologists, no matter how dedicated to scientific objectivity, neither conduct research nor theorize in a social vacuum. Psychologists, like anyone else, are selective and make value judgments about what they do. It is hoped that this and subsequent chapters serve to illustrate this important point.

In this chapter, four broadly defined approaches to human development and behavior are discussed: humanistic, behaviorist, cognitive-developmental, and psychodynamic. For each approach, the attempt is made to provide an appropriate definition, to describe its general characteristics and implications, and to offer some of the authors' reactions.

HUMANISTIC PSYCHOLOGY

Definition

The central tenet or core feature of humanistic psychology is that it "accords man a measure of dignity and excellence consistent with his high evolutionary status and accomplishments." (19, p. 180) Coupled with this core goal, to study the best in man, humanistic psychologists stress affection for mankind, respect for individuality, and a passionate interest in people's behavior as human beings. As a prominent spokesman for humanism in psychology has put it: "There should be a stout affection for human beings coupled with a consuming interest in their emotions and evaluations, their imaginations and beliefs, their purposes and plans, their endeavours, failures, and achievements." (22, p. 5)

In short, humanistic psychologists are primarily concerned with man's potential, his uniqueness and dignity, behavior that is singularly human, and methods of study based on their affection for and joy in human nature. Man's higher "needs" — justice, order, and love — and his pursuit of intrinsic and ultimate values of perfection, goodness, beauty, and truth are taken as realities for study (20).

Characteristics of Humanistic Psychology

As though they were the spokes of a wheel around this core definition, a number of related characteristics of humanistic psychology can be distinguished (19). First, according to this view, man's behavior reflects more the operation of internal forces, or self-initiating tendencies, than the influence of external factors. The authors believe that to humanistic psychologists this means that individuals are basically self-determining, rational, and active in shaping their own growth and environments, rather than passive reactors to the conditions of their upbringing and the social forces that impinge upon them. This idea is similar to the religious and philosophical notion of free will, and is also related to the points made in Chapter 1 about children and youth as factors in their own development.

A second, related feature of the humanistic approach concerns the idea that conscious rationality, intent, and decision making characterize human behavior more than does the irrationality of uncontrollable, unconscious impulses. In other words, humanistic psychologists argue that human beings, even to some degree in early childhood and more fully in youth and adulthood, are thinkers and active planners; that their lives are more a reflection of thinking and planning than of their emotions, impulses, or instinctual makeup. It is true, however, that many humanistic psychologists accentuate the interaction of conscious rationality and emotionality, especially in regard to such "peak experiences" as insight, wonderment, or awe about a person's self or his experience. In fact, the role of "emotional–cognitive flashes" concerning intuition, hunches, new ways of experiencing, and understanding the self is highly valued for purposes of personal growth (20).

These first two characteristics of humanistic psychology are further illumined by the words of an exemplary protagonist of this approach. This statement also illustrates how democratic philosophy is intertwined with humanism.

Up to now the "behavioral sciences," including psychology, have not provided us with a picture of man capable of creating or living in a democracy. . . . They have delivered into our hands a psychology of an "empty organism," pushed by drives and molded by environmental circumstance. . . . But the theory of democracy requires also that man possess a measure of rationality, a portion of freedom, a generic conscience, propriate ideals, and unique value. (1, p. 100).

A third, related emphasis within humanistic psychology is that placed on man's uniqueness, both as an individual and as a species. To most humanistic psychologists, little is to be gained for an understanding of man by studying the white rat, the pigeon, or even the non-human primate. Indeed, the typical humanistic psychologist is likely to ask, "Is psychology the study of laboratory animals?" Thus, the preferred orientation, again, is man. If man is to be understood, his uniqueness and wholeness must be defined and used as a springboard for psychological study.

Humanistic psychologists are much more likely to stress the psychology of normality and excellence than they are to concentrate on abnormality and pathology. Theirs is a psychology of positive growth, prosocial rather than antisocial behavior, and "self-actualization" rather than depression and defeat. Phenomena of curiosity, creativity, imagination, and subjective experience intrigue them, although they often show a lively concern for social and cultural forces that debase human beings or otherwise prevent people from reaching their fullest potentials. This idea is expressed by the following quote:

Some theories of becoming are based largely upon the behavior of sick and anxious people or upon the antics of captive and desperate rats. Fewer theories have derived from the study of healthy human beings, those who strive not to preserve life as to make it worth living. Thus we find today many studies of criminals, few of law-abiders; many of fear, few of courage; more on hostility than on affiliation; much on the blindness in man, little on his vision; much on his past, little on his outreaching into the future. (1, p. 18).

A fourth major aspect of humanistic psychology is its accent on man's future orientation, his continuing sense of purpose, and his tendency toward psychological growth. This means that psychological growth, not decay, may well go on through maturity and until death and that, given the chance, man continues to grow toward successively higher levels of personal integration. This accent on successive growth implies that man is continually involved in the process of discovering his true self—defining his true sense of being and learning how to be fully human (20). Discovering both one's humanness and one's "specieshood" is implied by this aspect of humanism.

A comment on the role of motivation in development is pertinent in connection with this accent on continuing growth. To some degree, many psychologists of other persuasions (notably the behaviorist and the psychodynamic) embrace the classical notion of homeostasis in learning or development. According to one version of classical homeostatic theory, organisms (including human beings of all ages) are rewarded by or reinforced for tension that occurs because of some need, since they find it satisfying to have tension reduced. In this way, one can maintain or return to a physical or a psychological "balance" that consists of a relatively low level of organismic tension. But, in line with their emphasis on successive growth and achievement of higher levels of personal integration, humanistic psychologists vigorously reject such a notion of homeostasis. Ideas that are logically humanistic in source have led to theory and

research indicating that infants, children, youth, and adults are attracted by the novel, that they are curious and exploratory "by nature," that they prefer complexity to simplicity, that they like to be surprised, and that boredom (lack of sufficient stimulation) is unpleasant, even punishing. The humanists take such data to indicate that man is a seeker of stimulation, not simply one who strives to reduce tension. It is further argued that the more stimulus input an infant, a child, or a youth receives (short of being overwhelmed), the more he will demand and thus the more likely he will become an effective and knowledgeable force in shaping his own development.

In addition to the four major features of humanistic psychology just discussed, still other characteristics can be briefly noted. For example, more than in most other psychologies, humanistic psychology stresses the "spirit of man" and his brotherhood with all men. The development of an ability for self-understanding and the understanding of others, described as mankind's shared problem, is basic to this spirit of brotherhood.

Humanists have little patience for notions of predeterminism, as has been made clear earlier in this section, but take a lively interest in and maintain a strong advocacy for joy. Many developmental psychologists, including the authors (see text of Part I), take joy in children and youth as delightful beings, quite over and above (and perhaps even more importantly than) their fascination and value as subjects of study.

Humanistic psychologists are quite tolerant of ambiguity (that is, things do not have to be crystal clear and precisely measurable before they will agree to consider and study them). It is true of most humanistic psychologists that they do not see "much value in the behavioristic type of situational analysis . . . because it tends to oversimplify the subtlety and complexity of human interaction with the environment and restricts the range of stimulus meaning considered." (19, p. 166)

Implicit in what has been said earlier in this section is that humanistic psychologists are keenly interested in the study of the experience of the individual human being — in the study of the single, unique case. This approach is in contrast to most other schools of psychology (except some of the traditional and clinically oriented dynamic psychologists). The more usual psychological approach is to study large numbers of people, reducing data to what is true for the group and neglecting the individual. The study of the unique, single case is often termed the *idiographic* approach; the study of large groups, and statistical treatment of the data in terms of means, ranges, variances (heterogeneity or homogeneity), significant differences between experimental and control groups, and so on, is often called the *nomothetic* approach. While many humanistic psychologists are interested in group differences, they are more likely than most psychologists to study the single case or the person or two who do not fit with the group tendency. Individual differences, in other words, intrigue most humanistic psychologists.

From the preceding two points (tolerance of ambiguity and interest in the uniqueness of the individual), it follows that humanistic psychologists will be much more tolerant of subjective, clinical data than, for example, will the behaviorists and the cognitivists (see the following two sections of this chapter). Nor will the humanistic psychologists be so much concerned with the precision of their methods as they will be with the viability and

social importance of their ideas about growth and development.

Finally, implicit in much of what has been said in this section of the chapter, humanistic psychologists are an optimistic lot. They are also interested essentially in behavior that has important life significance and broad, long-term implications for personal experience. As such, it is tempting to link humanistic psychology with Rousseauian philosophy, a philosophy based on the assumption that natural man is good, is capable of self-direction, and is invested with an innate sense of freedom (12). To Rousseau can be traced the romanticism of the nineteenth century and beyond — a romanticism accompanied by devotion to nature, proud individualism, and obsession with liberty, freedom, and the rights of man. The pessimism and cynicism about man frequently attributed to other psychological perspectives, especially psychoanalysis, is not apparent in the writings of humanistic psychologists. Optimism bordering on idealism pervades these writings, owing in large part to the conviction that normal man and competence are the natural topics for psychological study.

Implications of a Humanistic View of Human Development

It seems appropriate, and certainly plausible and defensible, to propose a set of implications about how human development is viewed under the perspective of humanistic psychology.

1. A major motive for the study of human development at all ages is the pleasure, even the joy, the psychologist derives from such study. Accordingly, the principal orientation for humanistic study of development is normality, health, and

positive well-being (versus pathology). For example, creativity is viewed as a natural condition of man in his healthy state of psychological development. But humanistic psychologists are likely to neglect what can be learned from the study of distorted development (for example, from the study of the retarded, the delinquent, the emotionally disturbed, the organically impaired) or from the study of nonhuman organisms. Consequently, such humanists arbitrarily limit or close off possible sources of understanding the broad spectrum of human development.

2. Within humanistic psychology, emphasis is placed on the individual's potential for constructive growth and ever higher levels of personal and social integration. A belief in man's power to develop his innate potential underlies this emphasis. No person, however unpromising he may appear, is written off in advance. It is possible that the concern for ultimate, longer term development may result in some neglect of the here and now. However, there undoubtedly is agreement among the humanists about the futurity issue (see Concluding Remarks).

3. The humanists express a strong interest in the *unique individual* of whatever age, with less emphasis being placed on the group or the average. Uniqueness and honesty in modes of expressing internal growth forces are encouraged and respected.

4. Humanistic psychologists focus on behavior and traits that are "big and important," such as *self-actualization*, *creative self-awareness*, and *constructive growth tendencies*. Unfortunately, these global terms are often not well defined, a fact that may lead to communication and research difficulties. Related to such ab-

sence of precision is the idea that, as in psychoanalysis, behavior is best understood in relation to an individual's feelings, fears, and motivations at any given moment. In practice, this leads to a preoccupation with *affect* (versus cognition), despite the strong theoretical concern for man's rationality.

5. Humanistic psychologists express a strong concern for ethics and values. Values that promote the "good life" as perceived by humanists (personal freedom, for example) are endorsed. Values that it is believed may "hurt" people (competition for status, for example) are usually rejected. Openness, nonauthoritarianism, autonomy, and freedom from anxiety are examples of other valued concepts of behavior. Some intolerance of any other view of what human beings should be often accompanies this concern.

6. Humanistic psychology leads to an interest in human welfare, with an attendant strong concern for understanding and correcting environmental forces and conditions that distort or impede constructive growth. This is often extended to include efforts to eliminate allegedly intrusive educational practices and restrictive child-rearing practices. Many humanistic psychologists may even be preoccupied with dramatic, sometimes revolutionary, means for achieving ideal ends—liberation movements, free schools, encounter groups, and the like. Occasionally this may reflect impulsiveness, expediency, opportunism, or simply a popularistic orientation to psychological study.

7. This flair within humanistic psychology for generalized ideals, global human traits, and social reform may be accompanied by a neglect or even a rejection of taut, carefully specified methods of studying human behavior and of those

who develop and evaluate programs for improving individual psychological functioning. Some humanistic psychologists show a rather cavalier approach to the scientific method, for example, and are impatient with or indifferent to the slow, tedious, painstaking process of making bit-by-bit additions to scientific knowledge.

8. This final point is perhaps not so much an implication as it is a question: "Where do most humanistic psychologists stand today in relation to the issue of the *being* (and/or?) *becoming* person?" Traditionally, humanistic psychologists have been preoccupied with long-range goals, plans, and ever higher levels of personal–social integration. For example, G. W. Allport's classic work is titled *Becoming: Basic Considerations for a Psychology of Personality*. A central theme of "becoming" is that man continually strives for unattainable goals in the sense that he is never completely fulfilled or never completely achieves unity of purpose.

The current humanistic position about *being* is perhaps less clear. For the authors, the psychology of *being* is as important in today's complex and harried world as the psychology of *becoming*. There are times in all lives (probably some time during each day, lifelong) when simply enjoying the here and now seems vital if the human condition is to be sound and happy. Moreover, it is plausible to argue that the best indication of *becoming* human at later ages is the degree of *being* human at earlier ages. There are indications that humanistic psychologists are now concerned with being. For example, two of the most prominent, Carl Rogers and the late Abraham Maslow, have had close affiliations with Esalen, one of the leading groups working to help people

simply *be* more happily, and with concurrent interests in happy, easy interpersonal relationships and group sensitivity.

Concluding Remarks

It should be obvious by now what the authors' judgment of humanistic psychology as it bears on human development is: They would not care to do without a healthy infusion of humanism. It makes the study of human development more fun, it induces the enjoyment of each infant, child, or youth worked with or studied; it leads to a healthy regard for and appreciation of individual differences; and it motivates the pursuit of important rather than trivial issues to think about, organize, and study.

However, the authors would not like to let a too blithe humanism interfere with scrupulous empiricism and precise research methods, nor let it lead them to careless analysis of concepts and development of definitions. They do not wish humanism to cut them off from sources of knowledge about development that come from the deviant, the pathological, and the nonhuman subject of study and concern. Nor do they desire an urgent humanistic position to lead to shortsighted "remedial" action or to expediency. But the humanist's emphasis on study of the *whole person*, how man seeks fulfillment through love and creative accomplishment, and the conflicts he experiences along the way (see Chapter 10) make humanistic psychology an appealing perspective on human development, especially in societies condemned as dehumanizing.

The points just made about humanism are well illustrated in the summary and brief discussion of a research study (23) with strongly humanist goals (see Example 2.1).

2.1 Humanistic Influences: The Study of Prosocial Behavior

The topic of the paper summarized here "Honesty and Altruism among Pre-adolescents," fits well with the goals of humanistic psychology. The purposes are positive, not negative; the authors investigate prosocial, not antisocial, behaviors; and they are concerned with health, not disease. The issues are gutsy and socially relevant. The methods are those of the pragmatist. The authors do not, however, represent the extreme humanist approach, since they adopt a deterministic point of view and their method is empirical, not clinical. Their assumption is that the foundation and future direction of honesty and altruism are set in early childhood by way of child-rearing methods. Thus, the authors take the determinist history-of-the-organism position that, as is seen in Chapter 3, is also held by behavioristic and psychodynamic psychologists.

Forty-six boys and forty-nine girls were studied. All were sixth-graders from California public schools, all were white, and most were from lower-middle-class background.

The subjects' popularity within their classrooms was determined, and tests were run to measure their self concepts, their altruism or generosity, and their resistance to temptation (their refusal to cheat in order to gain a prize when, as far as they knew, it was entirely safe to cheat). Finally, mothers were interviewed about, and made semiformal evaluations of, their children. The mothers also provided information about their child-rearing practices.

Results of this study are complex. Briefly, honest and altruistic girls were likely to come from homes where there was a warm, intimate interaction with their mothers, and such girls were likely to be high in self-esteem. On the other hand, boys who showed themselves honest in the "play" situation more often came from homes where their relations with their parents were not gratifying. Such boys were not very popular with their peers; and the honest boys did not possess high self-esteem. The boy cheaters, as a group, were high in initiative and independence. The altruistic (unselfish) boy was likely to have high ego strength (personal self-assurance and "toughness," or resistance to stress).

Recommended Readings for the Humanist Perspective

Allport, G. W. *Becoming: Basic considerations for a psychology of personality*. New Haven, Conn.: Yale University Press, 1955.

Bugental, J., (ed.). *Challenges of humanistic psychology*. New York: McGraw-Hill, 1967.

Buhler, C., and M. Allen. *Introduction into humanistic psychology*. Belmont, Calif.: Brooks/Cole, 1971.

Combs, A. W., (ed.). *Perceiving, behaving, becoming*. Washington, D.C.: Association for Supervision and Curriculum Development, National Education Association, 1962.

Hamachek, D. E., (ed.). *The self in growth, teaching, and learning*. Englewood Cliffs, N. J.: Prentice-Hall, 1965.

Hamachek, D. E. *Encounters with self*. New York: Holt, Rinehart and Winston, 1970.

Maslow, A. *Toward a psychology of being* (rev. ed.). Princeton, N. J.: Van Nostrand, 1968.

May, R. *Love and will*. New York: Norton, 1969.

Murray, H. A. Preparations for the scaffold of a comprehensive system. In S. Koch (ed.), *Psychology: A study of a science* (Vol. 3). New York: McGraw-Hill, 1959.

Rogers, C. *On becoming a person*. Boston: Houghton-Mifflin, 1961.

Severin, F., (ed.). *Humanistic viewpoints in psychology*. New York: McGraw-Hill, 1965.

THE BEHAVIORIST POINT OF VIEW

Definition

According to current psychological thought, one can consider himself a behaviorist "if he believes psychology to be the study of observable behavior and that the methods employed are the methods of science, namely, controlled systematic observation including experimentation. . . . The behaviorist identifies himself with carefully controlled and executed experiments in which the stimulus variables are appropriately manipulated, exact controls are executed, and the resulting behavior can be accurately observed and measured" (18, p. 258).

The roots of behaviorism in American psychology extend to John Watson. Watson (33, 34) was instrumental in turning psychology away from "mentalism" (theories involving propositions or assumptions about the mind not subject to open verification through objective ob-

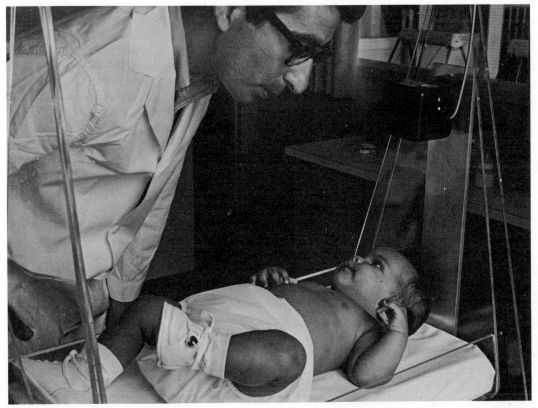

This photograph illustrates the experimental approach, with all data being public, that is the core of the behaviorist approach to human development. Professor Lewis P. Lipsitt is shown doing two things—checking the well-being of his infant subject and making sure his apparatus is working. The apparatus is designed to test the effects on quieting of different rates of rocking. (Courtesy of Professor Lewis P. Lipsitt and the Child Study Center, Walter S. Hunter Laboratory of Psychology, Brown University.)

servation) and philosophy. In so doing, he championed the idea that psychology should be a science dealing only with natural events (human and animal behavior) whose occurrence can be observed and empirically stated. Watson also clung stoutly to the scientific principle that psychology and its data were public, not private, endeavors.

Moreover, Watson maintained that within psychology, as within all science, the ultimate objective is prediction and control. Again, in psychology behavior is the subject of prediction and control. This objective is not without its philosophical issue, however, as seen in Chapter 3. Finally, Watson and his followers agreed that the name of the game in behaviorism, as in all science, is that the scientific or technical language employed be designed to achieve unambiguous communication among those who work in the field (28, 29).

Characteristics of Behaviorism as a Way of Viewing Human Development

As in humanistic psychology, a number of characteristics distinguish behaviorism from other major approaches to human development. But also like humanistic psychology, "suborientations" exist within the behavioristic framework. That is, even though behaviorists share many convictions in general, they differ among themselves about certain aspects of psychological study. These differences range, for example, from the extent to which inference is involved in explaining behavior to the exact nature of data sought. However, the authors consider the following characteristics generally applicable to behaviorism, omitting details and disputes within behaviorism itself.

Perhaps the principle about which behaviorists most closely agree is that, to an overwhelming extent, human behavior is learned. It changes primarily as a result of experiences within the environment. Learning has already been defined (Chapter 1). The following quote from a representative behavioristic view of development (3, pp. 20–21) further illustrates this strong learning emphasis:

. . . psychological development refers to progressive changes in the behavior of a biologically changing organism in response to a succession of environmental events which, for the most part, are products of the culture. Progressive changes in behavior may take many forms simultaneously: (1) changes in terms of the *number of responses to the same object.* When presented with a cube, a young infant will most likely put it in his mouth. Later he may also throw it on the floor, put it in a box, and stack it on other cubes, etc. (2) Changes may be increases in the *length of the sequence of behavior* (chains) which defines the ultimate response. The tinkle of a bell may produce a turning of the infant's head toward the object. Later the same stimulus will bring about head turning, grasping, and bringing-to-the-mouth behavior. (3) Progressive changes may be increases in the *number of other responses in operation* at the same time. In the initial stages of walking, practically all the child's responses are engaged. Later he walks with ease and at the same time talks and uses his hands effectively to do other things, as in fielding a baseball. (4) Developmental behavior changes also include *increases in skill* (shaping of the topography) in any of the behaviors described above. Compare, for example, the awkward gait of a two-year-old and the smooth strides of a six-year-old.

A second characteristic of behaviorists is their preoccupation with precise methods, their clear behavioral and situational definitions of concepts, and their insistence that a concept has no meaning unless it can be anchored to an operation. The concept *dependency*, for example, is at a very high level of abstraction. A behaviorist, if he uses the concept at all (and these days many do) ties it carefully to behavior. For example, dependency in a 3-year-old may be defined in terms of (1) frequency of his attempts per unit of time to sit on his mother's lap when he is in a strange situation; (2) frequency per unit of time that he wishes to hold the hand of the responsible adult in specified situations; (3) duration of crying when he is separated from caregivers; and so on. Note that both the *situations* and the behavior are defined so that observers possess clear ground rules for their observations. Thus two or more different observers, operating according to these situational and behavioral definitions, can achieve perfect or near-perfect agreement between each other about how many dependent behaviors occurred of each kind and in each situation; finally, the data are gathered in such a way that an indication of frequency (or "amount") can be made quantitatively and then subjected to statistical treatment. It follows from this illustration that behaviorists are empiricists. "The facts, ma'am, and only the facts." They depend first on experience *and* experiment and only then on theory and conjecture, often reluctantly and sometimes little or not at all.

Third, behaviorists are likely to concentrate on comparatively simple situations and simple behaviors. Their belief is that only situations and behavior that can be precisely manipulated experimentally will in the long run lead to the goals of prediction and control that behaviorists espouse. Understanding, prediction, and control will be most economically achieved by working from the simple to the complex. Behaviorists also believe that the laws and interrelations they find while working with simple phenomena will also apply to more complex phenomena (2).

Fourth, even as behaviorists are prone to work with simple rather than complex phenomena, they are also given to working in laboratory situations where they (typically) manipulate one variable at a time to see what occurs, rather than carry out their studies in the natural environment with all its complexity and unpredictability. We must recognize, however, that in recent years "applied behaviorism" has become increasingly popular. That is, many behaviorists have taken up the study of children in applied settings, especially the school.

Fifth, for much the same reasons (simplicity and feasibility of control), many behaviorists prefer to work with animals rather than human beings. This traditional pattern has changed much in recent years, however. Many behaviorists today are intently involved in working with human subjects of all ages. Many have also moved toward involvement with complex, "real life" phenomena such as language learning and the treatment of severe behavior disorders.

A sixth and closely related characteristic is the idea that behaviorists are often more interested in the usefulness of their data for advancing the state of psychological *science* than they are in applying their findings to pressing social problems. Historically, the behaviorist has been happiest, not when he has helped a child to read, but when he has discovered an empirical law or has formulated a more comprehensive theory that serves to integrate several empirical laws. Exceptions to this value, of course, are becoming more numerous; many "new wave" behaviorists are intent upon demonstrating the relevance of scientific concepts of behavior and development for society's needs (5).

Seventh, almost all behaviorists exhibit a burning interest in the learning history of the organism with which they are working, whether it be a pigeon or a preschooler. It is an article of faith with behaviorists that the behavior of every organism at a given time depends partly on the environmental context in which it occurs and partly on the organism's learning history. Of particular interest is a person's history of *reinforcement*. Simply stated, this means the individual's past experience with rewards and punishments, including the frequency and consistency with which given behaviors have been rewarded and/or punished (or ignored).

It is instructive to pause here in order to identify the variables in which most behaviorists are interested. These variables can be broken down into three categories (30, pp. 9, 10):

R (Response) variables: Overt, observable behavior.

S (Stimulus) variables: The properties in the environment that affect behavior. More formally, stimulus variables are defined as "events in the social or physical environment of the organism that are contemporaneous with the behavior being observed or that have occurred in the past" (30, p. 9).

O (Organismic) variables: Briefly, the state of the organism. This concept includes anatomical and physiological properties.

In view of the three major variables that the behaviorists study, the seventh characteristic of behaviorism raises two points: (1) How does one go about handling the reinforcement history of the organism conceptually so it can be related to the situation in which behavior occurs? (2) How does one understand apparently contradictory or erratic behaviors in the same individual as he moves from one situation to another?

In the first instance—reconstructing reinforcement history in order to predict current behavior—research exists indicating that as a group children from poor families are more harshly disciplined than children from advantaged families. If this is true, it follows that a sharper experimental manipulation of the here and now will be required to change or affect the behavior of poor children than will be required for advantaged children. Such predictions have been made, tested, and supported (24).

The situational context also affects behavior in what seem to be unpredictable ways. The authors have seen adolescent boys who are tough, swaggering, and delinquent in the open society and in the presence of their peers, but who, placed in a situation with friendly adult males, often become passive, uncertain, conforming, and dependent. Similarly, an independent, autonomous little girl at home may, in strange surroundings, become a thumbsucking, reticent child, glued to her mother's skirt. Or, children who have been subjected to severe parental discipline during their upbringing may be savagely aggressive with their peers when unsupervised, yet behave with obedient decorum in the presence of effective authority figures. These changes in behavior from one setting to another seem incongruous unless one considers reinforcement history, as well as the cues (stimuli) and reinforcements present in these different settings for behavior.

This brings us to consider here an eighth and final characteristic of behaviorists: Behaviorists are more interested in general laws than in individual differences. Behaviorists do not deny the importance of individual differences, but

The behavioristic tradition has fostered developmental interpretations that have three primary emphases—environmental (stimulating) events, observable behaviors (seen as imitation in this scene), and the present physical state of the person. (Photo by Hella Hammid)

not many devote much attention to such differences. In other words, the behaviorist typically searches for generalizations, principles, and "laws" that are universally applicable to behavior. This, it will be recalled, is in sharp contrast to the humanistic perspective in which a lively interest is taken in the individual case. When behaviorists *do* deal with individual differences, they bring in the O variables, such as the reinforcement history of the individual and his present state—for example, excitement or hypoglycemia (low blood sugar). It should be further noted, however, that certain outgrowths of behavioristic psychology—programmed learning and other technological advances in education—are oriented toward the individual. That is, these techniques are designed primarily to promote individualization in instruction.

Implications of a Behaviorist View of Human Development

Given the preceding features of behaviorism, the authors wish again to suggest some implications for the student of development who chooses to view behavior from this perspective. It is recognized, of course, that a certain amount of risk is involved in drawing implications and that shades of meaning may not be considered in the same way by other authors.

1. Since learning is the preeminent concern within behaviorism, one taking a behaviorist perspective is vitally concerned with how learning occurs, including the conditions that promote and interfere with it. This concern encompasses all kinds of learning, from the comparatively simple pecking behavior of pigeons to the complexities of formal academic learning. To study the learning process and the conditions affecting it leads to a focus on environmental influences (patterns of reinforcement and models of behavior for imitation learning, for example). It is, after all, the environment that is most subject to manipulation or change; the individual's biology generally is not. For any individual's behavior, whether considered "good" or "bad," the environment is essentially the unit for analysis. Just as the environment can produce desirable behavior, so can it produce undesirable behavior.

2. A closely related point for behaviorists is that all behavior is lawful. If all the facts were or could be known, all behavior could be understood, predicted, and controlled. This means that the behaviorist point of view about behavior is deterministic. It then follows that man is not a free agent. On logical grounds, the behaviorist is compelled to reject the philosophical and religious notion of free will. Man *is* controlled by the forces in his environment. The issue involves seeking an understanding of *how* man is controlled and how control can be exercised for positive ends. For such reasons, many think of behavioristic psychology as mechanistic and devoid of idealism.

3. Behaviorists take a strict view of the concept of science. In general, they believe that if something is not observable, it is not a matter for science and cannot (perhaps should not) be studied. Accompanying this view is a strong preference for meticulousness and precision in research methodology and definitions of terms. This preference may lead to intolerance of the humanists, for example, and of those who study relatively ineffable concepts such as imagination, imagery, the creative process, or loosely defined aspects of personality development. Accordingly, the behaviorist's interest is a child's behavior—what he *does*—not what may

exist "under the surface." In short, behaviorists are data bound and may not give the role to "the dream and the spirit" that many would like. The tendency to reduce the study of human development to its lowest common denominator and to avoid "gutsy" issues because of their lack of conceptual clarity has also resulted in criticism of behaviorists. For example, behaviorists are often indicted for atomism (failure to consider meaningful wholes or important, large segments of behavior) and for being limited, if not simplistic, in their approach to human development.

4. Perhaps because behaviorism is deterministic and demands that clarity and precision prevail in research, behaviorists are likely to be attracted to formal, structured, didactic training approaches to human development and education. Such approaches can be defined and are subject to manipulation so that their effects can be observed. Thoroughness, efficiency, and clarity prevail, although occasionally at the expense of excitation or inspiration. Some argue that behaviorists have too strong a concern for control and shaping of behavior toward predetermined outcomes as opposed to freedom and self-determination. On the other hand, behaviorists who work in applied settings often provide effective means for achieving important behavioral goals where other approaches have failed. This is notably the case in the schools and institutions for the retarded and emotionally disturbed.

5. While the humanistic perspective applies mainly to corner B (personal–social) in the model of development advanced in Chapter 1, it seems that a behavioristic approach offers greater promise in understanding corner A (academic–cognitive–achievement).

6. Since understanding leads to prediction and control, behaviorism may provide a great thrust forward in developing competence of an Apollonian nature among human beings (by Apollonian is meant thinking, cognizing, symbolic, achieving, and appreciating man). Competence is essential (although not sufficient) for a satisfactory, workable life in United States culture.

If behaviorism can help to promote competence while at the same time not interfering with happiness (a difficult word to define), then behaviorism can make tremendous mental health as well as competence development contributions to the science guidance of human development. However, these contributions will be made by the interaction of the behaviorist's work in corner A of our triangular schema and not by direct attack on the complex social, personal variables grouped in corner B. Referring to the three short life stories in Chapter 1, it should be noted that James, Judy, and Matthew could not have "made it" if they had not possessed a good behavioral foundation of competence.

Concluding Remarks

The authors have both come from a professional psychology background based on the empirical study of child development and the philosophy of science known as logical positivism. They therefore feel quite at home with the behavioristic tradition, including its strengths and weaknesses. It is their opinion that the contributions of behaviorism to the understanding of behavior and development are both numerous and significant. Most recently, for example, the development of behavioral modification techniques has resulted in a genuine breakthrough in terms of how children, youth, and adults may be better helped to develop effective behaviors, both social and academic. More is said about these techniques and their application throughout the book.

Despite the authors' general affinity for behaviorism in psychology, it is incumbent upon them, briefly but explicitly, to consider the major criticisms levied against this approach to human development. These criticisms can be grouped into at least three categories (18). First, behaviorism is often charged with reflecting a narrow, simple approach to the study of human behavior. That is, by focusing primarily on responses or response patterns that are amenable to empirical investigation, the behaviorists have missed the larger, fuller spectrum of behavior that is uniquely human. It should be understood that this preference is simply an outgrowth of the behaviorists' concept of scientific study. The behaviorists argue, quite legitimately the authors believe, that it makes better sense to start with comparatively simple behaviors that can be objectively studied and over which some control of environmental conditions can be established. In so doing, the relationship between environmental events and behavior may more clearly be observed. Once these relationships are described, one is likely to be equipped for the task of studying successively more complex behavior. Few, if any, human activities are mastered successfully by jumping in at a complex level before having developed necessary background skills. The study of human behavior would seem to be no exception. Admittedly, however, the progress may be slow and frustrating.

A second criticism of behaviorism is that the behaviorist has invested heavily in animal study. Critics often maintain that information derived from such study either is restricted in value or is irrelevant for the understanding of human behavior. In a historical sense, this criticism is at least partly justified. The authors know of no serious student of behaviorism who equates human behavior to animal behavior or who actually believes that information gained from the study of less complex organisms automatically applies to human beings. However, there seems to be no sound reason to deny oneself the possible insights that may come from animal study. If for no other reason, animal studies provide rich hypotheses for the study of human behavior. Even more important is the fact that many basic principles coming from laboratory animal studies hold very precisely for human beings of all ages (18, 27). But behaviorists have a responsibility always to communicate the limitations of data gathered in controlled laboratory and other experimental settings.

The third criticism deals with the behaviorists' concern only for overt behavior and their neglect of covert, internal behavior or "under the skin events" (18). This apparent neglect is further taken to imply that behaviorists do not care about feelings and the like. From the authors' experience, it is not lack of concern for human feelings that prevails among behaviorists. Rather it is a matter of dealing with abstract concepts of behavior that have little, if any, counterpart in objective space and time. For example, in terms of behavior, what do we actually mean when we use terms such as "the unconscious," "feeling of inferiority," "conscience," and the like? Further, are such terms really necessary to describe and explain behavior? If such concepts cannot be defined in behavioral terms, the behaviorist has little recourse but to abandon them for further study or work to objectify them so that scientific methods of study can be applied. It is notable that many behaviorists are now grappling with this task in promising ways (for example, 16, 31).

The oft-criticized emphasis within behaviorism on formal mechanistic determination at the expense of attention to the development of the "the whole, creative, flexible person" can perhaps be tempered by making a clear distinction between *response-dependent reinforcement* and *response-independent reinforcement*. The former involves a classical behavioristic principle: A response followed by a reinforcing stimulus is strengthened in the sense that it is more likely to occur again under similar conditions, whereas a response not followed by a reinforcing stimulus is weakened in the sense that it is less likely to appear again under those conditions. This principle has been taken as a tool for changing behavior. For example, if one wishes a child to continue his "cooperative behavior" in a group setting (sharing, compromising with others), cooperative behaviors should be reinforced. But reinforcement should be *contingent* or *dependent* upon the emission of cooperative responses; reinforcement should not be provided for responses incompatible with cooperative behavior, such as competitive behavior.

The study of response-dependent reinforcement has dominated behaviorism. Few behaviorists have written systematically about response-independent reinforcement (actually, *unplanned reinforcement*). In real life, such reinforcement is almost certainly always given when a child is being "good," or "lovable," or "funny," for example. A more proper distinction may be between *carefully planned* (contingent) and *spontaneous* reinforcement. Reinforcement that is totally response independent may influence the development of bizarre behaviors as sug-

gested by the study of "superstition" in pigeons (27). Here the experimenter reinforced (rewarded with food) his pigeons every fifteen seconds regardless of what they were doing. In other words, whatever the birds were doing at the time of reinforcement was strengthened, with the result that some soon were walking around in circles, some were grooming themselves "compulsively," others were craning their necks oddly, and so on.

Obviously, the authors have no interest in producing such behavior in people and do not mean to imply that response-independent reinforcement should be utilized capriciously. But they have begun to think about the concept of response-independent reinforcement in a way that may have important implications for human relations and may also attenuate the belief among critics of behaviorism that only the cold application of response-dependent reinforcement should prevail in the home and school. Specifically, what the authors are suggesting is this: Regardless of his behavior, each person in a given setting (a sixth-grade class, for example) is reinforced *simply for being himself*. The old nursery school teacher's admonition: "I like *you*, Johnny, but I don't like what you are doing!" expresses the difference between response-independent and response-dependent reinforcement. Regardless of his behavior, the teacher is telling Johnny that he is a valuable person, is of worth in her own eyes, and is not to be downgraded. At the same time, she is telling him that she does not like the particular piece of behavior he has shown. In effect, she is punishing him for this behavior in an informative way, not a very threatening way. She is employing response-dependent reinforcement. Her aim is to keep Johnny secure, happy, certain of his place in her esteem; but at the same time to have him behave differently and in a more socially adaptive way from the way he had been behaving.

Characteristics of response-independent reinforcement, the authors believe, are such behaviors as liking and being interested in children, youth, and people in general; showing a sense of humor and fair play with reference to all three groups; thinking of their rights as well as one's own; urging people of whom one is "in charge" to take part in decisions affecting their welfare; and so on. In short, response-independent reinforcement amounts to a "group climate" that is on the whole pleasant and nonthreatening and in which the individual is permitted to be himself as long as he does not interfere unduly with others and goes along personally with the overall, defined purposes of the group.

Such climates in homes or classrooms, the authors believe, can be quite logically created by behaviorists, can be studied carefully and, the authors speculate, can be effective in improving self concepts, in increasing motivation, in reducing anxiety, in fostering creativity, and in resulting in many things that go along with making good, productive, happy human beings.

In short, the authors are sympathetic to a behaviorist point of view. They consider themselves behaviorists, although they are not purists. The authors know that many behaviorists are limited in their approach to human development, if indeed they attend to it at all. But when they *do* attend to it, the authors consider them to have been a remarkably productive group. Behaviorism is more to the authors' liking than to their disliking, but the authors have tried to give a fair and objective survey of its characteristics and the implications of adopting it as a means of viewing human development. As they

did for humanism, they have chosen an exemplary behaviorist study (4) for summary and comment (see Example 2.2).

2.2 Behavioristic Influences: The Study of Reinforcement

This study is an example of work done by reinforcement theorists of the behaviorist orientation. These theorists applied their laboratory approach to the problem of different reinforcement histories, the sort they believe characterize advantaged children compared with disadvantaged children. The authors believe that advantaged children are better at concept attainment (abstract learning) than disadvantaged children, because their reinforcement histories have been logically consistent; that is, advantaged children have regularly been rewarded for logical, problem-solving sorts of behavior, whereas their disadvantaged peers usually have not.

The authors worked with sixty first-grade children, one half from affluent or advantaged homes, one half from very poor homes. Half the subjects in each group were boys, half were girls. The task to be learned was which of two different figures presented at the same time was the correct one. The figures were a triangle and a circle, and on any given learning trial the colors of both the figures and the backgrounds on which they were presented could be either green or red. The color of the figure and the background was at no time relevant for learning. Regardless of the color of the figure or its background color, the child was supposed to learn simply that the triangle was always right. A penny was given for each correct response.

Both the disadvantaged and the affluent children were divided into three groups of ten children each. The first research treatment group started immediately on learning, and a correct response was always rewarded. In the first forty-two trials the affluent children made a total of fifty-six errors, the disadvantaged children a total of 145. The latter were clearly and significantly inferior to the former.

In the second research condition, both the advantaged and the disadvantaged children, before they were put into the regular learning trials where the correct response was always rewarded, were given six random (erratic) reinforcements that had no relation to whether their choice was correct or incorrect. They were then put into the regular or (logical) learning condition. In the first forty-two trials of consistent reinforcement, the advantaged children averaged 151 errors, the disadvantaged 172 errors; the advantaged children still performed somewhat better, but their degree of superiority had decreased greatly, presumably because of the experience of a random or senseless reinforcement that had been introduced prior to regular learning trials.

In the third research condition, twelve random or erratic reinforcements were given before regular, logical learning conditions were initiated. This number of erratic reinforcements completely wiped out the superiority of the advantaged children. In their first forty-two logically rewarded trials, they averaged 179 errors; in the same number of logically rewarded trials, the disadvantaged first graders averaged 180 errors (no difference between the groups at all).

There were no sex differences revealed. The title of this article, "Chaotic Reinforcement: A Socioeconomic Leveler," embodies the main conclusion to be reached from the study. The study also clearly illustrates the importance behaviorists attach both to the history of the organism (reinforcement history) and to the study of the learning process.

Recommended Reading for the Behaviorist Viewpoint

Baldwin, A. L. *Theories of child development.* New York: Wiley, 1967. (See Chapters 14, 15, and 16.)

Bandura, A. *Principles of behavior modification.* New York: Holt, Rinehart and Winston, 1969.

Berlyne, D. E. Behavior theory as personality theory. In E. F. Borgatta and W. W. Lambert (ed.), *Handbook of personality theory and research.* Chicago: Rand McNally, 1968, 269–290.

Bradfield, R. H. (ed.). *Behavior modification: The human effort.* San Rafael, Calif.: Dimensions Publishing, 1970.

Gewirtz, J. L. Mechanisms of social learning. Some roles of stimulation and behavior in early human development. In D. A. Goslin (ed.), *Handbook of socialization theory and research.* Chicago: Rand McNally, 1969, 57–212.

Langer, J. *Theories of development.* New York: Holt, Rinehart and Winston, 1970. (See Chapter 3.)

Pitts, C. E. (ed.). *Operant conditioning in the classroom.* New York: Crowell, 1971.

Skinner, B. F. *Beyond freedom and dignity.* New York: Knopf, 1971.

Skinner, B. F. *The technology of teaching.* New York: Appleton, 1968.

Staats, A. W. *Child learning, intelligence, and personality.* New York: Holt, Rinehart and Winston, 1971.

THE COGNITIVE-DEVELOPMENTAL VIEW

Definition

Cognitive psychologists devote their attention to human development primarily in matters of intelligence, thinking and logic, language, and competence or efficiency. They may be said to be preoccupied with corner A of the triangular schema described in Chapter 1. Humanists, as stated, concentrate on corner B (personality and social) but many show great interest in corner A. Behaviorists seem to be divided between corners A and B, but seem to pay more attention to A, while, as will be seen, psychodynamic psychologists stress corner B almost exclusively.

The cognitivist way of viewing human development can be approached in several ways. Language is largely a cognitive matter, so the authors could have focused on language in this section. Because language has an immense substantive content, however, Chapter 4 is devoted to language development. Moreover, the topic of language and its development is in the midst of so much lively controversy that it does not seem logical at this time to talk of a linguistic way of viewing human development.

Those who develop theories about and who study intelligence can also be called cognitive psychologists. By tradition the discussion of intelligence is kept as a substantive rather than a methodological matter, and the authors have chosen to treat it as such.

Finally, many behaviorists are also cognitivists in that they are intensely interested in how symbol-using human beings learn and solve problems. Such behaviorists frequently organize their research around concepts that have been originated to account for mechanisms of human thinking and problem solving. Usually, however, their approach is only one of many in the armamentarium of their basic behaviorism.

These are the reasons the authors have chosen to organize this section around the developmental psychology of Jean Piaget, whose approach is largely cognitive. As such, this approach stands in contrast to the approaches championed by behaviorists and other psychologists interested simply in selected aspects of cognition. Piaget is an authentic epistemologist, interested in understanding the origin, nature, methods, and limits of knowledge, particularly with reference to human thought. But he and his students have extended their thinking and research so that the cognitive aspects of moral development and socialization are being brought to our attention (11, 13).

The overview of Piaget's cognitive-developmental perspective represents something of a departure from the format of the preceding two sections. Yet this seems to the authors the best way to convey the distinctive quality of a cognitivist's view of human development. Accordingly, they are not too much concerned with the correctness or incorrectness of this point of view, but rather in the degree to which it is useful in guiding observations and understanding of human development. Piaget's views are especially interesting, because they consist of a theory in the making and are focused on certain aspects of human development that in the past have not been examined extensively by American psychologists, whatever their persuasion. Piaget's way of viewing human development has rapidly attracted many followers, both in the United States and abroad, and must be considered one of the most influential perspectives on children and youth in contemporary psychology.

Characteristics of Cognitive-Developmental Psychology

First, for Piaget, mature intelligent behavior is the ability to reason and think critically in objective, abstract, and hypothetical terms. When a youth or an adult reaches this level of thought, Piaget regards him as being at the peak of a developmental pyramid—hierarchy—the lower levels of which have emerged sequentially and in progressively more complex form. In infancy, these subordinate hierarchical elements (the very foundations of thought) are sensorimotor coordinations. In a cumulative fashion, thought forms then move through a concrete level to the abstract level that we associate with formal logic.

Second, four factors act in concert in the progression of the development of thought (or moral judgment, or social development. For the most part, however, the discussion here is confined to the development of thought). These four factors are biological maturation, experience with the physical world (including one's own body and the bodies and physical actions of others), social experience (experience in interacting with other people), and *equilibration*. By equilibration, the authors understand Piaget to mean achievement by the individual of greater cognitive balance or stability at successively higher levels as he reconciles new experience with past experience.

The active reconciliation represented by successful equilibration can be more specifically defined by introducing two mechanisms of behavior change that interact with each other: *assimilation* and *accommodation*.

Assimilation refers to the child's or the older person's comprehension of a new experience. Any new experience must be plugged in as best as one can to fit with what he has already experienced and understood. In a 3- or 4-year old child, experience and understanding may lead him only to the point where the concept *life* is represented by anything that moves. To him, then, his new windup toy has life. This is the logical best he can do in line with his existing level of comprehension. Time and experience, however, move him along. Eventually he is put into *disequilibrium* about the concept *life* and the nature of his windup toy. He eventually learns that mechanical toys are not alive. Disequilibrium, we must assume, is at least mildly unsettling or, perhaps better, one wishes to eliminate it by learning what has produced it. An individual is curious about his disequilibrium. Removal of disequilibrium in the direction of ever more accurate perception and plugging in of experience is what Piaget calls *accommodation*.

In short, a child must frequently transform and develop, or else he is conceptually very wrong about experiences and stimuli. Of course, he must plug new ones in to where he is developmentally at any given moment. But the environment is insistent, stimuli have unalterable and undeniable qualities of their own, and, eventually in human development, stimuli and experiences "insist" that they be plugged in accurately, according to their true properties. When a person realizes that incorrect plugging in (assimilation) has occurred, disequilibrium results; to dispel it, accommodation (accurate plugging in) must be made. We must note that assimilation is not always the incorrect mechanism for learning, nor is accommodation always accurate. It is simply that interactions that culminate in accurate accommodation are those which mark developmental progress in thinking. Note the similarity of accommodation to Freud's *reality principle*, discussed in the next section.

Of course, countless such interactions are necessary for human beings to represent physical (or social) reality accurately. Piaget believes these interactions make up the core of age-related experience that, as it cumulates, eventually and through evolution results in logical thought.

Piaget's Sequence of Development

For Piaget, the evolution of logical structures begins with a state or stage of egocentrism and, ideally, terminates in a state or stage of perspectivism (17). The egocentric child is unable to conceive that his view of the world is not the only one that exists; he believes that the world exists for his sake and that his feelings and wishes are shared by everyone. For example, the kindergarten-age child goes to school for the first time fully expecting that his teacher knows all about his pets, toys, and friends, and that the teacher feels as strongly about these things as does the child. Changes in this orientation gradually occur, however, and the child comes to distinguish between his and others' viewpoints. Thought becomes more reflective. Eventually, when (and if) the child matures, he is objective in the sense that he both recognizes and accepts multiple viewpoints and feelings.

"That buzzing-noise means something. You don't get a buzzing-noise like that, just buzzing and buzzing, without its meaning something. If there's a buzzing-noise, somebody's making a buzzing-noise, and the only reason for making a buzzing-noise that I know of is because you're a bee. . . . And the only reason for being a bee that I know of is making honey. . . . And the only reason for making honey is so as I can eat it." ,From the book Winnie-the-Pooh *by A. A. Milne. Decorations by E. H. Shepard. Copyright 1926 by E. P. Dutton & Co., Inc. Renewal by A. A. Milne, 1954. Published by E. P. Dutton & Co., Inc., and used with their permission; also reprinted by permission of The Canadian Publishers, McClelland and Stewart Limited, Toronto, and of Curtis Brown Ltd., London.*

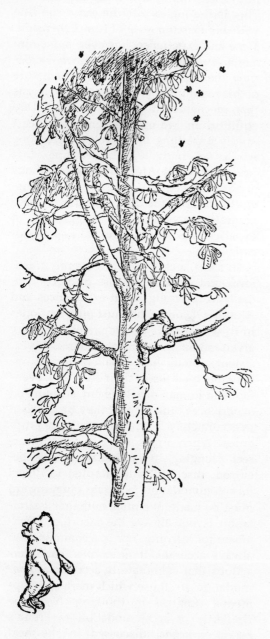

An Example of Egocentric Thought Characteristic of the Preoperational Stage of Cognitive Development.

Piaget has spent the greatest amount of his prodigious efforts in describing the sequence through which a child moves as he progresses toward perspectivism. Accordingly, cognitive-developmental theory is based on a sequence-relevant concept of development (see Chapter 1); but, as we shall see, it is also tied to general age periods. Piaget's notion of sequence is also *invariant* (that is, development proceeds in a fixed order, even though individual differences in developmental rate are acknowledged).

Piaget divides his invariant, hierarchical, and pyramidal sequence into four qualitatively distinct periods: the sensorimotor stage (birth to 18 months or 2 years), *preoperational thought* (about 2 to 7 years), *concrete operations* (ages 7–11) and *formal operations* (11 years and beyond). Convenient labels have been provided which perhaps point more clearly to the central characteristics of these stages than do Piaget's terms (6). During the sensorimotor stage, the conquest of the object is made. In the preoperational stage, the task is the *conquest of the symbol.* The task within the concrete operations stage is *mastering classes, relations,* and *quantities.* Finally, in the formal operations (most mature) stage of thought, the central task is *conquest of thought.*

Although these periods are age linked, the ages assigned are approximations and should not be regarded as rigidly correct or invariable.

Sensorimotor Period Sensorimotor behavior (such as looking at things heard and felt, grasping things seen and felt) provides the action basis for eventual symbolic thought. The primitive reflexive, passive, respondent characteristics of very young infants are quickly followed by goal-seeking behavior and by primitive concepts of time, space, and causality; that is, the child learns that by shaking himself in his crib, he can make the mobile (which is beyond his reach) move. One of the most important learnings during the sensorimotor period is *object permanence.* A child has the sense of object permanence when he has learned that things continue to exist whether or not he can see them. All subsequent logical thought obviously depends on this basic information.

Another important learning during the sensorimotor stage is the realization of *invariance despite change;* that is, objects or people may appear in different contexts or circumstances, but their basic identity stays the same. Still another major conceptual feat is learning that *certain acts result in reliable effects on the environment* (the above example of a child's shaking himself in his crib to make his mobile move reveals a primitive notion of causality and prediction of effect).

Furthermore, during the sensorimotor stage, the child seems to learn to distinguish between "me" and "not me." A primitive notion of the self as independent from the environment thus emerges. Toward the end of this stage, improvement of skill in remembering is increasingly demonstrated by deferred memory (imitating the act sometime after the model has demonstrated it).

Preoperational Thought In the second year of life for many children and by age 2 for almost all children, sensorimotor interactions with the environment are augmented and made more powerful and complex by the child's growing ability to use (including to understand) language. Language mushrooms in the third year of life. During this period, the child learns the difference between the signifier (the

Table 2.1 *Piaget's Stages of Intellectual Development*

Stage	Approximate Ages	Characterization
I. *Sensorimotor period*	Birth to 2 years	Infant differentiates himself from objects; seeks stimulation, and makes interesting spectacles last; prior to language, meanings defined by manipulations, so that object remains "the same object" with changes in location and point of view.
II. *Preoperational thought period*		
Preoperational phase	2–4	Child egocentric, unable to take viewpoint of other people; classifies by single salient features: if A is like B in one respect, must be like B in other respects.
Intuitive phase	4–7	Is now able to think in terms of classes, to see relationships, to handle number concepts, but is "intuitive" because he may be unaware of his classification. Gradual development of *conservation* in this order: mass (age 5), weight (age 6), and volume (age 7).*
III. *Period of concrete operations*	7–11	Able now to use logical operations such as *reversibility* (in arithmetic), *classification* (organizing objects into hierarchies of classes), and *seriation* (organizing objects into ordered series, such as increasing size).
IV. *Period of formal operations*	11–15	Final steps toward abstract thinking and conceptualization; capable of hypothesis-testing.

* Ages for 50 percent passing, according to Kooistra (1963). The ages given by Piaget and Inhelder (1941) are generally higher.

From "Piaget's Stages of Intellectual Development" in *REVIEW OF CHILD DEVELOPMENT RESEARCH*, Volume 1, edited by Martin L. Hoffman and Lois Wladis Hoffman, © 1964 by Russell Sage Foundation, New York.

word, usually nouns at first) and the significant (the object, event, or characteristic for which the word stands); that is, the word *chair* is not itself what one sits on. This recognition opens the way for symbolic mental activity (the beginning of thought).

However, children's thought is limited during this developmental phase, probably because of both maturational level and limited experience. Preoperational thought is apparently dominated by "before the eye reality." This means that the child's perceptions dominate his conceptions. A preoperational child who sees six marbles closely grouped and another six marbles widely spread will say there are more marbles in the dispersed than in the tight grouping: "This pile has more because it is bigger." The same behavior is likely to occur among preoperational children even when the piles are at first identical and close together and later one pile is altered and spread out *while the child watches*. It is as though the child does not comprehend that contextual appearance can change with no effect on quantity. This, in Piaget's terms, means that the preoperational child cannot *conserve number through irrelevant transformations*. The same failure to conserve occurs for weight, length, volume, and other general characteristics of objects, things, and classes.

A second limitation in thought that is characteristic of preoperational children (21) is their apparent inability to categorize objects and events along more than one dimension or according to more than one criterion: a drinking cup must be tall *or* wide, but does not possess *both* height *and* weight at the same time. More complexly, a balloon may be big or red, or blue or small; but a cluster of balloons will not be conceived along the multiple dimensions of big, red and small, blue balloons. Multiple classification seems to be beyond the preoperational child's power of combinatory thought—he attends primarily to one object at a time. He also has problems with regard to "superordinate conceptual classification." For instance, while he may acknowledge that a doll is a toy, his logic is also such that he will likely indicate that if all dolls in the world were burned, there would be no more toys. In other words, the subordinate class, *doll*, and the superordinate (more general and abstract) class, *toy*, are dealt with as equivalent.

Despite such limitations in his thought, the preoperational child moves rapidly through this stage of the "conquest of the symbol" in the direction of more sophisticated symbolic functioning. Growth is particularly rapid in the last two years of the preoperational stage (from about 5 to 7). Basic clarification rules, concept integration, and elementary quantitative thinking become apparent as one watches the behavior that accompanies children's thinking. However, preoperational children rarely verbalize their rules and strategies. For this reason, Piaget envisions preoperational thought as *intuitive*.

Concrete Operations   The intuitive thought of the 5- or 6-year-old is a transition to the next higher rung in the developmental ladder. Typically, the transition is achieved around age 7, which roughly marks the beginning of the period of concrete operations. The distinctive features of thought during the period of concrete operations is that logic and objectivity progressively characterize the child's thought. As Elkind says, this stage includes the conquest of classes, relations, and quantities. The child is now able to think deductively: If 1 foot equals 12 inches, then 12 inches put together equal 1 foot. If *all* dolls are toys, then *this* doll is a toy. In other words, logical operations—acts of reasoning—are performed in relation to real, or concrete, events and objects. Thus, the name of this stage, *concrete operations*.

Among the capabilities developed throughout this stage are multiple classification and conservation. Underlying these capabilities are understanding of *equivalence.* Objects of varying size and texture can be equal in weight. Changes in one dimension, such as height, do not necessarily mean that other dimensions, such as weight, change (the child learns to *covary*). The child also becomes capable of *reversibility.* Transformational sequences can be traced back to their point of origin in order to account for changes in appearance; actions can be canceled by counteraction. One of the simplest cases of reversibility is learning that the number of fingers on a hand, counted sequentially from thumb to little finger, is the same as the number counted from little finger to thumb. Another instance: When poured back into a tall, thin glass, the liquid that was judged less in quantity by the preoperational child when it was poured into a short wide glass can be seen to have remained the same despite its apparent transformation as it went from one glass into another.

Transitivity and *associativity* also come to be understood during the concrete operations stage of cognitive development. Transitivity refers to *seriation.* One can arrange a series of events or objects in continua such as greater than, less than, more than, fewer than. Understanding of this operation is essential if children are to understand number and size relationships.

A child may demonstrate his understanding of associativity by showing that parts of a whole may be combined in different ways without effecting a change in the whole. To produce a given shade of brown paint, for example, requires only that constant quantities of red, yellow, and black paint be combined. It makes no difference whether one puts the black paint in first, second, or third, as long as all three shades are put in in the prescribed amount.

However, the abstract derivations from such processes are not yet understood. Concerning transitivity, the child cannot solve the problem: "If $A > B$, and $B > C$, and $C > D$, which is heavier, A or D?" Only as he enters into the stage of formal operations can the abstractions from principles be formulated and employed in thought. Then, the child or the youth becomes able to generate hypotheses and to arrive at logical deductions performed on a symbolic level without assistance from concrete props.

Formal Operations The average child–young person is thought to move from the stage of concrete operations to the stage of formal operations at the age of 11 or 12 years. Hallmarks of the formal operations stage are the abilities to formulate and execute symbolic plans of action based on hypothetical events, and considering simultaneously the effects of more than one variable in a problem situation. The prepubescent child and the early adolescent youth have become able to examine logical form independent of the actual situation. Thus, the term *formal* operation. Potential relations among objects or events are imagined. Thought is not limited only to actual observances or occurrences, and logical incongruities in hypothetical contexts can be detected. Ideas of justice can transcend actual events.

Equally important, the human being of this age can reflect on himself. He is able to think about his own thoughts. This, one presumes, is a reflection of the true emergence of the self and the beginning of the time when *logical* (not emotional) egocentrism disappears forever. In such *reflective thought,* the young person can evaluate the quality or logic of his own thinking.

Implications of a Cognitivist Point of View of Human Development

1. If one is a cognitivist, he is likely to look first and mainly at the rational and the prerational variables of human development and behavior. Thus, he may neglect or overlook entirely the social, emotional, personal, and biological human being. The cognitivist, in other words, is likely to think mainly about Apollonian, rather than Dionysian, man (see Chapter 9, pages 329 and 330 for a discussion of these terms). Moreover, the cognitivist will often think less about human motivation than about describing problem-solving processes. Yet he will ultimately attend to the explanation of behavior, especially intellectual behavior, in pursuit of a principal goal of psychology.

2. The cognitive-developmental position, at least Piaget's version of it, includes an emphasis on the natural environment— the informal, unarranged learning experiences presumably common to all mankind. Cognitivists frequently concentrate on man's relation with the physical, rather than the social and psychological, world. Piagetians, in particular, prefer to think of informal and universal experience, not arranged experience and teaching. In fact, structured, organized, didactic approaches are not much favored by most Piagetians; they prefer to have the child actively order his own concrete experience. Consistent with this orientation is that their philosophical position about human development is also more akin to Rousseau's than

is the behavioristic view, for example.

3. A psychologist with a cognitive-developmental approach to human development is likely to favor invariant and perhaps biologically determined sequences of development that apply to all of mankind, while neglecting or overlooking individual and cultural differences. While this is valuable in pointing out transcendent commonalities for all people and all cultures, the unique case so well liked by the humanist and the psychodynamicist, and the joy of dealing with the unique case, are likely to be lost to the cognitivist.

4. For about the same reasons the cognitivist psychologist pays little attention to individual and cultural differences, he pays little attention to sex differences. In research literature, it is not surprising that we find few sex differences in the behaviors with which Piaget and his followers are concerned, but many sex differences in the behaviors that are of most interest to humanists and psychodynamic psychologists. Only in research areas such as paired associate and discrimination learning are we as unlikely to find sex differences as we are in the kinds of thought in which Piagetians are most interested.

5. The cognitive developmentalist typically thinks in terms of fixed stages and categories rather than of flexible processes and agents for developmental change. Thus, as has been stated, he is likely to neglect some important forms of human learning and the potential for change that is characteristic of human beings of all ages. In Chapter 1, the authors suggested the implications and potential of alternative and more economical sequence-relevant approaches to human development. Cognitivist psychologists are likely not to place much value on the potential of such approaches.

6. From paragraph 5, it follows logically that cognitivists are not likely to think much about intervention as a way of "improving" or speeding human development, because, basically, cognitivists believe an individual will profit from experience only when he is maturationally ready for it to be functionally plugged in (that is, when a child's assimilation readiness is developed to somewhere near his ability to accommodate). In other words, the traditional cognitivist believes that one cannot (and should not try) to accelerate the developmental process through arranged experiences (learning). Maturation, general age-related experience, and self-directed equilibration, essentially, are the key factors (14).

7. Similarly, cognitivists are more likely to be observers and testers of behavior (looking for *capacity*, as it were), than experimental manipulators of behavior. Neither are they much interested in the history of the organism. Rather, cognitivists concentrate their attention mainly on the behavior of the infant, child, youth, or adult when he is faced with a problem to be solved.

Concluding Remarks
In the authors' judgment, cognitive psychology provides a good and necessary foil for traditional psychodynamic psychology. Many cognitive psychologists may, however, go as far in dramatizing the rational, problem-solving, and, loosely speaking, intellectual aspects of human development and behavior as do the psychodynamically inclined (see following section) in emphasizing the instinctual, emotional, and noncognitive aspects. On the other hand, cognitive-developmental psychology seems to fit well with the humanist position. Humanists proclaim a strong interest in, but pay relatively little attention to, the rationality of human life and the transcendence of man's mind over his biology, instincts, and emotions.

Behaviorism and cognitive-developmental psychology have overlapped all too little (8). To date, psychologists from these schools of thought have not often brought their mutual skills to bear on the study of developmental processes, although much constructive cross-fertilization has recently occurred. It is now clear, for instance, that both behaviorists and cognitive developmentalists profess interest in a sequence-relevant concept of development. It seems to the authors, however, that behaviorists are less age conscious in their study of children and have less interest in *invariant* growth sequences or chronologically fixed developmental stages based on gross concepts of maturation and general age-based experience. Fortunately, many behaviorists have now recognized the appeal and descriptive validity of Piagetian developmental stages; accordingly, they have begun to examine areas of Piagetian theory for purposes of empirical investigation. These aspects include concept definition, how change from one Piagetian stage to another can be defined and how it occurs, and whether the change from one to another Piagetian stage can be speeded up or slowed down. Many behaviorists and behavioristically oriented educators are eager to prove that intervention designed to improve the human intellectual condition *will work*. Piaget has given them excellent motivation and an intriguing set of descriptions of the development of human thinking which they can use in their work.

Finally, it is helpful to keep reminding ourselves that Piaget is less a developmental psychologist than a biologist turned epistemologist and that he has most certainly given the field of developmental psychology interesting provocation and much liveliness.

Cognitivist-developmental psychology, like humanism and behaviorism, is made clearer if one looks at some research that represents it [see Example 2.3, (25)].

2.3 Cognitive-Developmental Influences: The Study of Reasoning Abilities

The authors chose the research paper summarized here for three reasons.

1. The study is characteristic of a major approach to research employed by cognitive-developmental psychologists. These psychologists analyze the concepts that they believe represent a developmental stage of thought. They then translate their analysis into operations that are frequently put in the form of tests. Finally, they give the tests to (measure) sizable samples of children and youth of different age levels. This is the cross-sectional (as opposed to the longitudinal) research strategy.

2. This piece of research extends our knowledge of children's reasoning from the later years of the concrete operations stage (see accompanying text) well into the formal operations stage. For reasons that are not entirely clear to the authors of this text, the intriguing years of later childhood and very early to middle adolescence have attracted the attention of psychologists less than the preschool and early school years.

3. The authors of this research have performed no environmental manipulations. They have not experimented; rather, they have taken their subjects as they found them in their natural environment.

The authors developed tests to measure basic principles of *class reasoning* and *conditional reasoning*. Under each of these two major headings, there were further subdivisions of items into those which were *symbolic* in nature and those which were concrete in form. Finally, each item had to be given some type of *context*, or type of *referent*. The authors made the contents of one third of the total items *concrete–familiar*, one third *suggestive*, and one third *abstract*. The child or the youth who took the test was to answer each item *yes* or *no*.

Examples of the different types of item are given below (quoted from Roberge and Paulus, format changed):

Class Reasoning
  Symbolic Form *All A's are B's; x is an A; therefore, x is a B.*
  Concrete Form *All of Joan's friends are going to the museum today. Pat is a friend of Joan's. Therefore, Pat is going to the museum today.*
Conditional Reasoning
  Symbolic Form *If p, then q; therefore q.*
  Concrete Form *If Joan goes to the museum, then she will meet her friend Sue. Today Joan is going to the museum. Therefore, today Joan will meet her friend Sue.*
Content Dimensions
  Class Reasoning
  Concrete–Familiar *All of the green coats in the closet belong to Sarah. The coat in the closet is green. Therefore the coat in the closet does not belong to Sarah.*
  Suggestive *All pittles are cloots. This is not a cloot. Therefore, this is a pittle.*
  Abstract *All $'s are *'s. This is a $. Therefore, this is a *.*
  Conditional Reasoning
  Concrete–Familiar *If the hat on the table is blue, then it belongs to Sally. The hat on the table is blue. Therefore the hat on the table does not belong to Sally.*

SUGGESTIVE   *If mice can fly, then they are bigger than horses. Mice can fly. Therefore, mice are bigger than horses.*

ABSTRACT   *If there is a *, then there is a #. There is a *. Therefore, there is a #.*

These tests were given to 263 Connecticut public school children enrolled in grades four (average age, $9\frac{1}{2}$ years), six, eight, and ten (average age of tenth-graders, 16 years). The children from the different grades were all of about the same average IQ; boys and girls had about equal IQs; and average IQ for the entire sample was at the national norm, or a little higher. As is usual in studies of the Piaget type, no sex differences were revealed in the results. The authors discuss the implications of this state of affairs in Chapter 5, when they take up the topics of fluid and crystallized intelligence, and deal with arranged and unarranged experiences in more detail. From the practical point of view, this typical result implies that there are no particular boy–girl differences in regard either to grade, kind of reasoning, or content of the reasoning (what is being reasoned about). These factors play an important part in how children's logical reasoning abilities develop.

Class reasoning (see preceding examples) seems relatively simple at all the age levels studied. This would have been predicted from Piaget.

On the whole, *class reasoning* is easier for children than *conditional reasoning,* but the difference is not strikingly large. Significant growth in both *class reasoning* and *conditional reasoning* occurs from the fourth to the tenth grades, but is most striking between grade six (average age, a little less than 12 years) and grade eight (average age, a little less than 14 years). These years, it was noted in the text, are the early years of the stage of formal operations. Finally, reasoning seems easiest about concrete and familiar material, then somewhat less easy about suggestive material, and most difficult for abstract content. However, there is little difference in difficulty between suggestive and abstract content in *conditional reasoning.*

Implications from these findings are that instruction of children as young as fourth-graders can include both class and conditional reasoning. Also, any teacher should be aware of the differences in difficulty of different types of content in reasoning. It is easier to reason about concrete and familiar things. Thus, it is well to start off instruction that demands either *class reasoning* or *conditional reasoning* with concrete and familiar material. Only later should the teacher move to suggestive and abstract material, after the learner–reasoner has mastered the *process.* In this case, *content* can make *process* easier.

Recommended Readings for the Cognitive-Developmental View of Development

Ammon, P., W. Rohwer, and P. Cramer. *Intellectual development: Three viewpoints.* Hinsdale, Ill.: Dryden, 1973.

Baldwin, A. L. *Theories of child development.* New York: Wiley, 1967 (see Chapters 5–9).

Elkind, D. *Children and adolescents.* New York: Oxford, 1970.

Flavell, J. H. *The developmental psychology of Jean Piaget.* Princeton, N.J.: Van Nostrand, 1963.

Furth, H. *Piaget for teachers.* Englewood Cliffs, N. J.: Prentice-Hall, 1970.

Ginsburg, H. and S. Opper. *Piaget's theory of intellectual development: An introduction.* Englewood Cliffs, N. J.: Prentice-Hall, 1969.

Kamii, C. K. Evaluation of learning in pre-

school education: Socio-emotional, per-
ceptual-motor, cognitive development. In
B. S. Bloom, J. T. Hastings, and G. F. Madaus
(eds.) *Handbook on formative and summative
evaluation of student learning.* New York:
McGraw-Hill, 1971, 281–344.
Kohlberg, L. Early education: A cognitive-developmental view. *Child Development,* 1968,
39, 1013–1062.
Kohlberg, L., and R. Mayer. *Early education:
The cognitive view.* Hinsdale, Ill.: Dryden,
1973.
Lavatelli, C. S. *Piaget's theory applied to an
early childhood curriculum.* Boston: American
Science and Engineering, 1970.
Piaget, J., and B. Inhelder. *The psychology of the
child.* New York: Basic Books, 1969.

While the authors have not mentioned
Jerome Bruner in this section, selections of his
work should be read, because he is one of the
leading cognitive psychologists. As a bare
beginning for Bruner, the following reading is
suggested:

Bruner, J. S. The growth of the mind. *American
Psychologist,* 1965, *20,* 1007–1017.
Bruner, J. S., R. R. Oliver, and P. M. Green-
field. *Studies in cognitive growth.* New York:
Wiley, 1966.

A PSYCHODYNAMIC VIEW

Definition
In this final section of the chapter, the
authors have chosen to concentrate on
classical Freudian psychodynamic psychology. The historical influence of this
psychology, technically called *psychoanalysis,* has been enormous. Its impact on
psychological thought is still clearly perceptible in many discussions of human
development. It is true that certain de-
partures from classical psychoanalytic
theory have occurred which have resulted
in the so-called *neoanalytic* psychologies,

but the authors mention only in passing
some of the concepts that have come into
psychoanalysis after Freud.

The following excerpt provides a workable definition for the authors' commentary on Freudian psychology:

Psychoanalysis began . . . in a therapeutic
setting. It was characterized from the beginning by a specific method of observing human
behavior (i.e., the physician listens to the
verbal expression of the patient's flow of
thought, and attempts to comprehend em-
pathically what the patient wishes to communicate about his psychic state) and by a
specific mode of theory formation (i.e., the
physician attempts to bring order into the
data which he has obtained about the inner
life of his patient). . . . Therefore it can be
said that psychoanalysis is a science based
predominantly upon a method of clinical
observation. It interprets empirical data, and
thus its starting point is always observation
of people: of things people say, things people
say they feel, and things people say they do
not feel. . . . Psychoanalysis is not a method
of "pure" observation — if such a thing actually
exists in science — but observation and theory
are closely interwoven: *observation forming the
basis of theories and theories influencing the
direction and focus of observation.* (15, pp. 113–
114, italics added)

To this description must be added that
observation of children's behavior during
both arranged settings and free play is
typically made by psychodynamic de-
votees for purposes of both therapy and
research. For youth and adults, use is
made of behavioral data other than speech
content, such as style of speech (blocks
and hesitations, for example), bodily pos-
ture, gaze meeting and avoidance, blush-
ing, perspiring, trembling, relaxation, and
so on.

In practice, many psychodynamicists
apparently believe that theoretical knowledge and observational attitude are so

completely integrated that an awareness of any dichotomy between theory and observation disappears (15). Yet they also maintain that psychodynamic hypotheses must be checked against both direct observations and verbal reports of persons being studied. Ostensibly, the latter commitment serves to identify the scientific component of psychoanalysis. But the fusion of theory and observation opens up the real possibility that subjectivity rather than objectivity will prevail in the study of behavior. Evidence gathered from this perspective may therefore represent art or intuition more than science.

Characteristics of the Psychodynamic Perspective

On the basis of data obtained from people through methods such as those just described, an extraordinary point of view was derived about man and his development. The discussion is focused first on the general orientation represented by psychoanalysis and then on some of its developmental features.

First, psychoanalysis traditionally has involved a marked preoccupation with aberration and disease, not normalcy and health. Regardless of this, data taken from the study of disturbed human beings have been organized to explain normal as well as abnormal behavior. Furthermore, psychoanalytic theory and therapeutic practice are essentially grounded in the clinical rather than the experimental method of studying behavior. Subjects for clinical study have most typically been advantaged middle- and upper-class adults whose childhoods are reconstructed in the clinical setting. It should be recognized that many variations from this approach have occurred, particularly from adherents of neoanalytic theories. Yet many of the basic data from which classical psychoanalytic

theory was built came from the clinical study of prosperous, but disturbed patients. Free verbal associations of adults and (more recently) the play enactments of children have been primary sources of such data.

Second, the attendant focus on childhood experiences is marked by the psychoanalytic conviction that early life experiences, notably parent–child and sibling relationships, are fundamental in determining the quality of personality development. Regarded as particularly significant are emotional experiences and the early socialization of human instincts. These instincts, including sexual energy, self-preservation, and aggression, constitute the raw material for motivation and much of behavior.

Third, and consistent with the first two characteristics, is that psychoanalytic adherents are more likely to concentrate on the individual than on the culture, on events that have been traumatic rather than on positive growth experiences, and on the way in which personality is structured than on how change occurs in human development. Since the affective characteristics of personality are viewed as so important, the intellectual components of behavior often become secondary. Even so, it is generally maintained within psychoanalysis that the principal goal of therapy is the development of rational thought. Rationality, however, seems to psychoanalysts a matter of developing control over one's instinctual tendencies and coming to terms with emotional conflicts. In fact, some view psychoanalysis essentially as a psychology of conflict and anxiety.

Fourth, much of the conceptual structure of psychoanalytic thought is based on the notion of unconscious mental life. Phenomena such as dreams, hypnotic behavior, slips of the tongue, selective forgetting, and sudden flashes of insight (the "aha" experience) are usually taken as evidence for the existence of a mental life that is beyond awareness. The issue involved here is twofold: (1) whether one needs to invoke the idea of an unconscious in order to explain behavior, and (2) in the absence of behavioral definition, how one possibly can study the unconscious in any sort of scientific fashion.

Fifth, psychoanalytic psychologists, like behaviorists, are deterministic. Freud was one of the first to argue that all behavior has a cause (is determined) and is capable of being explained by general principles of behavior.

Sixth, and specifically in relation to development, behavior is viewed within psychoanalysis as progression through a series of distinct, predictable stages. This progression is universal in that it purportedly holds for all people in all cultures and represents a gradual transformation from a narcissistic pleasure-seeking, impulse-dominated infant to a reality-oriented, self-controlled adult. This transformation may not occur successfully, however, if the circumstances for development are not "right." In other words, it is possible for a person to become fixated at one or another stage of development, after which his subsequent development is stunted. The central task for the developing individual is learning to modify basic impulses, most of which are in conflict with organized society.

Readers unfamiliar with or further interested in the details of psychoanalytic stages are invited to consult the recommended readings at the end of this section. The authors wish only to indicate that conflicts, frustrations, and satisfactions experienced during these stages of psychosexual development are the most decisive determinants of personality, according to psychoanalysis. These experiences revolve successively around *oral, anal,* and *genital* functions in the early years. Such functions are associated respectively with problems of dependency, aggression, and interpersonal relations (17).

Seventh, and finally, it is important to note that the *dynamic* aspect of the psychoanalytic perspective comes from the idea of fluid, incessant interplay among components of personality within the person and between these components and the person's environment. Through inference, three basic components of personality have been constructed: the *id* (seat of biological drives); the *ego* (basis for reality contact and problem-solving behavior); and the *superego* (the moral "watchdog" of personality). Dynamism occurs as the id constantly strives for expression (one's instincts exert constant efforts for gratification); as the ego seeks practical, socially acceptable ways to delay, substitute, or otherwise handle basic motivations and conflicts between the id and the superego: and as the superego, acting as one's conscience and ideal self, acts as a check on the id and monitors the ego processes.

This brief statement is, of course, an oversimplification of the process. The important point to note is that internal forces are constantly at work to produce behavior, however bizzare it may be. As the reader has probably guessed, the id dominates infant behavior—it is the biological given. Ego and superego development are slow, complex processes, the outcome of which will be largely determined by experiences during the first six years of life. Of penultimate significance are experiences that lead to the resolution of conflicts about sexuality in relation to one's parents and resultant sex identification.

Implications of a Psychodynamic View of Human Development

1. Within classical psychoanalysis, a bias exists toward the abnormal and the pathological. This seemingly sensitizes its followers first to look for developmental problems, conflicts, and anxieties and then to infer the possible motives that underlie variously unproductive or nonconstructive behavior. The psychoanalytic person is therefore a sort of trouble shooter with regard to the analysis of behavior. It is further implied within psychoanalysis that few if any people are truly healthy in a psychological sense. Rather, there are simply degrees of psychological ill-health.

2. If one takes the psychoanalytic view of human development, he is likely to concentrate on interpersonal intervention for emotional first aid (such as mental health service or psychotherapy) rather than on broader social intervention (such as better academic practices within the schools or a guaranteed annual wage). Within psychoanalysis the emphasis seems to be much more on adjusting the individual to things as they are than on promoting social reform that will make individual life and development less arduous. Psychoanalysis seemingly has been a status quo theory, socially speaking.

3. A person taking the psychodynamic point of view will be inclined to think of the developmental course, in the most important sense, as terminating with the resolution of basic sexual conflicts and the accompanying repression of early childhood experiences (at around the ages of 6 to 8 years). Thus, within the psychoanalytic school of thought, there is some pessimism about the possibility of fundamental change during later childhood, youth, maturity, and old age. If change occurs, deep therapy is required to produce it, a luxury unavailable to most of us.

Adolescence, with its vortex of new drives (libidinal and aggressive), is a stage that is excepted by many psychodynamicists from this pessimism. They consider it a time when the problems of sexual conflict may be reactivated and possibly healthily resolved.

4. Within psychodynamics, the tendency is to hold the parents and their child-rearing practices responsible for all aspects of the psychological development of the child. The often dramatic and constructive, but sometimes destructive, role of the individual in his own development is neglected within psychodynamic theory.

5. Personality formation is determined, mostly by historical (infancy and early childhood) forces. Thus, psychodynamics, like behaviorism, leaves no room for free will; but, more than behaviorism, the psychodynamic position may result in reasoning such that the person justifies his own abdication of responsibility for his personal development.

6. Within psychoanalytic theory, one is likely to approach human development in such a way as to neglect or underemphasize an individual's (or a group's) interpersonal relations, with the exception of his transactions with his parents and possibly his siblings. Dynamic psychologists seldom seem to direct their attention to the peer group or to sociological factors, although there are conspicuous exceptions (for example, 7, 32).

7. Implicit in the dynamic position (and most particularly in classical psychoanalysis) is a preoccupation with data and phenomena consisting only of verbal reports (and overt behavior, including words, shown by children in play). This may lead to neglect of nonverbal behavior and has the possible effect of making the entire psychodynamic system (including therapy) inappropriate for those who are

relatively nonverbal (for example, many disadvantaged delinquent youth and those of borderline or lower intelligence).

8. If one is a psychodynamicist, he is likely to be equally interested in the individual case (a clinical understanding) *and* general theoretical principles of explanation. However, he is not much given to gathering data from large samples of people, in good part because the basic psychoanalytic technique is exceptionally time-consuming, complex, and expensive. Erikson (7) is the only eminent psychoanalyst (and he is very far from Freud) whom the authors know who works with disadvantaged young people, for example.

9. Finally, derivation from psychoanalysis about child rearing seems to include more emphasis on *what not to do* rather than on *what to do*. Do not deprive the infant of the breast, do not schedule feedings rigidly, do not wean or toilet train "too early," do not separate the child from its mother until at least the age of 3, and so on. Although psychoanalysis is rich in its emphasis on explanatory matters, particularly for *post hoc* analyses of how development has gone wrong, few specific cues for positive behavior management can be extracted from this theory. In fairness, however, a general principle of management derived from psychoanalysis should be mentioned: Help the developing individual to express or channel his instinctual impulses in ways that are socially acceptable, or in ways that are at least not destructive to the self and to others.

Concluding Remarks

This brief treatment of the psychodynamic way of looking at human development has been provided because, historically, the psychodynamic (and especially the Freudian) way has been so important. From psychodynamic practice and theory, few hard facts about either development or behavior have emerged. Some ridiculous practices have been introduced for a time, such as *every mother a breast feeder, no child under 3 in day care,* and the state of affairs where for a time the cocktail party conversation of a stylish person was not complete without allusions to "*my analyst.*"

Some abuses have also been perpetrated in the name of dynamic psychology. The mother who had to put her child in the care of others or in day care, and who is aware of psychoanalytic ideas about the mother–child relation, is left with no alternative but guilt. The development of good day care facilities for young children, an economic necessity whether or not a good idea, was underplayed. At the same time, mothers were given so much responsibility for the course of children's development, determined in early childhood, that they had no recourse about motherhood but to feel alarmed. The onus of adjustment was put on the individual, while social disorganization and abuse that may actually have produced his difficulty were ignored. Individuals, told by dynamic psychologists that their personalities had been molded in their preschool years by their parents, were thus able to surrender personal responsibility for their destinies. Within psychodynamic psychology, there has been a remarkably passive acceptance of the socioeconomic status quo, accompanied by the luxurious (literally and figuratively) delving into the individual's psyche in order to adjust him to the world *as he finds it.* As a corollary, the disadvantaged—the not very bright, the not very rich, and the not very verbal—have been seriously neglected within this school of thought. Psychodynamic theory is also inimical even to moderate women's liberation movements.

On the other hand, it is hoped for the better, dynamic psychology has played an important role — many say the most important role — in stimulating research concerning the experiences of earliest childhood. Freud was vitally important in establishing the notion that all behavior is caused and is thus lawful. Dynamic psychologists have succeeded in interesting the intelligent lay public in psychology to a degree equaled by no other school of psychology. Many areas of human behavior, previously taboo for research, have been opened (or vital assistance has been given to opening them) by dynamic psychology — for instance, sexuality in general and childhood sexuality in particular — and the phenomena of death and grief. Dynamic psychology has exerted an important effect on the harder headed psychologies and has been instrumental in making them more inclusive in their scope and more relevant to real-life human problems. The statement may also be hazarded that dynamic psychology has played an important role in making people more aware of themselves and the implications of their own behavior. As psychologists, the authors must assume that this is good. Finally, psychoanalysis must be commended for its enlightening views on matters such as psychological conflict, the nature of anxiety, and the acting-out behavior of children and youth (see Chapter 10). In these areas, psychoanalysis has generated much research and a healthy ferment among psychologists of different theoretical persuasions.

Recommended Readings for the Psychoanalytic Perspective

Baldwin, A. L. *Theories of child development.* New York: Wiley, 1967 (see Chapters 10–13).

Bettelheim, B. Psychoanalysis and education. *School Review,* 1969, 77, 73–86.

Brown, J. A. C. *Freud and the post-Freudians.* Baltimore: Penguin Books, 1961.

Field, K., and E. Schour. The application of psychoanalytic concepts of personality development in the educative process. *American Journal of Orthopsychiatry,* 1967, 37, 415–416.

Freud, S. *An outline of psychoanalysis.* New York: Norton, 1949.

Grossman, B. D. Freud and the classroom. *Educational Forum,* 1969, 33, 491–496.

Tyler, L. L. Psychoanalysis and curriculum theory. *School Review,* December 1958, 446–460.

Tyler, L. L. Utilization of psychoanalytic concepts for assessing classroom transaction. *Journal of Educational Research,* 1967, 60, 260–266.

In Example 2.4 (26, 35), a piece of research is discussed that arose from psychoanalytic theory and in which psychoanalytic theory was tested. The authors of these studies believe that their findings are not well accounted for by Freudian notions, and advance a cognitive and power theory as a better explanation.

2.4 Psychoanalytic Influences: The Study of Sex Role Identification (26, 35)

In the discussion of classical psychoanalysis, the authors have seen that decisive tests of the accuracy of the theory using the traditional psychoanalytic method of verbal report are difficult if not impossible. However, psychoanalytic theory suggests many hypotheses that can be tested in other ways. The studies summarized here are examples. Like many of those who work from psychoanalytic concepts, the authors of these studies were concerned with a condition of deprivations, possible conflict, and social distortion. In this case, the concern was with father absence from the home for at least two years during the preschool ages, including the year that preceded and included the time of the study.

Thirty-three poor black boys and thirty-three poor black girls, about 5 years old on the average, all of whom had experienced such a two-year period of father absence, were studied. The mothers of these children were interviewed, and the interviews were carefully rated by experts for the child's masculinity–femininity, aggression, and dependency. (35).

The children were also given doll play interviews. These too were scored for masculinity–femininity, aggression, and dependency. Doll play is a projective technique. It is inferred that one is really acting out his own desires while playing with dolls, or is telling stories about pictures. Projective techniques are often favored by psychodynamic and humanist research workers.

From psychoanalytic theory it is predicted that father absence will not make too much difference to girls of the age studied here, but that boys' masculinity will be interfered with because it is necessary to have a parent of the same sex in the home before a child can resolve his psychosexual conflicts normally. Thus, boys cannot make an appropriate masculine identification unless the fathers are around. The general Freudian prediction is that father-absent boys will be relatively feminine, relatively unaggressive, and relatively dependent (in other words, their overall masculinity will suffer if they experience father deprivation). This Freudian prediction had been tested earlier by comparing many of the poor black father-deprived children in this study with carefully matched poor black children who had not been father de-

prived. It was clearly shown that the father-absent boys had indeed suffered in precisely the way predicted, but that the girls had been little affected. (26).

In this study (35), however, the investigators went a step further in their theorizing and prediction, and hypothesized that the presence of an older brother in the home would to some degree compensate for the absence of a father. This prediction moves this study away from a test of a conventional psychoanalytic theory to an enrichment of the theory by adding to it a theory from another system—cognitive and power theory in this case.

The results from the study are reasonably clear and for the most part in the predicted direction. The results provide stronger support to learning and modeling than to classical psychoanalytic theory. The authors conclude (p. 132) that "The presence of one or more older brothers offsets the father-absence effects on aggression and dependency in both boys and girls. Those effects, together with the negligible effects of the older sister, are most consistent with . . . cognitive theory and social power theory, and the least compatible with Freudian theory . . . some of the behavioral consequences do not appear to depend on the presence of a regular adult male partner for the mother, as Freudian theory seems to require."

The way in which one views human development affects what he sees, the meaning he attaches to it, the conclusions he draws, and what he does about these conclusions in both a practical and a theoretical or philosophical sense. It is thus important to examine the diversities in how scholars have viewed human development. For the discussion in this chapter, four of the more influential theories or systems for looking at human development and behavior have been chosen.

1. The humanistic theory.
2. The behavioristic theory.
3. The cognitive-developmental theory of Jean Piaget.
4. The dynamic theory, particularly that of Sigmund Freud and his classical psychoanalysis.

For each approach, four things have been done: (1) A definition has been given. (2) Major characteristics have been described (but details about the content of the system have been provided only for Piaget). (3) Implications have been drawn that, for the most part, are related to important practical and scholarly outcomes that depend on how one views human development and what he does about it *if* he adopts the stance of the particular system being discussed. Finally, (4) for each system, a rather personal summary of the authors' reactions has been given. By necessity, the authors' comments about these four approaches are tentative and concern the general state of each. These perspectives on development should not be taken as mutually independent or necessarily incompatible.

In this summary, only a few of the most striking things about the four systems can be listed. For example, humanists look at the *best* in man, are optimistic, and take delight in the individual case and large, purposeful, real-life issues. The authors believe strongly in man's ability to shape his own destiny.

Behaviorists are deeply concerned with the issue of methods in studying development and behavior. The core of

their approach is the study of how environment (stimuli, events) affects behavior (the learning process). Behaviorists and dynamicists are deterministic in their view of behavior and development. ("Everything is caused. The past shapes the present according to the context of the present. There is no free will.") Behaviorists prefer to work with small units of behavior that can be handled by clearly defined and observable methods. Principles that emerge from the "clean" or "pure" study of simple behavior can then be employed to understand more complex behavior. Behaviorists stress that psychology, like all science, must be a *public,* not a *private, endeavor.*

Cognitive developmentalists, like behaviorists, are likely to be preoccupied with rational, problem-solving processes, but, also like behaviorists, are extending their attention to other types of behavior, such as social and moral development. Cognitivists and dynamicists view development as progression from one stage to another. Humanists and behaviorists are most likely to think of development as continuous, and are usually at least as, and often more, interested in change than in status, in manipulation of development than in its description.

Finally, humanists build their thinking about people optimistically and concentrate their attention on excellence. Psychodynamic psychologists, particularly traditional Freudians, build normality (if indeed they admit there is such a thing) on pathology and conflict. Behaviorists and cognitivists are more likely simply to take the human being at whatever age he is and study the stages through which he goes (cognitivists) or the conditions of his developmental progression, particularly those related to learning (behaviorists).

REFERENCES

1. Allport, G. W. *Becoming: Basic considerations for a psychology of personality*. New Haven: Yale University Press, 1955.
2. Bijou, S. W., and D. M. Baer, *Child development*. Volume I: *A systematic and empirical theory*. New York: Appleton, 1961.
3. Bijou, S. W., and D. M. Baer. *Child development*. Volume II: *Universal stage of infancy*. New York: Appleton, 1965.
4. Bresnahan, J. L., and W. L. Blum. Chaotic reinforcement: A socioeconomic leveler. *Developmental Psychology*, 1971, *4*, 89–92.
5. Dollard, J., and N. E. Miller, *Personality and psychotherapy*. New York: McGraw-Hill, 1950.
6. Elkind D. Egocentrism in adolescence. *Child Development*, 1967, *38*, 1025–1034.
7. Erikson, E. H. *Childhood and society* (2nd ed.), New York: Norton, 1963.
8. Evans, E. *Contemporary influences in early childhood education*. New York: Holt, Rinehart and Winston, 1971.
9. Flavell, J. *Developmental psychology of Jean Piaget*. Princeton, N. J.: Van Nostrand, 1963.
10. Gage, N. L. Paradigms for research on teaching. In N. L. Gage (ed.) *Handbook of research on teaching*. Chicago: Rand McNally, 1963, 94–95.
11. Keasey, C. B. Social participation as a factor in the moral development of preadolescents. *Developmental Psychology*, 1971, *5*, 215–220.
12. Kessen, W. (ed.). *The child*. New York: Wiley, 1965.
13. Kohlberg, L. Development of moral character and moral ideology. In M. L. and L. W. Hoffman (eds.), *Review of child development research*. Vol. I. New York: Russell Sage Foundation, 1964, 383–481.
14. Kohlberg, L. Early education: A cognitive-developmental view. *Child Development*, 1968, *39*, 1013–1062.
15. Kohut, H., and P. F. D. Seitz. Concepts and theories of psychoanalysis. In J. M. Wepman and R. W. Heine. *Concepts of personality*. Chicago: Aldine, 1963, 113–141.
16. Krumboltz, J. D. (ed.). *Learning and the educational process*. Chicago: Rand McNally, 1965.
17. Langer, J. *Theories of development*. New York: Holt, Rinehart and Winston, 1969.
18. Lundin R. W. Personality theory in behavioristic psychology. In J. M. Wepman and R. W. Heine (eds.). *Concepts of personality*. Chicago: Aldine, 1963, 257–290.
19. Maddi, S. R. Humanistic psychology: Allport and Murray. In J. M. Wepman and R. W. Heine (eds.), *Concepts of personality*. Chicago, Aldine, 1963, 162–203.
20. Maslow, A. H. Some educational implications of the humanistic psychologies. *Harvard Educational Review*, 1968, *38*, 685–696.
21. Moely, B. E., F. A. Olson, T. G. Halwes, and J. H. Flavell. Production deficiency in young children's clustered recall. *Developmental Psychology*, 1969, *1*, 26–34.
22. Murray, H. A. Preparations for the scaffold of a comprehensive system. In S. Koch (ed.), *Psychology: A study of a science*. Vol. 3. New York: McGraw-Hill, 1959.
23. Mussen, P., S. Harris, E. Rutherford, and C. B. Keasey. Honesty and altruism among preadolescents. *Developmental Psychology*, 1970, *3*, 169–194.
24. Ostfeld, B., and P. A. Katz. The effect of threat severity in children of varying socio-economic levels. *Developmental Psychology*, 1969, *1*, 205–210.
25. Roberge, J. J., and D. H. Paulus. Developmental patterns for children's class and conditional reasoning abilities. *Developmental Psychology*, 1971, *4*, 191–200.
26. Santrock, J. W. Paternal absence, sex typing, and identifications. *Developmental Psychology*, 1970, *2*, 264–272.

27. Skinner, B. F. *Science and human behavior.* New York: Macmillan, 1953.

28. Skinner, B. F. Critique of psychoanalytic concepts and theories. *Scientific Monthly,* 1954, *79,* 300–305.

29. Skinner, B. F. Teaching machines. *Science,* 1958, *128,* 969–977.

30. Spence, J. T. Learning theory and personality. In J. M. Wepman and R. W. Heine (eds.), *Concepts of personality.* Chicago: Aldine, 1963, 3–30.

31. Staats, A. W. *Child learning, intelligence, and personality.* New York: Harper & Row, 1971.

32. Sullivan, H. S. The collected works of Harry Stack Sullivan. New York: Norton, 1953.

33. Watson, J. B. Psychology as the behaviorist views it. *Psychological Review,* 1913, *20,* 158–177.

34. Watson, J. B. *Behaviorism.* New York: Norton, 1930.

35. Wohlford, P., J. W. Santrock, S. E. Berger, and D. Leberman. Older brothers' influence on sex-typed, aggressive, and dependent behavior in father-absent children. *Developmental Psychology,* 1971, *4,* 124–134.

3 Dilemmas in Human Development

In Chapter 2 four different ways of viewing human development were discussed. The fact that there are four such diverse views of behavior and development leads directly into this chapter in which are discussed some dilemmas that, among other things, lead to diversities in theory and viewpoint. As already seen, controversy, dispute, and debate exist among psychologists about how development proceeds and how it can best be explained. Such controversies pervade society, of course, and are by no means confined to psychologists. Discussions, interest, and concern about the nature of childhood and adolescence, reasons and causes for human behavior, needs of children and youth, and the desirable end results of human development are pressing concerns for all thinking people. Such concerns also reach into public life (government and the schools, for example). Debate about schools, children, youth, and society often reaches such intensity that it seems agreement can never be reached even on the broadest generalizations.

In this chapter, several matters of unresolved dispute or conflict are examined. The authors call them *dilemmas* about important aspects of human development and society. The first half of the chapter examines dilemmas faced by all members of society who are concerned about human welfare, but particularly parents and teachers (current or prospective). The second half of the chapter is devoted to dilemmas confronted more specifically by students of developmental psychology.

There are at least two reasons for focusing on dilemmas in human development. First, many textbooks on developmental psychology are mostly catalogues or compendiums of facts and theories. Since this is an era much marked by concern for relevance, the authors think it is useful to go beyond such a cataloguing function and to comment on broader issues concerning the relationship of developmental psychology to social problems.

Second, as both psychologists and citizens, the authors are deeply concerned about many current issues and problems in development and education that demand decision making by parents and teachers. Accordingly, they find it impossible to limit the discussion solely to a treatment of the "cold facts" of human behavior and development.

THE NATURE OF DILEMMAS

✳ Two Types of Dilemmas

Our thinking has been organized around two basic and closely related types of dilemmas, *philosophical* and *procedural*. Philosophical dilemmas involve questions of value about the goals for human development in society. Procedural dilemmas, in contrast, occur around decision points about how to achieve preferred goals and to put strategies into effect for pursuing stated values.

In other words, once the dilemma of goal choices or value determination has been faced and dealt with and a commitment has been made to the resulting goal or values, one faces the dilemma of implementation. Procedural dilemmas also typically involve value judgments: What strategy or method is "best or most effective" for reaching a desired goal?

Levels at Which Dilemmas Are Experienced

Both philosophical and procedural dilemmas about human development occur at different levels of social involvement. Most broadly, one can talk about the "collective goals of a society." This involves a person in much the same thinking that went into the definitions of culture discussed in Chapter 1. At least in a democracy, collective goals are presumably established for the welfare of all members of a society. Broad societal goals are clearly

stated (or at least are defined by operations) in terms of national priorities. In a democracy (or perhaps any other form of government), national priorities are seldom established to everyone's satisfaction. Value judgments about health, education, national defense, foreign trade, welfare, and international relations, among others, are reflected by the national priorities that are established. At the time this book was being written, the philosophical and economic dilemmas of ecology versus technology were (and still are) creating agonized debate about national goals and priorities.

At another level of involvement, closer to everyday experience, are the philosophical dilemmas faced within social institutions such as schools. Priorities for learning, for example, are established within each school. These priorities always reflect value judgments about what is important—academics? aesthetics? athletics? —and what constitutes "the educated person." At the risk of oversimplifying, a dilemma increasingly faced in schools is the product–process dilemma. In some schools and communities, it is argued that learning basic subject matter content is supremely important. Others argue that content is secondary: It is skill in the processes of thinking, problem solving, and conceptualizing that should be put first among educational goals.

At a third and very personal level of experience, philosophical dilemmas are faced within every family unit. Goals for child rearing, implicit though they may be in some families, nonetheless reflect dilemmas about what parents *desire* for their children on the one hand and, on the other, what they believe *is necessary* for the child to succeed in our society. A mother and a father, for example, may prefer their child to be gentle, cooperative, and deferent to elders. At the same time, the parents are aware that it is very often the aggressive, competitive, and dominant individual who fares best in American society.

At a fourth level of experience are the philosophical dilemmas an individual faces about the course of his own life. Earlier, the importance of the individual as a factor in his own development was stressed. The choices one makes shape his life pattern. These choice points, often critical for later development, frequently present acute dilemmas. Let us consider an adolescent seeking to define his personal philosophy of life. In the process, he finds himself in conflict with two strong but opposing values, altruism versus materialism. His personal dilemma may be whether to make a commitment to social service or to personal material gain. Whichever he chooses or if he compromises, as many of us do, his choice will certainly influence his future development profoundly.

At this point, it is well to turn to *procedural* dilemmas. In the case just cited, once the commitment is made, there remains the dilemma of implementation. For most adolescents, many alternative pathways of goal or value implementation exist. In the above case, if the commitment is to altruism, the adolescent can consider alternatives that range from low-paid overseas or domestic service through social work to the Salvation Army. Whatever the choice, later development will be importantly affected.

In like manner, the way family procedural dilemmas are faced and resolved often results in great changes in developmental conditions for a child or an adolescent. Two sets of parents, both committed to achievement as an ethic, may select entirely different procedures for encouraging achievement in their children. One set may take the common position that excellence is its own reward, thus rarely praising the child for doing well but punishing him for behavior that does not meet their standard of excellence. A second set may choose to reward any sign of high-quality achievement behavior, while choosing simply to ignore poorer quality achievement behavior. One can confidently expect very different outcomes in terms of attitudes about achievement and parent–child relations between the children of the two families.

Procedural dilemmas must also be resolved within the schools. For example, if *process* is chosen over *product* within a given school system, how does one go about organizing the school so that process is the number one goal? Decisions about in-service training of teachers, instructional methods, and teacher behavior are critical. How the decisions are made will certainly affect learning and morale.

At a different educational level, state and federal procedural dilemmas are faced by executives, legislators, and courts. These groups must somehow act together in initiating (or not initiating), detailing, and implementing (legislating, financing, and administering) official educational priorities. The decision in 1971 that the Supersonic Transport (SST) program would be terminated illustrates action preceded by a procedural dilemma. The resolution had profound effects on children whose parents' income depended on continued SST funding. The failure of national leadership to assure that equal and nonsegregated education was available for all has profoundly affected many generations of black and white children. The present, often agonizing beginnings of resolving this dilemma

The answers to philosophical and procedural dilemmas about human development are not easily found. (Cartoon from Phi Delta Kappan, *1967, 49 (3), 147. Reproduced by permission of artist, Sidney Harris.)*

according to the Constitution rather than continuing to refuse to face it are affecting very large numbers of today's children, and will probably continue to affect them, their children, and their children's children.

In summary, there are basically two types of dilemmas, philosophical and procedural. It has been illustrated how resolving these dilemmas affects human development. The problem of dilemmas is discussed throughout this book. To provide a foundation for later discussions, examples of persistent, often troublesome dilemmas that are common in both homes and schools are now discussed.

CHILD-REARING DILEMMAS

Since the beginning of the twentieth century, dilemmas about child rearing seem to have become more intense and widespread. One author (49) gives three main reasons for this situation. First, there has been a steady, gradual, but increasingly

obvious emphasis on children as extensions of parental ambitions and as symbols of their parents' status in society. Such children are *extrinsically* valued (3). It is, of course, a rare parent who does not take pride in seeing his child develop successfully and secure social recognition. Within quite broad limits, there is nothing wrong with such eminently normal behavior. But if this is *all* the child means to the parents, both parents and child may suffer.

Second, it is argued that man has become more convinced of his power to control his environment and to shape his future, an argument that extends to the belief that to an important degree children can be molded by their environments. This view of the malleable child leads directly to concern about conditions in the environment that affect him.

A third trend that has apparently intensified dilemmas about child rearing is the strong need for personal direction (values, ideals, and the like) that comes on the heels of rapid and extreme cultural change. As established patterns of living are disrupted by such variables as technological change, accelerated urbanization, social mobility, and philosophical ferment, new patterns must take their place. The dilemma lies in deciding how to select new patterns that are appropriate, valid, and satisfying. Not only families, but also church, school, community, and broader state and national groups are faced with such dilemmas.

Some Persisting Dilemmas about Socialization in Human Development

Socialization has two faces—one a product, the other a process. As product, it is subject to cultural norms and value judgments. We say a child or a youth is well socialized (to follow Erikson as one example), when he is trusting, autonomous, possesses initiative along socially approved lines, and incorporates at least a moderate degree of the work ethic, in that he enjoys the "business" as well as the pleasure part of his life (17).

Socialization as process can refer to the child-rearing and educational methods that are adopted by parents and teachers and by those in the broader society. As has already been pointed out, with reference to socialization as both process and product, there are many procedural and philosophical dilemmas. In this section, several such persistent dilemmas are presented. The authors proceed on two fronts. First, they select and discuss a dilemma that faces those who are rearing the child (usually parents). Second, they select an analogous dilemma faced by those who are charged with education (teachers, administrators, and other education-related persons).

The three dilemmas chosen for discussion are (1) concept of control, (2) standards for behavior, and (3) nature of early experiences.

The Control of Behavior: An Age-Old Dilemma

A basic dilemma in human life is whether and how systematically to control behavior. The dilemma can take many forms. Many young parents, for example, express keen conflict about the value of creativity versus social conformity in their children. Most value both goals: They want their children to be creative, spontaneous, and individualistic, but not to go so far with such behavior that they are discourteous, disrespectful, impulsive, unpopular, and perceived by others as deviant or wild or silly. This dilemma probably arises so sharply in our culture because of our inclination to equate divergency with abnormality (50).

The philosophical dilemma about creativity versus conformity begets a procedural dilemma about control, namely, freedom versus restraint. Many parents, particularly the "now" generation of bright, articulate, well-educated, and a bit rebellious parents, seemingly believe that ample, almost total freedom is a necessary condition for the development of creativity. On the other hand, they also fear that freedom can result in self-centeredness. Such parents reason that a certain degree of social conformity is necessary, both for their child's welfare and the welfare of those with whom he associates. Still, they fear that if too many restraints are placed on children, they will become anxious, dependent, and short in creativity.

The issue of behavioral control is also found in more formal child development theory. In developmental psychology, for example, the dilemma is often associated with the schism between supporters of "naturalistic, indigenous growth" theories of development, and those who hold the "cultural competence" or environmental determination point of view (18). As seen in Chapter 2, supporters of the natural growth viewpoint believe that maximum socialization benefits can be gained by placing children in an enriched, benign, accepting, permissive, informally arranged environment (low control). The highest value is placed on self-expression in children, especially expression related to creative growth forces.

In contrast, those who espouse the cultural competence viewpoint place greater emphasis on the shaping power of experience. Arranged experiences and collective teaching forces are assumed to be necessary and potent. Skill development and environmental mastery are viewed as the means for achieving maximum development. Therefore, protagonists of this view are not willing to leave development to chance.

The authors cannot say which of these two views of development is most nearly correct or whether either is correct. Yet the contrast between the two illustrates the dilemma of control quite clearly. Philosophically, the dilemma is related to the goals toward which, and the values around which, control is to be exercised (40). This philosophical dilemma extends to a question of the right to self-determination. Procedurally, such a dilemma concerns what kind of and how much control should be exercised. Is the child capable of determining his own goals and values, or does he need systematic help from outside?

Interested readers should further explore the dimensions of this dilemma by examining sophisticated arguments on both sides of the question (24, 27, 40, 46). The authors cannot resolve the matter

here, although they believe that the evidence from socialization research is such as to conclude that child rearing cannot be left to chance alone. Conditions of development over which parents can exercise some form of control seem to make too important a difference.

To illustrate the importance of the control issue, a series of studies of individual differences in young children's competence is summarized in Example 3.1. The goal of these studies was to identify conditions, including parent behavior, that apparently contribute to differences in children's competence. Readers should think particularly about the questions that follow the summary of the research.

✳ 3.1 Socialization for Competence: The Issue of Control

Diana Baumrind (5, 6) conducted a series of studies of child-rearing practices and their relation to competence in young children. Specifically, her concern was to identify individual differences in *instrumental competence* among young children. Baumrind defined instrumental competence in terms of two dimensions: *social responsibility* (achievement-oriented, friendly, and cooperative child behaviors) versus irresponsibility (not achievement-oriented, hostile, and resistive behavior toward peers and adults); and *independence* (dominant and purposive) versus tractability (submissive and aimless in behavior). Early in her series of studies, Baumrind documented a wide range of differences in instrumental competence among both boys and girls of nursery school age.

Baumrind continued by reasoning that patterns of parental authority are major variables in the development of instrumental competence in children. Thus, another of her research tasks was to determine if different patterns of parental authority could be observed and described. By way of procedures too involved to describe here, three basic patterns were identified.

✳ *Authoritarian.* This pattern is characterized by a high degree of parental control, stress on obedience, absolute standards, tendency to utilize forceful, punitive disciplinary measures, and strong emphasis on respect for authority, tradition, order, with little verbal give-and-take between parent and child. This pattern may or may not involve rejection of the child.

A major child-rearing dilemma confronting developmental psychologists—and parents—is the issue of behavioral control. (Photo by Bruce Roberts)

✳ *Authoritative.* Firm rational control characterizes this second pattern. Both autonomy and disciplined conformity are valued for the child with a full recognition and respect for his interests. Encouragement and affirmation of the child's present qualities prevail, but standards for future conduct are clearly communicated. Both reason and power pervade methods of parental control, but verbal give-and-take occur freely and overrestrictiveness is avoided. This pattern may or may not include the explicit promotion of nonconformity in children.

✳ *Permissive.* This pattern represents an attempt by parents to behave non-punitively toward the child. Positive acceptance of the child's impulses, desires, and actions prevails. The parents consult the child about family policies and make few demands for order and household responsibility. The parents seek to be a resource for the child rather than a director of his activities. Self-regulation by the child is encouraged: Low control and emphasis on obedience to externally defined standards are preferred. The exercise of power over the child is avoided. This approach may or may not combine direct encouragement of nonconformity with laxity in discipline. Some permissive parents may stress high performance for the child in *some* areas, however.

Many specific findings have emerged from Baumrind's research, including a strong relationship of measured intelligence to instrumental competence. But the results of her most recent study serve to illustrate the relationship of parental authority and instrumental competence. In comparison to other patterns, *authoritative parental behavior* was most clearly associated with inde-

✳ *Laissez-Faire — let things go*

pendent, purposive behavior in girls and strong indications of social responsibility in boys. This pattern was also clearly associated with independence in boys when parents were nonconforming, and with high achievement (but not friendly, cooperative behavior) in girls.

In view of these and other findings, Baumrind argues for the following idea *in general:* "A matrix of parental values that lay stress upon individuality, self expression, initiative, divergent thinking, and aggressiveness should promote independence *if* not accompanied by lax, inconsistent discipline and an unwillingness to place demands upon the child. . . ." Similarly, the general importance of "modeling desired behavior, firm control and enforcement policies, fairness, open verbal exchange, acceptance and positive reinforcement . . ." has been stressed in relation to social responsibility.

The concept of instrumental competence most clearly represents what many associate with middle-class values in our culture. Further, Baumrind has derived her generalizations about the antecedents or correlates of this behavior from the study of literate, cooperative, "normal" parents and children, most of whom are reasonably secure financially. Our question is twofold. Is the goal of instrumental competence desirable for all children in all quarters of society? If so, should parents everywhere attempt to emulate the pattern of parental authority most clearly associated with this behavior in children?

The dilemma about behavioral control is as central in schools as in homes. Who shall resolve the dilemma is a matter of philosophical decision and commitment. Shall it be school boards, school superintendents, parents, teachers, the children themselves or, to be hoped for, some happy blend of all concerned and involved parties? Procedurally, dealing with this dilemma involves control of curriculum, including its content, methods of instruction, and policies and practices about evaluation.

In recent years, the dilemma about control in education has been characterized by efforts of parent and student groups to gain client control of education. Theoretically, parents already possess such control, because as voters they elect the school board. However, this control is clearly apparent mainly in small town and rural communities. Even there, much of the power to shape curriculum, to set standards and choose methods for behavior control, and to retain or discharge teachers rests with school administrators. Currently, demands for increased or even total parent control of the schools is most obvious in urban, minority group settings. Such demands are based on the charge that education is designed and implemented by professional educators who are usually white, Protestant, and middle class and, as such, do not do justice to poverty and minority groups. The demand for greater educational relevance and efficiency for special group populations is insistent. Another vigorous and growing dissent comes from "intelligentsia"—for the most part young, free-thinking, intent parents and youth who believe that national and educational priorities are wrong, that schools are failing, and that something else (the free school? the Montessori method?) is urgently needed. Many such people from all over the country, most frequently in the Northeast and the West coasts, have united and now operate their own schools outside the public domain.

At this point, however, our concern is consumer control—student control—versus professional control. This dilemma revolves around how much voice children and adolescents should have in deciding their own educational goals and experiences, designing their own curriculum, selecting their own teachers, and deciding whether to attend school at all. The dilemma also extends to the instructional staff, including the degree to which teachers are directive, employ didactic methods, structure both content and time allotted for learning, place sanctions on student behavior (disciplinary techniques, rules, and regulations), and evaluate student progress (grading and reporting).

Dilemmas are most clearly illustrated by taking extreme cases. At one end of the control dilemma is the traditional United States classroom where educational activities are prescribed to the last detail by teachers and administrators. Such prescriptive approaches are based on the belief that adults know better than children what kinds of learning are necessary for a person eventually to assume a responsible adult role in society. Critics argue that such prescriptive teaching more than anything else reflects the belief that students cannot be trusted to select their own learning (39).

At the other extreme can be found the ultrapermissive approach to education, where students determine exclusively what they will learn, when and under what conditions they will learn it, how long they will spend with any given learning activity, and with whom they will learn. The growing *free school* movement mentioned above reflects at least some conviction among parents and their children that a free approach to education is best. The rationale seems to be that a truly democratic society should offer its members alternatives to conventional public education, with freedom to choose among

them when desired. Moreover, self-determined learning is believed to be the most meaningful and therefore the most effective learning. Only when a student is allowed to choose will he be truly motivated to learn in a satisfying, self-fulfilling way. Critics of this view, as might be expected, maintain that such an approach is a royal road to anarchy.

3.2 Summerhill: A Radical Approach to Child-rearing and Education*

In the latter part of the eighteenth century, Jean Jacques Rousseau advanced an extreme maturational point of view about education and development during the life span preceding puberty. In the essay *Emile*, Rousseau advocated that no arranged or formal experiences should be imposed upon the child. Natural growth is best. Children should not be spoiled by corrupting them with adult ideas. When the child is mature is time enough to begin training for competence. Previous to that time, let him simply learn about life.

Working from similar philosophy, in addition to concepts of development from psychoanalysis, A. S. Neill, an Englishman, some fifty years ago founded a private school in England that he called Summerhill (36). Neill has long believed that formal approaches to education are repressive and are based on values that breed disturbances rather than contribute positive experiences for constructive development. The principle of freedom — freedom of belief, dissent, and self-governance — on which Summerhill is based comes through clearly in this excerpt from Neill's major work.

*From SUMMERHILL: A Radical Approach to Child Rearing by A. S. Neill, copyright 1960 by Hart Publishing Company, New York.

When we began this school, we had one idea in mind: to make the school fit the child, instead of making the child fit the school. . . . We set out to make a school in which we should allow children to be themselves. In order to do this we had to renounce all discipline, all direction, all suggestion, all moral training, and all religious instruction. . . . All it required was . . . a belief in the child as a good, not an evil being. . . . If left to himself without adult suggestion of any kind, he will develop as far as he is capable of developing . . . lessons are optional. Children can go to them or stay away . . . for months if they want to. There is a timetable, but only for teachers. The children have classes usually according to their age, but sometimes according to their interests. We have no new methods of teaching for we do not consider that teaching in itself matters very much. Whether a school has or has not a special method for teaching long division is of no importance for long division is of no importance except to those who want to learn it. And the child who wants to learn long division will learn it no matter how it is taught (36).

Among the most basic issues involved in the matter of total educational freedom is the relationship of schools to the society in which they exist. Also involved is the question of the outcome of such an "education" on one's personal development: the effects of a Summerhill experience over the long term. Neill, of course, has argued that his school is generally successful; otherwise, it could not have survived through these many years. He admits, however, that Summerhill has become increasingly dependent for its existence on enrollments of American children and youth. Oddly enough, almost no research is available to indicate the impact of Summerhill on its students. What little follow-up information is available indicates that some graduates are very successful as adults and are grateful for their experience with freedom. Others question the ultimate value of the experience and would do things differently if it were possible to relive their childhood. Still others are apparently less successful and less fulfilled as adults than they would like to be. These self-reports suggest that the value and net effect of Summerhill vary greatly from person to person. It is difficult to argue that Summerhill-type schooling or any other one approach to education is a panacea for human development. Yet if one truly believes in pluralism as a necessary condition for human welfare, alternatives such as Summerhill must be supported.

The authors believe the issue of prescribed versus free curricula is too easily conceived as an either–or dilemma. Various combinations of structured and free learning experiences at different periods in the individual's development may be more desirable than simplistic approaches from either extreme point of view. Furthermore, the authors know of no evidence whatsoever that indicates the superiority of any one educational (or child-rearing) approach for *all* children. The important question is whether or to what extent self-determination in an educational—or a home—setting contributes usefully to a given individual's functioning within society. This dilemma also extends to the question of whether students, especially young children, are capable of judicious self-determination and selection of experience.

It can be argued that the personal needs of parents exert considerable influence on their preferences for their children's education. For example, parents and young people not yet parents who espouse Neill's famous free school, Summerhill, are likely to deify childhood. Parents who

relative — Honest

resent, but who did not actively rebel against, organization and authority during their own childhood may receive vicarious satisfaction from seeing their children in an antiauthority school setting. The authors have observed that parents who are "on their way up"—are upward socially mobile—stress competence training for their children more than parents who have arrived.

NO PREMARITAL INTERCOURSE
— Honesty

Absolute versus *Relative Standards*

Related to behavior control is a second dilemma: What should be the nature of the standards (if any) that an individual takes as guidelines for his own behavior or that are imposed on him by parents and teachers? This dilemma permeates moral training—in fact, moral training is at the heart of the dilemma. Some authorities have even suggested that the ultimate concern in socialization is the moralization of the individual (31). This important matter is discussed in Chapter 8, but the authors wish to anticipate a bit by focusing on the dilemma faced by both parents and their individual children in selecting standards for moral behavior.

Consider the parents first. Consciously or not, parents indicate to their children their beliefs about what is and what is not moral in several important ways. First, parents (by default if nothing else) are necessarily models for their children. Some talk about what constitutes morality, but do not set a model; others both talk about morality *and* model it; still others do not talk about it, but model it. Second, parents selectively reward and punish behavior in ways that convey moral judgments. The pattern of rewards and punishments that parents employ is a good indication of which behavior they consider "good," which "bad." Parental confusion and inconsistency in talk, mod-

eling, and selective reinforcement may be disastrous for children.

One school of thought labels standards as absolute. Standards are intrinsically and unquestionably right, are enduring, and apply to all particular situations. The parent who tells his child, "You must *never* break your word or break a promise you have made to another person" is advancing an absolute standard based on the value and need of maintaining trust among people.

Standards can also be flexible and variable from one situation to another, depending on the context, or valid at one point in time but not later. Such standards are types of *relativism*. Current standards about premarital sex often reflect relativism. Whereas premarital sexual intercourse has traditionally been and by many is still regarded as *absolutely* wrong, today's young and not so young are likely to view it as all right if one is "in love" (7). Some do not place even this qualification on premarital sex (38). For the relativist, the judgment about whether premarital sex is right or wrong depends on the nature of the situation in which it occurs, *not* on an absolute moral standard.

Many parents are bewildered, facing severe personal dilemmas, about what moral standards to try to develop in their children and how to go about developing them. The rapidly changing nature of the times and conflicting views about child development deepen the dilemma. Some do nothing, thus abdicating their responsibilities. Many want to leave the problem to the schools or the church, or to both. Most parents, however, approach moral socialization with *some* goals in mind. An example helps to set the dimensions of both the philosophical and the procedural dimensions of the dilemma about morality. The area of sex has been selected because so many of our moral structures are built around it.

Two 5-year-olds, a boy and a girl, are playing doctor and nurse in the family garage of the boy's home. Each child demonstrates keen interest in the other's body. Eventually, the boy, as patient, must be examined for some disorder of the penis. At this moment, the boy's mother comes in to find her son with his pants down and his penis prominently displayed in front of the absorbed girl. This may be considered a critical moment in socialization. How should the mother respond?

The mother's response will usually depend both on her views about child development in general and on her feelings about sexual exhibitionism in particular. Her dilemma is both philosophical and procedural. What are her goals about socialization of sex and modesty? In view of her goals, how is she to handle this particular incident?

Some parents will employ absolute standards. Sexual exhibitionism is wrong for *everyone!* Then, many alternatives exist for enforcing the standard. Some parents will spank, deprive of privileges, or scold. Parents who employ absolute standards for their children often display guilt orientations toward their children's misbehavior. For example: "You have disappointed me greatly. You know this is wrong. I do not at all like what you have done. Go to your room and think about how badly you have behaved. We will talk more about it later."

By such behavior, a mother appeals to the relationship between her and her son. Her disapproval is a form of love withdrawal. Love withdrawal has been shown to produce guilt in children, both because they have violated standards that they have been taught are important and correct, and because they have disappointed and hurt their parents. Many argue that a guilt orientation is necessary and right, because eventually children so reared learn to police themselves. The consideration of an act known to be wrong arouses anticipatory guilt. *Anticipatory guilt can be avoided only by not performing the forbidden act*, a method whereby the individual acts as a check on his own behavior. No punishment is needed from others, because he has punished himself, even in advance. Guilt can be an internalized absolute standard for behavior that guides one across situations and events.

Inducing guilt can be very risky, of course, because at some point guilt feelings may become overpowering and even destructive. Guilt, at least excessive guilt, has long been considered a breeding ground for neurosis by many psychologists, particularly those with a psychoanalytic bent (see the section on dynamic psychology in Chapter 2).

Some parents respond by introducing a *shame orientation* as an alternative to a guilt orientation. The mother who has discovered the two children in doctor–patient sexual play may say to her son, "You should be ashamed of yourself. What would people say if they knew that you were exposing yourself to this girl? Stop it immediately before someone sees you!" This technique for socialization and behavior control is different from guilt induction, because the absolute standard for behavior is not made explicit. In fact, the underlying message is that the behavior itself is not so bad as long as the person is not caught.

Still another mother may see this incident as an opportunity to explain, enlighten, and promote self-understanding. She simply asks the children to explain what they are doing, then proceeds to discuss matters of sex differences with the children at a level they can comprehend. Here, the emphasis is more on "informal" education than on specific standards for behavior.

For some relativists, standards for behavior exist only according to group norms. Whatever one's reference group believes is right and wrong is used by the individual as the standard for his own behavior. As group norms change, so does the individual's behavior.

Dilemmas about morality also occur in schools and are associated with attempts at moral education and policies for classroom behavior such as cheating. Absolute as opposed to relative standards enter into student evaluation. Student evaluation is surrounded by more important philosophical and procedural issues than one is likely to recognize at first glance. The student's evaluation by his teacher and his school is the major feedback the student gets about his competence as a learner in the major achievement arena during his formative years. Thus, school evaluation touches central aspects of socialization and self concept.

Dilemmas about student evaluation consist of such questions as *how* and *for what* does one evaluate students. Related procedural dilemmas include matters of letter grades versus interviews or written reports, evaluation on "the curve" in comparison with classmates (relative) or an absolute standard (90%+ = A, 50%− = F, and so on); at what age should parents no longer be informed about the student's grade? should grades be a matter of public knowledge or privileged privacy? and under what circumstances may outside school personnel or agencies be given access to evaluations?

The reason that so much time is devoted to the discussion of evaluation is because, as has been implied, evaluations have profound implications for how students come to view themselves as learners, the kinds of relationships they develop with teachers, and the nature of the attitudes they develop toward school and authority. The arbitrary nature of most evaluation procedures should be clearly realized, as should also the implications of the effect arbitrary and sometimes very unfair procedures have on students. Educators, parents, and students need to examine other sides of the evaluation question: Is any kind of formal evaluation needed? Should students do their own evaluation or play an important role in the process? Should students be called in to help evaluate other students? Do teachers really have any right to evaluate at all?

The Nature of Early Experiences

The third parental and educational dilemma consists of issues about caregiving and education in early childhood. For infants and toddlers, superficially there appear to be few philosophical dilemmas. Everyone agrees that he wishes his children to be well adjusted and happy, healthy, clean, well fed, and so on. Procedural dilemmas beset such matters, however, and the question of education in early childhood is almost lost in the polemic storms created by those who advocate one or another, often flatly opposing, procedure for educating or not educating preschool-aged children.

Freud, as suggested in Chapter 2, was instrumental in calling to parents' attention the impact of infant and preschool experiences on later personality development. Historically (before Freud), the early and particularly the prelanguage years were not considered very important as long as the infant was fed, kept dry and clean, and got plenty of rest and fresh air. The urgency for personality development

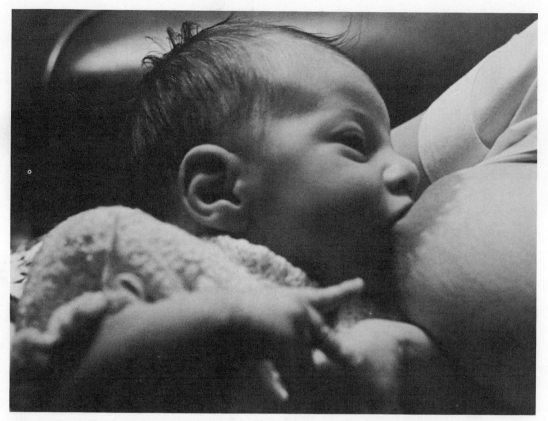

The developmental importance of early childhood experiences has been a persistent dilemma since the writings of Freud. Even the issue of breast feeding versus bottle feeding has not been convincingly resolved.

put on this period by Freud and his disciples changed the picture dramatically, affected all layers of society, and has created a host of dilemmas for parents and scholars alike.

Nursing and other feeding practices can be taken to illustrate some of the procedural dilemmas that must be handled during infancy and early childhood. For example, if a new mother is physically able, she must immediately face the issue of whether to breast-feed or bottle-feed her baby. Dynamic psychologists have taught that method of feeding is pro-

foundly important for security and other central aspects of personality, and favor breast feeding. Thus, the mother who chooses not to breast-feed may have some problems with her own anxiety and guilt. A related issue (dilemma) is *when* and *how* to wean the infant from breast or bottle to cup and spoon. Still another issue is *demand feeding* (when the child wants it) versus *scheduled feeding* (the traditional every four hours).

Much research has been carried out in efforts to resolve these issues by facts rather than pronouncements (11, 37). Research about mothers and infants presents enormous difficulties. How does a researcher reach mothers and their babies? How can a researcher measure personality in infancy and the preschool years? How can a researcher distinguish effects of feeding from effects of other child care practices? From the mass of studies, it must be reluctantly concluded that up to this time no clear relationships have emerged between infant and child behavior and the kind and the schedule of feeding (11). Our best estimate is that parent attitudes, rewards and punishments, and the nature of the emotional bond between parent and child are more important than a single technique of child care.

As children grow older, dilemmas about how to proceed in their socialization grow more frequent, complex, and often intense. Toilet training is the first time in most children's lives that they have had to sacrifice their own will, pleasure, and convenience to social custom and demand. Important questions about toilet training are: When does a mother initiate it? How does a mother go about it? What is the relation of bowel to bladder training? What is the relation between elimination and sex and modesty training? As in the case of nursing practices, much research effort has gone into understanding how variations in elimination training affect children's behavior. Disturbances in bowel and bladder functioning are often associated with punitive and/or premature training (11). Moreover, early elimination training based on coercive methods is often related to a mother's anxiety about sex and "need" for orderliness (34). Yet, different children respond differently to the same technique, whether benevolent or harsh, thus making it almost impossible to predict long-term

effects of elimination training. The authors suggest again, as they did for feeding, that the emotional climate in which elimination training occurs is more influential than the specifics of timing and methods (although extremes in timing and method may make important differences).

3.3 Behaviorist View of Toilet Training (48)

First, in accord with the principle of successive approximation and gradualness in training, it is suggested that the training should begin long before the time the parent expects the child to be completely trained. This seems necessary to enable all the stimulus-response (S-R) relationships to be developed without undue haste or stringent training methods. The parent must also expect very slow progress at first, and then only in simple general behaviors that set the stage for the specific training.

A first step might be to observe the usual times of bowel movement of the child. When this has been ascertained, the child could be placed on the potty-chair at a likely time. Without some source of reinforcement, however, the child may attempt to escape or may start to cry. The sitting period should therefore be short at first, and some reinforcers—games with the parent, play with toys, and so on—might profitably be introduced.

Through this procedure, a necessary adjunct to successful total toilet behavior, sitting in the appropriate place, may be brought under the control of the stimuli of the toilet situation through the use of positive reinforcement. The period of sitting on the toilet may also be gradually increased through reinforcement procedures, and the child can then be trained to spend some time on the toilet without being attended by the parent.

Furthermore, the behaviors involved in evacuation must undergo conditioning—but only as a by-product of the above procedure. If the child sits on the toilet each day at a propitious time, a certain proportion of "successes" should occur. Specific reinforcement of this behavior by the parents would then be expected to bring the operants (such as straining) under the control of the situational cues. Through classical conditioning, the respondents involving the lower intestines should also tend to be elicited on future occasions by the stimuli of the situation.

Verbal training may also play an important part in the process of toilet training. The verbal training may commence long before the other toilet-training procedures. For example, the parents may simply say "B M" (or some such term) whenever they see the child in the act of evacuation. By pairing the auditory stimulus with the respondents involved, the term B M should to some extent come to be a conditioned stimulus that elicits these respondents. This verbal stimulus may then be used in the child's training to increase the probability that he will evacuate during the time he is on the potty.

In time, in accord with the relevant principles of language learning, the child should himself come to say B M. After he learns to say the word and the parents prompt him to say it as he evacuates, the child's response of saying B M should start to come under the control of the stimuli produced by the distended bowels and other conditions until finally it occurs sufficiently prior to the act for the parent to have time to take him to the potty before elimination

of the kind of training previously discussed.

Verbal training of a slightly aversive nature may also be used when the appropriate verbal repertoire has been established. If the parent says, "Don't go B M unless you are sitting on the toilet," this will have the effect of making the act aversive unless the child is on the toilet. Thus, the act of evacuation in the absence of the toilet should become a conditioned aversive stimulus on the basis of language conditioning.

Dollard and Miller (14) discuss some other advantages of language for training the child in these behaviors.

*The reinforcement of the act of defecation itself will fix the correct series of responses into place. This will happen whether the course of the training has been stormy or smooth. However, in the case of the smooth, verbally aided learning there is much less danger of arousing furious anger or of creating maladaptive habits such as retention of feces and lack of control. Extremely strong anxiety reactions do not occur and feelings of excessive worthlessness are less likely. The end result is the same so far as mere cleanliness training is concerned. The difference lies in the fact that the . . . verbally aided method of getting out the response has much less risk of violent side reactions and character distortions (p. 140).**

Feeding and toilet training are only two of the many early experiences that present dilemmas to parents. Parents' widespread concern about such dilemmas continues to produce a good market for professional advice givers. Example 3.3 should not be taken as an example of professional advice; rather, it represents a behavioral analysis of how bowel training might be

* From COMPLEX HUMAN BEHAVIOR: A Systematic Extension of Learning Principles by Arthur W. Staats, with contributions by Carolyn K. Staats. Copyright © 1963 by Holt, Rinehart and Winston, Inc. Reprinted by permission of Holt, Rinehart and Winston, Inc.

arranged consistent with behaviorist principles of learning. The specificity and learning basis of this analysis illustrates clearly the scientific orientation of behaviorism.

Most parents, and rightly so, are concerned about their children's overall development. For the early childhood years, this concern is most obvious for health and emotional adjustment. Professional child developmentalists are equally concerned about such matters, but are also directly involved in early cognitive and language development. The current wave of early childhood education programs in our society reflects this concern (18).

The authors can illustrate what they mean by philosophical and procedural dilemmas in education by considering preschool intervention programs. Such programs are often described as compensatory education for economically disadvantaged children. The rationale of many programs is based on the idea that early school failure, so frequent among disadvantaged children, can be minimized and perhaps prevented by organized preschool experience. Such experience usually includes training in language and other preacademic skills that are basic to school success. Other programs reflect less a concern for specific school prepara-

The controversies whirling about the preschool and early-intervention programs are many and exceedingly complex. Is the intervention to serve the individual's or the society's needs? And what are the ultimate, long-term outcomes of such efforts? (Photo by Hanna W. Schreiber)

tion than for the general enrichment of children's social experience.

If the authors advocate professional intervention, they imply that educators can do a better job than many parents in providing skills and attitudes that lead to adequate school achievement. This point is debatable. Even so, a basic philosophical dilemma linked with preschool education is *intervention for what?* What should be the goals of preschool intervention programs? What *exactly* can educators do better with young children than can their parents? To say that disagreement among educators and parents exists about the goals and purposes of preschool education is a gross understatement. Preferences range from the direct, systematic training for language competence to informal, loosely organized discovery learning environments in which there are ample amounts of free play. Other early education dilemmas are more clearly procedural, such as determining when intervention should occur. In the past, most intervention programs have been directed toward children between the ages of 4 and 5. Some authorities now suggest that this is too late to exert any lasting or large effect on children's intellectual development (see the discussion of the critical-periods dilemma later in this chapter). The emotion-packed decision about who will conduct intervention programs must also be faced, as must the question of the qualifications and training of early education personnel. Other dilemmas include: where intervention programs can best be conducted, how long they should last, and how extensively parents should be involved.

Identification of dilemmas related to early education is useful for three reasons. First, the way the dilemmas are handled by adults can conceivably make important

differences in the quality of young children's existence. Accordingly, the quality of development over time can be affected, depending on the nature of what occurs during the preschool years. Even though we have a long way to go before we possess adequate knowledge about early education, the evidence clearly indicates that some programs are better than others for producing changes in rate and level of cognitive development and achievement of specific skills (18).

A second advantage to identification of dilemmas in early education is that they point toward broader questions about who possesses the authority to make decisions about intervention and the nature of preschool education. Whence is this authority derived? Third, the philosophical and procedural dilemmas about full day care for children of all ages and income levels are rapidly becoming more pressing, as welfare mothers are urged or required to go back to work or into work training regardless of the ages of their children; and as more economically advantaged women seek places for themselves outside the traditional wife and mother role, even at the time when their children are very young.

→ DILEMMAS FOR THE STUDENT OF DEVELOPMENTAL PSYCHOLOGY

Up to this point in the chapter, persisting dilemmas about socialization and development common in our culture have been discussed. In addition to such problems, scholars of developmental psychology face more specific dilemmas related to advancement of knowledge in the field. These dilemmas can also be classified as being philosophical and/or procedural. They include conceptual dilemmas concerning what is the truth about development. In this second half of the chapter, some representative dilemmas confronted in the search for truth in developmental psychology are examined.

Philosophical Dilemmas

Among the first dilemmas confronted by a developmental psychologist is, "What aspects of developmental psychology shall I study?" This choice will necessarily reflect value judgments about what the developmentalist thinks is important and why. For some, the selection of topics for study is made in response to social problems within society that require attention, such as delinquent and criminal behavior or mental retardation. It is obvious, of course, that the study of human development is the study of people. People must consent to be studied or to have their children studied. Access to large populations of children and adolescents must be gained in order to pursue most questions profitably (for example, underachievement, attitudes toward sex, drug use). Such studies are frequently difficult to conduct and expensive in time and money and require the careful examination of research proposals by committees of professional workers and parents.

In Chapter 1, it was often stated that "The answer to this question is not yet known;" or "Little is actually known about this phase of development." Such admissions, frustrating as they are to authors and readers alike, are often due to the fact that they touch on sensitive topics. People are reluctant or refuse to disclose information concerning either themselves or their children about many such topics. Sometimes, research workers (a respectable, middle-class group on the whole) are timid about treading on taboo ground. Human sexual behavior is a prime exam-

ple. It was not until 1948 that a major and scientifically respectable study of sexual behavior was published (30). Even now, we know little about how sexual behavior is socialized during childhood and early adolescence.

There have been other taboo topics—death, suicide, homosexuality, parapsychology (clairvoyance, extrasensory perception), and religion—as noted earlier (19). Imprecise methods of investigation further complicate the problem of the taboo topic. Above all, the student interested in researching a topic, however delicate and urgent its nature, must maintain professional ethics. Violating ethical standards or treating ethical issues in a cavalier fashion does injustice to a person's entire profession.

Once the research worker has chosen a topic for study, he faces many procedural dilemmas. But the point here is that a critical philosophical dilemma exists in addition to the choice of a topic for study. This dilemma is deciding what and how to report controversial findings to one's colleagues and the public.

Let us suppose that a person scrupulously studies race and violence, for example, and after taking infinite pains comes inexorably to the conclusion that those with more than 50 percent of racial component A are more violent than those belonging to races B and C; and that race A is one against which strong prejudice already exists in the society. What does the researcher do with his finding? Is the advancement of science to be gained by publishing more important than the increased impetus toward race prejudice that is likely to follow publication? And what should journal editors decide about publishing possibly inflammatory articles, even though they are scientifically impeccable?

The following are some of the dimensions of the ethical dilemmas posed: Should a scientist suppress data? Does not the individual have a free right of expression, whether he is a scientist or not? Is it not the scientist's duty to contribute to knowledge, because "truth suppressed is falsehood"? Should not data be put in the public domain so they can be scrutinized and perhaps replicated or invalidated?

On the other side of the dilemma are such issues as possible, perhaps probable, misuse of the data by racists; the fact that the data may add heat to the cauldron of race relations that is already near the boiling point; the personal risk the scientist runs of being labeled a racist and of alienating his liberal colleagues and friends; the possibility that the journal and its editor(s) will be faced with charges of racism; the possibility that publication of the findings will serve as a sanction—a semipermission, as it were—for members of race A to become even more violent than the research in question has shown them to be, because, after all, their violence is genetic–constitutional; or the risk that publication of such findings will reflect discredit and bring a bad name to the science. In other words, scientists, like all citizens, are sometimes faced with agonizing moral dilemmas that have both urgent philosophical and procedural aspects.

Procedural Dilemmas
Just as the scholar encounters philosophical dilemmas in his work, so also does he encounter procedural dilemmas. How can he go about his research without creating undue hardship for others, unnecessarily, illegally, or unethically invading their privacy, such as in psychological testing; using instruments for data collection the

validity of which is unknown or seriously in question; or violating the ethical principle of privileged communication when deeply personal information is gathered through interview or questionnaire procedures? Precautions about protecting the identities of children, youth, and their parents must be taken, and possible consequences on one's research for both short- and long-term development and behavior of his subjects must be considered.

3.4   A Statement on the Ethics of Testing (1)

Concern over the uses and misuses of tests in psychological research, education, and industry has increased markedly in recent years. Many of the issues raised, in the final analysis, are ethical. Some fear that tests lead psychologists and educators unfairly and negatively to label children and youth. Others point out the possibility of exercising Machiavellian control over human destinies by using test results as the criterion for decision making (grading, selection for educational programs, referral for therapy, hiring and firing, and the like). The professional psychologist is well aware of these issues. He seeks to discover ways in which tests may serve salutary, not negative and limiting, purposes in terms of both human welfare and the advancement of knowledge about development and behavior.

To illustrate this concern, the authors present a position statement about psychological assessment recently adopted by the American Psychological Association. The four guidelines contained in this statement apply equally to ability and personality testing.

1. Guaranteed protection must be pro-

vided for every individual against unwarranted inferences by educational personnel ill-equipped with necessary background knowledge and skill in testing.
2. Obsolete information (dated test results, for example) that might lead to unfavorable evaluation of an individual must be periodically culled from personal records in order to protect the individual.
3. Unnecessary intrusions into one's privacy must be avoided; irrelevant tests and questions have no place in a well-designed assessment program.
4. Given the aforementioned modes of protection, procedures should be established to facilitate continual investigation of new and improved techniques of assessment.

The long-term development of subjects highlights an important procedural issue; namely, to experiment or not to experiment. It is widely believed, and there are data to support the belief, that severe school underachievement is typically accompanied, and may actually be caused, by personal social maladjustment. A large hypothetical junior high school (we will call it "Boxwood") includes a high percentage of intellectually normal but seriously underachieving seventh- and eighth-grade boys. The counseling and psychological staff, as well as the Boxwood principal, is interested in cooperating with the local university in an experiment that has two goals: (1) to see if counseled underachieving students improve more than uncounseled students, and (2) to see if group or individual counseling is more effective.

Dr. Highland, the senior man in counseling and guidance at Boxwood, is assigned the task of coordinating the school and the university efforts. After plans for the research have been made and the names of the boys selected for participation in the research have been noted, Dr. Highland communicates with all the boys' parents to obtain their permission to have their sons take part in the study. He explains the study accurately to each parent. The first parent he reaches replies, "Absolutely not! I do *not* want my son to be a guinea pig for some psychologist! How is poking around in my son's private life going to affect his school grades? In my experience, counseling just makes people goofier than they were to start with."

This parent's argument is essentially that experimentation may be unethical, especially if all possible side effects of such treatment are not fully known. Most parents and psychologists agree with this position. On the other hand, the ethical psychologist will go to great pains to ensure that an experimental procedure will not have permanent or, it is hoped, even temporary negative effects. The parent's guinea pig argument can perhaps be countered by the argument that *not* to experiment is unethical. That is, the deliberate avoidance of activities that may result in increased knowledge and understanding about development, especially when the topic under study has promise for improving the human condition, is unethical. The authors *do* suggest that at the present state of their knowledge, conclusions that can be very helpful to underachievers might be reached by a study such as that planned at Boxwood Junior High School.

As mentioned earlier, the question of whether or not to intervene educationally with economically disadvantaged children often arises. Head Start is the best-known example of an intervention, compensatory education program. Many have argued that Head Start and other similar programs, intended mostly for 4- and 5-year-olds, are too little and too late. The Parent Child Center (PCC) movement is an extension downward in age and outward in scope, where mothers are trained in principles of child development and cognitive stimulation from the time their children are infants until they reach the age of 3 or so. The PCC is preventive rather than remedial, and is designed to prevent deleterious effects of disadvantaged conditions on children by "optimizing" their environments (learning opportunities) from about the time of birth onward. Results from the PCC's and other like programs are promising at this time, but cannot yet be said to be definitive.

Dilemmas around intervention or prevention, as stated briefly earlier, center on whether or not "white middle-class standards" are being imposed on poor Black, or American Indian, or Hispano children. Our belief is that great care should be taken not to interfere with the cultural values and principles of *any* co-culture, as long as they are not demonstrably damaging to either the members of the co-culture or the broader society (as would be true, for example, with a delinquent gang, or a drug co-culture). The authors can see no very serious risk—and vast potential advantage—to augmenting the problem-solving skills of severely disadvantaged children above what they may otherwise develop within the context of their disadvantageousness. In fact, we can think of few if any populations that would not benefit from augmented "intellectual power."

Few will argue against the need to maintain ethical standards in psychological research, although maintaining such

standards sometimes places limits on potentially useful research. The study of maternal deprivation provides a good example. Psychologists have long been interested in assessing the effects on infants and children of being deprived of or separated from a consistent mother or mother surrogate. However, it is ethically impossible to *experiment* with human beings concerning this issue. We cannot deliberately separate mothers from their offspring to see the results. Thus, we settle for "experiments in nature," and study characteristics of children in cases where for one reason or another maternal separation and deprivation have occurred "naturally." Obviously, studies in the open community can never be as well controlled and clearly defined as laboratory experiments. Thus, our results are unlikely to be as clear as they would be if we could ethically do experimental work.

Ethical questions obviously arise even from studies of nature, conducted in the open community. If psychoeducational findings suggest, for example, that institutional living is in some way harmful to children, are responsible people not obligated to take action either against institutions as institutions or toward institutional change designed to eliminate the damage to children? Of course we are obligated, but in so doing, we contaminate our own research by introducing uncontrolled procedures and thus further dilute and obscure our findings. However, almost all of us believe this is the way it must be if we are to work with human beings.

Questions such as this are extremely important for social policies concerning adoption, placing of infants and children in institutional settings or day care, and awarding custody of children in the event of divorce or loss of a parent.

The Search for Truth

Let us now move to the set of dilemmas in which questions and issues are raised that involve the search for truth about human behavior and development. The development and testing of theories of development and behavior (see Chapter 2) are examples of the search for truth. However, the authors' purpose here is to highlight conceptual dilemmas that often transcend any given theory. Such dilemmas sometimes lead to significant implications for designing an environment for human development. In the following pages, the authors discuss the classical dilemma usually called the nature–nurture controversy, the critical-periods hypothesis, stability versus change in human development, the nature of "developmental problems," and the question of normality in behavior.

The Nature–Nurture Controversy *Essay*

A basic issue for developmental psychology is to what degree nature (heredity) on the one hand and nurture (environment) on the other contribute to behavior development. Like the mythical flying Dutchman doomed forever to sail the seven seas without ever coming into port, this dilemma has historically seemed to (and may still) be fated to exist forever. One reason for so discouraging a state of affairs is the way in which psychologists have approached the issue. In the thirties and forties one of *the* burning psychological questions was, *"Which* human traits or characteristics are determined mainly by heredity and which by environment? *How much* of a given trait or characteristic is determined by heredity and *how much* by environment?"

For some things (eye color), the answer is very simple—heredity. For others, such as mechanical or musical skill, keenness of abstract thinking, or personal adjustment, the answer is murky.

As their scientific sophistication grew, most psychologists abandoned such *which* and *how much* questions, realizing that heredity is a necessary condition for environment, and vice versa. To ask which is most important for human development, heredity or environment, is like asking which is more important to water H_2 or O or, as another author has put it, like asking if length or width is more important in calculating the area of a rectangle (16). Today, we have mostly moved to thinking about how heredity and environment combine and interact in behavior and development, although there is often logical and practical merit in trying to calculate degree of influence exerted by one, the other, and both. Since there is little or nothing we can do about selective breeding (the only clear way now known to influence heredity), we are now mainly preoccupied with discovering what environments permit optimum growth for individuals of all types of heredity.

The time, energy, and emotional commitment devoted to heredity and environment have not been totally wasted. We now know that identical twins, for example, are much more like each other than fraternal twins, who, in turn, resemble each other in some characteristics (for example, intelligence) more closely than nontwin siblings. Remarkable similarities continue to exist for identical twins, even when they have been reared apart, but, on the whole, for psychological characteristics, they are less similar than identical twins reared together. Thus, we have evidence that both genetics and learning strongly influence many human characteristics (23, 44).

Even more striking evidence is provided by studies of animals, the conditions

At what ages, if any, are the maximal and the minimal forms of environmental experience necessary for optimal mastery of learning skills—for example, playing the piano? (Wide World Photos)

of whose rearing and breeding can be more tightly controlled. For example, one authority reports that boxers and Scottish terriers differ markedly from many other breeds in aggressiveness and fearlessness. This difference is commonly considered to be constitutional (genetic). However, when rearing circumstances are sharply altered for these breeds, their normal fearlessness is markedly decreased (33).

Perhaps more significant still is a generalization, also based on animal research, that identical environmental treatment may result in very different outcomes for animals of different genetic makeups.

Example 3.5 contains a summary of research bearing on this generalization (21). As can be seen, such results lead most of us now to concentrate on the question of genetic–constitutional and environmental–learning *interaction*. Few still construe the classic dilemma as nature *versus* nurture.

3.5 A Study of Genetic–Environmental Interaction

D. G. Freedman (21) conducted a fascinating experiment to examine the effects of "indulgent" and "disciplinary" training strategies among four breeds of dog: beagle, basenji, wirehaired fox terrier, and Shetland sheep dog. Dogs from each breed were subjected to both strategies, beginning daily from the third week of life and continuing through the eighth week. *Indulged* pups were never punished and were encouraged to engage in exploratory and other active forms of behavior. In contrast, *disciplined* pups were restricted and were taught to sit, stay, and come at the trainer's command.

At the end of the eighth week, a test situation was applied to each pup. This test consisted of placing a bowl of food in front of a pup, but preventing him from eating for three minutes, during which time a slap on the pup's hindquarters and a shouted "no" were administered by the experimenter. After this, the experimenter left the room and the elapsed time until the pup began to eat was recorded. This test situation was repeated for eight days.

Results of this experiment are that training strategy effects were large for beagles and terriers. For both breeds, the indulged pups delayed their eating

Substantiate Hereditary Theory

behavior much longer than did their disciplined same-breed counterparts. In contrast, kind of training seemingly had little effect for the other two breeds. All Shetland sheep dogs avoided the food entirely; all basenji pups ate quickly. These effects occurred regardless of whether an indulgent or a disciplinary approach to training had been taken.

Anyone who has children or who has worked with children has made informal observations that support the research reported in this study. Johnny will react calmly to a firm "no"; Bill will become physically agitated and often openly emotional in response to the same firm "no." Such individual differences in re-activity demand more individualization of education (including types of control) than is typically provided in schools and often in homes for the different children in a family (12).

The nature–nurture dilemma is by no means resolved or even fully understood. The authors' preferred approach is inter-actionism. Given normal heredity, some behavior may depend on experience; or given normal environment, some behavior may depend on heredity (26). Regardless, the two determinants are interdependent. One writer has summarized the inter-dependence in this simple equation (13):

Genotype × Environment = Phenotype,

where genotype refers to the sum of the individual's genetic endowment, and phenotype is the class name for the in-dividual's observable qualities. All in-dividuals except identical twins differ in genotype. This equation permits the ob-vious conclusion: Genetic potentialities of one person may be fully realized in en-vironment A, moderately well in environ-ment B, and not at all in environment C. James, whose life story was sketched in Chapter 1, would almost certainly not have fared well in the boxing arena, which opened up a new life to Matthew, whose life story was also summarized there. James, sexually timid and a clinger to his mother, would probably not have emerged well from the long love affair with an older woman, as Matthew did.

The Critical-Periods Dilemma

In the nature–nurture discussion, it was suggested that neither heredity nor environment yields behavior (2). Rather, heredity yields structures which, under certain environmental conditions and depending on their state (for example, how mature are they? have they been damaged by disease or accident?), are capable of a certain range of behavior (16). This notion of interaction leads us to an-other dilemma. Is the *timing* of environ-mental influence on genetic structure im-portant? If so, in what way? Most of us these days ask the question: "Are there periods during human development when the environment may affect the course and outcome of development in critical ways?"

Many of our ideas about critical periods have come from embryology (10), al-though, as shown in Chapter 2, Freud was also a "critical periods man." (Also see 41, 42.)

One theme in the theory of critical periods is that *organisms can be totally indifferent to, or resist certain forms or patterns of, stimulation after a critical point in time.* For example, the fetus is thought to be safe from danger of damage from rubella from three to four months after conception, but exceptionally vulnerable before that time. The idea of indifference or resistance following the critical period is supported within embryology (25). However, we have only beginning notions about whether the critical-periods hypothesis holds for almost any aspect of postembryological human development, and particularly psychological development.

We *do* have one related principle to the effect that organization inhibits reorganization (43): *The more organized and established a set of responses becomes, the more difficult it is to change them.* It was speculated earlier that Americans typically wait too long to start their children on a second language; underachievement after about the fourth grade has proved to be spectacularly resistant to remediation; the person trained on a manual typewriter has great difficulty learning the electric typewriter, and so on.

A second theme in the mixed body of facts and theory that surrounds the critical-periods hypothesis is the notion of *maximum susceptibility.* If a child is too *young* or if he is too *old,* a set of experiences will have little effect on him. Again, this hypothesis is supported by research from embryology, but we are not at all sure *how* it works or *if* it works in psychological development. Montessori, for example, believes that ages 3 to 6 years are the critical period for muscular training (18); ballet teachers seem to agree. An authority on perception holds that 4 to 6 years are the critical age period for perceptual training to facilitate later higher order cognitive development (22). It seems implicit in Piaget's thought (see Chapter 2) that a child must have a rewarding and rich set of experiences during his sensorimotor stage to move along well through his later stages in development of thought. Erikson (who was mentioned briefly in Chapter 2 as a dynamic psychologist) clearly believes, for example, that the first two years

of life are the critical period for the development of trust among human beings.

An associated, moderately well grounded principle is that experience has more effect on an organism the more rapidly the organism is growing and developing (9). The evidence for this principle is best for physical growth (see the research included in Example 1.3, Chapter 1, where the devastating effects of early nutritional deprivation are shown).

A third important principle within the critical-periods literature is the *cumulative deficit* hypothesis (4, 28). By this is meant that deficiencies or distortions of experience pile up—cumulate—and progressively interfere with future development. This interference may be geometric, that is, more and more severe with time. For example, the consensus of research seems to be that at the end of the second grade, disadvantaged children are but a few months behind their advantaged counterparts in academic achievement; but after ten to twelve years of schooling, they are several years behind on the average. The cumulative-deficit notion lies behind much compensatory and early childhood education. Head Start, for example, is specifically designed to provide children of an appropriate age (many now think too late) enriched experiences so as to prevent cumulative deficit.

In a moral society, we must ask these further questions. Can cumulative effects of debilitating early experience be reduced or eliminated by enriching a child's later environment? Can "normal" development be restored without permanent after-effects? When traumatic or debilitative early experience includes nutritional deficiency so severe as to interfere with neurological development, reversal or complete compensation is probably not possible. However, we are only beginning to gather sufficient firm data to permit us to move soundly in the area of compensation. The authors hold firmly that a moral society should be so constituted that compensation is not necessary. Compensation for early deprivation–debilitation is a bit like compensation for one's house and furnishings after they have been burned — is by definition inadequate.

The critical-periods hypothesis raises a number of questions that are important, even crucial, in any industrial society. For example, at what ages are what minimum and maximum amounts and types of environmental experience necessary for optimum social–personal development? intellectual–academic development? physical–motor development? After what time is it too late for adequate experience to produce optimum development or to remedy inadequate development? When is the best time to introduce a given type of learning skill (for example, learning to read, learning a second language, learning to play the piano)?

We have also seen that stage theories of development are to some degree critical-period theories (again, refer to Piaget and Erikson, Chapter 2). It may also be that events in the environment, such as death of a parent, *create* critical periods; and it should not be forgotten that *"all* periods in development are critical, but some may be more critical than others" (10).

The Dilemma of Behavioral Stability

The question "Is human development continuous and predictable, thus stable; or is it in constant flux, thus unpredictable and labile?" has long intrigued students of human development. Some believe the developmental system is closed. Hereditarians and constitutionalists are likely to adopt the idea of development as a closed system (15). Hereditarians admit (this is an extreme statement) that genetic forces, relatively unaffected by variations in experience, persist and overwhelmingly determine major components of personality, cognition, and intellect. Given *adequate* nutrition and freedom from disease and accident, most of us are closed-system people as far as physical growth and timing of physical (sexual) maturity are concerned. Environment will not affect these conditions much. Psychoanalysis, as noted in Chapter 2, is a relatively closed system. The course of personality development is partially determined in the first six or seven years of life. Humanism and behaviorism are much more open systems. Learning, rationality, and, in humanism, the concept of free will can result in major change at any time in the life span. In short, endorsing the open system viewpoint means that one believes that major components of personality, for example, can be changed during all of one's life.

The dilemma about behavioral stability is closely related to the critical-periods hypothesis that was discussed above. Proponents of an open system of human development will be less likely than proponents of a closed system to endorse critical periods for personality and intellectual development.

If we are to be sure of our position about stability and lability of human development, we must conduct longitudinal studies. Such studies are expensive, however; the "state of the science and the art" of measurement and theory changes from one decade to another; and human subjects grow weary of being studied and drop out of the longitudinal project. Thus, information about stability versus (stability *or,* stability *and*) lability has come to us very slowly.

Stability and lability may be construed in two ways. First, and most acceptably, a trait or some other aspect of development may be considered stable if members of a group keep the same ranking over their developmental span. If the most aggressive 2-year-old is still the most aggressive 14- or 44- or 84-year-old in the group and if other members of the group all keep about their same rankings, one is inclined to say that aggressiveness among humans is stable. If our most aggressive 2-year-old is our least aggressive 44-year-old and if all other individuals shift their ranking in the group as much as the most aggressive 2-year-old has done, we are likely to think of aggression as a "labile trait."

Lability–stability may also be thought of in absolute terms. Our hypothetical 2-year-old has exactly the same amount of aggression at ages 14, 44, and 84. Such an absolute definition brings in horrendous problems of measurement, since aggression among 2-year-olds is a very different matter from aggression among 84-year-olds. How can one ever say (because no "yardstick" is available) that the amounts of aggression are the same from one age to another?

To a considerable extent, any of the statements made at this time about the lability–stability question must be qualified by stating that our instruments for measuring complex human behavior are limited. Within such limits, research workers have found modest evidence of stability from preschool ages through adolescence for passivity–activity, social extraversion, and responsiveness (20). But girls are reasonably stable in their dependency behavior, and boys are not (29) (society does not take kindly to a dependent adult male, but will allow a little boy to hold his mother's hand and sit in her lap). Social expectations, then, also affect stability. From what has been said earlier

(organization inhibits reorganization), it follows that any set of behaviors which have been well learned (that is, how to deal with your aggressive, or your dependent, or your sexual, feelings) is likely to be persistent. Such persistence leads to behavioral stability. On the other hand, one is bombarded by social change. If he too does not change, he is lost, and thus, instability results.

The reasonable position is that both genetic and experiential factors determine behavioral stability–instability. A child can be "born" hyperactive. His calm, unflappable parents are not bothered. Eventually, not having been seriously frustrated and punished, the child learns the behavioral controls necessary for him to live without disturbing other people unduly (for example, as a young man in business, he learns to pace around his desk, or to excuse himself frequently from long and confining meetings in order to "get a drink of water" or to make a quick telephone call). He copes constructively, or at least in a socially neutral manner. Another, equally hyperactive child, handled oppressively, can conceivably learn to handle his problems through violent delinquency or to retreat from them—one way of handling them passively—by using drugs.

Environmental consistency is certainly related to behavior consistency. When parents are calm and predictable and when home life is well organized, it is logical to predict that the children in a family will show greater behavioral consistency than children in a home where one day cannot be predicted from the preceding day. Since rapidly changing cultures affect all families, it is also logical that there will be less behavior consistency in cultures that are changing rapidly than in those that are changing slowly (15).

Some cultures are continuous, some discontinuous (8). In a continuous culture, expectations for children have much in common whether the children are 2 years old or 12. The 2-year-old boy in a hunting culture is given a toy bow, at 12 he is given a more serious instrument more appropriate to his age; and in another year or so, he is expected to be able to handle an adult hunting bow. Or at ages 2, 5, and 15, boys and girls are expected to be interested in each other's genitals. The interest — mild to indifferent at 2 if we believe Freud, keen but nonfunctional at 5, and keen and functional at 15 — is matter-of-factly accepted within a continuous culture at each age, whatever its manifestations. With reference to sex (but not achievement), United States culture is discontinuous. Children and unmarried adolescents are required (but not really expected) to be asexual, to suppress the whole thing. But the first night of the honeymoon is presumed to be one where each partner gives the other great joy and in return experiences profound satisfaction.

To summarize, the question of behavioral stability is related to many other issues we have discussed: to determinism versus free will; to nature and nurture; to critical periods; and to the theory of measurement. With reference to behavioral stability, the authors must conclude in much the same way they did for nature–nurture. Stability and change are functions of both the nature of the individual human being, including his sex, and the experiences and circumstances of learning through which he goes. Thus, the variations and potentials are enormous.

Developmental Problems: Permanent or Phasic

There is always the question whether or not to take a developmental problem seriously (3). If one takes it lightly, he manifests his conviction that the "problem" reflects the developmental phase through which the child or the youth is going. The problem is thus only one aspect of a normal developmental stage, and it will go away when the stage is finished. This issue about the permanent or phasic nature of behavior is clearly and closely related to the previous topic, behavioral stability.

In considering this issue, one is first faced with the question, "What is a problem?" (51) The answer to the question depends partly on the situation. Aggressiveness on the playground, for example, is usually considered less a problem than aggressiveness in the classroom. A person's theoretical or practical orientation often determines whether he labels a given behavior a problem. Teachers, concerned about discipline and order, as they must be for practical reasons, are more likely than psychologists to consider aggressive and noisy behavior in class as problem behavior. This is because they are held accountable for the behavior of an entire class, which is thrown off by the aggressive child; the psychologist, on the other hand, is more likely to be involved with the single child and not the group.

Problems, in other words, are very much in the "eye of the beholder." However, there is some degree of general social agreement that children and youth who are constantly subjects of concern and conflict to a sizable percentage of their caregivers and peers are almost certainly manifesting problem behavior that should be attended to.

Normative data are particularly helpful in promoting objectivity about problem behavior. If a mother knows that almost all 2-year-olds are given to shouting "no!" in response to reasonable requests and that almost all 5-year-olds have at some point in their lives taken ("lifted") something from the supermarket or the hardware store, she is much more relaxed and better able to deal with her own 2- or 5-year-old who exhibits such behavior. Bed wetting is fairly common among 6-year-old males. The parents who are distraught because they think it is pathological for their 6-year-old son to bed-wet should be reassured by the knowledge that bed wetting is common. Thus, they should be better able to work with their son in helping him learn to sleep dry. On the other hand, random soiling (defecation) among 6-year-old physically healthy males is considered an indication of a rather profound disturbance in adjustment. If this disturbance is not faced and coped with, the child may go from somewhat disturbed to very disturbed.

In addition to norms about problem behavior, we need to know more about the frequency, intensity, and generality of the behavior. If the behavior is very frequent, very intense, and very general (that is, in all situations), the normal negativism of the 2-year-old may be a serious problem with disturbing developmental potential. On the other hand, *one* temper tantrum by the much older 10-year-old may mean nothing other than that he had had a singularly difficult day following a night with little sleep.

In general, the authors recommend that parents and teachers "roll with the punches," because they believe that human beings are almost infinitely flexible and subject to change; and also think that a general practice of rewarding positive and ignoring negative behavior is likely to result in a preponderance of positive behavior and a reduction of negative behavior (see Chapter 2). Even so, the dilemma needs to be clearly recognized.

We cannot predict whether or to what extent a given behavior problem will continue to develop in seriousness over time. Many people prefer to believe that most children will "grow out" of their problems. However, whether "growing out" provides an adequate solution to a developmental problem is often questionable. Certainly it will depend on many factors, including the extent to which physical maturation is a variable in the behavior, an individual's learning environment, his intellectual and social competence, and the like.

The authors believe that any parent or teacher needs to keep a radar system going about real trouble. When either is convinced that the trouble looms for a given child, he should seek expert help. Parents and teachers normally have too many other things to do with children to devote the time to work with deep behavior problems; nor do they usually have the skill to do so.

3.6 A Study of Children's Developmental Problems (32)

A portion of the classic Berkeley Growth Study, a longitudinal research that began with the study of infants born in the late twenties, provides an informative view of developmental problems—their nature and relationship to age during the first fourteen years of life. Data for this segment of the Berkeley Study were obtained from mothers at four periods of the children's lives: ages 21 months, 5 years, 10 years, and 14 years. Briefly, the results can be summarized as follows:

A. Problems that declined in frequency with increased age.
   1. Difficulties with *elimination* controls disappeared early and rapidly.

2. Speech difficulties (for example, stuttering), fears, and thumb sucking declined later and somewhat more gradually.

3. Disappearing still later and more slowly were problems related to hyperactivity and destructive aggressiveness. Temper displays were particularly notable among boys, many of whom were still "exploding" at age 13.

B. Problems that increased with age. Only one such problem, nail biting, increased systematically with age. The peak for nail biting for girls was around the time of puberty.

C. Problems that reached a peak and clearly diminished in frequency prior to puberty.

1. Insufficient appetite (strongly associated with high incidence of communicable diseases during childhood).

2. Lying.

D. Problems that showed early and high frequencies, early declines, then later reappearance.

1. Restlessness during sleep, dream disturbances.

2. Physical timidity, attention seeking, and irritability. (Peak elevations of frequency for these problems were the preschool period and late pubescence.)

E. Problems unrelated to age once established.

1. Oversensitivity (stable for girls throughout the period; stable for boys until about age 11, when it diminished dramatically).

2. Overdependency.

3. Somberness.

Several points should be made in connection with this study. First, the terms used to describe "problems" are those used by the mothers and indicate problems as mothers perceive them; few of these terms are much used by psychologists. Second, these data are descriptive. The research workers have offered their interpretations of the various patterns, but the reader is invited to speculate on the possible "causes" of these behaviors and their apparent change through time. Finally, these data were collected largely during the thirties and early forties. Can one expect the "typical" problems of similarly aged children today to be about the same? Or, is it more likely that the nature of developmental problems changes somewhat with time and social conditions?

The Dilemma of Normal Behavior

The issue of what is normal is essentially opposite to the dilemma of developmental problems discussed immediately above. First, *normality* is a matter of culture. In medieval England, the parents of the 14-year-old bride and groom proudly pulled aside the canopy of the marriage bed to display the bloodstained sheet to demonstrate that son–daughter had indeed consummated their marriage. In contemporary America, such behavior would result in a neighborhood consensus of eccentricity and perhaps perversion. Normality is also situational: the cursing driver in 5:30 P.M. urban traffic is acting in a rather normal way. The same language at his child's baptism would be considered deviant, to say the least.

Normality has at least two general meanings, the first being statistical (45). That which is shown by most people or (as mentioned in Chapter 1) which is within one standard deviation above and/ or below the average or mean is considered normal; it is a characteristic of "most people." The second meaning of normality is preferential: that which is well rather than sick is normal, that which is good rather than bad is normal, that which is superior rather than inferior is normal. Any decision to classify anything as normal is thus, to a degree, arbitrary. Consensual social values are the usual criterion.

What everyone does in subculture

A third meaning, often reflecting social change but closely related to the first, is often given to normality. After World War II, smoking marijuana was not considered normal. Perhaps jazz musicians and other very different groups did it, but not the sons and daughters of suburbia. Today, even though adults may be bothered by marijuana and even though the evidence about its effects on human development is by no means final, many consider marijuana smoking "normal" in the sense that many, many youth and more than a few adults smoke it. In the straitlaced cultures of the authors' childhoods, drinking martinis was bizarre, thus abnormal behavior. In their contemporary social settings, it is, if anything, abnormal or bizarre *not* to have an occasional martini (or martini substitute). Situationally, however, drinking martinis is normal at 5:30 or 6:00 P.M.; drinking martinis before breakfast is abnormal or problem behavior.

In arriving at a definition of normal, psychologists, psychiatrists, and social workers usually employ some combination of the three overlapping criteria of normality listed above. For example, let us take three 12-year-old girls of 85, 100, and 115 IQs respectively. Each is considered intellectually normal, because all are in the arbitrarily set range of intellectual normality. However, the first is "low" normal (here the criterion of social desirability enters), the second "average," and the third "high average," or "somewhat

above normal." All three girls occasionally defy their mothers and have "temperamental spells," during which they retreat to their rooms, brood, mope, cry, and sigh. This behavior is so frequent among girls approaching or only recently arrived at pubescence that it, too, is considered normal. But the third girl also loses control in such places as church services, and must leave the church, sobbing quietly. We worry about her "abnormality."

Other models of normality are based on possession of the characteristics needed to cope successfully within society. One author says it is normal when a person has good self-control, is personally and socially responsible, takes a democratic social interest, and follows ideals of principled conduct (45). Another author believes it is normal if by the time a person is 21, he is trusting and autonomous, shows initiative and industry, has a clear notion of his identity, and is capable of unguarded, intimate interactions with friends and loved ones (17).

Defining normality, then, is not easy. In arriving at a definition, the authors are faced with the dilemma discussed earlier of absolute versus relative standards and tight versus loose control (or at the least, stringent versus relaxed regard for, and evaluation of, behavior). Many say that schools adopt a definition of normal that bores the superior, frustrates the inferior, and perpetuates mediocrity for all. Schools are conservative enough about the behavior permitted within their walls that many say they savage creative, original, and autonomous children.

All societies, however, set up some sort of broad or narrow band within which behavior is tolerated—that which falls within the band is normal, that which falls outside is abnormal. It behooves us all to think carefully of the criteria for setting up the "band of normality," to make the best possible judgment of whether it fits with democratic traditions and individual rights, to ask whether it allows for the planned (or unplanned) heterogeneity that most of us believe should ideally be characteristic of American life, and to make sure that it does not systematically work to the detriment of other than privileged majority groups. In general, the authors believe the band of normality should be broader, not narrower.

In this chapter, human development has been considered according to the sorts of problems—the dilemmas—it poses in an *applied* sense, particularly for parents and teachers. Dilemmas within human development faced by students of development have also been considered.

Dilemmas usually have both a *philosophical* and a *procedural* side. Philosophically speaking, a dilemma must be analyzed for the issues it raises about personal, social, and educational goals and values. When a dilemma is solved philosophically, developmental and behavioral priorities and alternatives have been decided. After that, procedurally, one must choose how to achieve these priorities and hold fast to these values.

Practical child rearing and educating of children and youth both include three major, long-persisting, and pervasive dilemmas. The first is the question of behavioral control. Briefly, shall the child or the youth be handled with a tight rein, a loose rein, or possibly no rein at all? The second dilemma is focused on absolute versus relative standards of behavior, including morality. This is basically a question of universal, unquestionable "rightness" versus the point of view that all behavior must be judged within its social and psycho-

logical context. Extreme relativism is saying, "What the group does is about right, and that is what I will do." The third applied parent–educator dilemma concerns early childhood experience, such as breast or bottle feeding, time of weaning, timing and style of toilet training, and resolving the question whether or not to provide special or arranged experiences (including formal educational experiences) for children in infancy and the preschool years.

More formally, students of child development face philosophical and procedural decisions about a number of dilemmas. Each dilemma possesses theoretical and practical urgency. While the authors have primarily had psychologists in mind in mentioning students of human development, students in many other disciplines are deeply involved with the study and application of principles to human development, such as educators, home economists, nurses, pediatricians, psychiatrists, and social workers.

Whether to take a hereditarian (genetic–constitutional) or an environmental (learning–experience) point of view about how human development is patterned is a long-enduring, often emotional issue. The former may be thought of pretty much as a closed system, the latter as an open system.

The question about critical periods— that longer or shorter span of time in life when an individual is most affected by a particular kind and amount of experience—is very important. For example, some believe the first four or five years of life, starting in infancy, are the critical period for developing optimum intelligence. The social and educational implications of such a position are enormous.

Another dilemma is concerned with

behavioral stability (predictability, thus constancy and resistance to change), versus lability (quick response to different developmental phases or to environmental impact). Related to this dilemma is the important practical question, "What is a behavior problem?" Once behavior problems are defined, it is further questioned, is the problem a normal one that will likely go away when the next phase of development is reached (like excessive negativism among 2-year-olds); or is the problem pathological (like frequent soiling in a physically normal 10-year-old girl)? If the latter, intervention is advisable.

The question of developmental versus phasic problems leads naturally to the issue or the dilemma of defining *normal behavior*. One set of implications exists if we adopt the definition, "That which is *average* is normal." The implications are vastly different if we say, "That which is excellent, or optimum, or ideal is normal."

REFERENCES

1. *American Psychological Association* Psychological assessment and public policy. *American Psychologist*, 1970, 25, 264–267.
2. Anastasi, A. Heredity, environment, and the question, how? *Psychological Review*, 1958, 65, 197–208.
3. Ausubel, D. P. *Theory and problems of child development.* New York: Grune & Stratton, 1958.
4. Ausubel, D. P. How reversible are the cognitive and motivational effects of cultural depreivation? *Urban Education*, Summer 1964, 16–37.
5. Baumrind, D. Socialization and instrumental competence in young children. *Young Children*, 1970, 26, 104–119.
6. Baumrind, D. Current patterns of parental authority. *Developmental Psychology Monograph*, 1971, 4, No. 1, Part 2.

7. Bell, R. Parent-child conflict in sexual values. *Journal of Sociological Issues*, 1966, 22, 34–44.
8. Benedict, R. Continuities in cultural conditioning. *Psychiatry*, 1938, 1, 161–167.
9. Bloom, B. S. *Stability and change in human characteristics.* New York: Wiley, 1964.
10. Caldwell, B. M. The usefulness of the critical period hypothesis in the study of filiative behavior. *Merrill-Palmer Quarterly*, 1962, 8, 229–242.
11. Caldwell, B. M. The effects of infant care. In M. L. Hoffman and L. W. Hoffman (eds.) *Review of Child Development Research* (Vol. I). New York: Russell Sage, 1964, 9–88.
12. Caspari, E. W. Genetic endowment and environment in the determination of human behavior: Biological viewpoint. *American Educational Research Journal*, 1968, 5, 43–55.
13. Dobzhansky, T. Heredity, environment, and evolution. *Science*, 1950, 111, 161–166.
14. Dollard, J., and N. Miller. *Personality and psychotherapy.* New York: McGraw-Hill, 1950.
15. Emmerich, W. Stability and change in early personality development. In W. W. Hartup and N. Smothergill (eds.) *The Young Child.* 1967, 248–261.
16. Endler, N. S., L. R. Boulter, and H. Osser. *Contemporary issues in developmental psychology.* New York: Holt, Rinehart and Winston, 1968.
17. Erikson, E. *Childhood and society* (2nd ed.). New York: Norton, 1968.
18. Evans, E. D. *Contemporary influences in early childhood education.* New York: Holt, Rinehart and Winston, Inc., 1971.
19. Farberow, N. L. (ed.). *Taboo topics.* New York: Atherton Press, 1963.
20. Ferguson, L. R. *Personality development.* Belmont, Calif.: Wadsworth-Brooks/Cole, 1971.
21. Freedman, D. G. Constitutional and environmental interactions in rearing of four breeds of dogs. *Science*, 1958, 127, 585–586.
22. Frostig, M., and D. Horne. *The Frostig pro-*

gram for the development of visual perception. Chicago: Follett, 1964.

23. Gottesman, I. I. Genetic aspects of intelligent behavior. In N. Ellis (ed.) *Handbook of mental deficiency.* McGraw-Hill, 1963, 253–296.

24. Grunbaum, A. Causality and the science of human behavior. *American Scientist,* 1952, *40,* 665–676.

25. Hamburger, V. Trends in experimental neuroembryology. In *Biochemistry of the developing nervous system,* 1954, 52–73.

26. Hebb, D. O. *A textbook of psychology* (2nd ed.). Philadelphia: Saunders, 1966.

27. Hitt, W. D. Two models of man. *American Psychologist,* 1969, 24, 651–658.

28. Jensen, A. R. Cumulative deficit in compensatory education. *Journal of School Psychology,* 1966, *4,* 37–47.

29. Kagan, J., and H. A. Moss. The stability of passive-dependent behavior from childhood through adulthood. *Child Development,* 1960, *31,* 577–591.

30. Kinsey, A. C., W. B. Pomeroy, and C. E. Martin. *Sexual behavior in the human male.* Philadelphia: Saunders, 1948.

31. Kohlberg, L. Moral development and the education of adolescents. In E. D. Evans (ed.) *Adolescents: Readings in behavior and development.* Hinsdale, Ill.: Dryden, 1970, 178–196.

32. MacFarlane, J. W., L. Allen, and M. P. Honzik. *A developmental study of the behavior problems of normal children between twenty-one months and fourteen years.* Berkeley, Calif.: University of California Press, 1954.

33. Mahut, H. Breed differences in the dog's emotional behavior. *Canadian Journal of Psychology,* 1958, *12,* 35–44.

34. McCandless, B. R. *Children: Behavior and development* (2nd ed.). New York: Holt, Rinehart and Winston, 1967.

35. McClearn, G. E. Behavioral genetics: An overview. *Merrill-Palmer Quarterly,* 1968, *14,* 10–24.

36. Neill, A. S. *Summerhill: A radical approach to child-rearing.* New York: Hart Publishing, 1960.

37. Orlansky, H. Infant care and personality.

Psychological Bulletin, 1949, *46,* 1–48.

38. Reiss, I. L. The sexual renaissance: A summary and analysis. *Journal of Sociological Issues.* 1966, *22,* 123–137.

39. Rogers, C. R. The facilitation of significant learning. In L. Siegel (ed.) *Instruction: Some contemporary viewpoints.* San Francisco: Chandler, 1967, 37–54.

40. Rogers, C. R., and B. F. Skinner. Some issues concerning the control of human behavior: A symposium. *Science,* 1956, *124,* 1057–1066.

41. Scott, J. P. Critical periods in behavioral development. *Science,* 1962, *138,* 949–958.

42. Scott, J. P. *Early experience and the organization of behavior.* Belmont, Calif.: Wadsworth-Brooks/Cole, 1968.

43. Scott, W. A. Concepts of normality. In E. F. Borgatta and W. W. Lambert (eds.) *Handbook of personality theory and research.* Chicago: Rand-McNally, 1968, 974–1006.

44. Shields, J., and E. Slater. Heredity and psychological abnormality. In H. J. Eysenck (ed.) *Handbook of abnormal psychology.* New York: Basic Books, 1961, 298–343.

45. Shoben, E. J., Jr. Toward a concept of the normal personality. *American Psychologist,* 1957, *12,* 183–189.

46. Skinner, B. F. Freedom and the control of men. *American Scholar,* 1956, *25,* 47–65.

47. Skinner, B. F. The phylogeny and ontogeny of behavior. *Science,* 1966, *153,* 1205–1213.

48. Staats, A. W., and C. K. Staats. *Complex human behavior.* New York: Holt, Rinehart and Winston, 1963, 378–379.

49. Sunley, R. Early nineteenth-century American literature on child-rearing. In E. D. Evans (ed.) *Children: Readings in behavior and development.* New York: Holt, Rinehart and Winston, 1968, 2–19.

50. Torrance, E. P. *Rewarding creative behavior: Experiments in classroom creativity.* Englewood Cliffs, N. J., Prentice-Hall, 1965.

51. Woody, R. H. *Behavioral problem children in the schools.* New York: Appleton, 1969.

Part II
The Development of Symbolic Behavior and Special Factors in Cognition

In Part I of this book, the authors have tried to provide a broad view of human development during childhood and adolescence, including the theoretical filters through which such a view can be taken. It is now time to move from the broad view—the mediators, the implications and consequences of different theoretical perspectives, and the dilemmas of development—to the specifics.

Among all the species of the earth, human beings are unique in their use of symbols and reasoning in attacking the problems they face as they and their societies evolve. It seems sensible, therefore, to devote Part II of this book to the symbolic nature of man: his use of language; intelligence—the acuity with which he attacks problems; and other special aspects of his cognitive processes. In so doing, the authors also touch upon some elements of man's motivational makeup in the attempt to illustrate how all aspects of development interact.

Thus, Part II is devoted primarily to the symbolic and problem-solving aspects of the infant, the child, and the young person, and how these aspects are influenced by social experience.

4
Language
Development

This chapter consists of an overview of language development during childhood and some dilemmas associated with such development. Introducing the discussion of language development at this point suggests the importance the authors attach to language and its role in development as a whole. For one thing, most activities that occur in daily life require language communication of one sort or another. There is little reason to doubt that communication skill is a significant factor in one's cognitive, emotional, and social dealings with others. For another, the role of language in almost all forms of learning can hardly be overemphasized. For example, learning self-governance, the exercise of foresight, the ability to profit from experience, and complex memory functions all depend heavily on language.

DEFINITIONAL CONSIDERATION FOR LANGUAGE DEVELOPMENT

In the broadest sense, the term language development refers to the increasing quantity, range, and complexity of lan-guage and speech over time. As such, the formal study of language development includes a concern for the sequence, rate, and factors that affect language acquisition from infancy onward throughout life. However, in order to provide a more specific view of language development, it is important to note at least three basic points.

First, as implied above, a distinction can be made between language and speech. Language is generally viewed as a complex system of grammatical and semantic properties, whereas speech refers to actual utterances. Certainly language and speech are closely related, but they should not be considered the same for reasons that will become apparent throughout this chapter.

Related to this distinction is a second distinction: one between *receptive* (understanding) and *expressive* (producing) language. The ability of children to understand and act on the language communications they *receive* is not equivalent to the language communications they are able to *express*. For example, a 3-year-old child may be quite adept at following a simple story line and give every indication that he understands generally what is going on; yet this same child may be quite unable to repeat the story events clearly, in sequence, and with the same grammatical constructions used in it. This means that at any given point after infancy, children are able to understand words and sentence forms that they have not yet incorporated into their own expressive repertoire. Adults can be easily deceived about children's language development if their expressive language is taken as the only indication of competence with words and sentences.

Similarly, the mere mouthing of words cannot be taken as evidence of conceptual understanding. The young daughter of one of the authors, for instance, described her classmate's "allergic condition" in a very articulate manner, but when questioned by her father it became clear that she had not the foggiest notion about what an allergy is. This sort of "empty verbalism" is particularly important for classroom teachers to recognize to avoid misjudging the depth of conceptual understanding reached by a child in the course of academic activities.

Finally, the "self-communication" or "inner speech" aspect of language must be noted. This concerns the use the child or the youth makes of language "inside his head," as in daydreaming, planning how to solve problems, giving direction and organization to his movements. This aspect of language is important because, during the early years, learning becomes increasingly controlled by language, especially formal classroom learning. In fact, many early childhood education programs are focused on the principle that language skill development is a necessary part of the foundation for academic success. The "inner language" function is also well illustrated in thinking based on *formal operations* during adolescence and beyond (see Chapter 2).

Linguistic competence is not always manifested in expressive language. (Cartoon from Phi Delta Kappan, *1972, 53 (8), 572. Reproduced by permission of artist, Bardulf Ueland.)*

"After 'like' and 'man' – what do you articulate guys do for an encore?"

WAYS OF VIEWING
LANGUAGE DEVELOPMENT

Traditionally, the study of language development by psychologists has mostly involved *normative–descriptive* and *correlational* approaches. By normative–descriptive, the authors mean study that results in a charting of language behaviors as they are related to age changes: such things as the age of onset of speech, age of first spoken word with meaning, vocabulary size at successive ages, and number of words per sentence used by children as they grow older. In contrast, the correlational approach has involved the description of relationships between various aspects of language behavior, both with themselves (vocabulary size and average sentence length, for example) and with other factors (vocabulary size of child correlated with that of his mother, age of onset of speech with later measured intelligence, or level of language skill with social status among peers, for example).

These two approaches to the study of language development have been augmented by the study of factors associated with individual differences in language development. For example, generally faster rates of development during the early years have been observed for girls than for boys, children from smaller versus larger families, singletons as opposed to twins, and higher social class children compared to lower social class children (29). As a vast storehouse of descriptive information about this aspect of development began to take shape, it became apparent that better ways of organizing and interpreting such information were needed. In other words, the storehouse rated high on factual data, but low on explanatory and analytical armament.

Because of the gap in understanding language development and increased communication between psychologists and students of language phenomena in other disciplines, and because it has become respectable (even fashionable) to study language, a broader range of approaches to the study of language has gradually appeared. Among the more promising of these approaches in terms of generating new insights into language development are those which are inclined toward *linguistics*. Psychologists have been particularly stimulated by the insights of linguist Noam Chomsky. Chomsky has argued persuasively that language is structured by a generative grammar that permits the individual to create and understand sentences he has never heard before.

Linguistics, according to Chomsky (14, 15) and to those of other theoretical orientations, is the study of the structure and content of language, including grammar, sound combinations, and meaning. From this foundation of linguistics have developed variations in the study of language, at least three of which should be noted. (1) *Biolinguistics* is concerned with the maturational factors (anatomical and physiological) that set the stage for language development (27). (2) *Psycholinguistics* is the study of the relationship of language to the characteristics of the language user; this includes a concern for how the individual uses his capacity for language acquisition and his knowledge of the language to understand and produce utterances (31). Most psycholinguists are interested in discovering the rules that seemingly govern language behavior and how these rules are developed. (3) *Sociolinguistics*, a newly emerging field, is the study of language or dialect differences associated with ethnic group, geographical, and social class factors. The sociolinguist, to a greater extent than his biolinguist and psycholinguist peers, focuses on the social origins of linguistic codes, attitudes toward language, and various social implications of language use (21).

It should also be mentioned that, within psychology, behaviorists have exerted much influence on the study of language. As the reader will recall from Chapter 2, the behaviorist is basically concerned with learning conditions in the environment that affect development. This concern has specifically led to an examination of the role of imitation learning, stimulus and response generalization, and selective reinforcement in language acquisition. Scholars of humanistic psychology and psychoanalysis have not been much interested in, nor have they contributed in major ways to, the study of children's language development. The interests and concerns of cognitive developmentalists mesh almost completely with the psycholinguistic approach to language study, although, as has been indicated, behaviorism has exerted a strong influence on psycholinguistics.

Collectively, the points of view explained above have provided us with many insights, most of which have had an impact in shaping both the formal study of language and the current thinking about the social aspects of language behavior. Before we proceed with the discussion of specifics in language development, at least four insights from psycholinguists (17) should be mentioned. First, students of language development have now come to realize that children do not simply speak a "garbled version" of the adult language in their surroundings. Formerly, it was widely believed that children's language was essentially an erroneous form of adult language because of

children's "handicaps" in memory span, attention, and thinking. Today, most authorities believe that children more accurately are speaking their own language, a language with unique structural characteristics and patterns. Clearly, this language changes during the course of development, and the sequence of these changes has captured the interest of many scholars (particularly psycholinguists) in contrast to a cataloguing of language "errors" as defined by adults.

A second insight that has influenced recent studies in language development involves an analogy between the child and the linguist. That is, many authorities now view the child's principal task—language development—as essentially the same as the one faced by the student of linguistics. Both must discover underlying rules for creative language production from a morass of utterances provided by people. One of the most striking things about language development in children is that they quickly become proficient in generating novel sentences to communicate their thoughts and feelings, sentences that have not been "learned" or even been heard before in that exact form. Through exposure to verbal stimulation from others, children apparently develop a rule system for grammar, sound production, and meaning that is precisely the goal of the linguist interested in the formal analysis of language. This analogy has led to the psycholinguistic concern for understanding the processes by which *children accomplish their analysis of language.*

Third, it now seems clear that all languages are structurally complex and that no one language is structurally superior to any other (3, 25). This is an important point, since prejudice often manifests itself in the belief that one language or one form of a language is "better." Therefore, if you talk ghetto English or the dialect of *any* language, you are not as good a thinker as if you speak the formal language. The authors do not consider this to be true.

Fourth, applied Skinnerians (the behavior modification people) have demonstrated that nonlanguage users can be helped to talk and that speech can be improved through the systematic application of reinforcement contingencies (39, 41). Such demonstrations do not necessarily say anything about normal language development, but behaviorists generally maintain that reinforcement is a basic influence on both the frequency and the quality of expressive language.

THE DEVELOPMENT OF LANGUAGE

With the above definitions and insights in mind, five basic aspects of children's language development have been chosen for discussion: grammar, pronunciation, vocabulary, rate of talking, and communication style. Subsequently, some dilemmas in the study of language, including the interpretation of individual differences in language behavior, will be discussed. The authors recognize that "nonverbal," "sign," and "body" language is currently a topic of great interest. Such language is little understood, and the authors have decided not to discuss it here, because they do not have firm information about it.

Grammatical Development

What is commonly called grammar is a complex system of rules for organizing sentence and word form. The internal structure and form for sentence or phrase construction is known as *syntax;* the internal structure and form for words is

known as *morphology*. To illustrate, consider this sentence: "Mary bought ripe cherries." Syntactically, this is a simple declarative sentence, including a subject noun (Mary), a verb (bought), and a predicate noun (cherries), which is modified by an adjective (ripe). Morphologically, *Mary* is a proper noun (a given name), *bought* is the past tense of *bring,* and *cherries* is the plural of *cherry.*

Compare this with the syntactic and morphological complexity of "Not understanding her mother's orders, Mary had bought cherries instead of bananas, all the while planning how she would spend the money so saved the next time she went to the toy store." Very young children grasp both sentences amazingly well.

Learning this complex rule system is accomplished by children with amazing facility, yet the course of their learning is marked by characteristics that clearly differentiate early from "mature" language production. For example, compare the following common expressions of infants and preschool children with their mature adult versions:

Child's Utterance
a) "Allgone cookie."
b) "That a nice kitty was."
c) "I'm are here, Daddy!"
d) "Lookit mine feets in the water!"

Mature Version
"The cookie is all gone."
"That was a nice kitty."
"I am here, Daddy!"
"Look at my feet in the water!"

The child utterance examples represent a mix of normal grammatical construction related to sentence and word form. Examples (a) and (b) involve sentence form (syntax), while examples (c) and (d) involve word form (morphology). By adult standards these utterances represent grammatical "errors." But it should be noted that such constructions are normal and typical of the young child's system for expressive language.

Perhaps the most impressive feature of grammatical language development concerns the rapidity with which the child incorporates grammatical rules into his language system during the early years of life. Generally speaking, a child's grammatical development is well advanced by school age and closely resembles full adult form by the middle elementary grades. In the higher grades (grade five and beyond) advances in the control of syntax are much

more apparent in writing than in speaking (34). However, it is during the preschool period that the most rapid acceleration of grammatical development occurs.

The rapidity of this acceleration can be illustrated by a brief reference to the apparent sequence of grammatical development (30). *Holophrastic* (one-word) utterances around age 1 mark the beginning of grammatical development (and, as will be seen, the onset of vocabulary development as well). These holophrastic utterances are related to actions by the child or actions that he desires of other people or objects. For example, the 1-year-old may say "Dink" ("drink") to mean a number of things—his act of drinking, his desire for

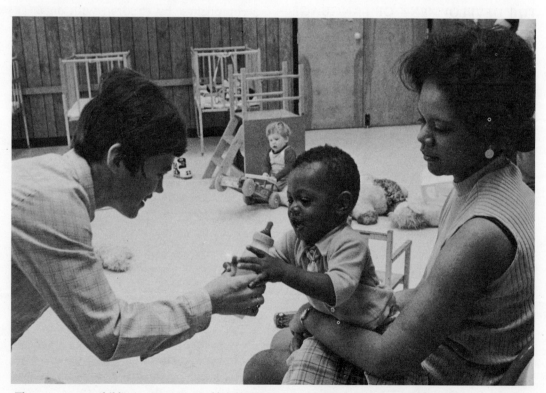

The very young child's utterances may be holophrastic—*only one word is used ("Drink")— but the meaning of his communication is clear. (Wide World Photos)*

a drink, or his reference to someone else's drinking. Awareness of the context in which such utterances occur is necessary to understand the child's communication at this point.

In general, two-word "sentences" begin to appear around age 1½. For example, the child now will say, "Baby drink," "Want drink," or "Doggie drink," to communicate his needs or observations. This use of two- and three-word sentences marks the period of *telegraphic* speech, so called because utterances typically contain only the necessary contentives (nouns, verbs, and adjectives) for communicating ideas. Gradually, function words such as prepositions, conjunctions, and articles (up, to, on, in, an, the, and) are added to form complete sentences. By age 4, most children demonstrate competence with fairly complex sentences, including the appropriate application of inflections (16).

Again, it should be noted that a child's recognition of grammatically correct language forms generally occurs before the child produces such forms on his own. This is important in distinguishing between language competence and language performance. Competence refers to the child's grasp of the abstract properties of language and his means for interpreting and generating language; performance refers only to that which is produced. This distinction can be illustrated by the child who remarks on Saturday, "I go to school and see teacher," when referring to something that occurred the preceding day. If the child understands and knows how to discuss past experiences but neglects to use the past tense, his performance is at issue, not his competence. If, however, he is unable to translate verb tense from present to past in order to describe a previous experience, or otherwise indicates

that he does not understand the difference, both performance and competence are at issue (11).

Although children's ability to understand grammatically correct language forms generally precedes their spontaneous use of such forms, their ability to *imitate* complex grammatical contrasts often exceeds their understanding of them. For example, a young child may be perfectly able to imitate the sentences "My bonny lies over the ocean," and "The ocean lies over my bonny," yet may show no understanding of the profound difference in meaning between these two constructions.

Finally, the application of sentence form rules (syntax) in expressive language generally precedes the application of word form rules (morphology), at least in English-speaking populations (37). For example, a child may say "two mouses," instead of "two mice," and almost everyone will understand; the child's meaning would be most unclear, however, if he said "mouses two."

Some Implications of Grammatical Development

To most of us, it seems logical that a child's grammatical development will depend to some extent on such things as the quality of his language models (parents, older siblings, teachers), amount of general language stimulation (conversation at mealtime, stories read to the child, extended conversations on walks), and the extent to which the child's language obtains his desired goals (reinforcement). Yet the exact contribution of these factors to grammar acquisition is not known. Neither has the process of grammatical development been identified to everyone's satisfaction. Our best information to date suggests that children achieve the rule system for grammatical language constructions on an inductive basis. Perhaps some mechanism of hypothesis forming and testing is involved (16). Example 4.1 represents a summary of some important work on this matter and indicates a possible system by which children accomplish the learning of grammar (8). It is notable that even though children come to design their language on the basis of a rule system for grammatical language, they are unable to explain the rules they use formally (for that matter, neither are most adults).

4.1 Some Hypothesized Processes of Syntactical Development

In recent years, some particularly important work in developmental psycholinguistics has been carried out at Harvard University (8). Much of this work has involved the exacting observation of a small number of children and their parents over the course of these children's early years of life. Of particular interest to the Harvard group has been the relationship of child utterances to parent utterances (and vice versa) during the course of parent–child interaction. Some early results of these interaction analyses are presented as they pertain to the child's acquisition of syntax. These results have been taken by the Harvard group to suggest three fundamental processes in syntax acquisition.

One process, *imitation and reduction*, involves the child's imitating a model, usually a parent, where such imitations are marked by a striking pattern: a reduction in the length of the model utterance; but where word order is clearly maintained, there is no cor-

responding increase in imitation when the model utterance is increased and when the words imitated are generally the large, "open" parts of speech (nouns, verbs, occasionally adjectives). A few examples will illustrate.

Model Utterance

"This is a pretty green coat."
"That's not the Lundin's dog."
"Grandma is coming on the plane tomorrow."
"No, you cannot go outside when it's raining."
"Want some milk?"

Child's Imitation

"Pretty coat."
"No dog there."
"Grandma coming."
"No go outside."
"Want milk."

A second process, *imitation with expansion*, concerns the nature of adult imitations of child utterances. The nature of the expansion technique is indicated later in this section (see page 131). The important features of an expansion are that they preserve the word order of child utterances, contain parts of speech omitted by the child, and are appropriate to the context. The following are examples.

Child Utterance

"Go store."
"Pat kitty."
"Daddy drink."

Adult's "Imitation"

"We are going to the store."
"Andrea is patting the kitty."
"Daddy is pouring a drink."

The third process described by the Harvard group apparently involves induction of the rule structure for generating language. That is, the child utters phrases that are ungrammatical and are not imitations of phrases he has heard from someone else. These ungrammatical utterances are thought to indicate the child's search for regularities in the syntax of his native language. Gradually the child's expressive language indicates that he has arrived at these regularities. It is suggested that this represents an inductive learning process whereby basic grammatical rules are "discovered" from among the regularities in speech the child hears from his models.

An example of such a rule is that for generating a noun phrase (NP). This rule governs the way in which a noun and its modifier are combined to form a phrase. Some common initial constructions by children illustrate this.

"More milk."	"Black bag."
"That Daddy."	"My bed."
"Big boat."	"My ball."
"More cookie."	"Funny face."
"Dirty foot."	

Nouns: milk, Daddy, boat, cookie, foot, bag, bed, ball, face
Modifiers: more, that, big, dirty, black, my, funny

The master rule for generating a noun phrase can be formally stated in this way: In order to form a noun phrase of this type, select first, one word from the small class modifiers and second, one word from the large class nouns. Gradually, the child comes to differentiate correctly all noun variations (for example, common, proper, singular, plural) and to operate consistently according to rules such as this. He also comes to elaborate on such phrases to form complete and subtly different sentences: "May I have more milk, please?" "Do you want more milk?" It is apparent that young children are either unaware of, unable to state,

or both unaware of and unable to state, the grammatical rules they use. It is the mystery of such rule induction that continues to intrigue most psycholinguists.

It has been suggested that the overall qualities of a child's language environment, including ample encouragement and opportunity for self-expression, are important factors in grammatical development. However, many authorities have been concerned with more specifically isolating the events in the language environment that affect the nature of this development. Three aspects of the language environment that are currently being studied illustrate this point: expansion and extension techniques for interacting with children, selective modeling, and the use of occasional questions.

Expansion and Extension Techniques

A possible way that adults influence children's grammatical development concerns the "natural" transactions that occur between most adults and children, transactions that build on the child's expressive language (12). One kind of adult response to a child's language has been called the *expansion* technique. This technique can best be illustrated by an example.

Child's Utterance
a) "Cindy wash?"
b) "Daddy no run!"
c) "See horse eat."
d) "Red bike there."

Expansion (adult
response to utterance)
a) "Cindy is washing the dishes."
b) "Daddy is not running now."
c) "I see the horse eating."
d) "Yes, the bicycle is red."

As these examples indicate, the adult responses to the child's utterances represent *complete* and *grammatically correct* versions of the child's presumed ideas. The expansion technique can therefore be defined by two characteristics. First, expansions deal with the *structure* of the child's utterance. The syntactical elements introduced by the adult are generally limited to those used by the child. Second, expansions are generally confined to the meaning that the adult believes the child has in mind.

It is possible, of course, that adult expansions can be confusing to a child if the adult infers a different meaning from that intended by that child. In example (b) above, the expansion, while grammatically correct, is not suitable in meaning if the child really was asking, "Can Daddy run?" This again illustrates the importance of carefully considering the nature of the situation in which a child speaks in order to communicate appropriately with him. It is also possible that children could be bombarded with so many expansions that they stop paying attention to them (9). This leads to the intriguing possibility that *contingent* expanding—that is, expanding only those child utterances that are clear and intelligible—may be preferable (and more influential) than expanding upon everything a child says (19).

A second technique, *extension*, can also best be illustrated by example.

Child's Utterance
a) "Cindy wash?"

b) "Daddy no run!"

c) "See horse eat."

d) "Red bike there."

Extension (adult response to utterance)
a) "Yes, but we can play again after I wash the dishes. What would you like to do?"
b) "Yes, but Daddy is tired and wants to rest. Shall we go talk to him?"
c) "The horse is eating some hay to make him strong and fast. How would you like to eat some hay?"
d) "The red bike is in the street. What might happen if someone doesn't move it?"

In these examples, the adult has contributed a related idea, one that carries the child's idea into a wider range of meaning and experience. Thus, extensions are characterized (1) by grammatically correct elements (as in expansions) and (2) by an additional idea (or ideas) that serves to maintain a conversational sequence.

The actual power of expansions and extensions for promoting children's grammatical language development is not precisely known. However, both techniques are probably superior to limited adult responses, such as the ubiquitous and simple yes or no answer. Such techniques are also probably preferable to the practice of correcting children's language unnecessarily. In the authors' experience, it seems that adults, especially teachers, are compelled immediately to label a young child's ungrammatical utterance as wrong and then to correct it. By so doing and without aiming to, adults often discourage children from expressing themselves spontaneously and may even make children feel insecure and incompetent. In fact, the pains taken by adults to "correct" children prematurely (before children have had sufficient opportunity to incorporate a new grammatical form) often have little, if any, constructive effect. The following exchange between a 4-year-old girl and her nursery school teacher will illustrate:

Child: "That man digged some hole."
Teacher: "No, say, 'That man *dug* some holes'!"
Child: "That man digged some hole."
(Four repetitions of this exchange)
Teacher: "Now listen *very* carefully! Say, 'That man dug some holes'!"
Child: "Okay! That man *digged* some *holes.*"

Selective Modeling

Closely related to the use of "natural interaction" techniques such as expansion and extension is a second component of a child's language environment that may influence grammatical development in positive ways. The authors refer to how basic grammatical structures may be modeled for children routinely (but in a planned way) by parents and other adults during the day and in the context of spe-cial, albeit informal, educational activities. Selective modeling is an integral part of some contemporary approaches to early childhood education (26), but the question of what grammatical structures should be emphasized is preeminent.

Research related to this question has provided us with some extremely interesting cues (4). These cues concern some grammatical structures that are simultaneously important for good interpersonal communication and apparently difficult for many children, especially those from various ethnic backgrounds whose experience with formal English has been limited. (See Example 5.2 in Chapter 5 for a commentary on this issue.) The authors believe that it is instructive to consider some examples of these important grammatical structures. Although it is perhaps most crucial that a child understand the differences involved in these grammatical contrasts, his ability to use them appropriately in his own expressive language is also important.

4.2 Some Important Grammatical Contrasts for Early Language Development (4, 26).

a) Basic noun–verb relationships, such as in active and passive sentences.

(Active)

The mother kisses the baby.
The baby kisses the mother.

(Passive)

The baby is kissed by the mother.
The mother is kissed by the baby.

b) Singular and plural forms.

(Singular)

"Pick up the toy."
"The dog runs."
"The block is wooden."
"This is a shovel."

(Plural)

"Pick up the toys."
"The dogs run."
"The blocks are wooden."
"These are shovels."

c) Possessives.

(Positive form)

"This is the brother's sister."
"This is the sister's brother."

(Negative form)

"This is not the brother's sister."
"This is not the sister's brother."

d) Affirmative and negative statements and questions.

(Affirmative)

"This dog has a collar."
"What can you wear on your feet?"

(Negative)

"This dog doesn't have a collar."
"What can't you wear on your feet?"

e) Adjective–noun relationships with prepositions involved.

"Find a green car in the red box."
"Find a red car in the green box."
"Put the little triangle under the big tray."
"Put the big triangle under the little tray."

(Other important prepositions include over, next, behind, on, above, below, and the like.)

f) Prefix and multiple negation

(Prefix)

"Which shoe is *un*tied?"
"The children are *un*happy."

(Multiple negation)

"Which shoe is *not untied*?"
"The children are *not unhappy*."

g) Various embedded sentences
(Two or more ideas in the same sentence)

"A boy jumps and another boy climbs."
"The dog sees the cat running."
"The girl who is sitting there laughs."
"Mother does her sweeping with a broom."

h) Use of tense

(Present)

"The ice cream is melting."
"Johnny is crawling."

(Past)

"The ice cream melted."
"Johnny has crawled over the chair."

(Future)

"The ice cream will melt."
"Johnny will crawl over the chair."

Example 4.2 portrays only a few of the more important grammatical forms most of us take for granted that children understand. Careful observation and questioning of children by professionals often reveal that some children behave as though they do not understand such forms. Consequently, it may be helpful to model forms such as these for children. This can be done as adults describe what they are doing, will do, or have done in the normal course of daily events. For example, a nursery school teacher who says in the presence of the child, "I am picking up the toy(s)" and "I picked up the toy(s)" as she performs these actions is modeling forms involved in (b) and (g) above. The teacher may also wish to check (by pointing or verbal description) on the child's ability to distinguish between pictures that show objects and events. Suitable for this purpose, for example, are items such as the mother–baby situation in (a), brother–sister in (c), footwear and non-footwear in (d), or similar situations. Countless opportunities for informal interactions such as these occur in the normal course of a child's day.

Occasional Questions

Still another kind of informal adult–child interaction or exchange may be of some help to very young children as they go about the discovery of certain grammatical rules—that is, the use of occasional questions. At least two kinds of occasional questions have been identified (9). One kind, the "say again" type, can be illustrated by example. *Child:* "I like canny!" *Mother:* "You like what?" *Child:* "Canny." *Mother:* "You like candy?" *Child* (nodding his head): "I like canny!" In this example, we see that the mother's questioning actually amounts to a request for the child to "say again" the main subject of his utterance. It is possible that such exchanges help the child to understand the relationship between grammatical forms used in declarative statements and those used in *wh*-questions (where, who, what, when). Moreover, such responses on the part of a parent are good indications to the child that someone important to him is interested in what he says.

A second kind of occasional question is a means of both *prompting* a child to respond and *demonstrating* that differ-ently worded *wh*-questions can be used for achieving the same purpose. These two contributions can also be illustrated by example. *Mother:* "Which cookie will you choose?" *Child* (no response). *Mother:* "You will choose which cookie?" or *Mother:* "Where should we hide it?" *Child* (no response). *Mother:* "We should hide it where?" Again, the examples show how a parent continues to show interest in a child while modeling different grammatical forms and prompting a meaningful response.

Pronunciation Skills — *Articulation*

A second important component of language development is the child's ability to pronounce words correctly so that he can be understood by others. This ability falls under the technical heading of *articulation.* Development in articulation includes at least three things: learning (1) the contrasting speech sounds of one's language, (2) how these sounds are produced, and (3) the rules of sound usage. However, the term articulation is used here without differentiating the complexities of these various tasks, and only to highlight the general aspects of development in this area.

Differences in immature and mature articulation can be illustrated by contrasting the normal speech of very young children and that of most adults.

Child's Utterance
"I wanna jewwy fancy!"
"Wash for a aggigator."
"Bibin pill, pease Daddy?"
"I going fathwoom wight now!"

Actual Words
"I want a jelly sandwich."
"Watch for an alligator!"
"Vitamin pill, please Daddy?"
"I must (will) go to the
bathroom right now!"

Obviously, articulation skills require facility in coordinating the various tools for speech production (that is, tongue–lower jaw). Thus, biological factors play a central role in articulatory development. The gross differentiation of vowels (a, e, i, o, u) and consonants (b, d, t, and so on)— the two basic English phonemes (basic units of sound)—is thought to represent an early landmark in articulation development during infancy (23). *Auditory discrimination*, or the ability to tell the difference between sounds, is also an important element in such development. For example, it becomes necessary for children to discriminate classes of sound (phonemes) that are paralleled by different meanings, as in the case of "pin" and "tin" or "lake" and "rake" (43). Sound imitation and simple word production— other important developments during infancy—provide still another portion of the foundation for progress in articulation.

Some Implications of Articulation Development

Several features of articulation development that are important for parents and teachers should be noted. As with grammar, the receptive ability of speech sound discrimination develops ahead of speech sound production. For instance, children generally recognize correctly articulated sounds even though they may not be able to produce these sounds themselves. This is illustrated by the following exchange between a 2½-year-old and his baby-sitter:

Child: "I having chitchun choop!"
Baby-sitter: "You're having what?"
Child: "Chitchun choop!"
Baby-sitter: "Chitchun choop?"
Child: "No! *Chitchun choop!*"
Baby-sitter: "Oh! Chicken soup?"
Child: "Yah! Chitchun choop!"

It is also important to recognize that *misarticulation* among children in the late preschool years is not necessarily a cause for alarm. Young children typically have difficulty with various sounds, and will often substitute one for another, as in "*wabbit*" for *rabbit*, or "*soos*" for *shoes*. Difficult consonant blends such as *st, str, dr,* and *fl* are often among the last to be mastered. Pronunciation difficulties such as these and other sounds may even persist until age 7 or 8.

A related point concerns the mild stuttering frequently observed among children between the ages of 3 and 4. Stuttering at this time is not usually a danger signal; rather, it is typically a "phasic" problem (if indeed one chooses to call it a "problem" at all). Stuttering during the later preschool years apparently reflects a wide gap between what children are able to understand and what they want to talk about. They may not yet have the words under their command for satisfactory self-expression. Excitement brought about by new experiences may also affect a child's speech at this time. Thus, a 3- or 4-year-old at the circus may stutter and stammer for some time before he is able to communicate intelligibly his thoughts about the lion tamer or the aerial performers.

Fortunately, most children's articulation difficulties indicate no serious pathology. Such difficulties more frequently involve faulty speech habits or incomplete learning. By age 5, most children are speaking clearly, although they may still mispronounce some sounds. For the more severe problems, of course, referral to a speech specialist and/or a medical expert is advisable. Example 4.3 is a study of diagnosing of articulation difficulties early in the child's school experience for the purpose of making decisions about special services for children (44).

4.3   An Example of Articulation Research

It is generally believed that the earlier a potentially serious speech problem can be identified and treated, the more likely it is that the problem be attenuated or perhaps averted completely. However, except for alert parents and pediatricians, it is unlikely that children's speech behavior will be examined closely until school age. At this time, resources of the school and community can be brought to bear with children who need help. Speech therapy is an expensive matter even when a school district or community has the resource available. There is the further possibility that some children whose speech suggests the need for special help may neither be helped by nor require therapy. The question therefore becomes one of determining, if possible, which children are likely *not* to improve their articulation without special help and then concentrating therapeutic efforts only on such children.

This is precisely the question that underlies the work of Van Riper and his colleagues (44, 45). Van Riper set about to design an objective testing procedure suitable for use with misarticulating first-grade children. His purpose was to use this procedure to predict which children from among these misarticulators might eliminate their speech problems *without* speech therapy. A predictive screening test consisting of nine subcomponents was assembled using cues from the literature about articulatory development and disorders. These subcomponents ranged from an emphasis on skill in producing single consonant sounds (*r, s, z, th, ch, j*), consonant blends (*cr, sp, tr*), and articulating sounds in specified syllables (for example, *puhtuhkuh*) to the ability to move one's tongue independently of the jaw and lips (as in producing the syllable "la" in "lalala").

Van Riper administered this test battery to 293 beginning first-grade children *all* of whom were previously diagnosed as having some functional articulation disorder serious enough to indicate a need for therapy. However, none of these children was referred for speech therapy. Rather, all were observed over the course of the following two years. At the end of this period (entering third grade), these children were again retested with an inventory of phonetic skills. Samples of their spontaneous speech were also taken. Together, these data were used to determine the articulation status of these third-grade children.

Results of this longitudinal investigation indicated that the earlier predictive test of articulation ability could discriminate among children who do and do not eliminate their articulation problems after one or two years *without* therapy. Specifically, 25 percent of the misarticulating first-grade children were error-free by the second grade, and 47 percent were error-free by the start of the third grade. In short, nearly one half of the children initially identified for speech therapy by language specialists had spontaneously mastered normal articulation within two years. Moreover, Van Riper discovered that the most effective predictors of self-mastery in articulation were the tested articulation skills themselves (versus motor skills, phonetic discrimination ability, auditory memory span, and the like). In other words, Van Riper reports that the best predictors of articulation mastery are to be found in speech itself.

Vocabulary Development - *Semantic*

Technically speaking, the child's compilation of his "word dictionary" is best described by the term *semantic development*. This term includes the development of word meaning, the influence of meaning on syntax, and the relationship of meaning to action (30). As such, there is overlap. The less technical term, vocabulary development, is used here to refer in the simplest way to major trends and some practical aspects of this phase of language.

It is generally agreed that by age 10 or 12 months, the infant normally responds to simple commands like "No," "Come here," and "Give," especially when such commands are accompanied by gestures. By the end of the first year of life, the infant usually utters his first word with meaning. Vocabulary development then

Very early in life the individual learns that particular sounds ("sock") apply to particular objects. (Wide World Photos)

proceeds rather slowly until about 18 to 24 months, when a rapid acceleration in word acquisition begins. For example, while the recognition vocabulary (words the child understands but may not use regularly in his own speech) of a typical 2-year-old contains about three hundred words, the average first-grader knows thousands of words (29). As in the case of grammatical development, the period of most dramatic vocabulary development typically occurs between ages 18 and 36 months. In fact, some authorities (27) refer to this period as the "naming explosion." It is likely that encouragement for children to learn labels useful in describing their actions and objects in their environment is especially important during this period.

Some Implications of Vocabulary Development

It is difficult to overestimate the importance of vocabulary development. For one thing, it is likely that the child who is adept at describing his needs, feelings, and experiences richly will receive more positive reinforcement from his environment than his less verbal peer. For another, range and complexity of one's vocabulary has long been considered a good, if not the best single, indicator of general intelligence (see Chapter 5). However, the process of vocabulary development is not well understood. It is clear that the growth and stimulation of vocabulary differ from grammatical and articulation development (10) in at least two basic ways. First, while development in grammar and articulation are practically complete by the primary grade years, vocabulary development continues throughout life. Second, vocabulary development is apparently influenced to a greater degree by informal and formal educational experiences. For parents and teachers, this suggests that thoughtful assistance can profitably be given to children in acquiring new words and in sharpening the meaning of words they have already learned.

One strategy for this purpose is the famous Montessori three-period sequence for vocabulary development (33). Period one, *naming*, is initiated by the adult, generally during a demonstration phase of learning. For example, a child manipulating color chips may be shown (by pointing) which ones are green, blue, yellow, or red ("This is red," "This is blue."). During phase two, the *recognition* period, the child is required to respond to identity statements that take the form of a request. The teacher may say, for example, "Give me the red," or "Give me the blue." Subsequently, the child enters phase three, the *pronunciation* period, and responds to such questions as "What is this?" (caregiver pointing to a red or a blue chip). A basic purpose of this strategy is to help the child become more precise in describing his environment and his experiences.

As in the case of grammar and articulation, the availability and quality of a child's language models (parents, brothers and sisters, teachers) are extremely important to vocabulary development. This importance is illustrated in several ways in the research literature about children's vocabulary. According to one study, for example, the best single indicator of a preschool child's vocabulary is the vocabulary test score obtained by his mother on an adult test (42). Other important early aspects of vocabulary development include the extent to which (1) children are rewarded for their naming behavior and question asking (for example, "What's that, Mommy?") and (2) adults use verbal description to specify actions and events occurring in the child's environment (for example, "This is the way we brush our teeth!" kinds of games).

It is reasonable to assume that the larger a child's vocabulary, the better (especially to the extent that word knowledge facilitates learning). This belief has long been reflected in the enrichment practices of nursery schools and kindergartens, many of which are designed expressly to increase vocabulary. As has been seen, however, word knowledge is only one aspect of language competence. Moreover, some argument exists over the limitations of vocabulary training per se as a way to foster language growth and thinking in children. In the past, most approaches to language improvement have involved mainly vocabulary enlargement, presumably because vocabulary is viewed as the principal unit of language. The question is whether "mere exposure to the basic units (of language) will 'lubricate' the entire language system" (7).

This question is especially important in the case of children whose language may be undeveloped as a tool for structuring or guiding thought, a purpose perhaps ill-served by simply adding more words to a child's vocabulary. For example, simply teaching a child words like apple, orange, grapefruit, bean, potato, and parsley is no guarantee that he will classify these objects into their appropriate categories (fruit, vegetable), further group them as all belonging to the class *food*, and then be able on command to name objects that are food but *not* fruit or vegetable. In other words, many authorities believe that language training should be designed specifically to help children develop their "inner speech" or their "self-communicative" language so that greater use of language in problem solving and logical thinking tasks is achieved.

Rate of Talking

Another important component of language behavior is the rate or frequency with which a child expresses his thoughts and feelings, asks questions, and initiates conversations with others (word fluency). This dimension is especially important for children who do not express themselves when it is appropriate or desirable for them to do so. At the extreme, one may encounter a nontalking or a mute child who, because of physical or emotional insult, is unable or unwilling to talk. We are concerned here, however, with the more general case of children, otherwise not handicapped, whose rate of talking is so low that it may interfere with normal progress in social development based on language interactions with others. Furthermore, in the absence of talking, it is often difficult for an interested adult to determine what a child may or may not have learned.

Implications of Talking Rate

There are many possible reasons why a child may not choose, or is unable, to speak or express himself frequently. The reasons may range from a sincere belief that what he has to say is unimportant, to severe emotional disturbance. It is not the intent here to focus on causation, diagnosis, or remedial techniques concerning a child who seldom talks. These are matters for specialized professional training. Rather, the focus is on one aspect of the language environment that is associated with individual differences in talking rate and is more directly under the control of adults concerned about such rates: positive reinforcement.

The concept of positive reinforcement was first introduced in Chapter 2. The discussion of positive reinforcement stressed the consequences for behavior that one wishes to maintain or increase in frequency. In the present context, the concern is with the extent to which a child or a youth generally associates pleasant consequences with talking. Some pleasant consequences are "natural"—for example, most children like to hear themselves talk. A sort of aesthetic pleasure is therefore involved. Other consequences include the sense of self-importance that children may experience by using language to influence others. Adult recognition, acceptance, and praise of children's talking are also important. Perhaps the most effective and natural reinforcement is simply showing an interest in what children have to say.

Fortunately, there is ample evidence from the literature concerned with language that positive reinforcement makes a difference in rate and frequency aspects of language behavior. For example, it has been demonstrated that both vocalization rate during infancy and continuous speech during early childhood are influenced by positive reinforcement (38, 40). Psychologists also report a salutary effect of reinforcement on verbal fluency, vocabulary usage, the nature of topics one discusses with others, and verbal mediation, or the "inner speech" that serves to coordinate motor behavior (18). Moreover, the reinforcing consequences of higher talking rates apparently may "spill over" into other facets of a child's existence. For example, a positive relationship between popularity with peers (social acceptance) and rate of talking in play interactions has been reported (28).

While information such as this is encouraging, it must be added that the influence of reinforcement on the quality of children's expressive language and the adequacy with which they respond verbally to requests by others is by no means clear. Nor has the influence of reinforcement on sound production and grammatical development been demonstrated decisively (18). In fact, some authorities (30) do not believe that reinforcement is very important in affecting the course of children's native language development. Yet, the data concerning reinforcement effects on rate of verbalization indicate that systematic efforts by adults can lead to beneficial results in certain areas of language behavior. Example 4.4 is included here to illustrate the practical implications of this idea.

4.4 The Impact of Contingent Reinforcement on Language Behavior

Hart and Risley (22) conducted a study to determine what procedures, if any, might be helpful in increasing the language skills of preschool children from disadvantaged backgrounds. This objective was based on reliable observations that the expressive language of such children is not often characterized by rich use of descriptive words — words that indicate both knowledge of important environmental characteristics (color, shape, number, size) and effective communication with other people. Hart and Risley first carefully and extensively observed each child within a group of preschool-aged disadvantaged children to obtain an idea of how frequently these children used descriptive adjectives in their speech throughout the course of a preschool day.

After charting the average frequency with which the children used descriptive terms in the preschool setting, Hart and Risley set about to assess the effect of selected aspects of the environment on the initially low rates of spoken adjec-

tives. Their analysis revealed both general and specific features of the environment that could be manipulated experimentally. Throughout and after the experimental period, these children were observed for changes in the extent to which they used descriptive words both. spontaneously during free play and in organized group learning situations.

Briefly, the results of this study follow. First, the low rates of descriptive word use (size and shape adjectives) were not affected by gross factors such as time spent in school, intermittent teacher praise, or general social and intellectual stimulation. Second, group teaching activities (including direct prompts and questioning) were associated with marked increases in rate of using color and number noun combinations *in the group situation*; but such teaching was not effective in altering the rate at which children used such combinations spontaneously away from the restricted situation. The only effective procedure for increasing the rate of adjective–noun combinations in the children's spontaneous vocabularies involved operating directly on the children during free play where access to materials (toys, paints and water, and other "manipulatables") was made contingent upon the child's language. That is, only when children used appropriate adjective–noun combinations were they permitted access to play materials. For example, a child simply could not take a toy or obtain one by pointing or grunting. He was required to specify in detail what he desired ("*red* car" or "*three* blocks"). In this study, preschool materials — dispensed freely and noncontingently in many traditional nursery school settings — apparently served as powerful reinforcers for desirable language behavior that, it seems likely, will extend beyond the preschool environment.

Communication Style

The four aspects of language thus far discussed—grammar, articulation, vocabulary, and talking rate—operate together to help produce unique communication style for every individual. By communication style is meant the way in which one uses his language to express thoughts and feelings, to relate socially to other people, to clarify ideas, and to describe things that have been experienced. One important dimension along which individual differences in language style can be observed is the degree to which language is used for elaborative (versus restrictive) purposes. The following example illustrates this point: The situation involves 5-year-olds who have discovered a jack-in-the box in the corner of a day care center.

1.   *Caregiver*
a) "What's that you have?"
b) "What?"
c) "What?"
d) "What is it?"
e) "Can you do anything with it?"
f) "Have you tried turning the handle?"
g) "What happened?"
h) "Do you like it?"

Child, Ronnie
a) "I got this thing!"
b) "This thing!"
c) "You know. This thing in that box."
d) "I dunno."
e) "I dunno."
f) "Hey!"
g) "This man come out!"
h) "Yeh."

2.   *Caregiver*
a) "What's that you have?"
b) "What?"

c) "What is it?"
d) "Can you do anything with it?"
e) "Have you tried turning the handle?"
f) "Do you like it?"

Child, Beckie
a) "A box from the toy chest."
b) "This box. I think it's a toy."
c) "A box with different colors on it."
d) "Well—I s'pose I could use it to build something with maybe."
e) "Look! When you turn this little handle a tiny clownman pops up!"
f) "S' funny, but I was kinda scared at first cause it 'prized (surprised) me. I think I'll go and scare Sharon and see what she does and then____(Child leaves).

This example illustrates a marked contrast in the degree to which two children express and describe their impressions. Ronnie is much more restricted in his comments, quite apart from the use of nonstandard pronunciations. Although it should not be inferred from this that Ronnie's actual thinking about the jack-in-the-box event is lacking, it would be difficult for an observer to tell just what his impressions were. In the case of Beckie, it is clearer that she is able to express her reactions more elaborately and completely.

Patterns of communication style have often been associated with social class and ethnic group variations (6). While the exact impact of socioeconomic factors or ethnicity on such patterns is not clear, it seems likely that the kind of early language environment a child encounters will strongly affect how he learns to use his language. Again, we stress the value of language models—adults and older children who elaborate ideas and feelings for younger children. To illustrate further, consider the following example. The situation involves mothers and their children riding together on a bus in heavily congested traffic. In each case, a 3-year-old child is sitting on her mother's lap (6).

1. *Mother:* "Hold on tight."
   Child: "Why?"
   Mother: "Hold on tight."
   Child: "Why?"
   Mother: "Hold on tight!"
   Child: "Why?"
   Mother: "You'll fall."
   Child: "Why?"
   Mother: "You'll get hurt!"
   Child: "Why?"
   Mother: "I told you to hold on tight, didn't I?"

2. *Mother:* "Hold on tightly, Alicia."
   Child: "Why?"
   Mother: "If you don't, you will be thrown forward and fall."
   Child: "Why?"
   Mother: "Because if the bus suddenly stops, you'll jerk forward onto the seat in front of you."
   Child: "No, I won't."
   Mother: "You won't if you hold on tightly."

As can be seen, the "styles" represented above differ along several dimensions including the degree of elaboration in syntax and vocabulary, in focus on clarifying ideas, particularly cause–effect relationships, and in amount of redundancy, or unnecessary repetition. The mother in (2) above is perhaps more consistent with the style that we associate with formal language, particularly the language of most American classrooms.

Concluding Remarks

To summarize briefly, five principal features of language development in childhood have been considered: grammar, pronunciation, vocabulary, talking rate, and communication style. The intent has been to highlight major trends in these areas as well as the environmental factors

that may influence development. The latter task is always hazardous, but particularly so in the case of language development, because the locus for language development is so strongly "built into" the child. Although the general course of language development is remarkably similar for young children, individual differences in language proficiency among them are also remarkable. The authors believe that general language stimulation, the quality of children's language models, and the nature of the reinforcement they receive for talking are extremely important contributing factors to these differences.

While the features of language development have been discussed separately, it should be noted that all features interact in complex ways. As will become more apparent throughout this book, language, social, and intellectual development are closely interrelated. The features of language development that have been discussed are also closely related to academic development (29). For example, children who do not early demonstrate satisfactory progress in reading are frequently children whose linguistic behavior is marked by the absence of elaborated sentences, a high proportion of short sentences (three to four words), an absence of connectives, and redundancy in vocabulary. Strong interrelationship between (1) the length, elaboration, and complexity of children's speech units and (2) the accuracy of children's speech sounds has also been observed (29). Moreover, normal progress in vocabulary development and both oral and silent reading is less likely among children having functional articulation defects. Although the causal factors involved in such matters are not clear, such findings further illustrate correlated development.

Finally, in the preceding section the

focus has almost entirely been on the early years of human development. The reason for this is simple. The preschool years are the period of most rapid native language development, and progress in such development (except for vocabulary increase) apparently ceases after about age 12 or 13, after puberty (27). This observation has led to the contention that species-specific biological factors are critical determinants of language development. In this connection, it is interesting to note that the period of "maximum ability" to acquire language tapers off dramatically about the time the normal brain reaches full weight (27).

DILEMMAS CONCERNING LANGUAGE DEVELOPMENT

In Chapter 3, the concept of dilemma was introduced, suggesting that it refers to a matter of dispute or puzzlement, often accompanied by questions of value. Here and in succeeding chapters, the authors present a sampling of dilemmas associated with specific aspects of human development. In the present context, they are concerned with dilemmas related to language development. Although many such dilemmas could be discussed, only three are examined for illustrative purposes. These dilemmas concern the nativist versus environmentalist interpretation of language development, the relationship of language to thought, and the interpretation of language differences among children from different cultural backgrounds.

The Nativist–Environmentalist Dilemma
In Chapter 3, the authors explored the nature–nurture controversy and suggested that various forms of this controversy would be encountered through the book. Such is certainly the case for language development. The nativist–environmentalist controversy (often referred to as the rationalist–empiricist debate) can be summarized briefly at the risk of oversimplification. At one end of this polar dilemma is the nativist or rationalist. He maintains that a satisfactory explanation of language development depends upon some important biological givens. These include certain innate structures or capacities such as the concept of a sentence. That is, children are prepared by their biological makeup to develop language in a sequential fashion; prelinguistic and early linguistic behavior are determined primarily by maturation processes. For example, as one spokesman for this position has put it: "Children everywhere begin [their language development] with the same initial hypothesis: Sentences consist of single words . . ." (30, p. 2). The rationalist finds too many linguistic universals—commonalities in language development from culture to culture—to believe that experience has very much to do with native language development during the early years. Obviously, *some* experience is necessary—a child must hear a language in order to speak it—but only to "activate" the child's innate capacity (17). Once activation has occurred, language is developed rapidly and rather effortlessly despite the enormous complexity of the task. It follows that the rationalist is most interested in marshaling evidence for this position, including the identification of universals. At the very least, he questions the adequacy of concepts like imitation and reinforcement for "explaining" basic language development (15).

In contrast, environmentalists assume that experiential factors are powerful determinants of language development and that such factors, once thoroughly analyzed in terms of learning principles, will account for much of the mystery surrounding language acquisition. The idea of innate linguistic structures is not taken as seriously as the notion that social forces shape the course of language development in much the same way that they shape other aspects of development. A species-unique, highly specialized ability to learn language is seriously questioned.

It is easy for us to paint a portrait in extremes. The truth is that the conflict between nativists and environmentalists is more a matter of degree than irrecon-

cilable difference (17). Some points of convergence between the two positions even exist. For example, representatives of both groups agree that language is acquired in a social context, that individual and group differences in linguistic performance exist, and that certain methods of studying language development are more appropriate than others (35). But a dilemma remains. No one really knows the extent to which either point of view is more correct, and proponents of neither position can account satisfactorily for all aspects of language development.

Our pragmatic environmental orientation leads us to consider first how experiential factors are involved in language

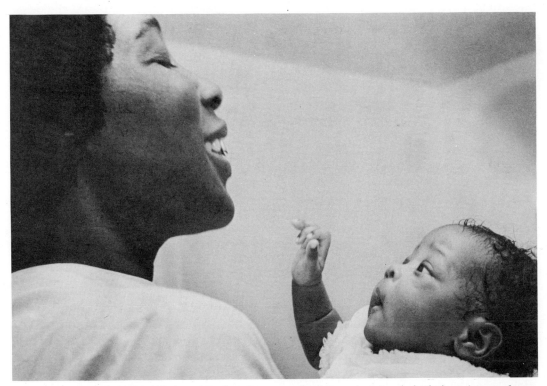

Convincing evidence exists that language development proceeds both from innate characteristics and from the need to communicate in social contexts. This mother and her baby obviously have much to communicate to each other. (Photo by Hanna W. Schreiber)

phenomena. That is, biology is fixed for every child, the environment need not be. To the extent that early experience, even to the point of planned education, can facilitate language, the recommendation of the authors is to capitalize on learning. Yet as theoreticians, they also commend the pursuit of understanding for the sake of understanding, and cannot close their eyes to either the rationalist or the environmentalist position.

The Language–Thought Dilemma

Based to some extent in the rationalist–empiricist distinction, and certainly in the specifics of contemporary psychological theory, is the dilemma of the language–thought relationship. With rare exception, psychologists agree that language plays a crucial role in thinking, but the exact contribution of language to thought is a matter of debate. Can one think without language? In what way does language control thought? Can reasoning power be improved through refined language skills? Does thought precede or follow the acquired language that is necessary for the content or processes of thought? These are a few of the teasing questions that are associated with the language–thought dilemma.

Again, it is convenient to refer to extremes in viewing this dilemma. For instance, according to the *linguistic-relativity* hypothesis, thought is shaped by the particular language through which it is processed (46). That is, language shapes ideas and serves to guide mental behavior. Both the pattern and the direction of thought are functions of the linguistic structure of a given language. If one takes this view, language is obviously much more than simply a servant of communication.

Another extreme is Piaget's contention that the development of logical thought

structures (those related to classification and conservation, for example) does not depend on language (see Chapter 2). Rather, language is structured by logic and serves only to express thought. Piaget argues that since developmental characteristics of logical thought are not linked in definite ways to successive advances in linguistic ability, it is not likely that language greatly affects thought. Most certainly language is not a sufficient condition for the emergence of thinking operations (20).

It seems fair to say that most psychologists fall somewhere between these two extreme positions. The issue is much debated, however, and various distinctions between thought and language appear throughout the literature on psychological development. Most basically, the dilemma here is related to the search for truth (see Chapter 3). The evidence accumulated to date requires a review far beyond the scope of this chapter. Thus, our immediate concern about this dilemma is the implications associated with it, specifically implications for early language training and intellectual development.

For example, if one leans toward the linguistic–relativity hypothesis, he might argue that systematic language training must be an integral if not a central feature of any attempt to improve children's intellectual functioning. This will be particularly true for children from impoverished backgrounds whose qualitative language development has been affected adversely. "Compensatory" early education programs variously based on such an argument have in fact been devised and implemented. One such program, for example, is focused on refining the structural features of language as a means for improving reasoning ability (5). Another has involved the training of functional language; that is, how existing language can better be used to promote improved abstract thought (7).

On the other hand, those who lean toward the Piaget end of the language–thought dilemma continuum argue that formal didactic and tutorial language training approaches are misguided, if not potentially harmful. As suggested in Chapter 2, supporters of Piaget's cognitive-developmental views argue that there is no substitute for self-initiated and self-arranged experiences as far as developing reasoning ability is concerned. Children must be allowed to construct their own reality out of their sensory experience. During this period, language may gradually be introduced as a means to abstract such experience, but *not* to determine thought.

The authors caution against the either–or trap implicit in discussions such as this. Not surprisingly, supporters of contrasting persuasions are usually able to provide some kind of support for their arguments. Concerning the matter of early educational strategies, it is most accurate to say that the jury is still out. What evidence is available to date seems to indicate fairly strong support for organized, systematic approaches, in terms of both facilitating language and intellectual skill development. However, the authors know of nothing to indicate incontrovertible support for either *extreme* view of the language–thought relationship. And the contribution of organized experience may well be more apparent in some aspects of intellectual behavior than in others. This idea is further explored in Chapter 5.

Language Differences

Earlier in this chapter, the authors stressed the idea that individual and group differences pervade the study of children's language development. For example, in-

dividual children and youth differ in such dimensions of language behavior as verbal knowledge (words and grammar), abstract reasoning ability involving the use of language, fluency with words and ideas, oral speech ability, and articulation (10). But children and youth in American society also differ among themselves in dialect and native language (13). For example, many children from rural New England, Appalachia, and parts of the South (Creole and Black English) will speak grammars that differ in striking ways from standard, formal, English. Yet these children may all have achieved comparable levels of language competence in their respective dialects. The following examples illustrate some common differences in standard and nonstandard English forms. These examples represent a variety of grammatically different additions, deletions, and word combinations as compared to their "grammatically correct" standard English versions.

Standard Construction
"We were sitting and talking."
"Jeff needs those clothes."
"I went to the kitchen to get an orange."
"Lisa's brother lives upstairs."
"Do you have a match? I don't have any."

Nonstandard Dialect
"We was sittin', an' we talkin'."
"Jeff, he need them clothes."
"I done went to kitchen to get a orange."
"Lisa, she brother live upstairs."
"Do you got a match? I don't got none."

In addition to dialects, many Americans speak some language other than English, and incorporate many of the rules of that language into their English. Examples include the English spoken by children and youth who come from Indian tribes, areas near French-speaking Quebec, and communities close to Spanish-speaking Mexico. Children of migrant workers often speak a different language, as do some children of immigrants who settle in our large cities.

Perhaps the most important aspect of group language differences is that children and youth whose principal language form is a dialect or a first language different from standard English may be handicapped in the public schools. That is, if one's native dialect or language is accompanied by a limited command of standard English, academic tasks that require facility with the standard form may pose difficulties (it seems clear that the language of the American classroom *is* and will probably remain standard English).

Unfortunately, there is a danger that language-based learning difficulties will be taken by teachers to indicate social or intellectual inferiority, language retardation, or a primitive linguistic system. Such a position is at best uninformed, and at worst destructive to children and youth. As indicated earlier in the chapter, there is good reason to believe that no language system, whether it be French, Spanish, or Black English, actually is superior to any other in terms of indicating more sophisticated thinking skills. A recognition of this, however, does not eliminate the basic problem of children or youth whose natural language is different from Standard English—learning to negotiate successfully in an educational environment and as adults in a society based on the standard English form. This leads to a procedural dilemma: How best to solve this problem?

What are the alternatives for dealing with the reality of standard English? At least three possibilities can be mentioned. Although the idea seems impractical in the long run, all formal schooling for children and youth could be conducted in their native dialect or language, whatever the form. This approach has its advantages but would be very expensive, and schools are already underfinanced. There is also the danger that American society would become even further fractionated by such an educational approach. An equally problematic approach would involve absolute conformity to the standard English model, including, if possible, the elimination of variant dialects or languages. This is now common practice in many if not most United States schools. Rigid and intolerant insistence on standard formal English, accompanied by derogation of any variant, has, the authors believe, done harm to countless children: immigrant children from non-English-speaking countries and Chicano, Appalachian, American-Indian, and poor Black children, among others. The authors prefer a third approach: helping all children and youth to use standard English competently when appropriate or necessary for their own welfare. Certainly this should include a policy of helping children learn to discriminate when and where the use of either native dialect or standard English is more or less functional. Neither does this exclude a policy of conducting the early years of school in the child's own dialect, then shifting gradually to standard English. This may possibly indicate greater acceptance of children "as they are" during the crucial first years of formal schooling. It can also represent an explicit commitment to the value of linguistic and cultural pluralism. To the authors' knowledge, however, no studies of the effects of such a practice, beneficial or otherwise, have yet been conducted.

It seems to the authors that culturally based language differences can be viewed as an asset both in schools and within

American society generally. Such differences can be employed to promote cultural identify and learning of respect for individual and group differences. However, educators and others must first abandon the idea that language differences somehow represent a continuum of inferior-to-superior language and thinking abilities. Genuine respect for the cultural heritage represented by different language systems also seems important.

In addition to the general issue of dialects and native languages that differ from standard English, many specific and related issues or dilemmas can be identified. Currently, the linguistic capabilities of economically disadvantaged children (especially black children) are a matter of intensive study and debate (2). Some authorities, for example, view the language of many such children as either dysfunctional or underdeveloped for formal academic learning and prescribe elaborate language therapy or special training experiences, including intensive pattern drill, for "remedial purposes" (5, 36). Others disagree, explain differences on alternative grounds, and suggest less "deficit-oriented" procedures for use with disadvantaged children (3, 25). As yet, no view of the language of these children has emerged as the correct one. Evidence continues to accumulate, however, to indicate that important differences between advantaged and disadvantaged children exist. These differences need to be examined carefully in relation to educational and social practices.

4.5 Social Class Factors and Language Behavior

One of the most reliable generalizations regarding language development concerns social class differences in communication effectiveness, word knowledge, and general proficiency with standard English (1, 24). The study described here represents recent explorations of social class factors and language (32). Two groups of kindergarten and first-grade children, forty-nine from advantaged circumstances and fifty from economically disadvantaged homes, were selected for study. Each child in both groups was read individually a story about an adventurous monkey, "Curious George." Pictures that illustrated the story action were pointed out by the reader during this activity. Subsequently, the examiner returned to the beginning of the story and invited the child to retell the story. Each child was permitted to have access to the illustrative pictures during this time. All children's responses were recorded verbatim by the examiner.

Once the children's protocols were assembled, they were scored independently by two trained personnel according to four categories: (1) total number of words, (2) total number of sentences (each new thought expressed by a child was considered a sentence), (3) total number of relevant sentences (sentences that conveyed ideas from the original story), and (4) total number of thematic units (credit was given for any correct approximation of each of the story's twenty-two basic themes).

Analysis of the protocol scores by group indicated that the advantaged children were superior to their disadvantaged counterparts on all four measures. Interestingly, these statistically significant differences were greater for the linguistic (total verbal output in words and sentences) than for the thematic (basic content) criteria. Analyses by sex and race (Black–white) within the disadvantaged sample indicated no significant differences. The main results of the study were therefore interpreted in terms of disadvantaged status, regardless of sex or race.

The reader is invited to consider possible explanations for these findings. Many things come to mind. For example, have advantaged children had more practice with this kind of verbal activity in their own homes? To what extent are differences in memory skill involved in a story-retelling performance such as this? Would the group differences be affected if children were not allowed to review the pictures as they told their version of the story? To what extent might differences in language encoding and decoding be implicated? The point is that studies such as this usually generate further questions that deserve further research. This study, in particular, dramatizes a difference in school-relevant behavior that can favor only the more advantaged child.

Still other persisting dilemmas can be identified, including the search for appropriate ways to measure language development and proficiency, especially with reference to children from different cultural backgrounds. The relationship of verbal and nonverbal language is only beginning to be explored systematically and is an area about which little is known. Questions about the precise relationship of language to learning to read continue to be explored by psychologists and educators. When and how best should we formally teach a second (or third) language to children in the schools? These matters are mentioned only to indicate that much remains to be learned about many aspects of development that have a language component, and to convey some of the many intriguing areas for further study.

Broadly speaking, language development refers to the increasingly complex elaboration of receptive (understanding) and expressive (production) language through time. While, in the past, psychologists have focused largely upon the task of describing age changes in language behavior and relationships between language production and demographic variables, the discipline known as linguistics has become a major influence in guiding the psychological study of language development. Drawing on data from the total range of language study, the authors have discussed five basic components of children's language development: grammar, pronunciation, vocabulary, rate factors in talking, and communication style.

Grammatical development involves the generation and application of rules for both sentence formation (syntax) and word form (morphology). Such development is very rapid during the early years. By school age most children comprehend and speak "adult" sentence and word forms; the developmental sequence involves a simple-to-complex progression of *holophrastic* (one word) utterances about age 1, *telegraphic* speech (cryptic sentences void of prepositions, conjunctions, and other "fillers"), and finally elaborated speech. Syntactic development generally precedes morphological development; however, both grammatical phenomena are influenced by aspects of the child's language environment, particularly his association and interaction with language models (for example, parents and older children). In this connection, several processes and techniques involved in native, or first, language learning have been identified. These include imitation, expansion and extension, selective modeling, and occasional questions.

Development in pronunciation skills, technically grouped under the concept *articulation*, consists of learning the speech sounds within one's native language, how these sounds are produced, and the rules for sound usage. The child's ability to recognize correctly articulated sounds generally precedes his ability to produce them for himself; misarticulation of the more difficult consonant blends is common, even as late as the year the child enters school, and does not necessarily indicate any pathology in speech production. Even so, it is important for language specialists in the school setting to be alert to exceptional cases that may warrant some form of remediation. Normally, the full range of articulation skills is mastered by the middle childhood years.

In general, the development of vocabulary—the child's word dictionary—proceeds slowly until about age 18–24 months, after which time a rapid acceleration in word acquisition begins and continues throughout the preschool years. Unlike grammatical and articulatory development, growth in vocabulary continues throughout life and presumably is influenced by educational experiences, including direct instruction, much more extensively than many other aspects of growth. Several examples of strategies for increasing children's word power have been discussed, including the famous Montessori three-period sequence.

Rate factors in language (including the frequency with which a child expresses himself, asks questions, initiates conversations, and makes ample use of adjectives in describing objects and events) have captured the interest of behaviorists who believe that reinforcement is a crucial variable in language development. A particularly illustrative

study of how contingent reinforcement may enhance preschool children's rate of descriptive language production was provided.

Communication style encompasses all the foregoing dimensions of language development—grammar, pronunciation, vocabulary, and rate factors. It can be conceptualized along several dimensions—for example, *elaborative* (full, rich, grammatically formal, and descriptively varied) versus *restrictive* (often including nonstandard grammar, and more elliptical and stereotyped). Communication style is strongly affected by the nature and the quality of a child's language models and is significant to the extent that skill in the elaborative mode is desirable, if not essential, for successful communication and verbal discourse in formal settings such as the school.

Several dilemmas in the study of language development can be highlighted. One, the nativist versus environmentalist (or rationalist versus empiricist) interpretation of language development is akin to the broader nature—nurture controversy discussed in Chapter 3. In the case of language, the dilemma concerns the degree to which one views language as affected more by biological than by experiential variables; the ultimate issue is perhaps the origin of language itself. A second, related dilemma concerns the relationship of language to thought. Again, this dilemma involves arriving at a clear understanding of the degree to which a given language form shapes, or is shaped by, thought. The dilemma is more than academic, since it is associated with opposing schools of thought about what the appropriate methods for language training are in early childhood education programs. Finally, the dilemma of sorting out the developmental and qualitative structural–semantic differences in various languages and dialects has been discussed. It has become increasingly clear that no one language necessarily affords its speakers a general superiority in thinking and communication. Yet faced with a wide diversity of dialects (and in some cases bilingualism) among children of different racial and ethnic backgrounds, American educational authorities are now grappling with the question of how best to accommodate to this diversity and simultaneously encourage proficiency with standard English.

REFERENCES

1. Baldwin, T. L., P. T. McFarlane, and C. J. Garvey. Children's communication accuracy related to race and socioeconomic status. *Child Development,* 1971, *42,* 345–358.
2. Baratz, J. C. A bi-dialectical task for determining language proficiency in economically disadvantaged Negro children." *Child Development,* 1969, *40,* 889–901.
3. Baratz, J. C. Teaching reading in an urban Negro school system. In F. Williams (ed.) *Language and poverty.* Chicago: Markham, 1970, 11–24.
4. Bellugi-Klima, U. *Evaluating the child's language competence.* Urbana, Ill.: National Laboratory on Early Childhood Education, 1969.
5. Bereiter, C., and S. Engelmann. *Teaching the disadvantaged child in the preschool.* Englewood Cliffs, N. J.: Prentice-Hall, 1966.
6. Bernstein, B. Social structure, language, and learning. *Educational Research,* 1961, *3,* 163–176.
7. Blank, M., and F. Solomon. A tutorial language program to develop abstract thinking in socially disadvantaged children. *Child Development,* 1968, *39,* 379–390.
8. Brown, R., and U. Bellugi. Three processes in the child's acquisition of syntax. *Harvard Educational Review,* 1964, *34,* 133–151.
9. Brown, R., C. Cazden, and U. Bellugi. The child's grammar from I to III. In J. P. Hill (ed.) *The 1967 Minnesota symposium on child psychology.* Minneapolis: University of Minnesota Press, 1968, 28–73.
10. Carroll, J. B. *Language and thought.* Englewood Cliffs, N. J.: Prentice-Hall, 1964.
11. Cazden, C. B. On individual differences in language competence and performance. *Journal of Special Education,* 1967, *1,* 135–150.
12. Cazden, C. B. Some implications of research on language development for preschool education. In R. D. Hess and R. Bear (eds.) *Early education.* Chicago: Aldine, 1968, 131–142.
13. Cazden, C., J. Baratz, W. Labov, and F. Palmer. Language development in day care programs. In E. Grotberg (ed.) *Young child in America.* Washington, D. C.: U.S. Government Printing Office, 1971.
14. Chomsky, N. *Syntactic structures.* The Hague, Holland: Mouton, 1957.
15, Chomsky, N. *Language and mind.* New York: Harcourt, 1968.
16. Clifton, C., Jr. Language acquisition. In T. D. Spencer and N. Kass (eds.) *Perspectives in child psychology.* New York: McGraw-Hill, 1970, 127–164.
17. Dale, P. S. *Language development: Structure and function.* Dryden, Hinsdale, Ill., 1972.
18. Ervin-Tripp, S. Language development. In L. W. Hoffman and M. L. Hoffman (eds.) *Review of Child Development Research, Vol. II.* New York: Russell Sage, 1966, 108–143.
19. Feldman, C. F., and M. Rodgon. *The effects of various types of adult responses in the syntactic acquisition of two-to-three-year-olds.* University of Chicago: Department of Psychology, Unpubl. paper, 1970.

20. Furth, H. G. *Piaget and knowledge.* Englewood Cliffs, N. J.: Prentice-Hall, 1969.

21. Gumpery, J. J., and D. Hymes. *Directions in sociolinguistics.* New York: Holt, Rinehart and Winston, 1972.

22. Hart, B. M., and T. R. Risley. Establishing use of descriptive adjectives in the spontaneous speech of disadvantaged preschool children. *Journal of Applied Behavior Analysis,* 1968, *1,* 109–120.

23. Jakobsen, R. *Fundamentals of language.* The Hague, Holland: Mouton, 1956.

24. Jeruchimowicz, R., J. Costello, and J. S. Bagur. Knowledge of action and other words: A comparison of lower- and middle-class Negro preschoolers. *Child Development,* 1971, *42,* 455–464.

25. Labov, W. The logic of nonstandard English. In F. Williams (ed.) *Language and poverty.* Chicago: Markham, 1970, 153–189.

26. Lavatelli, C. S. *A Piaget-oriented approach to early education.* Boston: American Science and Engineering, 1970.

27. Lenneberg, E. H. *Biological foundations of language.* New York: Wiley, 1967.

28. Marshall, H. R. Relations between home experiences and children's use of language in play interactions with peers. *Psychological Monographs,* 1961, *75,* No. 5.

29. McCarthy, D. Language development in children. In L. Carmichael (ed.) *Manual of child psychology* (2nd ed.). New York: Wiley, 1964, 492–630.

30. McNeill, D. *The acquisition of language.* New York: Harper & Row, 1970.

31. Menyuk, P. Language theories and educational practices. In F. Williams (ed.) *Language and poverty.* Chicago: Markham, 1970, 190–211.

32. Milgram, N. A., M. F. Shore, and C. Malasky. Linguistic and thematic variables in recall of a story by disadvantaged children. *Child Development,* 1971, *42,* 637–640.

33. Montessori, M. *Dr. Montessori's own handbook.* New York: Stokes, 1914.

34. O'Donnell, R. C., W. J. Griffin, and R. C. Norris. *Syntax of kindergarten and elementary school children: A transformational analysis.* Urbana, Ill.: National Council for Teachers of English, English Research Report No. 8, 1967.

35. Osser, H. Biological and social factors in language development. In F. Williams (ed.) *Language and poverty.* Chicago: Markham, 1970, 248–264.

36. Raph, B. Language and speech deficits in culturally-disadvantaged children: Implications for the speech clinician. *Journal of Speech and Hearing Disorders,* 1967, 32, 203–214.

37. Rebelsky, F. G., R. H. Starr, Jr., and Z. Luria. Language development the first four years. In Y. Brackbill (ed.) *Infancy and early childhood.* New York: The Free Press, 1967, 289–351.

38. Rheingold, H. L. Social conditioning of vocalizations in the infant. *Journal of Comparative and Physiological Psychology,* 1959, *52,* 68–73.

39. Reynolds, N. J., and T. R. Risley. The role of social and material reinforcers in increasing talking of a disadvantaged preschool child. *Journal of Applied Behavior Analysis,* 1968, *1,* 253–262.

40. Salzinger, S. Operant conditioning of continuous speech in young children. *Child Development,* 1962, *33,* 683–695.

41. Schiefelbusch, R. L. (ed.). *Language and mental retardation.* New York: Holt, Rinehart and Winston, 1967.

42. Stodolsky, S. *Maternal behavior and language and concept formation in Negro preschool children: An inquiry into process.* Unpublished Doctoral Dissertation, University of Chicago, 1965.

43. Templin, M. C. Research on articulation development. In W. W. Hartup and N. L. Smothergill (eds.) *The young child.* Washington, D. C.: National Association for the Education of Young Children, 1967, 109–124.

44. Van Riper, C. *A predictive screening device for children with articulatory speech defects.* Washington, D. C.: U. S. Office

of Education, Cooperative Research Project 1538, 1966.

45. Van Riper, C., and R. Erickson. A predictive screening test of articulation. *Journal of Speech and Hearing Disorders*, 1969, 34, 214–229.

46. Whorf, B. L. *Language, thought, and reality*. New York: Wiley; and Cambridge, Mass.: MIT Press, 1956.

5 Intelligence

Among the proudest but also the most disputed contributions made within the science of psychology have been research, theory, and practice about human intelligence. In Chapter 1, the life sketches of three young people, James, Judy, and Matthew, were given. The fact that each was quite intelligent contributed positively to his life pattern. In complex industrialized societies such as ours, intelligence is an important index of competence. As has been stressed, competence is a necessary but not a sufficient condition for human happiness and well-being in such societies (probably all societies); and a competently administered sophisti-catedly interpreted test of general intelli-gence yields one important measure of problem-solving competence.

Again in Chapter 1, intelligence was discussed as one of the eight most im-portant mediators of human develop-ment. In this chapter the authors expand the discussion begun in Chapter 1 about intelligence as a developmental mediator. Included are definitional problems and ways of viewing intelligence, measure-ment of intelligence and types of intelli-gence tests, intellectual growth and factors that seemingly influence such growth, uses of intelligence tests, and some cautions and dilemmas about

intelligence. It will be recalled that one view of intelligence and its development has already been dealt with in some detail: Piaget's cognitive-developmental approach. The discussion in this chapter is concentrated more on the study of intelligence from a psychometric point of view. In the psychometrics of intelli-gence, a child or a youth is typically given a standardized series of testing tasks or items. From his passing or failing these items, one or more scores are assigned to him that constitute an index of his intelligence or general problem-solving ability. This index is generally referred to as an intelligence quotient, or *IQ*.

DEFINITION

Many volumes have been written about intelligence, and dozens of definitions have been given—ranging from the dryly operational "Intelligence is what intelli-gence tests measure" to the general, not well defined "Intelligence is the ability to do abstract thinking and solve prob-lems."

The authors' preferred definition, for-mulated here at a very general level, is that intelligence is learning aptitude, coupled with abstract thinking and problem-solving ability. In determining the level and kind of intelligence, the authors certainly grant the importance of genetics, at least to the degree that its nature and perhaps its level are determined within broad limits by the structure of the nervous system. The nervous system is genetically determined, at least by species. The human nervous system differs from the nervous system of the chimpanzee or the white rat in the level of intelligent behavior it permits, for instance. In this sense, intelligence is "native ability" and "unfolds." However, the authors endorse an environmental or a nurture point of view in that they believe intelligence develops as a function of the interaction of the person and his environment—very rich environments will result in more intelligent people than very poor environments. In this sense, intelligence is viewed as "achievement," as a "learned" constellation of skills and abilities.

For students of human development, the important problem is, as one author has put it: How is cultural experience translated into cognitive behavior and academic achievement? In other words, the question is not *whether*, but *how* (2, 20).

FACTOR THEORIES

There has long been a scientific argument about whether intelligence is unitary or whether it is made up of more than one factor, or kind of operation. Is there a single intelligence, or are there several different kinds? Some of the more influential factor theories are reviewed here.

Classical, Two-Factor Theory

The pioneer theory of intelligence contained a g (for general) factor that included intelligent, problem-solving, sen-

tient behavior (37). It was considered to be the core of intelligence. Many specific or special factors (s) were also included. Some, such as number ability, were closely correlated with (overlapped and included common components of) g. Others (such as music or motor ability) bore little relationship to g.

Other Factor Theories

Wechsler A different two-factor theory is employed in one of the most widely used individual intelligence tests (the three Wechsler scales for measuring intelligence of (1) preschool children, (2) young children to adolescents, and (3) adults) (39). The Wechsler scales include a series of tests designed to measure *verbal* intelligence and *performance* intelligence. Items that measure verbal intelligence are such things as the number of words that can be defined and ability to give logical answers to reasoning questions—for example, what to do if you find yourself lost in the subway system of Paris. Performance items include constructing geometric designs with the use of small, wooden blocks in conformity with a model and identifying missing parts from pictures of common objects.

Many group intelligence tests (pencil and paper tests such as those most readers of this book will have taken in high school and college) are also often broken down according to two factors, a *verbal factor* tested in much the same way as described above, and a *performance* (or *quantitative*) *factor* that has to do with number and space concepts.

Cattell In another two-factor definition, intelligence is thought of as being *crystallized* or *fluid* (10, 21). Underlying both the crystallized and the fluid operations that make up intelligent behavior are the *anlage* (or preparatory, or foundation) behaviors, such as elementary perception and memory. Attention is the base for all intelligent behavior. A reasonably pure anlage function is memory span for digits. The tester tells the testee, "Listen carefully, I am going to say some numbers. Listen carefully and, when I am finished, say the numbers just as I did." Numbers are read in a monotone at the rate of one per second: 3–1–4 for very young children and up to nine or ten digits for adults at the upper limit of their attentional ability. Sheer "holding power" or immediate memory is the skill most involved in this task. Obviously, the ability to attend carefully, concentrate, and resist distraction is basic to such an anlage function.

Crystallized intelligence is made up of skills involved in mastering common elements of the culture. "The major educational institutions of a society (including the home and its substitutes) are directed at instilling this intelligence in the persons (the young) who are expected to maintain the culture. The anlage capacities of individuals are thus harnessed, as it were, by the dominant culture for the purpose of maintaining and extending the 'intelligence of the culture'" (21, pp. 246–247). This process is built from a base of simple experiences and concepts, becoming ever more complex and abstract with age. When experiences are so limited that these apparently simple skills are not developed, later development of crystallized intelligence is sure to be retarded. For example, in almost all middle-class homes, teaching very young children that two-dimensional pictures represent three-dimensional objects is so taken for granted that we think of the skill almost as a given — something that occurs without teaching. However, among the severely disadvantaged, such teaching–learning may not occur. Many disadvantaged children

enter school not realizing, for example, that the picture of a chair "stands for" or represents a real-life chair. The effect of this on learning to read is obviously disastrous, given our teaching methods for reading. Crystallized intelligence, in other words, develops through experiences that have been arranged (but not necessarily systematically planned) for the child, literally from his birth.

Fluid intelligence, on the other hand, develops relatively independently (but not entirely so) from the arrangements others make for the child. In any normal arrangement for a baby, his environment is full of movement. Soon after birth, when he can track with his eyes, he follows movements (the beginning of visual attention). If he is in any way reinforced for this following or tracking (and it may be that the sensation of tracking is in and of itself reinforcing), it leads to more tracking and eventually to systematic attention. Such systematic attention underlies perception, meaning, and thus all intellectual behavior. Unarranged experiences also seem to contribute to many of the cognitive thought functions that so interest Piaget (see Chapter 2). For example, almost all children, regardless of this culture and their advantages–disadvantages seem to master such concepts as object permanence, conservation, reversibility, and so forth. Life, as it were, forces such learning on a person when he is ready, although it is likely that deliberate arrangement of experiences (teaching) influences the rate at which these learnings are accomplished.

Fluid intelligence, in other words, is less dependent than crystallized intelligence on planned, deliberately presented learning experiences. Piaget's conservation (see Chapter 2) is probably an example of fluid intelligence. By age 6 or 7 some forms of conservation are present in normal children from all cultures and social classes—forms that develop through spontaneous and necessary dealings with their environment. Fluid intelligence, of course, does not develop completely independently from environment. In very barren environments, its development is slowed; in very rich environments (and probably also as a result of planned teaching) it is accelerated. However, it is less dependent on environment than is crystallized intelligence.

Guilford's Theory: The Structure of Intellect Guilford (18) thinks of intelligence as problem-solving ability, but rejects the hierarchical theories, such as *g* and *s*, or Piaget's stages of thought. Guilford conceives of intelligence as consisting of many factors—to be precise, 120 factorial cells. In simplified terms, a factor is a commonality among a set of relationships, all expressed in statistical terms. It is the name for the common element that links a number of components together (in this case, performance on intelligence test items of different kinds). Guilford's theories are widely enough held and influential enough that they must be presented in some detail. This is done in Example 5.1.

5.1   The Structure of Intellect

Guilford's Structure of Intellect (SI) is conceptualized as a rectangular cube. His model is shown in Figure 5.1. On its face in "layers" from top to bottom are six *products*. Cutting back at right angles from the face in "slices" or "layers" are *contents*, four in number. Intersecting these in vertical slices from the front to the back of the cube and parallel to the face are five *operations*.

What one sees in manifest human

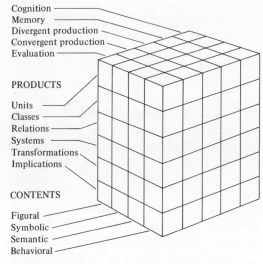

OPERATIONS

Cognition
Memory
Divergent production
Convergent production
Evaluation

PRODUCTS

Units
Classes
Relations
Systems
Transformations
Implications

CONTENTS

Figural
Symbolic
Semantic
Behavioral

Figure 5.1 *Guilford's model of the structure of Intellect. (From J. P. Guilford, "Intelligence," American Psychologist, 21, 1966, 20-26. Copyright 1966 by the American Psychological Association and reproduced by permission.)*

behavior is thus some combination of the *content* and the *product* (the forward face of Guilford's schematic cube). One must infer the *operation* that has produced such overt behavior. The meaning of these two statements will become clear as the three components of Guilford's structure of intellect are defined and illustrated.

A. *Guilford's "products."* From the simplest to the most complex, Guilford's six products (the horizontal "layers" from top to bottom of the face of his cube) are:

1. UNITS. Units are basic, and thus appear at the top. A unit can be an integer, such as the number 1, or it can be a musical note.

2. CLASSES. According to Guilford, classes are next in order of complexity. A class is a more complex concept than a

unit. The musical scale is a broader concept than a single note. The number system is broader than any single number or combination of numbers.

3. RELATIONS. To Guilford (18, p. 64) a relation is a connection between two things having their own character, such as prepositional phrases beginning with "belonging to" or "higher than."

4. SYSTEMS. The next complex among the products is system. An outline or a mathematical equation is a system.

5. TRANSFORMATIONS. "Changes, revision, redefinitions, or modifications, by which any product of information in one state goes over into another state" (p. 64) are transformations. Participles (verbs in noun form) are chosen by Guilford to illustrate transformations, for example, "reversing" or "coloring."

6. IMPLICATIONS. The most complex (the highest order) of the products is implication, by which Guilford means "something expected, anticipated, or predicted from given information" (p. 64): One thing suggests another. The term association is relevant to implication. An implication is less specifiable and verbalizable than a relation. In an implication, one thing, it is suggested, may derive from another. Guilford's usage is quite like that of regular speech.

B. *Guilford's "contents."* There are four types of content:

1. FIGURAL. This first content refers to conceptions of space.

2. SYMBOLIC. Here the referent is to number or to letter tests (p. 61).

3. SEMANTIC. Semantics refers to meaning, and this type of content is usually measured by verbal or word tests.

4. BEHAVIORAL. Guilford (p. 61) states that this category was arrived at on purely logical grounds, while the first

three categories came from previous findings about test construction. Behavioral content refers to gathering and formulating information about the behavior of people. Thorndike's notion of social intelligence also influenced Guilford in setting up this category. Guilford's illustrative test unit for behavioral content consists in selecting from a set of four pictures representing common human gestures the one picture that most closely matches the stem item in meaning.

C. *Guilford's "operations."* Guilford postulates five operations.

1. COGNITION. This first operation is recognizing, knowing, or discovering the basis of what one knows. Recognition also seems to belong here.

2. MEMORY. The second operation is memory, without which none of the other facets of the SI can work.

3. DIVERGENT PRODUCTION. This operation implies fluency, flexibility, and elaboration. The emergence of originals also belongs to this operation, implying creativity.

4. CONVERGENT PRODUCTION. The fourth operation refers to logical induction or deduction, usually from possession of a relatively complete set of facts and according to a formal logical procedure. Convergent production "must satisfy a unique specification or set of specifications" (p. 62).

5. EVALUATION. Evaluation involves judgment (placing a value on, or allocating a place for, values).

Now one can look logically at how Guilford's contents and products combine into behavior from which the operations can be inferred. If a six-sided figure is presented to a seventh-grader and he is asked to name it, he says it is a hexagon. The tester infers, first, that the operation of cognition has occurred (the testee knows what the figure is), and further, that memory is involved, since the testee must at one time have learned it and summoned memory to recognize and name it. Conversely, the testee may look at it, seem momentarily alert and insightful, then stumble and say he does not know. The tester infers that the testee has recognized it, but his rapidly changing expression says that memory has failed him and he has forgotten the name.

Guilford is steadily building tests to tap the various factorial cells, but has no single set of tests such as the Thurstones' Primary Mental Abilities Scales. He believes that different kinds of information come into experience at different times and that ability to handle them progresses at different rates, a position similar to Bayley's (4). Guilford points out that figural and behavioral information are present almost from birth, whereas symbolic and semantic information come much later. The brain, he believes, develops different ways of processing information and its products, as well as different mechanisms for the five types of operation.

Both the environment and the body, or soma, feed into the SI. Bodily information may be motivational and emotional, as well as purely informational. Both the brain and the sensory receptors provide input. Filtering and screening occur, varying from age to age, from individual to individual, and, within an individual, from time to time or situation to situation. Some sorts of input are shut off, others facilitated. Attention is closely related to the concept of filtering. The human organism is always evaluating, checking, and self-

correcting. Such checking is not the final stage of problem solving, but occurs throughout the process. Being aware of a problem, identifying it, and structuring it, Guilford believes, are cognitive operations that call for memory and evaluation of cognized information. In the process of problem solving, the individual is often motivated to seek new information, both from memory and from direct new experience. Guilford also thinks that the factorial structure of intellect may be complex from birth. Piaget's formulation of the sensorimotor stage of development during the first two years seems to be in agreement with such a position.

Ferguson's Overlearned-Skills Theory
Ferguson has proposed a learning theory of intelligence in which most emphasis is placed on environmental impact, little on genetic and constitutional factors (13, 14). His theory fits well with much current research in the field, lends itself to current thinking about intervention and prevention of cognitive disadvantage, and is a plausible way of "explaining" Cattell's concept of crystallized intelligence. Briefly, Ferguson believes that intellectual ability consists of correlated kinds of overlearning.

Overlearning means that an individual has practiced a skill to the degree that he applies it "automatically" and beyond the point of initial proficiency. For physically normal people after about age 21 months, walking and perception of circles are illustrations of such skills. Overlearning, interacting with the biological heritage, results in different asymptotic levels of the separate abilities that, grouped, are called intelligence (an asymptote is the highest point of a developmental curve).

In other words, once an individual's intelligence has developed, no matter how much the individual tries or others encourage and stimulate him, he will become no more proficient in performing intellectual tasks. Conversely, regardless of how seldom these tasks are practiced, the individual will lose little efficiency in performing them. Ferguson would say that a score from an intelligence test is useful in predicting success in school simply because the overlearned skills represented by an intelligence quotient (IQ) transfer in large part to the kinds of learning an individual must master in school. Ferguson also thinks that the abilities necessary to adjust satisfactorily and competently in any given culture increase regularly up to perhaps age 17 or a bit older. The abilities that are *not* necessary to adapt in a particular culture will increase more slowly. Indeed, they may not grow at all or may reach only a very low level. By such reasoning, Ferguson accounts for the differences in measured intelligence between people who live in different countries, in rural rather than urban areas, in impersonal and unstimulating institutions rather than in their own homes, and in circumstances of cultural disadvantage or isolation rather than cultural advantage. The marked differences in tested intelligence scores between the different socioeconomic classes, favoring higher socioeconomic levels (see Chapter 1), can be accounted for in a similar way.

In contrast to the factor theories of intelligence discussed above, Ferguson's theory is essentially a unitary learning theory. Thus, his is a process, rather than a structure, theory. However, Ferguson's learning (or better, overlearning) is applied to many kinds of skill, all of which can be subsumed under the heading of intelligence. Intelligence, in turn, Ferguson seems to think of as problem-solving ability and efficiency in learning. Finally, if we follow Ferguson, and this is an important point, *what is intelligent behavior in one setting or culture may not necessarily be intelligent behavior in another setting or culture.*

A Definitional Point of View

From what has been written so far, it is clear that there are many ways of construing or defining intelligence; but it is *not* clear that one is any more right or wrong than another. As the authors have gone through the literature about intelligence, have given intelligence tests to children, youth, and adults, and have observed themselves and others working cognitively, they have decided that Cattell's two-factor theory is as useful a way of viewing intelligence and cognition as any they have found. The theory makes sense in accounting for the data from intervention and prevention studies in which the authors have been involved. The theory is flexible enough to allow for the strong influence they believe learning exerts on intellectual development, yet the inclusion of the anlage functions and the concept of fluid intelligence allow a place for the genetic component that surely must enter into intellectual growth and development. Finally, the authors think Ferguson's ideas about intelligence as overlearning are quite plausible, particularly when they are applied to something like crystallized intelligence.

MEASURING INTELLIGENCE

Many present-day intelligence tests have been shaped according to theories of intelligence. While the chances are good that the most efficient prediction of problem-solving behavior will eventually be made with tests designed according to theory, intelligence tests originated because of practical need.

Alfred Binet, the French psychologist, is commonly but not entirely accurately given the credit as the father of intelligence testing, introduced early in the twentieth century. The French government assigned to him a very practical problem to solve: Why are so many young French children failing school? This led to the broader question of predicting which children would succeed in school, as well as which would fail. As one author puts it (33, p. 718):

First-grade teachers told Binet that most children had opportunity to learn many things before starting school. Those children who had learned many of those things, later learned well in school. Binet made a test of many of those things-which-most-children-had-opportunity-to-learn [see the authors' earlier discussion of crystallized intelligence], and found that the test gave a fair prediction of success in school. Binet's test—and useful subsequent IQ testing—was dependent upon:

1. Item content:
   a) Whether similar to material and processes to be learned in school.
   b) Whether background material useful for learning in school.
2. How much opportunity a child had had to learn the item content.
3. How much was learned, when the child did have the opportunity.

The author of this quote believes that one must keep his eye on such *functions* of intelligence testing. He argues that if functions and background are kept in mind, confusion about "the nature of intelligence" will diminish, and the often mischievously used terms *intelligence* and *mental ability* will either disappear from the arguments or be sensibly anchored to behavioral realities and learning opportunities.

Types of Intelligence Tests

There are many different types of intelligence tests and many different versions of each type. The *Sixth Mental Measurement Yearbook* (9) includes reviews of 130 different intelligence tests or instruments like intelligence tests. Intelligence tests range from those designed for infants upward to those which give pause to the most superior and well-educated adult. There are individual intelligence tests, such as those which must be given to infants and very young children (and are often given to older children and adults when a thorough study of intelligence is needed). Most tests that are given from age 5 or 6 upward, however, are group or pencil-and-paper intelligence tests. They yield a useful score but, as will be seen, not always a fair one.

There are tests of so-called verbal intelligence, such as verbal reasoning analogies (note the crystallized intelligence nature of the following item): "*Good* is to *bad* as *love* is to _____." One of the most frequently used and most useful verbal items is a reasonably simple test of vocabulary: How many words one knows, from a very simple word such as *pen* to a relatively uncommon and difficult one such as *pejorative*. There are also performance tests that deal with spatial relations, memory span, and visual–motor abilities. Seemingly, such items include elements of fluid intelligence. Performance tests, as implied in the term, do not involve the use of words to make a response, although most people guide their behavior by thoughts expressed to themselves in words. Examples of performance test items are solving paper mazes by tracing through them with a pencil, with a premium awarded for speed and accuracy; fitting jigsaw puzzles together; or selecting from a set of choices the choice that fits with what has been "cut out" of a whole picture or pattern.

There are tests and individual items within tests that are based on speed. The faster one works, the higher his score. Other items tap power, such as in solving ever more difficult verbal reasoning problems with no time limit imposed. Still other kinds of items stress a mixture of breadth and depth or power, such as the range of vocabulary or information. Still other tests measure simple reactivity, as in infant items that call for the infant to follow a moving object with his eyes or turn his head in the direction of a sound. For older children, youth, and adults, number facility tests (Q for quantitative) are widely used.

Infant Intelligence Tests

Some researchers think that the term intelligence has no place in the psychology of infancy, because the items used to test intelligence have little in common with items in intelligence tests for older children and adults. The authors believe that infant tests (tests for children under 2 years) can be useful if the score from them is not confused with the IQ score that is quite a good predictor of a number of useful things for individuals of age 5 or 6 years and older. Some infant tests, such as the visual tracking test mentioned earlier, seem to have no relation to intelligence as a problem-solving ability — learning aptitude. Other items, such as learning to use the string to pull the object to which it is tied within the baby's reach, seem truly to tap general problem-solving ability.

The following are the principal things

we now know about infant intelligence testing.

1. Seriously mentally defective babies can be distinguished from normals.

2. Babies who live in institutions anything like the old-line orphanage score lower than children living in homes with either their true parents or their foster parents.

3. Scores from intelligence tests given to children less than 18 months old are often quite unrelated to scores they earn when they are 3 or 4 years old and older. Some dispute this conclusion, maintaining that infant tests predict better than the authors are willing to admit. This lack of correlation between infant and older child intelligence test scores may be due to either or both of the following:

a) The items used to measure infant intelligence do not measure ability to solve problems. Many of them, for example, are essentially sensorimotor tasks.

b) The rate of development varies widely, so that an infant who is well ahead of his age mates may move more slowly through the developmental tasks of later childhood. Consequently, he may compare less favorably with others of his age when he, for example, is 7 years old.

4. Only with very severe deprivation, including malnutrition, does socioeconomic status seem to affect infant intelligence test scores below the age of about 18 months (that is, the children of the poor and the ill-educated score about the same as the children of the affluent and the well-educated up to about $1\frac{1}{2}$ years). Some authors place this age level higher, and say that social class level exerts little effect up to perhaps $3\frac{1}{2}$ years (28).

5. A sensitive, well-trained tester can

detect infant difficulties such as defects in social responsiveness, vision, or hearing. Like a good physical examination, an infant intelligence test provides a fairly good picture of the child as he is at the time of the test.

6. When an infant is tested when he is in a good mood, his test score predicts later tests scores better than when the infant is in a bad mood (as judged by the tester).

7. The different tests of infant intelligence often provide sharply different results for the same baby.

Further documentation to these points is given in (26).

An individual's performance on a test of intelligence must be interpreted with great care. Many factors can influence his performance at any given time or on any particular test form.

Tests for Preschool-aged Children

Intelligence tests for children up to about age 5 must be given individually. Both verbal and performance tests exist for children of these ages, and are fairly widely given for both research and clinical reasons. Goal directedness seems to play an important part in success with test items designed for the preschool years, whereas sensory alertness is more involved in items designed for infants.

The older a child is, of course, the more reliable is his intelligence test score, and the more will the items or processes included in tests be like those that he takes later as an adolescent or adult. In one of the most ambitious studies of prediction of IQ, California children were followed from birth to age 18 (young adulthood was taken as 18 years [3]), and many intelligence tests were given over the years. Test scores for the 6-month-olds actually showed a slight *negative* relationship to young adult IQ, although the correlation was not statistically significant. Tests given at age 1 year had a low positive, but not a useful, correlation (.25) with tests

for 18-year-olds. For tests given at ages 2 and 3, the correlation moved up to about .50 (respectable and modestly useful as predictor, but only at a low level of confidence). By age 4, the correlation was in the high .60s, moving to the middle .70s for tests given at ages 5, 6, and 7.

In other words, some prediction of young adult intellectual status is provided by preschool tests; but the prediction is a very long way from perfect, and there is much individual variation. Thus, one should be exceptionally careful about telling the parent of a 4-year-old that "Your child will be lucky to make it through the eighth grade." (No ethical or sensible professional person would make such a statement, even if prediction were much better than it now is.)

The topic of testing preschool-aged children is particularly important. Such testing, carefully done, holds promise for useful guidance of young children, particularly the disadvantaged. If factors that will interfere with later school and life success can be identified during the preschool ages when, it is presumed and

"I DON'T CARE IF HE DOES HAVE AN I.Q. OF 169 — I STILL THINK HE'S FAKING."

Parents and teachers alike can often underestimate the intellectual capabilities of young children (Cartoon from Phi Delta Kappan, 1969, 51 (2), 96. Reproduced by permission of artist, Sidney Harris.)

hoped, the child is malleable, it may be possible to correct them. (See the earlier discussions of intervention and prevention, as, for instance, in Head Start or the Parent Child Centers.)

The two authors whose work is summarized in Example 5.2 have taken a somewhat novel approach to intelligence testing of 4-year-olds (36). They employed tests based on Guilford's Structure of Intellect theory (see Example 5.1). Their aims were (1) to see how the Guilford model holds up for young children and (2) to investigate race, social class, and sex differences among children of about age 4 years.

5.2 Some Sources of Individual Differences in Measured Intelligence

Sitkei and Meyers (36) tested twenty-five children averaging about a month over age 4 years in each of four groups: black lower class, white lower class, black middle class, and white middle class. Approximately one-half the members of each group of twenty-five were boys, the other half were girls. The results were treated statistically, employing factor analytic methods for the most part.

The average IQ of the total group was 93; for all lower class children it was 84, for all middle-class children 101. A difference of 15 points favoring white children was found between the black and the white groups (white average was 100, black average 85), but this difference is exaggerated, because more black children were from the lowest socioeconomic class. What few sex differences there were appeared among the black children and favored the girls.

Insight into social class and race differences in tested intelligence is pro-

vided by the results. First, the superiority of the middle-class children over those of the lower class lay almost entirely in verbal comprehension. This is understandable, closely related as verbal comprehension almost certainly is to crystallized intelligence and "arranged experiences" (or teaching).

Second, the only race difference that clearly and consistently favored the white children was their performance on tests that demand facility in standard English. Black children, despite the fact that their average social class was lower than that of the whites, were superior to the white children in "memory for symbolic systems," the common term for which is memory span. Earlier in the chapter memory span was linked with fluid intelligence, and digit span (memory for digits recited at the rate of one per second) was used as an example of an anlage function.

Tests for Older Children, Adolescents, and Adults

As soon as children reach an age when they can follow instructions, can inhibit distractability, and can use a pencil, group intelligence tests can be used. As a general rule of thumb, individuals do about as well on group intelligence tests as on individual tests. However, a person with a reading problem will obviously do very poorly on a group test. So will one who does not speak English well (like many Hispano or American-Indian children). Individuals high in anxiety often go to pieces and do badly in the group intelligence-testing situation but do better in an individual testing situation where a skilled examiner can put them at ease. People who have trouble working against time typically do better on individual tests, since many group tests are timed for

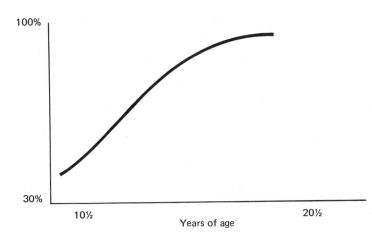

Figure 5.2 *Intellectual growth from 10½ to 20½ years. (From Mc-Candless, Children, 1967.)*

those who work at an "average speed." Thus, test administration can be fitted into an organized testing program embedded in the school day.

To summarize briefly, it is clear that different intelligence tests measure somewhat different specific behaviors. A given test must be examined closely if the tester wishes to know what aspects of "intelligent behavior" are specifically being tapped. Second, it is equally clear that intelligence tests measure somewhat different behaviors at different ages; the

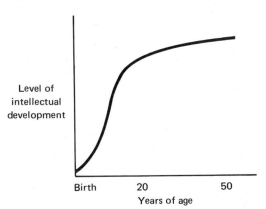

Figure 5.3 *A hypothetical composite age curve representing the growth of intelligence from birth to the middle years. (From McCandless, Children, 1967.)*

content of an infant intelligence scale and that of a scale to measure intelligence in early adolescence are simply not the same. It is also true that at successively higher age levels, intelligence test content becomes more homogeneous. Most tests at these higher levels are heavily loaded with verbal items. Finally, intelligence tests are designed for either individual or group administration. Ordinarily, the individual test is more comprehensive and relies very little on reading ability for performance. Generally speaking, however, relationship between a person's performance on an individual test and his performance on a group test is remarkably close.

INTELLECTUAL GROWTH

Figures 5.2 and 5.3 are curves showing intellectual growth, as indicated by intelligence test results.

We can see in Figure 5.2 that a little more than 40 percent of mature intellectual status has been reached by 10½ years and that growth from this age on is progressively slower. It should be noted that the criterion for determining "percentage of growth" at any point during development is a person's ultimate test performance at maturity. Such information on intellectual growth by necessity must come from longitudinal study.

As can be seen in Figure 5.3, the curve for intellectual growth from birth to the late teens is in the shape of a very shallow, steeply slanted **s**. During infancy and the early preschool years, growth is rapid and positively accelerated (faster as the child grows older). At school age, growth becomes negatively accelerated (slower year by year—this can be more easily seen in Figure 5.2). From the late teens on, growth is slow. Traditionally, we have believed that intellectual performance (power?) began to drop slowly and slightly in the mid-twenties and rather rapidly from the forties on. Now, it seems clear that most of this drop is not in power, but in speed. Indeed, there is some evidence, not all of it undisputed (1), that growth in some intellectual functions does not reach its asymptote (highest point) until ages 50 to 60 (17, 32). Kinds of items or scores that are thought to show gain until the middle years or later are verbal meaning (peaks at age 55), number "intelligence" (peaks at age 50), educational aptitude (a composite score, peaking at 55), motor cognitive flexibility (peaking at 60), and social responsibility (peaking during the five-year period between 50 and 55) (32).

Finally, girls gain less than boys in intelligence from adolescence to adulthood, and the brightest girls at adolescence make the least gains (7). Further, girls who gain show signs of personal–social maladjustment, while boys who gain are better adjusted than those who stand still or lose (19). The authors suspect that these sex differences can be attributed to sex role stereotype factors (which, it is hoped, are now changing)

that penalize competent women in United States culture.

In summary, most studies of intellectual growth indicate that a disproportionate amount of such growth occurs during the prepubertal years. Some authorities (for example, 6) believe that much of one's basic intellectual status is determined before age 8. In any case, any information about "growth curves," "peak performances," and the like, is a function of our measures of intelligence. To the extent these measures are faulty, our understanding of intellectual growth is also faulty. It is entirely possible that developmental phenomena related to intelligent behavior are not measured by conventional tests. In fact, the traditional emphasis on *product* in intelligence testing has led some authorities recently to focus on *process*, that is, the developmental study of changes in how a child or a youth goes about dealing with intellectual tasks (12, 35).

SOME FACTORS AFFECTING INTELLECTUAL DEVELOPMENT

Throughout the course of development, some children and youth are losers in IQ, some remain remarkably stable, while others are gainers in relation to their age mates. What may be some reasons?

Anxiety and Curiosity

Anxiety (see Chapter 10) typically inhibits curiosity and is negatively related to performance on both intelligence and achievement tests. It is probable that curiosity facilitates intellectual growth (25). Moreover, it is clear that low-achieving children and high school dropouts are withdrawn and passive as a group (16). The authors advance the hypothesis that children who are helped to become less anxious, at least down to the level of only moderate anxiety, will in turn become more curious. Thus, they may not only *perform* better on intelligence and achievement tests, but, through new experiences gained by being curious, may also actually improve in intellectual prowess (see the discussion about assimilation and accommodation in Chapter 2).

Cognitive Style

One of the better documented dimensions of cognitive style is impulsivity versus reflectivity (24). The impulsive individual works quickly and with many errors. The reflective child works relatively slowly and deliberately, and his responses are freer from error. It seems logical that the more an individual analyzes and the less he jumps to conclusions, the more likely he is to profit from his experience (accommodate, perhaps, in Piaget's term); thus, the more likely he is to gain in intelligence. Most certainly, he will do better on tests, provided he does not have to conform to too close a time limit. The concepts of the reflective and impulsive child and youth are discussed in more detail in Chapter 6.

In the sense that the motive to achieve reflects (or affects) an individual's cognitive style, those who are high in achievement motivation including competitiveness, persistence, independence, and self-initiative) at ages 6 to 10 are likely to gain in IQ. This is also more likely to occur among boys than girls (23).

As one of the authors has said (25):

The over-all approach of highly competent children and youth to their environment seems to provide them with constant rewards, and successful experiences alter the structure of their intellect; their efficiency and power of function follow an accelerating, rather than a linear or declining, curve, as expressed by an increasing IQ, greater and greater subject matter mastery, and so on." (p. 228)

The converse may also be predicted. In other words, to plagiarize a sacred source: "Those who have get; and from those who have not is taken away."

Sex Differences

It has already been pointed out that boys are more likely than girls to be IQ gainers. Girls who gain in IQ often seem to "pay a price" in terms of less satisfactory personal adjustment, whereas, if anything, male IQ gainers show improved adjustment as well as improved IQ. As the authors have said, they believe that this sex difference is largely culturally determined. IQ is a major index of competence. As mentioned above, traditionally, competent females have not been well received in United States culture, while competent males have been richly rewarded. The authors hope that the times are changing.

It is possible that the traditional difficulties faced by females, highly competent or otherwise, is based to some extent on the doctrine of male superiority. The authors hasten to point out that the psychological study of intelligence does not support such a doctrine; significant differences in general intelligence favoring one or the other sex have rarely been reported. Part of this lack of sex differences can be accounted for by the fact that test builders have tried to use items that do not discriminate between boys and girls.

It is true, however, that the pattern of tested abilities differs reliably by sex. For example, males excel slightly in numerical reasoning and spatial judgment, females slightly in verbal fluency and rote memory (38). In individual cases, such differences may be important for vocational considerations; for the general case, sex differences in intelligence do not seem to have much practical significance. For the authors perhaps the most provocative

Fairly early in childhood there begins to appear a superiority favoring males in spatial judg-ment. Is this due to innate sex difference or to sex-specific reinforcement in spatial judgment tasks? (Wide World Photos)

aspect of sex differences in intelligence concerns variability in intellectual growth; that is, intellectual growth in females, in comparison to males, seemingly is less affected by emotional climate, especially early emotional experiences (4).

Father Absence

Boys, especially, often seem to suffer competence retardation and distortion when they have no fathers in the home (5, 25). A good many of the studies in which this has been demonstrated leave much to be desired in terms of methods. For example, authors often do not tell us when during the child's life the father was absent, how long he was away, or why he

was away. Other authors are very careful. But since all the results point in the same direction, it seems safe to say, for whatever reasons, that having a father at home is useful in developing competence, a "masculine-type mind," and a higher intelligence quotient. Even little girls of 2 years and under seem markedly affected in their cognitive development by their fathers (31). The more highly educated the father, the better the little girl is at several cognitive tasks, even at the early age of 2. The reader should note that this statement tells us nothing about *why* this should be true. The statement merely reflects association. In addition to genetic factors, perhaps highly educated fathers read more books to their daughters or talk more to them while taking walks. The authors have mentioned earlier the need to study process—that is, in what way do two things come to be related to each other.

Prejudice and Rigidity

There is some tantalizing but inconclusive evidence that race-prejudiced individuals are less likely to gain in (and perhaps even to hold) their intellectual level. This makes good sense if, as has been hypothesized, prejudiced people are more rigid than unprejudiced people (and thus, presumably, less open to new experience) (25). Moreover, energy consumed in maintaining prejudice may be diverted from more constructive approaches to life of the sort that conceivably result in intellectual gain. Example 5.3 contains a summary of some research that suggests how this may come about if, indeed, it does.

5.3 Intellectual Flexibility and Learning Potential

To link prejudice with IQ change or level requires some intervening variable —some link to explain *how* the association came to be. In 1968, Budoff and Pagell provided a possible link that gives rise to interesting, potentially constructive speculation (8). These researchers worked with forty educable mentally retarded subjects between ages 12 and 17 years and with two control groups. One control group consisted of fourth-graders of the same mental age, but younger chronologically. The other control group consisted of normal ninth-graders of the same chronological age as the retarded subjects, but much higher in mental age and IQ. Budoff and Pagell studied the relationship between

rigidity and learning efficiency. Their tests of rigidity were (1) satiation on a simple repetitive task (putting marbles in holes: the shorter the time worked, the quicker the satiation time); and (2) the ease and frequency with which an individual could change from one conceptual method of sorting cards to another. Among the retarded subjects, those who satiated most quickly and changed concepts most easily—those who were least rigid, in other words— profited most from instructions in how to handle a nonverbal reasoning task. The older normal IQ group, as might be expected, were the most flexible; and the gainers among the retardates closely resembled the normal group in their patterns of nonrigidity.

Background and Child Rearing

In Chapter 4, the importance of early verbal stimulation and enriched learning experiences for language development was stressed. Much of what was said applies also to intellectual development. Of course, the two aspects of development are not one and the same. As has been seen, verbal fluency does not guarantee skill in conceptualizing, problem solving, and critical thinking. Yet language *does* play an extremely important role in intelligence.

Technicalities aside, our concern at this point is for home-based experiential factors that influence intellectual growth. These factors can be discussed at several different levels. For example, children and youth from relatively disadvantaged backgrounds are typically less proficient with intellectual tasks than their more advantaged age mates; they are also more vunerable to educational influences such as schools (25).

More specifically, it is apparent that

both the intellectual and the emotional climates established by parents are important factors in the development of intelligence. Intellectual climate can be represented to some extent by the kinds of activities parents, during daily living, encourage for their children and the way in which parents "teach" their children informally (16). Sheer amount of interaction seems to be important. The children of parents who interact a great deal with them, particularly verbally, are more intelligent than those of parents who do not interact much. When such interactions center around problem-solving tasks, parents of more intellectually proficient children are more explicit in helping their children to define the problem and offer only subtle hints for its solution instead of a more intrusive, directive style of teaching—they guide, but do not tell how. Such parents are also more receptive of their children's errors.

But all these interactions need not be pleasant; they may assume characteristics of very firm standards and strong demands. For example, mothers who are strongly concerned with, and even "push" their children to excel in, intellectual achievement generally have children who perform well on intelligence tests (34). The earlier discussion of socialization for competence (Chapter 3) is relevant to this point.

Sex differences in response to variations in child-rearing practices also appear in studies concerned with intellectual growth. For example, boys who are given much early maternal love and acceptance seem to develop slowly early in life, but later reach high achievement in mental abilities; boys with punishing and rejecting mothers show the opposite pattern (4). Relationships for girls are less clear. Moreover, boys who work cognitively at a high conceptual level are more likely than low conceptual level boys to come from homes that are not very authoritarian, and from parents who are in closer agreement with each other about child rearing than is true of parents of low conceptual level boys (11).

An extensive study is devoted to the topic of background and child rearing (30). Children between the ages of 6 and 12 years from higher social status families were more likely to be gainers than children from lower status families. On the whole, the most striking gainers between 6 and 17 years were girls with brothers, boys with much older siblings, and firstborns in general. Gainers of both sexes regarded male social roles favorably, female roles unfavorably. Boys, but not girls, from broken homes were low gainers or losers. The patterns were over all clearer for boys than girls.

Because this short paragraph does not do this study justice, the subject is presented in greater detail in Example 5.4.

5.4 Some Factors Associated with Changes in Measured Intelligence

Regardless of the criticisms that have been directed against intelligence testing (and they have been many and often thoroughly justified), there is no doubt but that results from an intelligence test predict, often with distressing accuracy, how an individual will achieve in school *and* in United States society. The guess may be advanced that such results predict best for the groups for whom they were built (white children and youth whose language from birth has been standard English), although prediction is still moderately good (and distressing) for other groups as well. For such reasons, it is well to look at the factors that affect intellectual change, either to raise, to maintain, or to lower intelligence quotient.

Data were pooled from five major longitudinal studies of child development (three of them carried out in Berkeley, California, one in Denver, and one in Ohio). From each place, intelligence test scores for a sizable number of children and young people could be attained from tests administered when the research subjects were 6, 12, and 17 years old. Very many other data were also available. Ninety-one subjects (that is, those at ages 9, 12, and 17 years) had all possible scores; and many more (in some cases as many as 375 subjects) from 6 to 12 years, or from 12 to 17, but not from both groups) had some combination of scores. For the most part, the subjects were advantaged, white, and Protestant. Some subjects were born as long ago as 1921; the youngest were born as recently as 1951. While Rees and Palmer (30) do not give the information, it is probable that the average age of the subjects in 1971 was 40+ years.

Gains were most conspicuous for girls with brothers, boys with much older brothers or sisters, and firstborn children. Among the data were TAT (Thematic Apperception Test) stories. TAT is a protective test (see Example 2.1, Chapter 2). The stories told about the characters pictured on each TAT card are assumed to reflect (project) the person's own wishes, attitudes, and needs in more or less direct form. In the present study, the gainers told stories in which the pictured males showed up favorably, the pictured females unfavorably. The low scorers (nongainers and losers) showed the opposite pattern. Boys from broken homes showed less gain than boys from intact homes, but this factor made no difference for girls. Between ages 6 and 12, social status factors were closely related to IQ gain: the higher the status, the greater the gain. This is surprising, since on the whole there was not much range in social status (almost everyone was reasonably affluent and well educated). However, from 12 to 17, social class bore little or no relationship to change. This point perhaps indicates that by age 12 or so, youngsters become much more important factors in their own development (see the discussion of the role of the individual in his own development in Chapters 1 and 2).

Finally, all relationships between IQ gain and other factors were clearer, more consistent, and stronger for boys than for girls. This is not an unusual finding, but its meaning is not clear. Are females less susceptible to environmental influences? Certainly, there seems to be less variation based on environment among girls. Is the impact of environment equal for boys and girls, but are girls provided with a more homogeneous environment?

We have seen that intelligence is quite a direct expression of competence in United States society and that, at least historically and certainly while the subjects of this study were growing up, competence is valued highly among boys and men, but less so among girls and women. Thus, it may be that social forces impinged directly and strongly on boys in the area of intellectual behavior, but not on girls.

To summarize briefly, the pattern of stability and change in intelligence test performance over time is associated with a variety of forces. Among those mentioned are characteristics of the individual (anxiety, curiosity, cognitive style, sex, and prejudice) and characteristics of his environment (father absence, child-rearing practices, and the like). Genetic factors have been discussed earlier in this book. The characteristics mentioned, of course, represent an interaction that continually occurs between the individual and his environment. It is the overall quality of this interaction that is seemingly most crucial for intellectual development.

It has also been emphasized that marked gains or losses in IQ can occur for children and youth throughout the course of development. In general, however, the IQ (as an index of intelligence test performance) becomes increasingly stable with age, especially after the early school years. Even so, the fact of individual differences in intellectual growth rate cannot be underestimated. Differential growth rates result in a successively wider range of individual differences in intelligence with age. Among other things, this makes the educator's task of accommodating to individual differences increasingly complex as children proceed through the school grades. This point is discussed again later.

USES OF INTELLIGENCE TESTS

As noted earlier in this chapter, intelligence test results for infants are useful in about the same way that a careful physical examination is useful. Given and interpreted by sophisticated examiners, they present a picture of the child as he is here and now. Anomalies and strengths in development can often be picked up. The authors seriously question whether any attempt should be made to estimate later (after age 3, for example) stages of ability from intelligence tests given below age 2, although gross retardation due to neurolocal or genetic fault and possibly to severe malnutrition can typically be diagnosed.

More predictive power exists for tests given during the preschool years. Again, conscientious psychologists shy away from making firm predictions of later status. For infants, however, developmental anomalies, including special weaknesses and strengths, can often be picked up through a carefully given and interpreted individual intelligence test. Results from such tests, the authors think, can be used to place children (for example) in carefully planned remedial programs from which there is some promise that cognitive gain will result (however, to speak candidly, this matter is open to lively dispute).

During the years of elementary and secondary schooling, intelligence test scores are moderately effective in predicting school progress. Table 5.1, taken from (25), includes representative data

Table 5.1 *Correlations for boys and girls between a group intelligence test and teachers' marks in four basic subject matter classes*

School Subject	Boys	Girls
English	.56	.76
Social Studies	.48	.82
Science	.65	.75
Mathematics	.39	.68

(Adapted from Olson, *et al.,* Long-term correlates of children's learning and problem-solving behavior, *Journal of Educational Psychology,* 1968, *59,* 227–232; copyright 1968 by American Psychological Association, reproduced by permission.)

concerning the relation of test scores from a group intelligence test and marks assigned by teachers. For the seventh-grade Minneapolis boys, whose data are entered in this table, knowing their intelligence allows one to hit about 15 percent better than chance in predicting their math grades (this rough estimate is made by squaring the correlation of .39, and converting it to a percentage). From intelligence scores for boys, science grades can be predicted some 40+ percent better than if the prediction was made by sheer guesswork (or chance). Social studies grades for girls can be predicted from intelligence test scores some 67 percent better than chance. These are respectable enough figures and indicate that, wisely used and with the fact kept in mind that prediction is far, far from perfect, intelligence test scores *can* be useful in guiding students.

Relationships between intelligence, school learning as judged by results from standardized academic achievement tests, and the school marks assigned by teachers, however, vary according to the characteristics of the group. In one study, the authors found that, on the whole, the most accurate academic predictions at the seventh-grade levels were for poor black girls, the least accurate were for advantaged white boys (27).

Even though results from intelligence tests are almost universally used in deciding who should and who should not be admitted to college, great caution should be exercised. In one large, ambitious, and careful study, it was found that standardized achievement test results predicted grades during the first semester of the freshman year at the University of Illinois moderately better than could have been done by guesswork alone, 13 to 26 percent better, (22). However, the predictions for the last semester

of the senior year (which is the one that *really* counts) were negligible. The best of the tests given added only 8 percent accuracy above chance. The author of this study reports that results from intelligence tests showed about the same pattern except that they were even less efficient than the achievement tests.

In summary, it is often useful to attempt to predict the course of an individual's learning life and, where possible, provide information to individuals who, so equipped, may make better decisions about their own educational or vocational planning. Intelligence tests, among other assessments, offer possibilities in this area. Marked developmental deficits and conspicuous strengths among infants and preschoolers often show up in intelligence tests, and information gained from such tests can be used with caution in shaping programs that either remedy or take advantage of the behaviors so elucidated. Within limits, school success is predictable from intelligence test results. As described later, it is hoped that, eventually, general intelligence tests will no longer be used for such purposes, but rather that more efficient predictors will be employed. Intelligence tests will probably continue to be used as research tools as we seek answers to such questions as the nature–nurture issue raised in Chapter 3.

DILEMMAS AND CAUTIONS ABOUT HUMAN INTELLIGENCE

Intelligence: An Aid or a Hindrance to Decision Making?
The concept of human intelligence has long been reified—people have made a *thing* of intelligence. As has been seen, intelligence is an abstract concept, de-

finable only by the operations—the test items and observations—that are used to measure or observe it. To the extent, and only to the extent, that these items or observations are related to other important human behaviors, is intelligence a useful concept—a helpful index of the *process* of human problem solving.

The first dilemma, then, in employing and measuring the concept of intelligence as one aspect of human development revolves around how to use it to promote and optimize people's lives, not to classify and limit them.

For example, intelligence test scores are probably used more often to keep people *out of* training programs or occupations than they are to open up the way for them to get into the *right* training program or occupation. Practically speaking, it may be well to look for cutting scores for intelligence tests rather than for linear prediction scores. This is being done more often. For example, if your score is 80 for an intelligence test, 100 being average, your chances of success in a Ph.D. program in physics are 1 in 100; if your score is 135, your chances are 75 in 100. On the basis of such prediction coefficients, individuals interested in entering specific programs and those involved in operating such programs can proceed with odds much above chance. Even so, some who "could have made it" will be excluded, and some will be admitted who for one or another reason will not make it.

Intelligence Tests and Human Guidance
The question whether intelligence is an aid or a hindrance to decision making leads to a second closely related dilemma: How can we design predictors that are more efficient than the intelligence tests now employed? This is a matter for

research, of course. The authors recommend a "work sample" approach that has little relation to conventional intelligence testing and which draws heavily from ideas such as those of Ferguson about overlearning of skills and transfer of abilities from one to another situation. Is a high conventional IQ necessary to be a good fireman? a good lawyer? a good butcher? a good physicist?—that is the traditional question. More realistically, we should ask what *skills* are necessary for the occupations of fireman, lawyer, butcher, and physicist? When we have moved toward answering the measurement-of-skills question, we can turn away from the notion of traditional intelligence testing to the more useful practice of skills testing for human academic and vocational guidance. An ingenious piece of research that represents such an approach is summarized in Example 5.5.

5.5 An Experimental Approach to the Prediction of Vocational Success

As has been said, there is general agreement that conventional intelligence tests are not fair to disadvantaged children and young people, who often have not had the experiences necessary to develop crystallized intelligence in the conventional, middle-class sense of the term that is embedded in almost all individual and group United States intelligence tests.

Norman Freeberg became interested in the problem of predicting success within a work training program, and developed his somewhat promising test with the cooperation of 123 adolescent boys and 133 adolescent girls from eleven Neighborhood Youth Corps urban project centers in northeastern United

States (15). In Freeberg's test, a picture and a series of responses to the picture appear either on one page or on adjoining pages, so these unsophisticated test takers "do not get lost." The test is designed for administration to small groups of perhaps a dozen persons. The reading level is pegged at about the fifth grade.

In each item, a cartoonlike picture represents an adolescent figure in some situation that pertains to the variable being tested (for example, interaction with an authority figure). Four or five possible responses are provided, of which the testee chooses one. The areas tested for are knowledge about jobs; vocational plans, aspirations, and interests; attitude toward authority; self-esteem; ability to defer gratification; skills at job seeking and job holding; motivation for vocational achievement; and practical reasoning.

For the vocational aspiration part of the test, for example, the cartoon in one of the items shows a girl pushing a figure in a wheel chair into Ward B. The four possible responses range from "A great job; the kind of thing I would like," to "This is a rotten kind of a job. I wouldn't like it at all." (p. 231)

Results from the test were correlated with supervisors' ratings, and, in general, relations were low to moderate, although more promising than much that has previously gone on in this field. For boys, the sections of the test that were correlated best were job-seeking skills and practical reasoning. Nothing much showed up for the girls, except that their attitudes seem more important in training success than was true for boys. Freeberg concludes; ". . . the results of the present study hold at least some

promise for the application of needed assessment devices *within* culturally and economically deprived populations." (p. 239)

Intelligence and Race
The authors believe the evidence is murky, the social implications dramatic and potentially explosive, and the indications strong that learning overrides genetics in the complex matter of intelligent behavior among human beings. Thus, they see little of either theoretical or practical importance to be gained through research in the United States concerning race and intelligence. Racially speaking, for one thing, relatively few people in the United States are "pure." *Negro* is more a sociological term than a racial term, for example. This is not to say that studies such as the one summarized in Example 5.2 are not good and useful studies, and results from such studies perhaps justify a certain expenditure of time and energy on the question of race and intelligence. It will be recalled that the results from this study suggest that the major difference between affluent and disadvantaged children was in verbal reasoning, and the biggest difference between black and white in test items related to use of conventional, formal English. Such findings can very likely be translated into practical educational use.

For the present, however, the authors are inclined to believe that the question of race differences in intelligence is overstressed. We are dealing with similar distributions of measured intelligence by race, with lots of overlap, and with individuals, not with abstract averages. Nor does *genetic* mean fixed. One form of mental retardation (phenylketonuria) that would formerly have been inevitable can now be avoided through a special diet; children from retarded or dull, normal families, adopted early into advantaged homes, often reach about the same intellectual and educational level as their adoptive parents.

Intelligence Tests and Special Groups

Infants and Preschoolers

As has been said, the authors believe that intelligence test results should be employed *most* cautiously in making determinations about the future of infants and preschool-aged children: to suggest positive programs, yes; as a basis for negative sanctions, no. By this, the authors mean that for an infant shown to be low in social responsiveness, a program in increased social interaction should be recommended. But an infant with a low score on an infant test should not be denied access to a foster home rather than be placed in institutional care or arbitrarily be cut off from adoption without other strong evidence.

When English Is Not the First Language

The results from United States intelligence tests should be regarded with tongue in cheek for children or youth who grow up with any other language than English. This category of course includes a very large number of (and perhaps most) Hispanos, those of Chinese and Japanese ancestry perhaps into at least the third United States generation, many American Indians, and Black children and youth with ghetto upbringings—those who are brought up where other than standard, formal English is typically spoken. It must be added, however, that whether dialectical variations on standard English seriously impede intelligence test performance is a controversial matter. Some authorities maintain that administering

tests to a child in his own dialect will result in improved performance (2). Others have data to show that the language condition (as long as it *is* English) makes no difference (29). This is sure to be an issue of much study for the next several years. Investigations of the influence of race and sex of examiner on children's test performance are needed; also needed are studies of the familiarity and degree of reassurance present in testing situations.

Disadvantage and Isolation

Any child brought up with a minimum number of the sort of arranged experiences discussed in this chapter may not have had the chance to develop his crystallized intelligence. Thus, the results of any conventional test given to him are suspect. This includes the sort of isolated upbringing that characterizes some rural children. Furthermore, it may be that some disadvantaged children have not adopted the achievement strategy that underlies successful performance on intelligence tests, but which is so common among advantaged children that we take it for granted; that is, we assume that every child wants to do his best, to put his best foot forward. This may not be true for many disadvantaged children. These children may also be handicapped by minimal social skills, by anxiety, or by shyness as well. The fact remains, however, that to the extent skills measured by intelligence tests are critical for success in various activities, the disadvantaged child or youth will be handicapped and will be more subject to failure.

The Critical-Period Dilemma

The dilemma presented by the notion of *critical periods* was discussed in Chapter 3, and it is not necessary to discuss it in detail here. However, the notion is so important that it must be mentioned once again. Some research evidence exists, and a good many serious and honest scholars in the field of child development believe, that there is a critical period for intellectual development, and that it has partially passed by the age of 5 or 6, when the average American child first meets organized educational experiences outside his own family. If his family has not provided him with a good cognitive environment, his intellectual potential can never be reached, according to a critical-period hypothesis. It then becomes a pressing practical and even moral issue to see to it that each child during his first years of life receives the amount and kind of stimulation needed for optimum cognitive development.

The authors think of intelligence as learning aptitude, coupled with abstract thinking and problem-solving ability. It is genetic or inherited, at least to the degree that the human species nervous system is genetically determined and sets its limits. But intelligence is environmentally determined in that learning opportunities strongly facilitate or retard the development of cognitive skills.

Cattell's two-factor theory of fluid and crystallized intelligence seems to the authors to be as useful as any that has been promulgated. They consider Ferguson's theory of *intelligence as overlearning* a plausible explanation, at least of Cattell's crystallized intelligence. It is helpful to think of intelligence as a *process*, not a *structure* or a *product*.

Intelligence testing of infants is useful as a "here and now" description of their developmental strengths and weaknesses. After infancy—from about ages 2 to 3 years onward—intelligence test results can be moderately useful in planning educational programs for children and youth. In such planning, the emphasis should be on *promotion and facilitation*, not on *classification* and, often, *limitation of opportunity*.

The common types of intelligence tests are individual (for infants and preschool children, or for careful diagnostic procedures employed at any age) and group. Another classification is according to verbal intelligence and performance intelligence. In performance tests, language is not required for responses. Quantitative (number) ability is often measured apart from either verbal or performance intelligence.

Intellectual growth is very rapid and positively accelerated during infancy and the preschool years. It slows, and the curve to represent it becomes negatively accelerated, thereafter. Evidence has now accumulated that, except for items requiring speed of response, intelligence may continue to grow well into and beyond the middle years of life, or at least may hold its level until much later than has traditionally been thought. Apparently boys and men are more likely than girls and women to gain in intelligence from later childhood onward. The authors guess that this is due to United States culture's derogation of competence among women, and perhaps to their more sheltered (homebound, less cognitively stimulating) lives.

Anxiety, rigidity, impulsivity, femaleness (at least in this culture), father absence (particularly for boys), and deprived backgrounds are thought to interfere with maximum development of cognition. Their opposite numbers facilitate cognitive-intellectual development.

Intelligence test scores are moderately useful in predicting school (and thus life) achievement, but they are only one factor in such predictions. Extreme caution should be exercised in helping others to plan, and dogmatic predictions from IQ scores should never be made. IQ scores, for example, predict first-semester college freshman grades fairly well, but not *last-semester college senior grades*. Ideally, specific work sample tests instead of more general intelligence tests should be used for educational and career guidance. Special care must be exercised in using IQ scores to help individuals make life plans when they come from disadvantaged backgrounds, when they are very young, and when conventional English is not their first language.

If there is a critical period in intellectual development (and the authors are inclined to believe there is), it is both *a practical and a moral necessity* to see to it that every child is provided an environment in his preschool years, from infancy onward, that will assure his normal-to-superior— or at least, optimal—intellectual development. All in all, the results of research on child rearing and intellectual development in children can be tentatively although cogently summarized by the following quote: "In essence, given the undamaged genetic potential, mental growth is best facilitated by a supportive, 'warm,' emotional climate, together with ample opportunities for the positive reinforcement of specific cognitive efforts and successes." (4, p. 1203)

REFERENCES

1. Baltes, P. B., K. W. Schaie, and A. H. Nardi. Age and experimental mortality in a seven-year longitudinal study of cognitive behavior. *Developmental Psychology*, 1971, 5, 18–26.
2. Baratz, J. C. A bidialectical task for determining language proficiency in economically disadvantaged Negro children. *Child Development*, 1969, 40, 889–901.
3. Bayley, N. Consistency and variability in the growth of intelligence from birth to eighteen years. *Journal of Genetic Psychology*, 1949, 75, 165–196.
4. Bayley, N. Development of mental abilities. In P. Mussen (ed.) *Carmichael's manual of child psychology*. New York: Wiley, 1970, 1163–1210.
5. Blanchard, R. W., and H. B. Biller. Father availability and academic performance among third-grade boys. *Developmental Psychology*, 1971, 4, 301–305.
6. Bloom, B. J. *Stability and change in human characteristics*. New York: Wiley, 1964.
7. Bradway, K. S., and C. W. Thompson. Intelligence at adulthood: A twenty-five year follow-up. *Journal of Educational Psychology*, 1962, 53, 1–14.
8. Budoff, M., and W. Pagell. Learning potential and rigidity in the adolescent mentally retarded. *Journal of Abnormal Psychology*, 1968, 73, 479–486.
9. Buros, O. K. (ed) *The sixth mental measurements yearbook*. Highland Park, N. J.: Gryphon Press, 1965.
10. Cattell, R. B. Some theoretical issues in adult intelligence testing. *Psychological Bulletin*, 1941, 38, 592 (Abstract).
11. Cross, H. J. The relation of parental training conditions to conceptual level in adolescent boys. *Journal of Personality*, 1966, 34, 348–365.
12. Elkind, D. Piagetian and psychometric conceptions of intelligence. *Harvard Educational Review*, 1969, 39, 319–337.
13. Ferguson, G. A. On learning and human ability. *Canadian Journal of Psychology*, 1954, 8, 95–112.
14. Ferguson, G. A. On transfer and the abilities of man. *Canadian Journal of Psychology*, 1956, 10, 121–131.
15. Freeberg, N. E. Assessment of disadvantaged adolescents: A different approach to research and evaluation measures. *Journal of Educational Psychology*, 1970, 61, 229–240.
16. Freeburg, N. F., and D. T. Payne. Parental influence on cognitive development in early childhood: A review. *Child Development*, 1967, 38, 65–87.

17. Green, R. F. The age-intelligence relationship between ages 16 and 64: A rising trend. *Developmental Psychology,* 1969, *1,* 618–627.

18. Guilford, J. P. *The nature of human intelligence.* New York: McGraw-Hill, 1967.

19. Haan, N. Proposed model of ego functioning: Coping and defense mechanisms in relationship to IQ change. *Psychological Monographs,* 1963, *77,* Whole No. 571.

20. Haywood, H. C. Experiential factors in intellectual development: The concept of dynamic intelligence. In J. Zubin and G. A. Jervis (eds.) *Psychopathology of mental development.* New York: Grune & Stratton, 1967.

21. Horn, J. L. Organization of abilities and the development of intelligence. *Psychological Review,* 1968, *75,* 242–259.

22. Humphreys, L. G. The fleeting nature of the prediction of college and academic success. *Journal of Educational Psychology,* 1968, *59,* 375–380.

23. Kagan, J., and H. A. Moss. The stability of passive and dependent behavior from childhood through adulthood. *Child Development,* 1960, *31,* 577–591.

24. Kagan, J., B. L. Rosman, D. Day, J. Albert, and W. Philips. Information processing in the child: Significance of analytic and reflective attitudes. *Psychological Monographs,* 1964, *78,* Whole No. 578.

25. McCandless, B. R. *Adolescents: Behavior and development.* Hinsdale, Ill.: Dryden, 1970.

26. McCandless, B. R. *Children: Behavior and development.* New York: Holt, Rinehart and Winston, 1967.

27. McCandless, B. R., A. Roberts, and T. Starnes. Teacher's marks, achievement test scores, and aptitude relations by social class, race, and sex. *Journal of Educational Psychology,* 1972, *63,* 153–159.

28. Palmer, F. H. Socioeconomic status and intellective performance among Negro preschool boys. *Developmental Psychology,* 1970, *3,* 1–9.

29. Quay, L. C. Language dialect, reinforcement, and the intelligence test performance of Negro children. *Child Development,* 1971, *42,* 5–15.

30. Rees, A. H., and F. H. Palmer. Factors related to change in mental test performance. *Developmental Psychology Monograph,* 1970, *3,* No. 2, Part 2, 1–57.

31. Reppucci, N. D. Parental education, sex differences, and performance on cognitive tasks among two-year-old children. *Developmental Psychology,* 1971, *4,* 248–253.

32. Schaie, K. W., and C. R. Strother. A cross-sequential study of age changes in cognitive behavior. *Psychological Bulletin,* 1968, *70,* 671–680.

33. Schweiker, R. Discard the semantic confusion related to "intelligence." A comment on Social class, race, and genetics: Implications for education. *American Educational Research Journal,* 1968, *5,* 717–721.

34. Shepard, W. O. Intelligence: Development and correlates. In H. Reese and L. P. Lipsitt (eds.) *Experimental Child Psychology.* New York: Academic, 1970, 529–569.

35. Sigel, I. How intelligence tests limit understanding of intelligence. *Merrill-Palmer Quarterly,* 1963, *9,* 39–56.

36. Sitkei, E. G., and C. E. Meyers. Comparative structure of intellect in middle and lower class four year olds of two ethnic groups. *Developmental Psychology,* 1969, *1,* 592–604.

37. Spearman, C. *The abilities of man.* New York: Macmillan, 1927.

38. Tyler, L. E. *The psychology of human differences* (3rd ed.). New York: Appleton, 1965.

39. Wechsler, D. *The measurement of adult intelligence.* Baltimore: Williams & Wilkins, 1944.

6 Special Factors in Cognition

Cognition can be thought of as the process by which a person comes to know himself and his environment. As such, many abilities are involved. The person must attend to the features of his environment, organize and codify his sensations, store impressions in memory, and manipulate in thought the concepts and generalizations that he forms from these sensations and impressions. Language and its critical role in cognition have already been discussed, as has intelligence, in terms of learning aptitude and problem-solving ability. The discussion now turns to some additional, and in many ways inseparable, aspects of cognition and their relationship to affective or noncognitive behavior: attention, perception, intentional and incidental learning, expectancy, cognitive style, curiosity, and creativity.

Some of these special factors in cognition, notably attention, perception, and curiosity, could logically have been discussed before the discussion of language development and intelligence. However, the authors chose to discuss these basic cognitive components in relation to the other variables mentioned above for at least two reasons. First, they believe that these special factors are intimately intertwined and can be grouped together for clarity of discussion and analysis. Second, space considerations do not permit devoting separate chapters to each topic. Consequently, this chapter represents a potpourri of concepts involved in cognitive behavior and development.

Finally, as the reader will discover, no attempt has been made to apply an identical format to the discussion of each topic, because each special factor in cognition possesses unique properties related to the nature of research efforts, findings, and implications.

ATTENTION

Definition
"Carl, pay attention to me! Won't you ever learn to mind?" "Ludlow would learn in school if only he would pay attention in class." "All right, children, let's come to attention and get down to business." Such admonitions, explanations of behavior, and directives for children have surely been heard many times by the reader. The examples indicate a common preoccupation among parents and teachers with the

182

concept of attention. Likewise, attention is a concept with which psychologists and philosophers have been very much pre-occupied, especially until the days of be-haviorist supremacy. Long ago, William James, working with the problem of de-fining attention, remarked: "Everyone knows what attention is," and stressed the obvious point that without attention, experience would be utter chaos. To early behaviorists, however, attention was a mentalistic term, a construct for which operations could not be specified clearly. Thus it was not a proper matter for scien-tific study, because it was obviously pri-vate, not public.

Some descriptive behaviorists still hold to this view (although with more sophisti-cation), and define attention thus: "Atten-tion . . . (is) . . . the fairly general move-ments involved in placing the sense organs so they may be more effectively stimulated" (63, p. 421). Or, similarly, "Attention is essentially an unobservable, unmeasurable phenomenon which, when used to describe behavior, infers that the organism is under the control of some stimulus." (28, p. 1)

In recent years, many psychologists (perhaps particularly those who are in-volved with laboratory and school learn-ing) have turned again to the concept of attention, and it is now much considered, studied, and written about (10, 30). Al-though clear *developmental* aspects of attention are difficult to extract from cur-rent research, the attempt is made in this section to convey some idea of the basic importance of this concept to an under-standing of development in general and children's learning in particular.

The authors, like many others (52, p. 310), believe that a major phase of atten-tion is the selective scanning of informa-tion. The *identification* (meaning) of what

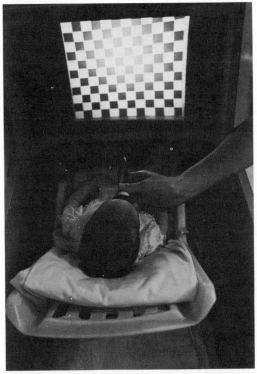

Increasingly, attentional behaviors in infants have been studied in laboratories. Close observations are being made here of the infant's eye movements as he gazes at this complex pattern. (Photo by Jason Lauré)

is scanned is *perception* (see following section). Attention is perhaps a central selective process that is intermediate be-tween the vast stimulus array to which a person is exposed at all times, and the responses he makes to this stimulus array.

Further, and again like many others (52), the authors think it is plausible to postulate two phases of attention. Phase 1 is the *orientation* (or the "What is it?") re-action. This may also be likened to alert-ness and vigilance and possibly to atten-tion span. An orientation reaction is a stance or a behavior designed to help one identify. Orientation reactions are such things as turning our eyes to the stimulus, or sniffing, or staying very still so as to "hear it again—or hear it better." An orientation reaction is preparation for additional stimulation and response. A logical definition of attention span is the range of stimuli our orientation reactions can encompass, in terms of either number or time (such as our example of remembering digits spoken slowly and monotonously).

Phase 2 of attention is the scanning, or searching, or selective process that makes up attention when we pick out a particular stimulus to "study" or when we are learning new things, doing abstract thinking, and solving problems. Thus, clearly, attention underlies what the authors have defined intelligence to be in Chapter 5.

Among other reasons, the authors prefer their definition to the bare-bones Skinnerian kind of definition (or denial of attention), because, within it, individuals can be seen as active selectors of the stimuli from which they wish to learn, rather than passive receptors and reactors to impingements of stimuli on them. The authors prefer to believe that individuals play an active, important role in their own development. In this, they are humanist in their orientation (see Chapter 2).

Role of Attention in Human Learning

First, the infant, child, youth, or adult who has learned to attend selectively and appropriately has acquired a base skill that can accelerate the rate of his later learning and can increase both the quality and the quantity of later learning that he undertakes or which is thrust on him. If he is to be an efficient selective attender, he must obviously learn to select appropriate stimuli by which he, as an organism, is to be controlled as he functions first in one and then another learning and problem-solving situation. This point was

illustrated in Chapter 2, Example 2.2, in which a series of random reinforcements that did not fit their attention patterns—the efficiently learning, advantaged first-grade children with their well-established learning habits, or sets—were reduced to most inefficient learners.

As has been seen, advantaged children, by the time they enter kindergarten or first grade, have usually been well trained to attend to adults who are giving instructions. Such children "are under the control of verbal stimuli," as the Skinnerians might say. Such control gives them a tremendous foot forward in the educational setting. The common way of stating this is to say, "They have learned to listen and to follow instructions." Such training is almost automatic in advantaged homes. Attention is elicited from infancy: "See the rattle." Attention is brought under control by pairing the statement with waving the rattle and then rewarding the child for his attentive response by giving him the rattle to play with. Thus, very early, children learn that people provide interesting things: If you pay attention to these things, you learn what they are; and if you follow verbal instructions or suggestions, you receive a payoff. Curiosity and docility (teachability) are thus learned, or at least reinforced and consolidated as life strategies, selectively in favor of advantaged children. In this context, advantaged means "stimulatingly mothered—or caregiven."

Direction of Attention

Attention in the form of the orientation reaction, one of the earliest forms of attention, may be elicited in several ways. In infancy, any noticeable change in stimulus (a loud noise, a sudden silence, a movement in the field of vision) elicits an orientation reaction. The parents of a runabout child (1½ to about 2½ years old) work away, oblivious to the bangings and clatterings of the child in another room. But the minute he falls silent, they respond with an orienting reaction.

The teacher's bell, pitch pipe, hand clap, or *"Children!"* is designed to elicit orienting reactions from all members of the group so they can direct their attention according to her verbal or other instructions.

Second, attention is "stimulus compelled." Stimuli that stand out, such as those mentioned above, produce orientation reactions. Such stimuli are "interesting"; they elicit more extended attention. As has been seen, novelty and change in stimulation are stimulus compelling. Some stimuli more than others have what is called "collative properties" (7). By this is meant that the individual must study the properties to understand them; they represent a degree of unexpectedness or uncertainty. The individual must therefore compare and collate information about these properties before they can be fitted into his experience. To return to the description of Piaget (Chapter 2), such stimuli present difficulty of assimilation; to be assimilated, some accommodation must first be made—thus, the attention-compelling properties of high collative property stimuli.

Examples of stimuli that are strong attention compellers in this sense are those which are new, or surprising, or incongruous, or complex, or uncertain (ambiguous, either because they have not yet been recognized or because they are not clear).

Third, attention is directed by *set*. This concept is so important it must be discussed in some detail.

Set The first level of set is *perceptual set:* What among competing stimuli do we attend to at once and "automatically"? It has been seen that some stimuli are compellers. They are not the ones that come under the heading of "response due to perceptual set." Rather, perceptual set is learned. It is a readiness, or a signal, to see things in a certain way or to see certain things that to others might be lost in the competitive array of stimuli. The bird watcher is perceptually set to see a flicker of brown as a song sparrow maneuvers through greenery. His nonbirder companion has real difficulty seeing the song sparrow, even with verbal and gestural instructions for identifying him. Through different training, the geologist sees one thing in a cliff, the artist another.

Set, in a sense, is a ready signal, and it can be and probably is most usually taught, either deliberately and formally, as in the cases of the bird watcher and the geologist; or informally and through incentive, as in the case of the mother of the runabout, who is set to hear what may endanger her child. This is not to say that there are no incentives for the bird watcher, the geologist, and the artist.

Sets, of course, can also be social and emotional. Benignly reared children and youth will probably be "set" to perceive that which is friendly, open, and good in others; the opposite may be the case for those who have grown up in hostile surroundings. Imitation, sometimes a most useful thing, may also be a learning set. (See the later discussions of *Perception*, the following major section, and of *Expectancies*, the fourth major topic in this chapter.)

Set also results from immediate previous experience. This is clearly illustrated in the following drawings and related text.

Finally, set may result from the *state of the organism.* In the first instance, motives and needs may act as *preparatory sets.* The

hungry person may perceive and attend to ambiguous but potentially food-related stimuli as food, while the person who has just eaten will not. The sexy person may see ambiguous but potentially sex-related stimuli as sexual in nature, and so on (instructions are also a way of setting up preparatory sets).

In the second instance, to take an extreme case of the state of the organism, the blind child will not be set toward visual stimuli, or the deaf adolescent toward sound stimuli. Less dramatically, most of us probably have sense preferences that may be inborn or may be learned. Some of us have sets that favor vision, others hearing, still others perhaps touching or smelling or tasting.

Set, then, is a function either of past experience, the state of the organism, or both. The concept of the state of the organism, of course, is hopelessly intermixed with the organism's learning history.

Sets may be perceptual, of the kind just discussed. They may also be *performance* or *learning*.

The second level of set to be discussed is *performance set* (52). There seem to be six kinds of performance set, each useful in coping with situations from early child-

The development of a mental set. Most people glancing at the cartoons at the left will describe the last as "an old man." People seeing only the cartoons on the right will very likely describe the bottom figure as "a rat" or "a mouse." In each case, the bottom figures are the same. We tend to see what we expect to see—and what we expect to see depends on prior experience (see B. R. Bugelski and D. Alampay, The role of frequency in developing perceptual sets, Canadian Journal of Psychology, *1961, 15, 205-211.) (Reproduced by permission from B. R. Bugelski* The psychology of learning applied to teaching. *Indianapolis, The Bobbs-Merrill Company, Inc., 1964.)*

hood onward during the developmental process.

Type 1 can be called *warm-up*. Formally, warm-up can be defined as a postural adjustment that facilitates performance; it is most conspicuous in motor learning and response. An athlete about to run the 200-meter race in a track meet jogs a bit, stretches and flexes, kneels at the blocks and straightens up again. The typist about to use a new typewriter takes a sheet of scratch paper and rapidly bats off "The quick brown fox . . . ," or runs through the keys, as *a b c d e f g h i* and so on, before he starts typing a letter that he wants to go out error free. Warm-up seems particularly related to rhythm.

Type 2 of performance set is *development of exteroceptive observing processes.* Here we cock our head so as to hear better, or turn our nose in the direction of the elusive scent, and sniff.

Type 3 is *development of internal attentional responses.* We tell ourselves that the trouble the next-door neighbor is having with his lawn mower is none of our business, and we will shut out the erratic noises, *pay no attention to them.* Or we tell ourselves, as we read, that we must organize a particular section of text into points 1, 2, and 3 so that we can remember them; or we say, "As I go out the front door, I will remember to check my pocket (or purse) to be sure I have the key."

Type 4 is *reduction of emotionality.* Emotion, particularly strong emotion, produces responses that interfere with most complex performance. Thus, we work to "play it cool," or help those for whom we are somehow responsible to "be less anxious, or less angry, or less frustrated."

Type 5 is *development of appropriate attending and performance techniques.* These are the strategies by which one approaches a task, some using mnemonic devices. If a telephone number is 739–1493, one holds the first three digits by rote memory, remembers the last four by "one year later than Columbus discovered America." Another strategy is to rehearse in between, whether this *in between* is between trials in a laboratory experiment, between course tests in the third or the ninth grade, or between rehearsals for a play. Others formulate and test hypotheses: "If the wire doesn't go there, it must go here."

Finally, type 6 of the performance sets is *discrimination set:* "I will look for differences." "I will notice which is 1 and which is 4." It should be noted in passing, and we will return to this point, that it is well to give children easy discriminations first, since such training facilitates handling later, more difficult discriminations.

With reference to performance set, it should be noted that none of these six processes is confined to any particular stimulus value. All (except possibly 5) can be developed in one kind of task and transferred to another (52). The practical implications from this section about performance sets are clear: From very early ages, we should help children develop such sets, and employ them appropriately.

The third level of set is *learning set* (52). This has also been called *learning to learn.* Essentially, the result of a learning set is that one performs better across a series of problems that have a common basis for their solution, but the contents (stimuli) of which are different; that is, if a person has a discrimination learning set, he will learn to tell the difference between an oval and a circle more quickly than if he does not; and the difference between red and pink circles more quickly than if there is not a discrimination set. The song One of These Things Is Not like the Others, from the television program "Sesame Street," illustrates nicely an approach to teaching a discrimination learning set.

The ultimate in a *discrimination learning set* is one trial learning or "insight." If a child is trained always to look for the "right one," soon his learning will be amazingly rapid, requiring only one trial in a choice between two alternatives. For example, we present the child with a choice between a cross and a circle, and tell him he is to learn the correct one, rewarding him for each choice of the circle (which is arbitrarily set to be correct). As soon as he has had a few trials at this, we move him to a square versus a rectangle; then to color, purple versus green. With amazing rapidity, even very young children will learn the "win–stay, lose–shift" strategy (that is, if you were correct the first time, *stay*; if you were wrong the first time, *shift*). For consistent reinforcement, a child will soon come to the point where he never makes more than one mistake in a two-choice discrimination (he may be wrong the first time, but shifts, and is right from there on).

Another interesting thing about discrimination learning is the form it takes. In one basic study of discrimination learning, preschool-aged children required an average of 20.4 trials to learn to discriminate randomly presented collection of "junk" correctly, fifth-graders required an average of 10.8 trials, and college students needed only 6.7 trials (52, pp. 271–272). These changes with age illustrate changes in efficiency of attention and problem-solving strategy. However, a fourth group of old people, ranging in age from 61 to 97 years, required an average of about 120 trials to learn the discrimination (they may not have been very much interested, it should be added).

However, the *way* learning came about was very similar for all four groups: rela-

tively slow at first (and others have found that, as a subject begins to "get the idea," he attends much more closely to the stimuli, staring fixedly first at one, then at another, stimulus before he makes his choice). Then, when some strategy approximating the correct one was arrived at by a subject, his performance shot up rapidly, and he soon reached the criterion of learning. In the study being discussed, the initial period for the aged was slowest, and it was shortest for the college-aged subjects.

A final, important point should be made about set. Many believe that there are two kinds of memory, short term and long term. Short-term memory can be illustrated by the example of the intelligence test item, digit span, mentioned in Chapter 5: holding onto a span of digits intoned at one per second by the tester, and repeating them. For almost everyone, memory of the digits—which ones they were and the order in which they came—disappears as soon as they are repeated back to the examiner (or indeed, before they can be repeated back and, for long series, even before the testee begins to speak them). This is short-term memory. Long-term memory is what is required when one passes an examination, remembers his telephone number when he lived in San Francisco five years ago, or recalls a joke that he heard last week in St. Louis.

In short-term memory, there seems to be no organization, no "coding." Long-term memory is more like a filing system with appropriate categories of subject matter content relating to political science, as in the example of the classroom examination; or familiar and useful data that have been much practiced, as in the example of the San Francisco telephone number; or of matters of personal and/or social pleasure, as in the case of the St.

Louis joke. The long-term memory storage file for both children and adults is enormous, often mystifying, often inefficient, sometimes awe inspiring.

It may be that set is the process by which much coding and filing of material that goes from short-term memory into long-term memory is done. The bird watcher of our earlier example files his song sparrow appropriately. His non-birder friend, not much interested in or informed about song sparrows, loses the song sparrow from his immediate memory bank almost immediately. Instead, he files the whole experience as "a morning spent under pleasant but frustrating experiences with a friend with a hobby." Much coding is done by verbal labels, but coding can almost certainly be done by visual images, smells, and, presumably, any of the perceptual and experiential avenues. Long-term memory storage thus involves "clearing up perception," or "removing ambiguity from percepts" (see the following section about Perception).

To illustrate the development of orienting behavior and the nature of discrimination learning, the authors have chosen to summarize a study in Example 6.1, the subjects of which were advantaged children who ranged in age from 3 years 3 months to almost 5 years.

6.1 A Study of Young Children's Orienting Behavior

James E. Turnure conducted two studies of young children who ranged in age from 3 years 3 months to almost 5 years (71). All were advantaged, and all were enrolled in middle-class and upper-middle-class nursery schools. Each child was to learn which of a pair of black geometric forms, available on slides in pairs, was correct. The correct form was arbitrarily chosen, and a red light went

on to give the child feedback when he was correct in his choice. The children were taken from their nursery school group (in experiment 1) during the free play period, and were told simply that they were going to play a game with the experimenter. All testing was done individually. In a noise condition, a tape of typing noises at about 70 decibels (decidedly noisy) was played during all the time the children were trying to master the discrimination learning task. In the control condition, the noise level was about 40 decibels (the noise made by the fan that cooled the projector for the slides). The measures taken were correct responses (an index of learning) and glances away from the task (evidence of distractibility).

There were no differences between boys and girls, but the older group of children (averaging about 4.8 years) did conspicuously better than the younger group (averaging about 3.8 years). The 3-year-3-month-olds were distracted by the noise, more frequently glancing toward it. If anything, the 3-year-9-month-olds and the 4-year-9-month-olds performed better under noise than nonnoise conditions—their learning was enhanced during noise, and they were less distractible. The explanation of this advantage is unclear. Some would advance *arousal* as an explanatory variable: Under noise, the children were stirred up, as it were, and "tried harder." This would include more intense concentration.

Turnure, a careful man, was skeptical about his results from experiment 1, because he had taken his children from a free-play period (that is, they moved into his experimental noise-and-control conditions from the exceptionally noisy environment that almost invariably exists during the free play of a group of normal, happy children). To control for this, Turnure ran a second experiment, using children from a Montessori school, where the classroom is ordinarily very quiet. The results with the Montessori children were about the same as those with the children in the first experiment, so Turnure (and the present authors) has great confidence in them.

Practically speaking, the results from this study lead us to think that very young children are not nearly as distractible as the public has been led to believe. Indeed, remarkable control over distractors (strong attention and concentration) is shown by children as young as 3 years 9 months. Distractors, in the form of noise, may even improve their learning performance (although, one suspects, at the cost of some strain to the learner, and also wonders if such improvement will hold only for short periods. Performance might be interfered with by hours, days, or weeks of noise).

Concluding Remarks

To conclude this section on attention, it is evident that attention is a basic process underlying human learning. It is itself learned, probably by environmental impacts on original, perhaps "biologically given" orientation reactions. Without adaptive and selective attention, experience, as William James said, would certainly be chaos. It can also be easily seen that adaptive attention underlies all development of the language and other intelligent behaviors discussed in Chapters 4 and 5. Further, it is clear that certain attentional *sets*, broadly speaking, facilitate linguistic and intellectual behavior development, others are neutral in impact, and still others exert a limiting effect.

Attention habits, including sets, should be both *open* and *closed*. They should be open to the degree that an individual is alert to new and meaningful stimuli of either an emergency or an enriching-useful type; and that he is flexible enough to change sets appropriately so as to try new strategies and change from one to another activity as needed. Attention habits should be closed, or closable, to the degree that an individual can concentrate on one thing at a time and resist distraction until the job is done (see Example 6.1, and the third major section on Intentional Learning and Incidental Learning). Finally, it is worth repeating that early learning of appropriate attention- and set-forming habits or skills greatly facilitates later learning that the individual wishes or is required to do.

PERCEPTION

Definition

Perception can be defined as a process of organizing, coding, and interpreting raw sensory input or experience—things seen, heard, felt, tasted, and smelled. Such sensory experience provides the stuff on which a child builds an understanding of his world. Consistent with the orientation in previous chapters, the authors consider perceptual development to be a complex function of maturation and environmental impact. The study of perception and perceptual development in psychology has a long, complicated history replete with theoretical controversies. However, the authors discuss only the importance of perceptual factors in learning and development and some general trends in perceptual development, and also touch upon some issues and implications of perceptual development for education.

Importance of Perceptual Factors in Learning

It cannot be denied that perceptual abilities are crucial for learning. For example, learning the identity of things such as salt, sugar, gasoline, water, toothpaste, clay, alarm clock, and whistle depends upon one's ability to (1) perceive the basic qualities and (2) determine the difference and similarity between these substances and objects. Sensory attributes relevant to the learning of these identities include color, texture, form, odor, and the like. Perceptual skills such as form perception and symbol recognition are also basic to many academic tasks, most notably reading. The successful pursuit of aesthetic activities also involves the development of refined perceptual skills.

Consider, for example, the subtle pitch, intensity, and rhythm matching required by members of a choral ensemble, or the subtle shading of color hues and form characteristics required by the professional oil painter.

These skills seem so obvious that it is easy to overlook the importance of perceptual skills in responses that most of us take for granted. Walking is a good example of how perceptual abilities influence the learning of "natural" behaviors (14). For the infant, success in beginning to walk depends on his accuracy in making visual judgments about the spatial dimensions and arrangement of objects that exist in his walking area. Success in walking also depends upon the infant's perceptual awareness of the location of his feet and the speed at which his feet move. Gradually, of course, walking becomes an almost automatic motor response in that children move about without being so dependent upon this kind of visual input. But perceptual efficiency is extremely critical during the initial stages of this developmental milestone (14).

The complex network of perceptual (and motor) skills involved in learning and performing many "simple" tasks can be further illustrated by example—copying a square (35). Before proceeding, the reader is encouraged to pause to itemize the subskills involved in this relatively elementary task.

For a beginning, it is clear that to copy a square, the child must be able to sit erect with his head up; coordinate finger, hand, wrist, and arm movements; and demonstrate sufficient muscular control and dexterity to move his pencil. Eye–hand coordinations are also basic. Eye movement must be coordinated with hand movement (sensory integration). The child must also be able to distinguish between his left side and his right side in order to locate a starting point with reference to his own body (right side, left side, or center). He must next determine a direction in which to move so that a line similar to that in the copy can be made. Movement must be initiated with enough pressure to make a mark (kinesthesia). The child must also be able to change direction while movement is in progress, thus matching his motor movements with the visual impressions he receives as he marks the paper. Visual cues must be used to determine when to stop (and start again), particularly if a mistake is made. While the child deals one at a time with the parts of a square (four sides), he must keep in mind the whole. The square must be perceived as a form on a background with separate lines and angles existing for the child simultaneously and in relation to one another (35).

This analysis of square-copying behavior is intended only to highlight the general perceptual components of such a task. It seems clear that more sophisti-

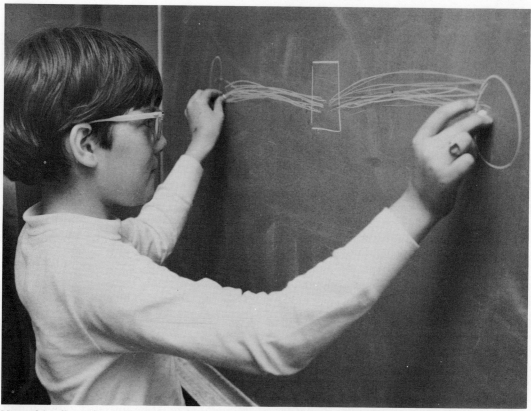

Normal intellectual growth of this girl has been hampered by poor visual–motor control. One aspect of her therapeutic program involves this exercise, in which she is learning to control the movement of her arms in a sidewise fashion while she concentrates her eyes on a fixed point. (Wide World Photos)

cated tasks such as brain surgery, radar navigation, and watchmaking involve a host of complex perceptual skills that develop with maturation and experience. Failure in these tasks, as in copying a square, could therefore be due to any number of things, including visual perceptual inability and difficulty in coordinating kinesthetic and visual sensory input.

Perception and Thought

In addition to the basic role of perceptual factors in learning and performance of most human tasks, the authors should acknowledge the foundation that perceptual experiences provide for thinking. The reader will recall from Chapter 2 that Piaget strongly emphasized the role of early sensory experience and its meaning for the evolution of logical thought structures. Possibly the most explicit treatment of this relationship in practice can be found in the Montessori method (45). Montessori's thesis, although not yet tested to the authors' satisfaction, is that the more refined and acute are a person's perceptions, the more refined and acute is his thinking, at least thinking that involves concepts built on meaningful sensory experience (activities involving color, form, shape, time, space, temperature, and the like). Montessori believed that perceptual refinement could best be accomplished by providing children with carefully sequenced activities, on the basis of their sensory attributes, beginning first with the *identity* of objects. Following the identity stage, *differences* among two or more objects or experiences are stressed, after which *similarities* are emphasized. Subtle *gradations*, such as blue, bluer, bluest in color perception cap the educational sequence. The basic role of visual perception is apparent in the Montessori program. All activities begin first with the task of visual discrimination.

Finally, the reader will recall the discussion of egocentrism in Chapter 2, that is, the apparent inability of children below about age 7 to take the viewpoint of others. Closely related to this phenomenon is a perceptual characteristic called *centering*. This refers to the child's tendency to "center" or focus his attention on one aspect of a situation or an event. It also involves the child's apparent inability to take into account other aspects of a situation or to shift his attention from one aspect to another. For Piaget, centering influences thought in that the young child's thinking is dominated by his perceptions and, among other things, contributes to his inability to conserve and appreciate invariance. Other authorities dispute this, however, believing that such behavior is more a function of insufficient experience and practice in detecting invariants (26).

Basic Trends in Perceptual Development
The study of perceptual development has been profoundly influenced by psychologists interested in visual perception.

Among the topics most frequently explored are developmental factors in depth perception, shape perception, size constancy, shifts in preference for color and form stimuli, and the like (30, 78). Rather than review the literature for these topics, the authors have chosen to discuss only broad interrelated trends in perceptual development. They recognize that some risk is involved thereby. That is, not all psychologists agree on trends and their interpretation, nor have all the perceptual components of behavior been studied sufficiently so that definitive trends can be stated.

Specificity
First, it is apparent that, with age, children become increasingly specific in their perceptual discriminations. This increased specificity is accompanied by a reduction in the amount of time it requires the child to make a response once something has been perceived (26). For example, the infant first will discriminate between other people only broadly—mother and not-mother. Gradually, however, he will come to discriminate between members of his own family and outsiders and to make subtle discriminations among outsiders. The 5-year-old child of one of the authors, for example, is better at discriminating between a set of identical twins who live nearby than her father is. This trend toward increased specificity in discrimination is also marked by a decrease in stimulus generalization (26). That is, younger children typically overgeneralize on the basis of perceived similarity. For one 3-year-old friend of the authors, all flying insects are "bees." Gradually, this child will reduce her generalization so that bees are distinguished from flies, moths, wasps, and other insects.

Selectivity

A second age-related trend in perceptual development is that children become increasingly more selective in their perceptions (26). Selective attention, which is, of course, necessary for something to be perceived, has already been discussed. This selectivity comes about through more and more extensive and systematic perceptual exploration with age. The child becomes more adept at picking up relevant information and discarding unwanted or irrelevant information, although the mechanisms involved are not clear. The older child also becomes more able to exercise perceptual exclusiveness — listening to a peer and tuning out the teacher when both peer and teacher are talking, for example. Also involved in perceptual selectivity is an apparent preference for, or at least a greater salience of, novel (versus familiar) stimuli as children grow older. (See the relation of this to Curiosity discussed later in this chapter.)

Economy

A third age-related trend in perceptual development is that information pickup becomes more economical (26). Children become more skilled at detecting the distinctive characteristics of objects and events — things that distinguish one thing from other things *and* features of things that remain constant (invariant) over change. For example, water has characteristics that distinguish it from other liquids, *and* a cup of water frozen, then thawed, will still contain the same amount. This trend is also characterized by increased ability to perceive the higher order structure or pattern inherent in much of what is perceived (26). This is well illustrated in reading, where the child comes to perceive groupings of letters within words as units and groupings of words as sentences.

6.2 Children's Perception and the Task of Learning to Read

An extensive series of research studies has provided David Elkind (19) with a springboard for studying the complex relationship of perceptual activity to reading. "Elkind argues that two of our most predominantly used methods of reading instruction may be inconsistent with perceptual development, at least in terms of teaching the "average 6-year-old" without having first provided perceptual pretraining. The "look–say" method, according to Elkind, requires of a child responses that are inconsistent with development in schematization. It is not until about age 7 and beyond that children are normally able to coordinate part–whole relationships (such as letter–word) so that each maintains both its identity and its interdependence. Neither does the phonics approach escape Elkind's analysis unscathed. Elkind believes that successful phonics learning depends on the spontaneous ability to reverse figure and ground (perceptual reorganization in the Piaget system). In other words, a child must come to terms with two related phenomena: (1) more than one sound is represented by one letter (letter "a" for example) and different letters can represent the same sound (letter "s" and "c" as in "snake" and "circus," for example); and (2) learning the equivalences of upper- and lower-case letters and manuscript and cursive letters."* As Elkind states,

In all of these instances, the real problem lies in the recognition that the same element can repre-

* From E. D. Evans CONTEMPORARY INFLUENCES IN EARLY CHILDHOOD EDUCATION. New York: Holt, Rinehart and Winston, Inc., 1971.

sent different things and that different elements can represent the same thing . . . (this) is then directly analogous to that faced by the child in reversing figure and ground when viewing an ambiguous figure (such as the famous Rubin-Vase Profile). That such an assumption is not fortuitous is shown by the fact that slow readers are deficient in the ability to reverse figure and ground in comparison with average readers of comparable mental ability. (19, p. 360)

The implication of Elkind's work is that training in perceptual reorganization and/or schematization may facilitate the reading process. At the least, assessment of perceptual behavior may be dictated for children who experience reading difficulties early.

The apparent advantages of perceptual training are shown by a recent study of inner-city second-grade black children (20). The children in one group were engaged in a program of nonverbal perceptual exercises over a period of fifteen weeks. A second group of children, matched with the perceptual trainees on the basis of reading achievement and initial perceptual ability, underwent training for the same period with a conventional reading series. At the end of the training period the perceptual training group demonstrated a significantly higher level of word and word-form recognition skills than did the control group. These data are taken to supply validity for the training techniques developed by Elkind from Piagetian thought.

Sense Modality Preferences

A fourth trend in perceptual development concerns changes in sensory modality preferences. By sensory modality is meant a system (visual, auditory, kinesthetic) for carrying on transactions with the environment through a basic sense (9). Most children seemingly progress from a kinesthetic modality preference during their early years to preferences for visual and then verbal (auditory) modalities when older. One team of investigators has described this age-related transition in terms of changes that occur in the way children represent their environment in thought (12). According to this view, early environmental representations are established through motor patterns. At a later stage the child represents his world primarily through visual imagery. In the final stage, representation occurs *symbolically* (verbal and nonverbal language).

Integration and Coordination

A final trend in perceptual development to be mentioned here involves an increased degree of sensory integration. With age, the child becomes successively more capable of "coordinating and relating information obtained through the various sensory modalities" (9, p. 133). Increased intersensory coordination enables older children to improve on their understanding of things heard or seen by feeling them and vice versa. The importance of intersensory coordination is nicely illustrated by our earlier example of copying a square. Performance of this task requires that a child "get it all together"; normatively speaking, the sensory integration necessary for success in this specific task does not occur until about age 5.

Concluding Remarks

To summarize briefly, five basic and related trends in perceptual development have been discussed. With age, and reflecting both maturation and learning, children become (1) more specific in their discriminations, (2) more selective in their perceptions, (3) more economical in picking up information, (4) more oriented toward visual and auditory modes for representing their experience, and (5) more capable of integrating and coordinating sensory input. With these trends in mind, the implications of perceptual development for learning and for interpreting behavior are now discussed.

Some Implications of Perceptual Development

Many implications for parents and teachers can be drawn from perceptual development. They range from general to specific, and only a few are presented for illustrative purposes. For example, at a very general level, it seems clear that it is desirable to provide a variety of rich concrete sensory experiences and ample opportunity for motor exploration during the early years. This is extremely important for optimum perceptual development and cognition. This point has been stressed in previous chapters and it need not be elaborated, except to state that overstimulation that results in a child's "tuning out" his environment may be just as adverse as understimulation. Fortunately most children and most youth find their own optimal level of stimulation when appropriate opportunities are provided.

More specifically, implications can be drawn about individual differences in perceptual development and functioning. It is clear that individual differences exist in sensory modality preference (9). This means that not all individuals will prefer the same modality for learning, whether it be visual, auditory, kinesthetic, or some combination. Neither are all individuals likely to learn as well through a sensory modality that is not preferred. Even at the college level, some students seem to prefer

material presented in lecture form, and do better when it is so presented; other students prefer the same material presented in written form, and learn more effectively when it is so presented. The measurement of sensory modality preference has not yet been perfected. Thus it is difficult to match individual preferences and modality input during classroom instruction. However, varying sensory input and providing opportunities to augment one modality with another are sensible guiding principles for teachers. The new "multimedia" approaches to learning fit well with these notions.

Related to the above is the matter of individual differences in discriminative capacities among children. For example, as late as age 6 or 7, many children will have difficulty in discriminating among complex forms such as numbers and letters of the alphabet. This is particularly true for the fine distinctions involved in "p" and "q," "b" and "d," and the like. This means that discrimination skills may have to be taught to children in the course of their learning to read, but usually these skills are the concern of sound reading readiness programs.

Many normal children have difficulty with form discrimination. The result is often failure to detect differences between similar letters or reversing letters (for example, Ǝ for E). Other children (and adolescents) suffer from serious perceptual dysfunctions that impede academic progress, especially reading. In recent years many developmental and remedial perceptual–motor training programs have been designed for such children and youth. Most such programs are based on the idea that retraining basic perceptual processes is necessary before perceptually handicapped persons can learn to read. The point is that such approaches may be helpful, although the early evidence about their effectiveness is quite mixed (21). At the very least, these programs must be carefully scrutinized, especially in relation to an individual child's specific perceptual problems, before any program is implemented in a given situation.

A final perceptual implication, also mentioned in the discussions of attention and set, concerns the influence of motives, values, and desires on perception. This phenomenon can be illustrated by the story of three persons—a sailor, a physician, and a recently engaged coed, all of whom simultaneously view a fleecy cloud in the sky. When asked by a psychologist, "What do you see?" each replies differently. The sailor sees a battleship, the physician a hospital bed, and the coed the profile of her lover. The point is that, objectively, the stimulus perceived is not different. Each apparently projects something of his or her own current motivational state into the situation. Such tendencies are notably true when ambiguous stimuli are involved and this dynamic is precisely that which underlies projective testing (see Chapter 2).

In addition to the projective quality of perception, interests, motives, and values often have an effect on selectivity in perception. That is, from among an array of stimulus properties, different individuals select different features for information processing. For example, one of the authors recently took six kindergartners to the circus. While all six took note of most of the big events, the details of their reports of perceptions were amazingly different. Anecdotes, of course, do not prove a point. But the fact is that ample research evidence can be marshaled to substantiate the phenomenon of selective perception (78). This evidence relates most clearly to motives and needs as

preparatory sets (see earlier discussions of attention and set).

The meaning of the projective and selective aspects of perception for such things as classroom learning is extremely significant. For example, the same teacher behavior is likely to be interpreted differently by different children and youth, depending on their needs and interests. Moreover, no teacher can assume from merely presenting material to a group of students that all students will perceive the important aspects of that material equally well. Unfortunately, many teachers reportedly *do* operate on the assumption that presentation equals learning (55). Only by seeking continuous feedback from students about their learning is a teacher likely to gain insight into student perceptions.

It may be conceptually useful to try to tie Piaget's ideas of *assimilation* and *accommodation* to the construct *perception*. A new stimulus can be perceived (plugged in) only according to the learning history of the individual. If the learning history includes nothing like the new stimulus, the stimulus will be most inaccurately perceived in the sense of its "objective reality." The San Francisco-reared 3-year-old who sees her first snow cries out excitedly, turns over hypotheses in her mind, and tells her parents "Cotton is coming out of the sky."

With repeated experience, reality forces its way in, as it were. Our 3-year-old assimilates more and more things about snow: it is cold, it is wet, it melts, it packs down, and so on. Finally, her percept "conforms with reality." In other words, an *accommodation* to the nature of the stimulus has occurred, and, cognitively, this child can never operate quite the same again, in that never again will she perceive cotton coming out of the sky.

INTENTIONAL LEARNING AND INCIDENTAL LEARNING

Definitions

The concepts of intentional learning and incidental learning were introduced earlier in our discussion of attention. Specifically, *intentional* learning involves a "closed" attention system, or set. A child or a youth purposefully works to master something that he wants, needs, is rewarded for, or has been coerced to learn. Formal classroom learning consists mostly of intentional learning in that specific goals are usually established and academic evaluation is done on the basis of such goals. Teacher instructions to learn certain aspects of academic material usually have the effect of inducing an intentional learning set through which material studied is filtered.

The importance and effectiveness of intentional, or directly purposeful, learning cannot be denied. However, much *incidental learning* hopefully occurs in the process of intentional learning. As the term is used here, incidental learning has two meanings. The first and more technically correct is the sort of learning that occurs "out of the corner of one's eye" while one is engaged in intentional learning. For example, a tenth-grade student may be studying an ungrammatical essay on life in Borneo specifically to detect grammatical errors and formulate their correction. But in the process he learns something of the economy and the native life on this island—items quite incidental, even irrelevant, to his original purpose. Such learning presumably results from a more "open" attention system, including set. This is commendable, although, in the extreme, an inclination toward incidental learning becomes "distractibility" and is self-defeating in many situations.

A second meaning of incidental learning is technically not quite so correct as the first given, but it is useful also to regard incidental learning as that which occurs when one learns things from free experience. In other words, incidental learning can also be thought of as learning that occurs with no apparent purpose or long-term goal in mind. For example, consider the high school senior with a free Saturday morning who visits the city library for information about the military draft. As he browses through the shelves, his attention is caught by a book on dream interpretation. For the next several hours, this student is engrossed in the book about dreams, an activity remote from his original purpose and only vaguely associated with any long-range goal, if at all. In a sense, *epistemic curiosity*, a topic discussed later in this chapter, is related to this second definition of incidental learning.

Implications Drawn from Intentional Learning and Incidental Learning

In all societies, it is often necessary to be purposive and task oriented—to be efficient at intentional learning, to concentrate on one thing at a time, to resist distraction, to "get the job done." To survive, however, a person must be sufficiently flexible (open in attention) so that environmental stimuli that may be important but *not* goal related are perceived and can be acted on as necessary. Moreover, incidental learning, appropriately coded and stored, may be useful in guiding future behavior. Finally, if a person is so goal directed (so intentional) as to ignore all incidental stimuli, he runs the risk of missing emergency cues that range from subtle ("My friend is a bit depressed and perhaps needs my sympathetic help") to obvious and even blatant ("That fire siren means that *this* building is on fire!").

The authors suspect that what is generally called social sensitivity is largely a matter of an open, but people-oriented, attention set and of incidental observation and learning. The egocentrism of adolescents is likely to make them intentional learners, in the sense that they concentrate almost entirely on what affects *them*. They often miss the more subtle, incidental cues about the behavior of others. The social insensitivity attributed to adolescents may be due to such tunnel vision.

Too intense motivation probably reduces incidental learning, because it leads to the exclusive study of and preoccupation with how to get to the goal; task-relevant cues become the exclusive targets for attention and perception. If one is "cut off" from incidental learning by excessive motivation for specific task accomplishment, he may become rigid and not open to new experience (see Chapter 5 for the earlier discussions of factors that favor intellectual growth).

Much of the fun in life comes from incidental learning. A person encounters many fascinating, fun, and often useful things when his attention simply wanders —when he opens himself up to incidental learning in the sense of the second definition given above, and simply takes in anything that comes along. This implies that one may give free reign to his curiosity, a motivational state that facilitates both incidental and intentional learning. However, as has been suggested, an adjustment in which one does all incidental and no intentional learning (if this is possible) could indicate diffuse or poorly channeled motivation or difficulty in sustaining goal-directed behavior.

The relationship between incidental learning and creativity should also be noted, although this topic is discussed more thoroughly in the final part of this chapter. Creative adolescents and young adults seem to accomplish more of both incidental and intentional learning in certain clearly structured situations.

Finally, although developmental studies in this area are rare, there is evidence to suggest a curvilinear relationship between age and incidental learning (27, 59). That is, through about age 12, children of both sexes seem regularly to increase the range of their incidental learning responses. After this time, there may actually be a mild decline in incidental learning, although this should not be taken to indicate that young children are superior to adults in incidental learning. This phenomenon is perhaps best explained by increased attentiveness with age up to a point where the ability to disregard irrelevancies and the cumulative effect of intentional learning set formation combine to dominate an individual's learning style. The authors believe, however, that the nature of a learning task and the reinforcement contingencies extant in a given situation have much to do with determining the extent of incidental learning that occurs, regardless of age. We will see later that much of the learning that goes into appropriate (or inappropriate) sex role behavior can be thought of as incidental.

Dilemmas Posed by Concepts of Intentional Learning and Incidental Learning

It has been suggested that different benefits are obtained from incidental and intentional learning and that both have their place in human development. Depending on our strategy, a stress on the virtues of incidental learning as opposed to intentional learning will lead to espousing and adopting different educational procedures. In turn, the frame of reference we take in viewing human development is likely to lead to attaching different values to incidental and intentional learning in the educational and developmental process. (See the discussion of developmental dilemmas in Chapter 3, and the treatment of ways of viewing development in Chapter 2.)

Behaviorists and psychodynamicists are likely to view human development in ways that lead them toward stress on intentional learning and arranged experiences: training and teaching in the formal sense. Humanists and cognitive developmentalists, in contrast, are likely to put more emphasis on unarranged experience, assuming that from such experience the developing organism, largely through incidental learning, will acquire the cognitive skills and emotional freedom that lead to "the good life."

What is education likely to look like when primary stress is laid on intentional learning? It seems logical that such an emphasis will lead to clearly planned goals, with formal, curricularly anchored prescriptions that stress intentional learning as a way of arriving at those goals. Guidance may be pervasive and perhaps even authoritative. The product aimed for may be more like Cattell's crystallized intelligence than like his fluid intelligence, and more like Guilford's convergent operations than like his divergent operations (see Chapter 5). Emphasis may be placed more on product-oriented teaching rather than process oriented. More stress may be laid on planning *for* the child or the youth than on letting him find out for himself. A preschool classroom may look more like Bereiter and Engelmann's tightly planned developmental, remedial curric-

ulum than like the British Infant School or the "Discovery Method." (21)

In contrast, when stress is laid on incidental learning—learning that occurs when the individual is left to his own devices even though the caregiver or teacher may have clearly formulated goals —very different child-rearing and educational practices may result. The inference made by those who stress incidental learning is that giving a person the opportunity to learn—exposure to developmental and educational opportunity—results in *his learning that learning is fun.* In other words, if one is given freedom and rich potential exposure, he will develop intentional learning skills on his own. The skills will not need to be imposed on him from above.

The free schools, for example (see Chapter 12), have clearly formulated goals, but employ free or incidental-learning *means* for reaching those goals. The modern humanists and the cognitive developmentalists who follow Piaget (see Chapter 2) may all favor an emphasis on incidental learning. This is also what Rousseau advocated for *Emile* up to approximately the age of puberty. Those who emphasize incidental learning are likely to be freer and more permissive in their guidance and control techniques. They are likely to lay emphasis on providing opportunities for experience, with the child or the youth finding his way through such experiences in his own way and in his own time. Thus, they stress unarranged experiences and process rather than product. Again, it seems likely that cognitive developmentalists would regard Cattell's fluid intelligence as the more important of his two factors in intelligence, and facility in Guilford's divergent (creative) operation as more valuable than in his convergent (logical, deductive) operation.

Concluding Remarks

To conclude this section, the authors believe that, as with almost all complex human behavior, a person should probably hit a happy medium between intentional learning and incidental learning. When the situation calls for it, at any age after infancy one should be able to settle down and focus sharply on a task. He should be capable of behaving as a concentrated, efficient, intentional learner. He should remain open enough, however, to be able to change strategies, receive new and useful or emergency stimuli that are incidental to the task, and at times open himself totally to experience simply so as to see what happens because he is curious. From such conclusions, it is obvious that the authors believe child rearing and more formal education should include provisions for developing proficiency at both kinds of learning.

EXPECTANCIES

Definition

The concept of expectancies can be construed in at least three ways.

1. (The reader may wish to refer back to the earlier sections of this chapter devoted to *attention* and *set* and to *perception*.) Perceptual sets, possibly several of the forms of performance set, and certainly learning set are all expectancies. In the examples of the series of frames where one, looking down, finally saw a rat or an old man, the expectancy (or better, expectation, in this case) for the bottom frame is different depending on which of the columns the individual first began looking at (perceptual set). After warm-up, the expectancy held by an individual is that he will perform better than if he had not warmed up (an example of set). In learning sets, if the individual expects that two stimuli will differ, he is more likely to perceive the differences than if he expects them to be alike (an example of learning set).

2. A second construction of expectancy is that it is *an estimate of probability of occurrence* (57). We have learned multitudinous expectancies about the outcomes of processes. They range from expectancies of danger if we cross a street against a red light or expectancies of success (an A grade) in a college course.

3. The authors believe that expectancies held about children and youth by their parents, teachers, peers, and other significant figures in their lives, strongly affect their behavior. If a parent, teacher, or peer expects one to fail, that expectation is betrayed in many subtle and not so subtle ways and is almost certain to affect the behavior of the person about whom the expectancy is held. This will be equally true if the significant other expects the individual to succeed.

Implications from the Three Constructions of Expectancy

When Expectancies Are Thought of as Sets

One implication from the definitions given above is that we perceive what we have been trained to perceive. In one classical experiment, tribal Zulu children who grow up in a world of circles—round houses, round cattle pens (kraals), and even a rounded landscape—fail to see the illusion of the Ames window (1), shown in Figure 6.1. The Ames window is so proportioned that, as it rotates, the length of the longer edges is always greater on the retina than the length of the shorter edge. For those who have grown up in cities, full as they are of squares and rectangles, the rotation of this window is usually seen as a sway back and forth in an arc. The cube in the figure is usually seen to detach

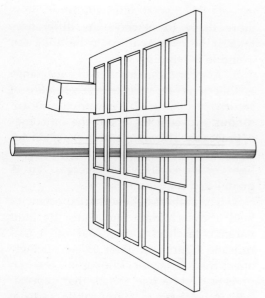

Figure 6.1 *The Ames window, with cube and rod attached, in rotation is likely to produce the illusion of sway. (Courtesy of Dr. Hadley Cantril.)*

itself and "swing without support in a ghostly fashion in front of the window. . . . Similarly, the rod bends, twists, or 'cuts through' the mullions in order to accommodate itself to the phenomenal oscillation. The observer finds the bizarre effect both amusing and inexplicable." (p. 105)

Tribally reared Zulu 10-to-14-year-old boys seldom experience the illusion. City-reared Zulu boys and almost all city-reared European boys *do* experience the illusion.

The results reported above illustrate a consequence of perceptual set induced by learning. Implications from performance and learning sets are similar: We continue to employ performance and learning sets that have worked for us before.

Expectancies as Determiners of Goals

To move to our second construction— expectancy as a probability estimate—

motivation for one form of activity or goal over another depends to a great degree on our expectancies of success in the activity. A slow-learning child or adolescent in a regular classroom of average and bright students estimates his chances of success in academic competition in the ratio of 0 to 100. Expecting failure with complete certainty, he does nothing and continues to fail.

For such a child or a youth, this pessimistic expectancy, though distressing, may be accurate. Because of special learning circumstances, however, expectancies may be inaccurate. The authors know two brothers, two years apart in age, who will be called Joe and Bill McKinley. Joe, the elder, is a high school senior at age 16. He delights in academic pursuits, is very bright, learns easily, and has been double promoted because of his scholastic excellence. He is a competent enough athlete, but not competitive or very much interested in athletics. Bill, at 14 and in the ninth grade, shows promise of being an exceptional athlete. Academically, he is an average performer, although his ability as judged by IQ is the same as that of his elder brother, Joe.

In talking with the boys, one discovers how this state of affairs possibly came to be, even though neither brother consciously planned it that way. Joe is the firstborn to academically inclined parents. They had given him everything he needed to begin school. He entered first grade and was off to a flying start, and he has never faltered in his progress. Bill came along two years later and, as it were, saw the area of academics preempted by his brilliant elder brother. In many ways, this information had been conveyed to him by his parents, his teachers, and his peers who had elder brothers and sisters in Joe's classes. Thus, Bill had a relatively negative set of expectancies about his probability of success in academic competition with Joe.

Joe, however, was only moderately successful in sports. Because everyone seeks his place in the sun as best he can, younger brother Bill chose an area *not* preempted by his elder brother. In Bill's case, an idiosyncratic (based on his special set of personal circumstances) and inaccurate set of expectancies steered him out of academics into athletics.

Expectancies and Effects of Reinforcement

Expectancies such as those just discussed are obviously learned. They are based on the individual's best information, whether it is correct or incorrect. They clearly reflect his history of perceptual learning (as in the case of the tribal Zulu boys and the Ames window illusion) or of reinforcement, depressingly but accurately, as in the case of the slow-learning boy in the normal classroom, who had never succeeded in competition with average children; and distortedly, as in the case of Bill, the younger of the McKinley brothers. Bill had never been successful in academic endeavors when compared with his efficient elder brother. Thus, he chose another field to pursue in which, according to his personal equation, he would have a higher probability of success.

Individuals who have always succeeded through amiable, cooperative, and courteous behavior will establish high probabilities of success for that behavior in the future. Individuals who have always succeeded when they have acted aggressively and fought for what they desire will likely follow an aggressive pattern in the future if it is at all appropriate.

There may be different effects of reinforcement for high and low expectancies of success (57). To a youngster with a high expectancy of success, one more success may possess little reinforcement value. He is, as it were, habituated to success. To the youngster who has a low expectancy for success, on the other hand, success may change his whole self concept. Thus, it may be that criticism will often work wonders with chronically successful children and youth, and success and praise will equally work wonders with chronically failing individuals. When expectancies are disconfirmed, in other words, assimilation of the experience (to use Piaget's term) is made doubly difficult, and, to be assimilated, profound accommodation (of self concept) must occur. (For an account of the role of expectancies in morale and motivation see 62.)

In this section, we find many implications for management and control. However, we should be careful, for example, not to conclude that criticism is *always* a method to use for efficient individuals and youth, never a method to use for those who are chronic failures. It may be that praise is *always* a safer and in the long run a more effective motivator than criticism. All the data, in other words, are not yet in. It is important to recognize, however, that different reinforcements work differently for those who have differing reinforcement histories and different previous experiences with and expectancies for success.

Expectancies Held for One by Others

It is common-sense experience that the expectancies we know others hold for us affect our behavior. If we are sure (rightly or wrongly) that someone regards us as a boor, we are likely to behave boorishly. We are at our best for a fond grandparent who believes we can do no wrong.

The influence on behavior of expectancies for an individual that are held by others has been extensively studied. Results are not altogether clear about the effects on classroom learning, for example, of expectancies held by teachers (13, 23, 56, 66). The authors believe, however, that there is modest evidence to support the conclusion that children and youth will achieve better and attain higher self-esteem when their parents, teachers, or other significant persons hold positive rather than negative expectancies about their behavior and who translate those positive expectations into actual behavior. The authors have selected one study of the influence of expectancies on behavior that they know was carefully done. They use the method often as a demonstration teaching technique in college classes and have replicated it many times. The summary in Example 6.3 speaks for itself.

6.3 The Issue of Teacher Expectancies and Classroom Behavior

Beez, studying the effects on tutoring behavior of expectancies about performance, carried out the following study and obtained the results indicated (4). To experienced teachers who were attending summer school classes at Indiana University he assigned for tutoring a random group of Head Start pupils. Quite without regard for the actual ability of the children who were to be tutored in a simple learning task, Beez gave one-half the teachers information suggesting that their tutee was a slow learner. To the other half of the teachers, he gave the opposite information (also quite without basis in fact): "This child will be a school success." The results of the study follow.

1. The tutors tried to teach more items from the learning task to the "fast learners."

2. The "high ability" children actually learned more items, although they were no more accurate than the "low ability" children.

3. The tutors rated the putative high-ability children more favorably than the putative low-ability children for achievement, social competence, and intellectual ability.

4. The teachers cued the children about their expectations for them, apparently quite unintentionally. They gave the low-ability children more explanations of the learning items they were teaching, they presented more examples to the low-ability children, and they spent more time with the low-ability children on *non*teaching activities.

5. Although there was no real difference in the tutees' ability to learn (intelligence), only one tutor rated the task to be taught as too difficult for a child in the high-ability group, while 63 percent of the tutors judged the task to be too difficult for the low-ability group.

The implications of the Beez study are profound and bear directly on the teaching of advantaged and disadvantaged children and youth. It seems that teachers are likely to feed the former group expectations of success and achievement, and try harder with this group. The latter, disadvantaged children and youth, may receive less teaching impact and are likely to have betrayed to them the sincere belief that they may fail. This idea has support from another recent study in which it was disclosed that teachers demanded better performance from first-grade children for whom higher expectations were held, and were more likely to praise such performance when it occurred (11). In contrast, teachers were more likely to accept poor performance from children about whom low expectancies were held, and were less likely to praise these children's good performance even when it occurred.

It must be added, of course, that expectancies for children and youth can also be unreasonably high. Where this occurs and when those for whom excessive expectations are held are simply unable to meet them, frustration and failure are the usual result. This state of affairs can be as unfortunate as underestimating the capabilities of children and youth or the subtle expression of "no confidence" by teachers and parents. Occasionally, students of the authors have remarked that perhaps no one really has the right to hold expectancies for the behavior of anyone else. Rights notwithstanding, the authors believe that expectancies inevitably *are* held by people for other people and thus should be examined carefully in terms of their source and validity.

Expectancies as Self-fulfilling Prophecies

The implications about expectancies drawn in the last several pages lead to the tentative conclusion that expectancies may indeed be self-fulfilling prophecies. For instance, as seen in Example 6.3, there is a strong likelihood that, when teachers think of children or youth as being low in ability, they do not try as hard with them, they may patronize them, and, usually unconsciously, they may in many ways tip their charges off to their belief that "what needs to be done, you cannot do." Inevitably students (or one's own children) will react to such expectations by discouragement and lowered effort. This, coupled with less teacher impact, results in precisely what was predicted: the students do

not learn. The prophecy has been self-fulfilled, if you will.

The plain girl who thinks no boy will ask her to dance adopts a defensive stance and is cool to the boys. She snubs them before they can snub her. As a result, no boy approaches her, and she goes home, confirmed in her expectancies about herself. She has thus fulfilled her own prophecy.

Issues about Expectancies

Aside from the questions of a "right" to hold expectancies for others, there are perhaps no real philosophical dilemmas about the concept of expectancies. Almost everyone agrees that it is well to rear children so that they possess realistic expectancies of success; that factually based expectancies are more useful than inaccurate expectancies; and that, on the whole, one's personal adjustment will be better if one holds positive rather than negative expectancies about himself. The question is, "How does one deal with children and youth so as to teach them realistic, preponderantly positive expectancies about the outcomes of their own behavior?"

In this connection, one specific issue often arises. The issue is presented here, but no sure-fire recipe is given for handling it. Specifically, many schools, quite objectively, are poor schools, attended largely by students of low- to medium-learning aptitude and academic motivation. A student who is graduated from high school in such a school and who stands at the head of his or her class is almost certain to hold high expectancies for future success in college. Actually, he will probably not do very well in college, although he may get through. How does one prepare him realistically for the future?

Conversely, many exceptionally able

students are enrolled in some of the high-powered public and private college preparatory schools. The student in the middle of or even toward the bottom of the class may think of himself as doomed to academic mediocrity or failure if he ventures into college, whereas he is actually a good college prospect. The task of realistic counseling for such a student is easier, of course, than it is for the class valedictorian from the poor school.

The dilemma suggested here illustrates how one's relative position in a group may serve to shape his expectancies and indeed, his self concept (see Chapter 11). As such, it is related to the more general dilemma of absolute versus relative standards discussed earlier in this book (Chapter 3).

The final comment in this section concerns an often expressed question raised by students in the authors' classes, many of whom plan to work with children or youth in some professional capacity: "What should I expect about the behavior of (preschoolers, fifth-graders, junior high students, or high school juniors—as the case may be)?" This question usually indicates a concern by students for the capabilities, interests, fears, and behavior problems that characterize children and youth of specific ages and in selected settings, such as school, scouting group, or church. Such a question is apparently motivated by the belief that resultant information will provide a better basis for personal interaction and decision making about the children or youth with whom one works. Answering such a question is not easy, for several reasons. For one thing, the wide *range* of abilities, interests, and general developmental status found at any given age level makes accurate generalization about behavior very difficult. One usually ends up in an attempt

to describe the "average" 6-, 9-, or 14-year-old, the result of which may not soundly describe any real person.

Another difficulty encountered in answering individual student questions about "what to expect" is that children and youth simply do not behave the same way in the presence of all adults; nor are same-aged children and youth likely to behave identically in the presence of the same adult. For one teacher, a group of seventh-graders may act in marked contrast to their behavior in the classroom of another; and the intereactions between these seventh-graders and their teacher will vary widely, depending on the unique characteristics of the individual child and his teacher. Our point is that satisfactory predictions about what might be expected from children and youth in this or that situation are problematical. Accordingly, prospective teachers and youth workers usually must content themselves with general probability statements about unknown persons.

Of course, age norms (see Chapter 1) can be a helpful source of information to unexperienced adults who wish to become more generally familiar with the physical, social, and intellectual characteristics of children and youth. Age-based and stage-concept theories of development can be consulted for their descriptions of broad, developmental trends. Taking Piaget's cognitive-developmental perspective, for example, a nursery school teacher should not expect to observe conservation abilities among her 4-year-old charges; a second-grade teacher, in contrast, should expect that most of her 8-year-olds will be capable of conservation and teach accordingly. As another example, a counselor who takes the psychoanalytic perspective will expect that young adolescents are experiencing certain sexual conflicts that are based in early parent–child relationships, and design his counseling strategy with this in mind. Age norms charted by pioneer researchers, such as Arnold Gesell in his books *The Child from Five to Ten* and *Youth: The Years from Ten to Sixteen,* also serve as points of reference for many parents and teachers, even though the data were gathered several decades ago and may not be valid for children and youth of the seventies.

Although age norms and stage theories may be useful as general points of reference for expectancies, the authors advise extreme caution in using them for this purpose. This caution includes the use of age norms and stages to determine what is normal at given points in the course of development (see Chapter 3). They also advise that, whenever possible, the study of age norms be accompanied by direct experience with the children or the youth in question across a wide variety of situations.

COGNITIVE STYLE

It has been repeatedly stressed that the course of development during childhood and adolescence is marked by great diversity among individuals. Individuals differ in their language competence and performance, learning aptitude, problem-solving skill, and motivation (their incentives). They also differ in *cognitive style*. The following definition of cognitive style sets the tone for the discussion of this aspect of individual differences.

Definition

"Cognitive styles can be most directly defined as individual variation in *modes* of perceiving, remembering, and thinking, or as distinctive ways of apprehending, storing, transforming, and utilizing information. It may be noted that *abilities* also involve the foregoing properties, but a difference in emphasis should be acknowledged: Abilities concern *level* of skill—the more and less of performance—whereas cognitive styles give greater weight to the *manner* and *form* of cognition." (36, p. 244)

The psychological study of cognitive styles is a comparatively recent phenomenon, although various dimensions of such styles have been related to a wide variety of important behaviors, including vocational choice and forms of pathology (48, 77). Example 6.4 includes descriptions of nine cognitive styles that have been labeled and studied by psychologists (44). It is not yet known exactly how separate or independent these various styles are from one another. Perhaps most are simply different labels for the same general components of cognitive behavior. However, some of these cognitive styles have been so thoroughly researched that there is good reason to believe they are reliable sources of individual differences among children and youth. One of these styles, reflectivity—impulsivity, seems particularly significant to the authors (item 6 in the list). Consequently, they have chosen to discuss this behavioral dimension to illustrate the way in which style influences cognitive development and behavior.

6.4 Varieties of Cognitive Style

Nine Cognitive Styles

1. *Field independence versus field dependence.* An analytical, in contrast to a global, way of perceiving (which) consists of a tendency to experience items as discrete from their backgrounds, and reflects ability to overcome the influence of an embedding context.

2. *Scanning.* A dimension of individual differences in the extensiveness and the intensity of attention deployment, leading to individual variations in the vividness of experience and the span of awareness.

3. *Breadth of categorizing.* Consistent preferences for broad inclusiveness, as opposed to narrow exclusiveness, in establishing the acceptable range for specified categories.

4. *Conceptualizing styles.* Individual differences in the tendency to categorize perceived similarities and differences among stimuli in terms of many differentiated concepts, which is a dimension called conceptual differentiation, as well as consistencies in the utilization of particular conceptualizing approaches as bases for forming concepts (such as the routine use in concept formation of thematic or functional relations among stimuli as opposed to the analysis of descriptive attributes or the inference of class membership).

5. *Cognitive complexity versus simplicity.* Individual differences in the tendency to construe the world, particularly the world of social behavior, in a multi-dimensional and discriminating way.

6. *Reflectivity verus impulsivity.* Individual consistencies in the speed with which hypotheses are selected and information is processed, with impulsive subjects tending to offer the first answer that occurs to them, even though it is frequently incorrect, and with reflective subjects tending to ponder various possibilities before deciding.

7. *Leveling versus sharpening.* Reliable individual variations in assimilation in memory. Subjects at the leveling extreme tend to blur similar memories and to merge perceived objects or events with similar but not identical

events recalled from previous experience. Sharpeners, at the other extreme, are less prone to confuse similar objects and, by contrast, may even judge the present to be less similar to the past than is actually the case.

8. *Constricted versus flexible control.* Individual differences in susceptibility to distraction and cognitive interference.

9. *Tolerance for incongruous or unrealistic experiences.* A dimension of differential willingness to accept perceptions at variance with conventional experience.*

Reflectivity – Impulsivity

The problem-solving process can be broken down into at least five major components: *encoding* (selective attention to and preferential perceptual analysis of an event), *memory* (information storage and retrieval), *hypothesis formulation* (producing alternative hunches), *evaluation* (examining the quality or the validity of one's hunches), and *deduction* (implementing hypothesis or arriving at conclusions) (32). It is the fourth component, *evaluation,* for which the reflective–impulsive cognitive style is most relevant – the tendency of children or youth to think carefully about their problem solutions or hypotheses before volunteering a specific response. Some people are characteristically deliberate and reflective about their problem-solving activities and the way they approach new tasks. They examine new information or materials carefully and systematically. Others respond impulsively or quickly and thoughtlessly in new situations. They do not take

* From "The Criterion Problem in the Evaluation of Instruction: Assessing Possible, Not Just Intended, Outcomes" by Samuel Messick, in THE EVALUATION OF INSTRUCTION: ISSUES AND PROBLEMS, edited by M. C. Wittrock and David E. Wiley. Copyright © 1970 by Holt, Rinehart and Winston, Inc. Reprinted by permission of Holt, Rinehart and Winston.

sufficient time to think carefully about the nature of the information and the materials or the alternative responses that they might make.

An example illustrates how reflectivity or impulsivity appears as early as the preschool years. Suppose two 3-year-old children enter for the first time a room full of unfamiliar toys and games. One child pauses to look about the entire room, taking note of the various alternatives for activity. He then selects a marble game, which occupies his attention for the next ten or fifteen minutes. After looking about still further, he next chooses to play a block-building game, and so on. In contrast, the second child does not look over the many possibilities for play. Rather, he runs immediately to a jack-in-the-box, which, in a few seconds, he discards in favor of a set of toy train cars. After a minute or two this child picks up some nesting blocks, only to drop them in favor of a ten-piece wooden puzzle. Then, instead of completing the puzzle, he moves to still another toy. This example suggests a basic difference in the way two children survey, approach, and engage in various activities.

An important result of this difference in terms of learning is that children prone to respond impulsively are more likely to make unnecessary mistakes than children who first reflect on the quality of their tentative answers. It should be noted that the greater number of mistakes made by impulsive children does not necessarily mean that such children are less bright or knowledgeable about their world (31). Rather, it is a matter of a difference in timing or tempo and of how this difference shows up in behavior. Most of us have observed that some children engaged in group recitation or discussion activities raise their hand to answer questions, apparently without thinking about whether their response is right or wrong. Some children volunteer answers even before they hear the entire question. In some situations, such as pretend quiz shows and guessing games, such behavior may be appropriate. In others, such as working independently on a perceptual matching task (matching pairs of pictures of letterlike forms on the printed page) or responding to a test where one must choose from among many different answers, impulsive behavior may be harmful. In fact, one authority reports that male children who are retained in the first grade are more often impulsive than their promoted peers, even though the two groups of children are not different in measured intelligence (43).

Developmental Aspects of Reflectivity–Impulsivity

Long-term studies of children's problem-solving tempo or style have led to two important findings: (1) that individual differences in this aspect of cognitive style may appear as early as age 2; and (2) that children generally become more reflective with age through adolescence and beyond (32). It is also possible that some children change little in impulsivity with age. Some may even become more impulsive. Constitutional factors such as general activity level may be involved, although developmental changes in tempo are undoubtedly affected in important ways by children's social and academic experiences. For example, some teachers and parents may place a greater value on speed than on accuracy of response in task situations, and may reinforce behavior accordingly. Various links between problem-solving tempo and several important academic-related behaviors have been made. Reflective children, for example, seem to demonstrate longer attention spans, greater persistence with difficult tasks, fewer errors of recognition in beginning reading (especially girls), and less distractibility or fidgety behavior in formal learning situations (31, 60).

Armed with the above information, one might easily make a value judgment to the effect that reflectivity is good and impulsivity is bad. Impulsive children, however, have been observed to be more active socially, more likely to interact spontaneously with peers and adults, and to enjoy such interaction more (31). In certain stages of the creative process, it is also possible that some degree of impulsivity may be valuable. It has also been suggested that reflective children may be more anxious about making errors or displaying incompetence (42). However, impulsive children often find themselves handicapped in formal learning situations, including those where making mistakes results in faulty learning or disapproval and criticism from others. Arithmetic is a good example of a subject about which it is typically a mistake to be impulsive. Impulsive tendencies may also interfere with the development of successful problem-solving skills, including the style of thinking needed for reasoning about problems. In this connection, it should be noted that reflectivity–impulsivity is most apparent in tasks that involve some degree of response uncertainty —tasks where methods of accomplishment and finalized solutions are not immediately apparent (34).

Some Implications of Reflectivity–Impulsivity

Consider first the implications of conceptual tempo for everyday adult–child interaction. Adults may rarely attend to a child's style for approaching conceptual problems. Rather, children are more often categorized by adults as bright (dull), responsible (irresponsible), outgoing (shy), and the like, rather than careful in their work (reflective) or hair-trigger (impulsive) (31). Accordingly, adults may even be deceived by impulsive, quick children in that such children may be looked upon as being "brighter" than their equally intelligent peers who take more time to examine data and organize their responses. The point again is that quickness does not necessarily indicate brightness, although it is clear that it is good (adaptive) to be alert. By the same token, deliberating and pondering do not necessarily indicate slowness or indecisiveness. Moreover, in some learning situations (for example, reading-readiness activities), a child's errors may be due less to "slow maturation," "sensory impediments," or "low intelligence" than to conceptual tempo. If tempo is important for success in a certain activity, helping a child to adopt the most appropriate tempo under the circumstances may be desirable.

One Possible Dilemma

Finally, let us consider the matter of changing or modifying an impulsive (or reflective) tendency where appropriate— that is, where one or the other response styles interferes with educational progress. This cannot be thought of as an easy task. As has been said, impulsive or reflective tendencies possibly appear in the form of a general habit as early as age 2 or 3. Several attempts have been made to develop strategies for changing conceptual tempo. These attempts range from general to specific and vary in the degree to which they incorporate learning principles such as imitation and reinforcement. In one study, for example, a direct tutoring procedure for impulsive first-grade children was implemented to help them learn how and when to inhibit fast responses to problems. The tutoring procedure was generally effective for this purpose, although little improvement in the quality of these children's intellectual performance was noted (33).

Other studies suggest the value of two conditions: planned positive reinforcement for reflective behavior and prolonged exposure to more and less reflective adult models in order to influence children's conceptual style (3, 79). The modeling procedure is particularly important. Anyone who has observed extensively in classrooms has probably noted differences in conceptual tempo among teachers themselves. Some teachers proceed rapidly with the presentation of activities, are constantly mindful of time limitations, encourage children to respond quickly, verbalize instructions and ideas rapidly, and generally operate at a high rate of speed. Others are more concerned with deliberations and alternatives and move at a moderate pace. The point concerns the possible effect(s) that teacher tempo may have on the conceptual tempo of children in a given classroom, in addition to the pattern of reinforcement for impulsive or reflective behavior and explicit, relevant task-appropriate instructions for performance.

CURIOSITY

Definition

Curiosity is a form of exploratory behavior. Its purpose is to change the stimulus field within which one operates, either by "finding out something about a specific object or event, or by searching for an interesting environment that enables one to achieve a preferred level of stimu-

lation" (52, p. 355; 16). The authors suspect that curiosity, like attention, originates with the orientation reaction (see the earlier section in this chapter about *attention* and *set*). Orientation reactions are typically reinforced, as has been seen. From these reinforced reactions, attention develops. Attention is in turn reinforced by novelty, among other things, and eventually novelty itself can become an incentive for behavior. In fact, novelty, in the sense of variation of sensory input, may even be a native reinforcement.

In formal settings for learning, such as the classroom, several criteria may serve as useful indicators of curiosity among children and youth. These include a learner's reaction to new, incongruous or complex situations and his persistence in exploring such situations (16). For example, the curious child or youth is one who shows an interest in new topics for classroom discussion, asks questions, and investigates such topics personally. He also frequently reads about exotic subjects that are often unassigned. He thinks about and discusses various topics introduced in class or items brought to school by classmates, and he persists with his explorations or manipulations until he reaches higher levels of understanding or insight. Most important, this pattern of behavior seemingly occurs without continual praise, recognition, or material reward from others (16).

It is plausible to regard curiosity as a well-established response set or a well-learned (overlearned) set of expectancies, perhaps across most, or at least the higher, animal species. Very early in the life of higher organisms, their "natural" activities have resulted in positive consequences. By wriggling closer to mothers, infants have found warmth or nourishment. By pawing, grasping, and mouth-

Curiosity is self-reinforcing

ing, they have secured food more easily. The authors might postulate a general expectancy or set: "Something interesting happens (changes) as a result of shifting attention and trying out new things." This "something" may be good, neutral, or painful at various times, but a law of partial reinforcement operates. For most children and youth, positive rewards occur often enough as a result of exploratory behavior that "curiosity" is reinforced and remarkably enduring.

Implications of the Concept of Curiosity

No one questions the basic role of curiosity in much of human learning. It is especially crucial in the "experiential learning" preferred by proponents of humanistic psychology (see Chapter 2). It therefore seems reasonable to encourage curiosity behavior by allowing its expression and reinforcing such behavior when it occurs. Of course, such a strategy may present certain problems; for example, recall the dilemma of the parent, discussed in Chapter 2, who wants his child to develop both curiosity and conformity. Beyond this, six specific conclusions from studies of curiosity are merited (16, 40).

First, it is clear that new or novel things arouse more curiosity than do the old and the familiar. However, novelty to the point of total unfamiliarity or threat inhibits curiosity. Ideally, a point of maximum novelty with just a touch of the familiar will draw out maximum curiosity. Similarly, novelty in the form of surprise seems particularly effective for evoking explanatory questions among older children and adolescents. The involvement that a skilled sleight-of-hand artist can elicit in a group of children or adolescents is a good example of this point.

Second, when something is taken away temporarily with some assurance that it will eventually reappear, interest in that something is evoked. This is reminiscent of the "I want most what is hard to get" phenomenon that almost all of us have experienced at one time or another.

Third, children and youth are particularly curious about things in which adults show an interest. In fact, the enthusiasm for activities demonstrated by adults seems to have a contagious quality that generally contributes to active, well-motivated learning among children and youth. Curiosity and enthusiasm for exploration continually show up as basic ingredients in effective teaching (22).

Fourth, certain personality characteristics frequently differentiate high- and low-curious children and youth. For example, individuals low in curiosity are typically more anxious, less socially responsible, less tolerant of ambiguous situations, and have less favorable self-images than their highly curious counterparts. Among other things, this means that children and youth will not respond to arousal techniques in the same way. Individual differences in curiosity behavior must therefore be recognized.

Fifth, boys often are more obviously interested in newness and novelty than girls. It is difficult to find a plausible biological explanation for this apparent difference, although it may be rooted in the slightly greater tendency toward activity and aggressiveness in males, both of which have biological underpinnings. A more likely explanation of this difference in arousal can be expressed in terms of the greater cultural stress on independence and initiative for boys and on conformity and obedience for girls.

Sixth, and finally, as children increase in age, they show successively stronger preferences for novel (versus old and familiar) stimuli. One implication of this generalization is that children (and youth) will attend more fully (and therefore will be more affected by) activities and learning materials that are new and different or contain some element of surprise or change from routines of the past. Insufficient attention to this principle by teachers may account for some of the school dissatisfaction and boredom expressed by older children and adolescents. Whether "change for the sake of change" in teaching methods and materials is wise can be debated; and one should keep in mind the possibility that overstimulation, disorganization, or ill-conceived gimmickry may impede rather than facilitate classroom learning. Yet the authors believe that it is the rare classroom that could not profit from a "spicing up" through the introduction of well-planned novelty and change.

Epistemic Curiosity and Diversive Exploration

The concept of epistemic curiosity is important in both formal and informal education (8). When one is epistemically curious he seeks to gain, code, and store information "in the form of symbolic responses that can guide behavior on future occasions" (7, p. 31). Question asking, free reading, "casing the environment," are all forms of epistemic behavior presumably motivated by this sort of curiosity. A child or a youth whom one observes to be "intellectually curious" across a wide range of situations can be described as epistemically curious.

It is believed that epistemic curiosity is motivated by conceptual conflict or conflict due to discrepant thoughts, beliefs, attitudes, or observations. Because of conceptual conflict, the individual seeks information to buttress, support, develop, or refine his prevailing thought (6). An example based on the principle of contradiction in teaching concepts to children or adolescents will illustrate. Suppose first that learners are somehow told or discover how plants use chlorophyll to perform the photochemical processes on which they depend for life. A bit later, these same children learn that plants exist that lack chlorophyll (fungi) and live in the absence of sunlight. The conceptual conflict prompted by this apparent contradiction can serve to emphasize these learners' incomplete concept of plant life. Hence, both the idea that the way of life for green plants is not the only possible way within the flora kingdom and the critical attributes of fungi can be reinforced (6). Resolving conceptual conflict thus is considered as intrinsically reinforcing.

Diversive exploration occurs when one combats stimulus deprivation or boredom (52). Boredom, which results from stimulus deprivation, occurs when a person is awake and when he has nothing to do, nothing to experience. A young and sophisticated friend of the authors, who may have borrowed the thought from someone else, remarked aptly that boredom comes only from within, which is true enough. On the other hand, few of us have enough inner resources to amuse ourselves endlessly in the midst of austere surroundings. Brainwashing, as we have seen from the Korean and the Vietnamese wars, may occur quite easily in circumstances of stimulus deprivation (acute boredom).

The lives of very young children without much inner life may be very boring if they do not have opportunity to shift the scene frequently. The lives of many older children and adolescents in barren life surroundings (bland suburbs, small, quiet towns, or impoverished ghetto apartments) can also be exceptionally boring.

A search for kicks—for something to do that changes the scene and introduces novelty—is undoubtedly behind many cases of classroom discipline and much delinquency, including abuse of drugs and liquor.

Some Final Thoughts about Curiosity

It is pathetic to see how little the average parent or classroom teacher uses the principles of curiosity, how little is done to arouse it, how little is done to satisfy it, and how little is done to take advantage of it. Parents and teachers rarely introduce gimmicks or plan for novelty and variety. In homes and schools, the same arrangements, the same bulletin boards, persist day after day and week after week. Toys are not alternated, routines are not varied, surprises are not introduced, new things are not tried.

It seems that curiosity in older children and adolescents often threatens parents and teachers. For example, sexual maturity is a new organism state reacting to a new set of reinforcers (sexual outlets) that bother adults greatly. Adolescents talk with their peers, they pore over pornography, they girl watch or boy watch, they avidly read sex-education and sex how-to-do-it books. They attempt to (and *do*) get into X-rated movies. They also seek to satisfy their curiosity directly, and many heterotic and homerotic explorations, casualties, or near casualties occur, often followed by guilt and fear.

Adolescents have other intense incentives, arising from their search for their own identity, including values. Thus, curiosity exists or can be aroused easily about religion, values, ethics, vocational guidance, and self-understanding. Most schools do depressingly little to take advantage of this vast motivational reservoir. This state of affairs seems very much related to the current, and long-overdue quest for "relevance" in the schools.

Implicit in the foregoing discussion, of course, is the belief that curiosity is a "good thing" and should be cultivated in the interests of positive cognitive and affective development. The reader who desires to learn more about the role of curiosity in instructional settings should find the references cited throughout this section well worthy of further study.

CREATIVITY

The six topics already discussed in this chapter are related to creativity and its development. Attention deployment perception, intentional and incidental learning, expectancies, cognitive style, and curiosity are all factors that appear variously throughout the creativity research. The study of creativity has also occupied the interests of psychologists from every major theoretical persuasion. As the reader has learned, humanistic psychologists generally maintain that creativity is a natural growth state of man and serves as an indication of positive mental health. According to one humanist, for example, there are three crucial elements of creativity—openness to experience, spontaneity, and an internal locus of evaluation (54). Behaviorists have been much concerned with environmental factors that affect the rate of one's creative output. As such, the behaviorists have usually considered creativity as a *product* (41). In contrast, psychoanalytic thinkers have concentrated most on the creative *process*. One such thinker, for example, views creativity as psychological regression in thought whereby the id is allowed to provide the ego with primary, uncensored material with which to deal (37). Finally

Humanist,
Behaviour,
Psychoanalytic
Cognitive - Developmental   *Piaget - Cognitive -*
Cognitive - Dev   215   *Developmentalist*

Special Factors in Cognition

One characteristic of the creative person is the ability to use common objects in novel or original ways. This child has discovered that a road marker serves as an excellent landing strip for his airplane. (Photo by Robert de Gast)

the cognitive-developmentalist's concern with creative development is aptly conveyed by Piaget's contention that the basic goal of education is to produce men who are capable of creativity, invention, and discovery (51).

Definition

But what, exactly, is creativity? Taking their cues from the major approaches to the psychological study of creativity, the authors use the term here to mean behavior that represents both a process and a product. As a *process*, creativity can be considered complex thinking that re-

quires as yet unknown proportions of knowledge, the ability to see new relationships among objects or events, radar-like attention to the environment, a willingness to engage in fantasy in thought, hypothesis formulation and testing, and skill in communicating one's thoughts to others. According to one authority, the "core" of a process definition of creativity comprises associative fluency and uniqueness (components of *divergent thinking* as discussed in Chapter 5). These processes are most likely to occur in response to tasks on which only very broad restraints and nonstringent evaluation by others (if any) are operating (73). Also implicated in the creative process are attention deployment (incidental cue utilization) and introspective sensitivity.

Creativity can also be discussed in terms of *a novel* or *an original product* that is usually satisfying, meaningful, and valuable to the creator, to his culture, or to both. Usually, such a product is a modification or a rejection of previously accepted ideas, represents large amounts of motivation and intellectual energy, and is prompted by an initially ambiguous and ill-defined problem (47).

Assumptions about Creativity

General though the foregoing definition is, the following discussion is built on five basic assumptions. First, it is generally assumed that creativity is an aspect of intelligent behavior that can be expressed in a variety of ways at a number of levels. For example, just as a nuclear physicist or a jazz composer can be creative in the laboratory or the music room, so can a cook in the kitchen and a kindergartner during "Show and Tell." Second, it is assumed that all children and youth possess creative abilities to some degree. One person may demonstrate his creative abilities more frequently than another, but no person completely lacks them.

A third assumption is that creative abilities can be developed under the "right" conditions. The exact nature of these facilitating conditions may not be the same for any two children or adolescents, but it seems clear that some general conditions apply to most people. This point will be discussed momentarily.

Fourth, the authors assume, with Piaget, that development of creative abilities is (or at least should be) a prime educational goal. This assumption raises some

sticky issues, including how to achieve a balance between necessary intellectual conformity in a society and individual deviation toward the unconventional. It also requires that one have clearly in mind the specific behavioral components of creative expression so that independence and meditation are not confused with destructive rebelliousness and indecisiveness. Nevertheless, the authors believe that creativity is a valuable part of human development that must be nourished and encouraged within the schools.

Finally, the authors assume that creativity (with its central component of divergent thinking) and measured intelligence (with its central component of convergent thinking) are not one and the same. In fact, some children and youth who score high on conventional intelligence tests often do not show their creativity as well as children and youth who score lower on such tests (64). What this may mean is that certain abilities important for creative expression are (or may be) different from those important for intelligence test performance. In short, the point is twofold. First, while creativity is surely an aspect of man's intelligence, high scores on intelligence tests and elevated levels of creativity do not necessarily go hand in hand. Second, higher levels of creativity probably involve factors over and above learning aptitude and problem-solving skills, including curiosity and other personality characteristics (15, 17).

The Psychological Study of Creativity

Although creativity has been an object of armchair analysis for centuries, scientific approaches to creativity began fairly recently. Much of the impetus for the study of creativity by psychologists was provided by Guilford's Structure of Intellect model (see Chapter 5). Since Guilford proposed this model, creativity research has been conducted along at least four related courses. Let us briefly consider each.

Mental Measurement

The avenue most directly associated with Guilford and his colleagues has involved *psychometrics*, that is, devising instruments to measure differences in creativity or, more accurately, *divergent thinking* abilities. Perhaps the biggest single problem for this line of research work has been to find measures that are truly distinct from traditional measures of general intelligence and achievement. Nevertheless, much success has been achieved, particularly in the measurement of fluency in generating a variety of original ideas in situations involving only moderate amounts of structure (73). A wide range of individual differences during childhood and adolescence has been revealed by using psychometric instruments such as Guilford's. It has also been discovered that test conditions make a difference in creative performance. Indexes of creativity are often higher when time limits are removed, a gamelike atmosphere is established, and people are allowed to share ideas (67, 69). This suggests that creativity may more likely flourish in situations where stress, anxiety, and social isolation do not prevail.

Personality Differences

A second avenue of creativity research has also been explored or at least opened by the first: investigations of personality differences between extremely creative and less creative children and youth. The results of these investigations are difficult to summarize for at least two reasons. First, the sheer number of such studies is virtually overwhelming to the student of creativity. Second, results are often con-

flicting, perhaps because of different ways of defining and measuring creativity. For example, some psychologists use ratings of children and youth by teachers or other "experts" to identify more and less creative individuals. Others use psychometric devices of the Guilford type. Still others infer creativity level by less direct means, such as projective test data.

Despite these obstacles, it is fair to say that some commonalities run through the studies concerned with the creative person. The weight of the evidence generally suggests that the creative child or youth is often highly self-confident, intellectually curious, independent in judgment and behavior, less concerned than most with social convention, genial (although not necessarily intimate with his parents), favorably disposed toward complex and novel activities, tolerant of ambiguity, persistent, sensitive to problems, neither dogmatic nor authoritarian, willing to entertain and sometimes express impulses, strong in disciplined effectiveness, and prone to value and cultivate a strong sense of humor (5, 18, 49, 65, 75). In short, these findings suggest that creativity and characteristics normally associated with positive development and adjustment go together. It should be noted that no cause–effect relationship is indicated by these data. "Good" personality adjustment does not necessarily guarantee creativity, nor can it be said that creativity does not occur in the absence of such characteristics. However, the authors believe that the data contraindicate popular myths that equate creativity with maladjustment and emotional disturbance or undisciplined thinking and social alienation (24, 72).

Background Factors

A third line of creativity research involves the search for background factors in creative development, including cultural and family influences that may contribute to individual differences in creativity. For example, in one of the few cross-cultural studies of creativity among elementary and junior high school children, creative expression was judged as more frequent in cultures characterized by less authoritarian attitudes toward child rearing and social relationships (2). It is argued that the dominant pattern in some cultures is one of restrictiveness, conditional acceptance, and failure to stimulate free interplay of differences among children and youth. Thus, an individual who grows up under the influence of such a pattern is less likely to become creative, especially since creativity implies communicating the truth as one sees it.

Social Class   As the reader should expect, the relationship between creativity and social class factors has also been explored. For the authors, the most provocative findings that have come from such exploration point to the stronger relationship between social class factors and creative output during the preschool and early school years than during the later school years (39, 61). That is, in contrast to developmental data regarding intelligence, creative performance apparently is not affected as much by socioeconomic background, especially in later childhood and adolescence. A related finding is that youth who drop out of high school, many of whom come from lower socioeconomic backgrounds, often score higher on creativity tests than their stay-in counterparts (29). The authors do not mean to suggest that social class factors are irrelevant to the study of creativity, but only to point out that the relationship of these

factors to creative development requires much more investigation.

Child-rearing Practices   A third cluster of studies concerned with background factors in creativity cannot be overlooked: studies of child-rearing practices. Most frequently, these studies have involved a comparison of parents whose offspring are high in creativity (or creative potential) with parents whose offspring show less creative promise. In an early study of adolescent creativity, for example, parents of high creatives were found to be comparatively less critical of their adolescent offspring and their schools; more liberal and tolerant in general outlook, tending to focus on their child's values; and open to experience, interests, and enthusiasms (25). These findings suggest that a child-centered orientation, along with creative parental models, facilitate creative development. This interpretation is reinforced by still other data. Parental characteristics associated with higher rates of divergent production in children are (1) low degree of punishment in the home, (2) low pressure for conformity, (3) absence of intrusiveness, (4) emotional support of and satisfaction with the child, and (5) self-acceptance (58).

As is the case for cultural and social class factors, data about child-rearing practices cannot be taken to prove causation. That is, the establishment of conditions such as those described cannot be thought to guarantee high creativity in children. It is possible that such parental behaviors occur after a child's creative potential becomes apparent rather than before. The child's very creativity may lead to such behavior. The point is that no one knows for sure what conditions in the home facilitate creativity for a given child. In general, however, overall *attitude* toward child rearing implied by these findings seems like a promising exploratory factor.

How Can One Encourage Creativity?
The question of what conditions best facilitate creativity is central to the fourth and last avenue for creativity research to be discussed. Psychologists concerned with facilitating conditions have concentrated largely on studying specific environmental factors that are subject to manipulation in the laboratory or the classroom. Because this concern is so directly relevant to educating for creativity, a virtual explosion of research into facilitative conditions has occurred in recent years. Some authorities began by attempting to identify characteristics of teachers and classrooms where low rates of creative production among students prevailed (68). As the reader might predict, classrooms characterized by low creative output are often those where challenging activities are rarely pursued, sanctions are established against questioning and exploring, a strong division is made between work and play (for example, "The fun's over now children; it's time for arithmetic."), and pressures for absolute intellectual and social conformity are applied (for example, "Johnny, only girls write love stories in English composition. Why don't you write about football or deep-sea diving?" or "Whoever heard of a green Santa Claus? Do your picture again and color Santa red!").

Subsequent research has revealed that teachers who are rated by their superiors as resourceful and pupil centered increase creative behavior among their charges (70). Another research worker found that a consistently indirect teaching style (accepting and clarifying student feelings, praising and encouraging student ideas, using student ideas to build and develop classroom discussions) was associated with growth in verbal and figural creative expression over a four-year period (74). Example 6.5 represents some recent research on specific training conditions.

6.5 Training for Creative Thinking
Ridley and Birney (53) were interested in any effects that specific training procedures might have on creativity. They measured creativity by performance on two tests from Guilford's original test battery: *Unusual Uses* (advancing plausible, but unconventional uses for common objects such as a brick, a light bulb, or a piece of paper) and *Plot Titles* (writing as many appropriate titles as possible for two stories during an allotted time period). These measures lend themselves to analysis in terms of both fluency and originality.

Ridley and Birney began by reasoning that certain task-relevant principles exist for creative thinking tasks and that if such principles are highlighted through a systematic training procedure individuals should be able to increase their creative performance beyond that shown in the absence of such training. Two similar experiments involving 159 college male freshmen were performed to test this idea. The classical experimental-control group design was used whereby one-half of these freshmen were assigned to the training procedure and the other half received no special treatment. Creativity test performance between the experimental and the control groups was compared subsequent to training.

Briefly, Ridley and Birney found that three training variables could be linked to increases in creative thinking. The first variable concerned instructions to be original on the tests themselves (for example, "Try to think of things that no one else will think of."). This variable constitutes a *set*, as this concept was discussed earlier in this chapter. A second effective training variable was practice in word association. For example, a list of twelve words was presented to the trainees six times. Each time through the list the freshmen were asked to provide a different association to the same stimulus words. Finally, training in the use of problem-solving heuristics seemed a fruitful strategy. An example of this involved encouraging thought about transformations or actions that might be performed on common objects.

The results of the Ridley and Birney study are similar to a subsequent study by Levy (38). Levy's thesis is that originality (creativity) is a matter more of role-defined behavior than a personal characteristic or trait. Through a combination of instructions and reinforcement for unusual responses, Levy was able substantially to increase the frequency of "original" responses among a group of volunteer college students. Such results, of course, are of considerable importance for those interested in "educating for creativity." It should be noted that originality per se cannot be the only criterion for judging creativity. The act of throwing one's peanut butter sandwich into the bell of a tuba during the school band concert is certainly highly original and "different," in the sense that such behavior occurs infrequently. But few would seriously consider such behavior as a creative act. It seems that additional criteria such as productivity, communicability, and some degree of social value are probably involved in most of what is called creativity.

As this book is written, there is nothing to contraindicate the potential value of a cluster of teaching techniques for encouraging creativity. It is clear that this cluster represents neither a prescription nor a substitute for general humane and competent teaching. The authors offer these suggestions, however, for the reader's consideration: (1) leading the student to question, (2) using analogy, metaphor, and the free association of ideas, (3) permitting logical analysis to come late in the discovery process, (4) encouraging skepticism, (5) permitting moderate disorder, (6) leaving blocks of time free for thought, (7) furnishing aesthetic experiences, (8) reinforcing creative expression, and (9) relating material that is studied to other subjects or to broader concepts and problems of relevance to learners (80). Specific activities relevant to this cluster of techniques are described elsewhere (46, 50, 76).

To summarize briefly, the authors have considered the nature of creativity in terms of both processes and product, have made explicit some basic assumptions that underlie contemporary thinking about creativity, and have examined four lines of research into creativity and its development. Many dilemmas associated with the psychological study have been omitted from the discussion because of space considerations. It should be recognized that these dilemmas range from the definition and measurement of creativity to procedures for promoting creative developments within the formal academic setting. It is interesting that some of the authors' own students maintain that creativity is such a personal and individual matter that it either cannot or should not be studied scientifically. The authors respect this view, but believe that a search for understanding human development and behavior is incomplete without paying serious attention to creativity, a unique characteristic of man. Also, the potential value is vast of the insights reaped from discovering conditions that maximize rather than minimize or subvert the creative potential of children and youth.

In this chapter, the authors have treated briefly seven interrelated topics that bear on language, intelligence, and cognition, as they were explored in some detail in Chapters 4 and 5.

The first topic was attention and set. Attention is probably learned from the orienting reaction: the what-is-it response, which is almost certainly also the foundation of curiosity. Set often directs attention and is of at least three types: perceptual, performance, and learning. Attention and set seem to be the processes by which human beings move perceived stimuli from short-term to long-term memory by coding and storage process. They are also necessary for retrieving such material, which is used later in guiding behavior.

Once a person has attended to something, he is ready to perceive it, that is, to organize and interpret his sensory input. The authors discussed the significance of perception for learning and highlighted some basic, age-related trends in perceptual development. As children grow older, they become increasingly more specific, selective, and economical in their perceptual processes. They also develop sense modality preferences and demonstrate greater degrees of intersensory interpretation and coordination.

Third, intentional (purposeful) learning and incidental learning were discussed. Incidental learning, as the term was used, is of two types. The first occurs "along the way and out of the corner of one's eye," as he engages in intentional learning. The second occurs simply because the individual is engaging in free activity, pursuing his interests of the moment, and, in general, experiencing without being formally "taught."

Fourth, the authors moved to expectancy. An expectancy can be a set, it can be a prediction about the outcome of our own behavior based on probabilities that we have learned during the course of our life, or it can be a generalized expectation about an individual that is held by someone else. When a teacher, for example, regards a child as a slow learner, he is likely to betray his expectancies to the child in subtle and obvious ways, and often expends less effort in teaching him. Thus, teachers often help to "fulfill their own prophecies." Similarly, individuals often behave in such a way as to guarantee that their expectancies about themselves will be realized (self-fulfilling prophecies).

Next discussed, under the heading Cognitive Style, was the phenomenon or manner or form of cognition. Many cognitive-style dimensions have been researched, but the authors chose to focus on reflectivity–impulsivity to illustrate the role of this aspect of cognition in human development. Reflectivity in cognitive style seems to increase with age, although a wide range of individual differences in reflective or impulsive behavior is apparent throughout the course of development. In general, reflectivity is associated with more successful accomplishments, especially in the formal academic setting. However, cognitive impulsivity may be important for many valued activities, including the early stages of creative production.

Curiosity was treated as the sixth major topic for the chapter. As mentioned, curiosity probably results from orienting reactions and from reinforcement of many forms of attention. Curiosity is considered a well-learned (or overlearned) habit. The curious child or youth often threatens authority, but curiosity is facilitative for cognitive—intellectual growth. As such, it should be encouraged. Epistemic curiosity is the storing of knowledge in order to guide future behavior. It is a hallmark of the creative, constructive, and contributing mind.

Finally, issues and research strategies involved in the psychological study of creativity were discussed. The treatment was built around the notion of creativity as both process and product. The authors recognize that controversy about the meaning of creativity is the rule rather than the exception in American society. A number of assumptions that underlie most conceptualizations of creativity were identified. They range from the idea that creativity can occur at different levels in different forms to the notion that creative development is a desirable educational goal. Several different pathways of creativity research were also discussed, including those involving mental measurement, personality differences in more and less creative individuals, background factors in creativity, and the dilemma of promoting creative growth and expression.

REFERENCES

1. Allport, G. W., and T. F. Pettigrew. Cultural influence on the perception of movement: The trapezoidal illusion among Zulus. *Journal of Abnormal and Social Psychology*, 1957, *55*, 104–113.

2. Anderson, H. H., and G. L. Anderson. A cross-national study of children: A study in creativity and mental health. In I. J. Gordon (ed.) *Human development: Readings in research*. Glenview, Ill.: Scott, Foresman, 1965, 307–315.

3. Baird, R. R., and H. L. Bee. Modification of conceptual style preference by differential reinforcements. *Child Development*, 1969, *40*, 903–910.

4. Beez, V. Influence of biased psychological reports on teacher behavior and pupil performance. Paper presented at the meeting of the American Psychological Association, San Francisco, September, 1968.

5. Berelson, B., and G. Steiner. *Human behavior*. New York: Harcourt, 1964.

6. Berlyne, D. E. Curiosity and education. In J. D. Krumboltz (ed.) *Learning and the educational process*. Chicago: Rand McNally, 1965, 67–89.

7. Berlyne, D. E. Curiosity and exploration. *Science,* 1966, *153,* 25–33.

8. Berlyne, D. E., and F. D. Frommer. Some determinants of the incidence and content of children's questions. *Child Development*, 1966, *37*, 177–189.

9. Bissell, J., S. White, and G. Zivin. Sensory modalities in children's learning. In G. Lesser (ed.) *Psychology and educational practice*. Glenview, Ill.: Scott, Foresman, 1971, 130–155.

10. Blum, A., and C. Adcock. Attention and early learning: A selected review. *Journal of Education*, 1968, *150*, 28–40.

11. Brophy, J. E., and T. L. Good. Teachers' communication of differential expectations for children's classroom performance. *Journal of Educational Psychology*, 1970, *61*, 365–374.

12. Bruner, J. S., R. R. Oliver, and P. M. Greenfield. *Studies in cognitive growth*. New York: Wiley, 1966.

13. Claiborne, W. L. Expectancy effects in the classroom: A failure to replicate. *Journal of Educational Psychology*, 1969, *60*, 377–383.

14. Cratty, B. J. *Perceptual and motor development in infants and children*. New York: Macmillan, 1970.

15. Cronbach, L. J. Intelligence? Creativity? A parsimonious reinterpretation of the Wallach-Kogan data. *American Educational Research Journal*, 1968, 5, 498–511.

16. Day, H. I., and D. E. Berlyne. Intrinsic motivation. In G. Lesser (ed.) *Psychology and educational practice*. Glenview, Ill.: Scott, Foresman, 1971, 294–335.

17. Day, H. I., and R. Langevin. Two necessary conditions for creativity. *ERIC: ED 026 673*, 1968.

18. Eisenman, R., and H. O. Cherry. Creativity, authoritarianism, and birth order. *Journal of Social Psychology*, 1970, 80, 233–235.

19. Elkind, D. Piaget's theory of perceptual development: Its application to reading and special education. *Journal of Special Education*, 1967, 1, 357–361.

20. Elkind, D., and J. A. Deblinger. Perceptual training and reading achievement in disadvantaged children. *Child Development*, 1969, 40, 11–20.

21. Evans, E. D. *Contemporary influences in early childhood education*. New York: Holt, Rinehart and Winston, 1971.

22. Evans, E. D. Student activism and teaching effectiveness: Survival of the fittest? *Journal of College Student Personnel*, 1969, 10, 102–108.

23. Fleming, E. S., and R. G. Anttonen. Teacher expectancy or my fair lady. *American Educational Research Journal*, 1971, 7, 241–252.

24. Garfield, S. J., H. A. Cohen, and R. M. Roth. Creativity and mental health. *Journal of Educational Research*, 1969, 63, 147–149.

25. Getzels, J. W., and P. W. Jackson. *Creativity and intelligence*. New York: Wiley, 1962.

26. Gibson, E. J. *Principles of perceptual learning and development*. New York: Appleton, 1969.

27. Hale, G., L. K. Miller, and H. W. Stevenson. Incidental learning of film content: A developmental study. *Child Development*, 1968, 39, 69–78.

28. Haring, N. G. *Attending and responding*. San Rafael, Calif.: Dimensions Publishing Co., 1968.

29. Janssen, C. Comparative creativity scores of socioeconomic dropouts and non-dropouts. *Psychology in the Schools*. 1968, 5, 183–185.

30. Jeffrey, W. E. Perception, attention, and curiosity. In T. D. Spencer and N. Kass (eds.) *Perspectives in child psychology*. New York: McGraw-Hill, 1970, 75–97.

31. Kagan, J. Impulsive and reflective children: Significance of conceptual tempo. In J. Krumboltz (ed.) *Learning and the educational process*. Chicago: Rand McNally, 1965, 133–161.

32. Kagan, J., and N. Kogan. Individual variation in cognitive processes. In P. Mussen (ed.) *Carmichael's manual of child psychology*. New York: Wiley, 1970, 1273–1365.

33. Kagan, J., L. Pearson, and L. Welch. Modifiability of an impulsive tempo. *Journal of Educational Psychology*, 1966, 57, 359–365.

34. Kagan, J., B. L. Rosman, D. Day, J. Albert, and W. Phillips. Information processing in the child: Significance of analytic and reflective attitudes. *Psychological Monographs*, 1964, 78 (1, Whole No. 578).

35. Kephart, N. C. *The slow learner in the classroom*. Springfield, Ill.: Charles C. Thomas, 1960.

36. Kogan, N. Educational implications of cognitive styles. In G. Lesser (ed.) *Psychology and educational practice*. Glenview, Ill.: Scott, Foresman, 1971, 242–292.

37. Kris, E. *Psychoanalytic explorations in art*. New York: International Universities Press, 1952.

38. Levy, L. H. Originality as role-defined behavior. *Journal of Personality and Social Psychology*. 1968, 9, 72–78.

39. Lichtenwalner, J. S., and J. W. Maxwell. The relationship of birth order and socioeconomic status to the creativity of preschool children. *Child Development*, 1969, 40, 1241–1247.

40. McCandless, B. R. *Children: Behavior and development*. New York: Holt, Rinehart and Winston, 1967.

41. Maltzman, I. On the training of originality. *Psychological Review*, 1960, *67*, 229–242.

42. Messer, S. The effect of anxiety over intellectual performance on reflection-impulsivity in children. *Child Development*, 1970, *41*, 723–735.

43. Messer, S. Reflection-impulsivity: Stability and school failure. *Journal of Educational Psychology*, 1970, *61*, 487–490.

44. Messick, S. The criterion problem in the evaluation of instruction: Assessing possible, not just intended, outcomes. In M. C. Wittrock and D. E. Wiley (eds.) *The evaluation of instruction*. New York: Holt, Rinehart and Winston, 1970, 183–202.

45. Montessori, M. *Dr. Montessori's own handbook*. New York: Stokes, 1914.

46. Myers, R. E., and E. P. Torrance. *The ideabooks*. Lexington, Mass.: Ginn, 1961–1966.

47. Newell, A., J. C. Shaw, and H. A. Simon. The processes of creative thinking. In H. E. Gruber, G. Terrell, and M. Werthermer (eds.) *Contemporary approaches to creative thinking*. New York: Atherton, 1962, 65–66.

48. Osipow, S. Some cognitive aspects of career development. In E. D. Evans (ed.) *Adolescents: Readings in behavior and development*. Hinsdale, Ill.: Dryden, 1970, 224–234.

49. Parloff, M. B., L. Datta, M. Klemen, and J. H. Haudlon. Personality characteristics which differentiate creative male adolescents and adults. *Journal of Personality*, 1968, *36*, 528–552.

50. Parnes, S. J. *Creative behavior guidebook*. New York: Scribner, 1967.

51. Piaget, J. Development and learning. In R. E. Ripple and V. N. Rockcastle (eds.) *Piaget rediscovered*. Ithaca, N. Y.: Cornell University Press, 1964, 7–20.

52. Reese, H. W., and L. P. Lipsitt. *Experimental child psychology*. New York: Academic Press, 1970. (See Chapter 8 for Set; Chapter 9 for Attentional Processes; Chapter 10 for Motivation.)

53. Ridley, D. R., and R. C. Birney. Effects of training procedures on creativity test scores. *Journal of Educational Psychology*, 1967, *58*, 158–164.

54. Rogers, C. *On becoming a person*. Boston: Houghton Mifflin, 1961.

55. Rogers, C. The facilitation of significant learning. In L. Siegal (ed.) *Instruction: Some contemporary viewpoints*. San Francisco: Chandler, 1967, 37–54.

56. Rosenthal, R., and L. Jacobson. *Pygmalion in the classroom: Teacher expectations and pupils' intellectual development*. New York: Holt, Rinehart and Winston, 1968.

57. Rotter, J. B. *Social learning and clinical psychology*. Englewood Cliffs, N. J.: Prentice-Hall, 1954.

58. Sears, P. S. The study of development of creativity: Research problems in parental antecedents. *ERIC: ED 021 279*, 1969.

59. Siegel, A. W., and H. W. Stevenson. Incidental learning: A developmental study. *Child Development*, 1966, *37*, 812–817.

60. Siegelman, E. Reflective and impulsive observing behavior. *Child Development*, 1969, *40*, 1213–1222.

61. Solomon, A. O. A comparative analysis of creative and intelligence behavior of elementary school children with different socio-economic backgrounds. Final progress report. *ERIC: ED 017 022*, 1967, 212 pp.

62. Spector, A. J. Expectations, fulfillment, and morale. *Journal of Abnormal and Social Psychology*, 1956, *52*, 51–56.

63. Staats, A. W. *Learning, language, and cognition: Theory, research, and method for the study of human behavior and its development*. New York: Holt, Rinehart and Winston, 1968.

64. Stein, M. I. Creativity. In E. F. Borgatta and W. W. Lambert (eds.) *Handbook of personality theory and research*. Chicago: Rand McNally, 1968, 900–942.

65. Taft, R., and M. B. Gilchrist. Creative attitudes and creative productivity: A comparison of two aspects of creativity among students. *Journal of Educational Psychology*, 1970, *61*, 136–143 (April).

66. Thorndike, R. L. Review: R. Rosenthal and

L. Jacobson. Pygmalion in the classroom. New York: Holt, Rinehart and Winston, 1968. *American Educational Research Journal*, 1968, *5*, 708–711.

67. Torrance, E. P. Curiosity of gifted children and performance on timed and untimed tests of creativity. *Gifted Child Quarterly 13:* 155–158, Autumn, 1969.

68. Torrance, E. P. *Education and the creative potential.* Minneapolis: University of Minnesota Press, 1963.

69. Torrance, E. P. Stimulation, enjoyment, and originality in dyadic creativity. *Journal of Educational Psychology*, 1971, *62* (1), 45–48.

70. Turner, R. L., and D. Denny. Teacher characteristics, classroom behavior and growth in pupil creativity. *ERIC: ED 011 257*, 1967, 14 pp.

71. Turnure, J. E. Control of orienting behavior in children under five years of age. *Developmental Psychology*, 1971, *4*, 16–24.

72. Walberg, H. J. Varieties of creativity and the social environment of high school. Paper read at meeting of the American Educational Research Association, New York City, 1971 (February).

73. Wallach, M. A. Creativity. In P. Mussen (ed.) *Carmichael's manual of child psychology.* New York: Wiley, 1970, 1211–1272.

74. Weber, W. A. Relationships between teacher behavior and pupil creativity in the elementary school. *ERIC: ED 128 150*, 1968.

75. Williams, F. E. Helping the child develop his creative potential. *ERIC: ED 026 113*, 1968.

76. Wilson, R. Creativity. In *Education for the gifted.* Chicago: University of Chicago Press, 1958, 108–126.

77. Witkin, H. A. Psychological differentiation and forms of pathology. *Journal of Abnormal Psychology*, 1965, *70*, 317–336.

78. Wohlwill, J. Perceptual development. In H. W. Reese and L. P. Lipsitt (eds.) *Experimental child psychology.* New York: Academic, 1970, 363–510.

79. Yando, R., and J. Kagan, The effect of teacher tempo on the child. *Child Development*, 1968, *39*, 27–34.

80. Zahn, J. C. Creativity research and its implications for adult education. *ERIC: ED 011 362*, 1966, 43 pp.

Part III
Social and Personal Development

In the final sections of this book—Chapters 7 through 12—the authors view social and personal areas of human development during the first one-third of the life span.

All human beings must accommodate to their gender, their sexual needs, and their sexual identification as they move from infancy through childhood to maturity. All human beings must eventually assume moral and political stances. All human beings must accommodate themselves to other human beings—older, younger, and same-aged—throughout their life spans. Within the context of human relations, conflict and stress inevitably occur. Through interactions

with others—pleasant, conflictual, and neutral—each child, youth, and older person eventually develops a rather clear picture of "who he is"—he comes to have a quite well-defined self concept.

These social processes of sexual identification, moral and political definition, social relations, ways of handling social conflict and stress, and self-concept development are all quite well set up by the time one is in his early 20s. The learnings that go into human adjustment are infinitely complex, and occur for the most part in two arenas: (1) home and family and (2) school. The first eleven chapters are devoted, directly and indirectly, to the family. Like most modern

227

developmental psychologists, the authors believe they must also deal in detail with the second arena of human development—the school. Thus, the final, long chapter is devoted to children and youth in schools. A range of school experiences from preschool through college is treated, and special school problems that result from being male or female, affluent or poor, and minority or majority affiliated are discussed.

7 Psychosexual Development

Psychosexual development refers to the psychological ways in which one adjusts to his biologically defined sex role and learns his sexuality in the broadest social sense of the term *sexuality*. At maturity, such development can be measured in terms of how one behaves with reference to his gender. Included in the study of psychosexual development are developmental features of sexual and reproductive behavior, attitudes toward sexuality in oneself and others, and attitudes toward one's social sex role, including the pattern of one's interests and often his vocation. In this chapter some major concepts and interpretations of psychosexual development are discussed briefly. Also reviewed is sexual *behavior* as distinguished from the *social aspects* of gender. The chapter concludes with a consideration of some basic dilemmas about sexual behavior, including the question (or perhaps the problem) of sex education as it is related particularly to the nation's schools.

PSYCHOSEXUAL DEVELOPMENT AS PRODUCT AND PROCESS

Like all other aspects of human socialization, psychosexual development is both a product and a process. In the *product* sense, consider terms about people such as heterosexual, homosexual, manly, feminine, promiscuous, and frigid that are used freely in our society. These terms generally refer to a set of responses that characterize a person's social and sexual relationships with others. As a *process*, the authors think of psychosexual development as only one specific category within the broader domain of human socialization—the way in which one acquires psychosexual characteristics. As previously indicated, their preferred frame of reference for viewing socialization processes is one of social learning, behaviorist in type. But important contributions to the study of psychosexual development have come from other points of view, notably the psychoanalytic and cognitive-developmental perspectives.

SEX TYPING AND IDENTIFICATION

The psychological literature concerned with psychosexual development reflects specifically the strong influence of two major concepts, *sex typing* and *identification*. By sex typing is meant the acquisition of behavior associated with the male and the female sex roles at various ages during the course of development. Sex typing can occur consistently with a person's biological gender, or it can occur inconsistently. Regardless, the truth is that wide individual differences in "masculine" or "feminine" behavior exist among members of either sex.

Such individual differences are particularly notable in a complex, industrial society such as ours. For example, few women are "totally feminine," few men are "totally masculine." It seems almost essential for women to possess some attitudes and behaviors commonly considered to be masculine, and vice versa. This overlapping in sex roles appears to be greater in middle- and upper-social-class groups than it is toward the less advantaged end of the social scale, and may well reflect differential educational opportunities. Perhaps because of greater overlapping of interests, marital satisfaction also is often higher in the upper socioeconomic groups (43).

In terms of sexual behavior, most individuals manifest behavior that is directed toward persons of the opposite sex. This, too, reflects a degree of sex typing. However, many individuals find both sexes sexually appealing, and some come to restrict their sexual interests and behavior exclusively (or almost so) to their own sex. Individual differences in sexual preference aside, it is one's sexual orientation (object choice) toward the opposite sex that is the most essential and (in the reproductive sense of normalcy) biologically the normal aspect of adequate sex typing (39).

A second major concept from the literature about psychosexual development is *identification.* A more polymorphous concept than sex typing, identification can be construed in any one of at least three ways

(38). First, identification can be thought of as behavior: When we say someone identifies with another, we are saying that that person behaves like the other person at a high level of generality and abstraction. The behavior may include mannerisms, language habits, values, interests, and even thought processes. Second, identification often refers to a motive. Consciously or unconsciously, a person is moved toward, or wishes to be and usually then becomes like, someone else. This is the sense of the term as most commonly used in psychodynamic theory. The well-adjusted adult has identified with the parent of the same sex; he has, as it were, incorporated within him the father image if male, the mother image if female. Such incorporation, the Freudians say, is essential for the development of true masculinity or femininity, and is also the basis of the superego (loosely, conscience and morality).

Third, identification is a process, "the mechanisms through which the child comes to emulate the model" (38, p. 19). In classical psychoanalytic theory, it is held that identification is typically completed (or has failed) by the time a child is 6 or 7 and has resolved (or failed to resolve) his Oedipal conflict. The authors' own attitude toward sex typing and identification is more that of the social learning theorist who says that "a more adequate conceptualization of personality must deal with man's extraordinary adaptiveness and capacities for discrimination, for self-regulation, and for constructive change as he copes with a changing environment" (38, p. 58). The authors would add that it is also necessary to cope with the aging process: How does one adapt to his own changing, maturing, and eventually declining body? This point of view, of course, is one that is as much humanist as behaviorist (see Chapter 2).

THE ROLE OF SOCIAL STEREOTYPES

It seems to the authors that whether one chooses to focus on either sex typing or identification as a principal concept of psychosexual development, he cannot overlook the impact of social stereotypes on such development. In Chapter 1 a representative set of research evidence (see Example 1.2) about social stereotypes of masculinity and femininity was reviewed (45). This evidence is extremely pertinent to the present discussion. The reader will recall that, according to this evidence, girls and women in United States culture are both expected and desired to be warm, interested in preventing social and family disruption (strong human relations orientation, nurturant, obedient, sweet, and the like). This has been described elsewhere as the *expressive* role expected and valued for women (41).

In sharp contrast is the *instrumental* role expected and valued for the male in United States culture. Independence, physical and psychological toughness, self-sufficiency, and initiative characterize this role. These are characteristics that underlie the notion of competence in a competitive, free-enterprise, industrial, and technical society such as our own. They are *instrumental* characteristics for achieving goals of security recognition and material success.

Sex role stereotypes tend to be global, semantically vague, and difficult to examine empirically; but they are also widely generalized across diverse situations and remarkably persistent in the thinking of individuals throughout our society (38).

The authors believe that such stereotypes clearly affect behavior, in that people often govern and judge their own behavior according to them, and judge and react to others in terms of these stereotypes.

In this sense, sex role stereotypes are related to the concept of *expectancy*, particularly expectancies held for a person by others, as explained in Chapter 6. Differential expectancies seemingly are held for children by their parents as early as infancy, and thereafter influence the course of psychosexual development.

For example, there is much evidence that mothers begin to apply child-rearing techniques differentially by the sex of their children almost literally from birth (2, 20). Mothers of male children cuddle their infants less than do mothers of female children. The authors hasten to add that this is a two-way street, because male babies are generally more active and less cuddly. It may therefore be that the male infant socializes his mother to behave in a way disposed to make him act in stereotypic male fashion, and conversely for a girl baby. In other words, socialization is not simply a matter of one-way parent influence.

Although the influence of sex role stereotypes on socialization practices is evident and is supported by controlled research, the authors wish to point out at least two problems with the general concept. First, it is not difficult to overdramatize the impact of role expectancies as determinants of sex role behavior. There is little question that sex roles are socially defined and pervasive, but their normative properties are not completely consensual in American society. For example, many social analysts believe that black women are more likely than their white counterparts to have "family power" and control over economic resources in the home; women from the middle- and upper-social classes are typically expected to be less subservient than lower-class women; and differences in girls' willingness to "play dumb" in deference to their male suitors are associated with geographic region (13). The point is that sexual differentiation depends upon a complex interplay of biological and social forces, many of which are not yet clearly defined.

A second problem is that social stereotypes such as those that ascribe sex role behaviors have come increasingly under

Humanists and many others believe that too great cleavage in sex roles handicaps both sexes, and suggest that each sex should be encouraged to keep the "best of its traits" while learning the best of those of the opposite sex (a benign unisex). (Photo by James Sudalnik)

attack. This is especially true of many humanistic psychologists who believe that stereotypes for "appropriate" male or female behavior pose an obstacle to personal growth. That is, these ascriptions work to deny girls and women roles of competence, self-esteem and -respect, and social equality. Similarly, they work to deny males freedom for emotional expression, intimate interpersonal relations (particularly with their own sex), and the privilege—or safety valve—of admitting vulnerabilities such as loneliness, fear, and anxiety. This notion is discussed again in the section on Implications and Dilemmas.

WAYS OF VIEWING SEX TYPING AND IDENTIFICATION

Classical Psychoanalytic Theory

As seen in Chapter 2, Sigmund Freud's thought has profoundly affected theories of development and personality. Freud considered sex typing only incidentally, but devoted much attention to identification (17). To oversimplify, he saw two processes in identification, the first a strong dependency and love relation with the mother (anaclitic identification) that begins in infancy and occurs for both boys and girls. This is the only process, or at least the major one, for girls. With age, mother's attention is diverted to some degree from her growing child. The girl develops her conscience or superego to please her mother so as not to lose her love. Boys are thought to seek to recapture the mother and to have sexual fantasies about her. A second factor is threat: The father is a threat—a potential castrator. Through fear of castration, the normal boy eventually makes a defensive identification with his father. He "identifies with

the aggressor." This is analogous to the adage, "If you can't lick them, join them." During his Oedipal, or sexual fantasy, seductive stage, a boy becomes intensely hostile to his father, as well as fearful. The resulting anxiety is so painful that both the sexuality and the aggression are repressed, the Oedipal dilemma is resolved, and the boy becomes like his father and thus appropriately masculine.

Freud postulated a weaker superego for women than for men because of the less harsh process through which girls go to identify. As might be imagined, this theory has entered into social stereotypes about women and is vigorously rejected by the "liberated woman." The authors know of no convincing evidence to support the Freudian thesis of a weaker feminine superego, and they themselves reject the hypothesis.

Cognitive Developmental Theory

Cognitive developmentalists do not agree on how sex role development occurs. Most generally, however, these theorists strongly emphasize the idea that commonly held social stereotypes define what is masculine and what is feminine for almost all members of a culture (25). These stereotypes therefore provide cues for the child who actively selects and organizes his own experience relevant to them. Sex typing begins by the child's being labeled "boy" or "girl." This label, presumably associated with positive interactions in the home, provides the gender identity basis of an "abstract self concept" and is also used to label others (30). Gender identity of sex self concept thereafter serves as both an organizer and a determinant of social attitudes and values. Masculine or feminine values arise from the need to assimilate things that are consistent with gender identity. Hence, as the reader would anticipate, cognitive consistency, or equilibration, is a prominent explanatory concept for the cognitive-developmental approach to sex typing.

According to cognitive developmentalists, sex self concept stabilizes around the beginning of the concrete operational period (see Chapter 2), at which time genuine identification usually takes place. Just as the child now understands that physical properties such as quantity, volume, and weight are invariant, he also understands that his gender identity is invariant. Subsequently, the child assimilates and accommodates important cross-cultural stereotypes of sex-appropriate behavior (stereotypes) that reflect perceptible sex differences in biological structure and function (30).

In short, sex typing may be viewed from a cognitive-developmental perspective as a natural accompaniment of maturation and cognitive development. It is considered to be independent of specific training or organized learning experience. Some degree of observational learning is, of course, essential for sex role acquisition. But the critical factor is the child's own role in the process—a "motivated adaptation" to physical and social reality combined with the need to maintain a positive, stable self-image (30). Unlike the psychoanalytic interpretation, sex typing is seen as the forerunner, rather than the product, of identification.

Combinatory Theory

Many modern personality theorists and developmentalists have attempted to achieve various "mixes" of psychoanalytic and cognitive-based interpretations of sex role identification. As an example, one authority has distinguished between parental identification and sex role identification.

Parental identification is the internalization of personality characteristics of a given parent and . . . unconscious reactions similar to those of the parent . . . (while) sex role identification refers to the internalization of aspects of the role considered appropriate to a given sex and to the unconscious reactions characteristic of that role. (31, pp. 18–19).

According to this view, a child conceivably could identify with a cross-sex parent or not identify at all with a parent, yet identify with the appropriate sex role. However, the authority referred to believes that all the following conditions must be considered in the development of both parental and sex role identification (31). (1) Parental preference (presumably, appropriate parental and sex role identification result from preferring the parent of the same sex). (2) Sex role preference. (Obviously, it is easier to make an identification with the parent of one's own sex and with one's own gender if the girl or the woman prefers being female; and if the boy or the man prefers being male.) (3) Perceived parental similarity ("To what degree am I like my mother or my father?"). (4) Perceived sex role similarity ("I am like other boys or other young or old men," or "I am like other girls or other young or old women"). (5) Parental behavior adoption (behaving like one's mother or father). (6) Sex role adoption (behaving like a boy, a girl, a man, a woman).

The cognitive aspects of this view of identification and sex role development concern sex differences in the actual process *and* outcome of identification. Specifically, it is argued that the girl learning to be a woman (through identifying with her mother and identifying as a female) very directly learns through interacting with and observing her own particular mother, who is constantly with her in the home. The boy, on the other hand, whose father works—thus is not much at home, must go to the broader society and abstract the principles (1) of what *his* father is all about in order to identify with him, and (2) of what masculinity is all about in order to make a male sex role identification. Thus, for girls, parental and sex role identification are "lessons to be learned," while for boys, they are "problems to be solved." Implications about personality are then drawn: the expressivity of women discussed above and the conclusion that girls and women will be inferior in problem-solving skills to boys and men and will also have weaker superegos. The converse will be true for boys and men who, while "solving their problem" of identifying with their fathers and identifying with males, also learn the instrumental masculine social role and will at the same time become superior to girls and women in problem-solving and conscience development.

These contentions have yet to be proved, although admittedly the rationale for them is provocative and insightful. Meanwhile, the authors are inclined toward a simpler or a narrower view of sex role and identification based on behavior principles. Indeed, they are not even sure about the value of the concepts—sex role typing and identification—with their related network of assumptions and theoretical explanations.

Behavioral Theory

The authors favor a behavioristic interpretation of sex role development based on principles of modeling and reinforcement. Children very early learn their gender and what is expected of, and valued for, people of that gender. Rewards and punishments seem to be given in about even mixture to boys who develop congruently with the male sex role stereotype held within a given culture (sex role stereotypes vary widely from one culture to another); that is, they are punished when they act girlishly, rewarded when they act boyishly. The nature of the punishments varies (35, 36). They may range from severe parental and particularly paternal discipline or criticism for "sissy" behavior through to self-correction: "This is how boys should behave. This is how I behaved. My behavior does not fit what is expected of, and valued in, boys. Thus, I should not behave this way again." It is obvious to the reader that this sort of "self-correction" is akin to cognitive-consistency theory held by cognitive developmentalists. The concept of incidental learning as discussed in Chapter 6 is also relevant to a behavioral interpretation of sex role development.

Rewards to boys for being masculine are plentiful, particularly (it seems) from their fathers and their masculine peers. However, the instrumental role for boys often leads to nonconformity, disobedience, and classroom discipline problems. Thus, it is often discouraged in schools, even as early as the nursery school years. Example 7.1 is an example of how teachers encourage stereotypic feminine behaviors in both boys and girls while discouraging stereotypic male behavior (14). However, it is also seen how the male peer group rewards boys for their masculinity, while inoculating them against the effects of teachers' rewards for "feminine" type behavior.

7.1 Sex Role Behavior in the Nursery School

In this study, the authors tested three hypotheses.

1. Sex differences in play behavior exist among 3-year-old children.
2. Female nursery school teachers reinforce feminine behaviors for all children, regardless of their sex.
3. Like sex peers reinforce each other in appropriate sex role behavior.

The authors of the study observed reliably and extensively in two nursery schools, and developed a sex role behavior checklist. Items that were clearly preferred by boys in both nursery schools were block-building and transportation toys. In both nursery schools, more girls than boys preferred painting and artwork. The authors also classified the consequences of children's activities according to the following ten categories. (1) The teacher initiates a new behavior after the child starts his activity. (2) The teacher comments favorably. (3) The teacher joins in the activity. (4) The teacher criticizes. (5) The child imitates another child. (6) The child joins another child in parallel play (doing the same thing, but not necessarily interacting in any cooperative way). (7) The child joins another child in interactive play. (8) The child stands and watches another child. (9) The child continues alone. (10) The child criticizes another child.

Overwhelmingly, children engaged in the preferred activities for their sex. Girls, for example, spent less than 8 percent of their time in "boyish" activities, boys 13.5 percent of their time in "girlish" activities.

When a tally was made of how often the four women teachers in the two nursery schools rewarded children for sex-preferred activities, 232 instances were found for boys, and, of these, 199 of the reinforcements were for feminine behaviors. In the case of girls, there were 363 rewards for sex-preferred activities. Of these, 353 were for feminine activities. Thus, the teachers were *rewarding both boys and girls* for doing things found to be "feminine" in nature. "Teachers are reinforcing both sexes for the same behaviors — feminine. Feminine-preferred behaviors constituted 83 percent of the sex-preferred behaviors that received positive teacher reinforcement (comment favorably, initiate, or join behavior)." (35, p. 566)

However, the boys did not become more feminine during the school year. The reason for this seems to lie within the peer group. Boys reinforced other boys a total of 359 times during the observation periods, but reinforced girls only 71 times. Girls reinforced other girls a total of 463 times, but reinforced boys only 63 times.

Of the children who were observed for this study, one boy was decidedly feminine in his play activities. His peers criticized him more than any other child in the schools (14 percent of the time compared with an average 1 percent of the time for other children), and played with him less (7 percent of the time compared with an average of 21 percent of the time with other boys).

In this study, we see the active role played by the peer group in maintaining "appropriate sex role behavior," to the degree that, for the boys, the peer group overrode the influence of the teachers. In the case of the one different child, peer reinforcements seemed to be consolidating his differences, even though the teachers did not differ in their behavior toward him from the way they acted toward other boys.

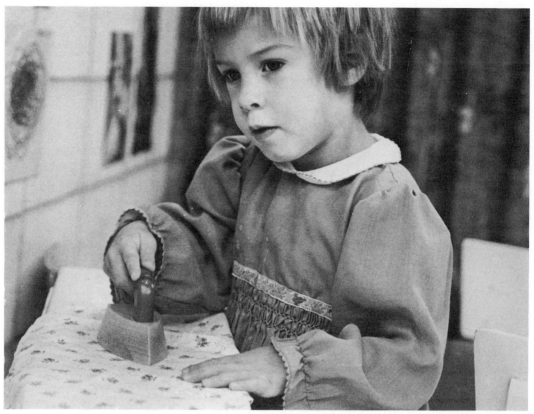

The introduction of "sex appropriate" toys into the child's life plays an important early role — for better or worse — in the socialization of sex identification. (Photo by Lynn McLaren)

Girls apparently learn feminine stereotypic "sex role appropriate" behavior principally through rewards, probably from fathers more than mothers, and certainly from girl peers, teachers, and, at least by adolescence, from male peers. The evidence is plentiful that girls are not punished for boyish behavior to the degree that boys are punished for girlish behavior. Thus, it can be predicted (and evidence supports the prediction) that girls do not identify with their gender role as early and perhaps not as firmly as boys. As might be expected (and some evidence supports the expectation), they *do* identify with their sex role more congruently than boys, perhaps because their learning occurs more through reward and less through punishment. The evidence to support this is normative and consists mainly of the fact that there appear to be fewer women than men who misidentify in their sex role. That is, there are fewer women homosexuals, transvestites, and transsexuals. On the other hand, this normative state of affairs conceivably results from the greater activity and tendency to explore that exists among boys and men, for whatever reasons. Learning seems to play a more important role in shaping the sexual behavior of males (16).

From a very early age, children learn to imitate. Imitation is a helpful way of learning to solve problems and to secure information. It is often rewarded ("You're just like your mother—or your father," a comment that is typically given as a compliment). More directly, behaving like a model often obtains for you the same rewards it obtained for your model. Other things being equal, imitation or modeling is greatest for models (1) who are like you (are perceived to be similar, as mothers and other girls are for girls, fathers and other boys are for boys); (2) who possess characteristics you desire (a favorite teacher, or, for girls, the most popular girl in the class); (3) who have rewarded you in the past (warm and loving fathers for boys, warm and loving mothers for girls); (4) who are accessible and thus provide ample opportunity for personal association; and (5) who are powerful (that is, who control the things you want, or who have the capacity for one reason or another to punish you effectively). Obviously, for most children, parents possess much power. Parents are physically big, control many resources that children want, usually demonstrate expertise in various important aspects of life, and are sources of needed affection and recognition for children. The authors believe that because of these factors, parents are generally powerful models for their children, especially parents who are nurturant and competent in dealing with younger children. Similarly, older siblings, peers, and other adults (teachers, athletes, clergymen, and the like) all possess characteristics on which children and youth model as they develop and mature.

In summary, the authors believe that at the present state of our knowledge, identification and sex typing can appropriately be likened to *generalized imitation* (19). That is, the learned tendency to imitate across a wide variety of situations can be extended to the development of "maleness" or "femaleness." Maleness and femaleness are conceptions of social behavior, attitudes, and interests as much as they are of gender and sexual behavior. It must be added, however, that much remains to be learned about this very complex aspect of human behavior. For example, at least some research suggests that *generalized imitation* is neither a powerful nor a valid enough concept to account for gender identification in human learning and development (19, 57). Meanwhile, the concept appears promising to us in terms of guiding further investigation.

SOME GENERALIZATIONS FROM SEX TYPING AND IDENTIFICATION RESEARCH

In this section are presented seven generalizations in the form of tentative conclusions that have emerged from the research on sex typing and identification. These conclusions come from a variety of sources. Interested readers will wish to consult these references for more detailed information: (5, 7, 9, 21, 22, 23, 24, 36, 38, 51, 55).

Briefly, the conclusions follow, in approximately the order of the firmness of the findings.

First, both an awareness and a manifestation of "sex appropriate" behavior are apparent among children as early as age 3, and most certainly by nearly all children by age 5. In fact, some authorities have suggested that the first two years of life represent a "critical period" in sex typing. Boys, especially, express very early and clear preferences for masculine toys, games, activities, and same-sex peers.

Second, boys are more clearly affected by father absence; the earlier in a boy's life his father leaves the home, the more likely will the boy's development be affected adversely. Specifically, when there has been reasonably prolonged father absence, boys are less efficient in school and do not show as advanced moral judgment. Boys with fathers absent also more often demonstrate "feminine cognitive development" in that they score higher for verbal than quantitative intelligence (see Chapter 5).

Girls with fathers present are more evenly balanced cognitively. Their quantitative intelligence scores are closer to the same level as their verbal intelligence scores than is true for father-absent girls. Father-absent girls are also reported to be either extremely shy heterosexually or inclined toward overeagerness in their courting behavior. When very young, father-absent boys seem to be rather feminine in their attitudes and behavior, but there is no clear evidence, for example, that being without a father is more likely to result in a boy's having a homosexual adjustment. On the whole, for both sexes but more clearly for boys, social adjustment is better when fathers are in the home. Of course, this may not be directly related to the father per se, but simply to the fact that life is likely to be more difficult in homes where only one parent is present. So few homes are without a mother or mother surrogate that we have no data about what mother absence does to the psychosexual and other social development patterns of children. However, it appears that boys from fatherless homes whose mothers are competent and strong and who like men will develop normally psychosexually.

Third, children and young people with appropriate sex role typing and identification seem on the whole to have better self concepts than those with less appropriate sex typing. There is evidence on both sides about the personal–social adjustment of young men and young women who are openly homosexual in their sexual preferences. Apparently, those who are functioning reasonably successfully vocationally in the open society (that is, who are self-determining and not in psychiatric care) are neither better nor worse adjusted than comparison groups that are heterosexual.

A fourth generalization is that parental warmth and power are both important in determining parental identification. It seems ideal for children's psychosexual development for the parent of the same sex to possess qualities of both warmth and power, although the evidence is clearer for boys than for girls. Boys identify maximally with fathers (and here the evidence is clear) who are loving toward them and who are also powerful in the sense that they exert leadership roles in their marriage and family situations.

Fifth, girls whose mothers identify with them (who are informed about their daughters' interests) identify more closely with their mothers than girls whose mothers are unaware of their interests. At the college level, girls who identify with their fathers seem to be at least as well and perhaps better adjusted than those who identify with their mothers. It is thought that the most competent girls are those who are moderately distant from their mothers, but reasonably close to their fathers. The most competent boys are moderately distant from their mothers but by no means estranged, and close to, but also rather firmly disciplined by, their fathers (who evince warmth toward them but are not nurturant and overprotective).

A sixth generalization concerns the differentiation by sex of general behavior patterns. Much research about such sex differences has been centered on aggressive and dependent behavior. The former *dependent* is considered to characterize males, the latter females. No really solid evidence has accumulated, however, to indicate that there are general traits of aggressiveness or dependency. Girls, for example, usually show more prosocial aggression than boys (that is, they hit less and in general show less physical aggression, but are equally or more verbally aggressive in the sense of saying, "That is not a nice thing to do"). However, when anonymity is guaranteed, these differences partially disappear, and girls are as capable as boys of meting out aggressive consequences such as administering electric shocks to others in laboratory experiments.

It is important also to note that boys, girls, young men, and young women are more reluctant to aggress toward females than toward males, when the aggression takes the form of administering electric shock. (It should be noted that in almost all studies such as this, the apparatus is rigged so that, while the subject thinks he is administering electric shock, nothing is actually happening to the "victim".)

Seventh and finally, appropriate sex role behaviors are more *consistent* than inappropriate sex role behaviors. For example, aggressive little boys are likely also to be aggressive as young men, dependent little girls still dependent when they grow into young women. But there is no absolute relation between being a dependent

little boy and later a dependent young man, or an aggressive little girl and later an aggressive young woman. This notion is related to the concepts of stability of behavior and discontinuities in development discussed earlier in this book.

IMPLICATIONS AND DILEMMAS

The area of sex typing and identification is, of course, social dynamite. Research into homosexuality, transvestism, and transsexualism was included among the taboo topics discussed in Chapter 3. Yet most of us are acquainted with persons who have one or another of these adjustments. Some of our most constructive citizens and some of history's outstanding figures have not been conventional in terms of sexual interests and activities. Many have suffered social ostracism because of their adjustment. The authors believe that legal sanctions exist in most of the United States against homosexual transactions between males, regardless of the circumstances or the age of the participants.

Being sexually different, particularly when the object of one's interest is his own sex is, then, at the very least inconveniencing and typically illegal. A child-rearing, educational, and legal dilemma, then, is related to the child-rearing practices that produce children, youth, and adults with "different" sexual adjustments. Once such different adjustments are manifested, what does one do? Certainly, the different child, youth, or adult is not to be cast into limbo. Expulsion from school, parental rejection, and prison are certainly neither humane nor effective "therapies." Deep social change will be needed if the homosexual, transvestite, or transsexual is to be given his or her matter-of-fact place as an equal and a respected person in society.

A second issue concerns the perpetuation of the "appropriate sex role stereotype." It was suggested earlier that such stereotypes perhaps operate so as to deny girls and women opportunities to become competent and boys and men opportunities to express themselves or to enjoy to the fullest interpersonal, emotional relations. Should these stereotypes be altered, expanded, or broken down completely? Students in classes of the authors have often agreed that they should. Appealing as the idea may be, any success in doing so may well depend on the degree to which stereotypes are social implementations designed to accommodate male–female biological differences. For example, in an overwhelming majority of cultures, boys are more likely to be involved in overt aggression and conflict with others; males in most all cultures have greater authority and execute the more physically demanding, risky tasks (12). In a word, the *instrumental* role of males is a near-cultural universal. Similarly, girls in most cultures are more likely to be nurturant, sociable, and responsive to others, characteristics relevant to the *expressive* role discussed earlier in this chapter. This is most certainly not to say that what *is* is what *should be*.

Despite these regularities, it is difficult to argue that sex role differences arise directly from biological givens (39). Striking exceptions to these regularities have been observed (see Example 7.2). Yet the strong hormonal and other physiological factors that differentiate the sexes seem sufficiently implicated in sex role differences that it is unrealistic to deny them. Perhaps what is needed is a greater appreciation of and respect for sex differences, coupled with a relaxation of rigid

guidelines for the socialization of sex role behavior, particularly those only remotely related to biological factors.

Still another dilemma concerns what to do about a system of formal schooling that

Recent social movements, coupled with changing technological and economic structures of the society, may lead toward a breakdown—or at least a diminution—of traditional sex-role stereotypes. (Photo by Bonnie Freer)

seems more tailored to the needs and life styles of girls than to those of boys. In fact, the charge that schools are designed, intentionally or not, to feminize children and youth is not infrequently heard. Early education environments are especially vulnerable to this charge, operated as they are almost exclusively by women. And as has been seen (Example 7.1), girls seem to receive preferential treatment. In study after study, it is reported that boys are perceived more negatively by their female teachers, are criticized more frequently by them, and usually perform less well in school (perhaps as a direct result of these factors) (15). The source of this problem may be not so much female teachers as it is the very nature of the formal classroom per se. Nevertheless, the past and the current state of affairs concerning this problem is unsettling to many parents and professionals.

Among the most common strategies designed to ameliorate these conditions, recommended by concerned parents and professionals, is to bring more men teachers into day care and elementary school settings. Another recommendation suggests placing male adolescents in day care centers or in nursery schools, to serve as caretakers and as teacher aides. Both ideas are promising, yet the recruitment problem is staggering. Men are not easily attracted to work with young children, nor, without extensive training, are they often skilled in the nurturance and unique communication abilities so essential in working with infants, pre-schoolers, and primary grade children.

A final dilemma to be discussed here concerns the validity of the identification concept for teachers and other child–youth workers. Theoretically, it could be argued that effective learning can be facilitated through a student's identification

with a teacher. That is, assuming that the teacher is himself a "good learner," he can serve as a model for identification and thus promote better academic behavior among those who identify with him. This is a plausible idea and the conditions cited earlier concerning what promotes parental identification conceivably also apply to teachers as well. Yet this idea has not yet been provided with firm research support. Moreover, it poses an immense research problem; namely, measuring strength of identification between a student and his teacher. At the very least, the authors believe that the kind of behavior a teacher or a child–youth worker models for his charges is critical, whether or not identification occurs. Especially significant is the importance of congruity between what an adult model does and what he says, together with expectations for student behavior that neither convey a lack of confidence nor represent unrealistic demands.

SEXUAL BEHAVIOR

Physical growth obviously occurs also for the reproductive system. Up to this point in this chapter, the psychological accompaniments of such growth have been discussed. As the authors have said, these are strongly influenced by culture; for example, what is considered masculine in one culture is not necessarily considered masculine in another. The liberated woman of the 1970s, currently quite well accepted, might well have been run out of town in 1900. Certainly, her behavior would not have been considered desirable within the acceptable range of feminine behaviors. However, we have also seen that stereotypes about sex role appropriate behavior are remarkably widespread among both men and women, that men and women agree with each other about what is masculine and what is feminine, that stereotypes hold tenaciously, and that they influence behavior.

Less subject to cultural influence are what one author has called psychobiological sexual development (1). Regardless of a youth's culture, he must make certain behavioral adjustments to increased size and strength, to maturation of primary and secondary sex characteristics, and to the biological rhythms and pressures that follow puberty (as in the menstrual cycle for girls and the insistent pressure toward sexual outlet for boys, with attendant erections, wet dreams, masturbation, and heterosexual and other sexual explorations).

In one way or another, sometimes freely and openly, sometimes covertly and in a suppressed and secret way, all forms of human social organization provide for sexual behavior. We will turn now to the topic of sexual behavior. How do children, youth, and adults accommodate to the procreative drive in terms of their behavior?

Put another way, into terminology that fits the authors' theoretical frame of reference more closely: With age, children become youth, and from pubescence onward, the state of the organism is such that sexual reinforcers operate in a very different way from that for prepubescent children. Different sexual reinforcers are sought, although prepubescent children often engage in much sexual behavior.

Biological Aspects of Sexuality

In the discussion of biological sex, both the structure and the function of sex must be included. First, how do we define maleness and femaleness biologically? At least five factors are involved (8):

1. Chromosomal composition (XX in the female, XY in the male).
2. Composition of the gonads (ovarian tissue for females, testicular tissue for males).
3. Hormonal composition (the estrogen–androgen balance, estrogens being the female hormone, androgens the male hormone).
4. Internal accessory structure (vagina, uterus, ovaries, and fallopian tubes for females, seminal vesicles and prostate for males).
5. External genitalia (clitoris — internal and external — and labia for females, penis and scrotum containing testicles for males).

Additional male–female differences include size, body conformation, distribution and ratio of fatty and muscular tissue, distribution and amount of body hair, and so on. For normal people, a congruence of all these factors results in clear biological maleness and femaleness so that a glance at an individual (with or without clothing) clearly tells the observer the gender.

Three other genetically controlled reflexive functions of the neuromuscular system accompany maleness and femaleness (26). The first is the capacity for tumescence. For example, complete male genital erection is possible during the neonatal period. This reaction may accompany bladder distention or may result from penile manipulation.

A second reflex component in sexual behavior is orgasm and ejaculation. According to the Kinsey data, orgasm (sexual climax) can be produced in human infants of either sex. However, ejaculatory power in the male is not acquired until puberty, and the production of normal sperm (or eggs in the case of females) is often delayed until later in the cycle of pubescence. For the sexually mature male, orgasm and ejaculation occur together; for females, orgasm is not accompanied by the ejaculation of any sort of fluid.

Finally, the capacity for rhythmic, pelvic thrusts is a neuromuscular component of sexual behavior that facilitates the mating act.

If one considers the total cluster of biological components of sexuality, it is apparent that different segments of sexual behavior mature at different rates. Aside from the possible influence of nutrition, there is little to indicate that environmental factors have much effect on sexual maturation rate. As has been said, apart from biological underpinnings of sexual behavior, it seems clear that the form of sexual expression is heavily, if not completely, determined by learning. In this connection, it should be noted that learning the forms of sexual expression is inseparably linked to learning of sex roles and sexual identity discussed earlier in this chapter.

Furthermore, while puberty dramatizes an individual's sexuality and, for most persons in United States society, marks the beginning of mature sexual behavior, the authors believe that sexuality is a product of cumulative development. It is not something suddenly achieved with puberty, the first orgasm, or the first sexual liaison. Sexuality, it seems to them, is determined strongly by one's attitudes toward himself and others. Nor does it seem to the authors that sexuality is something separate from a person's total personality. That is, with the possible exception of sexual pathology, sexual expression usually will reflect an individual's prevailing personality characteristics. For example, a male who is generally aggressive, hostile, and inconsiderate toward others will likely be aggressive, hostile, and inconsiderate in his sexual relations. Similarly, a passive, dependent, and anxious male is likely to manifest this general social orientation when engaged in the sexual act. In short, sexuality is but one aspect of socialization.

Cultural Variations in Sexual Behavior

No one seriously questions the universality of psychosexual development or the power of sexual motivation as a source of energy for a wide range of human behavior. But the form and the tempo of sexual development and behavior vary greatly within and between cultures. So do the style and the frequency of sexual practices, marital or otherwise, and the degree of tolerance for sexual "deviation" (16, 33). The wide cross-cultural variation in sexual practices strikingly indicates the influence of social factors, or cultural learning, on sexual behavior and attitudes. This variation illustrates both the malleability of human behavior and the power of social influences to mediate a basic human drive (54).

To illustrate this variation and its significance, the authors have drawn on anthropological studies of sexual behavior. In one of the classic anthropological analyses of such behavior, societies have been arranged along a continuum of restrictiveness–permissiveness about sexual practices and the socialization of sexual behavior (16). In extremely restrictive societies, for example, ultrasecretive and limited sexual contact usually occurs between adults; young children and adolescents are denied access to sexual knowledge and are prevented from expressing sexual interests in any form. Methods of enforcement for this restriction may include strict segregation of the sexes until marriage, continuous adult chaperonage of girls, and threats of severe disgrace, physical punishment, or even death (16).

In contrast, other societies take a permissive approach to sexuality. Sex play among children and adolescents may occur in public, apparently in the absence of adult sanctions. Children are not restricted from observing adult sexual activity in the home, and may even be sexually stimulated by their parents or caregivers through masturbation (16). The point is that, in addition to wide variation in sexual practices, widely different beliefs (even superstitions) usually underlie punitive or tolerant approaches to this aspect of human behavior. Belief in a malevolent god and fear of social retribution are often associated with restrictiveness. Where open sexuality among the young is encouraged, beliefs include the notion that children must exercise themselves sexually early in life in order to achieve fertility or that girls will not mature without benefit of sexual intercourse (16). In still other cultures (for example, the Turu in Tanzania), a system of adultery for adults, which has tenuous support by law, is supported to make romantic love possible without endangering the institution of marriage (46). Thus, one cannot overlook institutionalized legality in determining what things facilitate or inhibit sexual behavior.

Cross-Cultural Regularities

While cross-cultural variation in sexual behavior obviously affects sexual attitudes and behavior, it is important also to note certain regularities surrounding sex and marriage from culture to culture. These regularities illustrate the controls that cultures find necessary for economic and ecological survival. No culture is without laws, both written and "unwritten" (sometimes unenforceable and unen-

forced), that pertain to sexuality, regardless of how permissive or how restrictive the culture may be. For example, sanctions against incest, rape, and sexual relations between adults and children exist in virtually every organized society (33).

Values apparently related to preservation of the family unit, personal hygiene, and the control of property are reflected in still other cross-cultural regularities. For example, one authority reports such universals as the general expectation (or at least preference) that mothers should be married; that marriage is not undertaken for a specified, short-term period; that mothers should live in the same domicile as their children; and that sexual intercourse should not occur during the menstrual period (52). Such universals or near universals suggest that even in the face of marked cultural diversity, there are some regularities in human existence that govern family life and sexual behavior. While every society must exercise control of sexual behavior that is disruptive, clearly such control is achieved in a variety of ways. Example 7.2 contains an outline of the range in sexual roles provided by different cultures and can serve to summarize much of what has been said (37).

7.2 Sexual Roles in Cultural Perspective

1. The role of wife and mother is the most common in United States culture. Indeed, it is the "normal" function. Preparing for and achieving this role is at this time seemingly a major preoccupation of adolescent girls of all social classes and ethnic backgrounds in the United States. It is the career of the married female who will bear and care for children. Though normal and desired,

it is viewed with mixed emotions by many women, as indicated by the frequent response to a question about occupation—a sigh and "I'm just a housewife."

2. The role of the adult male who will beget and provide for his children is modal for males, but, according to recent studies, less a preoccupation among adolescent boys than is wifehood and motherhood among girls.

3. The third role is that of the adult male who will not marry or beget children, but who will exercise some sort of prescribed social function. Across cultures, such functions may be celibacy with or without religious connotation, sexual abstinence, renunciation of procreation, specialized forms of ceremonial sexual license (such as have been described in tribal life, most particularly for religious leaders such as witch doctors), or exemption from social restrictions placed on other men.

4. Many adult females neither marry nor produce children, but are accorded status in a religious context, for example, nuns. Other roles may be ceremonial prostitution. The spinster, the bachelor girl, or the old maid is a recognized minority in our culture.

5. In some cultures, adult males assume institutionalized female roles, including transvestism, where such an adult sexual career is open only to males. This role was not uncommon for actors in early Grecian society.

6. In some societies, females assume male roles, including transvestism, where such a career is open only to females.

7. In other cultures, nonprocreative ceremonial roles are important. These may involve transvestism and adoption of the behavior of the opposite sex; in such cases, genital construction is ignored or denied. Margaret Mead gives interesting accounts of selecting *shamans* or *berdache* among the American Indians and training them for their roles.

8. There are some sexually mutilated persons. The mutilation may be congenital or socially created, as it has been through the centuries for eunuchs and at times in history for boy sopranos. In such cases, society clearly expects nonmarriage and nonparenthood and allows a relaxation of the ordinary relations between the sexes.

9. Professional or commercial prostitution is recognized in a very large number of societies. In the United States, commercial prostitution is practiced more frequently by women than by men, although cases of male prostitutes are by no means uncommon in this country, and are frequent in others.

10. A role that is presumably rare in the United States is zoolagnia, or sexual preference for an animal. Pornographic movies frequently are concerned with such sexual interactions (37). In most cultures, chronological age is differentially related to expectations for sexual behavior. Homoerotic behavior of adolescents is forbidden in this culture, but it is openly expected in other cultures. Elderly heads of households may be expected to withdraw entirely from an active sexual role. In many societies (rather openly for males in this culture, increasingly openly perhaps for females) a period of license is allowed before marriage, but chastity after marriage is expected. The reverse may be true in other cultures. In some cultures, widows are not expected to remarry or to indulge in further sex relations of any kind.

ADOLESCENT SEXUALITY IN UNITED STATES CULTURE

The sex drive and its psychological accompaniments (or the new state of the organism and its new reinforcers) unquestionably act as major forces on behavior during adolescence. However, sexual behavior is not unique to the time of puberty and the years that follow it. Sex interest and sex play are common among preschoolers and preadolescents. Boys and girls exhibit to each other, within and across sexes. Doctor–nurse games, such as the one mentioned in Chapter 3, often result in mutual genital inspection. "Peepee places," to use one version of the term, are much talked of and looked at. Preadolescents are fascinated with nudity and peeping. Males especially incorporate sex-related slang words and jokes into their repertoire within and often outside the peer group.

The motivational basis (or reinforcing basis) for prepubescent sexuality, however, seems to be curiosity rather than the more mature form of reinforcer such as an orgasm or romantic love (1). To be sure, some preadolescents, probably more girls than boys, engage in sexual intercourse, usually initiated by adults, although their behavior is not typically a search for sexual gratification (18).

Age Trends and Sex Differences in Adolescent Sexuality

As they move into later adolescence, more young people engage in some form of sexual activity — masturbation, heterosexual petting, and intercourse. Although percentage figures vary according to sampling procedures, most surveys indicate that almost all adolescent males masturbate at some time during adolescence. Their average number of outlets is somewhere between two and three a week (26). Masturbation among adolescent females is apparently less frequent and widespread. About 60 percent of adolescent girls admit to masturbation and about one-half of these masturbate only after having experienced orgasm in situations involving others. It is not until the late 20s that the incidence of orgasm for females, through masturbation or other means, typically reaches the frequency that it does for males at age 16 (49). Regardless, using a statistical concept of normality (see Chapter 3), masturbation during adolescence cannot be considered anything but normal.

Sex differences in sexual outlet are also reflected in the incidence of premarital intercourse. Roughly 85 percent of adolescent males admit to intercourse before marriage with at least one partner, whereas about 50 percent of females so report. These percentage figures vary according to social class. A greater incidence of premarital intercourse is found among adolescents from lower socioeconomic backgrounds (43). The typical lower-class adolescent of either sex also experiences intercourse at an earlier age than does his middle-class counterpart. In the case of the lower-class male, intercourse is more likely than masturbation as a major sex outlet. Intercourse for such males occurs more frequently and with more partners than for the average middle-class male. This difference is commonly explained in terms of the greater value placed on "manliness" and masculine status accorded by exploitative sexual conquests (18).

It may be that the male youth who is the son of poor and ill-educated parents has few other ways to prove his worth than by showing that he is a man with a penis that, as it were, triumphs over all and thus proves his importance. Young males from homes where parents have more money and are better educated may have learned that there are other ways of asserting their importance, both as persons and as males. Whatever the reasons may be, disadvantaged youth seem to be less inhibited about sexual contact than advantaged youth.

Other sex differences in adolescent sexuality have also been reported (50). For example, in their sexual relations, males are more easily and frequently aroused solely for physical gratification as compared with love expression. In contrast, females are generally more concerned and satisfied with the romantic aspect of love making and usually demonstrate a less erotic sexual orientation than males. Reactions to pornographic film content also vary by sex. In one study, for example, both males and females reported comparable arousal levels after viewing a film depicting sexual intercourse, but males were aroused more and females less by a film depicting oral–genital sex (32).

Significance of Sex Differences in Adolescent Sexuality

The consistency with which sex differences in attitudes and behavior concerning sexual expression have been found suggests a basic difference in male and female orientation during sexual development (18). In general, males begin their sexual lives earlier, often with masturbation. This private self-gratification may foster a detached kind of sexuality, even when self-gratification is accompanied by elaborate fantasies. Masturbatory activity is an activity whose principal reinforcement is physical. The sexual commitment is almost entirely genital. It

is from this private, physical commitment that the male must move toward a broader sociosexual orientation—one in which a commitment to romantic love is made. This necessitates training in the language and actions of romantic love and the ability to deal appropriately with the emotional aspects of a genuine heterosexual relationship.

For females, the pattern is usually reversed. Girls seem to be better and earlier trained for a commitment to and capacity for romantic love and the subtleties of emotion that lead to strong heterosexual attachments. For females, sexual experience, including orgasm, is more likely to occur first in the context of a relatively stable love relationship. Thus for many, perhaps most, females, commitment to sexuality begins on a sociosexual foundation. The typical girl will more often continue to seek the romantic qualities of heterosexual affiliation, whereas the male continues to seek the erotic and the physical. It is no wonder that heterosexual involvements, particularly those which occur early in adolescence, are often marked by conflict, misunderstanding, and disappointment. But the importance of developing a healthy sociosexuality can hardly be overestimated in view of its importance for family formation, adult roles and obligations, and self-definition (49). This point is again considered in Chapter 11. It should be added that this clear sex difference in seeking physical sexual gratification may be disappearing; the data are not yet in.

Socialization Practices and Adolescent Sexuality

Little is known about the nature and the effects of socialization of adolescent sexual behavior and attitudes. Clearly, sexual problems often accompany personal maladjustment during adolescence and beyond, but what contributes to such maladjustment can rarely be stated precisely. Possibly, sexual problems are more frequently a symptom rather than a cause of maladjustment. It is not unreasonable to postulate a relationship between childhood socialization practices and adolescent sexual beliefs and attitudes. For example, attitudes toward sexuality revealed in parental behavior concerning nudity in the home, responsiveness to children's questions about sex and childbirth, children's masturbatory behavior, and the like, are sure to affect the sexual outlook of the growing child. Yet sufficient evidence cannot be marshaled to indicate how extensive the effects may be.

In one of the few studies of sex and modesty training in United States families, a large group of mothers from middle and low socioeconomic households indicated four basic short-term goals. Each of their goals suggests avoiding rather than facilitating accurate sexual orientation. The mothers' goals seem to be: (1) internalization of the incest taboo, (2) training to avoid masturbation, (3) training to avoid heterosexual sex play, and (4) information control (47). In general, mothers strongly disapproved of sexuality in their children, but few indicated that they regularly punished in order to restrict sexual activity. Where punitive measures were taken, they were more often applied in lower-class homes than in middle-class homes.

If such sex-training practices are an indication of a general approach to sex and modesty training in United States culture, at least two points can be made. First, such disapproval of sexuality (however tacit it may be) and emphasis on delimiting sexual activity in children suggest a generally restrictive approach to sexuality in American society. Second, such data highlight the discontinuity in socialization concerning sex in this culture. The authors know of few parents who seriously and consciously intend to deter their children from attaining the goal of a successful adult sex life. Yet in the early stages of socialization, most parents seem to expect their children to be asexual

A child's attitudes and understandings about sex begin to form very early in life. Parents vary widely in their ability to deal with their children's curiosity about this fascinating topic. (Niépce-Rapho Guillumette)

and discourage any overt sign of sexuality. This restrictiveness is replaced with the often subtle, yet powerful, encouragement of heterosexual relations during adolescence as a preparation for marriage. Thus, an about-face in socialization occurs precisely at the time when sexual urges are intensifying.

The dilemma for the student of human development, of course, is whether such discontinuity interferes in any way with satisfaction of adult sexual relations; again, the evidence is indirect and fuzzy. As an example, one authority reports that the reason most frequently given by men for unsatisfying marital sex relations is that their wives are too inhibited sexually. Women complain about dissatisfaction with sex in marriage because of their husbands' lack of sensitivity and concern for general romance and sexual foreplay (26, 27).

It is possible that restrictiveness and discontinuities in socialization are somehow implicated in such reports. The authors do not presume to suggest, however, that a continuing, permissive approach to the socialization of sexual behavior in United States culture is necessarily good or even possible. Tacit or active approval of childhood and adolescent heterosexual behavior can conceivably have profoundly adverse ramifications for individuals and for society. For example, the easy availability of birth control techniques has never deterred the frequency of paternity during adolescence, nor has access to prophylaxis had much impact on the incidence of venereal disease among adolescents (53). The point is that a change in orientation toward premarital sexual activity needs to be examined carefully in the light of our unique cultural framework and the broader spectrum of values around which American life is organized.

For example, does easy, early sex gratification reduce the need for fantasy and dreaming, and thus reduce the value of people of the opposite sex as *people?* What effect does early, easy, frequent sex gratification have on the achievement motive (that is, many people work and achieve in order to be able to marry and support a family)?

Psychological Impact of Adolescent Sexual Behavior

Sexual behavior among adolescents is often accompanied by and results in intense emotions, some pleasant (for example, excitement, a sense of fulfillment, and joy) and some unpleasant (for example, fear, guilt, and hostility). The nature of the emotional experience associated with sexual outlets depends on an individual's attitudes, expectations, and current motivations. It is the rare adolescent who does not frequently experience ambivalence about the form of his or her sexual expression, whether masturbation, petting to climax, or actual coitus. In some cases, the possible negative consequences of coitus—venereal disease, pregnancy, loss of one's "reputation" if discovered, and guilt over violating an internalized moral standard—may inhibit sexual behavior altogether or limit sexual satisfaction. As suggested, this reaction currently seems more likely to occur among females than among males. This notion is buttressed by the fact that few males express regret about their premarital sexual relations, whereas unmarried females often experience some feelings of remorse. Girls' attitudes are often centered around the feeling that the male partner is more interested in them as a sex object than as a person (50). Not unrelated are other data that indicate a negative relationship between self-esteem and sexual promiscuity among females in late adolescence (10). Interestingly, however, in a major study of female sexual behavior, over three-fourths of the *married* women interviewed indicated no regret over having indulged in premarital coitus (27). It is realistic to suggest that sexual intercourse before marriage is enjoyable for many girls and carries no negative overtones, and that this state of affairs is growing more common.

The central question may be what short-term and long-term emotional value or harm accrues from adolescent sexual practices. We cannot speak to the matter of value or positive effects with confidence. Release from sexual tension (physical gratification) is certainly pleasant, and the maintenance of a bona fide mutually satisfying interpersonal relationship in which sex plays an important role seems unlikely to harm the participants, unless they suffer socially or feel guilty. There are simply too few data to permit even reasoned inference.

On the other hand, the potential negative effects of sexual outlet during adolescence are more easily documented. Perhaps this reflects in some indirect way the influence of Puritanism ("sex as sinful") on psychologists. It has already been indicated that the remorse and self-depreciation occur mostly among females. Emotional conflict arising from using sex dishonestly may also occur. Certainly the emotional cost of bearing a child out of wedlock must be recognized, although again this is more obviously applicable to the unmarried female (and her parents) than to the father of an illegitimate child. Unmarried fathers seem to suffer more because they have not been men enough to assume responsibility for their "woman and child" than because they have engaged in premarital sex. Aside from the

obvious socioemotional and health problems involved with pregnancy and venereal disease during adolescence, probably guilt and anxiety most affect adolescents (1). For example, the adolescent male who has learned that it is wrong to masturbate and that dire mental or physical consequences can result from this practice (impotence, cancer, warts, halitosis, ulcers, insomnia, and even insanity) but who yields to the sexual impulse to masturbate may be so racked with anxiety and guilt that his social and school life suffer. Medical evidence does not indicate that masturbation per se is harmful. It is the adolescent's perception of this sexual activity that is significant.

Although guilt and anxiety are unpleasant emotional states, perhaps a more potentially serious outcome of masturbation or heterosexual petting is canalization (1). By this is meant the development of a preference for such sexual outlets that, in reality, are merely substitutes for heterosexual intercourse. Where canalization occurs and when it interferes with the development of a heterosexual relationship involving intercourse, the satisfaction of one's sexual partner may be impaired. It is interesting to note, however, that a more powerful total physiological response has been observed from orgasm induced by masturbation than from orgasm resulting from intercourse (34).

The emphasis on the potential negative effects of adolescent sexual outlets should not be taken as an exhortation against such outlets. Adolescents have expressed their sexuality, openly or secretly, and will continue to do so. The authors simply desire to clarify some possible consequences of adolescent sexual behavior and point out that the consequences are largely mediated by the customs about premarital sexual behavior. In a permissive society or in an even more restrictive society, the emotional consequences of sexual outlets during adolescence may be quite different from those that exist here.

Sexual behavior among older children can apparently also serve a number of non-sex-related purposes. Among adolescent girls, sex is sometimes used to gain at least the appearance of popularity. Girls also often seem to use their sexuality to strike back at their parents, perhaps particularly their mothers. And as suggested, boys can employ sexuality to enhance their prestige among their male peers or from motives of hostility and revenge (11).

There is no evidence known to the authors to indicate that sexual abstinence interferes with either physical health or personal adjustment.

Homosexual explorations and fantasies are so common in our culture that, statistically speaking, they cannot be considered seriously abnormal. More than one-third of American males and about one-fourth of American females have had at least one homosexual experience to orgasm, and another 15 to 20 percent have had fantasies about it (26).

In view of the inevitability of premarital sex among adolescents, a society seemingly has two basic options (6). One is to employ every legal and moral means possible to prevent premarital intercourse. If experience in United States culture is any indication, this option will probably result in a fairly high incidence of unwanted marriages, illegitimate births, abortions (illegal or not), and unmeasurable psychological stress among pregnant females. The other option involves the flat recognition and acceptance that premarital intercourse will occur and that everything possible should therefore be done to provide birth control information and contraceptive measures during adolescence. Obviously objections can be raised in relation to both options, hence a dilemma. This matter provides an appropriate transition to a discussion of some major dilemmas related to sexuality and psychosexual development.

Some Dilemmas Related to Sexual Behavior and Development

In this discussion of adolescent sexuality, the authors have tried to set the stage for discussing some prevailing dilemmas about sexual behavior and development. These dilemmas will be examined under three headings. First, the general philosophical dilemma of goals for socializing sexual behavior is considered. Second, the popular idea that United States society is undergoing a sexual revolution or renaissance is examined. Finally, dilemmas related to sex education in the schools are reviewed.

Socialization Goals and Human Sexuality

This part of our discussion can profitably be begun by asking a series of related questions. First, what should be the outcome of the socialization process for sexuality? Second, are parents (and teachers) committed to do everything possible to prepare children and youth for a "successful" adult sexual life? Third, what should parents and teachers (and society collectively) do to maximize the probability that "healthy" sexuality will be achieved? From the authors' point of view, the answers to these questions are neither clear nor consensual. The issues involved should be discussed from the standpoint of mental health and social interdependence.

Consider first the question of basic goals. It is apparent that society justly demands of its members a certain degree of self-control about sexual expression. Otherwise, the fabric of our social order could quickly be torn apart. At the same time, a sexuality interlaced with shame and guilt about one's sexual feelings, genital functions, and undue inhibitions seems to us equally undesirable. Thus the problem concerns what defines the "happy medium" between poorly controlled and overcontrolled, self-recriminating sexual expression. A person capable of both self-fulfillment and tender regard for others in the context of an emotionally honest (versus exploitative) sexual relationship perhaps represents an appropriate model for socialization.

Other aspects must be considered, however, many of which involve one's judgmental capacity and general respect for others. For example, sexual expression is appropriate at some times and in some situations, inappropriate at others. The matter of personal responsibility is also important. That is, although sexual intercourse can be endorsed as a most intimate and enjoyable form of communication between two people, in our culture it also implies the necessity that one take responsibility for the consequences of that communion. Where the consequences may be unwanted pregnancy or venereal disease, it seems that appropriate precautions are imperative. Otherwise, both society and the parties involved are faced with problems that complicate, rather than facilitate, mental and physical health.

The authors recognize that any discussion of goals and guidelines for sexual behavior contains moral issues. Much of our United States morality and law is built around sexual behavior and the nuclear family. Ultimately, the choice of goals and guidelines for an individual's sexual life and the choice of child-rearing practices

regarding sexuality are matters of personal conscience.

Concerning the second question— whether or to what extent adults are committed to facilitating healthy sexual development among the young—the authors can only speculate. From their experience it seems clear that most adults at least pay lip service to the value of healthy sexual attitudes for children and youth—for example, attitudes that indicate accepting one's sexuality and the capacity for sexual communication that is satisfying both to oneself and to one's partner. Yet, if one examines carefully what many adults do and say (or fail to do and say) to their children, he cannot help questioning the validity of this lip service. For example, it seems to the authors that accurate knowledge about one's body, its functions, and the dynamics of sex are an integral part of healthy sexuality. Survey after survey indicates, however, that as many as 50 percent of children and youth receive no information or instruction about sex in the home (42). Still other children and youth seemingly receive information that is totally or partially false. Moreover, the often violent opposition to organized sex education programs, either in the church or in the schools, suggests that many adults are themselves fearful or are in conflict about the socialization of sexual behavior.

This brings us to the third question. Even if a consensus about a healthy sexuality is obtained, what socialization measures can be employed to promote its achievement? Again, this is mainly a matter for reasoned speculation, since insufficient data concerning the socialization of sexual behavior are available. However, at least three general guidelines are helpful. First, it seems wise to avoid extremes in child rearing such as harsh, punitive, and restrictive methods, or a laissez-faire or a direct overstimulation approach to socialization of sex. It is plausible to argue that the former extreme can result in inhibitions, anxieties, and negative attitudes about one's body and sexual functions. By the same token, no guidance or overstimulation, particularly during the formative years and adolescence, can result in distortions of attitude. For example, in view of the growing eroticism reflected by the mass media, an emphasis on the physical aspects of sex can possibly dominate an individual's sexual perspective at the expense of the interpersonal.

A second guideline concerns the nature and quality of parent–child or parent–youth interactions. For the authors, such interaction should from the outset be based on honesty, truth, and openness in communication. There seems no valid reason for adults intentionally to promote discontinuity in sexual information. Children who first learn untruths about sex may be at once confused and disillusioned when they confront reality. Certainly, a willingness on the part of parents to discuss sexuality when the need arises seems basic to a sound parent–child relationship.

Finally, the value of modeling a healthy sexuality is stressed in both attitude and behavior, just as one tries to model other aspects of constructive personal–social and intellectual behavior. It is *not* suggested that parents should model the sex act for their children or flaunt their nudity in order to "prove" that no sexual inhibitions exist in the home. What is suggested are adult self-acceptance with respect to sexuality, natural expressions of physical affection for members of one's family, and an approach to sexual matters that is not overwhelmed by anxiety.

Sexual Revolution: Fact or Artifact?

Much ado has recently been made over a "loosening" of morals in American society, principally as reflected in standards for sexual behavior. Concerned writers often cite recent increases in the rate of illegitimate births, illegal abortions, and venereal disease as evidence that premarital sex, in particular, is more frequent than ever before. Other manifestations of changing patterns of sexuality are often linked with the mass media (18). That is, sexual representations in magazines, plays, and movies, which were not previously permitted or were censored, are now commonplace. These representations range from explicit, sex-related language to nudity and graphic depictions of sexual intercourse and male and female homosexuality. The remarkable sales of books about sex, including specific advice about how to become more sensuous and seductive, are also cited as testimony to a culture that is becoming successively more "obsessed" with sex.

There can be little argument that the state of affairs concerning sex and the mass media is more liberal in the 1970s than it traditionally has been. It is also difficult to ignore the sometimes dramatic increases in the incidence of gonorrhea and out-of-wedlock births among youth over earlier periods in recent history (56). These data are difficult to interpret, especially because official reporting procedures by medical and social service authorities are much improved in recent years. Yet the basic questions are whether such data actually indicate a genuine sexual renaissance in American society, and to what extent actual premarital (or extramarital) sexual contact has increased in comparison to "more sexually conservative" periods in this century.

The reasonably good data that are

This photograph is an illustration of the new open styles in sexual mores. (Photo by Jason Lauré)

available about this question indicate some increase in premarital sexual petting and intercourse, especially among white females from the middle- and upper-social classes (3, 44), perhaps because this segment of society traditionally has been lowest in sexual permissiveness and thus has had the "farthest to go" in matters of change. There is little convincing evidence, however, that today's youth are significantly more sexually active or promiscuous than were their parents (3). The available evidence suggests that change has occurred mostly in the degree to which (1) sexual practices among adolescents and youth are congruent with their professed attitudes and (2) candor is reflected in their discussions about sex. In other words, if a renaissance has occurred

among youth, it is in the direction of less hypocrisy and more openness about sex as compared to their parents and their grandparents (3, 44).

At least two other changes deserve mention because of their implications for the network of values that is associated with human sexual behavior. The first relates to technology (56). With advances in methods of contraception, it has been increasingly clear that the biological (procreative) and social (nonprocreative) functions of sexual intercourse can be separated. Through technology, individuals can now maintain a sexual relationship solely on social grounds, without fear of pregnancy or justifying sex on procreative grounds. Moreover, as birth control measures have become more reliable, many legal, economic, and social sanctions previously applied to discourage premarital sex have become irrelevant.

Of course, such sanctions are irrelevant only for those who take precautions and whose morality does not inhibit sexual contact. For many adolescent females in particular, there is some evidence that conscious planning for intercourse, including obtaining contraceptives, is often avoided because of the "I am not that kind of girl" syndrome (56). For such girls, premeditated sex is often taken as an indication of promiscuity or immorality, both of which may invoke guilt and anxiety. Thus, a girl, to avoid admitting to herself by taking precautions in advance that she desires sex with a boy, may enter a relationship "unprepared" for intercourse. In this way, the probability of pregnancy is increased. Possibly this unwillingness to recognize and accept one's sexual motives is one reason why the availability of contraceptives has not had any apparent impact on the incidence of teen-age pregnancy in American society. Attitudes, not availabilities, are involved.

Perhaps related to technological advances is a second factor that indicates a sexual renaissance—that is, the apparent shift in emphasis on sexual intercourse as an act to the quality of the interpersonal relationship that it can represent (28). Increasingly, many young people (especially females) seem to be developing a view of sex whereby intercourse is permissible, if not actively sought, under conditions of genuine affection. In other words, if an emotional relationship perceived as stable and genuine develops between male and female, this relationship can provide a necessary and often sufficient condition for extended sexual contact. It is suggested that this new code, labeled elsewhere as "permissiveness with affection"

(44), represents a substantial change from a more traditional sexual morality based on love and marriage, not just love, as the necessary condition for sexual relations. When adolescents believe that if there is love, there can be sex, and when their parents believe that only with love *and marriage* can there be sex, generational conflict is bound to result.

7.3 Generational Conflict in Sexual Values

One way to assess the extent of difference or similarity in sexual beliefs and values between generations is to ask parents and their adolescent offspring about such matters at various points throughout the high school and college years. Robert Bell and Jack Buerkle (4) were particularly interested in the degree to which mothers and their college coed daughters agreed about such things as virginity, premarital intercourse, and sharing of views about sex with their parent. These research workers obtained a sample of 217 coeds at different class levels in college. Data concerning values associated with the aforementioned topics were then gathered independently from both the girls and their mothers.

Bell and Buerkle found that similarity in the values of daughters and mothers toward the importance of premarital chastity was greatest among younger coeds and smallest among older coeds. Even so, rather striking differences were discovered. For example, 88 percent of the mothers reported that it was "very important" for a girl to be a virgin when she marries, while only 55 percent of the daughters thought so; 83 percent of mothers expressed the belief that premarital intercourse during engagement is "very wrong" as compared to 48 percent of the daughters; and only 37 percent of the daughters, as compared to 83 percent of the mothers, agreed that daughters should freely answer questions from their mothers about attitudes toward sexuality.

Taking these and other findings collectively, Bell and Buerkle suggest that mothers place far greater emphasis on the condition of virginity at marriage than their daughters do. These research workers also argue that the period of greatest liberalization among daughters is around age 20, when they are becoming engaged and experiencing intense heterosexual relationships. Daughters are then most likely to profess that love is a sufficient condition for sexual

involvement. Bell and Buerkle also argue, on the basis of their own and related data, that this liberalization subsides somewhat once marriage has occurred. It is then that mother–daughter values about sexuality again become more similar, although each generation professes somewhat increasing degrees of liberality about sex in general.

Finally, in a later paper, Bell (3) reflects on the broad spectrum of data concerning parent–child sexual values and the conflict that value differences can produce. Bell suggests that youth generally seek to minimize this conflict by spending an increasing amount of time away from home for social activities, by being secretive, and through

Young persons seeking guidelines regarding premarital sexual intercourse encounter a contradictory confusing array of moral codes and attitudes in their society. (Photo by Jason Lauré)

reducing communication with parents about heterosexual involvements. A sort of game is established, says Bell, whereby parents can assume that their children are abiding by traditional values, while youth go about developing their own modified standards. The following quote aptly conveys this notion: "For many parents and their children, the conflict about premarital sex will continue to be characterized by the parent's playing ostrich and burying his head in the sand, and the youth's efforts to keep the sand from blowing away." (3, p. 44)

Sex Education and the Schools

A final set of dilemmas to be discussed concerns one of the most complex and controversial aspects of American public schools: sex education. The most basic dilemma involved seems to be whether and for what reasons schools should attempt sex education at all. If the answer is "Yes, they should" and if it is based on sound reasons, many dilemmas are encountered. Notable among them is the dilemma of goals (see earlier section). What should be the outcome of a given sex education program? Some educators may take a pragmatic approach to this dilemma and suggest that the success of a sex education program is measured in terms of lowered rates of illegitimate births, venereal disease, and sexual maladjustment. Other educators may stress less tangible, idealistic goals such as an increased capacity for spiritual union through heterosexual relations and positive attitudes toward child rearing. In either case, however, it would be extremely difficult to link a public school sex education program directly to such outcomes, because so many other out-of-school experiences impinge upon the

individual to affect sexual behavior and attitudes.

Even when program goals are clearly specified and are logically sound, strong objections to the whole concept of sex education in the public schools are usually raised. Such objections range from rational to irrational. For example, some opponents of sex education argue sincerely that schools should be devoted to academics and intellectual pursuits. Education for mental health, sociability, or sexuality is rejected entirely on philosophical grounds. Others object because of the fear that sex education will lead to increased promiscuity. They argue that once the details of sexual anatomy and reproduction are revealed to children and

"If I had my life to live over again, I'd know just what to do!"

If and when to provide birth control information to adolescents is a matter of intense debate among parents and teachers. (Cartoon from Phi Delta Kappan, *1969, 50 (6), 404. Reproduced by permission of the artist, Herbert Goldberg.)*

youth, they will be tempted to experiment and sample the "forbidden fruit." The authors know of no evidence to support this belief.

Still other opposition to sex education reflects religious and moral values, especially those values related to birth control. Many people apparently believe that instruction about contraception is inevitable in a sex education program and that, once birth control techniques are disclosed, youth can and will enjoy sex without marriage. This condition, in turn, may result in lowered marriage rates with an eventual threat to the family as a social institution.

Again the authors cannot cite any data that support this argument, but this and other viewpoints are variously reflected in stands against public school sex education. Educators and parents who want some form of sex education in the schools should be aware of and prepared for such opposition.

Still other dilemmas associated with sex education include determining the content, sequence, and scope of a curriculum. For example, should a sex education curriculum be limited to factual biological information or should it be extended to include moral and ethical issues in sexuality? How should this content be programed? Should the curriculum begin with age-appropriate experiences, in the kindergarten or primary grades, in junior high school, or in senior high? Should the program be compulsory or voluntary? coeducational or segregated according to sex? Of course, the dilemma of personnel must be reckoned with. Who should be responsible for implementing a sex education program? What personal and professional characteristics are necessary for such personnel? How shall the personnel be selected?

The authors do not wish merely to bombard the reader with questions. Their purpose is to point out a few of the many genuine dilemmas that are involved. It would be nice if they could draw on clear objective data to facilitate the resolution of these dilemmas. Unfortunately, sex education programs, where they exist, have not been well researched. Moreover, their quality and scope are so variable that drawing sound generalizations about them is impossible. What few data exist, however, suggest that adolescents (1) are not receiving adequate sex education in the home, (2) desire sex education as part of their formal school experience, (3) show substantial increases in the amount of knowledge about sexual matters, having participated in them, and (4) may change their attitudes about sex in the direction of their instructors especially if nondirective instructional methods are used (29, 40, 48). The latter finding is especially significant in terms of highlighting the potential influence of educational authorities who communicate with involved, interested adolescents in the classroom. This relates directly to the notion of the teacher as a model for identification.

Finally, although it is rarely mentioned in the context of teacher education, the authors believe that teachers should be aware of the role of sexuality in their own relations with students. This is true for both a teacher's own sexuality that may be expressed toward students, and the sexual attitudes and impulses that exist and are at times openly shown by students. This dynamic deserves particular attention when students reach adolescence.

Crushes can at times help adolescents work through their own sex role identifications. At the same time, a crush inappropriately handled can be disastrous for both student and teacher. Nor is there any escape from the conclusion that, although we cannot expect all teachers to be ideally adjusted sexually, we must ask them to be well *behaved* sexually with all their students.

It is unlikely that the dilemmas mentioned will be easily resolved by school personnel and parents even when these groups work closely together in pursuit of quality education for children and youth. However, the authors believe that sex education *in principle* is a legitimate function of the schools—a belief based on the assumption that qualified personnel and a psychologically sound curriculum for such education are available.

A Psychologist's View of Sex Education
The authors' study of the literature concerned with psychology and sex has led them to view positively the general framework for sex education advanced by Ausubel (1). Ausubel, who is both a psychologist and a physician, sees the fundamental purpose of public school sex education as twofold: the provision of accurate sex information and the opportunity to establish an ethical perspective on sexuality. The authors agree with Ausubel that the development of a capacity for intelligent self-direction regarding sexual expression is unlikely without these factors. Concerning the matter of sex information, Ausubel suggests that careful attention be given both to the physiology and the psychology of sex. One's personal ethical perspective on sexuality, it is to be hoped, will develop through free and open discussions of the emotional and social goals of sex expression where guiding principles of honesty, respect, and consideration for the feelings of others are highlighted. Specific problems about sex practices, however, should be left to individual guidance and counseling by trained personnel.

Ausubel's framework for sex education is not uniquely psychological, but a sound developmental orientation is reflected in his recommendations for designing a sequential program in relation to changing interest patterns. For example, during preadolescence the principal focus for program content would be the physiology and anatomy of sex, including reproduction, conception, and the birth process. Factual education, in other words, should be complete before puberty. During early adolescence, when adult heterosexual behavior patterns are becoming established, such matters as psychosexual development, courting problems and practices, sex differences in sexual motivation, and moral–emotional aspects of sex will be emphasized. Finally, as the upper level of high school is reached, concepts and problems relating to marriage, family relations, child rearing, and homemaking will be stressed.

Ausubel, the authors believe, provides many helpful cues concerning the design of sex education programs for the schools. However, even with elaborate and well-executed sex education programs, it is probably unrealistic to believe that school experience alone will produce dramatic changes in adolescent sexual behavior. The authors' thinking is well summarized by the following quote:

Perhaps the most important contribution that secondary school sex education programs can make is to assist the individual with the development of an explicit cognitive frame of reference within which he may view himself. Those programs which are descriptive and allow the individual adolescent to make his own judgments concerning the personal relevance or import of various sexual topics and questions are likely to be more helpful in this process than those which attempt to take over this function. Finally, while it is necessary to keep in mind that any program or curriculum will achieve this result to different degrees . . . those which include the most diversity of content and format are those most likely to succeed. (42, p. 175)

Summary

By psychosexual development is meant the ways one adjusts to the reproductive aspects of his body from its childhood state through pubescence, adolescence, and adulthood to the years of decline. A most important aspect of psychosexual development is learning to live appropriately according to one's gender.

In the United States at this time, females are expected to be *expressive:* gentle, nurturant, adroit in social relations, and responsible. Males are expected to be *instrumental:* full of initiative, self-sufficient, task oriented, sexy, and psychologically tough. These stereotypes shape much of our behavior, yet often operate to deny females competence and males self-expression.

Sex typing is learning gender-appropriate behavior. Identification is learning attitudes that, in the statistically normal sense, first, are like those of one's same-sexed parent and, second and more broadly, are like those which are socially approved for one's gender. The authors view sex typing and identification as only one part of the broad range of behavior that is referred to as human socialization. They also think of sex typing and identification as both products and processes. In the *product* sense, they use such terms as heterosexual, homosexual, boyish, girlish, or manly, womanly. In the *process* sense, they believe that learning and modeling theory, at least at this time, offer most promise for understanding, predicting,

and controlling psychosexual development among human beings.

As a broad generalization, those who are appropriately sex typed and sex identified seem to be happier and more successful in American society, but there are many exceptions.

From a background of psychosocial aspects of sexuality, specific biological and cultural aspects of sexual behavior were examined. Maleness and femaleness were defined biologically, and some prominent neuromuscular capacities for sexual response were explained. From these biological givens, variations and regularities in form, style, and tempo of sexual practices were linked to cultural learning. This learning is clearly reflected in both the nature and the psychological impact of sexual practices during adolescence.

Although emergent aspects of sexuality serve as a powerful motivation during adolescence, it was indicated that very little is known about socialization practices in the home or the school at this critical stage in life. There is good reason to believe that attitudes toward sexual functions are shaped during childhood, many of which are the result of incidental learning rather than direct tuition. The actual working out of psychosexual development occurs within the peer group and seems currently to be clearly affected by the mass media. In our United States culture, premarital sex is negatively sanctioned by adults, especially for girls. These sanctions generally have not been successful in limiting the sexual behavior of adolescents. Many problems result, such as personal–social problems presented by venereal disease, out-of-wedlock births, and personal recrimination, that demand the attention of youth workers.

The discussion of adolescent sexuality can serve to highlight many philosophical and procedural dilemmas. Foremost among the philosophical dilemmas is: What should be the goals of socialization for human sexuality in American society? Related to this is evidence that a change of near-renaissance proportions has gradually occurred in United States culture, principally involving a relaxation of traditional Puritan attitudes and a trend away from secretiveness and hypocrisy about sexual behavior and attitudes.

Finally, the issue of sex education in the public schools was examined. Sources of controversy about such education were discussed, most of which have moral overtones that are unfounded in fact. The authors have taken the position that, in principle, sex education is a legitimate and essential aspect of formal schooling. Consistent with this orientation, they presented some guidelines for a developmental approach to sex education that appear to meet the criterion of relevance for today's children and youth.

REFERENCES

1. Ausubel, D. P. *Theory and problems in adolescent development.* New York: Grune & Stratton, 1954.
2. Bell, R. Q. Stimulus control of parent or caretaker behavior by offspring. *Developmental Psychology,* 1971, 4, 63–72.
3. Bell, R. R. Parent–child conflict in sexual values. *Journal of Social Issues,* 1966, 22, 34–44.
4. Bell, R. R., and J. V. Buerkle. Mother and daughter attitudes to premarital sexual behavior. *Marriage and Family Living,* 1961, 23, 390–392.
5. Biller, H. B., and L. J. Borstelmann. Masculine development: An integrative review. *Merrill-Palmer Quarterly,* 1967, 13, 253–294.
6. Bjork, R. M. International perspective on various issues in sex education as an aspect of health education. *Journal of School Health,* 1969, 39, 525–537.
7. Blanchard, R. W., and H. B. Biller. Father availability and academic performance among third-grade boys. *Developmental Psychology,* 1971, 4, 301–305.
8. Brown, D. C., and D. B. Lynn. Human sexual development: An outline of components and concepts. *Journal of Marriage and the Family,* 1966, 28, 155–162.
9. Carlsmith, L. Effect of father absence on scholastic aptitude. *Harvard Educational Review,* 1964, 34, 3–21.
10. Chickering, A. *Education and identity.* San Francisco: Jossey-Bass, 1969.
11. Cleaver, E. *Soul on ice.* New York: McGraw-Hill, 1968.
12. D'Andrade, R. G. Sex differences and cultural institutions. In E. Maccoby (ed.) *The development of sex differences.* Stanford, Calif.: Stanford University Press, 1966, 173–204.
13. Dornbusch, S. M. Afterword. In E. Maccoby (ed.) *The development of sex differences.* Stanford, Calif.: Stanford University Press, 1966, 205–219.
14. Fagot, B. I., and G. R. Patterson. An in vivo analysis of reinforcing contingencies for sex-role behaviors in the preschool child. *Developmental Psychology,* 1969, 1, 563–568.
15. Felsenthal, H. Pupil sex as a variable in teacher perception of classroom behavior. Paper read at the American Educational Research Association Convention, New York City, February, 1971.
16. Ford, C. S., and F. A. Beach. *Patterns of sexual behavior.* New York: Harper & Row, 1951.
17. Freud, S. *An outline of psychoanalysis* (1st ed., 1940). New York: Norton, 1949.
18. Gagnon, J. H., and W. Simon. *The sexual scene.* Chicago: Aldine, 1970.
19. Gewirtz, J. L., and K. G. Stingle. The learn-

ing of generalized imitation as the basis for identification. *Psychological Review,* 1968, *75,* 374–397.

20. Harper, L. V. The young as a source of stimuli controlling caretaker behavior. *Developmental Psychology,* 1971, *4,* 73–88.

21. Heilbrun, A. B., Jr. Identification and behavioral effectiveness during late adolescence. In E. D. Evans (ed.) *Adolescents: Readings in behavior and development.* Hinsdale, Ill.: Dryden, 1970, 70–79.

22. Hetherington, E. M. Sex typing, dependency, and aggression. In T. D. Spencer and N. Kass (eds.) *Perspectives in child psychology: Research and review.* New York: McGraw-Hill, 1970, 193–231.

23. Hoffman, M. L. Father absence and conscience development. *Development Psychology,* 1971, 4, 400–406.

24. Johnson, M. M. Sex role learning in the nuclear family. *Child Development,* 1963, *34,* 319–333.

25. Kagan, J. Acquisition and significance of sex typing and sex role identity. In M. Hoffman and L. Hoffman (eds.) *Review of child development research.* Vol. I. New York: Russell Sage, 1964, 137–167.

26. Kinsey, A. C., W. B. Pomeroy, and C. E. Martin. *Sexual behavior in the human male.* Philadelphia: Saunders, 1948.

27. Kinsey, A. C., W. B. Pomeroy, C. E. Martin, and P. H. Gebhard. *Sexual behavior in the human female.* Philadelphia: Saunders, 1953.

28. Kirkendall, L. A., and R. W. Libbey. Interpersonal relationships — crux of the sexual renaissance. *Journal of Social Issues,* 1966, *22,* 45–59.

29. Kirkendall, L. A., and G. J. Miles. Sex education research. *Review of Educational Research,* 1968, *38,* 528–544.

30. Kohlberg, L. A cognitive-developmental analysis of children's sex-role concepts and attitudes. In E. E. Maccoby (ed.) *The development of sex differences.* Stanford, Calif.: Stanford University Press, 1966. 82–173.

31. Lynn, D. B. *Parental and sex role identifica-*
tion: A theoretical formulation. Berkeley, Calif.: McCutchan Publishing Corporation, 1969.

32. Mann, J. Effects of erotic films of sexual behavior of married couples; sex guilt and reactions to pornographic films. Exposure to pornography, character, and sexual deviance: A retrospective survey. *ERIC: ED 043 076,* 1970. 35 pp.

33. Marshall, D. S., and R. C. Suggs. *Human sexual behavior: Variations in the ethnographic spectrum.* New York: Basic Books, 1971.

34. Masters, W. H., and V. E. Johnson. *Human sexual response.* Boston: Little, Brown, 1966.

35. McCandless, B. R. *Adolescents: Behavior and development.* Hinsdale, Ill.: Dryden, 1970.

36. McCandless, B. R. *Children: Behavior and development.* New York: Holt, Rinehart and Winston, 1967.

37. Mead, Margaret. Cultural determinants of sexual behavior. In W. C. Young (ed.) *Sex and the internal secretions* (3rd ed.), Vol. II. Baltimore: Williams & Wilkins, 1961, 1433–1479.

38. Mischel, W. Sex-typing and socialization. In P. H. Mussen (ed.) *Carmichael's manual of child psychology.* New York: Wiley, 1970, 3–72.

39. Mussen, P. H. Early sex role development. In D. Goslin (ed.) *Handbook of socialization theory and research.* Chicago: Rand McNally, 1968, 707–732.

40. Olson, D. H., and A. E. Gravatt. Attitude change in a functional marriage course. *Family Coordinator,* 1968, *17,* 99–104.

41. Parsons, T. Family structure and the socialization of the child. In T. Parsons and R. F. Bales (eds.) *Family, socialization, and interaction process.* New York: Free Press, 1955, 35–131.

42. Payne, D. C. Sex education and the sexual education of adolescents. In E. D. Evans (ed.) *Adolescents: Readings in behavior and development.* Hinsdale, Ill.: Dryden, 1970, 163–176.

43. Rainwater, L. Some aspects of lower class

sexual behavior. *Journal of Social Issues,* 1966, 22, 52–56.

44. Reiss, I. L. The sexual renaissance: A summary and analysis. *Journal of Social Issues,* 1966, 22, 123–137.

45. Rosenkrantz, P., S. Vogel, H. Bee, I. Broverman, and D. M. Broverman. Sex-role stereotypes and self-concepts in college students. *Journal of Consulting and Clinical Psychology,* 1968, 32, 287–295.

46. Schneider, H. K. Romantic love among the Turu. In D. S. Marshall and R. C. Suggs (eds.) *Human sexual behavior.* New York: Basic Books, 1971, 59–70.

47. Sears, R. R., E. E. Maccoby, and H. Levin. *Patterns of child rearing.* New York: Harper & Row, 1956.

48. Shipman, G. The psychodynamics of sex education. *Family Coordinator,* 1968, *17,* 3–12.

49. Simon, W., and J. H. Gagnon. On psychosexual development. In D. Goslin (ed.) *Handbook of socialization theory and research.* Chicago: Rand McNally, 1969, 733–752.

50. Staton, T. F. Sex education for adolescents. In J. F. Adams (ed.) *Understanding adolescence.* Boston: Allyn and Bacon, 1968, 248–271.

51. Stein, A. H. The effects of sex-role standards for achievement and sex-role preference on three determinants of achievement motivation. *Developmental Psychology,* 1971, 4, 219–231.

52. Stephens, W. N. *The family in cross cultural perspective.* New York: Holt, Rinehart and Winston, 1963.

53. Suggs, R. C. A critique of some anthropological methods and theory. In D. S. Marshall and R. C. Suggs (eds.) *Human sexual behavior.* New York: Basic Books, 1971, 272–287.

54. Suggs, R. C., and D. S. Marshall. Anthropological perspectives on human sexual behavior. In D. S. Marshall and R. C. Suggs (eds.) *Human sexual behavior.* New York: Basic Books, 1971, 218–243.

55. Thompson, N. L., Jr., B. R. McCandless, and B. Strickland. Personal-social adjustment of male and female homosexuals. *Journal of Abnormal Psychology,* 1971, *78,* 237–240.

56. Wagner, N. W. Adolescent sexuality. In E. D. Evans (ed.) *Adolescents: Readings in behavior and development.* Hinsdale, Ill.: Dryden, 1970, 44–52.

57. Waxler, C. Z., and M. R. Yarrow. Factors influencing imitative learning in preschool children. *Journal of Experimental Psychology.* 1970, *9,* 115–130.

8
Moral and
Political Development
and Behavior

It was pointed out in Chapter 2 that the era of objectivity and hardheaded methodology began for psychology with John Watson, the behaviorist, in the late 1920s. At that time, psychology as science moved away from its parent discipline, philosophy, and from anything that was irretrievably private or smacked of mentalism. This divorce resulted in long-time neglect or outright rejection of some of the legitimate and worthwhile preoccupations of psychology, such as the study of imagery and thought.

Concurrent with this emphasis on pragmatism—what *is*—scientific psychologists rejected consideration of what *ought to be*. Science, they said, is concerned with *facts*. Values are matters for philosophers and theologians.

This position is now much changed. As one psychologist puts it (29, p. 383): "The barbarities of the socially conforming members of the Nazi and the Stalinist systems and the hollow lives apparent in our own affluent society have made it painfully evident that adjustment to the group is no substitute

for moral maturity." Many psychologists have now adopted this point of view, have stopped "adjusting to the behaviorist norm," and have preoccupied themselves quite usefully, in the authors' opinion, with matters of values and morality. It is their thinking and research that are dealt with in the first half of this chapter.

In the second half of the chapter, the psychological study of political development and behavior during childhood and adolescence is considered. This kind of developmental study is newer than the study of morality. As such, the avenue is marked more by perplexing questions than by satisfying answers. However, it is increasingly apparent that moral and political development are linked in important ways, a linkage brought into focus by research into the motives for various forms of political involvement by youth. Certainly both moral and political development are prime examples of the larger, more encompassing socialization process. Hence, this is the reason for including discussions of both areas in this chapter.

MORAL DEVELOPMENT

DEFINITIONS OF MORALITY

The authors believe that it is necessary to look at two faces of morality. The two faces do not fit harmoniously in many instances, as will be seen. First, and most important in the long run, morality is the development, formulation, and expression of intentions or conscience that are internal and that focus a person's outlook on life. Morality also involves the direct representation of a person's personal construction of social values. Second, and sometimes more pressing than the first face, each of us must assume objective obligations and responsibilities to his community and the order of things in his society. The first face of our morality— our intentions or conscience—force us to judge our personal society. As we know, the norms of some societies are false or evil, and the highest morality is to reject and combat them (39).

Behind the second face of morality— adherence to social norms and responsibilities—also lie human values. The first face is the values themselves. If we decide to abide by the norms of any given group within which we live, we are implicitly agreeing that conformity to its norms makes possible the realization of values that lie behind them. We must then go still further—we must analyze the values and decide whether they are themselves sound. This makes it clear that statistical normality is not in and of itself an indication of morality. Some norms are abnormal or pathological when judged on the basis of moral principles that, as best we can judge, possess universal validity.

These abstract matters can perhaps be clarified by an example. Some years ago the authors knew a young man who was a prominent campus leader both politically and socially—he was president of the student council at his university and was also president of his fraternity (it was the best on campus; this was in the days when few questioned the underlying value of fraternities and membership automatically conveyed campus prestige). This young man was thoughtful and principled in that he did battle for civil rights, for full social and political rights for nonfraternity students, for freedom of press for the campus newspaper, and for other issues that for his day were indicators of high principles—and still are.

One night, after a fraternity dance, the young man, his girl, and some of his fraternity brothers and their girls were caught in a compromising situation in the local hotel. Penalties for these students would be set by the student council and the administration; possibilities ranged from expulsion to forfeit of a certain number of academic credits. The young man— persuasive, articulate, and well respected by the university authorities—was in a good position to help his male and female companions (and himself) because of his student council role, and his friends put heavy pressure on him to use his influence in their behalf.

His personal representation of the first face of morality in our definition was that under no circumstances did one use an elected office for personal gain or for the special interests of any group, including his own fraternity. His representation of the second face of morality was that fraternities are good things, that they promote social development, that loyalty to friends is important, and that he was indeed close friends with the others who were in trouble. Driven by this crisis of principles to analyze the values behind his fraternity, he came to the conclusion that for his group these values were basically those of personal aggrandizement, hedonism, and a loyalty to individuals that somewhat suggested gang psychology. The young man was forced to conclude that the values mentioned were less worthwhile than his principled dedication to the democratic process that had put him into the presidency of the student council.

Reluctantly, the young man resigned from both the fraternity and the student council (the latter resignation was not accepted) and worked with the council and the administration on appropriate penalties for his and his friends' behavior (penalties, parenthetically, that proved to be mild).

Reciprocity is perhaps the basic human morality: I see your point of view, I honor it and respect it, and I facilitate it so long as the integrity of others is not destroyed in my so doing. I also respect custom and law, but, ultimately, my orientation is "to conscience as a directing agent and to mutual respect and trust" (30, p. 7). In other words, reciprocity is essential if the value of human dignity is to be achieved. Together with a concern for equality and the welfare of others, reciprocity also provides the basis for *justice*, a universal human tendency (31).

DEVELOPMENTAL CONSIDERATIONS

Different Assumptions about Morality

Historically as well as currently, there are three major ways in which morality is construed, or assumptions on which its definitions are based. First, there is the conception of original sin, the "killer ape" view of man. Second, there is the notion of innate goodness, the "fallen angel"

view of man. Third, there is the *tabula rasa*, or wax-tablet, viewpoint. Nothing has been written on this tablet. In this view, the human infant is infinitely malleable.

The major monotheistic religions, Christian, Islamic, and Judaic, all include the notion of original sin. Classical psychoanalysis, as seen in Chapter 2, also embodies this concept: The libido is engaged in ceaseless struggle with the ego, policed and held in check mainly by the superego. Evolution—up from the ape—also lends itself to such a construction of morality.

Humanists from Rousseau onward seem to embrace the fallen-angel point of view: Given the chance to grow freely, man will seek to realize himself and will move toward self-fulfillment and the constructive. Many modern cognitive-developmental psychologists, including Piaget, also fit well in the fallen-angel school.

Learning theorists, including of course behaviorists, are at heart *tabula rasa* theorists. Their view of the nature of man is empirical and neutral. As has been seen, behaviorists have traditionally shied away from making value judgments. Such judgments are inevitable, however, if one seeks to apply behavioral modification techniques in the practical setting, whether it is the classroom or a juvenile detention home.

In fact, those who embrace the original-sin view and those who take the *tabula rasa* view are both likely to endorse active training and teaching programs for the developing child as far as both cognitive and moral developments are concerned. For the former, the original-sin people, such training is essential in morality "to keep the beast in check." For the latter, the *tabula rasa* people, teaching and training are essential so that the end product of development is a person who functions usefully in society. Both the original-sin and the learning theorists, in other words, depend heavily on learning (arranged experiences) as major shapers of the end social product. This is as true for sex typing and sex identification, as seen in Chapter 7, as it is for cognitive development (see Chapters 5 and 6) or for morality and political attitudes and behavior, as we see in this chapter.

Those who assume the innate goodness of man, on the other hand, place their faith in keeping "hands off"—in unarranged experiences. Rousseau, it will be recalled, advocated simply letting *Emile* grow naturally until about the age of puberty. Such thinkers as Piaget and his American disciple Kohlberg believe that moral development (like cognitive development) is in large part a function of maturation within a context of general age-related experience. The human organism acts on his environment, and his natural environment acts on him; he takes from it what he needs and what is suitable, and matures in accord with his biological nature interacting with his environment. Those who take this line of thought have little confidence in *teaching* either cognitive or moral development. This is not to say that they do not consider the environment important. A malign or unduly circumscribed environment, they know, can distort or retard either moral or cognitive development, but an artificially enriched or accelerated environment will accomplish little. Kohlberg, in particular, has advanced a general prescription for moral education that has faint overtones of programed learning (31).

Moral Development: Product and Process

Within a democratic society, satisfactory moral development as an end product

usually includes at least four characteristic ways of behaving (19).

First, the individual conforms behaviorally within sensible limits (these limits are often difficult to define, as we all know).

Second, the individual perceives authority as being rational and essentially well disposed toward all members within the society, including himself, and behaves toward authority accordingly.

Third, the individual is able to inhibit his impulses when necessary or desirable and to postpone immediate gratification for the sake of later, more important or greater satisfactions. He is planful, in other words.

Fourth, the individual is reciprocal in his orientation, as stated above under Definitions of Morality. He is considerate of others, respects their feelings, and wishes justice done for them as well as for himself.

Views of the Moral Development Process

In the authors' estimation, there are three major schools of thought about how goals such as those listed above are reached by the developing child: psychoanalytic, behavioristic, and cognitive developmental. Basically, the points of view about moral development within each of these schools of thought closely parallel their considerations about sex typing and sex identification (see Chapter 7).

This is especially true for psychoanalysis. The development of satisfactory psychosexual and moral development go hand in hand. An overwhelmingly important condition for both aspects of development is the same-sex parent, although ultimately both parents affect moral identification. This identification occurs in about the same way as sexual identification—it represents the incorporation of parental standards as one's own, in the form of the *superego* (this term is used here synonymously with "conscience").

Within psychoanalytic thinking, guilt represents a higher level of moral development than shame. Guilt is *internalized control*, shame *externalized control* (see the section on Dilemmas, Chapter 3). Moreover, moral identification is thought to be a universal trait. That is, one behaves with about the same degree of morality across all situations that call for moral judgment and action. In view of the strong role accorded identification models within psychoanalysis, it follows that the quality of a child's moral development will depend largely on the degree to which his parents and others important to him are moral. It must also be noted that, according to psychoanalysis, certain indications of moral identification should appear by age 5 or 6. For researchers, of course, this has meant that the behavioral components of moral identification must be specified. Example 8.1 contains a description of the components that have frequently been taken to indicate level or extent of moral identification. It should be noted that the behaviorists have been instrumental in pressing for such indicators.

8.1 Presumed Indicators of Moral Identification

Many psychologists, especially those with a psychodynamic bent, believe that morality is internalized: it is inside the person, and operates like a unitary trait. In this sense, it is like sex identification as the term was discussed in the previous chapter. In the interests of making all scientific endeavors public (see Chapter 2), psychologists have tried to specify human behaviors that they believed indicate moral identification (internalization). Most have employed one or more of the following four indicators (19).

1. *Resistance to temptation, such as refusing to cheat even though one knows he cannot be detected.* This suggests that one's moral code is inside himself, is not referred to anyone else (externalized). Thus it can be said to be internalized.

2. *Guilt over deviations.* An individual does something wrong. No one else knows about it, but he feels bad. This is taken as a sign of internalized morality. Judgment about this variable is usually made from stories told about pictures, on the assumption that the story reflects the feelings of the person who creates it.

3. *Independence of actions from external sanctions.* As far as one knows, he behaves morally because these are *his* standards rather than because someone else—*anyone* else he can think of—will disapprove or punish.

4. *Confession and assumption of responsibility for one's own actions.* The amoral person is not going to tell on himself unless his misdeed can be proved. Thus, he refuses to take responsibility for his own actions. The person who has internalized his morality will feel uneasy and often feels compelled to confess, thereby saying, "I am responsible and will assume the consequences for my behavior."

As the reader can see, these indicators are rather like principles by which one guides his behavior in situations where elements of "rightness or wrongness" prevail. They are basically independent of specific moral *values,* or the content of morality.

While some behaviorists have organized their work around the concept of moral identification, psychologists of this school more typically focus on established learning principles. Specifically, moral development is viewed as the process (and result) of progressive discrimination learning whereby judgments become finer and finer and responses are differentially reinforced. Consequently, the kind of specific learning experiences and opportunities that a child has will largely account for moral development as conceived by behaviorists. At the risk of oversimplification, an "immoral" person would most likely be viewed as one for whom the reinforcements for immoral behavior are greater or more consistent than are reinforcements for "moral" behavior.

Yet, it is unlikely that most behaviorists would even talk about something as general as the "moral" person. Rather, they would talk about responses within specific situations along a continuum of morality as defined by society. For example, a husband may be the model of fidelity in his home community and therefore moral in that setting. Yet, the same husband may engage in extramarital affairs while traveling alone on business trips. Many people (including his spouse) would likely label this husband's extramarital behavior as immoral. The behaviorist would view the two situations, home and travel, as representing different cues and reinforcement contingencies that govern the class of responses involved in fidelity. This position, of course, raises the issue of morality as a general trait or situationally specific set of responses. We again encounter this issue later in the chapter.

Finally, cognitive developmentalists are likely to view moral development both as a series of qualitatively distinct stages of moral reasoning and a unitary process of thinking that is involved in such reasoning. Unlike the psychoanalysts, the cognitive developmentalists believe that moral development is not the result of repressed drives (for example, aggression and sexuality), nor do they place much significance on reinforcement. Rather, they link moral behavior closely to rationality and consciousness as reflected by cognitive development and chronological age.

The position of the authors is a blend of cognitive developmentalist and behaviorist. However, before they can discuss their own position, they must provide further background information. Thus, they describe in greater detail the thinking of Piaget and Kohlberg, since these men best represent the cognitive developmentalist point of view.

Piaget's and Kohlberg's Sequences of Moral Development. Piaget believes that morality, essentially, consists of an individual's respect for the rules of his particular social order, in addition to his sense of justice (41). A mature sense of justice includes concern for reciprocity and equality among people.

The young child is egocentric. He is unable to see anyone else's point of view, and thus assumes that all points of view are the same—and are like his. He also operates in terms of moral realism. By this term, Piaget means that the child considers all rules to be sacred and unalterable. The young child's morality is heteronomous (determined by the rules laid down by others, typically his parents). Things are either black or white. Justice is immanent (that is, if you do something bad, then something bad happens to you —an accident or an unescapable, arbitrary punishment).

Autonomous morality occurs later and, Piaget believes, largely because of the give-and-take the child experiences in his peer group where he slowly learns others' points of view, and thus grows out of his egocentrism through role taking and participating in decisions. Piaget does, however, believe that equalitarian parents who handle their child through reasoning or induction can greatly facilitate moral development (19). Autonomous morality comes from within and, in its highest form, approaches the level of morality described above under Definitions of Morality. Moral relativism is substituted for moral realism (or absolutism). Laws are seen, not as sacred and immutable, but as social arrangements that come about through reciprocal agreement and that are for the good of all those affected by them. Thus, laws are modifiable in terms of human need, including social change.

Piaget postulates predictable changes with age in the process of moral development. Six of his predictions have been well supported across a number of cultures. (Consistent with his emphasis on unarranged experiences, Piaget and his followers believe that the progress of moral development, like that of cognitive development, is about the same regardless of culture or differential learning experiences.)

The six characteristics that seem to hold up well across cultures are regular changes with age in the following:

1. *Intentionality.* That is, acts are judged not so much according to their consequences as by the intention the person had. For example, the older child will regard it as worse to break a cup while stealing a cookie from the cupboard than to break a dozen cups by accidentally bumping into the tea cart. The younger child will judge the latter act, in which more was destroyed, as the worse of the two.

2. *Relativism in judgment.* The older child considers behavior in its context, the younger child in terms of absolute right and wrong.

3. *Independence of sanctions.* The older child behaves properly because of his own decision, the younger child because of fear of punishment or retribution.

4. *Use of punishment as restitution and reform.* Punishment should be meted in the form that makes up for the harm done or that helps the individual to learn to be better in the future.

5. *Use of reciprocity.* The points of view and the needs of others are taken into account in moral judgment and action.

6. *Naturalistic views of misfortune.* Ills that befall oneself and others are not necessarily the result of bad behavior, but occur for any one of a number of realistic reasons.

Kohlberg (29, 30) has carried out interesting and constructive systematizing and formalizing of Piaget's not always rigorous or clear thinking about moral development. Kohlberg has developed a scale of moral judgment that is quite reliable; that is related fairly strongly both with intelligence (correlations ranging from .31 to .53 have been reported) and with chronological age (correlations approaching .60); that has modest relationships to moral behavior as rated by teachers; and that can to some degree be predicted from peer group relationships, as Piaget postulated. This is to say, more popular children who are also leaders rank higher in moral judgment than their less popular, nonleader counterparts (24).

Kohlberg (29, p. 400), from his thinking and research (originally done with boys ages 10 to 16), postulates three levels of morality, with two stages within each level. These levels emerge successively from premorality, which is an early stage in which the child does not comprehend "goodness" or "badness" according to rules or authority.

Within level I, the "preconventional" level, are two kinds of primitive morality, each representing progressive stages of moral development. Stage 1 is the *punishment-and-obedience orientation* so typical of very young children. Conformity, for example, is largely a function of avoiding punishment: "I should not hit my baby sister because my daddy will spank me!" Gradually, and if moral development proceeds on course, this stage is abandoned for stage 2, what Kohlberg calls *naïve instrumental hedonism*. By this is meant that the child (or individual) behaves "morally" so as to obtain rewards, to have his own favors returned, to store up "brownie points," and the like. Such an orientation is egocentric and reflects no real insight into the broader bases for human moral behavior. A concern for what is "fair" may be present, but essentially in a self-serving way.

Level II morality, the "conventional" level, is also characterized by two stages. Stage 3 is conceived in terms of *interpersonal concordance*—the "good boy and nice girl" orientation. Moral behavior in this stage is good behavior if it pleases other people, helps them, or results in their approval. As such we might think of this as a morality of social reinforcement. Conformity to stereotypes or to the majority is often characteristic of this stage, presumably because it is "the thing to do." From this orientation emerges stage 4, or the *law-and-order orientation*. Again,

conformity is very strong, but apparently out of respect for authority, the "inherent" worth of fixed rules, and preservation of the social order. A person may argue, for example, that stealing is wrong because "It's against the law." or, "It is one's duty to obey society's rules." In a sense this is not unlike stage 1 behavior in that the person conforms to avoid being censored by authorities. But conformity in stage 4 is also motivated by the desire to avoid guilt that may occur if one is detected in the violation of acknowledged and accepted rights and duties.

Postconventional morality—level III—is marked by an adherence to moral principles whose validity and relevance are essentially independent of the authority of persons who hold them and the individual's personal association with such persons (or groups). Stage 5, the first stage of moral judgment and behavior within this level, is defined as the *social-contract legalistic orientation*. The person at this stage of development considers his contracts with others as morally binding matters. Moral action is viewed in relation to individual rights and standards for behavior that have been achieved by critical discussion and consensus with society. An individual accepts and abides by democratically accepted law. Conformity is less a matter of avoiding legal sanction than it is that of avoiding the loss of respect of impartial observers who judge behavior in terms of community welfare. Agreements between people, formalized through legal means or not, are considered obligatory. Even the law, however, is not considered forever absolute; it can be changed through rational means in the interest of social utility.

The final, and most advanced, stage in moral development (level III) is stage 6—

the *universal ethical-principle orientation.* At this pinnacle in moral development, abstract and ethical principles (for example, the golden rule) are taken as indications of universal morality. They are "self-chosen" in the sense that the individual selects principles to guide his behavior because they consistently and logically represent his belief in the sacred nature of human life and the ultimate value of respect for the individual. Conformity to these principles occurs to avoid self-condemnation: "I could not live with myself if I did (such and such)." Hence a form of judgmental behavior rendered by personal conscience rather than social convention and laws characterizes stage 6.

Having defined these progressive stages, Kohlberg further maintains that: (1) these levels and stages of moral development are strongly cognitively determined; (2) each is a unique emergent from the one preceding it, in that it is qualitatively different; (3) the sequence of moral development is invariant and goes on from the first through the sixth stages (although not all and perhaps not many people reach stage 6, or even stage 5); (4) the developmental process is similar in all cultures (although it may not go as high in some cultures as in others); (5) a greater consistency between one's moral beliefs and his actual behavior in situations involving moral conflict will occur at higher

Table 8.1 *Kohlberg's Levels of Morality*

Stage	Illustrative Behavior
Level I. Premoral	
Stage 1. Punishment and obedience orientation	Obeys rules in order to avoid punishment
Stage 2. Naïve instrumental hedonism	Conforms to obtain rewards, to have favors returned
Level II. Morality of conventional role-conformity	
Stage 3. "Good-boy" morality of maintaining good relations, approval of others	Conforms to avoid disapproval, dislike by others
Stage 4. Authority maintaining morality	Conforms to avoid censure by legitimate authorities, with resultant guilt
Level III. Morality of self-accepted moral principles	
Stage 5. Morality of contract, of individual rights, and of democratically accepted law	Conforms to maintain the respect of the impartial spectator judging in terms of community welfare
Stage 6. Morality of individual principles of conscience	Conforms to avoid self-condemnation

Source: Kohlberg L., *The development of children's orientations toward a moral order. I. Sequence in the development of moral thought. Vita humana* 6: 11–33 (S. Karger, Basel 1963). (Adapted from Hilgard, Atkinson, and Atkinson *Introduction to Psychology,* 5th edition, 1971, 78.)

stages of development (especially stage 6); (6) moral development is irreversible; and (7) each stage is unitary (that is, in all areas of morality, the individual will judge—and tend to behave—according to the general principle or beliefs of that stage (30, 31).

Comment on the Cognitive-Developmentalist Position. There seems to be no question that moral judgment is rather closely related to both intelligence and chronological age. To be moral, a person must be able to look at more than one side of an issue, regard the background and context of an act, and weigh one thing against another. All these processes are related to problem solving and require experience for their development—thus, their relationship to both intelligence and age.

But it is doubtful if moral judgment or behavior (morality, to use the most general term) is a unitary trait. For example, people often seem to apply different principles in their business and professional lives from those they use in their relations with their wives, sweethearts, children, and friends. The pressure of urban evening traffic can devastate the moral behavior of usually high-principled men and women, as can extreme internal and external stress of all sorts. The Kohlberg view of morality demands that an individual have full information about issues in order to behave concerning them in the ways demanded by moral development stages 5 and 6. Since it is humanly impossible to be well informed about all the issues that demand our moral commitment, it seems inevitable that our level of moral judgment and behavior will vary not only according to the pressures and temptations in our current situation but also according to our available information.

In other words, the authors think that individuals are likely to both judge and behave at different moral levels. They argue, in other words, for specific discriminative moral behaviors depending on the situation rather than for a unitary, universally generalized moral process.

The authors believe that there are regularities of moral development, just as there are regularities of cognitive or sexual development, but they suspect that morality varies widely from one culture to another. They do not believe that the Piaget–Kohlberg (cognitive-developmental) point of view allows enough room for individual differences or for the effects of needs and incentives on moral behavior.

The authors agree with Kohlberg (29) when, for instance, he postulates that repeated serious delinquency in almost all cases indicates retarded moral development. They agree that morality at times may transcend law, but that the instances (in a democratic society) are not frequent. They agree that the level of moral judgment tends to be related to level of moral behavior, so highly principled people usually behave accordingly and with considerable consistency from one situation to another.

The position has been developed that moral character is largely a function of ego strength (29). If this is true, the highest level of moral judgment and behavior should be expected from the following types of person: (1) one who is of good intelligence (average or well above); (2) one who can anticipate the future, is capable of both predicting consequences and choosing distant, larger rewards as compared with immediate, smaller rewards; (3) one who can maintain focused, steady attention for as long as the task in which he is involved demands it; (4) one who can control his unsocialized (or antisocial) fantasy (that is, can think about knocking someone's teeth down his throat but, for reasons of conscience, not fear, refrains from doing so); and, finally, (5) one who has a good deal of self-esteem and who is essentially satisfied with the environment in which he lives.

This seems to the authors an eminently reasonable position, and is basically the way they view the background dimensions of moral development.

SOME RESEARCH FINDINGS ABOUT MORAL DEVELOPMENT

Research about moral development stopped to all intents and purposes with the negative findings from the classical studies of honesty among children conducted in the 1920s by Hartshorne and May (16). From elaborate, ingenious, and generally carefully conducted research, Hartshorne and May found that it was virtually impossible to predict cheating from one situation to another; that there was no such thing as an honest child as opposed to a dishonest child, but rather a normal distribution of honest behavior around an average of moderate cheating. Caution as much as honesty was involved in cheating. Cautious children cheated less. The immediate situation influenced cheating behavior strongly, and cheating was much more frequent in classrooms where peers did not disapprove of it. There was not much correlation between moral knowledge and moral behavior as measured by cheating; and middle-class children cheated less than economically disadvantaged children (30).

Some later work done with these negative data shows that there was a bit more generality to their findings than Hartshorne and May believed (7). On the whole, however, their results cooled research

into moral development and behavior for many years. As has been said, interest has been recently rekindled by such writers as Piaget and Kohlberg and by the need to fit their points of view with those of psychoanalysts and behaviorists. This illustrates how research and advance of knowledge can result from theoretical conflict.

If moral development is indeed related to and derived from ego strength, the following predictions should be supported.

1. Older children and older adolescents should show more ego strength than younger children and younger adolescents. This should be manifested by older youth demonstrating more confidence in their original judgment of a situation in that they do not change it after having been fed false norms. They should, in other words, be less blindly socially conforming than younger adolescents.

2. Subjects with low self concepts should be more conforming (in the same sense of the word as in 1) than subjects with positive self concepts.

3. Subjects who work with those who are known to be exceptionally competent should be more conforming than those who work with partners reputed to be low in competence.

4. The most conforming of all should be the persons with a poor notion of their own competence who are teamed up with high-competence partners.

All four of these predictions obviously have clear social implications; and, as can be seen in Example 8.2, in which this study is summarized, all four predictions have research support.

8.2 Ego Strength and Morality
Predictions about moral development and ego strength (see text) were tested in

a study of 13- and 14-year-old boys and girls, all of whom were academically superior high school students, and a second group of older adolescents, 18-to-21-year-old college students about equal in intellectual ability as the younger students (32).

The subjects were paired off such that two people of the same sex and age group were seated back to back and were told that they were to be tested for their ability at working together with others in making accurate judgments. Their task was to judge the length of lines presented to them. Faked reports were then given to both members of each pair in each other's hearing. Some youth were told that they were below chance in accuracy (low competency), others that they were "terrific, very good" (high competency). In a second line-judging task, pairs were formed as follows (all boy–boy or girl–girl pairs): Within each age group, one-half the subjects believed they were low competence, one-half that they were high competence. One-half the low-competence subjects were paired with partners they believed to have the same competence as themselves, the other half were paired with partners they believed to be of high competence.

One-half of the two age groups who believed they were high competence were paired with low-competence partners, and the other half were paired with high-competence partners like themselves. Results are shown in Table 8.2. The higher the score entered in the table, the more the subject conformed to his partner's judgment in the task where the two were working together in pairs (that is, changed his original judgment of the length of a line in the direction of his partner's).

Table 8.2 *Results of Tests for Accuracy in Judgment (average scores)*

	High Self-Competency	Low Self-Competency
High partner competency	.36	.51
Low partner competency	.28	.31

The low-competency youths working with high-competency partners were the most conforming (mean score = .51).

The authors of this study report the following conclusions.

1. The early adolescents were significantly more conforming than the late adolescents.
2. Low-competency subjects were significantly more conforming than high-competency subjects.
3. Subjects who believed their partners were high in competence conformed significantly more than subjects who believed their partners were low in competence.

There were no sex differences in conformity, and knowing or not knowing beforehand who their partners were made no difference in the results. Results from this study fit well with the idea that ego strength and morality go hand in hand.

Child-rearing Practices

The dimensions of child rearing that seem most closely related to moral development are power assertion versus nonpower assertion (19). The power-asserting parent is exactly that: He manages the child by force, physical or emotional. The non-power-asserting person comes in at least two guises — the love withdrawer and the inducer. The love withdrawal technique is a punitive technique, in the same way that power assertion is usually punitive. But in love withdrawal, anger is more controlled, the variables are more psychological than physical or rawly emotional, and the time span is indefinite. For example, a child knows that if he is to be spanked (power assertion), it will be done and over with. But he has no idea when love withdrawal will end—in an hour, in a week, or, as in the case of one mother and her adolescent son the authors know, in five years. Power assertion ordinarily ends positive interaction between parent and child while it is going on, but it endures for a short period only. Depending on the parent and the child and on how forgiving each is, positive parent–child interaction may be resumed almost immediately after a spanking, for example. Love withdrawal also ends parent–child interaction (positive *or* negative) for its duration, and its duration is indefinite.

Induction means reasoning. It is a democratic way of dealing with moral behavior, and it may be self-oriented or other-oriented. In *self-oriented induction*, one may say "Don't cheat because sooner or later you will be caught in your own deception and cheating keeps you from learning what you are supposed to." In *other-oriented induction*, the child or youth is told, "Don't pull the puppy's tail, it will hurt him," or "Say thank you because Mrs. Smith's feelings will be hurt if she thinks you don't appreciate what she did for you." Other things being equal, other-oriented induction is logically more conducive than self-oriented induction to promoting moral development, since it is levied against egocentrism. It also seems likely that other-oriented induction techniques are more effective in developing empathy (feeling with others).

Cutting across these different ways by which parents rear their children is the variable of affection. Affection is less likely to accompany power-assertive techniques than non-power-assertive techniques of child rearing, but there is much individual variation. Some parents who use much physical discipline, for example, are also loving; and some equalitarian, induction-technique parents are often rather withdrawn and impersonal with their children. There are also social-class differences: economically disadvantaged and poor parents are more likely to be power assertive than better-educated and more affluent parents.

There are several reasons for this distinction. The great difficulties encountered in their lives may build up frustration and anger in poor and ill-educated parents. Such frustration and anger are then translated into hostile, power-assertive ways of dealing with their children. The poor are more likely than the middle class and affluent to work in a blatantly boss-bossed relation in which they are handled in a power-assertive manner, and they pass such treatment on to their children. A steady diet of power assertion through the exercise of raw power and threats of punishment may be successful in promoting a rule conformity that simulates morality. But the test comes when an individual reared on such a diet finds himself removed from the constraints of his parents. If, in the absence of authority, this individual does not apply learned principles of right and wrong, this method of moral learning can be seriously questioned.

Still other factors probably complicate the process of moral development among children of poverty. Their parents are likely to be less proficient than the affluent in general problem-solving skills and vocabulary. Thus, it is harder for these parents to employ reasonable problem-solving ways of handling their children. Compared with the affluent, the poor are likely to have more children and less time to reason with them. They often must work harder and longer for what they have, and thus may be too tired when they come home to spend the time and the energy required by such things as other-oriented induction techniques. Their homes typically are less adequate, so the children are more likely to be in the street. Child-rearing techniques are thereby diffused, and the peer group may have more influence than the parents. Finally, the poor are largely alienated from social decision making. They are outside the sociality and the power dimensions of the society. Thus they themselves may have developed morally to a lower level than the more powerful, participating affluent sectors of society. For such reasons, they may not possess the know-how to help their children in moral development (29, 30).

Some colleagues of the authors object to this tentative analysis of life among America's poor. They prefer to seek other reasons, as yet unclarified, for social-class differences in moral development. To be sure, considering the plight of poverty-stricken parents, many are remarkably adaptive and competent in dealing with constant adversity. The issue here, however, is the quality of moral development. For whatever reasons, the fact remains that lower levels of moral development have been consistently found the further down the social ladder one moves (19).

Social class, then, seems to be related to both child rearing and moral development. Other childhood factors that seem to be related (mothers have been more studied that fathers) are these (19).

1. Maternal (and probably paternal) power assertion is negatively related to moral development among children.
2. There is no research consensus about the effects of love-withdrawal techniques on moral development.
3. Maternal, but not paternal, inductive techniques are positively related to advanced moral development.
4. Affection and nurturance seem to accelerate moral development. Perhaps this is because these traits create a climate in which the child is likely to attend positively to the parent's modeling and tutelage.
5. High levels of parental education (a favorable environment for cognitive development) accelerate moral development.

Power assertion techniques block the child and frustrate his mastery and competence needs. The power-asserting parent provides an angry model for his child and, insofar as the child models on his parent and insofar as unpunished aggression on the part of a model disinhibits aggression in the modeler, power assertion techniques produce aggressive children. At least, these children are aggressive to those who cannot exert power over them (those who are younger or weaker), or are aggressive in circumstances where they will not be caught, as in many delinquent acts. In a situation where power is being asserted, the child's attention is focused on the parent and on himself, but *not on the consequences of his act.* This condition seems likely to retard the kind of learning required for advanced moral judgment. Finally, as we know, the high tension inherent in power-assertive situations is likely to provoke interfering anxiety and fear. It may also inhibit all responses, not only the punished nonmoral behavior but also other potentially constructive morally oriented responses. However, in real life "some power assertion may be needed for the voice of reason to be heard" (19, p. 341). The interested reader should consult Hoffman (19) for a sophisticated and much more detailed discussion of these points.

Experimental Evidence

The conclusions summarized above have come mostly from nonexperimental studies. Many rest on data gathered by interviews with mothers about their own behavior and that of their husbands and their children rather than on direct observation or experimental manipulation. The conclusions must, then, be regarded as general and tentative. The authors have some faith in these conclusions, but only as broad generalizations made with moderate confidence. But they do not think the data are solid enough, for example, to provide a manual on "How to rear your child to be moral."

In recent years, there has been a spate of studies of imitation and modeling as they relate to moral judgment and behavior. These studies are similar to those concerning sex typing and sex identification discussed in the preceding chapter. The results from the studies are by no means clear. There is evidence that love withdrawal in the form of isolation from adults may make children susceptible to adult influences, but only when an adult is present and the child is performing simple cognitive tasks. Thus, the laboratory evidence for any relationship between love withdrawal and moral development is meager. This is also true of the real-life studies summarized earlier.

Nurturance and affection have been shown to increase self-criticism for prohibited acts. So does providing cognitive labels for the act (a form of induction).

Modeling and imitation disinhibit children (for example, result in their behaving more aggressively); but it has not been demonstrated in laboratory settings that children will inhibit undesired behavior or resist temptation as a result of modeling and imitation. Modeling and imitation laboratory studies have provided results indicating that children can learn to delay gratification. They learn to choose delayed but larger rewards more often.

One overall conclusion from the experimental studies that seems to be justified is that models can more easily undermine past socialization (disinhibit) than they can promote further, more advanced moral development. However, there is some evidence that modeling and imitation can increase altruism and consideration for others (19). In justice to experimentalists, it is very difficult to reduce the big gutsy issues involved in moral judgment and behavior to dimensions that can feasibly or ethically be studied experimentally.

Sex Differences

As a group, girls are more conventionally moral than boys (that is, they conform more readily). There are probably several reasons for this state of affairs.

1. Social pressures for conformity are greater for girls than for boys (see the discussion in Chapter 7 of appropriate and valued sex role stereotypes).

2. Related to 1, girls are generally less willing than boys to admit unconventional or immoral thoughts and actions. There is some evidence (36) that when girls believe they will not be detected, they are as aggressive as boys (in the physical realm—in this case, administering electric shock in an experimental situ-

ation). The evidence is abundant that girls show at least as much, and usually more, prosocial aggression (moral strictures) than boys and more antisocial aggression in the form of gossip and backbiting.

3. Biological factors may enter the picture. Much conventional morality revolves around the issue of aggression. If boys are more physically active and restless than girls (and this seems to be clear), they are more likely to wander into trouble, to meet frustration and become angry, and so on. In general, the authors suspect that high-active children are faced with more impedence in moral development (at least as far as conformity is concerned) than low-active children.

4. The high sexuality of boys is likely to lead them into morally ambiguous sexual situations on the one hand, but, on the other hand, male transgressions in this area are taken more lightly than female transgressions. Thus, it may be that the sexes balance out in this area.

5. With the cultural expectations of initiative and self-sufficiency held for boys, boys are more likely than girls to be involved in moral transgressions. In America today, property is power, power in our culture is more important to males than females, and thus boys may be more likely to steal (property, money, cars) in order to gain power.

6. Dishonesty in school (cheating on tests, for example) does not vary much by sex. To the regret of the authors, it also seems to be normal behavior. Given the opportunity and freedom from risk, nearly 50 percent of both boy and girl groups cheat. These data come from many studies, from a wide age- and social-class range of subjects, and from both boys and girls. Interested readers should consult (19) and (38).

Religion and Morality

Sound evidence is scarce about the relations between religion and morality, even though morality is the core of most religions. Thus, a data-based discussion of the matter cannot be presented to our mutual satisfaction. Adherence to the ethical aspects of the three religions we know best—Christian, Jewish, and Muslim—should certainly promote and encourage moral development, but sound studies on the matter have not been conducted. In fairness, of course, it is very difficult to design research that will result in definitive data. Consider, for example, the methodological difficulties faced by a research worker who attempts to isolate the influence of religious experience from other socialization variables, including school, peer group, and mass media.

Among colleagues with whom the authors work there is moderate agreement that people only casually affiliated with churches or whose affiliation is extrinsic (for example, a desire for recognition and status, church as a means to meet and socialize with community leaders, or simply because "it's the thing to do") are less moral than both a-religious people and people who practice their religion intensely. At least those who are casually oriented or extrinsically motivated usually rank highest in prejudice and hawkish attitudes about war.

SOME DILEMMAS IN MORAL DEVELOPMENT AND SOCIALIZATION

Behavioral Conformity as a Moral Matter

Some of the essential questions relating to moral development and socialization are these.

When does conformity become mindless submission?

How can we bring up our children to conform in a reasonable way yet at the same time to be original and creative? By definition, originality and creativity constitute nonconforming behavior.

How can children and youth learn to conform to a reasonable degree, yet maintain their respect and tolerance for harmless but sometimes annoying nonconformities of others?

Derived from such questions is this issue: if we teach our children to conform—to respect law, order, and custom—are we at the same time denying them the opportunity to be spontaneous, original, curious, and creative? This dilemma, it will be remembered, was posed in Chapter 3.

In our society, we are given to punishing nonconformers. The lack of continuity in American life, the nuclear family structure built around the all-too-fragile husband–wife dyad, and the breathless pace of our protean American society may cause us to cling to conformity for reasons of personal security. If we are lost in the group, we cannot be singled out and held responsible. We may be lost, but we are secure in our anonymity. Nonconformity also threatens our bureaucratic, republican structure which, with all its unwieldiness, depersonalization, and other weaknesses, may still be necessary for a democracy to survive.

For such reasons, nonconformers are

Recent years have witnessed several volatile clashes between groups of people—not necessarily the young versus the older—having different moral codes. (Photo by Bob Combs)

likely to be punished by their peers and the authority figures in their lives. To be punished is to have one's integrity threatened. Anger and continued, often nihilistic, rebellion are the end result of nonconformity for many. Such people may be the ones who bomb, burn, and assassinate. Moderates — the ones who see the merits in both sides of the case — are often punished by those in the extreme groups at the left and the right. Moderate people are thus often forced into radical positions, probably driven more often to the right than to the left in our society, because, on the whole, leaning toward the right is safer and less controversial.

Rationality of Authority as a Moral Matter

The questions to be raised here are the same as those raised about behavioral conformity. If democracy is to survive, as the authors believe it must, those who administer it — the authorities — must be perceived by those in the ranks as rational, basically well-intended people. But what of urban slum and rural Black or Chicano children and youth whose depressing conditions are often revealed to authorities who are neither kind, rational, well disposed, nor fair? Among such authorities are many police, landlords, teachers, and welfare workers. They are the dominant power figures, more powerful than parents, to whom poor children are exposed.

More affluent children and young people are also frequently confronted with irrational authority: teachers who are grossly unfair; police who assume guilt; public officials who cheat, steal, and lie.

It may be that the disposition to see authority as rational goes back to earliest childhood, perhaps to Erikson's first stage of man, *trust* (11). If so, there is the danger of too much as well as too little trust. It is no better to be a gull than a cynic. Pollyanna cannot survive any more successfully in today's complex society than an utterly alienated, despairing, and cynical member of, for example, the hard-drug culture.

Impulse Inhibition as Moral Matter

We have seen that there is a consensus that one aspect of advanced moral judgment and behavior is the ability to delay gratification so as to opt for a later, larger reward rather than for an immediate, smaller reward. Carried to its extreme, as it sometimes is in this culture (where there is still a Puritan streak), this attitude may mean that you never have any fun *now.* Or it could also mean a denial of the impulsive, "spur of the moment" behavior that often makes life the exciting thing that it is.

The authors do some traveling. In their travels, they often encounter pinched, frail, little old ladies (more often than little old men) who have saved all their lives for "the chance to see Paree." But they have saved so painfully and for so long that they no longer have either the energy or the talent for enjoying *Paree* when they finally get there. Further, they have often waited until they lost the partner with whom they wished to share *Paree,* so they see it in loneliness.

On the other hand, the authors often see children and young people who greedily and recklessly grasp the here and now, much like Aesop's grasshopper in the fable of the grasshopper and the ant. Addiction to either drugs or alcohol, they believe, implies both inability to cope with the frustration and the denial that are part of the human condition, and inability to postpone immediate gratification.

How, then, do we bring up our children with a capacity for simply *being:* for having fun, for turning loose, for acting like happy, carefree Dionysian people sometimes, yet for the most part adhering to an Apollonian ethic? In the Apollonian way of life, planning is done, things are accomplished, and a central motive is to *do*. The Dionysian enjoys things now, and there are occasions when this is both useful and necessary. The Apollonian is more likely to wait to enjoy the larger thing later, but if he waits too long, he may lose it forever.

Some thoughtful youth (and some not so youthful) deplore the competitive, depersonalized, materialistic fabric of American life. A surprising number of our brightest young people on the highest moral development level carry their distaste for the conforming American way of life to the point of dropping out. This is a loss to everyone.

The authors believe that a major American task at all levels, from elementary school through to big business, industry, and government, is to modify the American system so as to allow more room within it for individual expression and happiness. In the long run, they believe that the culture will profit (even in terms of so crass an index as the gross national product) if everyone is a bit happier and is given a bit more leeway as a biological, emotional human being. In other words, unhappy workers, the authors predict, will produce fewer and poorer quality products than happy workers, even with all the technology in the world; and more of them will be social casualties.

Consideration for Others as a Moral Matter

Consideration for others is closely related to impulse inhibition, and needs little additional discussion. Consideration for others often, perhaps usually, demands impulse inhibition, because "What is good for me can be bad for you." The issue in child rearing and education is to develop respect for others and a lively sense of reciprocity and consideration, but not at the risk of losing personal autonomy and the occasional freedom to enjoy life on one's own terms.

Moral Education in the Schools

The above issues, in addition to many others, are most certainly involved in any consideration of the school's role in moral development and education. There can be no question that teachers are constantly involved in moral education, whether they realize it or not. It is perhaps fair to say, however, that moral education more often takes the form of exhortations and injunctions in the classroom than anything else. Efforts made by teachers to control cheating, aggression, and sexuality and the pressures they exert to induce conformity to values or virtues all have strong moral overtones. This approach often represents a system of aversive control ("If you do such and such you will be punished"). Further, the exact nature of the moral values is not always made explicit or consistent from one classroom to another. Some teachers the authors have known retreat entirely by stating that any attempt at moral education, indirect or otherwise, is "immoral," that is, constitutes an attempt to indoctrinate or impose the values of one person on another.

It should therefore come as no great surprise to the reader that there is little evidence to suggest that conventional school experience has much effect on the moral values and behavior of children and youth. By way of contrast, there is much evidence to indicate that the highly systematic Soviet approach to moral education is quite successful (6). This approach, however, is based on systematic techniques of social control, group pressure, competition, and peer censure, which are viewed dimly in the United States. Moreover, the Soviet system seems more directly based on moral indoctrination with the basic aim of promoting total allegiance to the state, individual rights and needs notwithstanding.

Thus, in addition to the dilemma of determining the goals of moral education within the school complex, American educators face a procedural dilemma: how to go about the matter of moral education in ways that are both acceptable to society and effective for their stated purpose.

As this book is written, the literature about moral development and education reflects a healthy ferment. Among the most clearly visible approaches to the problem is that taken by Kohlberg and his colleagues from the cognitive-developmental perspective (31). Briefly, this approach has as its central aim the stimulation of the individual student's moral judgment and character toward successively higher stages of development (see the earlier discussion of Kohlberg's stages). This, Kohlberg believes, simply consists of facilitating growth in a direction that students already are going but may not completely realize. For such occurrence, educational experiences must reflect real-life moral issues that concern students directly, either individually or collectively, as members of society. Association with persons whose moral judgments reflect at least one stage higher in the developmental sequence is necessary in order for a lower level student to experience cognitive conflict, engage in introspection, and equilibrate to a more advanced stage.

Obviously, translating such a general plan into classroom action is no easy task. Among other things, one must know at what moral level students operate at the outset, and must provide and, through group discussion, highlight suitable moral dilemmas that are capable of arousing conflict. He must also ensure that advanced levels of moral reasoning are clarified without resorting to didactic methods. There is some evidence that such an approach is workable. Combined with opportunities to model consistently moral behavior on the part of teachers and with the experience of positive consequences for moral behavior, this approach is promising indeed. (For details, see 30 and 31.)

✝ POLITICAL SOCIALIZATION AND DEVELOPMENT

DEFINITION

In Chapters 3 and 7, the overall concept of socialization was discussed. It was concluded that socialization must be viewed as both process and product. In political socialization, *process* concerns the ways in which children and youth are introduced to political attitudes, behavior, and roles (47). As a *product*, political socialization refers to the beliefs held about political ideals and the realities of political life, together with the affective orientation toward the political system(s) of his country (47). The "rational attitude toward authority," discussed in the first part of this chapter in connection with moral development, is a political as well as a moral matter. In democracy, the authors believe, authority is basically regarded rationally, while in totalitarian governments the attitude toward authority seems to reflect a heteronomous more than an antonomous morality. Logically, it is clear that espousing democratic systems demands a higher level of moral development than espousing totalitarian systems. Common terms for political socialization as product are liberal, conservative, racist, pink, activist, and so on.

A political system, in turn, is a pattern of human relationships involving power, authority, and rule. This pattern reflects basic value and moral commitments (8). As stated earlier, the morally mature person must examine the norms of his society (as they are reflected in political organization as well as otherwise), must decide whether they permit the realization of the values they are derived from, and, finally, whether or not these values are the correct ones. For such reasons, the discussion of political socialization logically follows the discussion of moral socialization.

In this section, developmental and background factors in political socialization are discussed. The authors believe that the current wave of student activism is so politically significant that a special subsection is devoted to it. Finally, a few basic dilemmas about political socialization are examined, especially as they are related to the schools.

DEVELOPMENTAL TRENDS IN POLITICAL SOCIALIZATION DURING CHILDHOOD

It has already been indicated that psychological data concerning religious and sexual behavior are scarce. The same is true for political behavior. Only since about the time of Sputnik has there been much psychological study of political development and behavior. Consequently, most of the information available at this time is tentative and incomplete. Fortunately, there have been a few major studies, largely descriptive, whose findings provide a baseline against which students may consider their own political development and design their own studies of political development in others. In this section, six baseline generalizations about political development are presented — generalizations that have emerged from these major studies: (14, 18, 20, 21, 23, 34, 43), and a brief comment is added on political ideology in adolescence.

National Feeling

First, patriotism, or national feeling, is apparent among children as early as the primary grades. This feeling and related understandings about the concept of nation become more differentiated and elaborated with age. But, in general, the sense of national feeling (in contrast to attitudes toward *government*) seemingly undergoes little change during the elementary grades. Young children focus more on concrete symbols of nationalism such as the flag and the Statue of Liberty, but by junior high school age national feeling is more often reflected by pride in freedom and the right to vote.

Formal Government

A second age-related generalization concerns the concept of formal government. Younger children personalize government and organize their views around people toward whom they show personal attachment (or rejection). Older children think at least as much of function and organization as of personalities in government. With age, a shift occurs from an early belief in the personal benevolence and protective power of governmental representatives, typically focused on the president

Schools are one of society's major socialization institutions. Thus, they play a dominant role in the formation of young people's political attitudes and understandings, although the exact contribution of such outcomes has been difficult to establish. (Copyright Paolo Koch)

in this country. Older children and youth are more likely to be concerned with official duties, qualities of leadership, and executive competence of those in government.

Positive feelings about government typically diminish as one moves from national to state to local government. This may be because teachers concentrate at the national level. "Familiarity breeds contempt" may be involved. Finally, among mobile Americans, ultimate political identification is likely to be American rather than New Yorker or Californian or Kansan. We are likely to be

United States citizens all our lives, but citizens of many states during the developmental span. Positive feelings (trust and confidence) shown by children are often much reduced in postadolescence. This seems particularly true of graduate student and many professional student populations.

View of the "Good Citizen"

A third generalization is related to how children and youth view the "good citizen." Young children value virtuous behavior, such as cleanliness and courtesy. As in moral development, older children and youth are more abstract and concentrate on altruism (reciprocity), voting responsibility, the power of the state, and the responsibility of *all* citizens to assure honesty and competence in governmental operations. However, obedience to law is stressed at all levels. This is understandable when one considers that compliance to authority underlies socialization in general (for example, the emphasis on duty to obey school rules and regulations encountered from kindergarten all the way to graduate and professional school).

Political Activity

Fourth, it is clear that age differences occur in the form of political activity in which children engage. With age, an increasing number of children engage in political discussion with parents and peers. Young children, however, are generally apolitical in terms of activities normally associated with politics, such as campaigning, taking sides on issues, and attending political rallies. This is not surprising. As compared with older children, younger children have neither the cognitive power nor the opportunity for meaningful political participation. Further, it obviously is not until a person reaches legal age that participation in society's political affairs can be complete, including the ultimate privilege of voting.

Knowledge and Attitudes

Fifth, children's knowledge about the kinds and the impact of political influence increases with age, and their political attitudes differentiate and become more sophisticated. For example, knowledge about personal political influence is generally limited among younger children to voting and perhaps rioting. Nuances of

influence such as behind-the-scenes pressure group activity, the exercise of personal power and the spoils system, and nonviolent protest are neither known nor appreciated until late elementary or junior high school age. Even then, political naïvete among children is the rule rather than the exception. This naïvete extends also to children's perceptions of the motivations of political candidates, the role of governmental representatives in promoting (or impeding) social change, and differences between the major political parties. Even as late as the high school years, uncertainty about political affairs and where to obtain information about political candidates is frequently expressed by youth. This may be because families, schools, and communities do a poor job of political education. This issue is examined in greater detail in the later section on dilemmas.

Political Affiliation

Finally, there is evidence to indicate that political party affiliation (partisanship) is often reflected in the verbal behavior of children in early elementary school years. Young children are likely to parrot their parents' political preferences and thus identify themselves with a given political party. Today, however, the trend, at least for older children and youth, seems to be away from partisan political affiliation toward independent status as voters. Perhaps because it is considered desirable in our society to make up one's own mind, increasing numbers of youth are placing candidates and issues above simplistic party affiliations and the traditional straight-party-ticket pattern of voting. Youth from 18 through 20 throughout the country have recently voted in national elections. Preliminary surveys indicate

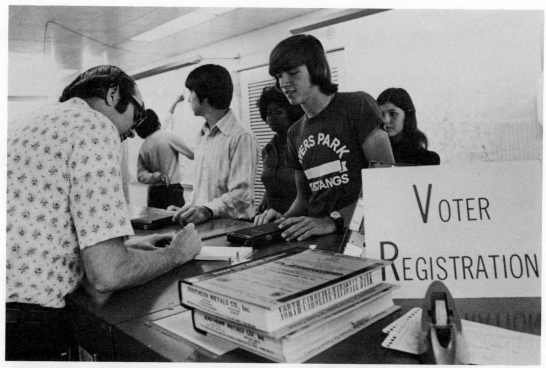

The admission of 18-to-20-year-old youth into the electorate may bring about significant changes in the character of local and national political activities. (Photo by Bruce Roberts)

that party affiliations did not predominate. Apparently, many new voters see themselves independent from traditional political parties.

SOME BACKGROUND FACTORS IN POLITICAL SOCIALIZATION

In this section some prominent background factors in political socialization are highlighted: family influences, social class, intelligence, and sex. Most comments about the role of political education within the schools are reserved for the later section on dilemmas about political socialization.

Family Influences

As for other aspects of socialization, family influence is probably the most salient mediator of political development. Children generally follow parental preferences, although parents apparently are most influential with respect to general partisan commitment and preference for major political candidates (47). Parental influence is often lower for partisan *issues,* especially abstract issues such as economic reform (47). Moreover, children perceive parents (along with teachers and the clergy) as exerting major influence on views about citizenship. The authors believe, however, that the peer group becomes a powerful reference group for political activity and beliefs, especially during early adolescence and beyond. The role of the peer group is discussed specifically in Chapter 9.

A popular belief among adults (and adolescents, the authors suppose) is that adolescent political behavior and attitudes represent a rebellion against the political beliefs of their parents. The facts are that not much evidence exists to support the rebellion hypothesis. As in childhood, similarity in political beliefs between parent and offspring is generally high throughout adolescence. In fact, growing evidence indicates that even radical political activism during later adolescence and young adulthood usually is not an indication of rebellion against one's parents, but is rather a continuation of a family tradition. Specifically, such activism is often linked to a family background characterized by strong parental dedication to ideological matters (46). Such parental behavior, combined with a permissive orientation to child rearing, seemingly sets the stage for many political activists to implement their ideology during adolescence and beyond. The potential power of parental models and reinforcement for active political behavior in the area of political socialization cannot be overlooked.

The specific matter of political activism will again be discussed shortly. Meanwhile, the authors wish only to reiterate that little evidence can be presented to support the idea of political rebellion against parents during adolescence. Where apparent rebellion *does* occur, it is more often against politically *involved* than politically *apathetic* parents (45). This suggests that the dynamics of rebellion may be less tied to political ideology per se (liberal or conservative) than to the quest among some adolescents for independence from parents who take a strong stand on anything. Even in their rebellion, for example, young left-wingers from conservative families seem often to be modeling on their parents' activism and dedication, though not its direction. The less frequent converse is also plausible.

Socioeconomic Factors

In Chapter 1, it was indicated that the nature and quality of formal school experience is generally more crucial for the academic development of disadvantaged children than for advantaged. This seems also to be the case for political development (47). The reason may be that less overlap exists between civic training in the home and school for children from disadvantaged circumstances. Parents and their children from lower socioeconomic status are more likely than their more advantaged peers to say that they have no control over their environment or that forces beyond their control (fate, luck, chance) govern their lives (35). Since a person is not likely to become politically involved unless he believes he can exert some influence on political affairs, it is plausible to suggest that a belief in external control is associated with political apathy.

Further, middle-class children more so than their lower-class counterparts report greater amounts of politically oriented discussions with their parents (18). It is likely that such discussions have the effect of both sensitizing children to, and promoting their interest in, political affairs. As pointed out in the first half of this chapter, the poor typically feel that they have no part in the political process (29). Thus, they are not often politically active and provide their children with no models for political attitudes and behavior.

Intelligence

The political savvy of bright children, as compared to their less bright peers, has been documented in a number of ways, just as it has been for moral development (47). For example, children of higher intelligence conceptualize the government earlier and more along abstract dimensions of structure and function (versus organizing their concept of government around specific people, such as the president). They also are less likely to view government officials as paternalistic and charged with the responsibility of preserving the status quo. Bright children also earlier recognize that government officials and institutions are not infallible and that elected officials may misrepresent or otherwise fail to account for the wishes of their constituencies (18). More intelligent children are also quicker to see the importance of a system for monitoring the activities of government and its officials, particularly in terms of organized citizen activity.

This information suggests that intelligence most clearly influences both the rate at which insight into political realities is achieved and the level of abstraction at which political phenomena are conceptualized. However, data also indicate a positive relationship between intelligence and political behavior, particularly political activism. This point is examined again in the following section about political ideology and activism among youth.

Sex

In addition to child-rearing practices, social class, and intelligence, there is some evidence that political behavior differs by sex. The data that are available indicate that males are more politically active than females as early as late childhood (18).

This sex difference is most apparent in matters related to partisanship, debate over conflictual political issues, and desire to change or improve the political system. This, of course, is consistent with the direction of sex differences in behavior reported elsewhere in this book. Sex differences in motivation are perhaps involved in still another area; namely, the fact that females are more often oriented toward the interpersonal aspects of political life, whereas males are oriented more to the abstract, problem-centered aspects.

From the above discussion it can be seen that various mediators of development, as first discussed in Chapter 1, are at work in the area of political socialization and development. While much more research is needed, including a clarification of the relationship of religion and other cultural forces to political behavior, a beginning into this complex area of development has been made. Let us now turn specifically to political ideology and activism among youth.

POLITICAL IDEOLOGY AND ACTIVISM AMONG YOUTH

In the above section about developmental trends, it was suggested that most limitations in political development during childhood are associated with or due to both limitations in cognitive ability and circumscribed political experience. Before age 14 or 15 (when adolescents have fully entered into Piaget's formal stage of operational thought), older children and young adolescents often possess only a vague sense of community and the law, are remarkably insensitive to civil liberties, and profess a preference for expedient and often authoritarian solutions to problems

(1, 2). At about age 15, however, new trends typically emerge: awareness of individual rights, recognition of the need to limit government control, and the understanding of the social contract with the state that is basic to the democratic process. The authors believe that this expanding awareness reflects adolescents' ability to conceptualize alternatives for political organization and to analyze the moral prescriptions implicit in political systems. In other words, older children and youth become able to examine their society to see if its organization permits its values to be realized and, ultimately, to judge whether these values are morally correct.

With adolescence, there also comes the ability to distinguish between what is real and what is ideal. Making this distinction is often disillusioning, and for young people who first recognize the distinction the result may and very often seems to be disenchantment with the political system.

Student activism and dissent are discussed in this context: a shift from comparative political naïvete and ignorance of political realities to a reasonably accurate perception of the implications of the American political system for human behavior. The authors believe that the increased involvement by youth in political affairs is very significant and that it represents a trend toward more complete implementation of civil liberties that is essential if democracy is to succeed fully. As this trend is discussed, the relationships between moral and political development are also more clearly illustrated.

Incidence and Sources of Student Activism and Dissent

Since the ''Berkeley incident'' of 1964, various forms of activism have become commonplace on the nation's campuses. It is perhaps even more significant that student activism, including dissent, has become more frequent in American secondary schools. For example, one national survey reveals that during 1969, some form of activism occurred in nearly 60 percent of American high schools and 56 percent of junior high schools. (48). Moreover, the school administrators involved in this survey indicated their belief that politically motivated student unrest will continue to increase in both strength and scope during the 70s. It is obvious that a careful examination by educators, psychologists, and sociologists of the causes of and procedures for accommodating student activism is imperative.

It was indicated earlier that political systems are patterns of human relationships involving power. It seems that much contemporary student activism and dissent is an attempt on the part of youth to achieve more decision-making power in school and, in some cases, local, state, and national affairs. A basic issue has thus emerged: how much collective authority for decision making should students exercise? Moreover, militant student activists, although they are a small minority of adolescents and youth, have often taken their dissent beyond the matter of how authority for decision making is exercised in the schools by teachers and administrators. Their radical dissent extends to challenging legitimacy of school authority itself. This is reminiscent of our discussion of the control of behavior and standards for evaluation in Chapter 3.

A closely related issue is that of which facets of school policy are legitimate domains for student participation and control. There is some evidence that the kinds of concern about school policy vary according to educational level. At the college level, student dissent typically revolves around curriculum relevance, grading policies, and the quality of instruction (including demands for a voice in personnel hiring and tenure decisions). In contrast, dress and hair regulations, cafeteria and smoking rules, censorship of underground newspapers, and the use of undercover narcotics agents on school grounds seem to be the hot issues in junior and senior high schools at the time of this writing (37, 48). Despite these differences, students in high school and college alike express concern about ecology, racism, war, and personal freedom for themselves and groups such as Fem Lib and Gay Lib (9). These issues concern basic questions about human existence that are explored more fully later in this section and that are intimately related to justice, and reciprocity in morality as these issues were discussed in the first part of this chapter.

In many ways, the school conditions under which protest flourishes are similar at high school and college levels. These conditions usually include low student involvement in policy determination, an impersonal climate for learning, and encumbered communication systems (5). A greater incidence of political activism is also found in larger, public educational institutions located in urban environments (4). This is apparently true whether the activism is *traditional* (for example, participation in Young Democrats or Young Republicans), *radical* (for example, disruptive protest), or *episodic* (for example, unique to a given event at a specific time).

Characteristics of Activists

The authors have observed that many adults, including some teachers and other youth workers, often think of student dissenters as a mixed bag of hotheads and maladjusted hipsters. Considering the current range and scope of student protest, student dissent cannot be dismissed as primarily an outlet for unrepresentative minorities of emotionally unstable youth.

The reason is at least twofold (44). First, as many as 40 percent of the 1969–1970 college population supported values that underlie student activism. In fact, many of these values are basic to the kind of personal involvement on which a successful democracy depends. Percentage figures for high school populations are not available at the time this book is written. However, data about high school protest presented earlier provide us with some indication of student support.

Second, research about the personal characteristics of active student dissenters results in a generally favorable picture. For example, activists, when compared to nonactivists, are more often high in academic achievement and measured intelligence, possess greater knowledge of political affairs, and more clearly recognize the political implications of social issues (27). Activists also are more likely to come from liberal families in which humanist values are stressed and which manifest strong patterns of principled moral reasoning (15). Again, these generalizations are mostly based on studies conducted in college settings, although the authors have no reason to believe that high school dissenters include a qualitatively distinct or less well adjusted body of students.

It should perhaps be noted that Piagetian and Kohlbergian notions account well for the intellectual but not the affective aspects of student dissent.

Personality Differences among Student Protestors

It has been noted that overall comparisons of activists and nonactivists reveal a generally positive or social desirable set of shared attributes among activists. However, these comparisons can be deceiving. Differences within the ranks of student dissenters are perhaps greater than those between dissenters and nondissenters. This is most apparent from analyses of distinct varieties of student dissent. One such analysis, for example, has resulted in the identification of at least two varieties of dissent: the politically active protestor and the culturally alienated student (26). The former group consists of students who are strongly influenced by basic social and political values inherent in a democracy. They are generally not estranged from their parents. Although the politically active protestor may experience anxiety about social policy and feelings of isolation, he believes that society can be improved and works to put this belief into practice. In short, this type of protestor is both committed to and engaged in a quest for social salvation.

In contrast, the culturally alienated protestor has usually rejected or otherwise discounted existing social values and is more likely to be estranged from his parents (especially the father). Moreover, the culturally alienated student's protest is typically accompanied by a whirlwind of experimentation and nonconstructive activities. It has been suggested that such a protestor is likely to turn to private psychopathology if "culturally permissible" means for the expression of alienation are not available (25, 26). In short, the culturally alienated protestor is seemingly more wrapped up in the pursuit of personal rather than social salvation. The alienated student may also be at a lower level of moral development, and may be more likely to resort to violence than the politically active protestor. For example, more radical and violent activists have been found to be at a premoral (Kohlberg's stage 2, level I) level of moral judg-

ment, and more nonviolent or liberal activists at the highest level (Kohlberg's stage 6).

Distinctions such as these obviously are made at the risk of oversimplifying the dynamics of political activism. In fact, it is perhaps most appropriate to think of the two "types" that have been discussed as extremes on one of the complex dimensions of protest. More elaborate typologies that include politically conservative and apathetic students have been proposed (3). The point is that activism springs from a variety of personal motives, responses to social experience, and levels of moral reasoning.

Levels of Student Protest and Political Ideology

It has been emphasized that the nature of student protest is both complex and pluralistic. It is appropriate to consider further the levels on which protest and activism are manifested. In this way, the authors believe a clearer perspective on the causes and the dynamics of protest can be achieved. To begin, at least *two* basic levels of protest can be identified: (1) responses to critical questions of *human existence in general* and (2) the ideology of protest among *adolescents specifically* (33).

Concerning critical issues of human existence, at least three basic interrelated clusters of response can be described (33). One response cluster constitutes a revolution for *survival*—that is, survival of mankind as a species. Current efforts to salvage and improve our ecology exemplify this cluster of responses. A second response cluster involves revolution for *equitability*—that is, protest about the extremely unequal distribution of resources and opportunities available to people throughout a society. The civil rights movement and pressures to achieve economic opportunity for all citizens are examples of this form of revolution. Finally, a third response cluster can be described as a revolution of _meaning_—that is, a cluster of responses for the purpose of broadening the range and quality of human existence. Specifically, this revolution is designed to overcome an existence limited to the "luxury of overabundance" (33). Here, youth and others are seeking more open, honest, and meaningful human relationships, including a search for ways of becoming a contributing member of a group without being submerged and lost in it (39).

It seems that much of the current student protest is focused on the revolution of meaning, particularly the protest that involves the college population. It is also apparent, however, that a common ideological position is not shared among all student protestors. In fact, the ideological basis for protest is seemingly affected by social class and racial factors. One authority suggests that protest based on materialistic values (revolution of meaning) is more likely to occur among privileged adolescents who can afford the luxury of seeking new frames of reference by which to shape their life styles (12). Disadvantaged blacks, in contrast, may not challenge materialistic values so strongly, because so few of them have experienced even economic security, let alone affluence. Rather, this segment of the youth population may be more concerned with finding ways quickly to obtain their share of the economic pie. They are more likely to take part in revolutions of equitability.

To the authors, the precise relationship between political ideology and the content of protest in the public schools is not clear. However, they believe that all three "revolutions" (survival, equitability, and meaning) are represented to some degree in the specific protests of adolescents and youth.

It is likely that these ideological bases culminate in at least three goals widely shared among student protestors (33). The first goal is a commitment to achieve congruity between the values inherent in the democratic idea and the behavior of people who ostensibly believe in democracy. In other words, youth are pressing to eliminate the hypocrisy that is so common and so inconsistent with the democratic idea.

The second is the desire to change the social system wherever possible in order to reduce the alienation that youth see as characteristics of both themselves and other large segments of the American population (including most minority groups). Third, youth are resolved to engage in concrete action, not just in abstract and detached theorizing from the traditional ivory tower. It is clear, however, that among youth there is no consensus about the *form* such action should take. Witness the difference, for example, between Vista and Peace Corps activity and the destructive violence of the Weathermen.

Since the violence-marked antiwar demonstrations of the late 60s, campus protests have been fewer and more restrained. This diminished dissent, contrary to many predictions for the 70s, is not easily explained. We can speculate that the growing scarcity of jobs for many college youth has induced among them a stronger career-oriented work commitment, with little time and energy left for protest activities. It is also possible that many young people have come to believe that violent protest is too often counterproductive, is not inconsistent with the professed ideals of political action in a democracy. Perhaps suffrage for America's 18-year-olds symbolizes a new era of participation by the young. Of course, it is also possible that we have merely observed a lull in extremist antiestablishment activity and that the forces of adamant protest are being remarshaled by student political leaders. As this book is written, however, it does not yet appear that a majority of America's high school or college and university students is dedicated to political protest against government policies, inhumane social conditions, or extant educational institutions—disruptive or otherwise.

SOME DILEMMAS ABOUT POLITICAL DEVELOPMENT

There are many dilemmas related to political development. Some are urgent and explosive. They range from discovering precisely how children become socialized politically to defining the political role of teachers in the schools. Because of space limitations, however, only two political socialization dilemmas are discussed, both of which are related to citizenship education. The first, more general, dilemma concerns how best to conduct such education in the public schools. The second, more specific, dilemma involves the response of educators to radical student activism.

The General Dilemma of Citizenship Education

The very small percentage of American adults who are positively active in politics at some level (estimated as 5 percent) has often been taken to indicate widespread public apathy in this arena of human affairs (28). Even among youth on our college campuses, political activity nowhere

"My guess is the surf is up."

To many adults, the commitment and involvement among a majority of youth appear to be fleeting and contradictory. Perhaps this is in part a function of the communication gap between youth and their observers. (Cartoon from Phi Delta Kappan, *1969, 50 (5), 263. Reproduced by permission of artist, Henry R. Martin.)*

involves a majority of students (4). Growing numbers of critics are now pointing their fingers at public institutions because of their role in promoting such apathy. For example, one critic has emphasized the paradox that while the rhetoric of democracy calls for a politically active citizenry, its institutions (particularly the schools) systematically but silently perpetuate apathy (40). This apathy purportedly is due to several factors (17, 40). One is that school children and youth are taught a concept of government as benevolent and nurturant, where the rights and needs of all are both guaranteed and served. Thus many young people may early believe that there is little need for activity to "keep the system honest." A second factor is that the social realities of politics—power struggles, interpersonal conflict, compromise, pressure group tactics, and the like—are not explored in most programs of political education. Thus the stage may be set for disillusionment (and subsequent withdrawal from political activity) among those who finally discover the discrepancy between political ideals and social realities. Still another possibility is that people are taught that the vote is the all-powerful tool for shaping political affairs, when, in fact, its individual power is limited. A power bloc is typically necessary (17). Finally, the hypocrisy of educating for democratic living within a basically authoritarian school system is seen by some critics as a counterproductive socialization strategy (47).

The authors cannot testify that these factors are directly responsible for political apathy and cynicism in American society. It is clear, however, that the institutionalized procedures for citizenship education are increasingly coming under attack by scholars who believe that more realistic and thorough approaches are needed to sustain a healthy democracy.

At least two questions come to mind about such criticism. One is the validity of the criticism itself. For example, have the schools actually failed to provide adequate citizenship education? Any answer to this question requires first a look at the basic task of citizenship education delegated by society to its schools. According to one authority, this task has been twofold (17): to transmit knowledge about the political system and its processes and to facilitate the adoption by children and youth of political values and traditions. Viewed in this way, citizenship education is perhaps more a matter of indoctrination than anything else.

One issue involved here is whether a society can afford to do anything but indoctrinate its members to its particular institutionalized way of life. In view of the fairly high political stability in American society over the past century, one can infer that indoctrination, if indeed this is what occurs, has been reasonably successful. Yet critics still maintain that this comes at the expense of a politically active citizenry both aware and capable of dealing with the nitty gritty of political life. Too much emphasis is placed on the ideals of democracy, they say; too little on its operation.

It is difficult to analyze this matter, because very little good research on the political impact of school experiences has been reported. It is particularly easy to make the schools a whipping boy for the ills of society when data either are vague or are insufficient. The dilemma of where the truth about citizenship education lies is further compounded by the paradox that, in our experience, many of the same adults decry *both* political apathy and political activism among youth.

8.3 An Example of Citizenship Education Research

One of the many questions that can be asked about political socialization has to do with the effect of the secondary school civics or social studies curriculum on political attitudes and knowledge. Although this is an extremely difficult area for research, some pioneering efforts have been made. Preliminary results have not been impressive, however. For example, data taken from a national sample of high school seniors suggest that the civics curriculum has little or no impact on political knowledge or attitudes. Still other data indicate that curriculum impact may be mediated by several variables or conditions, including the extent to which an "open atmosphere" for discussion and reasoned examinations of controversial issues (for example, Vietnam, race relations, partisan politics) is maintained in the classroom.

To check the possible influence of such classroom conditions on citizenship behavior, Ehmann (10) conducted a study of some 334 youth (grades 10 to 12) in a large, racially integrated urban high school. Specifically, Ehmann was interested in the singular or the combined effect on four aspects of political behavior and attitudes (1) of an open atmosphere for discussion, (2) of opportunity for the discussion of controversial issues, and (3) of the extent of exposure to social studies courses. The aspects are discussed below.

Political cynicism. A belief that the government tends to be wasteful, crooked, untrustworthy, and fumbling and is run for the benefit of a few.

Political participation. The extent to which one discusses politics with others,

persuasiveness (versus passivity) in political discussions, frequency of attendance at political rallies or meetings, and monitoring of the news media.

Political efficacy. A belief that one has or will have some influence on the outcomes of the political system and that the system is basically responsive to the opinions and actions of persons like himself.

Sense of citizen duty. A feeling of obligation expressed by a person to fulfill his future role as a citizen by voting.

The major findings of this study can be summarized as follows. First, Ehmann was unable to show that the social studies curriculum, whatever its content and climate for instruction, has a substantial impact on the political behavior and attitudes of high school students. The magnitude of effects, however, apparently varies by race. For example, greater curriculum impact was documented for blacks (versus whites), especially in the open classroom setting. Second, Ehmann noted a general tendency toward increased cynicism as students moved through the high school grades. Whether this can be directly attributed to school experience is questionable. Third, where consistently favorable *trends* in political attitudes were noted among this sample, they were associated with exposure to controversial issues in an atmosphere marked by inquiry and openness.

The study described in Example 8.3 is included to round out the discussion about the impact of school curricula on citizenship behavior. It also helps to bring into focus a second question in response to criticism about citizenship education. If past methods for such education are not suitable, what shall be done to make this form of education more effective? There is no dearth of recommendations. For example, one authority maintains that political education should proceed through the study of moral philosophy whereby the relationships among economics, politics, and ethics within social institutions are placed in perspective (28). Public school teachers better equipped with knowledge of history, politics, and philosophy are also called for.

Still other authorities stress the need for more realistic course work, including specific instruction about the various ways in which political power can be exercised in one's personal and political group life (40). Another favored strategy suggests removing citizenship education from the formal, often sterile classroom and conducting it within community institutions where social action programs can be directly implemented by children and youth (42). Finally, one could take a Summerhillian approach to such education (see Chapter 3). This approach is predicated on the belief that the best moral–political education is self-education within an open, permissive, peer-dominated environment.

Such approaches *are* being tried. Whether they result in education for democratic citizenship that is measurably superior to "traditional" methods remains to be seen. Meanwhile the authors can think of no better guidelines for public school practice than (1) ample provision for students to practice democracy in the schools, not simply have them read about it, and (2) opportunity to examine with candor and honesty the strengths and the weaknesses of social life in a democracy.

A subdilemma for those who would implement a meaningful program of political education in public schools is made up of questions of community disapproval and job security. Our public schools are on the whole authoritarian and conservative. Many of the same problems arise in the area of political education that come up in that of sex education (see Chapter 7). As with sex education, a very large number of school people have decided that it is "better to be safe than sorry." The result is little or no meaningful political education, just as there is currently little or no meaningful, or at least very useful, sex education in American public schools.

This subdilemma and its dubious resolution in most schools is easy to understand, although it may be hard to forgive. Think for a moment of a careful in-depth analysis of the government of any municipality, county, city, state, or the nation itself. In such an analysis, searching questions will have been asked about just *whose* values are being served, how, and why; and whether these values are those which are morally best. Some embarrassing answers are bound to emerge, and some important toes will thus doubtless be stepped on. Since schools are community controlled (typically by the more powerful and conservative people in the community), teachers and students who engage in such in-depth analysis—an analysis that is essential for *good* political education—are likely to find themselves on precarious ground and in the midst of conflict.

The Dilemma of Radical Student Activism

Any talk about practicing instead of merely formally studying the principles of any political system during the course of citizenship education inevitably raises the question of power—power to make decisions. More specifically, who will have how much power to make what kind of decisions? In Chapter 3, the dilemma of controlling behavior was discussed. The dilemma about behavior control is clearly involved in the current demands by many students that they be included in decision-making activities that ultimately affect their behavior, both immediately and in the future.

The authors have already noted some strong commitments among many youth to change the social system so that alienation is reduced or eliminated. Many of them also take concrete action to do so. As in society generally, these convictions may take a variety of forms in the public schools, ranging from mild pressure through normal channels to overt violence and disruption. The basic philosophical dilemma is: Can or should schools be operated (changed?) according to student vote or demand? Here, however, the authors are mainly concerned with the dilemma of how best to respond to demands.

For the authors, it is helpful to consider this dilemma of student participation and activism in relation to tactics often employed by radical student activists who seek to change the schools by whatever means are necessary. Example 8.4 includes an outline of these tactics (13), which constitute a series of steps or stages in dissent.

The authors cannot condone a policy that permits interest groups, student or other, to coerce, intimidate, or use violence successfully in attaining their goals. Reinforcing disruption, as seen in step 6, Example 8.4, is inconsistent with the democratic ideal and is contrary to principles of reciprocal morality. On the other

hand, neither are authoritarian, paternalistic, and unresponsive school administrations and faculties satisfactory democratic representatives to youth. Such behavior from power figures is not truly moral any more than violence is.

The authors do not profess to have a magic solution to the dilemma of dealing with dissent. What seems reasonable is an approach whereby the worth of changes proposed by students is considered in terms of their potential for improving the educational process (13). Furthermore, the authors believe in the need for accessible, open channels for student–faculty, faculty–administration, and school–community communication. Grievance procedures should also be established, and those who use them (students or anyone else) should be protected from open or covert censure for such use. The principle of student representation on school committees that deal with curriculum and instruction also has much to commend it. Finally, in-school experience should be provided concerning how institutional change can be effected. These experiences may take the form of seminars, workshops, or even formal courses for credit. In the final analysis, the authors believe that a school environment built on sound principles of learning and motivation, development, and reciprocally considerate human relationships is one that is unlikely to undergo attack by students, radical or otherwise.

8.4 The Tactics of Radical Student Activists

According to one authority on student activism, R. A. Gorton (13), the strategy for protest and power seeking among radical dissenters consists of several steps.

The continuities and the discontinuities of both moral and political development are perhaps most sharply illustrated in the phenomenon of student activism. (Photo by Lawrence Frank)

1. Identify an issue for which the support or sympathy of a majority of students can be marshaled, wherever possible including existing student body leaders.

2. Present the argument in the form of demands to school officials. If student support (step 1) has been obtained, this argument can be based on the grounds that in a democracy majority rules. If majority support is not forthcoming, the rights of the minority in a democracy must be emphasized. If school officials do not act, then take step 3.

3. Exercise every means possible to list approval and support from adults, especially parents and teachers. It is notable that student activists often capitalize on the conflict that frequently exists between school faculties and administrations. Thus, teachers are appealed to on the basis that the "administration is repressive and unreceptive." If no results occur, go to step 4.

4. Identify the "villains." Open and specific charges are addressed to specific personalities within the administration. The principal charge usually is that the administration will not listen. Often, however, step 4 is taken even when the administration responds. Dissenters are often dissatisfied with the rate at which a response is obtained, and/or fail to acknowledge that honest differences of

opinion may exist concerning the merits or validity of the original demands. Gorton also points out that radicals either ignore or fail to appreciate the idea that changes in one aspect of school operation often exert effects on other aspects of the operation, including implications for future program development. Thus, a cavalier approach to change must be avoided by responsible school authorities. If still no action, go to step 5.

5. Seek specific support from outside groups, including (if possible) the press, American Civil Liberties Union, and even the Parent–Teachers Association. The idea is to apply still more pressure on the school administration to "get off the dime." Sophisticated strategies of persuasion are usually employed at this stage, often accompanied by the contention that "A majority of students supports us," and that "It's high time the school places some trust in its students." If no action, proceed to step 6.

6. Achieve disruption of the school program by whatever means is expedient and effective—a sit-down strike, a boycott, or even violence. Step 6 behavior is usually rationalized on the grounds that "We have tried everything through established channels, but with no success. Therefore, we must take extreme action if these critical student rights are to be secured."

The authors know of no universally suitable counterstrategy for use by school officials in dealing with step 6 crises. However, it seems that educators must have at their disposal a carefully considered advance plan of action for dealing with disruption. Possibly the best insurance for school administrators in this regard is anticipating student needs and exerting leadership for posi-

tive change as against a status quo approach, which finally results in reacting to crises, often emotionally and inconsistently. In short, there may be no *cure* for step 6, only prevention.

However analytical and insightful this sequence of student protest behavior may be, a major question remains: Are the strategies and goals of protest sufficiently similar across situations to permit a meaningful, generalized description of activist behavior?

Finally, and perhaps anticlimactically, there is no substitute for common sense and sensible empathy (looking at and respecting others' points of view—the morality of reciprocity). In running a school, we certainly do *not* want to repress, frustrate, and alienate. On the other hand, faculty and administrators often *do* know best, and their expertness deserves to be used. Finding a happy medium seems to be the problem. If people's intentions are good and if they work at it, this happy medium can usually be approximated.

Summary

Morality has two aspects. The highest morality consists (1) of personal principles of reciprocity based on empathy, mutual respect, and regard for the integrity of human beings and of human life and (2) of realistic acceptance of social responsibility. The two aspects do not always mesh easily.

Three assumptions about morality prevail: the innate evil, or killer-ape, nature of man; the innate goodness, or fallen-angel, nature of man; and the *tabula rasa,* or neutral, blank-slate, nature of man. Humanists embrace the second; psychodynamic psychologists the first; behaviorists the third. The latter two depend heavily on training for moral development; humanists depend more on free experience.

Moral development parallels the other socialization processes and products, such as sex typing and identification. It is closely tied to cognitive development and ego strength. The authors regard Kohlberg's notions of moral judgment as promising. Kohlberg postulates three levels of development: (1) premoral (including preconventional), (2) conventional, and (3) postconventional or principled. Moral judgment is modestly related to moral behavior, and the relation should be closer the higher the level of moral judgment. Morality is not a unitary trait, as individuals vary in their moral behavior from situation to situation and according to personal needs. Needs and emotions as well as external pressures influence moral behavior and probably moral judgment.

Power assertion as a child-rearing tactic is negatively associated with level of moral judgment and behavior, and affection and reasoning are positively related. For complex reasons, children of the poor show lower levels of moral judgment and behavior. Girls' morality may be more conforming; boys', more principled. This is probably due to different social training for the two sexes. Little evidence exists about morality and religion.

Dilemmas about morality involve behavioral conformity (not too much, not too little); belief that authority is rational (one cannot be naïve, but must be somewhat optimistic about the nature of authority); control of impulse (plan ahead *but* remember also that you live only once); and consideration for others (a healthy and constructive amount, but do not become a martyr).

Moral education in the schools is a complicated matter; proper faculty and administration modeling of morality in the context of democratic educational practices makes for the best possible program for moral education, which, the authors believe, cannot be formally and didactically taught.

Like all other aspects of socialization, political development is both a process (how does it occur?) and a product (an end result, such as a political activist, a Republican, or a member of the League of Women Voters). The politically mature person will examine his political settings at all levels to see what and whose values they serve and facilitate, and how they do so. He will also examine carefully to see whether these values are moral and worthwhile. This can be a complex, painful, conflict-producing process, but is necessary for a good political education. The pain and the risk involved in so doing may account for the facts that few people examine their political settings in this manner and few schools provide such political education.

Like moral development, political development begins with concrete, personalized concepts focused on leaders, such as the president. It moves toward the abstract and the principled (what is *democracy* and how can it be made to work?). Before full political development can be attained, it seems likely that a person must have moved well into the formal operations stage of cognitive development and into at least the next highest of the six stages of moral development.

Children and youth model politically on their parents. Activists come from activist parents and, on the whole but with many exceptions, the children of conservative parents are conservative, those of liberal and radical parents, non-conservative. In general, politically activist youth are brighter, better informed, and at higher levels of moral development than nonactivist youth. However, some activists—a minority—are morally primitive (at the preconventional stage of development) and more destructive than constructive. Males tend to be more active politically than females, and children and youth from well-educated and affluent families are usually more politically active than those from poor homes with ill-educated parents.

Political activism is common and apparently occurs in some form today in well over one-half the nation's high schools and junior high schools. Activism is most usually centered on critical questions about human existence in general and adolescent ideology about activism in particular.

Finally, it was concluded that, while good citizenship education is essential, there is little of it; and a morality of reciprocal human relations was urged in the dealings of authority and power figures (such as police, politicians, school administrators and faculty) with children and youth.

REFERENCES

1. Adelson, J., B. Green, and R. P. O'Neil. The growth of the idea of law in adolescence. *Developmental Psychology,* 1969, *1,* 327–332.

2. Adelson, J., and R. P. O'Neil. Growth of political ideas in adolescence: The sense of community. *Journal of Personality and Social Psychology,* 1966, *4,* 295–306.

3. Block, J. H., N. Haan, and M. B. Smith. Activism and apathy in contemporary adolescents. In J. Adams (ed.) *Understanding adolescence.* Boston: Allyn and Bacon, 1968, 198–231.

4. Blume, N. Young Republican and Young Democratic college clubs in the midwest. *Youth and Society,* 1971, *2,* 355–365.

5. Brammer, L. The coming revolt of high school students. *Bulletin for the National Association of Secondary School Principals,* 1968, *52,* 13–21.

6. Bronfenbrenner, U. Soviet methods of character education: Some implications for research. *American Psychologist,* 1962, *27,* 550–565.

7. Burton, R. V. The generality of honesty reconsidered. *Psychological Review,* 1963, *70,* 481–500.

8. Dahl, R. A. *Modern political analysis.* Englewood Cliffs, N. J.: Prentice-Hall, 1963.

9. Education, U.S.A. *High school student unrest.* Washington, D. C.: National School Public Relations Association, 1969.

10. Ehmann, L. H. An analysis of the relationship of selected educational variables with the political socialization of high school students. *American Educational Research Journal,* 1969, *6,* 559–580.

11. Erikson, E. H. *Childhood and society.* (Rev. ed.) New York: Norton, 1963.

12. Friedenberg, E. Current patterns of a generational conflict. *Journal of Social Issues,* 1969, *25,* 21–38.

13. Gorton, R. A. Militant student activism in the high schools: Analysis and recommendations. *Phi Delta Kappan,* 1970, *51,* 545–549.

14. Greenstein, F. I. *Children and politics.* New Haven: Yale University Press, 1965.

15. Haan, N., M. B. Smith, and J. Block. Moral reasoning of young adults: Political-social behavior, family background, and personality correlates. *Journal of Personal and Social Psychology,* 1968, *10,* 183–201.

16. Hartshorne, H., and M. A. May. *Studies in the nature of character:* Vol. I, *Studies in deceit; Studies in self-control:* Vol. III, *Studies in the organization of character.* New York: Macmillan, 1928–1930.

17. Hess, R. D. Political socialization in the

schools: A discussion. *Harvard Educational Review*, 1968, *38*, 528–536.

18. Hess, R. D., and J. V. Torney. *The development of political attitudes in children.* Chicago: Aldine, 1967.

19. Hoffman, M. L. Moral development. In P. H. Mussen (ed.) *Carmichael's manual of child psychology.* New York: Wiley, 1970, 261–359.

20. Hyman, H. *Political socialization.* New York: Free Press, 1959.

21. Jahoda, G. The development of children's ideas about country and nationality. Part 1: The conceptual framework. *British Journal of Educational Psychology,* 1963, *33*, 47–60.

22. Jahoda, G. The development of children's ideas about country and nationality. Part II: National symbols and themes. *British Journal of Educational Psychology,* 1963, *33*, 143–153.

23. Jennings, M. K., and R. G. Niemi. The transmission of political values from parent to child. *American Political Science Review,* 1968, *62*, 169–184.

24. Keasey, C. B. Social participation as a factor in the moral development of preadolescents. *Developmental Psychology,* 1971, *5*, 216–220.

25. Keniston, K. Student activism, moral development, and morality. *American Journal of Orthopsychiatry,* 1970, *40*, 577–592.

26. Keniston, K. The sources of student dissent. *Journal of Social Issues,* 1967, *23*, 108–137.

27. Kerpelman, L. C. Student political activism and ideology: Comparative characteristics of activists and nonactivists. *Journal of Counseling Psychology,* 1969, *16*, 8–13.

28. Kirk, R. Political socialization in the schools: A discussion. *Harvard Educational Review,* 1968, *38*, 545–549.

29. Kohlberg, L. Development of moral character and moral ideology. In M. L. Hoffman and L. W. Hoffman (eds.) *Review of child development research,* Vol. I. New York: Russell Sage, 1964, 364–431.

30. Kohlberg, L. Moral education in the schools: A developmental view. *The School Review,* 1966, *74*, 1–30.

31. Kohlberg, L., and E. Turiel. Moral development and moral education. In G. Lesser (ed.) *Psychology and educational practice.* Glenview, Ill.: Scott, Foresman, 1971, 410–465.

32. Landsbaum, J. B., and R. H. Willis. Conformity in early and late adolescence. *Developmental Psychology,* 1971, *4*, 334–337.

33. Langton, S. Demythologizing the student revolt. *Phi Delta Kappan,* 1970, *51*, 540–544.

34. Laughton, K. Peer group and school and the political socialization process. *American Political Science Review,* 1967, *61*, 751–758.

35. Lefcourt, H. E. Internal versus external control of reinforcement: A review. *Psychological Bulletin,* 1966, *65*, 206–220.

36. Mallick, S., and B. R. McCandless. A study of catharsis of aggression. *Journal of Personality and Social Psychology,* 1966, *4*, 591–596.

37. Mallory, D. (ed.). *Student activism and the relevancy of schooling.* Melbourne, Fla.: Institute for Development of Educational Activities, 1970.

38. McCandless, B. R. *Adolescents: Behavior and development.* Hinsdale, Ill.: Dryden, 1970.

39. National Institute of Child Health and Human Development. The acquisition and development of values. Perspectives on research. *Report of a conference May 15–17, 1968, Washington, D. C.* Washington, D. C.: U. S. Government Printing Office, 1969.

40. Newmann, F. M. Political socialization in the schools: A discussion. *Harvard Educational Review,* 1968, *38*, 536–545.

41. Piaget, J. The moral judgment of the child. New York: Free Press, 1948. (Originally published, 1932.)

42. Raskin, M. Political socialization in the schools: A discussion. *Harvard Educational Review,* 1968, *38*, 550–553.

43. Sigel, R. Image of a President: Some insights into the political views of school children. *American Political Science Review*, 1968, 62, 216–226.

44. Skolnik, J. Student protest. *American Association of University Professors Bulletin*, 1969, 55, 309–326.

45. Sullivan, E. V. Political development during the adolescent years. In E. D. Evans (ed.) *Adolescents: Readings in behavior and development*. Hinsdale, Ill.: Dryden, 1970, 92–107.

46. Thomas, L. E. Family correlates of student political activism. *Developmental Psychology*, 1971, 4, 206–214.

47. Torney, J. V., and R. D. Hess. The development of political attitudes in children. In G. Lesser (ed.) *Psychology and educational practice:* Glenview, Ill.: Scott, Foresman, 1971, 466–501.

48. Trump, L. L., and J. Hunt. The nature and extent of student activism. *Bulletin of the National Association of Secondary School Principals*, 1969, 53, 150–158.

9 Children, Youth, and Their Peers

As an introduction to the complex topic of peer group relations among children and youth, consider the following exchanges. Each exchange is a segment from interviews held independently between one of the authors and three young people: Joanie, Roger, and Pat.

Joanie (10 years old; grade five; suburban, middle-class elementary school)

Interviewer: "How do you feel about kids who cheat in class?"
Joanie: "It's wrong, I guess."
Interviewer: "Should the teacher know when cheating happens?"
Joanie: "I guess so."
Interviewer: "What if one of your classmates copied from your paper? Would you tell the teacher?"
Joanie: "It depends on who copies . . . I mean, if it was Barby or someone I like I wouldn't tell. Nobody rats on a friend. But, if it was Randall or somebody like that I might tell."
Interviewer: "Why?"
Joanie: "Well, Randall is such a fink . . . nobody likes him!"
Interviewer: "Why?"
Joanie: "I dunno . . . he's just dumb . . . weird!"

Interviewer: "How does Randall feel about not being liked?"
Joanie: "How should I know? Anyway, who cares!"

Roger (12 years old; grade seven; large, urban, racially mixed junior high school)

Interviewer: "Are there any kids here at school that the other kids especially look up to?"
Roger: "Yeah, a few . . . let's see . . . there's Ken Craft, Bud Mance . . . and Sparkie Betz. Especially Bud, though . . . he's a ninth-grader, ya' know."
Interviewer: "Besides being a ninth-grader, what's special about Bud?"
Roger: "Well . . . he really knows where it's at, ya' know, and . . . uh . . . well, he ain't afraid of tellin' a teacher to go stick it in his ear, ya' know? Uh . . . I mean, Bud's cool . . . he makes it with the girls, too . . . I mean, uh . . . he'd just as soon rub 'em up as look at 'em!"

Pat (15 years old; grade ten; all-male parochial high school)

Interviewer: "Is there a class in school that you like least?"

306

Pat: "Yeah . . . English!"

Interviewer: "What do you find unpleasant about English class?"

Pat: "Mainly the teacher . . . he plays favorites and treats a lot of us unfair."

Interviewer: "Have you ever talked to the teacher about this?"

Pat: "Well . . . no."

Interviewer: "Do you think it might help?"

Pat: "Maybe."

Interviewer: "Will you do it?"

Pat: "I may . . . but I'd want to check with the other guys first to see whether they'd do it, too."

These interview segments, the authors believe, illustrate some typical social attitudes anchored in the peer group relationships of many children and youth. In Joanie's case, we see the operation of a group code ("Don't rat on your friend") common to most social groups, along with a callous indifference, if not outright rejection, of a peer thought of as "dumb" and "weird." For Roger, there is awe and near-idolization concerning the older, "cool swinger" on whom Roger and his friends may model themselves in their quest for social recognition. Finally, we see in Pat a peer consciousness that likely will affect the degree to which he acts autonomously or exercises independent judgment in social situations.

It is with these and other facets of the peer group experience with which this chapter deals. First, some definitions are given, notably a reference to the various strata of peer experience that influence social development. Subsequently, major categories of social development are discussed, including age trends in peer relations, leadership–followership, the issue of youth culture, and some dilemmas about children, youth, and their peers.

DEFINITIONS

Almost all children experience several layers of interaction with peers.

First, most children have siblings close enough to themselves in age that they have played, confided, plotted, and fought together, and have mutually influenced each other greatly.

Second, all but the most isolated children have in their neighborhoods playmates with whom they interact from their preschool years onward.

Third, almost all children attend school. They are enrolled in classes with other children of about their same age, and come to know all the members of their class very well in the classroom and on the playground. They are influenced by, and in turn influence, their classmates deeply.

Fourth, children are influenced by children and youth in classes other than their own. "The big kids"—those in the higher grades—are likely to exert more influence than those who are younger and in lower grades. Peer influence according to school segregation has not been thoroughly studied, but it seems likely that schools that are integrated by race, socioeconomic level from high to low, and sex (both boys and girls) provide importantly different peer influences from those existing in schools that are segregated according to one variable or another.

Fifth, there are generalized social expectancies about what children of different ages do. Such expectancies are likely to provide a form of peer group influence, albeit at a high level of abstraction. For example, we are given to saying, "Two-year-olds are negative." "Thirteen-year-olds are moody." "Fifth-graders are a delightful age." "Boys are noisier than girls." Such general social expectations are bound to influence behavior, although the effects may not be profound.

In this chapter, the authors are mainly concerned with the second and third categories mentioned above: the child and the age mates with whom he plays intimately in the neighborhood; and such children and the other peers with whom children attend school and are in close association, particularly classmates. Collectively, this association exerts immediate, constant, and profound influences on social, academic, and (later) vocational development.

The authors think of the peer group as a primary group (refer to the discussion of primary and secondary groups in Chapter 1). Among peers, first, there is much immediate, face-to-face, close association. Second, the norms of the group determine what behavior is accepted, rejected, approved, and disapproved. Third, the peer group is a leveler. That is, for most children, the peer group supplements and reinforces what has been learned at home, but typically in a more tolerant and a less emotional way. However, when customs and practices in the home differ sharply from the community norm, the peer group affords the child the chance to learn "how most people do it." This may be for the better or for the worse. Finally, the peer group provides a degree of emotional support for most children. One's same-age friends often understand the processes and the crises of development better than his parents.

For our purposes, then, peers constitute a primary social group. At least from kindergarten and first grade and for several years thereafter, influence is exerted mostly by children of one's own age and sex, although young boys interact with

and learn from young girls and vice versa. A good bit of segregation by sex continues into adolescence, but for normal adolescents, the peer group then becomes heterosexual rather than unisexual.

DEVELOPMENTAL TRENDS[1]

Very young children, until about the age of 18 months, are not truly social animals, although they react to their peers with interest and enjoy and need extensive social relations with caregiving adults (40). On the whole, however, their goals and needs are related more closely to maturation and learning, and interactions of the two, than to purely social relationships. Of course, maturational goals (such things as sitting alone, walking, and the other antigravity behaviors; motor skill; and speech) are all achieved in and facilitated or retarded by children's social contexts. Evidence is reasonably clear that such maturational goals are achieved more rapidly and efficiently, and may reach a higher level of competence, if the child's social environment is rich in stimulation and provides him with personal security.

It will be recalled (see Chapter 3) that Piaget conceives of the first 18 to 24 months of the child's life as the sensorimotor stage, in which the major developmental goal is to master the objective environment, the world of things. The available data about children's social interactions during this period fit well with Piaget's conceptualization. For instance, under about 18 months, children seem to regard other same-aged children as objects and manipulanda rather than playmates; for example, from 6 to 12

---

[1] In this chapter, the authors draw heavily on the work of Hartup (25) and Elder (17).

The extent of the social relationship between these two small children is limited to one interest they hold in common—the desire to ride the hobby horse. (Wide World Photos)

months, infants seemingly react to other babies as playthings. At about 1 year, two infants together often engage in conflict over playthings. At about 18 months, true social interest seems to arise, and the interest of two children in each other as social beings seems to become more important than an interest in playthings that are available to both infants (40).

Reasons for this kind of development seem clear. Young children are egocentric. They think of themselves, not of others, and find it difficult or impossible to take the points of view of others. Mature social relations depend, in part, upon the ability of one person to take the point of view of another; certainly this ability is important for genuine empathy with another human being. Social relations also depend heavily on communication with other people by both gesture and speech, but more on the latter than the former. Children do not have the representational tools (language and gesture) to communicate very fully with others before the ages of 2 or 2½ at the earliest. Socialization also demands foresight, and young children usually are not effective planners, because they have neither the tools nor the experience necessary for planning. Thus, young children have trouble anticipating the actions of others and equal trouble in delaying their own gratification, which must frequently be achieved at the expense of other people. Moreover, young children do not tolerate frustration easily, and social interactions are full of frustration.

In other words, because mature social interactions demand rather full communication, planning and anticipation, sacrifice of immediate personal gratification so as to preserve the social interaction, and a good deal of frustration tolerance, children during their early preschool years are not well socialized in the adolescent or adult sense of the word.

From about age 3 onward, developmental trends in peer-related behavior are about what is to be expected of children who gain in age, experience, impulse control, cognitive complexity, ability to play roles and see the point of view of others, and language and other forms of communication facility. For example, children become steadily more dependent on their peers, in relation to their dependency on adults, often to the dismay of parents and teachers. Physical aggression declines, almost to nothing among girls, and is replaced to some degree by verbal aggression (see Chapter 10). Prosocial aggression, often rigidly moralistic, appears, whereby children typically take the role of a moral authority and correct or reprimand those who deviate from the norm. Children become more able to share with others (altruistic), but at the same time also become more competitive.

Not surprisingly, sharp cultural differences exist in cooperative and competitive behavior among children. United States children, for example, are dramatically more competitive and less cooperative in structured strategy-demanding situations than are children from Mexican villages or Israeli kibbutzim (where the children have been reared in groups). Israeli urban children are more competitive,

less cooperative than kibbutzim-reared children; and children of Mexican national origin living in the United States in urban communities are less cooperative and more competitive than Mexican village children. In these studies, no ethnic differences between Black, Hispano, and white children living in urban areas was found (14, 15, 19, 31, 32, 39, 57).

On the whole, however, social interactions become increasingly more positive and less rancorous with age. Yet both the nature of the situation and the way groups of children are handled by adults will affect this phenomenon. For example, when reinforcements are given to children for social participation, constructive reactions to frustration, and cooperative and other high-level social play, these types of behavior increase in the group (24). It seems logical that the opposite can also occur and, indeed, to some degree such behavior has been repeatedly demonstrated. Classes where teachers are sharply critical, for example, are relatively high in disruptive social behavior (research in progress by the authors) at all age levels from first through eighth grades.

Play Behavior and Early Social Development

Classically, social interactions among young children in play have been classified as either (1) unoccupied, (2) solitary, (3) onlooking, (4) parallel, (5) associative, and (6) cooperative (50, 51). Full descriptions of these qualitatively different forms of play are presented in Example 9.1. Throughout the preschool years, from age 2 to 5, solitary and parallel play decrease, and associative and cooperative play increase (7, 50). Age changes for unoccupied (low at all ages), solitary, and onlooker behavior are less striking.

9.1 Forms of Play: A Developmental View

The careful observation of children (ages 2–5) at play in nursery school settings has led to the formulation of the following six classes or categories of social involvement during the early years (51).

Unoccupied behavior. Unoccupied behavior represents the smallest extent of social involvement. It is also the least frequent sort of behavior that occurs among children in most preschool groups. By unoccupied behavior is meant behavior that indicates no play in the usual sense of the word. Rather, the child apparently occupies himself with watching anything that may be of interest at the time. Random movement may also be present—getting on and off chairs, crawling under a table, following the teacher, or just standing around fidgeting with one's own body.

Solitary play. Solitary play refers to play in which the child acts alone and independently of others. He may play with toys different from those used by children nearby. No effort is made to initiate conversation or other association with others. The child seems simply to concentrate on his own activity, and play occurs without involvement with or reference to what other children are doing. This form of play is usually more frequent among younger children (ages 2–3). As children grow older, they normally spend less and less time in this form of play, as opposed to more social forms.

Onlooker behavior. In onlooker behavior the child spends his time watching others play. Conversations with other children may be initiated, including question asking and advice giving. But the child does not engage himself in the play he observes. Often the child will station himself close to a play activity so that he can see and hear what is going on. Onlooker behavior therefore differs from unoccupied behavior in that it usually represents a sustained interest in other groups of children and often establishes communication channels. Such behavior is similar to unoccupied behavior, however, in that it occurs rather infrequently among preschoolers, by comparison to solitary and parallel play.

Parallel play. Parallel play is also independent play, but the activity chosen by the child rather naturally brings him among other children. Here the child will play with toys similar or identical to those used by children near him, but he plays with them according to his own plan. Neither does he try to get other children to do what he is doing. Thus, the child plays alongside others and is compatible with them, yet he does not play *with* the others. This sort of play is very common between the ages of 2 and 3. Parallel play continues to be a fairly frequent form of play during the later preschool years, but associative and cooperative play usually become more prominent among older preschoolers.

Associative play. Social interaction based on play activity is involved in this form of play: "borrowing" and "lending" of playthings, leading and following one another with trains and wagons, and moderate efforts to control which children will or will not be "allowed" to participate. Children engage in basically the same activity; no attempt is made to divide play tasks or organize the activity. Children play as they wish and do not surrender their interests to the group. This form of play is perhaps most common among 3- and 4-year-olds, although 2-year-olds will often join in such fun.

Cooperative play. Two-year-olds are seldom observed in this form of play. Here, mostly older preschoolers play in a group organized for a purpose: making something material, competing to reach a goal, dramatizing adult or group life situations, or playing formal games. Children sense either that they do or do not "belong" to the group. Group control is in the hands of one or two members, who direct the activities of participants.

Specific tasks are usually assigned to children, either individually or in subgroups. Activities are organized so that children do not work at cross-purposes or duplicate the activity of others.

This classification of play behavior illustrates vividly the social character of play as children grow older. Physical–motor, language, and intellectual skills undoubtedly combine to bring about greater awareness and competence in social situations. The rate at which children develop their skills differs, of course. Partly because some children are more advanced than others, various pat-

Play behavior becomes increasingly more cooperative, complex, and rule-bound, as demonstrated by the activities of these adolescents. (Photo by Nicholas Sopieha)

terns of social development can be observed. And play activities most clearly provide the setting for these patterns— leadership–followership and peer acceptance–rejection, for example.

One research worker (7) believes that the nature of play, circa 1971, is markedly different from that observed four decades ago. For instance, in this more recent study, there was much less than one-half the amount of cooperative play among 3- and 4-year-olds that had been shown in the older study, more than twice as much onlooking behavior, and one-half again as much unoccupied behavior. The author suggests that smaller families, in addition to the enormous amount of time spent by today's children passively watching television, may be associated with these changes. Subjects for the earlier study were urban Minneapolis—St. Paul children, and those for the recent study were children from a Canadian town of 18,000 population. This factor must be considered in interpreting the findings. On the surface, however, there is little reason why living in a big town rather than a small town, or in Canada rather than in the United States, should affect cooperative play, onlooking play, or other social play behavior in any systematic way.

To summarize this section, children move along in their relations with their peers much as they do in moral development, cognitive development, or development of sex typing and identification. By the time they are in late adolescence, most children have learned to cooperate when appropriate, compete subtly and with some effectiveness when appropriate, make some sacrifices for the good of their close friends and broader peer group, show consideration for the moods and

troubles of others, focus their sexual interests heterosexually while preserving good friendships among members of their own sex, conceal fears and anxieties that they believe will interfere with their peer relations while at the same time finding close associates in whom they can confide their fears, anxieties, hopes, dreams, and ambitions. In late adolescence, there are few outbreaks of raw aggression in the peer group, although aggression against out-group members persists with distressing frequency.

Many children and youth, of course, are social casualties in their relations with their peers. Among late adolescents, this casualty rate is demonstrated in school dropouts, drug and alcohol addiction, early and unhappy marriages, emotional difficulties, and problems with the law. The socialization casualty rate approaches 25 percent and poses one of the most important problems within our society (41). Perhaps, considering the rapidity of change and the pressures to which children, youth, and adults are exposed, the rate is surprisingly low. Even so, the situation is horrendous, and calls for intelligent and urgent attention and action.

FUNCTIONS OF THE PEER GROUP

The peer group is central for much of human development, closely rivaling the influence of the family and perhaps even equaling it. For example, Piaget's early hypotheses (52) that moral development is learned in the peer group has received consistent support from research (34). Although parents set the stage for satisfactory social development, the action takes place in the context of peer interaction. In other words, it is in the peer group that the child develops, practices, and, for better or for worse, solidifies his techniques and skills of cooperation and competition, sex typing and courting behavior, autonomy and independence, and leadership–followership.

Moral Development

Moral development and political development have been discussed in detail in the previous chapters, so little needs to be added. It should be reaffirmed, however, that the topic of moral development must be placed clearly in the context of children, youth, and their associations with their peers. There is good evidence about the progression during human development from lower to higher stages of moral judgment and behavior, despite the fact that deviations from the optimum are distressingly frequent among children, adolescents, and adults all the way through to senior citizens.

Although the stages of moral judgment and behavior have been tentatively established, the authors know little about the factors that produce movement from one stage to another, or which prevent individuals from reaching the highest stages. The idea of cognitive disequilibrium as an explanatory principle has been advanced (36, 52). The reader will recall that cognitive disequilibrium results when the set of rules an individual possesses for construing himself and his environment at a given time does not account for new experiences and incontrovertible new data that will not fit into the old framework. Given favorable circumstances, processes of assimilation, accommodation, and new, higher level, and more complex equilibriums—in short, growth toward maturity—result.

Long ago, Piaget suggested that interactions with peers are prime sources of the disequilibriums that result in moral growth. Young children are morally absolutist—in a stage of objective morality. In this stage, they have a one-way respect for authority and believe that rules are sacred and unchangeable. Their rules are likely to be derived from uncritical acceptance of what their parents or other caregivers have laid down for them as being right and proper.

The leveling function of the peer group was described early in this chapter. This function can be clearly illustrated with reference to morality. For example, in their peer group, most children find exceptions from their parents' rules. For a child to be accepted by his peer group (a crucial condition for social development), he usually must move away from a one-way conception of rules toward reciprocity. The other fellow must be respected and sometimes given way to. Only then will he respect you and sometimes give way to you. For successfully socialized children and youth, mutual respect eventually emerges from this necessary reciprocity, much of which is learned in games. The child eventually learns that moral rules and laws are themselves, and probably should be, products of group consensus. Since rules and laws are derived from group agreement, they are subject to change and, as such, require analysis, thought, and action.

A number of predictions can be made from such a theory, among them being that children who are leaders within their peer group will be more successful in learning mutually respectful reciprocity than nonleaders, because of the centrality of the formers' group roles. This learned reciprocity will result in, and perhaps cause a higher level of, moral development among boys and girls who show high leadership than among those low in leadership.

Example 9.2 is a summary of a research paper in which evidence is presented to support this prediction (34).

9.2 Social Participation and Moral Development

Keasey (34) studied seventy-five boys and sixty-nine girls from fifth- and sixth-grade classes in a West Coast public school. Most of the subjects were white, although there were a few minority group members, mostly Hispano. The children were average in intelligence and from homes that could be characterized as lower-middle class.

All the children were given Kohlberg's *Moral Judgment Interview,* a test that measures level of moral judgment which was described in Chapter 8.

About two months after determining their levels of moral judgment, the children were ranked according to eight criteria of leadership and popularity. From their self reports, it was determined how many school clubs they had belonged to in the past, how many they belonged to at the time they took the test, and how many leadership roles (for example, president, secretary) they held at that time. From peer nominations, it was determined how many children regarded each child as their best friend; and all students were rated by both their teachers and their peers for popularity and leadership qualities. The highest and the lowest boys and girls according to each of these criteria for potency of social interaction and leadership were then compared on the basis of their level of moral judgment. For every possible comparison, high-leadership or high-popularity boys and girls ranked higher than low-leadership or low-popularity boys and girls in level of moral judgment. Thirteen of sixteen differences that were tested were statistically significant, and two of the other three approached statistical significance.

On the basis of this study, it appears that both the quality and the quantity of a child's social participation facilitate his moral development. For girls, the quality appears somewhat more influential than the quantity; but the relative influence of quantity and quality is not clear for boys.

Social Development

Thus far, a basic aspect of social development has been stressed: although parents and family members unquestionably set the stage for such social development, the action that produces it occurs among the child's peers and significant members of his family who are not his parents—for example, teachers, scout leaders, aunts, uncles, older sisters and brothers. It seems certain that profound influence is exerted by peers with whom a child most closely interacts, notably his classmates and particularly those among them who are his intimates. The circle of intimate friends— the "clique," loosely speaking—is almost as much of a primary group as the family. That it does not exert the same intense, long-time influence is probably due to the fact that children enter such peer groups later than they enter family groups, and that intimate peer groups change over time or because some members move away.

An intimate peer group is informal. Evidence indicates that children come together in such groups because of some common motive among members of the group, but not elsewhere (25). In other words, groups form because the members and the activities provide some kind of reinforcement that is needed or desired by the members. These reinforcements are provided by the interaction of the members with one another and progress toward mutually desired goals. If reinforcers change or become no longer effective or if other reinforcers from other sources become more effective, group cohesiveness usually diminishes and may break up entirely. This phenomenon is illustrated by the title of an old, popular song, "Wedding Bells Are Breaking Up That Old Gang of Mine." In this instance, other reinforcers (heterosexual) are supplanting the reinforcers previously supplied by the unisexual group.

Unlike more formal groups (the classroom, the scout troop, or other adult-controlled group setting), informal peer groups represent almost complete freedom for determining group membership, activities, and leadership. Inevitably, norms for behavior—a group code—are established which serve as guidelines for behavior within that particular group. Such norms usually reflect shared values regarding winning and maintaining group acceptance and status. Of course, consensual norms for group behavior are not limited to informal cliques or the larger, less intimate group known as the gang. Norms are also generated within formal groups; they may or may not be compatible with adult established values. For example, in one classroom, cheating may be frowned upon by group members, or such behavior may even result in rejection of a cheater by his peers. In another classroom, the degree of sophistication in cheating that a child demonstrates may be a criterion for group status. Conflict between adult values and peer group norms can be one of the most disturbing and difficult phenomena with which adult group workers must deal. Fortu-

nately, such conflict is less often a matter of basic value differences than it is a matter of how values are translated into behavior.

Cooperation and Competition

Earlier in this chapter, the authors remarked briefly about marked differences in children's cooperative and competitive behavior that are associated with cultural membership. Group-reared kibbutzim (Israeli) children, for example, have been found to be more cooperative and less competitive than urban Israeli children (39, 57); and Mexican village children more cooperative and less competitive than urban-reared Hispano, Black, or Anglo children (31, 32, 39, 57). Similarly, cooperation is generally higher among Russian children reared in day care centers than that among children in the United States (10). These differences seemingly reflect the differing emphasis placed on such behavior by parents and caretakers who act in concert as representatives of the broader culture for child-rearing purposes.

Differences in cooperative and competitive behavior among children are also related to age and sex (25). For example, competitiveness increases with age through the childhood years and is usually more marked among boys than girls. However, with age, both sexes become increasingly more capable of cooperative behavior, and the importance of cooperation for effective group action cannot be overemphasized. Critical variables for determining either competitive or cooperative behavior are, of course, the nature of a given task and the reinforcement contingencies that are operating in a given situation. One can expect cooperation to occur in relation to group-oriented, or collective, goals. If, however, individual goals are being sought, cooperation usually wanes. Finally, many authors (for example, 24) have demonstrated that the incidence of cooperative behavior can be increased by the systematic provision of adult reinforcement.

To conclude this brief section, the authors can say that cooperative peer group activity contributes both to group cohesiveness and to group productivity (although it is difficult to determine here which is cause and which is effect). When a peer group is threatened by outside forces, cohesiveness is likely to increase (an easily observable political, or gang, phenomenon). At least among preadolescent girls, cooperative intergroup interaction results in more favorable attitudes toward the out-group than competitive interaction between the groups (5, 25). The children of punitive, rejecting, or neglectful parents seem to be more closely tied to, dependent on, and influenced by, the peer group than are children of more loving and reasoning parents (45). Both broad cultural mores, then, (see Chapter 1 for the discussion of effective culture as a mediator of human development) and specific child-rearing and child-training practices mediate cooperative and competitive behaviors.

Sex Typing and Courting Behavior

Implicitly, one conclusion about peer relations and sex typing and identification emerged from the discussion of these topics in Chapter 7. The family, perhaps particularly the father, sets the stage for sex typing and identification, but the child plays out his role with his peers of about the same age and of both sexes.

It was mentioned in Chapter 7 that both boys and girls without fathers but with older brothers frequently are more masculine in their characteristics than fatherless children without older brothers. Further, a swaggering compensatory masculinity, often merging into delinquency (26) is often seen among fatherless boys as they move into public school age (in the preschool years, they are more likely to be passive, dependent, and "feminine"). This development seems almost certain to have been acquired from the peer group, among whom sissy behavior is not condoned. It has also been noted that girls without fathers may have heterosexual difficulties in adolescence; they incline toward one of two extremes—shy, inept withdrawal from males or bold heterosexual behavior that often verges on the promiscuous (26). While the issue has not been studied, it seems likely that the presence of older brothers, or congenial and cooperative peer groups including friendly males, would ameliorate this behavior. It was also observed in Chapter 7 how the male peer group reinforces masculine interests and activities in the face of discouragement of such behavior by female teachers (20). Reinforcement for girlish interests and behavior was found to be double in this study. Both the girl peer group and the teachers reinforced girls for being "girlish," but only the male peer group reinforced boys for being boyish.

Observation of adolescents quickly reveals the role of the peer group in affecting courtship and other sexual behaviors. For example, boys seem to band together in seeking out prostitutes and in "gang banging" behavior (35). Both young males and young females do much role rehearsal with each other in courtship behavior, ranging all the way from the rules for mild flirtation and obtaining dates to trading information about sexual and contraceptive techniques. Within a peer group where steady dating is the rule, it seems that every adolescent wants a steady. Where group dating—informal and shifting pairings—is the pattern, relatively little steady dating is found and, apparently, heterosexual involvement is less intense than in the steady-dating situation in the sense that fewer of the couples move into full-fledged sexual relations with others.

It is apparent that the peer group exerts the same leveling influence on children and youth in the development of sex-related behavior and attitudes that it does in other social development. Members of the group, regardless of their home background, move toward the central tendency of their intimate peer group (54). Yet it also seems that children and youth pick as intimates friends those who are more or less in the same attitudinal and behavioral ball park as their parents. A youth's friends, however, are perceived as more liberal than his parents, particularly in sex attitudes and behavior. Adolescents, for example, report typically that they are less liberal in their sexual attitudes and behaviors than their best friends, but are closer to their best friends than they are to their parents. On the other hand, the children of liberal parents have more liberal attitudes and behavior than the children of parents who are sexually very conservative. The former may also be expected to choose more liberal best friends, and indeed this seems to be the case.

Autonomy and Independence

One of the expected courses of human development is a steady progression from infancy to maturity in traits of autonomy (self-directedness) and independence, which is a closely related concept. In our culture, males are expected to be more autonomous and independent than females (42), but the concept of psychosocial

maturity includes a rather high degree of both kinds of behavior for older girls and women as well as for boys and men. For example, in later life, the average woman needs such capabilities at least as much as the average man. It may be argued that, if, on the average, wives are two years younger than their husbands and if, on the average, American men die seven years sooner than American women, the average married woman in our society will end her life having been a widow for nine years. As we all know, a single existence demands sturdy amounts of autonomy, self-sufficiency, and independence.

Parents are notoriously slow in granting their children autonomy and independence, probably more so among economically advantaged families than among financially ill-equipped ones. To be sure, we early encourage our children to walk and to tie their shoes for themselves, but we are remarkably slow in encouraging them to think independently, to set their own limits for when they shall go to bed, to decide what and when they shall eat, and to determine how they shall govern their courtship lives or their own standards of dress.

The authors possess few research data on which to base this subsection of Chapter 9, since the respective contributions of parents, teachers, and peers to helping children grow toward autonomy and independence have been little investigated. Thus, this section is based largely on their own subjective, clinical observations of the interactions with peers, teachers, and parents of the children they know and have watched grow up.

Socialization is a two-way street. Parents and teachers socialize those for whom they are responsible; at the same time, their "wards" socialize them (see 61, for

"His music has that certain something that manages to bridge the generation gap."

Authorities debate the nature of a generation gap but agree on the importance of improved communication between adults and youth. (Cartoon from Phi Delta Kappan, *1971, 52 (7), 412. Reproduced by permission of artist, Henry R. Martin.)*

example). The authors suspect there is no parent of a child of 5 and over who has not heard the statements, "All the other kids do it," or "All the other parents allow it." Parents become suspicious of such statements, and wise parents check them. But almost all parents listen, and when their checking out of the statement indicates that it is true, they are likely to change their own demands on their children, typically in the direction of relaxing the limits.

In short, the peer group serves as a lever for helping each of its members move toward greater autonomy and independence, at least with reference to parents. By feeding the child new standards, the peer group encourages him to put pressure on his parents to allow him more freedom to explore and grow (not always safely and not always wisely); and this pressure is likely to work so as to permit the child to move himself forward along his growth pattern.

Younger children also receive such benefits from their older brothers and sisters. Having got their older children through the various crises of growth, parents are inclined to relax a bit with the younger children in the family (sometimes they are merely tired, of course). This parental relaxation of controls may be the reason for the reported greater suggestibility and conformity of firstborn children when compared with later born children mentioned earlier. Be that as it may, almost any eldest child can recall annoyance with parents about their permitting younger brothers and sisters to do things that were denied him at the same age. This is typically put as "You made me toe the line, but you let Sue get away with murder!" Carried to extremes, as is sometimes the case with youngest and tagalong children, the degree of freedom allowed the child may reach the danger point, so that the child gets into situations that he is ill equipped to handle.

Children also learn autonomy and independence from formal and informal activities with their peers. Being "It" in a game of hide-and-go-seek surely is a rehearsal for autonomous and independent behavior, just as abiding by the rules in more formal games is an exercise in cooperation and functioning acceptably in a group. A youth's first drink with the peer group is an exercise in independence from parents; deciding to stay sober so as to be able to get the group home safely when other members have been drinking too much to drive safely is an exercise in autonomous and independent responsibility—a fidelity to one's standards that is constructive, reasonably mature behavior.

Sensible organization within school systems provides children and youth an opportunity to assume alternating positions of leadership and followership that promote the team behaviors of group cooperation and individual leadership. If schools do not provide such opportunities for growth of independence and autonomy for children and youth, they are guilty by default.

Many other organizations for children and youth—the church, the scouts, the 4-H, for example—provide contexts within which independence and autonomy can be and are developed. A well-run sports program provides chances for growth and development, as do the other extracurricular activities within schools. Smaller units, of course, usually provide more such opportunities than massive units (for example, see 59 and 60). The peer group, particularly for boys, is also a potent instrument for moving children in the direction of task orientation—getting the job done. This can be an excellent behavioral foundation for personal autonomy and independence.

Conformity

Although the supportive function of the peer group has been stressed in terms of practice for autonomy and independence, the issue of peer group conformity cannot be overlooked. Conformity—yielding to group pressures—seems to be viewed largely in a negative sense by American parents who profess strongly the values of independent judgment and personal autonomy. College students, many of whom are still in late adolescence, also more often than not decry the ills of conformity. Yet both parents and college students can be observed to conform, some slavishly, in various groups with which they are identified.

A certain degree of conformity, of course, is necessary for any group to maintain its distinctiveness; it is the collective support of consensual norms that provides a group with its identity and usually facilitates its effectiveness, whatever may be the specific goals. Further, without some degree of conformity to shared values, activities, and goals, it is unlikely that the cohesiveness necessary for effective goal accomplishment will be developed and maintained. The point is that conformity per se is not necessarily the ugly force that some persons might have us believe. For the authors, the prob-

A peer group demands conformity from its members at the same time it fosters autonomy and independence. (Photo by Bob S. Smith)

lem is primarily a matter of degree; that is, conformity to others at the expense of one's individuality and sense of self-direction, or conformity for the sake of social acceptance even when conformity means behaving contrary to one's beliefs, moral–ethical standards, or sense of truth, can be problematical.

Developmentally speaking, peer group conformity increases in intensity with age to a peak during preadolescence and early adolescence, after which it decreases (13, 38). In part, this reflects an age-related shift in the locus of children's dependency from parents and other adults to peers;

that is, children become gradually more dependent upon (and seem to prefer) peer recognition and approval. In fact, during preadolescence and beyond, it is the peer group that seemingly has the greater influence on children. Experimental studies with children and youth have revealed a high degree of acquiescence to majority opinion among age mates even when the majority is known to be wrong (9). Such conformity is most apparent in ambiguous situations where children are unsure about what they should do or are supposed to do.

Moreover, these same studies show

that, in matters of opinion changes, a teacher is usually less influential than the peer group. Specifically, when teachers attempt to persuade individual children to change their opinions contrary to the majority, some success is noted with children under age 10, but almost none with older children. Sex differences are also apparent, with girls more likely than boys to take their cues for behavior from the peer group (28).

It should be noted that peer group conformity is not always complete and permanent, nor is it always sincere (37). Occasionally, to conform is simply to do the expedient thing; at other times it represents a judicious way to avoid unpleasant and unnecessary conflict. There is indication, however, that some individuals are more general and persistent conformers than others. As compared to more independent and self-assertive persons, chronic conformers tend to be less intelligent, less able to cope with stress, higher in anxiety, more prone toward feelings of inadequacy, more passive, stronger in their desire for affiliation and social approval, more dogmatic, and less tolerant of ambiguity (37). It is tempting, therefore, to postulate a conformity-prone personality. But, in addition to personal attributes, many variables operate to affect conformity behavior. The apparent influence of age and sex role identification has been noted. To these factors can be added others, including a variety of situational variables.

Situational factors that influence degree of yielding to group pressure include group size and composition, extent of unanimity of group consensus, and the nature of pressure techniques applied by group members (1, 2, 3, 14, 53). For example, near-maximum levels of yielding occur in small groups where at least three or four persons oppose an individual; but some individuals seem to yield even to one opponent. Yielding is also extremely high in groups where an individual finds himself in a minority—the only stranger in a group of comrades or a member of a racial–ethnic minority group, for example. Typically, yielding is also influenced by the social power or status of those who exert pressure. For example, a high-status member of a group, a friend, or persons perceived as highly competent are more likely to effect yielding than are persons not so qualified (38) (see Chapter 8, Example 8.2). Finally, unanimity of group consensus is an important factor. Unanimity tends to produce greater yielding, but where an individual can elicit the support of at least one other person in the group (such as a partner with whom mutual agreement is recognized), yielding usually is lower. This bit of evidence suggests a profound social implication, as the following quote will indicate: "A dissident opinion, if expressed loudly and clearly, can have a tremendous effect in strengthening the independence of like-minded people. The expression of a dissident opinion may not *change* the majority's beliefs, but it can conserve the minority view" (37, pp. 514–515).

To conclude this section, the authors wish to emphasize that, however puzzling and frustrating marked peer group conformity may be to adults, it is a fact of life from middle childhood through adolescence. Certainly in a statistical sense, much peer conformity is "normal" (see Chapter 3); and, apart from extreme other-directedness, conformity to peer group norms that are generally consonant with accepted social values probably facilitates the socialization process. However, a problem can arise when conformity interferes with the development of autonomy or occurs in antisocial groups which collectively undermine constructive pathways of socialization. Finally, a provocative experimental study of conforming behavior is described in Example 9.3. This description will serve to illustrate both a methodology for investigating conformity and some likely dynamics that underlie such behavior.

9.3   A Study of Conformity Behavior

A long-standing premise in psychology is that the degree to which an individual conforms in a given situation is closely related to the amount of fear he experiences in that situation. In fact, conformity based on fear is often interpreted as a special case of dependency behavior, the antecedents of which can be traced to early socialization experience. In the general context of such thinking, John Darley (15) conducted an experiment to test two predictions about conformity: (1) that increased fear results in a higher probability of conforming behavior and (2) that a fearful person subjected to conformity pressures from others who share this fear will conform more readily to these persons than to persons with whom the fear is not shared.

To test these predictions, Darley arranged for four groups of paid volunteer subjects, each of which was composed of twelve college females. Elaborate procedures were devised to establish the following differences between the groups.

GROUP I. Subjects who believed that they were about to receive an intense electric shock (fear of physical pain), and who believed that all the other girls in their testing session would also receive

the shock and therefore were also highly fearful.

GROUP II. Subjects who believed that they would receive the electric shock but who also believed that none of the other girls in the session would receive the shock and hence would not be fearful.

GROUP III. Subjects who believed that they would not be shocked, but who believed that all the other girls in the session would receive the shock.

GROUP IV. Subjects who believed that neither they nor any of the other girls in the session would receive the shock.

Once these groups were formed, self-report measures of fear and affiliation were obtained from each subject. A test of conformity (yielding) was also administered. This test required that each girl count the number of tape-recorded metronome clicks that she heard through earphones. Each girl gave her answer after hearing the answers of three other girls, ostensibly fellow-participants in the study. In fact, however, these three other girls were confederates of the experimenter, and provided incorrect, but unanimous, answers for twelve of the eighteen separate metronome count trials. The confederates' responses were also delivered through tape recording, thus ensuring that each experimental subject heard identical conformity pressures. Degree of conformity was determined by the number of trials on which the experimental subject agreed with the collective confederate response.

Briefly, the results of this experiment supported Darley's original predictions. High-fearful girls more readily conformed than their low-fearful peers. Furthermore, greater conformity was observed among high-fear girls who believed that conformity pressures emanated from similarly fearful peers than among high-fear girls under pressure from unthreatened peers. Notably, a correlation of .67 was obtained between effects of fear and conformity behavior. Darley concluded that increased fear results in increased conformity and that such increase is greatest if conformity pressures originate from persons toward whom one feels affiliative.

Leadership—Followership

Developing leadership qualities and learning leadership roles obviously require at least two people; and the common conception of leadership is that it occurs in groups of three or more. Leadership emerges when the group has a common task. Common tasks may range from planning a game in a sandbox or a doll corner among preschoolers through managing a class outing or plotting a group-delinquent act among older children and adolescents. The qualities of leadership demanded vary greatly from one kind of activity to another. The leader in sports or social activities may not be the leader in academically related activities, such as the French Club. This suggests that leadership status is often situationally specific, although some talented individuals demonstrate general leadership potential across a wide variety of situations. A final criterion necessary before leadership emerges is some differentiation of roles and responsibilities within the group (25). However, there is some evidence that, even among preschool children, leadership qualities are somewhat consistent from one situation to another and from one group to another (21).

Qualities most important among leaders (as rated by male adolescents) are helpfulness, fairness, sociability, and expertness (55). Not surprisingly, in some crisis situations characteristics of fearlessness and physical strength are also considered important leader qualifications by many children and youth. As noted in the following section, the attributes of leaders are not very different from those of popular children and youth, although they are sufficiently different to justify the distinction between popularity and leadership. However, followership is distinctly different from unpopularity or isolation from the group. Unlike popularity, leadership is more likely to fluctuate according to the nature of the situation: The football leader with a bad accent is likely to be popular among both his teammates and his fellow members of the French Club, but it is likely he will be a leader only in the football crowd.

Leaders are commonly and correctly considered to be socially powerful children and youth, even as is true in adulthood. Power in this sense may be defined as "having something someone wants (or fears), coupled with the willingness to share it (or the ability to dispense it)." Leaders, in other words, have within their repertoire reinforcers that are important to other members of the group in one way or another, and are known to be capable of administering them.

Core Characteristics of Leaders. The core leadership descriptions encountered in developmental literature have mostly been provided by a group of professional people who are interested in both developmental psychology and group formation and function and who have long been centered at the University of Michigan. Their work can be conveniently summarized (and has been referenced) in the following paragraphs (25).

Intelligence is related to leadership, but not strongly. Presumably, intelligence is more important for leadership in academic undertakings. Socially powerful children are also usually popular children. Competence in the central task for the group is also a powerful determinant of leadership, as intimated above, and initiative—aptitude for starting an action—is also another important determiner of leadership. This finding certifies to the importance of developing autonomy and independence. Leaders typically like much social interaction and are more sociable (and well adjusted) than the average child or youth. They seem able to pick out central issues and argue them, or at least convince the group to follow them in their ideas about how to proceed on a course of action. This may be related more to social sensitivity than to high intellectual power. Among boys, aggressiveness (usually but not necessarily of a prosocial sort) is positively related to leadership, but not among girls. Apparently, this aggressive component in male leadership is more important among lower IQ children and youth than among higher.

Leaders also seem to be realistic about themselves (it is noted later that this is also true of children who are popular and who have positive self concepts). As might be expected, leaders "believe in themselves" and possess higher self-esteem than the average child or the chronic follower. Interestingly and not surprisingly, good leaders are also good followers when the circumstances are appropriate. This follows logically if, indeed, leaders are realistic, socially sensitive, and possess strong self-esteem.

This cluster of behaviors (intellectually able, sociable in an active and appropriate way, and reasonably assertive and aggressive, at least for boys) seems to hold for leaders in a wide range of situations and socioeconomic levels. As one reviewer cautions (11), however, all the relations reported above are modest: they are tendencies for groups, not rules for individual children. Thus some shy and somewhat withdrawn children and youth may be leaders, but more are not; some ill-adjusted children may be leaders, but more are not, and so on.

POPULARITY AND LEADERSHIP

Measurement

Popularity and leadership can be measured in several different ways, of which the most widely used is the *sociometric* technique (47). Such social measurement can be made by the following methods.

Choices. Ask a child or a youth to name in order his first three to five best friends. This may be done by using the general term, "Name your best friend," or according to specific behaviors; for preschool children, for example, one of the authors has successfully used the following technique. Clear pictures of all the children in a group are placed in random order on a bulletin board so as to keep them fresh in the child's mind. The child is asked to point to "The one you like to sit beside in story group," or "play with in the sandbox." Then, "Who else?" and "Who else?" for a total of three choices. The child most frequently named is considered to be the most popular, and children with few or no choices are considered to be least popular.

The technique can also be used for "rejects." "Who is not your friend" in order from first to third or fifth. Eliciting rejects, however, is often anxiety-evoking to children. The procedure may trigger action in the sense that a child who was not clearly aware of his dislikes is forced to formulate them, then acts on them with undesirable consequences for his "not friend" and possibly for himself. Thus, although valuable information about children's groupings is obtained by securing patterns of *dislike* as well as *like,* the technique raises enough ethical questions that the authors are reluctant to recommend it.

Leadership can be similarly measured: "Who is the outstanding leader in your class?" for example. As in measuring friendship, leadership can be made situation specific for a great variety of situations: "Whom would you like to have as chairman of the arrangements committee for your class party?" "Whom would you like to have head the committee for the Science Fair?" "Whom do you choose as class president?", and so on.

Ratings. As a substitute for choices of first through third or fifth, ratings may be made for leadership and friendship. A child or youth is given a list of his classmates and asked to assign a *1* to his best friend, or to the person he thinks is the best leader in the class, a *2* to a good friend or good potential leader, a *3* to "average," a *4* to "not a close friend," or "only a fair leader," and a *5* to "not my friend," or "would not be a good leader."

About the same overall ranking of friends and leaders is provided by the two methods, and a good picture of the social network of a class is provided by either method.

Paired comparisons. Paired comparisons is a reliable but cumbersome and time-consuming method suitable only for older children. In paired-comparison ratings, each child judges each other child in the class as to whether, for example, child A is a better friend, the same, or not so good a friend as child B; the same for child A versus child C, child D, and so on, until

every child has been compared with every other child.

Ranking. The ranking method may also be employed, although young children are not very good at rankings of a class, say, of twenty-five to thirty pupils. In this method, children are ranked from most popular to least popular leaders or best to poorest leaders.

Guess who. The "guess who" technique is another version of sociometrics. *"Guess who* is always willing to do his job as head of a committee?" is a question designed to reveal leadership. Each child is asked to list perhaps three names, and children or adolescents most frequently nominated are assumed to be the class leaders. This same technique can be used to elicit names of aggressive children, mischief makers, good followers, or almost any other social role one wishes to determine.

Teachers as well as pupils are often asked to make rankings, ratings, or choices concerning popularity and leadership. In one study of fifth- and sixth-grade boys and girls for a total of five classes (34), teachers and pupils agreed fairly closely in their ratings of leadership among girls (the correlation was .78), but were not close together in their judgments of leadership among boys (r was only .30). Teacher–pupil agreement about popularity was $r = .79$ for girls, $= .66$ for boys. This is probably a fairly common situation. Most elementary school teachers are women, and they are likely to understand the leadership and friendship dynamics among girls better than those among boys.

Concerning popularity during middle childhood and preadolescence, it is more meaningful to elicit choices, rankings, and ratings for boys only from boys and for girls only from girls, since the sex cleavage in friendship is sharp. However, the things that make for same- and cross-sex popularity are similar (27). For leadership, in contrast to popularity, it is useful to employ both sexes as choosers, raters, or rankers for each child, although sex differences may emerge. If opportunity and time are available, it may be well to assess leadership of boys among only boys and among both boys and girls, and the same for girls.

Observations may be used to check for popularity, but are not useful except when children are of an age to be relatively unself-conscious about being observed, and when they are in situations where they are permitted to choose freely the ones with whom they will be associated, such as the free play or story circle situations in preschools and elementary schools. Even so, observations may not yield an accurate picture of true preference. For example, an extremely popular child—a star—may be so much in demand that there is "simply not room" for all the children who would like to be with him actually to be with him. In such a situation, the more imaginative, resourceful, or assertive children will monopolize the star's company, sometimes when the star might possibly prefer to be with another child or a group of children. However, observations have much validity when checked with choices. Using the sociometric technique based on choices made from photographs (mentioned above as useful with preschool-aged children), the correlation between actual playground association of 3- and 4-year olds and their choices of best friends from pictures were correlated about .55; and the correlations of actual play with other children and the teachers' judgments of best friends were correlated .58 for girls, .44 for boys (43).

That teachers and children make closely related judgments of popularity is another indication of the validity of observa-

tion, because teachers' judgments are necessarily based on their repeated, although usually informal, observations of the behavior of their pupils.

A final measure of leadership is usually available, at least upward from the early grades of elementary school. This measure is simply a count of the number of offices a child or a youth holds in the different kinds of organizations to which he belongs: class president or secretary, captain of the football team, president of the drama club, and so on. Such a measure is obtainable from most school records, at least for school-related activities; and most children can easily provide the information about themselves if asked.

Relationship of Popularity and Leadership

The relationship of popularity and leadership may be expected to vary widely as a function of the situation. For a group cast on a desert island, among whom only one person is a carpenter and he is heartily disliked, the relationship may be strongly negative. The most-disliked individual becomes the leader because of his special skills. Where the group is homogeneous, where the climate is benevolently authoritarian, and where the goals of the group are all the same (and when most of them are set by the authorities), the relationship between popularity and leadership may be exceptionally high. In one study of freshmen in a Roman Catholic girls' school, for example, the correlation between leadership and popularity ranged from a high of .91, when the girls were just coming to know each other, to .72, after eight months' association together (48).

But on the whole, the overlap between leadership and popularity is great. From the earlier mentioned University of Michigan studies, it seems that relationships, as expressed by correlation coefficients, range from one to another situation from about .50 to about .80, with the most correlations clustering in the low .70s (25). It also seems certain that leadership choices will vary more according to the situation than will friendship choices.

In summary, about the same personal characteristics go into choosing a leader as go into choosing a friend, with one important addition: competence at the task concerning which leadership is to be manifested. Assertiveness seems to be more important in leadership among boys than among girls. The competency dimension leads to variation in leadership choice depending on the situation. A different leader—stronger, braver—may be chosen for dangerous situations than for benign situations, for academics and athletics or a social occasion, or for political action. However, one's friend is likely to remain one's friend regardless of the situation.

Uses of Friendship and Leadership Information

The uses that may be made of information about the popularity and leadership status of children and youth are many. To this point in the chapter, usefulness for research has been stressed. Indeed, the authors believe that any information about human development that expands our understanding of development is useful, even if no practical consequences of the information seem obvious. In addition to its research value, however, knowledge of friendship and leadership status adds much precision to our practical dealings with children and youth.

First, this information is useful in guidance. It is common sense as well as scientific knowledge that, within limits,

almost everyone likes to be liked. If we know who in a group is liked—a star or a well-accepted member—and who is disliked—an isolate or a reject—we may be able to work with children and young people who find no place in a group, to help them develop social and leadership skills that will give them a chance to operate more effectively within the group. By so doing, greater personal happiness and security may be gained. The group may also be guided toward tolerance and acceptance of "different" children who, despite or because of their difference, possess real potential for contributing to the group *if* they can be accepted within it. However, this task is not without its dilemmas, as we see later in this chapter.

Information about friendships and leadership roles, if we are careful to employ ethical safeguards, can be used to increase group morale and cohesiveness. In a rather dramatic case, sociometric information of the kind that has been described was gathered from adolescent, delinquent boys. These boys were living in one particularly disrupted, indeed out-of-control cottage in an institution for troubled youth. The two stars—boys who accumulated a plurality of votes for both best friends and leaders—were deeply antisocial boys according to the most tolerant standards. It seemed doubtful that even the cleverest guidance could bring the boys in the cottage back within the accepted limits of behavior in the institution without taking special measures with the two stars. Thus, they were removed from the cottage situation for individual counseling and residence in a different cottage, while cottage staff sought to develop new and better socialized leaders. The morale of the cottage improved quickly, the atmosphere of chaos and anarchy diminished, and within a few weeks, the two former stars were able to return to the cottage, more understanding of themselves and less disruptive (as well as less influential) leaders and associates.

In another case, the teacher of a class from which she felt estranged—"I am getting nowhere with this group"—found, as a result of obtaining friendship—leadership data, that the powerful-seeming, delightful boy whom she had thought of as her right-hand man was thoroughly rejected by the group. Her dependence on him made her, too, the enemy as far as the class members were concerned. She further realized that her partiality to the boy was possibly damaging him and estranging him from his group. Slowly and carefully, she attenuated her dependence on him, but without rejecting him, and spread her attention and favors more widely within the class, to the benefit of all.

In ways like those described above, valuable information can be gained about problems of racial integration, equality of the sexes within the group, and tying together the common aims of physical fitness (the athletes) and academic competence (the "quiz kids"). These groups are often estranged from each other, yet bridges between them usually exist that can be mapped by means of sociometric data.

Sociometrics and Socialization

It has been repeatedly stressed that popularity and leadership (competence or respect) are closely related to each other, but sufficiently different that one must think about them separately. The *popular* child or youth, by definition, is the well-loved child or youth—the one toward whom one feels warmth, with whom one is comfortable, with whom one enjoys relaxation and fun. The *leader* may also have these qualities, but his distinguishing characteristic is competence in getting the job done. Many things required in getting a job done are similar to those involved in comfortable, frank friendship; and most people want their friends to be not only comfortable, warm, loving, and reassuring, but also competent. However, the prime quality of friendship is interpersonal comfort; the prime quality of leadership is competence. One has fun with his friends, one gets things done with his leaders (or as one leads others).

These considerations suggest to the authors that there are both Dionysian and Apollonian qualities in human relations, an idea that has persisted for many years. To be Dionysian (after Dionysus, the Greek god of wine, vegetation, warm moisture—thus, fertility) is to be warmly, loosely, vividly alive and open to sensory experience. In other words, if we are Dionysian, we relish life as warm-blooded mammals. To be Apollonian is to sponsor competence in a wide range of activities. Apollo, another Greek god, was the father of the Pythian games (our modern Olympics); he was also the god of song, music, and poetry. He bested the satyr, Marsyas, before a jury of the nine Muses. The oracle of Delphi, the seat of ancient mythological wisdom, was his priestess. She knew the future of all who consulted her. Thus, Apollonian qualities are uniquely human characteristics of thought, creativity—of biological experience channeled through learning and technological skill to result in experiences that represent all that is uniquely, intelligently, and artistically human. Apollonian qualities are skill, expertness, and wisdom—in short, competence.

Possibly the ideal socialization product is a person who combines both Dionysian and Apollonian qualities—one who is warmly and emotionally alive and who rejoices in life, yet who is patient, who in our culture is achievement oriented, who is thoughtful, and who subjects himself willingly and eagerly to learning so that he may be competent. Further, it can be argued that the best socialized child or youth is one who is high both in friendship or popularity scores (which may represent Dionysian qualities) and in respect or leadership scores (which likely represent Apollonian qualities).

It is doubtful that a child or a youth who scores high for both friendship and leadership has anything seriously wrong with him, unless he lives in a pathological culture (all such scores reflect the culture— think, for example, of what would have gone into high friendship and leadership ratings in Hitler's *Jugend*). In fact, given a healthy culture—and no doubt there are many varieties of healthy culture as long as human rights and dignity are respected —the goal of socialization is probably to produce children and youth who are high in nominations both for best friends and for leaders. A necessary condition for this, of course, is a wide variety of activities that offer rich opportunities for the exercise of leadership potential. Those who are high friends but low leaders may, perhaps, be friendly slobs. Those who are high leaders but low friends may be emotionally barren friends. It is almost certain that those who are low friends and low leaders are missing the best part of the human developmental experience.

These are speculations about uses that may be made of sociometric techniques. If the speculations are followed by research, important additions to knowledge and practice may result.

The Ethics of Sociometrics

We live, and rightly so, in an era in which the rights to privacy should, indeed must, be respected. To paraphrase what Thomas Paine said, "The price of freedom is eternal vigilance." At times, admittedly, it is difficult to distinguish between rigorous vigilance and paranoia, but the need for vigilance is self-evident. Thus, some children, youth, and their parents object mightily to probing into their friendship and leadership nomination networks. As noted earlier, the ethical considerations of the authors now prevent them from working with *reject* nominations as they gather sociometric data.

But sociometric data about friendship and leadership are useful, even necessary, if we are to do a proper job of educating children and youth. Consider, then, the following conditions that are essential if we are to take such sociometrics.

1. Parental permission must be secured. This will be given in most cases if we and the system of which we are a part have a history of operating ethically and safeguarding the rights of individuals to privacy and confidentiality of information given to us.

2. A child or a youth must not be forced to provide such information if he is unhappy at doing so, even though his parents' permission has been obtained.

3. Such information must be used only for research purposes, with the identities of individuals carefully concealed; or for guidance, with the welfare of the individual and the group so guided kept as the paramount goal. To move back to

earlier examples: If the sociometric data elicited from the cottage oi delinquent boys had been used to punish the two youths who had been revealed as anti-social leaders, rather than to help them, ethics would have been violated. If the teacher who found she had been deputizing the wrong boy as her leader had, as a result, rejected the boy, ethics would have been violated. In brief, information gained through sociometrics *cannot* be employed to hurt or to penalize an individual, but can be used only to try to help all concerned to grow.

4. Particular care should be taken to explain to students, parents, and staff the uses, dangers, and ethics involved in gathering and using sociometric data; and the authors themselves must observe the ethics assiduously.

If these four points are observed, few parents and students will object to the gathering of sociometric data; honest responses will be secured; the rights of those who do not choose to provide such data will be respected; and science and the practice of human development in groups will likely be advanced.

PEERS "VERSUS" PARENTS

The heading peers "versus" parents is deliberately provocative. It sets an issue that often exists for individual cases and for most children and their parents at one time or another. For American parents and their children, however, the issue is more properly stated as "the coexistence of parents and peers."

Over all, children and youth seem to choose as their friends other children and youth of whom their parents approve: others of their own kind, if you will. Parents assure this by the places they elect for rearing their children. The "flight to the suburbs" is not all white malice toward blacks, but is often largely dictated by the parents' honest efforts to place their children in the best developmental surroundings. The *move to a better neighborhood* is usually motivated for similar reasons. As human beings we are shortsighted, however, and often exchange the cluttered but warm, vital, and stimulating city proper for a barren and homogeneous suburb that may be rich in greenery but poverty stricken in human relations.

Regardless, most children live in neighborhoods populated by parents much like their own parents and by other children much like themselves. The forces of economics and prejudice are at least as important, possibly more so, than the forces of rational choice. Thus, the case is seldom one of peers against parents, but rather of peers living together and providing one another with the learning experiences necessary to consolidate parental values, or to alter them only slightly.

The reader will recall the emphasis in this chapter on the peer group as a leveler. If parents are extremely conservative, the peer group is likely to liberalize the children, and vice versa. A degree of parent–child conflict is thus almost inevitable except for completely middle-of-the-road parents of whom there are few, at least for all issues. Perhaps the major victims of the peer group, at least in intensity of conflict, are parents of one socioeconomic level who are forced to live, because of de facto segregation, in communities where the majority are economically disadvantaged (as are many middle-class blacks, for example). To illustrate, the achievement motives that middle-class black parents instill in their children are likely to be attenuated by the youngsters with whom their children play and with whom they attend school. Regardless of the values of the American achievement motive, this result is almost certain to be deplored by middle-class parents and teachers.

Experimental evidence bears out the ancient saying, "You are known by the company you keep." Influence of an adult model who imposes strict standards on himself, demanding his own high quality performance, for instance, has been shown to be eroded by the experimental introduction of a child of the same age as the experimental subject. In this case, the child introduced sets an example of generous rewards for mediocre performance. The experimental children seemed to be as likely to follow the example of the low-standard peer as they were to follow the high-standard adult model (6).

A practical lesson to be learned by parents from the influences of peers is to encourage their children to associate with those who have about the same standards as the parents hold for their own children. This may be a mixed blessing, because in American life it is as likely to result in surrounding one's children with proper but mediocre companions as it is to surround them with true exemplars of an ideal democratic way of life.

The influence of peers on high school achievement and progression into college is marked (41). By the end of high school, the later plans of a youth's best friends seem as likely to shape his plans as do his parents' standards and aspirations. Standards held by his teachers, on the other hand, are not very influential at all. On the whole, however, the influence of peers is greatest on relatively superficial issues (current fads in dress and recrea-

tion) and least in important life issues such as college, early or late marriage, and so on. Thus, much superficial conflict may result between parents and children, but the old adage about the tree growing the way the twig is bent holds true for most children. However, there are enough exceptions, fortunate and unfortunate, that the adage should not be taken automatically as truth for any *individual* child or youth. Certainly, the influence of the peer group deserves the most serious attention from both theoretical and applied workers in the area of human development. In individual cases, the peer group can operate to dilute and distort influences of good home environments, to meliorate malignant home environments, and to assure that middle-of-the-road children generally remain in the middle of the road.

A Youth Culture?

A final, and perhaps a most general, question relevant to parents "versus" peers is whether adolescence in American society represents a cultural existence apart from the broader adult culture. This question of cultural separation is hotly debated among students of adolescence. For example, some authorities argue that genuine cultural distinctions exist; their arguments usually focus on the psychological functions of the peer group as discussed earlier in this chapter (11, 12, 58). Others argue that adolescent behavior more accurately reflects the prevailing adult culture, although frequently in exaggerated form (8, 18, 49). Evidence can be gathered to support both positions, a fact that has led still others (for example, 29) to declare the entire question a "pseudo issue."

The question of distinctiveness for an adolescent culture undoubtedly is based in a semantic discourse complicated by the way in which one defines culture (see

Chapter 1). The study of values shared by both adolescents and adults indicates, for instance, a substantial overlap in these two age groups (30, 49). Without such overlap there would be little if any generational or cultural continuity and, although value changes can be noted from one generation to the next, one does not see much evidence of value reversals and dramatic discontinuity among successive generations. In final analysis, then, what is at issue is perhaps the degree of generational continuity (or the absence of it).

A principal criterion by which to consider cultural overlap or distinctiveness is whether adolescent communication systems and behavior patterns truly distinguish youth from both the children they were and the adults they will become (23). Given this criterion, a strong argument can be advanced that youth culture has distinctive qualities. Immediately, such things as adornment styles, musical preferences, unique argot, and dance forms come to mind. These phenomena seemingly mark a trend during adolescence toward increasingly idiosyncratic tastes. Collectively, these tastes create a distinct image for adolescents, and moreover, may strongly influence the "adult culture." Witness, for example, the impact that youth's preferences for clothing syles have had on the clothing industry in recent years. However, this distinctiveness is perhaps most significant in relation to the task of clarifying both personal and peer group identity during adolescence (11, 58). The general matter of identity seeking is examined in Chapter 10.

Still another point concerning youth culture is in order. It has been noted earlier that the locus of interpersonal influence rapidly shifts from adults to the peer group during preadolescence. This pos-

sibly indicates that many young people prefer to base guidelines for their behavior on values and belief systems that they themselves generate. True, for many adolescents these values and beliefs may simply be extensions of those held by their parents. But the peer group seemingly operates as a testing ground for examining the validity of various values, ethics, and morals for individual adolescents. Ultimately, and ideally, a commitment to a set of values, ethics, and guidelines for morality will occur. For many adolescents, however, the teen years serve as a psychological moratorium during which differing degrees of conformity to peer group customs, alienation, insecurity, conflicts about life style, and self-awareness may be experienced. This common experience perhaps serves to accentuate the distinctiveness of youth culture, although there are vast differences in the degree to which individual adolescents identify with their peers.

For most parents and teachers, the question of youth culture is perhaps most crucial in relation to whether its values support or run contrary to the educational and intellectual goals of the school. Much evidence has been presented in the past decade or so to suggest that the value system of adolescents is nonintellectual, if not anti-intellectual (33). The exact effect of this state of affairs, if real, is difficult to determine. However, the consensus among researchers is that, faced with this value system, many adolescents somehow mask or disguise strong intellectual attainment goals for the sake of peer acceptance (33).

Yet for the authors, there remains a question whether youth groups collectively and deliberately conspire against academic excellence. To be sure, intellectual achievement may connote def-

Few of the older generation understand, and are easy with, such interests of youth as illustrated by this gathering at a rock festival (Wide World Photos)

erence to the adult establishment and may therefore create a source of conflict for an adolescent striving for emancipation (44). However, this need not result in persistent underachievement or a rejection of the value of intellectual competence. Rather than accept uncritically the idea that adolescents generally are nonintellectual or anti-intellectual, both the system of rewards and recognition and the existing avenues for the development of personal competence in the schools should be scrutinized. In some cases, for example, it may be found that adults, as well as adolescents, reward more quickly and strongly achievement in athletics and social activities than in academics.

To conclude this brief discussion, most authorities now agree that youth culture exists in various forms and as a distinct entity, although it may be more accurate to speak of youth *cultures* instead of a single, unifying youth culture (33). Authorities also seem to agree that the effects of such "cultural" membership can be powerful and diverse, extending to moral and religious beliefs, aesthetics, and educational plans and aspirations. As one source indicates, however: "Proposed explanations of the sources of adolescent subcultures are speculative and appear in all shapes and sizes, ranging from dynamics based upon 'contraculture' to 'being in the same boat.' A minority of researchers believe that adolescent subcultures are a myth and that, since they do not exist, searches for their sources and the nature and extent of their influence are meaningless" (33, p. 209). If there are youth cultures, they may develop because the adult world gives youth few meaningful roles in the world it has created.

One final note is in order. As this book is being written, the authors have heard much discussion among colleagues about a growing counterculture movement in the United States. This movement is said to represent a rejection of values that are reflected in the mainstream of American life: intellectual reason over emotion, self-reliance, personal responsibility, deferred gratification, and advance planning. The main progenitors of this movement are said to be white, upper-middle-class youth who have reacted against the in-authenticity or hypocrisy of adult-controlled social institutions. These youth are said to be joined in many instances by articulate black youth who seek a liberation from oppressive social conditions. It is tempting to suggest that these youth have come to champion elements of the Dionysian life style, including a focus on immediate sensory experience, the cultivation of deep interpersonal relationships, and a general "back to nature" calling. The present appeal for many youth of communal group life, drug use, organic food, and the occult might be taken as evidence of their alleged antirational, hedonistic orientation.

The authors cannot say how deep and widespread the undercurrents of this movement are, nor how persistent this form of counterculture will be. If this movement is a genuine manifestation of value conflict in United States culture, however, educators (and others) en-sconced in the role of fostering the domi-nant, more conventional values of hard work, rationality, and future orientation may find their work increasingly difficult. At the very least, this conflict may necessitate workable educational alternatives to a degree heretofore unknown in American society.

SOME DILEMMAS ABOUT CHILDREN, YOUTH, AND THEIR PEERS

Broadly speaking, only one dilemma about the young and their peer relations has so far been mentioned. This is the conceptual dilemma of youth culture, reality or myth. In this section, three common dilemmas that have both philosophical and procedural components are discussed. These are the dilemmas of control over social relations, goals for personal–social development within the peer group, and unisex versus coeducational schools—dilemmas that often arise in planning for the developmental progress of children and confront parents or teachers regardless of their degree of economic advantage or other characteristics.

The Dilemma of Social Control

Our first dilemma concerns the desirability of exerting close, even tight control over children's peer associations, or leaving them largely free to explore the peer group for themselves. Of course, some degree of control over peer associations occurs as a by-product of residential living—people *do* segregate themselves residentially. In many cases this segregation is intentional, based on socioeconomic, racial, and ethnic factors. As mentioned, many city parents—of all races, but most of them white—move to the suburbs or to the country. Among their reasons is likely to be this sincere one: "It will be good for the children; we are moving to a better place for them to grow up in."

Such parents apparently abandon the heterogeneity and the associated dangers and richnesses of city living for the homogeneity and tighter control of the suburbs or the countryside. Such planned homogeneity may provide greater physical safety and academically better organized schools. It may also provide insularity, provincialism, and superficiality— which add to a peculiar, economically advantaged form of cultural deprivation. On the other hand, such a move may provide children with an opportunity to be alone so they can cultivate their own inner resources. (One of the authors, who was born and reared on a farm, does not wish to undersell the virtues of space, isolation, and the need to combat one's own boredom and loneliness by developing his inner resources.)

The choice of residence, then, is for many a part of the socialization *process.* Growing up under such and such physical conditions, some caregivers believe, is likely to result in their children's becoming the kind of person they desire: a good *product,* at least by their standards.

Whether in the suburbs, in the countryside, or in the inner city, caregivers of children make many day-to-day choices about their children's companions: "I do not want you to play with (so and so)." The safeguards range from such explicit commands to more subtle disparagement of the kind of child with whom caregivers do not want their children to associate. Either technique comes under the heading of exercising control over peer associations.

Other caregivers exercise little censorship over their children's associates. The child plays with whom he wishes (which, of course, he is likely to do anyway, since caregivers have only the indirect "psychological" control over their charges' associations during the important hours of the day when children are in school).

The tightly supervising caregiver (typically, the parent) attempts to reduce the margin of risk for his child by keeping him from the influence of those who will lure him from the caregiver's way of doing things. The loosely supervising caregiver trusts more to the child's or the youth's inner controls. The authors know of no data bearing on the question of which policy is best, if indeed either is. They suspect that, as in most human affairs, some sort of golden mean is the best procedure. Responsible caregivers know where and with whom their children are, but give them a wide range for their individual tastes after, they hope, steering them firmly in the "right" direction.

Teacher Influence on Peer Group

A subdilemma worthy of consideration involves the form of influence that a teacher (or other group worker) should attempt in working with groups of peers. The earlier discussion of sociometrics and their use applies directly to this dilemma. At this point, however, we are more directly concerned with the role that a teacher or a group worker may take during the course of long-term interaction with the young.

First, it should be recognized that teacher influence on peer group norms and structure is much more likely to occur at the elementary school level rather than the secondary school level. Probably the most basic reason for this is that elementary teachers, as compared to their secondary counterparts, spend greater amounts of time with more intact groups composed of children generally more amenable to adult intrusions (56).

Second, adult social influence is usually effected more by modeling desired behavior than by exhortations to children and youth about social or authoritarian control. The dilemma here, of course, concerns the human values on which one chooses to model "desirable" behavior. The authors agree with others (for example, 56) that certain qualities of interpersonal relations are desirable in almost any group setting. These include acceptance of and respect for individual differences, equitable treatment of students (versus favoritism), enthusiastic involvement in group activities, forthright and constructive communication with children and youth, competence in facilitating group problem solving, and authenticity (versus masking one's true self). Group workers who wish to exert a positive influence on attitude development and change within a group setting must also be perceived as trustworthy by their charges. Finally, it is important to provide ample opportunity for group involvement in setting desired goals, in establishing rules for group conduct, and in arranging activities appropriate to such guidelines.

The authors cannot claim that conditions of positive interpersonal influence and regard will result in problem-free classroom or other social groups. Many forces work in opposition to harmonious group relations and the pursuit of academic development in the schools. Such forces, often represent competition for the attention and energy of children and youth. Example 9.4 is included to illustrate this latter point. A matter for consideration in this example is the desirability of adult control (including form and extent) over social dating during adolescence. The study described is also pertinent to the earlier section on courting

behavior and the subsequent discussion of coeducation.

9.4 A Study of Social Dating, Academic Orientation, and Peer Relations

Many students of youth culture have suggested that a strong dependence on peer functions for support and recognition during adolescence may impede the attainment of socialization objectives approved by adults. This suggested incompatibility between adult and youth culture goals can be traced to the psychoanalytic contention that a primary youth culture function is to provide a medium for adolescent rebellion. This contention has not been much tested empirically, but in part underlies Robert Grinder's (22) hypothesis concerning a relationship between strong social–sexual interests and involvement in educational activities during adolescence. Specifically, Grinder has hypothesized that student engagement in high school responsibilities is adversely influenced by a relatively high interest in the rewards of social dating.

To test this hypothesis, Grinder first approached the problem of defining and measuring social-dating interest. Social dating was defined as any situation in which the two parties involved are free agents and constitute an unmarried, unchaperoned, heterosexual pair. He further analyzed such dating in terms of four incentive categories: *sexual gratification* (dating as a sanctioned opportunity for heterosexual physical contact), *independence assertion* (dating as a context for autonomous behavior and deviating from accepted parental or societal standards), *status seeking* (dating as a vehicle for upward social mobility or widespread social recognition), and *participative eagerness* (intrinsic social rewards and the avoidance of loneliness, boredom, work responsibilities, and activities with parents or same-sex peers).

Grinder developed a questionnaire with which to measure adolescents' social-dating interest for each of these four incentive categories. This questionnaire was then administered to 393 boys and 346 girls from the tenth, eleventh, and twelfth grades of a large, urban high school. Also obtained from each subject was a set of personal data: actual dating activity, academic status and aspirations, peer relationships, and participation in high school activities. Both sets of data (social dating and personal) were collected so as to guarantee anonymity and confidentiality of information for all subjects.

Grinder's principal findings are as follows. First, a negative relationship between interest in all four aspects of dating and academic performance in school was revealed for boys; that is, the higher the expressed interest in dating, the lower a boy's academic achievement. A similar negative relationship was noted for girls, but only between academics and two social-dating aspects — sexual gratification and independence assertion. Second, a negative relationship also was observed between participation in adult-sponsored extracurricular activities and certain social-dating attractions (social status and participative eagerness for boys; independence assertion for girls). Finally, dating interest and peer relations were significantly associated. Interest in all four dating aspects was related to extensive involvement with numerous close friends (boys only); and clique membership was

reliably associated with the status-seeking (both sexes) and the sexual (girls only) aspects of dating.

These findings held for adolescents in all three high school grades, thus indicating a pervasive pattern of social and academic activity. Grinder's findings also suggest that the reinforcements of social dating may serve to draw many adolescents away from school-based educational activities; in effect, reinforcements for school achievement compete with peer reinforcements for dating. It is also likely that various frustrating and unpleasant aspects of school life repel still other adolescents who then seek compensation in social–sexual activity. For whatever reasons, perhaps the most telling feature of Grinder's study is that a strong interest in sexual gratification and independence assertion is consistently related to poor academic performance during the high school years.

The Dilemma of Socialization Goals and Group Involvement

A second dilemma faced by those who guide the course of human development is whether to aim for an adolescent and adult product who is "a good member of the group" or one who is an autonomous, independent individual who thinks for himself, regardless of what the conclusions of the group may be. As noted in the previous chapter, the highest level of moral judgment is basically individual, autonomous formulation of and acting on our choices according to our own conscience, *after* considering the welfare and the interests of the group, but *sometimes directly counter* to that welfare and interest. Such an exercise of moral judgment can be a lonely and difficult matter. Moreover, this dilemma of good group member versus independent and autonomous person is reminiscent of the dilemma discussed in Chapter 3 about whether to rear children to be creative or to conform.

The dilemma has been posed in many forms by many people for many years. For instance, we have heard it expressed as "organization man versus free soul"; group member versus loner; outer directed versus inner directed; introverted versus extroverted; and field dependent versus field independent (21). Henry Thoreau is said to have posed it to Ralph Waldo Emerson in a famous exchange. Thoreau, a man who valued his solitude but who also valued social justice, had been jailed for civil disobedience. When Emerson saw Thoreau in jail, he asked with concern, "What, my dear friend, are you doing in there?" Thoreau countered, "And what, my dear friend, are you doing *out there?"*

Over the long span of years, there seems to be little doubt that a rich inner life, a strong and reasonably self-sufficient ego, and a powerful but realistic conscience and sense of justice are the best recipes for reaching the integrity aspect of what Erikson has called the eighth Stage of Man: Integrity versus Despair (19). But such personal self-sufficiency and strength can almost certainly not be reached without deep respect and presumably affection for one's fellow man. Such respect and affection are likely gained as the result of intense and continuing social interaction of the sort that can be experienced only if an individual is willing to conform to a sensible degree. The total nonconformer is simply cast out. As a loner, he has little opportunity to experience the delightful and good aspects of his fellows, but can only watch their follies from a distance.

Another important and related issue is the degree to which peer acceptance or rejection affects children adversely. Teachers, for example, frequently express concern for socially rejected children on the basis that it interferes with classroom learning and mental health. Moreover, it is the rare parents who do not care about the quality of their child's social relationships. One authority (46) believes that at least two patterns of social behavior warrant judicious home and classroom care. These include the child (1) who persistently and strongly avoids peer relationships and rejects or ignores all friendly overtures from others or (2) who is highly motivated to establish friendships with peers but goes about this in a way that distresses or alienates others.

Obviously, one must make some basic value judgments in order to intervene in the lives of such children. Further, certain procedural problems must be solved, including the valid identification of such children, interpreting the meaning that social rejection or isolation has for the child, and selecting appropriate intervention strategies (see the earlier discussion of sociometrics). Certainly the persistent dilemma of establishing the goal(s) of intervention cannot be escaped. For example, should a parent or a teacher be content simply with reducing active rejection of a child by his peers? Or, should an effort be made to promote genuine acceptance and peer preference? In any case, what skills must the rejected or the isolated child develop in order to facilitate his own social acceptance? These are but a few of the nagging questions that face adults who act as agents in children's social development. Answers do not come easily and, according to some, may too often be influenced by the "cult of extroversion" that seems to pervade American society (4).

The Dilemma of School Composition

A third dilemma many caregivers face about the education of their children concerns unisexual schools versus coeducational schools. Today this dilemma is less often a serious problem in the United States than it is in other countries, but it remains a matter of concern for some who wish to keep their boys and girls from situations where early boy–girl attractions, steady dating, and the other joys and hazards of adolescent courtship behavior are likely to present themselves. Few United States public schools are now segregated by sex, but there remain many girls' and boys' boarding schools. Some are denominational, some nondenominational, and some (for boys) are military. Proponents of coeducation are likely to argue that life is full of associations among men and women and that the school years should be a preparation for the social system as it exists. Others worry that unisexual education is likely to lead to naïvete and impulsive, swept-off-one's-feet behavior when a youth is eventually exposed to the opposite sex. They are also concerned that unisexual schools may be dangerous to proper sex role development in that crushes on those of the same sex may occur and possible homosexual ways of managing sex outlets may be learned.

Proponents of unisexual schools may return the argument that boys and girls should be separated, not merely for reasons of sexuality, but because boys mature later than girls and are thus at a disadvantage when placed in classes with girls of the same age. The argument has also been made that boys are more restless, active, and aggressive than girls. Thus, when boys are placed in classes with the girls, their behavior looks relatively "bad." Because of the contrast effect, boys are given more punishment and rejection and receive less praise and approval than girls. In other words, in coeducational classes, boys become a "prejudiced-against minority group." Evidence to support this point comes from many sources, beginning as early as the preschool years (16, 20, 61). The much higher incidence of reading, speech, and disciplinary problems among boys when compared with girls may be further supporting evidence for the charge that boys are not fairly treated in school. In the one study known to the authors, where demonstrably equal treatment (both negative and positive) was given by teachers to first-grade boys and girls, there were no differences in reading level between the sexes at the end of first grade, although such a difference (favoring girls) is commonly found (16).

Again, no firm evidence about the respective virtues and drawbacks of unisexual versus coeducational education exists and, where the dilemma is activated for a given family, it is resolved by some mixture of availability of alternative kinds of school, family finances, religious inclinations of the parents, and (it should be hoped) the wishes of all concerned (parents and children). According to school enrollment figures, the overwhelming majority of American children attend coeducational schools. Thus, the climate of United States opinion seems to be more favorable to coeducation than to unisexual education at all grade levels.

In this chapter the authors have focused on various layers of peer interaction during the course of social development and the relationship of such interaction to the socialization process. The central developmental trends in peer interaction were highlighted, beginning with infancy and extending through preschool play behavior into the intimate peer group activity of preadolescents and adolescents. The related roles of culture, cognition, and sex role identification in social development were singled out for special emphasis.

Basic peer group functions, especially the leveling and the support functions, were discussed in relation to moral development and five important aspects of social behavior: cooperation and competition, sex typing and courting behavior, autonomy and independence, conformity, and leadership–followership. Age and sex differences, in particular, were noted for cooperativeness, competition, autonomy, and conformity. Children in United States culture generally become more competitive with age, although they also increase in their capacity for cooperation. Boys exercise autonomy earlier, but peer group conformity is especially apparent during preadolescence and early adolescence for both sexes. Both personal and situational factors affect competitiveness, independence, and conformity, including an individual's sense of personal competence, nature of a task, group size and composition, and unanimity of group consensus.

Leadership–followership can be conceptualized in terms both of the personal qualities that are characteristic of group leaders and of the relationship of leadership to popularity. Sociometric techniques have been used for a better understanding of these phenomena. The research and educational values of such techniques were stressed, especially in terms of gaining knowledge about the structure of groups and patterns of social power that develop among children and youth. However, the many ethical considerations of sociometry make it necessary for those in a position to influence children's social development to ensure that basic human rights are protected.

The idea of a "generation gap" is widely discussed in American society. The authors chose to discuss this idea in the context of parents "versus" peers. Studies have revealed that both generational continuity and discontinuity occur in our society. It is also apparent that parent–child value differences, as well as similarities, exist. In general, parents exert the single most powerful influence in determining what social values are adopted by youth, but peer group influences are extremely powerful during adolescence. The impact of the peer group typically has been explored in relation to the concept of youth culture; the utility of a youth culture for providing a basis for identity seeking and general emancipation from adults is supported by many authorities on adolescent development.

Finally, three widespread dilemmas about children, youth, and their peers were identified. Two of these involve both the "shoulds" and the "hows" of exerting social control over children and youth and imposing on them predetermined socialization goals. The dilemma of unisex versus coeducation was also examined.

REFERENCES

1. Asch, S. E. Effects of group pressure upon the modification and distortion of judgment. In H. Guetzkow (ed.) *Groups, leadership, and men.* Pittsburgh, Pa.: Carnegie Press, 1951.
2. Asch, S. E. Opinions and social pressure. *Scientific American,* 1955, *193,* 31–35.
3. Asch, S. E. Studies of independence and

conformity: A minority of one against a unanimous majority. *Psychological Monographs*, 1956, *70*, Whole No. 416.

4. Ausubel, D. P. Some misconceptions regarding mental health functions and practices in the school. *Psychology in the Schools*, 1965, *2*, 99–105.

5. Avigdor, R. The development of stereotypes as a result of group interaction. Unpublished doctoral dissertation, New York University, 1952.

6. Bandura, A., J. E. Grusec, and F. L. Menlove. Some determinants of self-monitoring reinforcement systems. *Journal of Personality and Social Psychology*, 1967, *5*, 449–455.

7. Barnes, K. E. Preschool play norms: A replication. *Developmental Psychology*, 1971, *5*, 99–103.

8. Bealer, R. C., and F. K. Willits. Rural youth: A case study in the rebelliousness of adolescents. *Annals of the American Academy of Political and Social Science*, 1961, *338*, 63–69.

9. Berenda, R. *The influence of the group on the judgments of children*. New York: King's Crown Press, 1950.

10. Bronfenbrenner, U. *Two worlds of childhood: U. S. and U.S.S.R.* New York: Russell Sage Foundation, 1970.

11. Burlingame, W. V. The youth culture. In E. D. Evans (ed.) *Adolescents: Reading in behavior and development*. Hinsdale, Ill.: Dryden, 1970, 132–149.

12. Coleman, J. S. *The adolescent society*. New York: Free Press, 1961.

13. Costanzo, P. R., and M. E. Shaw. Conformity as a function of age level. *Child Development*, 1966, *37*, 967–975.

14. Crutchfield, R. S. Personal and situational factors in conformity to group pressure. *Acta Psychologica*, 1959, *15*, 386–388.

15. Darley, J. M. Fear and social comparison as determinants of conformity behavior. *Journal of Personality and Social Psychology*, 1966, *4*, 73–78.

16. Davis, O. L., Jr., and J. J. Slobodian. Teacher behavior toward boys and girls during first grade reading instruction.

American Educational Research Journal, 1967, *4*, 261–269.

17. Elder, G. H., Jr. Adolescent socialization and development. In E. F. Borgatta and W. W. Lambert (eds.) *Handbook of personality theory and research*. Chicago: Rand McNally, 1968. 239–364.

18. Elkin, F., and W. A. Westley. The myth of adolescent culture. *American Sociological Review*, 1955, *20*, 680–684.

19. Erikson, E. H. *Childhood and society* (2nd ed.). New York: Norton, 1963.

20. Fagot, B. I., and G. R. Patterson. An "in vivo" analysis of reinforcing contingencies for sex-role behaviors in the preschool child. *Developmental Psychology*, 1969, *1*, 563–568.

21. Gellert, E. Stability and fluctuation in the power relationships of young children. *Journal of Abnormal and Social Psychology*, 1961, *62*, 8–15.

22. Grinder, R. E. Relations of social dating attractions to academic orientation and peer relations. *Journal of Educational Psychology*, 1966, *57*, 27–34.

23. Grinder, R. E. Distinctiveness and thrust in the American youth culture. *Journal of Social Issues*, 1969, *25*, 7–20.

24. Harris, F. R., M. M. Wolf, and D. M. Baer. Effects of adult social reinforcement on child behavior. In W. W. Hartup and N. L. Smothergill (eds.) *The young child*. Washington, D. C.: National Association for the Education of Young Children, 1967. 13–26.

25. Hartup, W. W. Peer interaction and social organization. In P. H. Mussen (ed.) *Carmichael's manual of child psychology*. New York: Wiley, 1970, 361–456.

26. Hetherington, E. M., and J. L. Deur. The effects of father absence on child development. *Young Children*, 1971, *26*, 233–248.

27. Horowitz, H. Prediction of adolescent popularity and rejection from achievement and interest tests. *Journal of Educational Psychology*, 1967, *58*, 170–174.

28. Iscoe, I., M. Williams, and J. Harvey. Modification of children's judgments by

simulated group techniques: A normative developmental study. *Child Development*, 1963, *34*, 963–978.

29. Jahoda, M., and N. Warren. The myths of youth. *Sociology of Education*, 1965, *38*, 138–149.

30. Johnstone, J., and L. Rosenberg. Sociological observations on the privileged adolescent. In J. F. Adams (ed.) *Understanding adolescence*. Boston: Allyn and Bacon, 1968, 318–336.

31. Kagan, S., and M. C. Madsen. Cooperation and competition of Mexican, Mexican-American, and Anglo-American children of two ages under four instructional sets. *Developmental Psychology*, 1971, *5*, 32–39.

32. Kagan, S., and M. C. Madsen. Experimental analyses of cooperation and competition of Anglo-American and Mexican children. *Developmental Psychology*. 1972, *6*, 49–59.

33. Kandel, D. B., G. S. Lesser, G. C. Roberts, and R. Weiss. The concept of adolescent subculture. In R. F. Purnell (ed.) *Adolescents and the American high school*. New York: Holt, Rinehart and Winston, 1970, 194–205.

34. Keasey, C. B. Social participation as a factor in the moral development of preadolescents. *Developmental Psychology*, 1971, *5*, 216–220.

35. Kirkendall, L. A. *Premarital intercourse and interpersonal relationships*. New York: Julian Press, 1961.

36. Kohlberg, L. Stage and sequence: The cognitive-developmental approach to socialization. In D. Goslin (ed.) *Handbook of socialization theory and research*. Chicago: Rand McNally, 1969.

37. Krech, D., R. S. Crutchfield, and E. L. Ballachey. *Individual in society*. New York: McGraw-Hill, 1962.

38. Landsbaum, J. B., and R. H. Willis. Conformity in early and late adolescence. *Developmental Psychology*, 1971, *4*, 334–337.

39. Madsen, M. C., and A. Shapira. Cooperative and competitive behavior of urban Afro-American, Anglo-American, Mexican-American, and Mexican village children. *Developmental Psychology*, 1970, *3*, 16–20.

40. Maudry, M., and M. Nekula. Social relations between children of the same age during the first two years of life. *Journal of Genetic Psychology*, 1939, *54*, 193–215.

41. McCandless, B. R. *Adolescents: Behavior and development*. Hinsdale, Ill.: Dryden, 1970.

42. McCandless, B. R., C. B. Bilous, and H. L. Bennett. Peer popularity and dependence on adults in pre-school-age socialization. *Child Development*, 1961, *32*, 511–518.

43. McCandless, B. R., and H. R. Marshall. Sex differences in social acceptance and participation of preschool children. *Child Development*, 1957, *28*, 421–425.

44. McDill, E. L., and J. S. Coleman. Family and peer influence in college plans of high school students. *Sociology of Education*, 1965, *38*, 112–126.

45. Medinnus, G. R., and R. C. Johnson. *Child and adolescent psychology: Behavior and development*. New York: Wiley, 1969.

46. Moore, S. Correlates of peer acceptance in nursery school children. In W. W. Hartup and N. Smothergill (eds.) *The young child*. Washington, D. C.: National Association for the Education of Young Children, 1967, 229–247.

47. Moreno, J. L. *Who shall survive?* New York: Beacon House, 1953.

48. Nemec, A. M. A study of the determinants of interpersonal attraction among females. Unpublished M. A. thesis, Emory University, 1971.

49. Offer, D. G. *The psychological world of the teenager*. New York: Basic Books, 1969.

50. Parten, M. B. Social participation among preschool children. *Journal of Abnormal and Social Psychology*, 1932, *27*, 243–269.

51. Parten, M. B., and S. Newhall. Social behavior of preschool children. In R. Barker (ed.) *Child behavior and development*. New York: McGraw-Hill, 1943, 509–525.

52. Piaget, J. *The moral judgment of the child.* New York: Free Press, 1932.

53. Radloff, R. Affiliation and social comparison. In E. F. Borgatta and W. W. Lambert (eds.) *Handbook of personality theory and research.* Chicago: Rand McNally, 1968, 943–958.

54. Reiss, I. L. America's sex standards—how and why they're changing. *Trans-action,* 1968, 5 (March), 26–32.

55. Rosen, S., G. Levinger, and R. Lippitt. Perceived sources of social power. *Journal of Abnormal and Social Psychology,* 1961, 62, 439–441.

56. Schmuck, R. A. Influence of the peer group. In G. S. Lesser (ed.) *Psychology and educational practice.* Glenview, Ill.: Scott, Foresman, 1971, 502–529.

57. Shapira, A., and M. C. Madsen. Between and within group cooperation and competition among Kibbutz and non-Kibbutz children. *Developmental Psychology.* In press.

58. Spindler, G. D. The education of adolescents: An anthropological perspective. In E. D. Evans (ed.) *Adolescents: Readings in behavior and development.* Hinsdale, Ill.: Dryden, 1970, 152–161.

59. Wicker, A. W. Undermanning, performances, and students' subjective experiences in behavior settings of large and small high schools. *Journal of Personality and Social Psychology,* 1968, 10, 255–261.

60. Willems, E. P. Sense of obligation to high school activities as related to school size and marginality of student. *Child Development,* 1967, 38, 1247–1260.

61. Yarrow, M. R., C. Z. Waxler, and P. M. Scott. Child effects on adult behavior. *Developmental Psychology,* 1971, 5, 300–311.

10 Areas of Psychosocial Conflict

This chapter has a parallel in Chapter 6. In both chapters are presented a variety of topics that are different enough from one another that they cannot easily be integrated into a cohesive whole. Each topic, however, is one of genuine importance within the psychology and sociology of human development. The topics are also related to one another in many significant ways. All have extensive, sometimes conflicting, theoretical backgrounds; but the limited space does not permit a detailed discussion of these theoretical considerations. Finally, the diverse nature of the topics is such that they cannot be put into a common format.

DEFINITION OF PSYCHOSOCIAL CONFLICT

Conflict results when an individual or a group is faced with things or situations that call for mutually incompatible behavior, either because of their nature or because of the learning history of that individual or group. The more important the possible outcome and the more equal the strength of the competing behavior cues, the more intense the conflict.

Conflict, moreover, can be comparatively minor and transitory, as for the preadolescent, for example, who struggles with a decision about how best to spend (or save) his weekly allowance; or, conflict can persist over time and can involve basic aspects of psychological development. From the humanistic perspective (see Chapter 2), for instance, two fundamental life conflicts can be identified. One is the perpetual conflict between a person's human propensities for pleasure–love–sex and the achievement of decisive, responsible life–world commitments. A second, perhaps more significant, lifelong conflict, according to humanistic psychology, is the motivational clash between complacent, security-seeking adaptation to life's status quo features and venturesome, creative, visionary action that has a potential for improving and enriching life in a changing world. The point is that the conflicts of our human experience can be viewed in terms of varying magnitude and depth throughout the full course of psychological development. These conflicts can also be viewed in terms of categories with varying implications for psychological adjustment, a consideration of which is now presented.

Three Categories of Conflict

A classical analysis of conflict includes three categories: (1) approach–approach; (2) approach–avoidance; and (3) avoidance–avoidance (47).

In approach–approach conflict, at least two alternatives exist, each of which is desired. A small child must choose between one of two toys because he does not have the money to purchase both. An adolescent may be forced to choose between the date with glamour and the date with substance as a companion for the junior–senior dance, because one cannot go with two people to the same dance. Approach–approach conflict, of course, has within it elements of avoidance–avoidance conflict. Which is the more painful—losing the chance to go out with the glamour date or losing the chance to go out with the substance date (by substance is meant all the solid qualities one looks for, for example, in a husband or a wife)?

Approach–avoidance conflicts are everyday occurrences. The second-grader goes to school because he truly wants to learn and because his parents want him to. However, his teacher is strict and the school day is often boring. Thus, he has a school approach tendency and a school avoidance tendency (or, as Lewin, 47, called it, valence) toward school. A teen-age boy and girl want to have sex with each other, yet fear pregnancy and believe that premarital sex is wrong.

Avoidance–avoidance conflicts are also common. Does the second-grader confess that he took his sister's candy, and face the consequences? or does he lie and face his own guilty knowledge that he has done wrong, fearing that his knowledge-able parents and sister will find him out and he will be doubly punished, once for stealing and again for lying? Does the teen-ager stay in a deadly authoritarian high school because he must be graduated in order to go on to college, or does he leave school and face the consequences of being a dropout for the rest of his life?

When the possible behavior choices are about equally strong, an individual may be immobilized for a time. He leans one way, then the other, but he cannot act decisively. The anxiety evoked by immobility often causes him to resolve the conflict: "I must do one or the other!" He may work out his choice rationally, he may literally or figuratively toss a coin and abide by the result, or he may wait until the impulses for one of the choices become sufficiently stronger than those for the others that he is free to act. Sometimes the conflict is resolved by panic: The person chooses the alternative behavior for which he has the first opportunity.

Time and distance attenuate avoidance responses more quickly than they do approach responses (53). The second-grader starts to school briskly, but takes a long, long time going up the steps to the door. The teen-age male approaches his dating situation avidly. He can hardly wait to pick her up, and for the evening to progress to a hoped-for outcome of parking alone with her. But finally, as he approaches the local lover's lane, he panics and rushes his girl home with embarrassment, propriety, and frustration. It may be that these differential gradients for approach and avoidance lie behind the ancient saying that "Anticipation is always better than realization."

Common Areas of Conflict

In the course of human development, conflict is often associated with or caused by

Prolonged or frequent indecisiveness is a common indicator of conflict.

anxiety, independence and dependence, and aggression, the first three topics discussed in this chapter. Clearly prosocial behaviors also lead to conflict. We are torn between trusting and mistrusting people, between being selfish and altruistic, and between cooperating and competing. Conflict, in a culture that has as much Calvinistic, Protestant ethic underpinning as ours, is bound to occur between our working, achieving life on the one hand (our Apollonian functions in society) and our playing and fun life on the other hand (the Dionysian needs we all share as members of the mammalian species).

In this chapter, the authors deal with the areas of psychosocial conflict listed above. Psychosocial conflicts should be distinguished from cognitive conflicts, although the former possess cognitive components, as will be seen, but are more tinged with emotion and purely social

interactions than are conceptual conflicts. However, like conceptual conflicts, psychosocial conflicts produce dissonance, efforts to solve problems and reconcile incongruencies, and, it is to be hoped, eventual growth (accommodation of greater, depth and breadth).

ANXIETY

The discussion of psychosocial conflict begins with an overview of the data concerning anxiety. The reason for this is simple. Anxiety is a common symptom of conflict and to some extent is an influence on several of the types of behavior discussed in this chapter. For example, as anxiety increases, dependency behavior is likely to become more frequent and intense, especially in younger children. Undue anxiety may interfere with the trusting relations so essential for human transactions, and may disturb altruistic, cooperative, and other prosocial behaviors. The high-anxious child, youth, and adult are often less effective in their work and learning than those with moderate or low levels of anxiety. Many of us feel aggressive toward each other, but at the same time experience anxiety because we know that open aggression is generally disapproved in our society and its consequences may be dangerous.

But what, exactly, is anxiety? The fact is that this term is among the vaguest in the psychological literature. Such imprecision prevails even though the study of anxiety has resulted in a voluminous literature. At least part of the definitional problem can be traced to diverse theoretical orientations toward the study of anxiety. As one authority has put it:

Almost everyone agrees that anxiety is an unpleasant feeling state, clearly distinguishable from other emotional states and having physiological concomitants. In addition to this common core of meaning, however, the term takes on other nuances and shadings of meaning, depending upon the particular theoretical orientation and operational criteria employed by individual researchers. (68, p. 461)

Thus, anxiety has been conceptualized variously as a personality trait or characteristic of the child (either as a chronic or a predispositional state), a descriptive label for measurable physiological responses, a drive or motive, a learned response or habit, and a multidimensional or a unidimensional construct. At the risk of minimizing important theoretical issues, the authors prefer to deal with the definitional problem by saying that anxiety is very similar to what is commonly called fear: a complex emotional state marked by apprehensiveness and height-

ened physiological reactions (including increased pulse, respiration, and perspiration rate) (46). The authors distinguish anxiety from fear by the clarity of the reference or cause. Fear is set off by objective stimuli such as a snarling dog, a great height, or "something that goes bump in the night," whereas the antecedents or stimuli for anxiety are typically vaguer or entirely unknown; they can seldom be well defined. Fear and anxiety share in common attributes of intense personal discomfort. We go to great lengths to reduce our fears and anxieties, and their reduction is exceptionally reinforcing. Many inappropriate responses are undoubtedly learned because they bring relief from fear and anxiety. Avoidance (including giving up or not trying at all) and aggressive attack are among common responses to fearfulness and anxiety.

Freud's great interest in anxiety and his inclusion of it as one of the most important motivating conditions in his psychoanalytic psychology have provided major impetus for modern theories of and research into anxiety. The close (if not complete) similarity of fear and anxiety is reflected in psychoanalytic perspectives. Freud identified three general emotional states based on the idea of fear or anxiety: (1) fear of the external world (reality anxiety), (2) fear of one's own impulses (neurotic anxiety), and (3) guilt (moral anxiety). Within psychoanalysis, the latter two forms of anxiety (in particular) are generally considered to be the breeding ground for psychological disturbances. Psychotherapy is in large part designed to help a disturbed individual recognize and come to rational terms with his anxiety and guilt.

The role of anxiety, particularly as the basis of neuroticism, has continued to appear in many studies as a central dimension of personality or temperament. According to one authority, for example, anxiety (along with extraversion) accounts for much of what personality tests measure (74). Still other authorities (for example, 12) suggest that anxiety is a master motive that underlies many other "acquired" motives such as need for achievement, need for power, dependency, and aggression. Regardless of how anxiety is defined, it seems that anxiety, as a diffuse and an unpleasant emotional state, is a universal human experience. Of course, some individuals are more generally anxious or prone to experience anxiety than others. There also exist individual differences in the extent to which anxiety is associated with specific situations, such as classroom tests. But it must be the extremely rare person who does not experience some degree of anxiety at one time or another.

The authors must state that the foregoing discussion does not provide a scientific definition of anxiety. Ultimately such a definition must be established if one intends to conduct research on this topic. Definitional issues about anxiety have received much attention elsewhere (for example, 12, 68), but for the present purposes the authors choose not to belabor the problem. They consider anxiety, in its most general sense, as fear, usually not clearly specified.

Developmental Considerations

Developmental views of anxiety are frequently organized around the apparent sources of anxiety responses that have been observed in longitudinal studies of children. According to one source (57), for example, one of the first reliable anxiety responses among American infants is *stranger anxiety*. This usually takes the form of crying and withdrawal from any unfamiliar person. It reaches a peak somewhere between the ages of 7 and 9 months and is closer to fear than to anxiety. By age 15 months, stranger anxiety normally has run its course. However, between 13 and 18 months, many infants manifest anxiety over separation from their mothers (or caretakers) with whom an attachment has usually been well formed. According to these same authorities (57), other general developmentally linked anxiety responses include anxiety over the lack of an adequate parental identification model (ages 5 to 6), rejection by the peer group (especially acute during preadolescence), and failure during adolescence to crystallize a firm sense of identity (see Chapter 11). In a more general sense, these situations may reflect anxiety over possible physical harm, loss of approval or affection from others, inability to cope successfully with the environment, and the like (58). In each case, it is the *anticipation* of dire although not clearly defined consequences that seemingly triggers anxiety.

Second, anxiety can be detected among children when they start school. Thereafter it is related to behavior in academic progress, especially reading achievement (70). Although school anxiety apparently decreases generally among American children during the years of middle childhood and beyond (64), children who show increases are often those whose academic development is slower. This is especially true for children who are average and below in intelligence (see Chapter 5). It is difficult to determine the extent to which increased anxiety causes academic difficulties. In fact, anxiety may be more the effect than the cause of such difficulties. The point is that investigator after investigator has revealed significant relationships between anxiety and academic performance, usually to the disadvantage of highly anxious children.

Third, in addition to school performance, many other correlates of anxiety have been documented during middle childhood and beyond (68). For example, increases in anxiety are associated with increased acquiescence to authority, susceptibility to annoyance, willingness to admit common failings, dependency, and conflict about overt aggression. Higher anxiety is also often associated with lowered self-confidence and risk taking, direct aggression, peer status, and a low level of curiosity. If nothing else, such findings indicate that emotionalism pervades the behavior of children and youth.

Fourth, it must be acknowledged that the relationships between measured anxiety and other behaviors, however pervasive, are usually affected by cultural and other factors, including sex. Even in similar cultures, such as the United States and the United Kingdom, differences in anxiety patterns have been observed (11). Such differences are probably partly due to variations in the opportunity for emotional expression and culturally based expectancies about behaviors such as timidity, adventuresomeness, and fantasy. In fact, developmental changes in anxiety have been explained in terms of cultural factors (3). It was indicated earlier that anxiety in American children generally decreases as they move from middle childhood through adolescence. The opposite pattern has been observed among Japanese children and youth (39). It has been argued that greater permissiveness toward children's aggression and sexuality characterizes Japanese child-rearing practices, as compared to American practices. While early restraint may give way to greater freedom of expression among American children and youth, in Japan it

is more likely that constraints appear after early childhood. These constraints typically take the form of increased pressure for appropriate sex typing, deference to others, and strong competition for success in school (7). Such cross-cultural data lend support to a plausible hypothesis about development of anxiety: "Anxiety follows a course parallel to that of societal restrictions or pressures which are imposed upon individuals in an age-linked sequence; individuals (therefore) manifest higher anxiety during those age periods when societal restrictions upon them are greater" (30, p. 946). This hypothesis conceivably could account for the developmental variations in anxiety discussed earlier in this section.

Cultural factors may also be implicated in the frequent finding that, throughout development, anxiety in girls is generally higher than in boys. Possibly this is because girls are allowed freer expression of almost all forms of emotion and, accordingly, admit to more anxiety than do boys. Constitutional factors may also be involved; and not all research workers report data consistent with this generalization about anxiety and sex. Some authors indicate no sex differences in anxiety (50). The point is that many variables must be taken into consideration if the role of anxiety in behavior is to be understood. For example, higher school anxiety (sex differences aside) has been linked to such diverse variables as authoritarian, directive teaching styles (77), defensiveness and other-directedness in parents (69), test (versus gamelike) situations (45), and inner-city public (versus private) school settings (34). Consistent with their theoretical orientation, the authors believe that cumulative learning, especially that which occurs in situations where children are being evaluated by adults and their peers, is more relevant for explaining anxiety than is the sex of the person per se. However, individual differences in emotional reactivity and conditionability are almost certainly important in the development of anxiety.

Parental Factors in Anxiety

As parents set models for children's fears, it is likely that they set models also for children's anxieties (31). For example, one author has shown that parents who are anxious about sexual behavior have sons who are guilty about sex and are anxious about asking others for help, as, in turn, were their parents (3). Furthermore, the more modest and anxious the parents were about sexual activity, the less sexual activity their sons demonstrated.

One fertile breeding ground for anxiety is the family headed by parents who possess very high standards for their children but who are at the same time permissive in their child-rearing practices. Apparently, the parental goals are perceived and incorporated by the child in such a home, but he does not know how to reach them. Thus, he feels threatened with loss of love because he simply does not know how to proceed to do what is expected of him by people who are very important in his life (52).

Some Implications and Dilemmas Concerning Anxiety

The discussion has so far been focused on the negative aspects of anxiety. It is not unlikely that this focus reinforces the idea that anxiety is all bad and should be avoided at all costs. Unless we avoid anxiety, some may argue, children and youth will develop into suffering neurotics who dream about impending doom instead of dancing sugar plums. There is little question that too high a level of anxiety can be personally debilitating. Many investiga-

tors have indicated that high anxiety interferes with learning and performance, especially on complex intellectual tasks or in ambiguous situations where guidelines for behavior are a matter of guesswork (53). But the authors prefer to view anxiety simply as a fact of life to be dealt with as constructively as possible—a phenomenon that has both positive and negative functions. On the positive side, for example, moderate levels of anxiety are often associated with maximum performance on a variety of psychomotor and cognitive tasks (46). The material in Example 10.1 is included specifically to acknowledge the rarely discussed social value of anxiety.

10.1 The Social Value of Anxiety

Eugene Levitt (46) has provided an extensive treatment of the psychology of anxiety. Following is an excerpt from his discussion.

The mental health professional regards anxiety as a painful, debilitating, even catastrophic condition that cries for alleviation. Anxiety as a malignancy is a limited concept. It considers the emotion only in the extreme intensity in which it disrupts behavior. Moderately intense anxiety, however, energizes the organism and improves performance. White (1952) suggests that moderate forms of anxiety not only are used to shape behavior in the child, but also may serve as a very definite incentive in the normal process of growing up. Psychological maturation is fostered by the drive to overcome the anxieties of childhood.

Some defenses against anxiety, like compulsivity and counter-behavior, seem to be constructive as long as they do not get out of hand. It is perhaps plausible that much human striving, much of the endless doing that we call progress, is in one way or another a consequence of anxiety. Stein (1964) summarizes evidence which indicates that learning in rats is seriously retarded if accompanied by stimulation of the limbic system pleasure sites. On purely logical grounds, hedonism and social progress are antithetical. We may conjecture that the advance of human society over the ages is, at least in part, a consequence of the human organism's capacity to experience anxiety. This view, which was expressed by such nineteenth-century philosophers as Kierkegaard, is summed up by Berthold (1963):

"But within all this they see an 'anxiety to. . . .' They read the signs as tokens of a desire to better one's lot and imply that without anxiety there would be no impetus to learning or improvement. Knowledge, in this connection, is the transformation of anxiety into fear — the identification of what is 'wrong.' But anxiety is the mother of the drive to know."

A few theorists have carried the philosophical speculation even further, suggesting that anxiety, or emotional maladjustment in the general sense, produces creativity. Even if we could define creativity for experimental purposes, the hypothesis is untestable. There have been, and are, geniuses who seemed extraordinarily well adjusted, and some who appeared equivalently mentally disturbed. What someone might have been if the circumstances of his life had been different is an unanswerable question. We can only wonder vainly what De Quincey or Poe or Van Gogh would have produced if he had been emotionally better balanced.

Thus, anxiety is a Janus-headed creature that can impel man to self-improvement, achievement, and competence, or can distort and impoverish his existence and that of his fellows. The distinction appears to be a sheer matter of degree, of intensity, as it is with many other phenomena of human life. The urgent need is to acquire the knowledge to utilize anxiety constructively, to be its master and not its slave. (pp. 199–200)

(From *The Psychology of Anxiety* by Eugene E. Levitt, copyright © 1967, by The Bobbs-Merrill Company, Inc., reprinted by permission of the publisher.)

The High-Anxious Child

Despite likely social values, anxiety in its extreme forms undeniably often inter-feres with the educational and personal–social welfare of children and youth. Accordingly, highly anxious children have been the concern of numerous psychologists and educators (14, 15, 54, 69). Gradually, a pattern of behavior generally characteristic of high-anxious children in settings such as the classroom has emerged from studies based on this concern. Specifically, highly anxious children are likely to behave in a self-defeating way to the extent: (1) that authority figures are present to make evaluations; (2) that test aspects of a situation are emphasized; (3) that efforts by these children to gain support and encouragement from others are ignored; (4) that speed in performance is emphasized, or strict time limits are imposed; (5) that directions for learning are unclear; (6) that past habits are incompatible with responses required for progress in learning; and (7) that children anticipate failure rather than success.

It is perhaps unrealistic to expect that all these conditions can be eliminated for the benefit of a highly anxious child. Yet teachers can avoid placing undue stress on the possibility of failure and can make a special effort to provide helpful cues or hints for learning. Noncontingent acceptance of the child (see Chapter 2) also seems important. Too often, the authors believe, children get the idea from teachers that being liked or accepted depends primarily upon the quality of one's academic performance. Hovering over a highly anxious child during a test may decrease, rather than increase, task-appropriate responses, popular belief to the contrary. Finally, as others have noted (for example, 69), glib reassurances (for example, "There's nothing to worry about! Relax, you can do it.") may be ill advised if such comments imply to the child a lack of understanding or concern about his feelings.

In sum, we undoubtedly know more about what conditions create anxiety than we know about how actually to reduce disabling anxiety among insecure children and youth. It is to be hoped that an awareness of the problem is a constructive first step for teachers and parents who desire to help such children and youth deal with their anxiety.

INDEPENDENCE AND DEPENDENCE

Personal independence is a strong value in American society. It is the rare parent or teacher who does not consider relative independence, including characteristics such as self-reliance, self-sufficiency, or autonomy, among the most desirable goals for socialization in our society. Obviously, an individual does not develop personal independence overnight. Even as adults, some individuals seemingly do not achieve a sense of self-security or a capacity for independence of judgment.

Clearly, the achievement of any real degree of independence involves a long, complex chain of learning experiences. This chain extends from infancy, when the newborn is totally dependent on others for his survival, through the childhood years, when alterations in dependency become crucial for peer relationships and scholastic achievement, through adolescence, when final emancipation from one's parents usually occurs.

A fundamental characteristic of the human being is a complete state of psychological and physiological dependence on his caretakers during earliest life. (Photo by Hanna W. Schreiber)

In this section three major aspects of the literature about independence are discussed: definitional considerations about dependency, developmental trends in independence behavior, and some general implications for independence training.

The Concept of Dependence

To begin, it is necessary to examine the concept of dependence. In lay circles, this concept is at best a general one. Because of the wide spectrum of meaning this term has for parents and teachers, it is helpful to identify the specific behaviors involved in the psychological study of dependence. Such study has revealed the following seeking and protest behaviors as most indicative of dependence among children and, to some extent, adolescents as well (24, 51):

Attention seeking (in both positive and negative forms).
Comfort and assurance seeking.
Recognition and approval seeking.
Seeking closeness to others.
Seeking to establish or maintain physical contact.
Protest over separation from adults or peers.
Seeking help to accomplish goals.
Passive reaction to frustration.

With this in mind, at least two points can made. First, care must be exercised in making value judgments about dependence. For example, while most seeking behaviors listed above can be desirable throughout life, their appropriateness depends upon the manner and direction of such seeking behavior at different ages. The affection seeking of a 3-year-old toward his nursery school teacher is usually considered typical, age appropriate, and even a healthy sign of emotional development; in contrast, the persistent,

overt, and intense affection seeking of a 15-year-old toward a strange adult usually is not.

A second point is that dependence behavior in childhood or in adolescence often differs according to the situation in which the individual is placed. Seeking help with a complex mathematics problem, for example, indicates a different sort of dependence than clinging to a teacher's skirt for comfort and emotional support. In fact, three different interpretations of children's dependence can be made (24). Each of these is explained below, not to encourage the reader to label behavior, but further to clarify the concept of dependence.

Interpretation of Dependence Behavior

A first interpretation of dependence behavior represents possibly the most common meaning of dependent behavior: *emotional dependence.* Generally, this refers to nurturance seeking (seeking affection and protection) among children and adolescents. Occasionally, nurturance seeking in young children can take a form that irritates adults (for example, clinging, tugging, or even whining for attention). Most adults, however, seemingly enjoy the fact that children seek their attention and affection, and may even encourage this, subtly or openly. It is thought that emotional attachments of one degree or another may be established between adult and child if both gain satisfaction through nurturant personal interactions. In fact, most children desire adult praise, approval, and affection. They will usually behave in ways directed by the adult if, by complying with adult desires, children receive such social reinforcement. When these conditions exist, significant adults (including teachers) usually find themselves in a position to influence young children strongly. They hope this influence will be positive and in the best interests of children.

While emotional dependence among children is generally approved of, if not encouraged, in our culture, the same cannot be said for older children and adolescents, especially males. Expressions of emotional dependence during adolescence are often discouraged by adults for several reasons. One is the tendency in American society to equate dependence with weakness and unmanliness. Males, in particular, are expected to demonstrate a bravado that does not include overt emotionalism. Another reason is perhaps related to the sexual overtones that accompany adolescent–adult emotional interactions, especially when they include expressions of physical affection. Whatever the reasons, it is clear that expectancies and reinforcements for emotional dependence change during the course of development, more so for boys than for girls. It also seems clear from a survey of the literature that extensive demands for emotional dependence on adults interfere with children's self-development and their relations with their peers. The child very high in emotional dependence has usually been found to be less popular than the child who is relatively low in his emotional dependence demands (see Chapter 9 for a fuller discussion of this topic).

A second interpretation of dependence involves *help seeking*. Help seeking may be inappropriate, as in children who consistently ask for help even though they can do the tasks in question independently (such as dressing, toileting, and eating for children 4 or 5 years old and older). This kind of help seeking is not really *instrumental dependence*, or means-to-end behavior (as contrasted with emotional dependence), but rather falls under the heading of seeking contact and attention. Thus, it may be more appropriately thought of as emotional dependence. True instrumental dependence is directed toward goals other than social reward. As the word *instrumental* implies, such dependence is directed toward getting the job done. Instrumental dependence is by no means always undesirable, particularly when it involves social interactions that result in the child's mastering difficult problems and learning new skills. Boys seem more likely than girls to indulge in instrumental dependence demands; girls are typically higher than boys in emotional dependence demands (33). This pattern may be changing, however, if indeed competence among girls and women is becoming more acceptable, even valued, in our culture. However, consistent, widely generalized, and successful instrumental dependence can easily interfere with the development of mature independence. In short, both the degree of such dependence and the situation in which it is manifested are important in analyzing the developmental significance of help-seeking behavior.

A third form of dependence concerns the extent to which an individual is passive or active across a wide variety of situations. Many of us probably link dependence with the reticent, quiet child and independence with the energetic, outgoing child. Yet the relationship between passivity–activity and the two foregoing forms of dependence is far from clear. This third interpretation of dependency is mentioned to highlight again the need for care in labeling behavior and inferring one characteristic of an individual's behavior from another. For example, one "retiring" child may be quietly independent—a child who efficiently, calmly, and happily goes about performing constructive tasks on his own—while another may do nothing until he is told precisely what to do and receives ample emotional support for doing so. Similarly, an "energetic" child may be actively involved in independent problem-solving activities, while his equally active peer consumes his energy by making demands for adult attention and direction.

Developmental Considerations

The discussion thus far may lead the reader to infer that dependence and independence represent opposite sides of the same question, or that independence is simply a "lack of dependence." Neither of these is a completely accurate statement of the case. In fact, the difficulties faced in determining acceptable definitions of dependence and independence have led some to prefer terms such as *attachment* and *affiliation* behavior (for example, 25). Whether this change in terminology will result in clearer conceptualizations of the behavior in question is not yet known. Meanwhile, the authors prefer to phrase their discussion in the more traditional terminology. They recognize, however, both the relativity and the global nature of such terms. Preschool children, in particular, may be alternately dependent and independent according to several variables, including characteristics of the immediate situation, the nature of their activities, their emotional states, and their relationships to individual adults and peers. Girls may be more dependent than boys only in situations that call for "masculine" skills; boys, faced with "feminine" tasks, may show themselves as more dependent than girls in the same situation. The average adult American male, for example, seems to be unblushingly dependent when faced with complex sewing or cooking tasks and today's urban male is as likely as today's urban female to exert dependence demands (often both emotional and instrumental) on his local mechanic when his car develops seemingly complex problems.

With such qualifications in mind, we next consider some general trends in independence development as reflected in the research literature (35, 51).

First, a trend in the direction of greater independence is apparent as early as the preschool years. This trend is affected by several factors including physical maturation, increased language competence, advances in problem-solving skills, and cumulative social experience. Even the 2-year-old is noted for his independence striving as demonstrated by increased mobility, sphincter and bladder control, and general assertiveness. In fact, the word "No" may seem to be the most frequent term in the vocabulary of many 2-year-olds.

A second and related trend concerns a gradual decrease during the early years in one form of emotional dependence: seeking physical closeness to others. However, attention-seeking behavior is generally maintained and may even increase during the preschool and early school years. This increase is frequently more apparent in relation to peers than to adults, particularly after social group activity becomes a regular part of children's routines. In other words, most children gradually come to prefer, and to be more influenced by, peer recognition than adult recognition in much of their development. A sensitivity to peer recognition and approval, as stated in Chapter 9, flourishes during preadolescence and adolescence. In fact, peer dependence commonly intensifies, at least temporarily, during this period of development and is generally manifested in looking to others for personal evaluation and "accepted" or "in" standards for conduct, dress, and even speech (19). This is probably based, at least in part, on the insecurity or uncertainty engendered by rapid change in biological development and the role expectations of others.

Third, during adolescence, the continued development of independence is especially crucial in relation to the family. Such development may occur variously along five dimensions (18, 52): (1) increased development of self-control, (2) definition of acceptable personal values, (3) achievement of freer mobility and decision-making power, (4) a gradual breaking of puerile emotional attachments to parents, and (5) (during late adolescence and early adulthood), economic independence. Of course, individual differences in these developments are striking throughout the years of childhood and adolescence. Sex role, familial experience, and constitutional factors are among the variables associated with such differences.

Fourth, the testing and criticism of authority is perhaps the most common indication of increased independence striving (19). To this may be added the pattern best described as "Please Mother. I'd rather do it myself." It is often difficult to distinguish between healthy independence—justified criticism, questioning, searching for better ways to do things, and the like—and rebelliousness. However, the latter often reflects hostility and destructiveness that is self-defeating and irrational. The authors take the position that independence striving is often misinterpreted by adults as defiance, when, in fact, it is more accurately a healthy response to environmental conditions that are unnecessarily restrictive. The reactions of adolescents to severely punitive

school disciplinary practices, for example, are often perceived as defiance by teachers rather than as efforts by students to maintain their personal integrity.

In summary, perhaps the soundest generalization that can be drawn about developmental trends in independence is that the form of dependent behavior changes with age, in terms both of the objects of one's dependence and of the frequency with which dependent behavior is manifest. There is probably no such thing as completely independent behavior: "No man is an island." Hence, it is appropriate to speak of *interdependence* in a complex society such as ours. Yet, a capacity for independent judgment and for self-sufficiency is extremely important for personal survival. Moreover, it seems that such a capacity is not only desirable but also necessary for the achievement of a sense of dignity and self-esteem. This point is again considered in Chapter 11.

Some Mediators of Growth in Independence

Most of the mediators of human development discussed in Chapter 1 clearly apply to growth in independence. For example, most bright children are less dependent and less influenced by social pressure than their less bright peers (20, 38, 39). Thus, intelligence is a relevant mediator of independence development. Cultural factors are also involved. For example, Dutch and Belgian adolescents reportedly are significantly different in social and emotional independence (66). Presumably, this difference is due largely to cultural values that are translated into opportunity structures and patterns of reinforcement. Further, it is clear that the pattern of growth in independence varies according to sex, with dependence a stabler characteristic of girls in United States culture (43). The authors have often referred to this phenomenon and it needs no elaboration. However, they wish to develop in more detail another mediator of growth in independence from which some basic implications for independence training can be drawn: child-rearing practices.

Child-Rearing Practices

Parental child-rearing practices are clearly associated with differences in children's dependence behavior. For example, at least three general patterns of parental behavior may be involved for children high in dependency (32, 35, 53): (1) parental rejection, (2) a combination of parental warmth regarding dependence and restrictiveness concerning independence, and (3) inconsistency in dispersing rewards and punishments for dependence behavior. In contrast, higher levels of independence behavior have been observed among children in families where opportunities for the exercise of self-reliance and parental demands for autonomous behavior exist (19).

Despite documented relationships between such practices by parents and persistent dependence in their children, the exact degree to which certain parental practices "cause" certain child behaviors cannot be stated. Different children react differently to similar environmental circumstances, be they child-rearing practices or teaching methods. It is therefore difficult to determine clearly why a given child may be more or less dependent. Consequently, it is probably less constructive for teachers, for example, to speculate about historical causes than to consider ways in which the school contributes to various forms of dependence (or independence).

Although very little work has been re-

ported concerning the subject, it is likely that conditions affecting dependence in adolescence are similar to those that foster such behavior during childhood. For both periods of development the impact of modeling, opportunities for and training in self-direction and self-assertiveness, variations in control techniques (especially related to restrictiveness and protectiveness), and parental warmth are important (19). All these interact with the child's "constitution." For instance, in identical situations, sturdy, well-coordinated, and early-maturing children should certainly have an easier time learning independence than their weak, awkward, and late-maturing peers.

Some Implications of Independence Development

The authors believe that most parents want their offspring to exercise a healthy independence in both academic and social settings, but on the basis of observations they question whether many of these same parents—and teachers as well—act consistently with this professed wish. In some schools, for example, teachers have been heard to pay lip service to the value of independence in learning, yet the same teachers often demonstrate an authoritarian teaching style that reinforces dependence among students. Of course, the dilemmas faced by adults concerning independence training are myriad. For example, when and how should independence training begin? What effect do developmental stage differences have on one's choice of activities and latitude for self-reliance and decision making concerning children and youth? What is, and how does one achieve, a "good" balance between instrumental independence and emotional dependence?

Again, no magic formulas exist to answer such questions. However, a few general guidelines for independence training may help the reader to formulate his own position concerning the matter. Perhaps the most basic of these is to help children early to help themselves. During the preschool years, for example, play activities, self-help activities, and practical life exercises such as cleaning, washing, sweeping, and polishing provide opportunities for parents to encourage and reinforce independent behavior.

Another guideline involves providing children with specific responsibilities that both foster independence and extend their learning in valuable ways. Responsibility for the care of plants and animals is a good example—an example of the concept that careful attention is necessary for the survival of these living things.

Respect for and patience with children who wish to do things on their own is also important. We overlook the value of encouraging and rewarding children who take the initiative in problem-solving tasks and who complete routine activities (for example, toileting and dressing) without unnecessary help.

Parents and teachers may also wish to avoid creating stressful, frustrating situations for children—prolonged periods of waiting, pressure on children to accomplish tasks for which they are ill prepared, and isolating children from others for prolonged periods, for example. Such conditions are often followed by increased dependence demands that can be difficult to manage (51). Finally, the authors can recommend emphasizing to children the sense of satisfaction or accomplishment that can be gained through independent problem-solving and task performance— for example, "Doesn't it feel good to do something well all by yourself?" This, of course, is related also to the achievement of a general sense of competence or mastery, of which independence training is a significant part.

Conflict about independence–dependence relationships typically intensifies as adolescence approaches. Moreover, the conflict may extend to parents, teachers, and adolescents alike. A parent, for example, may simultaneously wish to encourage and allow independent behavior, yet be reluctant to do so because of the fear that his offspring is not quite "ready" or that the risks of psychological and physical harm are too great. Such a parent can be described as ambivalent about permitting genuine independence. Similarly, the adolescent may simultaneously wish to exercise his independence yet continue to seek comfort in the dependency relationship that he has so long experienced within the family. Thus, the adolescent may himself be ambivalent about accepting responsibility and demonstrating independence that does, in fact, represent a certain amount of risk. This phenomenon has been described elsewhere as *dual ambivalence* (72). Both parent and adolescent are in conflict about independence and seek simultaneously to approach and avoid aspects of their relationship that involve assertiveness and succorance. Parents want to be needed, children want to be loved and nurtured; yet each is nervous about "too much of a good thing."

Dual ambivalence need not be limited to independence–dependence conflict. It can pervade other dimensions of interpersonal relationships, including heterosexuality and competitiveness. However, the authors' point is that adults and their youthful charges frequently may be unaware that ambivalence is dual. Further, such ambivalence often goes unexpressed. When this is the case, communication and understanding between adults and youth suffer to the disadvantage of both parties. In this regard, the authors agree with the humanists, who maintain that open, honest, and acceptant interchange of feelings between people is often the best road to mutual understanding and respect.

The conflict about independence represented by two philosophies of child rearing based on the Protestant ethic and the social ethic, respectively, should also be discussed (40). Rugged independence unquestionably has been part and parcel of the Protestant ethic. It is also, and not incidentally, associated with the idea of entrepreneurialism developed in Chapter 1.

In contrast, the social ethic is mainly based on the idea of "getting along." Cooperation and cordial compromise, perhaps imperative for successful bureaucratic life, are the cornerstones for socialization based on this ethic. The dilemma, of course, concerns what "mix" of experiences parents and teachers should provide for children and youth in order to equip them best for a future that is difficult to conceptualize in view of rapid social change. Perhaps it is the extremes that should be avoided—the chronic conformer, whose cooperativeness impedes a clear sense of personal identity, and the unyielding individualist, whose independence becomes irrational. In complex human affairs, the golden mean—an optimum but difficult-to-achieve position —is often the best answer.

✝AGGRESSION

The psychological study of aggression in children and youth is as complex as the study of dependence and independence. This complexity extends both to the definition of aggression and to the problems concerning the management of children's acting-out behavior. The management of children's aggression unquestionably is a major concern for most American parents and teachers (78). More often than not, teachers view aggressive behavior as disruptive, a threat to their efforts to maintain order and group control, and something about which direct action is usually required. Parents are likely to see such behavior as either a danger to their child or a threat to themselves, or both. In this section, the meaning of aggression is examined briefly, along with background factors and the relationship of frustration and punishment to aggression. Subsequently, guidelines for living with aggression are offered.

The Meaning of Aggression

There are at least two broad approaches to defining aggression (4, 5). One approach is based on observable behavior, including the effects or consequences of aggression. For example, acting-out behavior—either *verbal* (yelling, shouting, threatening, ridiculing) or *physical* (hitting, kicking, throwing objects at another person) can clearly be seen by any observer. Moreover, the effects of the behavior can usually be observed: pain or injury to another person, destruction of property, and the like.

The second broad approach to the definition of aggression is an extension of the first—the apparent *intention* or *motive* of the aggressor is included. One person, for example, may deliberately set about to cause pain to another. The inclusion of a judgment about intent or motivation requires that one *infer* such motivation from the aggressive behavior observed. Of course, intent cannot be directly observed unless one person admits verbally to another that his intent was to injure. Even then, a person must assume that such an admission is true. In other words, correct inference about the motives of others is a difficult matter. In children's play situations, for example, it is sometimes impossible to determine whether one child strikes another accidentally or intentionally. Knowing the exact social context in which the striking behavior occurs helps to increase the probability of correct inference. But the difficulties faced by a person who must resort to inference in explaining or analyzing behavior illustrate the need for caution in such matters. Otherwise, children may be unjustly accused, blamed, or punished for aggression that is, in fact, misinterpreted by an observing adult.

Another problem in defining aggression is to distinguish between aggression whose goal is harm to others for harm's sake, and aggression that is designed to achieve an instrumental goal (to get something done, to protect something, or to reach some desired outcome). Examples of instrumental aggression include aggression to gain possession of material goods, to win a prize in competition with others, or to achieve control or power over another's activities. Such instrumental aggression *may* include harm to others; it frequently occurs, however, when a child or a youth wishes to obtain desired goals quickly and perhaps because no constructive alternative to aggression exists.

Third, and finally, the notion must be considered whether aggression is *situational* (is specific to certain social settings and conditions) or *general* (represents a basic tendency for children or youth to show a certain level or kind of aggression across a wide variety of settings). For example, some children seem to behave aggressively wherever they are—school, church, or playground. Other children, in contrast, rarely behave aggressively and then only in certain stressful situations. The issue is whether aggressiveness is a pervasive personality characteristic or a

set of responses to very specific conditions. Behaviorists are inclined to accept the latter position. Psychoanalysts, with their emphasis on the instinctual nature of aggression, usually lean toward the personality trait viewpoint. This point is mentioned to illustrate once again the influence of theory in guiding one's interpretation of behavior (see Chapter 2). However, for the authors both possibilities are plausible and are not necessarily incompatible.

When general aggression seems to characterize a given child's behavior, many psychologists assume that strong feelings of hostility toward others are implicated, whatever the source of such hostility may be. Other psychologists (for example, 26), doubt that hostility is necessarily involved. Regardless, it is clear that "inner feelings" are difficult to assess just by looking at an individual's behavior. In the case of situational aggression, attention is called to the circumstances that lead to acting-out *and* any consequences of aggression that promote or maintain the behavior. For example, one might observe that a given child is aggressive only when other children make demands on him for sharing toys and other play equipment. This child may become quite successful in keeping what he wants by striking out or otherwise intimidating his peers. If so, he will probably continue to behave this way, because his aggressive behavior is often rewarded. Another child may behave aggressively only when attacked or abused in some way by other children. In such a self-defense situation, his aggression may be not only appropriate but also desirable.

Some Background and Developmental Factors in Aggression

In our society, it seems that most people value reasoning rather than brute force in solving personal conflicts. Certainly this belief is reflected in American child-rearing practices. At least, American parents generally discourage their children's direct aggression, or acting-out behavior, and encourage rational means for problem solving (53). However, the specific form that such discouragement takes varies widely. One source of variation is the age of the child (26). For example, very young children are often permitted occasionally to hit, bite, and throw objects during expressions of rage. These direct aggressive acts of older children are usually vigorously discouraged by their parents. Many parents, however, resort to physical punishment in dealing with children's aggression, ostensibly for the purpose of reducing or eliminating the undesirable behavior. Unfortunately, it is probably true that, in anger, adults often act out their own aggression on their children, sometimes with little or no justification (and by so doing, provide a model of aggression to their children with the effect of eventually increasing rather than reducing childhood aggression). The shocking incidence of child abuse, often called the "battered child" syndrome, is stark and depressing evidence of parental aggression directed toward their own offspring (28).

The effects of disapproval and various forms of punishment on children's aggressive behavior are not easily predicted. It is generally true, however, that physical aggression among children gradually decreases in frequency throughout the preschool years (especially for girls), whatever the reasons may be. This decrease does not mean that aggression subsides. Rather, verbal aggression (yelling, name calling, swearing, and threats of physical aggression, tattling, and reproving) becomes more frequent during the late preschool years. During the primary-grade

years, most children have learned how to substitute competitive striving for extensive verbal and physical outpourings of aggression. Yet some children, more often males than females, manifest a strong, stable pattern of aggressive behavior through childhood and into adolescence (43). During adolescence, of course, direct forms of aggression can become very serious for both society and the individual; for example, physical assault, property destruction, and theft qualify as criminal acts. This raises the issue of the relationship of aggression to delinquency. Delinquency is discussed later in the context of adolescent problems (see Chapter 12).

Putting aside for the moment criminal implications of aggression, a prolonged pattern of aggressiveness over the developmental years may indicate that parents tolerate, or even approve of and reward, their children's aggressive behavior. This can be a problem, especially in schools where acting-out behavior is neither desirable nor typically productive. For the child, home and school may represent a conflict in reinforcement contingencies, if not basic values. Acting out can also create difficulties in home–school communication. Of course, such conflicts and difficulties may also involve other matters, including the work ethic, and these matters must be recognized rather than denied. It is hoped that they can be dealt with satisfactorily through reasoned discussion with parents.

The Management of Aggression

The preceding discussion leads directly to a consideration of problems and guidelines for managing aggression. The problems are related both to the democratic idea and to normal social development. For example, it is clear that aggression often results in harm to others or otherwise interferes with the rights of others. Moreover, a child who frequently acts aggressively toward his peers often ends up being rejected by them. Peer rejection serves to cut off the aggressive child from many valuable social contacts, to say nothing of the implications of such rejection for a child's self-esteem. Retaliation (the vicious circle) is also often the result of aggression. Perhaps the most basic task for child and youth workers is to determine how aggression may be channeled so that both society and the individual benefit (if possible) rather than suffer.

Among other things, the accomplishment of this task requires a serious examination of the factors that may promote more or less aggressiveness in children and youth. Constitutional factors conducive to aggression, such as hyperactivity, low threshold or tolerance for pain, and strong emotional reactivity must, of course, be considered. Such factors are rarely subject to direct control, however, although acceptable coping techniques can often be developed. In contrast, more control can be achieved over other important factors. It was suggested earlier that opportunities to imitate aggressive models may actually promote aggression. Models in this sense refer to both adults and other children who are themselves violent and who threaten, coerce, ridicule, and manhandle other people. The effects of models can be particularly strong if the aggressive behavior modeled is successful—that is, leads to desired outcomes (26). Situations where aggression is allowed to go unchecked are also likely to foster higher rates of aggression among children. Included are situations where controls of basic standards for conduct are not applied clearly and consistently. Of course, direct encouragement and reward by adults or other caretakers for children's aggression is an extremely powerful method for shaping the course of aggression.

The Role of Frustration

To the above factors can be added frustration. Frustration is a term that can be used to describe an emotional state that results when an individual is unable to achieve some desired goal for whatever reason. Frustration may also involve physical pain and threats to one's self-esteem. A popular, long-standing view in psychology is that frustration frequently leads to aggression and that some degree of frustration probably underlies all forms of aggression (17). While this view does not fully explain the whole story of aggression, it is clear that when frustration leads to anger, aggressive behavior is a likely outcome.

An obvious practical implication of this statement is that one should avoid the proionged or excessive frustration of children if needless aggression is to be prevented. For example, conditions that typically produce frustration in young children, or at least serve as antecedents to aggression, include confining children to small spaces, requiring them to remain quiet or sit for long periods, prodding them always to "hurry up" their activities, providing inadequately for rest periods and snacks, changing routines frequently and unexpectedly, unfairly removing privileges, and inflicting physical discomforts, including corporal punishment.

Of course, like anxiety, frustration in various forms is a fact of life. Moreover, some degree of frustration tolerance is necessary for all children and youth. One approach to this matter is for adults to assist children to deal with their frustration in constructive ways wherever possible, rather than through outpourings of aggression. A key variable in such an approach, however, is the degree to which frustration is relevant (versus irrelevant) to a given situation or task (53). For example, many learning tasks, both in and out of school, are frustrating to children and youth because of their complexity and the practice that is required for mastery. This sort of frustration can even be described as normal and expected. Good teachers recognize this and provide leeway for changes in difficult learning tasks, especially in the initial stages of learning. But to "natural" frustration should not be added irrelevant sources of frustration. Vague, poorly organized presentation strategies by teachers, requirements of children for which they are not prepared, poor planning, distracting noise, and substandard lighting and room temperature control can all be sources of irrelevant classroom frustration.

Punishment and Aggression

The role of punishment in relation to aggression deserves further comment. Punishment by an authority figure, for example, often inhibits the direct expression of children while in the presence of the punisher; harsh punishment can often lead to greater amounts of aggressive behavior directed toward other objects or persons, especially when the punisher is absent (26). This phenomenon is sometimes discussed in terms of *displaced* aggression. That is, aggression (in retaliation to a punisher) may not be directed toward the original punisher, but toward some less threatening figure or object instead—another child, a possession, or an animal, for example.

Some authorities (for example, 2) emphasize the direct model of aggressiveness that a punishing adult provides in explaining displacement. This interpretation is reinforced by the research finding that parents who both permit and punish aggressive behavior frequently have highly aggressive children (26). It is also likely, however, that some degree of frustration is present, especially in children whose parents respond to aggression inconsistently.

Another danger lies in the consistent use of strong punishment. Punishment is likely not only to stop (or to repress or drive underground) the behavior toward which it is directed, but to stop *all* behavior. The net result may be an inhibited, passive, nonspontaneous child for whom constructive social, cognitive, and motor development is difficult because he so seldom displays behavior that can be rewarded. Constructive socialization probably proceeds best with selective reinforcement, with a predominant emphasis on positive or developmental, rather than negative and repressive, interactions with significant others.

Some Final Thoughts about Aggression

A widely held belief in American society (and psychology) is that aggressive behavior may be dissipated or reduced by means of *catharsis*. Catharsis refers to the free expression of aggression either vicariously (in fantasy or by watching others act aggressively) or through play, verbalizing one's feelings, or actual aggressive responses toward something—striking a Bobo doll or smashing a junk car with a sledge hammer, for example. Cathartic expression, it has been argued, serves to reduce one's tendency to perform other aggressive acts or otherwise results in feelings of satisfaction or relief from tension. At the practical level, this view of catharsis reflects a belief that aggressive children may be helped to become less aggressive (and hostile) by acting out their feelings in doll play, in shooting toy guns, in finger painting, in physical exertion, or in related forms of vicarious participation in aggressive acts (for example, watching cartoons in which the characters behave aggressively).

Appealing as this belief may be, there is little evidence to support its validity (8). In fact, such techniques of cathartic expression may even promote higher rates of aggression among children. Of course, most people agree that aggressive doll play or mild competitive games are less destructive than striking one's peers. It should not be assumed, however, that such activities will either necessarily reduce a child's "aggressive feelings" or cause him not to act out against other children. These and other "substitute" activities are best viewed as means for channeling aggression away from human targets.

A major point here is that an important distinction exists between constructive and destructive ways of expressing anger. The authors do not advise that children or youth "bottle up" their anger and be prevented from emotional catharsis. Not expressing anger very possibly has its own negative consequences, such as psychosomatic disorders, impaired cognition, and deceptive interpersonal relationships (37). But neither should one conclude that catharsis is a cure-all for undesirable aggressive behavior.

A clinical note should be added about self-awareness. It seems well for "each man to know himself." Thus, the authors believe it is wise for children, youth, and adults to recognize their feelings of hostility and anger, to accept their hostility and anger without anxiety and guilt, but, at the same time, to handle such feelings in personally and socially constructive ways. These are known as coping techniques. One cab driver, for example, diminishes the horrors of urban traffic by asking himself (or often his passengers), "I wonder what happened to that poor devil this morning?" when he is honked at or yelled at irrationally.

A final comment about aggression concerns the possible influence of violence in the mass media on aggression among children and youth. Definitive statements about this relationship cannot be made at this time. However, relationships between the amount and kind of aggressive behavior observed by children (as in television, movie cartoons, and general exposure to aggressive models) and the incidence of subsequent aggression in such children have been described by many authorities (for example, 10, 48, and 49).

This effect is particularly notable in competitive situations where children experience failure (26). Moreover, both physiological reactions (emotional sweating) and verbal expressions of fear among children have been linked to film content dealing with cartoon and human violence (63). Children exposed to filmed violence have also been found willing to hurt other children more than control children exposed to nonviolent TV sequences for an equal period. Example 10.2 is a summary of one current study in which the willingness of children to help or to hurt another child was checked (there was not really a child, but the children in the study were led to believe there was). The experimental children had watched a violent film; the control children, a filmed sports event.

10.2 A Study of Children's Aggression

Robert M. Liebert and Robert A. Baron (48) studied 136 Midwestern children from a wide variety of socioeconomic levels, four-fifths of whom were white, one-fifth of whom were black. About

Psychologists are not in total agreement about the possible influence of violence in television programs on aggressive behavior in young people; however, there is no disagreement that young people are exposed to a distressingly large amount of violence through this medium. (Photo by Bruce Roberts)

one-half the children were 5 and 6 years old when studied, about one-half were 8 and 9 years old. One-half the subjects were boys, one-half were girls. The children's parents had volunteered them for a study of the effects of televised violence, the conductor of which was a young white woman.

After coming into the experimental situation with their parents (or parent), the children went into a waiting room containing children's furniture and a television set. After each child was made comfortable, the set was turned on for six and one-half minutes, four minutes of which were taken up by humorous commercials, one about a paper towel and the other about a G-rated movie. The experimenter left the room after turning on the TV set. Then, children in the experimental group watched three and one-half minutes of a popular TV series in which a simple story line was preserved, and there were a chase, two fist-fighting scenes, two shootings, and a knifing. The control group watched three and one-half minutes worth of a very active sports sequence involving hurdle races, high jumps, and so on. Finally, for all subjects, the last sixty seconds of TV contained a commercial for automobile tires. The experimenter came in just as the last commercial ended and announced that she was ready to begin to work with each child.

The child was then taken to a room that he was told was next to another room where another child was playing a game involving turning a handle. The experimental child had in front of him a response box with a red button labeled HURT and a green button labeled HELP. He was told that when he pushed the green HELP button, the "other child" (there was not really another child) would be helped because his handle would turn more easily. When he pushed the red HURT button, the handle would get hot and the "other child" would have to turn loose of it. A signal light told the experimental child when the "other child" was working, and he was instructed that he must push one of the two buttons each time the signal light came on. After twenty trials, the experimenter came back, announced that this part of the work was finished, and took the child to a third room containing three attractive nonaggressive toys and one aggressive toy, in addition to two inflated plastic dolls. The child was left alone again, after being told he could play with anything he wished. The nature of the child's play was then observed through a one-way mirror.

The children who viewed the aggressive film, both boys and girls, hurt the presumed other child in the testing situation more (that is, pushed the HURT button longer) and played more aggressively after being moved to the room with the toys. This latter effect was strongest for the youngest boys.

A laboratory study such as this comes very close to real life, because all the experimental children apparently believed there was a real live child (but one whom they could not see) whom they were either hurting or helping. Thus, in the present author's view, the results should be taken quite seriously.

From this and other studies of aggression and the mass media has developed the belief that television and movie violence can often instigate increased aggression in social situations, such as play, especially among young male children. This, of course, says nothing about the further likelihood that filmed violence stimulates aggressive fantasies among children (and youth) of both sexes. While most children and youth seem not to act out antisocial fantasies at the expense of others, many do. The authors believe it is social folly to encourage such tendencies by providing an indiscriminate diet of violence to America's children. They thus urge parents to exercise caution in their children's television (movie) habits and in interpreting mass media accounts of studies about filmed violence and children's aggression. Such accounts are no substitute for the studies themselves.

The authors believe that such information serves to caution both parents and teachers about the nature of behavior observed by children and the conditions under which it is observed. At the very least, the authors strongly recommend that adults avoid placing children in situations where violence is glorified, as in much of the current television fare. Beyond this, professional opinion about how and when to introduce children to aggression is mixed. One authority (76), for example, has recommended that aggressive themes, appropriately designed for successive age levels, be deliberately woven into children's textbooks. In this way, it is argued, acculturation concerning the "realities" of human aggression in organized society might occur under reasonably controlled conditions. No one knows how effective such a strategy would be. Certainly such themes have existed in comic books and even fairy tales for years, although haphazardly placed and consumed. Essentially, then, the dilemma is how best to introduce children to the "facts of life" about aggression in human affairs.

The authors cannot offer a tested solution to this dilemma. However, they find much to admire in the humanistic concern for a reduced emphasis on aggressiveness in human affairs. Accordingly, their final suggestions for the management of children's aggression (where desirable and possible) include (1) diverting children from aggressive to non-aggressive activities, (2) use of reasoning or inductive techniques focused on the consequences of aggression for interpersonal relations, (3) explicit disapproval,

(4) removing rewards that might follow aggressive acts, (5) helping children to understand why others may be aggressive toward them, and (6) helping children substitute language for physical acting-out as a means for resolving interpersonal conflict. Of course, it is also advisable to note that aggression is occasionally both necessary and desirable, especially in defense of basic human rights. This suggests an important question for parents and teachers: Should children be helped to discriminate when aggression may be an appropriate response to destructive social conditions, including transgressions by others? If so, what is the best procedure? If not, why not?

PROSOCIAL BEHAVIORS

Prosocial behaviors are those which are socially constructive and which usually result in benefits for both the person who engages in them and for those who receive them. Examples are trust, altruism, and cooperation, which characterize groups as well as individuals.

Table 10.1 *Erikson's Eight Stages of Man*

Stages (Ages are approximate)	Psychosocial Crises	Radius of Significant Relations	Psychosocial Modalities	Favorable Outcome
I. *Birth through first year*	Trust vs. mistrust	Maternal person	To get To give in return	Drive and hope
II. *Second year*	Autonomy vs. shame, doubt	Parental persons	To hold (on) To let (go)	Self-control and willpower

Table 10.1 *Erikson's Eight Stages of Man (concluded)*

Stages (Ages are approximate)	Psychosocial Crises	Radius of Significant Relations	Psychosocial Modalities	Favorable Outcome
III. *Third year through fifth year*	Initiative vs. guilt	Basic family	To make (going after) To "make like" (playing)	Direction and purpose
IV. *Sixth to onset of puberty*	Industry vs. inferiority	Neighborhood; school	To make things (competing) To make things together	Method and competence
V. *Adolescence*	Identity and repudiation vs. identity diffusion	Peer groups and outgroups; models of leadership	To be oneself (or not to be) To share being oneself	Devotion and fidelity
VI. *Early adulthood*	Intimacy and solidarity vs. isolation	Partners in friendship, sex, competition, cooperation	To lose and find oneself in another	Affiliation and love
VII. *Young and middle adulthood*	Generativity vs. self-absorption	Divided labor and shared household	To make be To take care of	Production and care
VIII. *Later adulthood*	Integrity vs. despair	"Mankind" "My Kind"	To be, through having been To face not being	Renunciation and wisdom

Source: E. H. Erikson *Identity: Youth and Crisis* (copyright 1968 by W. W. Norton) 94, and *Childhood and Society* (2d ed.) (copyright 1950, 1963 by W. W. Norton). Reproduced by permission of W. W. Norton and Hogarth Press Ltd., London.

Trust

Erikson, one of the more influential of the neopsychoanalytic authors, postulates eight stages of man—eight developmental crises that each person must face in the total span of his development (23). The first and, in Erikson's theory, the foundation of all the others is the stage of *trust versus mistrust*. Erikson believes that the basic tendency for a person to be optimistic and trusting as contrasted with cynical and mistrusting is learned during the first year or two of life (Freud's *oral* stage). Trust seems to develop (the re-

A sense of trust in one's physical and social environment is considered to be the positive outcome of the child's mastery of the earliest developmental crisis. (Photo by Hanna W. Schreiber)

search is neither extensive nor high in quality) when the infant is almost totally accepted by his caregivers and when he lives in a partially consistent, safe, and comfortable world. The process by which basic trust is learned most probably parallels the notion of classical conditioning; that is, trust is an automatic thing learned from repeated pairings of comfort and relief (ministrations by friendly and loving caregivers), with signals of distress made by the infant. When he cries, someone soon comes to relieve his distress. When he is hungry, he is promptly fed. He is spared from arbitrary separations and abandonments. When he is curious, he is introduced to the stimuli that elicited his attention, and these stimuli are found not to be hurtful. From such treatment, a general propensity arises to the effect that the world is basically safe and people are generally good.

Learning to trust occurs during the developmental period that Piaget calls the sensorimotor stage (see Chapter 2). Babies exposed (with due regard to their safety and comfort) to more and more complex stimuli and situations that demand problem-solving skills indeed become "masters of the thing." They learn to deal autonomously with their physical world. Trust and competence, then, may well be closely linked, with one feeding the other in a benign cycle. It is easy to see that overprotective parents, themselves likely to be mistrusting by nature, lead a child to mistrust himself (that is, his radar tells him his caregivers do not think he can cope). Their behavior also leads to mistrust of his environment, which, because of the behavior of those who look after him, he comes to see as dangerous and unpredictable. Neglect, unpredictability, and rejection by caregivers would seem logically to produce the same result, as would sharp restriction of freedom for the child to explore the world around him.

In later childhood and adolescence, trust generalizes to interpersonal relations. One pair of authors states: "Interpersonal trust is defined as a generalized expectancy held by an individual or a group that the word, promise, or verbal or written statement of another individual or group can be relied upon" (44, pp. 657–658). These authors present evidence about college students to the effect that fathers may be crucial agents in developing trust in their children, particularly their sons. Fathers are typically the liaison agents between their families and the outside world, and sons of high school and college age must surely look partially to their fathers as models on whom to pattern their own trusting-mistrusting behavior as they negotiate with others. In this study, it was found that the fathers of highly trusting college men (as determined by the Interpersonal Trust Scale) were significantly more trusting than the fathers of low-trusting college men. Mothers' trust scores, on the other hand, bore little relation to the trust scores of either their sons or their daughters, and there was only a weak tendency (not statistically significant and thus, strictly speaking, not even a tendency) for the fathers and the mothers of trusting college girls to score higher on the trusting test than the fathers and the mothers of low-trusting girls.

This is a plausible enough finding for traditional American families, where the father is the breadwinner, the mother the housekeeper and caregiver. It will be interesting to extend this research to homes where mothers work, or where there is no adult male in the house. In such homes, it is logical that the mother will be the mediator of interpersonal trust for the children, or that her attitudes of trust and mistrust will be as influential on the children as the fathers', particularly if she has about the same vocational prestige.

Anxiety and trust probably are linked, although there is no firm evidence about the matter. It seems logical that highly anxious people will be less trusting than low-anxious people, both of themselves and of others. The relations between trust and dependency may well be complex. Does the dependent individual trust others but not himself? Does the excessively independent person trust only himself, and not others?

Trust has also been linked with sex role identification (for an example of this literature, see 75). For males at least, mistrust of a degree serious enough to be considered paranoia is thought often to result from sex role misidentification. Those with deep but unrecognized identification with the opposite sex (latent homosexuals) develop defensive fears of attack. These fears are manifested by suspiciousness that, carried to an extreme degree, becomes psychotic and potentially dangerous. The danger lies in that the defensively suspicious individual may attack those whom he erroneously believes plan to attack him.

Child-Rearing Dilemmas

Parents, teachers, and other caregivers are constantly faced with the dilemma of fostering *realistic* trust in children and adolescents. There are actually many dangerous things and people and situations. Children must be alerted to them, *but only alerted and not paralyzed with fear.* Little girls and boys must know that wandering alone in urban parks can be dangerous; that one does not accept gifts and rides from strangers; and that some people steal. On the other hand, children and youth of all ages receive more reward (and live more comfortably) if they are basically trusting. An open, friendly, confident social approach typically elicits similar behavior from others.

The authors know of no recipe other than their usual recommendation of the golden mean that applies to most complex human affairs. Children should learn, but without dramatics, about the dangers that lie in both urban and rural environments, and should be helped to develop techniques for dealing with the dangers as efficiently as possible. One set of parents known to the authors, trusting people themselves, gave the usual cautions, including instructions about what to do, to their 7-year-old daughter about strange men, candy, and cars in parks or lonely streets. The girl was approached one day as she walked home through a neighborhood park. She declined firmly and courteously the offer of a treat and a ride, retreated off the park road through shrubbery in the direction of the nearest residence, and, having memorized part of the automobile license, gave it to her mother, at the same time recalling as much as she could about the man who had approached her. With her evidence, the man was later located and found to be responsible for a series of child molestations that had occurred in the park.

By such a combination of information and coping techniques, children and youth are as well protected as possible (the world can never be entirely safe). They know what the most common danger situations may be, they are armed with a plan for appropriate behavior that presumably gives them some confidence in themselves, and yet they are not so fearful that they shy away from anything that is new, strange, or different.

Altruism and Empathy

Altruism and empathy are discussed in the same section because there is logical reason to believe that altruistic behavior seldom occurs before children develop the ability to empathize (1, 33). Experimental data fit well with the logic about the matter. Piaget talks of the egocentric view of the young child (see Chapter 2). An egocentric person cannot see the point of view of other people. Egocentrism is predominant in the preschool years, declines during the elementary school years, and can be and often is surmounted entirely (when necessary) from the time children are 12 or 13 years old and well into what Piaget calls the formal operations stage of cognitive development. Of course, as a practical matter, all of us sometimes display egocentricism throughout life. The point is that from about the time of puberty we are capable of operating in an allocentric (other centered) rather than an egocentric way if we need to. For adolescents and adults, reasons for behaving egocentrically are emotional and personal rather than cognitive, as is the case with the young child. He has not learned about the points of view of others and may be cognitively incapable of such learning.

Altruism is kindly, non-self-centered behavior, including sharing, from which no apparent reward is gained other than "feeling good." Altruism demands a certain amount of self-sacrifice. The development of altruism is one phase of moral growth, and thus much of what was stated in Chapter 8 applies to altruism and the other prosocial behaviors discussed in this section.

In the present context, empathy means "feeling with someone else." If we are moved to tears by the tears of another, we emphathize. If we are pleased when good

Altruistic behaviors—such as comforting another person in a time of distress—may be displayed by some children even in the preschool years. (Photo by Lawrence Frank)

things happen to someone else, again we are empathetic. Thus, logically speaking, in order to be altruistic, we must have developed far enough both emotionally and cognitively to appreciate the attitudes, emotions, and experiences of others.

It is doubtful if behavior that can truly be called either empathy or altruism occurs in the first two years of life. However, the authors have seen bright 2-year-olds whose parents have provided them with a wide range of social, intellectual, and emotional behavior, who at least seem to show empathy, and who express sympathy when they recognize the cues if the cues are obvious. For example, seeing a bandage on his mother's finger,

a 2-year-old pats his mother and says, "Poor mommy." In this case, he has had cuts himself that have been bandaged, and has had sympathy expressed by his mother. Similarly, we have seen very young children comfort both their caregivers and other children when they have shed tears or have fallen.

However, the evidence is that altruism increases very slightly during the preschool years (33). Altruism is not a widely generalized attribute among very young children, and probably appears only in somewhat dramatic situations with clear and familiar cues, as in the instances given in the preceding paragraph. From kindergarten onward, sharing behavior increases markedly. It probably parallels the cognitive development that results in decline of egocentrism, emotional development, independence, and widened experience, particularly of the kind that results in the child's receiving satisfaction from helping others and from sympathizing and sharing with them. Thirteen- and 14-year-olds are able to show selfless behavior, including the appreciation of points of view of others, nearly as well as college-aged young adults (29), and are much more like college-aged students than they are like 9- and 10-year-olds.

From the research literature about altruism (see 33 and 36), we know that altruism does not develop in a vacuum. Conducive to altruistic behavior are:

1. Altruistic models, who may be either adults or children; that is, the child who sees selflessness in others is likely to include it in his own behavior.
2. Clear information that altruistic behavior is appropriate for the situation. With sufficient experience, children and youth come to assess situations for

themselves and behave appropriately, but they learn only by stages and most typically, the authors suspect, from models who also explain the reasons for their behavior. For example, the authors predict that a child treated as described in the first instance below will be more likely to develop altruism than the child handled as described in the second instance.

In this first instance, Ralph, aged 4, struck his slightly younger and less agile guest, Teddy, who cried. The mother comforted the guest, at the same time telling Ralph: "You shouldn't hit other people to make them cry. See, he has a bump there, and he is crying and his nose is running. Remember how you were hurt and cried when you got a bump? Can you get me a Kleenex and help me make Teddy feel better?" Ralph does as he is requested, and his mother says "Good boy."

This second instance is an identical occurrence with Tom, the son, and Victor, the guest: *Mother:* "Tom, that was a bad thing to do. Get in that chair in the corner until I tell you to come out again!" at the same time saying to Victor, "Tom was bad. Come with me and I'll give you a sucker. That will make it feel better."

3. Opportunity to practice altruism. In the above examples, Ralph is given such an opportunity, Tom is not.
4. Direct or indirect reward for altruistic behavior. In the above examples, Ralph receives such reward, even though his altruistic behavior was by no means spontaneous.

Dilemmas in Altruism–Empathy Training

Again, as with all the behaviors discussed in this chapter, the dilemma about training for altruism and empathy is to strike the happy medium. None of us wishes his children to be patsies, yet we want them to have compassion for their fellows, to stand up for the helpless, and to lend a hand to the unfortunate. Since compassion, sharing, and friendship are rare commodities in human society, we may do well to train toward the selfless extreme of the altruistic-selfish continuum and to trust that our children, if they are secure, reasonably intelligent, and sensible, will know "when too much is enough."

A second dilemma concerns how one tells the difference between expedient altruism and what might be called intrinsic altruism. That is, much of what appears as "altruism" may simply reflect social conformity or a desire to reap certain rewards for oneself by behaving kindly toward others. Expedient altruism may also represent nothing more than a means of escaping social sanctions or punishments that may result from selfish or antisocial behavior. In contrast, intrinsic altruism occurs in the absence of external rewards or obvious personal gain; one may even give up valued personal possessions or privileges for the benefit of others without the slightest expectation for reciprocal behavior. It is likely that the casual observer of children and youth will have difficulty distinguishing between these two forms of altruism. However, the authors suspect that expedient altruism appears among children before intrinsic altruistic behavior occurs with any consistency. This sequence is roughly analogous to the developmental stages of morality discussed in Chapter 8.

Cooperation

Like altruism, cooperation may be considered one component in moral development. In Piaget's thinking, autonomous morality is a morality of cooperation or reciprocity (65). When such a stage of moral development is reached, children no longer view rules as rigid and unchangeable, but rather as set up and maintained by reciprocal social agreement. Thus, rules become subject to modification according to human needs and changing situations. Cooperation may be one aspect of moral relativism.

Cooperation includes an element of altruism: "I will give up some of my prerogatives for doing things my way and grant you the opportunity to do them your way." Cooperation is also often tinged with enlightened self-interest: "If we work together, we will get done what I want (which happens also to be what you want). Working alone, neither of us can accomplish his aims."

Cooperation and its cousin, altruism, are essential in a democratic system of government. Cooperation probably begins in infancy. Its first manifestations may be during the dressing operation, when the baby learns to move his body so that diapers may be more easily pinned or arms more easily inserted into sleeves. The most successful toilet training appears to be an instance of parent–child cooperation, with each accommodating himself to the other. More mature forms of cooperation are developed during children's games. In fact, the peer group has been posited as the agent of both moral development in general and cooperative behavior in particular (see the discussion in Chapter 8).

In American society, there is an uneasy compromise between cooperation and competition. Traditionally, we are a competitive society. Of necessity, we are an interdependent society, and interdependence demands cooperation. That this does not come easily for American children (or adults) was illustrated in the discussion of cooperation and the peer group in Chapter 9. Children in other societies often seem to be more harmoniously cooperative, less self-destructively competitive than children in United States society. The distinction between bureaucratic and entrepreneurial families has already been discussed. To review, breadwinners—family heads—in bureaucratic families are employed in multilayered institutions, such as large, stockholder-owned companies, school systems, and agencies of the government. Entrepreneurial families are in business or in practice for themselves and must thus be more ruggedly self-sufficient and competitive. Indications have emerged from one study that early adolescents (boys, in this case) from bureaucratic families incorporate more of the ethic of cooperation and reciprocity than adolescents from entrepreneurial families (9).

It has also been shown (see Chapter 9) that cooperative behavior is learned and that its incidence can be sharply increased when significant adults provide reinforcement when it occurs. We have also seen that cooperativeness is associated with leadership and popularity, and thus has implications for self-esteem and other kinds of learning that occur in social interactions.

It is logical to postulate that cooperativeness and trust are closely related. To cooperate with another person, we must be able to trust him. The greater the degree of our trust, the more frequently, it seems, we choose to coexist, or interdepend, or cooperate. Competence is also related to cooperation in that we are more likely to cooperate with those we believe know what they are doing than with those whom we believe to be inept. Competence can be more subtly tied to cooperative, socially constructive behavior. One trio of authors worked therapeutically with 15- to 17-year-old institutionalized delinquent boys (71). Their treatment was an academically oriented therapy, in which they tried to increase the boys' academic competence while giving them bounteous response-independent reinforcement. It was found that as the boys' academic skills improved, their self-esteem grew. With improvement in self-esteem, the boys' attitudes to authority also improved and their behavior (with particular reference to cooperativeness) became more acceptable. It is important to note that this change came in an orderly sequence: improvement first in competence, then in self-esteem, then in attitudes to authority—and finally, and only then, improvement in behavior.

It is clear that the principles for developing cooperation are about the same as those for developing any other kind of social behavior, namely: appropriate models, clear instruction, opportunity to practice, and rewards for cooperating.

The Cooperation–Competition Dilemma

The cooperation–competition dilemma goes to the heart of United States society. Traditionally, we are a society of competition and rugged individualism. Currently, the solutions to our many dilemmas (for example, problems of race tensions, urban chaos, environmental pollution) seem only to be solvable by cooperative behavior and a degree of altruism that is going to hurt, indeed to pinch very tightly, and for which American children, adolescents, and adults appear to be poorly prepared. Resolving the dilemma may very well be necessary for the nation's survival.

As developmental and educational psychologists, the authors content themselves with pointing out the crucial nature of this dilemma, and venture their subjective judgment about child-rearing and educational practices which they believe will help in developing cooperative behavior.

Considering the current state of affairs in United States (and world) society, the authors believe it is better to err on the side of training children to be very cooperative than to be very competitive. Granted, it is a fact of life—perhaps an innate characteristic of living organisms—to be competitive. Getting enough for your own survival is essential. However, the jungle law of getting first for yourself because there is not enough to go around is not appropriate in a country as affluent as the United States, or indeed in the world if distribution matters were efficiently and altruistically handled.

Perhaps an ethic of enlightened self-interest is the best one to follow. People are more likely to be altruistic and thus cooperative if they are able to see that what is good for them is also good for their neighbors.

The authors realize that this is a very high level goal abstraction, but they believe that an approach can be made to achieving it if the steps outlined above for developing cooperation in children and youth are followed.

EFFECTANCE, COMPETENCE, AND ACHIEVEMENT

As was true for the earlier discussion of empathy and altruism, the authors believe that effectance, competence, and achievement are closely linked concepts. One author believes there is a need for effectance (73). Effectance is doing something by oneself with the things in one's environment. Need for effectance is a need to *affect* things. Effectance, as so defined, is the core task in Piaget's sensorimotor stage of cognitive development (see Chapter 2). Effectance may well be closely linked to trust. Successful effectance breeds trust, trust leads to effectance.

It is logical to expect that the child who goes through his first eighteen months to two years of life and who has learned to manage the physical world around him with generally benign results will have developed attitudes and skills that lead to competence. Competence is the characteristic of doing well the things one attempts.

Finally, when put to work, competence leads to achievement. Achievement is the record of the things that have been accomplished. Such records may be in the form of scores on school achievement tests, of athletic skills mastered, of positive social relations, of artistic productions, and a host of others. In our Western society, as already stated, competence seems to be a necessary but not a sufficient condition for good personal–social adjustment.

We have already covered much of the pertinent literature about development of effectance, competence, and achievement. We have seen that these characteristics, at least historically, are more valued among boys than among girls, and have pointed out the disadvantages to both sexes of such evaluations. We have seen that authoritative (not authoritarian and not extremely permissive) child-rearing practices lead to child competence, at least during the preschool years (6). In this major study by Diana Baumrind, authoritative parental behavior was clearly related to independent and purposive behavior for girls and, when parents were both authoritative and nonconforming, their behavior was also associated with independent and purposive behavior in their sons. Parental authoritativeness is associated with a high level of social responsibility for boys, but its result for girls is more confined to high achievement. Parenthetically, parental nonconformity was not associated with social irresponsibility in the family's children.

It will be remembered that authoritative parents are reasonably sure of themselves and are able to give active and firm guidance to their children while at the same time allowing their children to work out their own solutions to problems. Authoritative parents guide their children, but they do not do all the work for them. Such parents are experts in residence, as it were, but they are not straw bosses and dictators.

In the following chapter, where self-esteem is discussed, we see further that parents who develop high self-esteem in their children (at least in their boys) are also authoritative, as the term has been defined. Such parents set specific goals for their children, they make sure the children understand the goals, they reward progress toward the goals, they do not fear occasional conflict with their children; but they give their children almost total acceptance, respect their rights to individuality, and allow them wide latitude in the methods they choose for pursuing approved goals (13).

A need for achievement among American youth has been widely postulated, widely researched, and much written about. The results from all this attention are cloudy, more so for girls than for boys (21). At the time of this writing, the authors doubt if need for achievement is a unitary trait. That is, a person's need to achieve is not generalized across all his life situations. One may desire to achieve in algebra, for example, while being indifferent to how well he does in creative writing. Boys may wish to achieve in settings they judge to be masculine, but not in things they think of as feminine. Girls, if they were studied in the proper situations (that is, situations that they construe as being valued and feminine), may well be found to be as achievement motivated as boys. They simply have not been studied with equal sophistication.

It is suspected that a need for achievement (whether it be situation and task specific, or a generalized, unitary trait) develops like all the other strands that make up human social and moral development (see the discussions in Chapters 7 and 8). To develop effective, competent, and achieving behaviors, children and youth need models, clearly articulated tutelage, prolonged practice across a wide variety of situations, and repeated experiences of success.

A Core Dilemma

American life is about equally made up of *doing* and of *being*, as has been repeatedly stated. As technology advances, more and more time becomes available to the average man and woman for being, and less and less time is taken up in doing. There are exceptions to this statement. The self-employed, a very large number of professional people, teachers whose duties can expand limitlessly depending on their motivation—all such people are exceptions.

There are indications that Americans do not at present know what to do with all this time left over from work. For example, one pair of investigators interviewed a random sample of 401 men about their work (56). The general consensus from the interviews was that "working gives them a feeling of being tied into the larger society, of having something to do, of having a purpose in life" (p. 8). When the men were asked the question "If by

some chance you inherited enough money to live comfortably without working, do you think you would work anyway or not?" an overwhelming majority (80 percent) answered that they would indeed continue to work (p. 8). One-third of these men gave only negative reasons for wanting to continue to work. Their reasons suggest they have little idea of how to go about simply living or being. Many said they would feel lost if they did not work. They "would go crazy with idleness." They "wouldn't know what to do."

The suggestion resulting from all this information is that children and youth need to learn both competent and achievement attitudes and behavior, and relaxation and "joy" attitudes and behavior. It seems as necessary to teach people how to be gleeful as it does to teach them how to be effective in school or in their jobs, and the former kind of teaching has been much neglected in America.

One last comment should be made. Many people are quite literally able to "play while they work." Any man or woman who truly enjoys his job is having a good time. He is *being* while he is *doing*. This leads to a social reform suggestion for industrial psychologists. In addition to concentrating on increasing production, they should be working on the problem of what conditions increase workers' pleasure in their work.

LOCUS OF CONTROL

The set of ideas that has led to a theory of internal and external locus of control has been around for a long time. In psychodynamic theory, these ideas go back to C. G. Jung (41, 42). Jung was a student of Freud's who, after disagreeing with the master, began his own school of psychodynamics and developed a central theoretical theme of introversion and extroversion.

The concept of locus of control bears on how an individual perceives the world he lives in. At one extreme, he may see it as chaotic and unpredictable; at the other, as orderly and reliable. The way in which a person's world is predicted is likely to play an important role in determining his behavior and its outcomes (61). Locus of control has been defined as follows:

When a reinforcement is perceived by the subject as following some action of his own but not being entirely contingent upon his action, then, in our culture, it is typically perceived as the result of luck, chance, fate, as under the control of powerful others, or as unpredictable because of the great complexity of the forces surrounding him. When the event is interpreted in this way by an individual, we have labeled this a belief in external control. If the person perceives that the event is contingent upon his own behavior or his own relative permanent characteristics, we have termed this a belief in internal control (67, p. 1).

In other words, when a child, a youth, or an adult believes he has primary control over his own fate — produces his own reinforcements — and thinks that he can determine the way things turn out by the way he acts, we say he is internally controlled. When he believes that the things that happen to him are the results of the behavior of others (or of the stars, or the fates, or luck), he is externally controlled.

Locus of control is a subjective concept, a very personal concept. As we move to the next chapter (self concept), we can see that it is intimately related to one's notion about himself. There is much variation in the nature of locus of control from one individual to another, and an individual may likely vary in the degree of internality or externality of his locus of control from one time to another. Human nature being what it is, the authors predict that a person will become more external following a chain of unfortunate behavior outcomes (after all, it is easier to blame others than oneself). Similarly, a person is likely to become more internal following a chain of successes. It is natural for a person to take credit for success to himself, thus to take an internal locus of control stance. To tie the concept of locus of control to the topics that have been taken up earlier in this chapter, the authors suspect that there are positive associations between an internal locus of control and the characteristics of trust, altruism, cooperation, independence, competence, and achievement. As seen later, some of their expectations are supported by relevant data.

Locus of control should be distinguished from expectation of success. Expectation of success is our prediction of how a given endeavor will turn out: "I have a 50–50 chance of making it — or a 90–10 chance — or a 5–95 chance." Such an objective prediction has little relation to locus of control. Similarly, locus of control should be distinguished from an accurate judgment of environmental arrangements. It is well known that the odds are stacked against black youth, for example. They have been found to score more external in locus of control tests than white youth (61). However, when the way they answer individual questions on the locus-of-control test has been checked, it has been found that the blacks' high scores are partially earned because they endorse items related to political power. The institutions of government, they believe, are outside their control. Government, they think, is an external agent, not responsive to their needs or efforts. But there is little difference between the blacks and the whites in answering questions that deal with areas seen as related to personal control. From what we know of government and prejudice, this is not an unreasonable or inaccurate point of view.

Measuring Locus of Control

Locus of control is usually measured by answering *yes* or *no* to items in a paper-and-pencil questionnaire. For example, one instrument for measuring locus of control, designed for children and youth through the twelfth grade, includes items such as the following (61).

"Are some kids just born lucky?" (A *yes* answer for this item is scored in the direction of *external* locus of control.)

"Most of the time, do you feel that you can change what might happen tomorrow by what you do today?" (For this item, a *yes* answer indicates internal locus of control.)

"Most of the time, do you feel that you have little to say about what your family decides to do?" (A *yes* answer is scored for externality.)

Still other authorities (for example, 16) have developed a locus-of-control measure for children more specific to the classroom situation or settings for intellectual achievement. Sample items include those listed below.

"Suppose you don't do as well as usual in a subject at school. Would this probably happen
a. because you weren't as careful as usual? or
b. because somebody bothered you and kept you from working?"

"When you remember something you heard in class, is it usually
a. because you tried hard to remember it? or
b. because the teacher explained it well?"

In both instances, choice of the "a" alter-native would indicate a more internal (versus external) locus of control and thus a greater tendency to take responsibility for one's own actions.

For self-report measures such as the foregoing, a person's score is usually determined by the number of internal control statements endorsed minus any external control statements that may also be endorsed. Thus, locus of control is viewed as a relative matter, one that represents a continuum from one extreme to another.

Findings about Internal and External Locus of Control

A summary of the extensive literature about locus of control includes the following findings: (22, 55, 59, 60, 61, 62). They are interesting for both theoretical and practical reasons.

Among young adults (most research including adults has been conducted with college students as subjects), those who score high in internal locus of control, when compared with those who are high in externality, have more realistic and adaptive levels of aspiration, are more involved in civil rights movements, and achieve better in school. They also recall more information that is relevant and useful to their future goals, are more likely to resist subtle attempts to influence them, and place a higher value on reinforcements that are contingent on personal skill. There are no practically important differences in intelligence between high and low externals. The severely mentally ill (schizophrenics have been studied) are less internal in scores than normals are. Blacks have repeatedly been reported to test higher in external locus of control than whites. However, when strict controls are imposed for socioeconomic level and type of question (that is, when matters of prejudice do not realistically enter the picture), the difference between blacks and whites is not always found.

Older children are more internally controlled than younger children, brighter children have often been found to be more internally controlled than children who score low on intelligence tests, although, as mentioned above, intelligence is not closely related to locus of control. Children and youth with high levels of internal control are found to be more popular than children and youth high in external locus of control. Children and adolescents who experience a predictable environment move significantly in the direction of an internal locus of control. This has been reported in at least two pieces of research, one involving a camp managed by behavior modification with strong emphasis on reward (59), and the other conducted with classes of economically disadvantaged black children from first through seventh grades (55). These classes were also conducted according to a "success environment" philosophy that included behavior modification techniques as a major method of dealing with pupils. Children who are high in socioeconomic status and whose parents have high levels of education usually test as more internally controlled than those with less advantaged parents. Those who are high in internal locus of control both achieve better in school (boys particularly) and have higher morale about school (27).

Implications from Locus-of-Control Research

From the evidence reviewed here, it seems that it is desirable to be internally controlled and not so desirable to be externally controlled. However, we must remember that most of the research about locus of control is correlational in nature. Thus, we can only talk of associations, not

causes. Furthermore, most of the correlations that have been revealed are low. For example, the highest correlation in one study is $-.45$ between a locus-of-control scale score and achievement test results for twelfth-grade young men (61). This correlation, however, is about as high as the one usually found between IQ and achievement. Even so, the locus-of-control score accounts for only about 20 percent of the variance for academic achievement. Regardless, anything that adds this much to our efficiency in guiding people is worth pursuing, as long as we remember that we are dealing with group trends and not with individual cases. If the authors were responsible for the guidance of one of the twelfth-grade males who took part in this study on the basis of the reported evidence, they would be derelict if they predicted flatly that a young man who was external would fail in college while another who was internal in his score would succeed. However, it would be legitimate to caution the first, externally scoring young man that he should pay particular attention to his work habits, and to encourage the second young man to continue to set his own high standards and adhere to them.

On the whole, it seems that parents and other caregivers should be urged to attend to the matter of developing an internal locus of control in children and youth. In Chapter 6, it was noted that an internal locus of control may well be associated with intellectual gain, and it is clear that high internal students are more efficient, academically speaking, as well as superior in other socially important spheres.

The central principle for guidance concerns environmental predictability or accountability. When people are informed in a consistent way about the consequences of their behavior, they move toward an internal locus of control. When they do not have accurate information about the results of their actions, they are more likely to be external in their orientation. Furthermore, more privileged people — those with more self-determination — seem to be higher in internality.

The authors have no information whether negative or positive information about behavior outcomes (that is, success or failure, praise or reproof) is more likely to produce internality of locus of control. The only two studies that bear on the issue known to the authors concern positive behavior management (55, 59). It seems logical that any accurate information about behavior outcome, whether positive or negative, should lead an individual to conclude that he is responsible for the outcome of his behavior. This is true, however, only if the person also knows that the determination of the outcome is fair and objective.

✱ *Summary*

In this chapter, a number of theoretically and practically important areas of human development have been discussed. Many of the areas are related to each other, but each deserves separate treatment and each represents possible psychosocial conflict of several sorts: (1) within the individual himself; (2) between the individual and society; (3) for the parent, teacher, and other caregiver as he tries to determine the goals for his interactions with children and youth; and (4) for the parent, teacher, and other caregiver as he attempts to reconcile his dealings with individual children and youth, or groups of children and youth, and their relationships to society at large.

The conflict areas included in this chapter differ from conceptual conflicts in that they are more emotion laden. They are similar to conceptual conflicts in that their successful resolution is growth promoting.

Three forms of conflict were defined at the beginning of the chapter: approach–approach conflict, between two attractive alternatives; approach–avoidance conflict, in which a behavior has both positive and negative consequences (for example, going to school is desirable, but unpleasant things sometimes happen in school); and avoidance–avoidance conflict, in which the child or youth must choose between two unpleasant alternatives. The six areas of conflict selected for discussion were (1) anxiety, (2) independence and dependence, (3) aggression, (4) prosocial behaviors, among which were included trust, altruism and empathy, and cooperation, (5) effectance, competence, and achievement, and (6) locus of control.

It is clear that constitutional factors enter into at least some of these conflict areas. For example, hyperactive children are more likely to be frustrated than more passive children; frustration predisposes a child toward aggression; thus, hyperactive children are likely to have more problems with aggression than are more relaxed, quiet children. Another theme that runs through the chapter is the notion of the golden mean. Too much anxiety, for example, interferes with almost all aspects of an individual's life, including his learning efficiency. On the other hand, in our culture anxiety serves as a motivator and may be helpful in promoting achievement and success when modestly present. It may also prevent transgressions against society.

Dependence falls into two categories, emotional and instrumental. A certain amount of emotional dependence seems necessary if a person is to have friendly or loving relations with others. Too much emotional dependence makes an individual helpless and is likely to result in his being rejected. A moderate amount of instrumental dependence seems essential. If we did not behave in an instrumentally dependent fashion, we would deny ourselves the benefit of learning what other people know about the things we try to do. On the other hand, too much instrumental dependence may result in our failing to develop autonomy and self-sufficiency. The picture is much the same with aggression. The problem with aggression, however, is to channel it into socially constructive channels (perhaps sports or sensible business competition) or at least to neutralize it, because open aggression seldom serves any useful social purpose and, indeed, is often dangerous. Others may be badly hurt by the aggressive action, and retaliation may result, which harms the individual who behaved aggressively in the first place.

Common learning experiences emerge for all six of the areas discussed in this chapter. For a person to be anxious, or dependent, or aggressive, or trusting, or competent, it seems four things are necessary. First, there must be models. Second, at least for most of the areas (perhaps not, for example, for anxiety, dependence, and aggression), there must be clear instruction about the behavior. Children, for instance, need to have altruism fully explained to them, and a philosophy of enlightened self-interest is recommended for such explanation. Third, there must be opportunity for practice. A person does not learn the effectiveness of either asocial behaviors (such as physical aggression) or pro-

social behaviors (such as altruism) unless he has a chance to practice them. He does not consolidate such behaviors into his personal repertoire unless he emits them socially and is rewarded for them. Thus, finally, children and youth must be reinforced in order to learn any given behavior. If nothing occurs as a consequence of anxiety, anxious responses may well be reduced in intensity and frequency. The same is true for dependence—independence, aggression, and the prosocial behaviors. For development of internal locus of control—a belief that by his behavior one can exert major influence over his environment—a predictable environment seems to be essential, as well as much freedom for self-determination.

REFERENCES

1. Aronfreed, J. *Conduct and conscience: The socialization of internalized control over behavior.* New York: Academic Press, 1968.
2. Bandura, A. *Principles of behavior modification.* New York: Holt, Rinehart and Winston, 1969.
3. Bandura, A. Relationship of family patterns to child behavior disorders. *Progress Report,* U.S.P.H.S. Research Grant M-1734. Stanford University, Palo Alto, Calif., 1960.
4. Bandura, A., and R. H. Walters. Aggression. In H. W. Stevenson (ed.) *Child psychology.* Chicago: University of Chicago Press, 1963, 364–415.
5. Bandura, A., and R. H. Walters. *Social learning and personality development.* New York: Holt, Rinehart and Winston, 1963.
6. Baumrind, D. Current patterns of parental authority. *Developmental Psychology Monograph,* 1971, 4, 1–103.
7. Benedict, R. *The chrysanthemum and the*

sword: Patterns of Japanese culture. Boston: Houghton-Mifflin, 1946.

8. Berkowitz, L. Experimental investigations of hostility catharsis. *Journal of Consulting and Clinical Psychology,* 1970, *35,* 1–7.

9. Berkowitz, L., and P. Friedman. Some social class differences in helping behavior. *Journal of Personality and Social Psychology,* 1967, *5,* 217–225.

10. Bryan, J. H., and T. Schwartz. Effects of film material upon children's behavior. *Psychological Bulletin,* 1971, *75,* 50–59.

11. Cattell, R. B., and F. W. Warburton. A cross-cultural comparison of patterns of extraversion and anxiety. *British Journal of Psychology,* 1961, *52,* 3–15.

12. Cofer, C. N., and M. H. Appley. *Motivation: Theory and research.* New York: Wiley, 1964.

13. Coopersmith, S. *The antecedents of self-esteem.* San Francisco: Freeman, 1967.

14. Cox, F. N. Some effects of test anxiety and presence or absence of other persons on boys' performance on a repetitive motor task. *Journal of Experimental Child Psychology,* 1966, *3,* 100–112.

15. Cox, F. N. Some relationships between test anxiety, presence or absence of male persons, and boys' performance on a repetitive motor task. *Journal of Experimental Child Psychology,* 1968, *6,* 1–12.

16. Crandall, V. C., W. Katkovsky, and V. J. Crandall. Children's beliefs in their own control of reinforcements in intellectual-achievement situations. *Child Development,* 1965, *36,* 91–109.

17. Dollard, J., L. W. Doob, N. E. Miller, O. H. Mowrer, and R. R. Sears. *Frustration and aggression.* New Haven, Conn.: Yale University Press, 1933.

18. Douvan, E., and J. Adelson. *The adolescent experience.* New York: Wiley, 1966.

19. Elder, G. H., Jr. Adolescent socialization and development. In E. F. Borgatta and W. W. Lambert (eds.) *Handbook of personality theory and research.* Chicago: Rand McNally, 1968, 239–364.

20. Emmerich, W. Continuity and stability in early social development: II. Teacher's ratings. *Child Development,* 1966, *37,* 17–27.

21. Entwisle, D. R. To dispel fantasies about fantasy-based measures. *Psychological Bulletin.* 1972, *77,* 377–391.

22. Eppes, J. W. The effect of varying the race of the experimenter on the level of aspiration of externally controlled inner city school children. Unpublished doctoral dissertation, Emory University, 1969.

23. Erikson, E. H. *Childhood and society* (2nd ed.). New York: Norton, 1963.

24. Ferguson, L. R. Dependency motivation in socialization. In R. Hoppe, G. Milton, and E. Simmel (eds.) *Early experiences and the processes of socialization.* New York: Academic Press, 1970, 59–80.

25. Ferguson, L. R. *Personality development.* Belmont, Calif.: Wadsworth, 1971.

26. Feshback, S. Aggression. In P. Mussen (ed.) *Carmichael's manual of child psychology* (Vol. II). New York: Wiley, 1970, 159–260.

27. Flanders, N. A., B. M. Morrison, and E. L. Brode. Changes in pupil attitudes during the school year. *Journal of Educational Psychology,* 1968, *59,* 334–338.

28. Fontana, V. J. *The maltreated child.* Springfield, Ill.: C. C. Thomas, 1964.

29. Fry, C. L. A developmental examination of performance in a tacit coordination game situation. *Journal of Personality and Social Psychology,* 1967, *5,* 277–281.

30. Gotts, E. E. A note on cross-cultural by age-group comparisons of anxiety scores. *Child Development,* 1968, *39,* 945–947.

31. Hagman, E. R. A study of fears of children of preschool age. *Journal of Experimental Education,* 1932, *1,* 110–130.

32. Hartup, W. W. Dependence and independence. In H. W. Stevenson (ed.) *Child psychology.* Chicago: University of Chicago Press, 1963, 333–363.

33. Hartup, W. W. Peer interaction and social organization. In P. H. Mussen (ed.) *Carmichael's manual of child psychology.* New York: Wiley, 1970, 361–456.

34. Hawkes, T., and R. H. Koff. Differences in

anxiety of private school and inner city public school elementary school children. *Psychology in the Schools,* 1970, *7,* 250–259.

35. Hetherington, E. M. Sex typing, dependency, and aggression. In T. D. Spencer and N. Kass (eds.) *Perspectives in child psychology.* New York: McGraw-Hill, 1970, 193–231.

36. Hoffman, M. L. Moral development. In P. H. Mussen (ed.) *Carmichael's manual of child psychology.* New York: Wiley, 1970, 261–359.

37. Holt, R. R. On the interpersonal and intrapersonal consequences of expressing or not expressing anger. *Journal of Consulting and Clinical Psychology,* 1970, *35,* 8–12.

38. Hottel, J. V. The influence of age and intelligence on independence-conformity behavior of children. Unpublished doctoral dissertation, George Peabody College for Teachers, 1960.

39. Iwawaki, S., K. Sumida, S. Okuno, and E. L. Cowen. Manifest anxiety in Japanese, French, and United States children. *Child Development,* 1967, *38,* 713–722.

40. Johnson, R., and G. Medinnus. *Child psychology: Behavior and development* (2nd ed.). New York: Wiley, 1969.

41. Jung, C. G. *The integration of the personality.* New York: Farrar, Straus, 1939.

42. Jung, C. G. *The psychology of the unconscious.* New York: Dodd, Mead, 1927.

43. Kagan, J., and H. Moss. *Birth to maturity.* New York: Wiley, 1962.

44. Katz, H. A., and J. B. Rotter. Interpersonal trust scores of college students and their parents. *Child Development,* 1969, *40,* 657–661.

45. Lekarczyk, D., and K. T. Hill. Self-esteem, test anxiety, stress, and verbal learning. *Developmental Psychology,* 1969, *1,* 147–154.

46. Levitt, E. E. *The psychology of anxiety.* Indianapolis: Bobbs-Merrill, 1967.

47. Lewin, K. *A dynamic theory of personality.* New York: McGraw-Hill, 1935.

48. Liebert, R. M., and R. A. Baron. Some immediate effects of televised violence on children's behavior. *Developmental Psychology,* 1972, *6,* 469–475.

49. Maccoby, E. E. Effects of the mass media. In M. L. Hoffman and L. W. Hoffman (eds.) *Review of child development research* (Vol. I). New York: Russell Sage, 1964, 323–348.

50. Maccoby, E. E. (ed.). *The development of sex differences.* Palo Alto, Calif.: Stanford University Press, 1966.

51. Maccoby, E. E., and J. C. Masters. Attachment and dependency. In P. Mussen (ed.) *Carmichael's manual of child psychology* (3rd ed.). New York: Wiley, 1970, 73–158.

52. McCandless, B. R. *Adolescents: Behavior and development.* Hinsdale, Ill.: Dryden, 1970.

53. McCandless, B. R. *Children: Behavior and development.* New York: Holt, Rinehart, and Winston, 1967.

54. McCoy, N. Effects of test anxiety on children's performance as a function of type of instruction and type of task. *Journal of Personality and Social Psychology,* 1965, *2,* 634–641.

55. Moore, T. C., and W. R. Brassell, Jr. The success environment: An approach to community educational improvement. Atlanta: Atlanta Public Schools, End of Budget Period Report, Fiscal Year 1971. Progress Report for grant from U. S. Public Law 89–10, Title III, Director: Marion Thompson.

56. Morse, N. C., and R. S. Weiss. The function and meaning of work and the job. In D. G. Zytowski (ed.) *Vocational Behavior.* New York: Holt, Rinehart and Winston, 1968, 7–16.

57. Mussen, P., J. Conger, and J. Kagan. *Child development and personality* (2nd ed.). New York: Harper & Row, 1963.

58. Mussen, P., J. Conger, and J. Kagan. *Child development and personality* (3rd ed.). New York: Harper & Row, 1969.

59. Nowicki, S., Jr., and J. Barnes. Effects of a structured camp experience on locus of

control orientation. Paper presented at the Southeastern Psychological Association meetings, New Orleans, May, 1971.

60. Nowicki, S., Jr., and J. Roundtree. Correlates of locus of control in secondary school age students. Unpublished Manuscript, Emory University, 1971.

61. Nowicki, S., Jr., and B. R. Strickland. A locus of control scale for children. Paper presented at the American Psychological Association meetings, Washington, D. C., September, 1971.

62. Nowicki, S., and C. Walker. Achievement in relation to locus of control: Identification of a new source of variance. Unpublished Manuscript, Psychology Department, Emory University.

63. Osborn, D. K., and R. C. Endsley. Emotional reactions of young children to TV violence. *Child Development,* 1971, *42,* 321–331.

64. Phillips, B. N. *An analysis of causes of anxiety among children in school.* Austin: University of Texas, Bureau of Research, USOE Project No. 2616, 1966.

65. Piaget, J. *The moral judgment of the child.* New York: Harcourt, 1932.

66. Pinner, F. G. Parental overprotection and political distrust. Annual American Academy of Political and Social Science, 1965, *361,* 58–70.

67. Rotter, J. B. *Social learning and clinical psychology.* Englewood Cliffs, N. J.: Prentice-Hall, 1954.

68. Ruebusch, B. K. Anxiety. In H. W. Stevenson (ed.) *Child psychology.* Chicago: University of Chicago Press, 1963, 460–516.

69. Sarason, S. B., K. S. Davidson, F. F. Lighthall, R. R. Waite, and B. K. Ruebusch. *Anxiety in elementary school children.* New York: Wiley, 1960.

70. Sarason, S. B., K. T. Hill, and P. G. Zimbardo. A longitudinal study of the relation of test anxiety to performance on intelligence and achievement tests. *Monographs of the Society for Research in Child Development,* 1964, *29,* Serial No. 98.

71. Shore, M. F., J. L. Massimo, and D. F. Ricks. A factor analytic study of psychotherapeutic change in delinquent boys. *Journal of Clinical Psychology,* 1965, *21,* 208–212.

72. Stone, L. J., and J. Church. *Childhood and adolescence* (2nd ed.). New York: Random House, 1968.

73. White, R. W. Motivation reconsidered: The concept of competence. *Psychological Review,* 1959, *66,* 297–333.

74. Wiggins, J. S. Personality structure. *Annual Review of Psychology,* 1968, *19,* 122–350.

75. Wolowitz, H. M. Attraction and aversion to power: A psychoanalytic conflict theory of homosexuality in male paranoids. *Journal of Abnormal Psychology,* 1965, *70,* 360–370.

76. Zimet, S. G. A rationale for the inclusion of aggression themes in elementary reading textbooks. *Psychology in the Schools,* 1970, *7,* 232–237.

77. Zimmerman, B. J. The relationship between teacher classroom behavior and student school anxiety levels. *Psychology in the Schools,* 1970, *7,* 89–93.

78. Ziv, A. Children's behavior problems as viewed by teachers, psychologists, and children. *Child Development,* 1970, *41,* 871–879.

11 The Development of Self

So far, the discussion about human development can be related to the idea of "self." *Self* includes self-knowledge, self-worth, and an understanding of one's place in the social world. Close relations between children's views of themselves and their independence and achievement have been discovered among children of preschool age (19); and the way kindergarten children view themselves has been shown to be related to their progress in reading in their later elementary school years. Later in this chapter are discussed other data in which relationships between a positive self-view (self-esteem) and general school achievement, effectiveness in social groups, curiosity, creativity, and low anxiety are revealed (61).

The purpose in this chapter is to examine theoretical and developmental aspects of the self. The authors' aim is to develop a picture of conditions that apparently affect the quality of self-development and to focus on the formation of personal identity associated with adolescence in our society. Moreover,

they continue their emphasis on dilemmas by advancing theoretical and practical issues that arise in the psychological study of the self.

The study of self-development is one of the most significant and the most confusing undertakings of psychology. Its significance lies in the fact that conscious, thinking man has always been concerned with self-awareness, uniqueness, and the purpose of his life. Such a quest is related to the notion of the soul that dominates much of religious life. Similarly, understanding the uniqueness—the selfhood—of man is a central goal of psychology.

Research and theory about *self* are sufficiently murky that many scientifically oriented psychologists become discouraged with the topic. The authors do not belabor the problems of work in the self area, but touch lightly on the problems that are particularly relevant to the self-development literature. Hardy students may want to look at some advanced sources (for example 102 and 103).

The various theoretical orientations

that have influenced study of self-development should also be mentioned. Theory and research about the self have mainly sprung from psychodynamic and humanistic psychologies (see Chapter 2). Freud's notion of the ego is one of the main anchoring points for a psychology of the self. Humanists have given *self* such a central role in behavior that many of them (for example, Rogers, Maslow, and Allport) are referred to as self theorists. There is really no way that people who are concerned with healing the sick (clinicians, psychodynamicists) or helping man find himself (humanists) can avoid the working concept of the self. After all, each of us *knows* he has a self. He lives with it all day, every day. The concept, it might be said, has compelling, immediate face validity.

Cognitive developmentalists and behaviorists have not been much involved in theory and research about the self. In recent years, however, some of the cognitively oriented psychologists have turned their attention to self-development. They have worked with gender identity (for example, 48), which is certainly an important aspect of the self (see Chapter 7). They have also considered the relations of cognitive development to self-development. For example, children who are more proficient in conservation than their age mates (see Chapter 2) are also likely to be more objective in their self-evaluations (32).

The subjective, hypothetical (mentalistic?) nature of self concept may have turned behavioristic psychologists away from this area of theory and research. Some of them have concerned themselves with spontaneous self-reference behavior and with internal and external locus of control. But most have been skeptical about whether one can investigate or even talk about the self clearly and with scientific rigor. This topic is treated later in the discussion of dilemmas.

DEVELOPMENTAL AND DEFINITIONAL CONSIDERATIONS

A major problem among psychologists who study self-development has been agreement about a definition of *self*. Without clear, consensual definition, scientific progress is impossible (see Chapter 2). The problem of defining *self* is not yet solved. One major disagreement has centered on "self as object" versus "self as process" (35).

When one talks about self as object, he deals with a person's attitudes, perceptions, feelings, and evaluation of himself as an object: what a person knows and thinks about himself.

A process orientation to self is different in that the self is considered an amalgam of active processes of thinking, perceiving, and remembering.

To illustrate the definitional problems still further, a standard dictionary of psychological terms gives seven different definitions of *self* (21).

When the definition of a construct is difficult, the desired measurement of the construct is difficult or impossible. Measurement is difficult enough even when a definition is conceptually clear. Most of the current techniques for "measuring self" involve self-ratings or self-descriptions. Occasionally, ratings of an individual by other people such as teachers or peers are used. There are two clear problems with the measures that have been used for *self*. First, many investigators devise their own measure of the self, since they have unique definitions of the construct. This means that the results from their research are not comparable. It is as though one person were to use a yardstick and another a meter stick, and we were then given the results of the measurement only as "21 units long," without being told that one reporter was talking about inches, the other about centimeters.

A second problem has been the value-ridden nature of many self-concept measures. In one frequently used measure, a maximum score for self concept is obtained if a child or youth rates himself at the highest end of the scale for seven dimensions: smart, happy, well liked, brave, attractive, strong, and obedient (11, 20, 54). From such a measure, we are as likely to obtain a measure of social desirability (how accurately the rater knows social norms about desirable behaviors and the degree to which he espouses them) as we are a measure of self concept.

Such reservations are kept in mind as the rest of the chapter is developed, and the reader should also remind himself of such reservations as he follows the discussion. The concentration is on three interrelated components of the self: self concept, self-esteem, and identity (39). The perspective on self, it should be clear, is more self as object than self as process. After treatment of these three interrelated components, some highlights of the research about these components are reviewed. Finally, some dilemmas about self-development are introduced in much the same way as dilemmas have been introduced in previous chapters.

Self Concept

Self concept refers to an individual's awareness of his own characteristics and attributes, and the ways in which he is both like and unlike others. The authors believe this awareness begins during the first year of life, when the child begins to differentiate himself from his environment. It is in the sensorimotor period (see Chapter 2) that the child seems to become aware of *me* and *not me*. By age 1, most infants indicate genuine self-recognition. This often shows up in mirror play (17). As he develops thought and self-awareness, the child comes to think of himself as tall, or strong, or talkative, or healthy, or slow, or dull, or awkward, or dirty. Obviously, he learns to make such referents because of his particular learning experiences.

Preschool-aged children cannot talk clearly about individual characteristics and differences. However, there is no doubt that by the time a normal child is 2 to 3 years old, he sees himself as distinct from his parents and other children. He uses "ego" or "self" and "other" words such as me, mine, you, yours, and sometimes we and ours. Some believe that the use of the first person singular—I—indicates that genuine self-consciousness has been achieved (3). Self-reactions then become more complex and allocentric (as opposed to egocentric). Children identify with others, they compete with others, they make self-judgments, and they manifest guilt (3). By the age of 3, most children know their sex, including knowing about the physical characteristics that distinguish girls from boys (see the discussion of sex typing in Chapter 7). As young as 3, most children also discriminate racial differences, and may come to think of themselves in terms of their skin color (91).

One important dimension of self-concept development is the extent to which an individual can describe himself objectively and accurately. We must also distinguish between self-descriptive behavior (relatively objective and free from value judgments) and self-evaluative behavior: how one *rates* or judges the worthwhileness or status of his appearance, abilities, and so on. This consideration leads us directly into a second component of self-development, *self-esteem.*

Self-Esteem

Self-esteem refers to the value a child or a youth puts on himself and his behavior. How does he feel about himself? How does he judge himself in terms of "goodness" or "badness?"

Although a nursery school child may have a limited vocabulary, it is certain that he sees himself as distinct from his parents and other children; he can already think of himself in terms of sex and skin color. (Photo by Hella Hammid)

Self-esteem is intimately related to the self concept, because value judgments are so frequently involved in what children learn about themselves from other people. It is unlikely that young children separate fact from evaluation when they hear such things as: "Say, aren't you a big boy!" "Where did you ever get all that red hair?" "Look at how that little scamp climbs that tree!" "I sure wish you looked more like your Daddy." "Algernon? What an odd name for a little boy!" "When are you going to learn that little girls just don't do that?" and "You can't do it? Well, perhaps it's too much to expect of a poor, black child."

Many studies reveal that individual differences in self-esteem are apparent at least as early as kindergarten age (77, 103). For reasons that are not entirely clear, children generally become less positive in their self-evaluations with age (47). It is likely that a broader base of experience, advances in cognitive development, school factors, peer evaluations, and a keener awareness of the ultimate in human development all combine to affect self-evaluative behavior. We return to this point shortly. Meanwhile, it is emphasized that self-esteem can range from low to high or from negative to positive. It reflects how a child or a youth regards himself across a wide spectrum of activities. Self-esteem also usually reflects a child's feelings about his group memberships of the sort that defines his racial, ethnic, sex, and religious identities.

Identity

A child's self concept concerns his image of himself as an individual. Identity implies future development: awareness of group membership and the expectations, privileges, restraints, and social responsibilities that accompany that member-

"TELL ME, ROMLEY, WHEN DID YOU FIRST BEGIN TO FEEL LIKE A NOBODY?"

A low or a negative self concept is usually associated with much dissatisfaction in life.

ship. For example, a young girl's recognition that possessing certain physical characteristics means being a "female" will normally come before her knowledge about what females are expected or allowed to do. Similarly, a young child's awareness of his skin color will occur before his understanding that this may designate him as a Chicano, Asian, or American Indian and that such groups face certain hardships in a society dominated by white Americans.

Identity formulation, then, can be thought of as a process through which a child gains knowledge of such matters as his name, race, sex role, and social class *and* the meaning these descriptions have for his life. These meanings are derived from the particular culture to which the child belongs, although young children may not understand the reasons that underlie them. For example, a young child may quickly learn that he and his family are not welcome in certain groups or situations because they are black. But it is not likely that he will understand why being black should result in social discrimination.

It is probably safe to say that identity formulation occurs throughout the total course of development. That is, events occur throughout life that effect changes in the nature of a person's personal freedom, obligations to others, expectations held for a person by others, and the like. "Become first a wife and then a mother," for example, implies role changes that relate to a girl's personal identity. So does a change in a person's occupation, say, from being a farmer to being an insurance salesman. Many psychologists think that the critical period for an individual's basic sense of identity is adolescence. Certainly, it is plausible that the stage of "formal operations"—the capacity for dispassionate self-regard and for reflecting on one's thoughts (see Chapter 2, Piaget)—must be reached before the person can deal with so complex an issue as "Who am I?" and its derivative "Why am I?" Because many regard adolescence as a time when the principal developmental task is the development of identity, a separate section of the chapter is reserved for a discussion of identity formation and consolidation in adolescence.

SOME FURTHER DEVELOPMENTAL CONSIDERATIONS

Some developmental aspects of self have been referred to in the definitions of self concept, self-esteem, and identity. To make additional comment about self-development is difficult for several reasons. One is that few longitudinal studies of self-development have been reported. Accordingly, findings from scattered cross-sectional studies must be pieced together. This is at best a risky task. Another reason is that variety in both theoretical orientations and measurement of self-constructs complicates any synthesis about self-development from research workers who deal with different aspects of self, descriptive and evaluative, and who employ different measurement techniques—ratings by the person himself or ratings of a person by others, for example.

Regardless, the weight of the evidence that can be marshaled about developmental aspects of self suggests at least five broad, interrelated trends (26, 38, 46, 51, 53, 64, 75).

Differentiation— *Looking at Samenesses & differences)*
First, it is reasonably clear that successively finer distinctions in self-knowledge and self-evaluation occur with age. That is, with age and advanced experience, the child becomes increasingly less global in his view and evaluation of self. For example, a very young child is likely to think about himself in absolute, unqualified terms: "I am a good boy." Gradually, this absolutism gives way to qualified, more detailed expressions about the self: "I am good most of the time and especially when I am rested, not hungry, and with people I like." Still later, self-knowledge and self-evaluation become even more precisely articulated and differen-

tiated across situations and tasks. Thus a person's self concept of ability, for example, may differ according to the class of activity involved (academics, athletics, or social contact) and even within a given activity class (reading, writing, or arithmetic).

Differentiation in the organization of self-knowledge and self-evaluation suggests an age-related increase in the capacity to form more specialized, complex impressions in an integrated way. This differentiation, however, is most certainly influenced by the steady stream of reactions from others that a child receives during the daily course of events. In fact, one of the lines of thought concerning self-development about which psychologists generally agree is precisely this idea: Development and change in self concept and esteem are determined largely by the way in which "significant others" react to a child's behavior (56).

Individuation— *allow me to be a different person*
A second, related trend in self-development concerns individuation. This means that the extent to which the child distinguishes himself from others increases with age. While very young children may represent themselves primarily as similar to or like other children, later, during the elementary grades, self-representation is more likely to be in terms of how one is *different* from one's peers. This trend seems to be accompanied by increased self-reliance, especially among boys, and an increase in the personal power that a child perceives in himself. Again, the cumulative experience that a child has with others is probably a key factor in promoting individuation. More frequent and varied contact with different people in different circumstances leads to individuation.

Complexity

Together, differentiation and individuation in self-development imply a third trend: increased complexity with age. It has been indicated earlier that the very young child's view of self is comparatively diffuse, global, and simple. Gradually, however, several dimensions of self begin to take shape, perhaps the most basic of which involves the distinction between self and ideal self. That is, in addition to a view of the self "as I am" (actual self), the child is thought gradually to develop a view of the self "as I would like to be" (ideal self). Some psychologists (for example, 82) believe that a wide gap between the actual and the ideal self is an indication of poor adjustment. In other words, dissatisfaction with self may lead to self-rejection. Self-rejection, in turn, impedes acceptance of others. A vicious cycle of unhappiness and interpersonal difficulties may therefore be established. However, the point here is that ever more complex perceptions are built upon the actual self–ideal self distinction (102). For example, one's actual self concept may eventually involve a view of both the social effects of his behavior (social self concept) and a view of his personal attributes that is largely independent of social relations with others (private self concept). Similarly, one may come to hold both an independent concept of the idealized self and a view of himself in terms of ideals that are held for him by other people, including parents and teachers. This kind of self concept has been called "mirror self-image."

Consistency

A fourth trend may be less clearly developmental than motivational: the tendency for a child or a youth to behave consistently with his image of self. As knowledge about one's self is acquired, including relative strengths and limitations concerning various activities and traits, certain expectancies evolve (see Chapter 6). As these expectancies become organized, they are increasingly reflected in subjective estimates about what one can or cannot do. If, for example, a child expects that he will be able to learn hopscotch readily, he is likely to engage in such learning confidently and persistently. In contrast, if he expects that hopscotch is too difficult and that failure is imminent, he may become only slightly involved, if at all, in learning the game.

Stability

The fifth and final trend to be discussed here concerns increased stability of the self with age. The concept of stability was introduced in Chapter 3. As maturity is gained, behavior in general becomes better organized and more stable. So it is with an individual's view of self, including self-regard. This leads to a greater capacity to resist and recover from disorganization in the environment and to ignore appraisals by others of oneself that are incongruent with his own view of himself. In an extreme form, stabilization of self concept may lead to rigidity, social insensitivity, and unrealism. None of this implies, however, that self-concept change does not occur as one grows older. Each new change in role (becoming a kindergartner or first-grader, or high school student; or having one's first car date; or becoming engaged or married, or having children; or retiring from a job at age 65 or 70) demands a change in self concept. Thus, self-concept theorists by definition hold an open system view of personality as do the humanists, behaviorists, and cognitive developmental people (see Chapter 2).

Rather than accept a closed system—complete stability of self concept—the authors argue only that organization inhibits reorganization (that is, the more you know about how to do something or about a subject, the more difficult it is to learn to do it a different way or to change your point of view about it). Few longitudinal studies of stability in self-concept development exist, but Example 11.1 is an illustration of work in this area. The study described introduces our discussion of identity during adolescence.

11.1 Stability and Change in Self-Concept Development

Rae Carlson (10) has taken the position that one important manifestation of identity formulation during adolescence involves self-concept changes that occur during the teen years. Her theorizing includes the premise that the process of identity formulation requires that a person somehow come to terms with culturally defined sex roles. As such, somewhat different channels for such formulation can be predicted for boys and girls.

From this background of thought, Carlson developed a questionnaire in order to measure two "conceptually independent" dimensions of the self concept: *Social-personal orientation* and *degree of congruence between self-description and ideal self-description*. Specifically, social orientation can be defined in terms of the extent to which a person's interpersonal experiences influence his view of self. Social orientation also involves the degree to which one is vulnerable to social appraisals by others. In contrast, personal orientation concerns self conceptions not contingent on the nature of one's social experiences. Rather, personal orientation purportedly reflects more of what we might call a private segment of the self concept. The following sample items from Carlson's questionnaire illustrate the difference in these two orientations. Letters in parentheses designate item classification:

I usually get along very well with my teachers. (S)ocial
I'd rather figure things out for myself before asking for help. (P)ersonal
My friends spend a lot of time at my house. (S)
I prefer difficult tasks to easy ones. (P)
People think I have a good sense of humor. (S)
I enjoy many different kinds of recreation. (P)

Carlson administered her questionnaire and another measure of role behavior to a sample of sixth-grade children. These instruments were administered again six years later when the subjects were high school seniors. In all, forty-nine persons responded at both points in time.

Analysis of the data resulted in several conclusions about self-concept development during preadolescence and adolescence. First, Carlson noted that very little change occurred among her subjects in their descriptions of self–ideal-self discrepancy. This was interpreted as an indication of general stability in self-esteem, independent of sex role. Neither was there a significant difference between the sexes in this dimension of self concept at either age level. As predicted, however, developmental sex differences in social–personal orientation were clearly observed. With age, girls became progressively more socially oriented and boys more personally oriented. Carlson suggests that this finding reflects the salient influence of sex role norm qualities on self-development. Apparently, these trends in social–personal orientation represent the still further impact of socialization during adolescence. In Carlson's words, this important dimension of self-development "mirrors the divergent processes of masculine and feminine character development among adolescents in our culture" (10, p. 573).

Such differential changes tie to the whole notion of valued sex role stereotypes, wherein competence and independence are devalued among females, social dependence and orientation are devalued among males. Earlier (see Chapter 7) the disadvantages of such extreme divergence of sex role expectations for those of both sexes were discussed.

FACTORS ASSOCIATED WITH INDIVIDUAL DIFFERENCES IN SELF-DEVELOPMENT

In the introduction to this chapter it was suggested that almost everything discussed thus far in this book can be related in some way to self-development. The fact that individual differences in all three components of self-development—self concept, self-esteem, and identity—can be observed during the preschool years indicates that important forces are very early at work to influence self-development. In this section, some of the more salient of these forces are examined: parent–child relationships, physical development, school achievement, disadvantages and minority group status, and other factors. Some of these factors cannot clearly be identified as direct causes of differences in self-development. In the case of school achievement, for example, it is likely that self-development both affects

and is affected by success and failure. The point is that the state of knowledge about self-development does not allow us to speak unequivocally about causation.

Parent–Child Relations

Most theorists believe the quality of parent–child relations is closely linked to differences in self-descriptive and self-evaluative behavior among children and youth. Surprisingly, however, few studies have been made in this area, although three recent research findings of relevance warrant our attention. One study concerns a positive relationship between self-concept measures of mothers and their children at time of school entry (92). Another concerns the finding that kindergarten children whose self-evaluations are comparatively more autonomous are more likely to manifest independence, achievement behavior, and stable aspiration levels than children whose self-evaluations are less autonomous; and the autonomous children are also more likely to come from homes not characterized by high maternal control (19). Still another finding is that deaf children whose parents are also deaf evaluate themselves more positively than deaf children whose parents have normal hearing (62).

Collectively, these findings suggest the possibility that parents whose self-development is positive, who encourage and reinforce their children's autonomy behavior, and who accept their children's failings or problems may do much toward providing "good" home conditions for their children's self-development. This implication fits nicely with studies of child rearing discussed earlier in the book (see especially Example 3.1 in Chapter 3). It is also consistent with the findings of one of the most extensive studies of self-esteem conducted to date (15). In this study, the home backgrounds of pre-adolescent boys whose self-esteem ranged from high to very low were examined. A most striking result of this study is that high self-esteem during preadolescence (and presumably before) was associated with two basic patterns of parental behavior: parental acceptance of the child and the style with which parents manage their children's behavior.

Acceptance as defined in this study refers to such things as parental expression of affection, demonstration of concern about the problems encountered by their children, general harmony within the home, friendly joint activities, and the availability of parents to provide well-outlined, confident help for their children when help is needed. Management style refers to such things as providing a set of clear and fair rules and demands, acting firmly and consistently in applying these demands, and respectfully allowing freedom (within defined limits) for children to act. The point is that higher levels of acceptance and management style as defined here were associated with higher levels of self-esteem. A cause–effect relationship cannot be advanced. However, it is probable that both parental behavior patterns—acceptance and management—influence the way in which children view themselves.

This notion gains some support from information about low-esteem preadolescents and their parents provided in the same study (15). For example, parents of children with low self-esteem made rather frequent use of corporal punishment (spanking and slapping) *and* love withdrawal disciplinary techniques (for example, "Mothers don't love boys who don't mind." "Your father won't love you

if you continue to behave this way." or "I don't see how I can possibly love a child who is so naughty!"). As suggested earlier in this book, this approach to discipline may be an effective way of communicating to a child that his acceptance is conditional—he is not accepted for himself, but only on the parent's terms—or that the child is valued on the basis of what he does (extrinsic valuation), not because of who he is.

A second point worthy of note concerns the observed tendency among parents of low-esteem boys to place greater importance on the punishment of "bad" behavior than upon rewarding (reinforcing positively) "good" behavior. As indicated in Chapter 2, a reinforcement pattern based on the principle "accentuate the positive" seems preferable to a concept of feedback couched in the negative.

In summary, it is plausible to conclude that child-rearing strategies of parents can make a substantial difference in their children's self-development, even though the direct evidence for this is meager. Parents provide not only the greatest and most consistent amount of feedback to children in the early years, but also a model for self-development that can be observed extensively by their offspring. Thus, the authors believe that the following quote, representing a set of hypotheses, deserves the careful attention of adults concerned with self-development:

Presumably, then, the parent can influence the development of such aspects of the self concept as (a) the generalized level of self regard (e.g., by being loved and accepted the child comes to love himself, and through acquisition of accepted—reinforced—behaviors he comes to respect his own functioning); (b) the subjective standards of conduct which are associated with his role and individual status (i.e., the development of the ideal self); (c) the realism of his view of his abilities and limitations, and the acceptance of them; (d) the degree of acceptance in the phenomenal self concept of inevitable characteristics (e.g., hostility, jealousy, sex); (e) the adequacy of his means of appraising accurately his effects on others (103, pp. 121–122).

Constitutional Factors and Self-Development

Self-development is almost certainly influenced by activities in which success is determined by body size and/or physical skills. The reactions from others that one receives concerning such success (or its lack) and physical appearance in general must also influence self concept (60). For example, physical attributes such as size, weight, strength, speed, and agility may either contribute to or interfere with the development of many socially approved skills. The tall, dextrous, fast-running adolescent usually has a substantial advantage over his shorter, less well coordinated, and slower peer in athletic games such as football and basketball. Both social recognition and opportunities for further athletic development—a high-status activity in most youth cultures—depend on basic physical prowess. Moreover, because a person's physical attributes may show varying degrees of conformity to culturally defined values or standards for physique and appearance, positive or negative feedback may be received from others. The obese adolescent female in American society is unlikely to encounter as favorable a psychosocial environment as her well-proportioned, trim, graceful peer. In fact, obesity may result in outright social rejection and set the stage for serious emotional problems.

The relationship between physical factors and self-development is best documented by studies related to three variables: body type or body conformation, maturation rate, and physical handicap. Each of these variables is considered briefly in order to highlight this relationship.

Body Type

Interest in the link between body build and personality has existed for thousands of years. This interest can be traced to Hippocrates' efforts to classify body type more than 2500 years ago. Modern psychologists have concentrated heavily on the interaction of body build and temperament and mental disorders. Among the most well known of the somatotype (body type) theories, one theory is based on a tripartite distinction involving endomorphy, mesomorphy, and ectomorphy (87). Although "pure types" are rarely found, the endomorph is one whose body is rounded in conformation ("pear shaped"), with comparatively wide hips, thick midsection, and a predominance of fatty tissue. Mesomorphs, in contrast, are more muscular, narrow hipped, and broad shouldered—the "athletic" type. Finally, ectomorphy is characterized by leanness (a large external body surface in relation to weight), less muscularity than the mesomorph, and a general "gangly" appearance.

Much controversy surrounds the idea that body build contributes directly to personality characteristics such as the self concept, sociability, and aggressiveness. However, there is little question that people react differently to persons of different somatotypes. This social reaction is perhaps most clearly involved in the body-build–self-development relationship. For example, male children as early

Social and Personal Development

The body type of an individual mediates, to a substantial degree, the reactions he receives from other people. Particularly for males, poor physique and late physical maturity seem to be associated with negative self concept and social behavior. (Photo by Enrico Natali)

as age 8 demonstrate strong, stereotyped concepts of behavioral characteristics in relation to body build (40). Specifically, it is the mesomorphic individual who apparently is perceived and reacted to most favorably. By comparison, endomorphs are consistently rated as socially unfavorable; and ectomorphs are generally rated as more socially submissive and personally unfavorable. If such ratings are any indication of children's attitudes toward somatotypes and if peer reactions actually do affect one's private or social

self concept, we can expect that somatotype is an important variable in self-concept differences among children.

Unfortunately, not many studies have been designed directly to compare the self concepts and self-esteems of children and youth whose somatotypes are distinctly different. What little evidence that can be mustered, however, suggests that children of different body builds also differ in self concept; for example, "heavy" children report less positive self concepts than do their "balanced" and "linear" peers (27). It should be pointed out that this finding applies largely to preadolescent males; the body-build–self-concept relationship apparently attenuates as pubertal changes occur (29). Furthermore, very little is known about girls in this area. As suggested above, however, there is good reason to suspect that somatotype mediates the reactions a person receives from others and the degree of success that a person has in physical activities, especially sports. Consequently, the body-build variable must be considered as one important constitutional factor in self-development.

Maturation Rate

A second constitutional variable important for self-development is the rate at which one approaches physical maturity. This seems especially pertinent during the sensitive period of adolescence. For example, several studies have been competently executed to illustrate differences between adolescents who are extremely early (accelerated) in their physical development and age mates who are extremely late (retarded) (44, 49, 65, 66). Bone ossification status is generally used as the criterion in determining maturation in such studies. The overall result of these investigations is an apparent advantage in self concept and peer status among early-maturing youth, especially males. Specifically, early-maturing males (as compared to their late-maturing counterparts) more consistently receive positive ratings from both peers and adults in terms of attractiveness, composure, and social sophistication. They are also more frequently chosen for positions of school leadership and identified as prominent participants in extracurricular school activities.

More directly related to the present discussion is the consistent finding that later maturing males, compared with their early-maturing peers, more often report inadequacy feelings, low self-esteem, and the belief that they are rejected. Perhaps to compensate or overcome these feelings in some way, late maturers also often demonstrate a pattern of attention seeking and rebellious autonomy. Such behavior seems more likely to increase than to ameliorate their social and personal difficulties.

Still other authors (for example, 98) indicate that late physical maturation is generally a handicap among males at the college level. Moreover, some of the psychological differences associated with maturation rate during adolescence, including those involving personal dominance, independence, and self-control, have been observed among males during the third decade of life. Of course, the apparent disadvantages of late maturation need not be inevitable. Physical development status is by no means the only factor associated with self and social development. In the case of girls, at least at the time, too early maturation may even be somewhat handicapping (45).

When very early maturing males are followed into their 40s, their conspicuous superiority to late-maturing boys largely disappears (43, 60). While they are still well off on the verge of middle age, the incipient failure of their bodies may have brought them to about the same level of personal leadership and well-being as the late-maturing boys, who were possibly never so dependent on their bodies. These late-maturing boys may be finding some payoff from their hard-earned lessons about being affable, lively, and self-examining.

The point, generally speaking, is that the value of early maturation may influence the psychological development of children and adolescents, most particularly in body image, social self concept, and social self-esteem.

The findings are clear enough that parents and teachers should take great care to help develop psychological resources among early maturers and self-confidence built on factors other than physical maturity among late maturers.

Physical Handicap

As in the case of body build and maturation rate, physical handicap is at least indirectly involved in self-development. Parent and peer reactions to a physically handicapping condition provide social feedback that influences a person's view of himself as a more or a less adequate or worthy person. In one important study, for example, preadolescent children demonstrated a strong tendency to consider physical handicap in establishing their preferences for other children (80). Girls seem more frequently to focus on cosmetic attributes such as obesity and facial disfigurement in this regard; boys, in contrast, apparently respond more negatively to functional impairments, such as amputation of an arm or a leg.

It is probably true, despite findings such as the above, that attitudes toward a given physical handicap or disability are not uniform among children and youth (1).

Self-esteem is especially difficult to develop among handicapped children. (The New York Times *photo*)

However, the collective impact of social isolation or rejection of physically handicapped children and the reduced opportunities they may have for participation in socially valued activities surely will affect the self. Moreover, related problems, such as chronic illness, may also negatively influence a child's self-development. This is particularly likely when chronic illness interferes with academic progress (88). We examine the self-development–school-achievement relationship more fully in a later section.

To summarize, body build, maturational status, and physical handicap all represent attributes that can influence both the degree of achieved competence in given activities and the social reactions one receives from other people. To the extent that success and positive social reinforcement are important to a child or a youth and serve to shape his self-evaluation, it is expected that these three constitutional attributes are strongly involved in self-development. It must be reemphasized that attributes such as physical handicap or body build do not inevitably lead to maladjustment; nor is it easy to demonstrate definite associations between specific physical attributes and the quality of behavior, including self-development (76). Yet the authors believe that such factors are too often overlooked and underestimated when it comes to assessing qualitative psychological development. They also wish to emphasize the importance of social attitudes toward constitutional factors that are conveyed to children and youth. For the authors, such attitudes mediate the quality of self-development to a large degree. Adults are therefore cautioned to avoid making prejudicial judgments about and discriminating against children and youth whose physical development and status deviate from the cultural ideal.

Disadvantage and Minority Group Status

The relationship between economic disadvantage and minority or ethnic or racial group membership and self-development has received increased research attention during the past several years. This increase is apparently the result of a number of factors, including intensified sensitivity to the problems of the poor and those who have been the target of social discrimination in American society. Particular attention has been focused on the schools. Many educators seem more concerned than ever before about their responsibility to foster self-development among their charges. This concern has probably been most strongly stimulated by the fact that federal programs for compensatory education reflect a top priority for enhancing the comparatively lower self-images of disadvantaged, minority group children (104).

That past research has usually demonstrated less positive self-development among the poor and racially different (for example, Black, Hispano, and American Indian) is not surprising in view of the distorted relations typical of majority–minority and rich–poor social contact in American society. What is especially disturbing is that less favorable self-development can be associated with race and economic disadvantages as early as school entry and continuing throughout the period of adolescence (34, 51, 52, 101). These data generally have indicated that black children and youth, for example, report consistently lower self-esteem than do their white peers; they also indicate that it is usually the child or the youth of poverty who is characterized by lower self-confidence and worth, regardless of racial identity.

For reasons yet unclear, however, some of the most recent investigators have found that this pattern may be changing. For example, in one study, no consistent differences in either self concept or feeling about peers were found between economically deprived black and economically advantaged white fifth-grade children (99). In another, negative self-perceptions or lower self-esteem could not be reliably associated with economic status (89). Still another study has led to the conclusion that disadvantaged school children report consistently *higher* self-esteem than their advantaged peers, regardless of race, geographical residence, or the extent to which their schools are racially mixed (93).

Such results run counter to the findings about ethnicity, economic status, and self-development that have dominated the past. Perhaps they are largely artifactual, that is, a function of peculiar sampling and measurement practices. But it is just as likely that changing social conditions are implicated. Some authorities (for example, 104) have suggested that society is gradually becoming more genuinely pluralistic with the result that minorities and the poor now receive more respect from the majority culture membership than in the past. Minority group liberation movements and increased emphases on racial ethnic distinctiveness and culture (for example, "Black is beautiful") may be affecting children and youth in positive ways. With respect particularly to economic disadvantage, it is also possible that more privileged children and youth experience from their parents (and teachers) greater pressures and higher expectations for achievement that in some way may adversely affect the self (93). This notion gains some support from a large comparative study of adolescents from different social class and ethnic backgrounds. Specifically, privileged youth of educated parents who were enmeshed intensively in academic work reported lower self-esteem (84).

It is recognized that these are speculations. To the authors' knowledge, no one has explained completely and satisfactorily the apparent shift in research findings concerning self-development, disadvantage, and ethnicity. Such factors are obviously important, but it is increasingly difficult to generalize about the direction of the interrelationships. Other factors, such as sex, serve to complicate this mixed bag of data even further. For example, there is some evidence to indicate that skin color is a more salient factor in self-esteem and peer preferences for girls than for boys (79, 89). Further, it is likely that differences in self-development occur within ethnic minorities themselves. As compared to Black children, for example, Puerto Rican children have been described as demonstrating lower self-esteem (105).

It will probably be some time before the complexities of this area of self-development research are untangled. Perhaps a few reliable trends have already emerged—a gradual increase in positive self-esteem among many minority group children, for example. Of course, it is hoped that shifts in self-development for one group do not occur at the expense of other groups; and also that knowledge of the possible effects of ethnic and economic status on self-development will be used constructively by all members of the helping professions.

To summarize, the data from older studies of self-development among the poor and the prejudiced-against fall quite consistently in the direction of distortion and debasement of self concept. Data from some newer studies support equality and in some cases superiority of self-esteem among the groups formerly found to be debased. No firm conclusions about the state of affairs in this area of research can be advanced at this time, but more study is clearly indicated. In the meantime, it is well to work toward an egalitarian society in which factors irrelevant to the human-being-inside-each-human-skin are genuinely treated as irrelevant. Then ethnicity, race, and economics will indeed have no negative bearing on self-development. This, the authors believe, is as it should be.

The Self and School Achievement

On purely logical grounds, it can be predicted that the quality of self-development—including degree of self-confidence in facing and mastering the environment—will affect and be affected by school performance. The school is a primary setting for academic and social experience. Unfortunately, this setting is not so benign for some children's self-development as might be hoped. Psychologists have consistently documented a significant relationship among such things as academic achievement, school satisfaction, self concept of ability, and self-esteem (77). This relationship has been reported for children as early as the primary grades and as late as the college years. There is an ample amount of evidence concerning the middle school grades as well (9, 15, 41, 42, 49, 90, 97, 100).

Taken together, the studies of self-development and school achievement indicate that it is the child or the youth with low self-esteem, poor self concept of ability, or negative identity whose academic progress is hindered. This relationship is perhaps best illustrated in studies of underachievement. Typically, these studies involve a comparison of pupils who are achieving close to their potential with their peers who are not. While achieving pupils may certainly feel inadequate in specific areas, it is the under-achiever who is likely to report more general feelings of inadequacy and negative attitudes toward the self (86).

The complexities and dynamics of underachievement are explored in more detail in Chapter 12. Meanwhile, the authors wish to stress the pervasiveness of the school-achievement–self-development relationship. Of course, the fact of relationship does not prove cause and effect. It is difficult, especially where young children are concerned, to determine whether successful school achievement results in, or is largely the result of, a strong positive self-image.

This difficulty highlights a persisting debate in education. For example, within early-education circles, it is often argued that a positive, clear self concept of ability is a prerequisite for successful academic progress. Therefore, early-education strategies should be designed first and foremost to promote self-confidence and self-esteem (25). Others argue that the best route to positive self-development is the mastery of challenging, meaningful tasks. Therefore, early education should be focused specifically on the development of coping strategies, problem-solving skills, preacademic competencies, and the like, with self-development as a by-product.

The authors believe both approaches are useful, even necessary. Every child has the right to be esteemed, liked, laughed with and enjoyed, and treated with good humor and fairness "for himself alone." In such a climate (the authors have called it one of response-independent positive reinforcement), the authors believe that curiosity, spontaneity, creativity, and high self-esteem are developed. Every child must also "be taught," and in the teaching of skills and knowledge, response-dependent reinforcement (behavior shaping) has a prominent space. There is nothing contradictory about generous administrations of both response-dependent and response-independent positive reinforcement.

Debates about self as related, or opposed, to skill development and the methods by which both may be encouraged are stimulating and frequently productive. However, the authors endorse the idea that the self-development–academic-achievement relationship is a two-way street (77). The two interact so as to influence each other directly and continuously. It also seems likely that this relationship is mediated by various expectancies for success or failure that are established through cumulative experience in school and in other formal settings for learning (see Chapter 6). Finally, it can be argued that a positive self concept of ability may often be a necessary, but is rarely a sufficient, condition for successful academic progress (76). School achievement, for the authors, represents the outcome of a complex variety of factors and cannot be traced to the existence of only one personal attribute. .

School Conditions That May Impede Self-Development

The relationship of school achievement and self-development is so basic that it has led psychologists and educational critics alike to look for factors within the school that are counterproductive in terms of student self-development. Even so, surprisingly few hard data relevant to this problem have been reported. Among the variables singled out for consideration are grading systems based on student competition (someone is always doomed to fail, relatively speaking), retention in grade, corporal punishment, and ability grouping (76). Polemics concerning such factors are the rule, although the accompanying empirical evidence is typically ambiguous and inconclusive. Studies of ability grouping, for example, demonstrate that children usually know in which stratum of achievement they have been placed, but the precise effects of differential placement on self-esteem are not clear (36, 70).

There is little ambiguity about the effects of consistent failure and rejection by others, however (102). It may well be the quality of the personal relationship between student and teacher, combined with teacher skill in individualizing instruction, that is the key variable in the school-achievement–self-development relationship. Neither must the effect of school practices and student behavior on the continued self-development of teachers be overlooked. As one might expect, teaching success, as determined by a supervisor's ratings, is linked to positiveness about self, including greater personal security, clarity in identity, and less self-conflict (30). But it is difficult to believe that even a secure, confident teacher can remain so in the face of continual failure to obtain satisfactory responses from, and to observe academic progress among, students. Conditions that may affect the self-esteem of both students and teachers are illustrated by the material in Example 11.2. As the reader will see, the themes represented in the comments of students and

their teachers are insightful and relevant to the general issue of self-development in the schools.

11.2 Self-Esteem in a Public School

Malcolm Meltzer and Bernard Levy (63) conducted extensive independent interviews with a group of ninth-grade students and their teachers in a large, inner-city junior high school. Their primary interest was to explore with these two groups the attitudes they held toward each other and the extent to which the general theme of self-esteem is implicated in student–teacher relationships. Once the interview data were obtained, Meltzer and Levy attempted to organize them into categories that highlighted both concern for self and perceptions of the school experience in general. Although the study, including the treatment of data, is subjective in its frame of reference, it illustrates conditions that probably impede self-esteem and general morale within schools of the kind studied.

Student responses mostly represented complaints about teachers and school practices that contributed to resentment and alienation. Included were the following "charges":

School is uninteresting.
Students are not sufficiently involved in class planning and discussions.
Low recognition by teachers of student ideas.
Unfair discipline, resentment of teacher control, being dismissed from the classroom, teacher's word always overriding that of students.
Teacher favoritism.
Teachers acting in a condescending manner, not taking a personal interest in students, acting too aggressively, and making students feel like children.

Meltzer and Levy presented these complaints to the group of teachers only to find that denial and amusement, rather than concerned acknowledgment and sympathetic understanding, were the initial reactions . . . perhaps as a defense or a genuine difference of opinion about what is going on in the school. As the teacher interviews proceeded, however, it was apparent that teachers, too, had complaints about their school orientation. These included criticism of the school curriculum as lacking relevance for many students, inadequate student participation in their own educational planning, obstacles and deficiencies in classroom management, insufficient training to deal successfully with the problems of inner-city children and youth, inconsistency in standards among faculty colleagues, and reluctance to experiment with and try alternative approaches to education. These teachers also expressed difficulty in being able to understand the motives underlying student unrest.

Perhaps more telling, however, are the criticisms of students voiced by these teachers; for example:

Students have no regard for law and order.
Students often attempt to coerce teachers through confrontation and threats.
Students misuse freedom, and often spoil teachers' attempts to make class enjoyable.
Low moral standards among students.
Problem students serve as "heroes" for others to emulate.
Failure to utilize recreational facilities of the school to "let off steam."
Students allow personal problems to interfere with learning.

These teachers also focused on the inadequate nature of many students' home backgrounds; for example:

Broken homes leave students insecure and rejected.
Conflict in home–school values.
Absence of home–school communication.
Low discipline in the home.
Decline of religious training in the home.

Meltzer and Levy suggest, in view of these expressed attitudes, that the school houses two "warring groups," each dissatisfied with the other at the expense of self-esteem among both groups. Both students and teachers apparently have insight into many of the problems that negatively affect school experience, but may not be sufficiently moved (or encouraged and supported) to do anything about it. It is difficult to say how widespread this problem is; but if these student and teacher perceptions are at all accurate, it is a situation that society cannot afford to tolerate.

Example 11.2 and the discussion that preceded it point to a complex balance and interaction of forces that affect self-development within the schools of both students and teachers. This balance and interaction are illustrated by three statements, none of which is soundly supported by data, but each of which is plausible (as are their converses).

When parents in a community are proud of their schools, morale of both teachers and students is likely to be high and positive self-development will be encouraged (and the reverse).

When the level of home security in a community is low (as in very low income areas), this condition is reflected in insecure students among whom learning deficiencies are prominent. This is likely to set up a vicious circle among parents, teachers, and students, with all of them coming to distrust one another and none of them reinforcing the other, so that morale sinks still lower, with consequent adverse results for both academic achievement and self-development.

When teacher–principal morale is high, academic achievement and self-development among students are promoted, and this situation in turn has a positive effect on parent–school relations.

Some Additional Correlates of Self-Development

Thus far, the discussion of self-development has concentrated on primary influences such as child–parent interaction, constitutional factors, and school achievement. A great variety of additional human attributes and conditions can be associated with self-development from childhood through adolescence. For example, it is clear that a positive relationship exists between self-development and intelligence and curiosity (59, 81). Children whose self-evaluations are low or negative are also characterized by higher anxiety and generally less favorable reactions from peers, and are more external in their locus of control (22, 28, 50). The latter relationship is particularly intriguing, as it raises the possibility that a positive self concept may cushion the sense of powerlessness often associated with membership in a "stigmatized" minority group (see Chapter 10) (22).

In early adolescence, it is reported that (for males especially) those who are high in sex role identification are higher in self-esteem than are their low-identification peers (13). This seems also to be true for parent identification (74), although the evidence is scanty. As two final examples, self-esteem is reportedly higher among college students whose vocational goals and plans are crystallized (versus vague) and also among those who possess a generally optimistic attitude toward inter- national affairs as well as their own immediate, personal world (72, 78).

These generalizations are mentioned to reinforce further the pervasiveness of experiential and constitutional influences on self-development. The authors can think of no other body of data about human development that better illustrates this principle: *all aspects of development interact.* It is perhaps this idea that has led many psychologists to view the self as the central, organizing feature of personality—a feature that is unique for every individual, but which is affected in similar ways by environmental conditions encountered by everyone. This concept of self can also be related to the notion introduced in Chapter 1 concerning the individual as a factor in his own development.

Example 11.3 is included to show one way of summarizing the interacting effects of experience on self-development.

11.3 A Longitudinal Study of Self Concept in Children

Robert Sears (85), of Stanford University, performed a study of self-evaluative behavior among sixth-grade children (eighty-four girls, seventy-five boys). For this study, positive attitudes toward the self were defined in terms of satisfaction with one's abilities, favorable comparison of self with others, general feelings of worth and success, and perception of others as friendly and respectful toward the self. In contrast, self-derogation, self-dissatisfaction, feelings of guilt and inferiority, painful self-consciousness, failure orientation, and self-aggression were taken as indications of negative attitudes toward self.

Sears administered five different self-concept scales in order to measure these various components of self-evaluation.

He also administered a measure of gender role (masculinity–femininity) in order to estimate degree and direction of sex typing. The resulting data were correlated with two sets of data obtained earlier in these children's lives. One set included interview data taken from the mothers of the children during the kindergarten year, a period of seven years preceding the self-concept study. These data were used to estimate such things as parental warmth and acceptance, family adjustment, permissiveness in child rearing, and father–mother dominance. Measures of intelligence and school achievement were also obtained when the children in this sample were third-graders. In all, Sears was interested primarily in the interrelationships of familial variables, school competence, and self concept among children over the elementary grade span, particularly any that might suggest antecedent–consequent relationships.

Briefly, Sears found that high self concepts (positive self-evaluation) were associated with high reading and arithmetic achievement, small family size, early ordinal position (birth order), and high maternal and paternal warmth. These associations held for both sexes. However, the father–mother dominance variable was linked only to self concept among boys; that is, high self concept in boys was related to *low* father dominance in marital relations, but not in girls. Sears also found for both boys and girls that femininity was associated with less positive self concepts. It is notable, however, that no overall sex differences in self concept were disclosed.

As these findings represent correlations only, one cannot assume cause–effect. Neither can one assume that family relationships remain qualitatively the same over so long a period as seven years. Yet, as Sears himself remarks, "the present data suggest fairly clearly that a child's self concept at age 12 is significantly related not only to his own academic competence (as measured 3 years earlier) but to several aspects of the family constellation which already existed when he was 5 years old" (85, p. 288).

IDENTITY IN ADOLESCENCE

Earlier in this chapter the definition of identity during childhood included awareness of group membership (such as sex, race, ethnicity, and social class) and the meaning such membership has for personal–social development. Identity formulation clearly has its roots in childhood, but the crystallization of identity is considered by many to be the central developmental task of adolescence: a period for integrating one's sexual identity, goals and aspirations, personal ethics, and other features of self-development. In a sense, this period of integration represents a reorganization of self—a reorganization provoked by pubertal changes, mounting cultural pressures for independence and decisive personal action, and the assumption of broader responsibilities to one's self and others.

In this section the authors examine briefly the ideas of a scholar who is perhaps the man most responsible for the current and widespread concern among psychologists for adolescent identity problems, Erik Erikson (23, 24). It should be noted that Erikson's frame of reference concerning identity formulation has been shaped mainly from psychoanalytic thought (see Chapter 2). However, he is notable among contemporary psychoanalysts for his attention to cultural and social factors that influence personality development.*

Definitional and Developmental Considerations

For Erikson, identity consciousness is the result of a continual process of personal reflection and observation—a process that involves much self-evaluation. A person subjectively compares himself with others and considers himself in relation to cultural forces and interpersonal relations. Identity is constantly subject to change, particularly in the direction of increased differentiation of awareness of others and societal problems. Thus, cognitive as well as affective factors are involved. It is during adolescence, however, that identity is subject to a *crisis*. In Erikson's words this crisis is "a necessary turning point, a critical movement, when development must move one way or another, marshaling resources of growth, recovery, and further differentiation" (24, p. 16). Moreover, this crisis involves the "final establishment of a dominant positive ego identity" (23, p. 306).

For positive ego identity development, Erikson maintains that the adolescent must arrive at a commitment, a genuine personal investment including both *occupation* and *ideology*. Choosing an occupation, of course, demands that one establish priorities, including occupational goals and ambitions, in such a way that he selects a direction for his life. Ideology commitment refers to the development of a consistent personal position on basic matters such as religion, politics, and ethics. The term identity crisis refers to a period of decision making, examining of alternatives, and active questioning. Once

* See Table 10.1 (pp. 368-369) for a review of Erikson's description of personality development.

occupational and ideological commitments are made, the identity crisis of adolescence is thought to be resolved and a firm sense of identity is achieved.

For Erikson, the developmental hazard of adolescence is identity diffusion, or role confusion. To illustrate, Erikson refers to the dilemma of Biff in Arthur Miller's "Death of a Salesman": "I just can't take hold, Mom, I just can't take hold of some kind of life." In other words, doubt, bewilderment, sexual insecurity, lack of autonomy, and failure to reach commitment combine to interfere with ego identity. Adolescent peer group phenomena, including the "overidentification" with folk heroes, general clannishness, and faddish conformity are, for Erikson, indications of a *defense* against prolonged identity confusion. This implies that adolescents actually may help each other through much developmental discomfort by forming cliques and stereotyping themselves, their ideals, and their enemies. Further, the common tendency for adolescents to pledge fidelity and to become virtually consumed by idealistic causes is seen by Erikson as a common manifestation of the identity-seeking process.

Erikson maintains that almost all adolescents temporarily experience a degree of identity confusion. As suggested earlier, failure to overcome this confusion eventually leads to a number of growth-impeding outcomes—for example, a persistent inability to "take hold," as in Biff's case, or the jelling of a negative identity. These outcomes may be accompanied, Erikson believes, by "devoted attempts" among adolescents to become precisely what culture, school, or parents do not wish them to be. But a person who emerges from the adolescent period with a firm sense of identity based on commitment is prepared for further personal growth, including growth that may occur during mature heterosexual involvement. In fact, for Erikson, the period of young adulthood represents a further developmental crisis, one that involves a readiness for genuine *intimacy* with another person. This requires that a person develop the capacity to commit himself to "concrete affiliation and partnerships and to develop the ethical strength to abide by such commitments, even though they may call for significant sacrifices and compromises" (23, p. 263). The negative counterpart of adolescent identity confusion during this period is isolation, that is, the persistent avoiding of relationships that involve or require intimate personal commitment.

Economically advantaged youth are often given more chance to work out their identity crisis "at their leisure" than are disadvantaged youth. Economically secure parents with solid places in the community, for example, are able to protect their children from drastic consequences of early delinquency. The youth caught in a delinquency but unprotected by such parental buttress may be booked, imprisoned, and thus forced into premature identity foreclosure (in this case, delinquency–criminality). Becoming illegitimately pregnant or marrying very young forces many girls and boys into premature identity foreclosure. Advantaged parents thus provide for their children what Erikson calls a *psychosocial moratorium*. To a degree, this moratorium has been institutionalized in the United States by such well-intended legal provisions as juvenile courts, youth authorities, and sanctions against publishing the names of those under a certain age who commit crimes.

In summary, then, the individual whose sense of identity is well developed as he approaches young adulthood knows who he is and where he is going, and is confident about his self-perception compared to the way he is perceived by others (4).

Identity Crisis from a Research Perspective

Erikson bases his ideas about identity formulation mainly on his clinical experiences with disturbed adolescents, although he has drawn on data from many fields, including cultural anthropology. His basic views are so widely shared among psychologists, notably the humanists and the psychoanalysts, that the idea of adolescence as identity crisis seems almost taken for granted in American society (and Western culture generally).

Some Correlates of Identity Status

There have been few direct, empirical tests of Erikson's thesis. Of course, part of the problem has been developing valid and reliable means for measuring identity along the achievement status–identity diffusion continuum. Another problematical factor has been the unraveling of the often abstruse and complex nature of Eriksonian thought. Despite these difficulties, protagonists of the identity crisis orientation have begun to supply data that generally support Erikson. In one early study, for example, the author set the modest objective of assessing the degree to which certain manifestations of identity diffusion exist in the same person (8). In general, it was disclosed that a cluster of behaviors consistent with Erikson's thinking about identity diffusion could, in fact, be observed among a sample of college women. These interrelated characteristics include a generally unstable sense of self (particularly concerning the relationship of past to present), relatively high anxiety, uncertainty about one's own dominant personal attributes, and evidence of great fluctuation in feelings about the self. In short, such data provide a degree of validity for the concept of identity diffusion.

Other studies of ego identity and diffusion also fit Erikson's theoretical pattern fairly well. For example, ego identity status is associated in predictable ways with academic achievement, anxiety proneness, and satisfaction with school (7, 16, 95). The latter relationship is particularly interesting in view of our earlier discussion of student activism (Chapter 8). Specifically, it has been reported that one important factor in student dissatisfaction is the association by students of a personal identity crisis with the college years (95). In other words, students who experience crisis in relation to occupation and ideology are less satisfied with school than their peers who have achieved full identity status. Example 11.4 contains a further discussion of individual differences in identity status and related psychological functioning.

11.4 Identity Crisis and Commitment: An Example of Research

One of the most active research workers concerned with identity achievement during adolescence is James Marcia (57, 58). On the basis of Eriksonian theory and his own exploratory research, Marcia has proposed four basic categories of ego identity: identity achievement, moratorium status, foreclosure status, and identity diffusion. Briefly, these categories can be defined as follows. *Identity achievement* is essentially the prototype status for the secure, well-organized person, one who has undergone a period of crisis (in the Eriksonian sense of the word) and has developed a

relatively stable commitment to some occupational endeavor and a consistent set of ideological beliefs. An individual currently experiencing a period of struggle and active questioning about occupation and ideology is said to be in *moratorium.* The third category, *foreclosure,* refers to the individual who has never experienced a genuine crisis, but is nonetheless committed with respect to occupation and beliefs. The *identity diffusion* category consists of those who neither demonstrate basic commitments nor seem actively involved in arriving at such commitments. A person so characterized may never have experienced a crisis or has engaged in a period of questioning without success in arriving at basic occupational and ideological choices.

In two separate studies, involving college males and females respectively, Marcia found that the above four identity statuses are distributed fairly evenly — that comparable numbers of late adolescents can be classified in each of the four categories (57, 58). However, there is apparently a slight sex difference in that proportionately more females have been characterized as identity achievers in Marcia's research. To put it another way, proportionately more males are found in the moratorium category. Perhaps more significant is the general finding that identity status is related to several patterns of behavior that are generally in line with Eriksonian theory. For example, Marcia has observed that identity-achieving males surpass their peers in other identity status categories in concept learning under stress. Moreover, males in the foreclosure group were observed more frequently to set unrealistically high goals for themselves on experimental learning tasks, and to endorse authoritarian values more completely when compared with other identity status peers. Marcia has suggested that foreclosure status reflects the strong, perhaps unduly strong, influence of parents concerning life's ambitions and values so that little room is left for individuality in their children. Admittedly, however, this is speculative in view of the tentative results from Marcia's research.

In a second study, similar elaborate interviewing and testing procedures were applied to a sample of college women. Of particular interest in the second study is Marcia's addition of sex (especially attitudes toward premarital intercourse) to the areas of occupation and ideology for females in order to determine identity status. Marcia reasoned that sex is a greater area of conflict for females than for males in our society. Therefore, it is a more relevant consideration in the assessment of ego identity. Unlike the male sample, Marcia found no significant differences in problem-solving performance among the females whose ego identity differed. It was found, however, that identity achievers were involved in more difficult courses of study in the college setting, especially in comparison to the identity diffusion group. As in the case of males, females in the foreclosure group were highest in authoritarianism, but, unlike the male subjects, foreclosure females were highest in self-esteem and lowest in anxiety. This finding was interpreted in terms of greater approval seeking among females or as a function of the adaptive value of this identity status for females in American society. Finally, the female identity diffusion group was characterized by comparatively higher levels of anxiety, a finding that could be predicted on the basis of Eriksonian thought.

Research of this kind suffers from methodological problems, such as selecting a sample and obtaining valid measurements. Yet it represents a worthy attempt to translate complex theoretical notions into an empirical framework. On the face of it, reliable differences in ego identity do exist among late adolescents, and these differences are associated with a number of important psychological functions. Equally clear is the fact of sex differences. This is especially true in regard to self-esteem. Whereas Marcia found clear-cut differences in self-esteem among females of differing identity status, no such differences were noted among males across status categories. It is possible that unreliability in self-esteem measurement is greater for males than for females, but this phenomenon needs to be clarified through further research.

Developmental Studies

If Erikson is correct, we can expect that the status of having achieved identity is more frequent with age. More and more individuals will manifest a firm, stable sense of identity as they move from early to late adolescence and young manhood and womanhood. Remarkably few attempts to demonstrate this tendency have been reported. However, what data there are lend themselves to such a conclusion. For example, in one study of nearly one thousand college students of both sexes, a consistent increase in "successful identity resolution" was noted from the freshman through the senior years (14). This pattern of increasing maturity was clearest among males, although females had been found to enter college with a more advanced sense of identity.

In interpreting these results, one must contemplate the dilemma in which American society places young women. An explicit choice is often forced on them of career *versus* wifehood and motherhood. To the authors, it is not surprising that a college senior girl faced with such a choice experiences acute conflict in resolving her identity successfully. For a male, on the other hand, graduation from college does not represent the possibility of giving up something he cherishes: his autonomy, independence, and competence. Rather, it is one more landmark he has successfully passed "in order to get where he is going."

At this time, it cannot be said how much the college experience per se facilitates or impedes the rate of identity development, and, unfortunately, next to nothing is known about identity development among noncollege youth.

In a study of college males, an expected shift toward positive identity status concerning occupation has been noted during the freshman year (96). In the same study, however, there was evidence of some "retrogression" in the area of ideology. In line with our earlier question about the function of college experience, it is possible that the variety and open interplay of ideas characteristic of most college environments may disrupt equilibrium in this area, especially if ideological commitment is tentative and premature.

The distinction between ideology and occupation and the fact that identity development may not be parallel in both areas are relevant to a third and final example of developmental research about identity. It is also germane to the persistent disclosure of sex differences in identity formation. The authors refer specifically to a massive study of some 3500 male and female adolescents, grades six through twelve, conducted by Douvan and Adelson (18).

On the basis of extensive interview, questionnaire, and psychological test data, Douvan and Adelson concluded that the process of identity formulation may be more difficult for girls in American society than for boys. Douvan and Adelson argue that, whereas the male's occupation serves a critical identity-defining function, in most cases the female must rely largely on her marriage for true self-definition. Accordingly, an adolescent male may begin to solidify his identity by

Research has suggested that the process of identity formation in American society may be more difficult for girls than for boys. (Photo by Christa Armstrong)

voluntarily choosing and preparing for an occupation. For Douvan and Adelson, this activity helps the male adolescent to "focus and stabilize" many transitional conflicts and problems. He has something fairly concrete to "hold on to." In contrast, the female's identity task is considered to be more ambiguous within this frame of reference. Marriage, for example, not only is a matter for the undefined future, but it usually depends in large part upon a decision by someone else. Douvan and Adelson believe this situation is not conducive to "rational planning" beyond the matter of cultivating one's personality and enhancing one's general attractiveness.

In line with findings presented earlier, it seems that as males seek specific occupational preparation in college, they may make comparatively more progress in identity formulation. Many girls may be less committed to a specific occupation and more dependent on the general idea of marriage and child rearing for a crystallization of identity. As indicated, the women's liberation movements may alter this general cultural pattern. Meanwhile, sex differences in identity development are reinforced by the further finding that males generally experience their greatest feelings of esteem through personal achievement (much of which is related to occupational development). Females, in contrast, more often report acceptance by others and gratifying, secure interpersonal relations as their greatest source of self-esteem (18).

Taken together, the studies cited can be interpreted as providing general support for the Eriksonian theme of identity crisis and commitment during adolescence and the early stages of young adulthood. They also fit quite consistently with the related research about self concept and self-esteem discussed earlier in this chapter.

There are many perplexities, however, that require careful study, including the matter of sex differences. The universality of the identity crisis also requires additional clarification. From the data presented in Example 11.4, it seems that not all adolescents experience an identity crisis (Erikson's views notwithstanding). Certainly the interpretation of crisis as turmoil (marked disruption of psychic processes with resultant disorganization of behavior) seems not to be tenable in light of recent research (69). Perhaps turmoil is more the outcome of the identity crisis gone wrong, although even this hypothesis requires a thorough and direct test.

Other questions are equally basic to the identity crisis theme. For example, is a crisis necessary for subsequent and maximum self-development? If it is, how intense and prolonged must the period of crisis be? Or, is the identity crisis phenomenon actually the most central task of adolescence in our society? As the reader will recognize, these questions represent conceptual dilemmas with which psychologists must deal in the search for truth about adolescent development. The necessity of a period of crisis for growth, particularly a period marked by "storm and stress," is still a matter of conjecture. Some psychologists, especially behaviorists, question whether identity formulation is the foremost developmental problem during adolescence. One authority, for example, rejects the idea that the adolescent is preoccupied with self-discovery (12). Rather, it is argued that the basic problem of adolescents in American society is gaining sufficient freedom to act autonomously while at the same time feeling clearly the consequences of their actions in order to learn better their roles in the larger social order.

The best learning has always proceeded in this way . . . one feels directly the consequences of his actions and, if necessary, modifies his actions to make these consequences beneficial. The critical problem for the adolescent in modern society is that the consequences of his actions are indirect and far in the future: thus they can have little impact on his current actions (12, Preface).

This line of thinking is clearly related to the nature of reinforcement and the extent to which reinforcements are either absent or delayed as adolescents test their skills in an ever-broadening social context. Such thinking is also relevant to the earlier discussion of locus of control (see Chapter 10) and opportunity failure, as discussed in Chapter 9. However, these phenomena are not *necessarily* incompatible with the identity crisis idea. In fact, they may reflect some of the environmental influences that contribute to identity diffusion. But the issue is largely a matter of the degree of parsimony that one wishes to achieve in explaining behavior and its causes. This idea serves to shift the discussion from conceptual dilemmas about the identity crisis phenomenon to a cluster of dilemmas about self-development in general.

SOME DILEMMAS RELATED TO SELF-DEVELOPMENT

In this section, two basic dilemmas about self-development are discussed. The first is clearly a conceptual dilemma and concerns whether the self is an objective reality suitable for psychological research (55). The second represents a mixture of philosophical and procedural dilemmas that consist of building, changing, and otherwise "educating" for self-development.

The Self: A Suitable Concept for Scientific Study?

To readers, this dilemma in question form may seem odd, if not illogical, because in the earlier discussion, text and references to psychological research have been interspersed. In other words, after basing an entire chapter about self-development on research findings, why is the picture confused by questioning the concept of self in psychological study? The reason is simple. Throughout this volume, the authors have always attempted to present the truth about psychological study as best they can. The truth is that psychologists have not developed a consensus about the meaning of self, much less perfected methods for its study that meet the standards of scientific method. They do not agree about whether the self is an object or a process. Is the self what the individual thinks it is as he describes himself according to one or another instrument? Or is self the way other people perceive and describe a person? Or is self the way a person thinks he is perceived and acted on by others (the mirror or social self)? Or is self the "self" constructed by experts from a series of psychological tests and observations to which the individual has been subjected? No one seems to agree.

Further, almost everyone who performs a study about the self seems to want to begin with a new or a modified instrument. This makes the comparison of results from one study to another difficult, if not impossible. Finally, many studies of the self are thoroughly mixed up with what is called social desirability. If one is asked to say whether he is brave, beautiful, honest, and thrifty, his answers are almost certain to be slanted toward what is socially desirable. Since it is "good" to be brave, beautiful, honest, and thrifty, the influence on a test taker is strongly toward indicating that indeed he is all these things. Thus, test takers are socially pushed toward positive self concepts.

To illustrate the absence of precision of meaning in the area of study of the self, let us consider six different notions about "self" that have been advanced by one thoughtful scholar in the field (55): (1) the self as knower whose function is to apprehend reality; (2) the self as motivator, or the entity that underlies self-assertion or self-actualization: "I must do well because it is important to me"; "I need to express my potentialities, as it is the nature of the human existence to do so"; (3) the self as an inner, private, and unique personal experience; (4) the organizing self, or the self that gives consistency to one's existence; (5) the self as a pacifier, or an adjustive mechanism that serves to maintain congruity between the self and the nonself; (6) the self as the subjective "voice of the culture," a purely social agent that views behavioral responses in terms of environmental conditions or inputs.

These meanings provide alternatives from which one can draw in order to conduct self concept research. But choice of one alternative means that the others must usually be rejected. For example, the self as motivator (2) and the self as pacifier (3) are contradictory. The former implies a concept of dynamism and growth, while the latter suggests a static condition or at least a state of minimum tension. Moreover, the self as social agent (6) implies a denial of the self as an entity; for example, behavioral consistency comes from consistency of events within the environment, and is not something that "resides" within the individual (55).

The old saying "You pays your money, you takes your choice" perhaps best summarizes this conceptual dilemma. Ordinarily, psychologists select the meaning that most nearly fits their theoretical perspective. The problem is, "Which meaning is most valid?", if in fact any of them is. The authors believe that something is to be gained by a serious study of the self. Otherwise, they would not have devoted a chapter to this topic. To deny completely the self is akin to denying our own existence. We all have feelings about what is important and what is not, what we can do and what we cannot do, what we do well and what we do not do well. These feelings, or beliefs, represent legitimate matters for psychological study, whatever their exact nature.

Anything common to almost all people demands thought and study. It will undoubtedly be some time before the conceptual complexities of research about the self are better clarified. Meanwhile, the authors find it useful to maintain the earlier distinctions concerning self and for psychologists to proceed with further study along these lines: the self concept (representing knowledge of personal attributes and effectiveness); self-esteem (self-evaluation and -acceptance along a continuum from positive to negative); and identity (awareness of one's role in relation to social groups, including ethnic, religious, political, and occupational groups). As such, the authors agree with others (for example, 102) who have explored the problems of self theory and research in greater depth. Rather than abandon vague, overgeneralized self-referent constructs such as the six discussed above, those who seek further insight into complex human behavior are better served by refinements of the six or more specific attributes (such as self-esteem).

The Dilemma of Strategies for Self-Development

Throughout this chapter it has been stressed that reactions one receives from significant others influence self-development. This means that children and youth incorporate into their self conceptions the appraisals of other people who are important to them, whose expertise is recognized, and with whom they maintain personal and "business" relationships. Several interesting studies have been conducted to demonstrate the influence of appraisal by others on both self-esteem and general self concept in children *and* adults (31, 60, 61). This evidence suggests that disapproval or approval from others exerts a measurable impact on self-esteem and self concept of ability. Other authors suggest that conditions can be set up that alter a person's view of himself or herself. These conditions include reinforcing an individual positively for behaving in ways that do not fit his existing self-image and then making public (for example, to parents and peers) the fact that such behavior occurred (61). Still other studies indicate that there is a relationship between self-concept change and both psychotherapy and educational strategies broadly designed according to self theory (83, 94). It has also been argued that bibliotherapy—a technique based on the idea that a person is influenced by what he reads—carries a strong potential for affecting self-development (37, 68). Finally, the reader must be reminded about the possible effects that expectancies held for an individual by others may exert on self-development (see Chapter 6).

The Role of Feedback

While a person normally strives to behave consistently with his concept of self, that concept is subject to change. The question is how extensive and permanent will this change be if it is based on the contrived efforts of those who work with children and youth. Perhaps more basic even than this important question is the pyramid of philosophical and procedural dilemmas that one faces in any consideration of self-concept change. This pyramid can perhaps best be represented by example.

Suppose you have good reason to believe that a child with whom you are working in school holds both a low self concept of his ability and a negative self-esteem concerning himself as a learner. The child seems to be saying to you, "I'm not very capable of learning school subjects and I feel inferior to others in my class." Should you attempt to change this state of affairs? If you should, on what grounds? Moreover, what should your goals be? If, for example, you decide that something should be done to help this child in order to promote better academic progress, and that the first priority is increased self-esteem and acceptance, how should you carry out your program for change? Immediately, we should rule out extensive psychotherapeutic measures for which one is not trained. Then, apart from this, what will you as a concerned and humanitarian teacher attempt to do?

Most teachers and college students with whom the authors have discussed this dilemma recommend ample praise and personal recognition for such a child. This encouragement, coupled with involvement in an activity (any activity) in which the child is interested and can perform adequately, they hope will improve self-esteem. In a general sense, this strategy is commendable. However, there exists the real possibility that it can lead to distortion in the way a child perceives himself.

As one authority has put it:

First, the child who realizes that his product or performance is lacking may become confused by the discrepancy between his own judgment and the feedback he is receiving. He may then alter his own judgment and standards to coincide with the feedback he has received, or he may become distrustful of the adult and discount his future pronouncements. . . . Another possible consequence of excessive praise is the establishment of the child's image of himself as infallible. The child who is lavishly approved or rewarded for any performance may have difficulty at a later time accepting the harsh reality that he, too, sometimes fails. Faced with failure, the child may become defensive and refuse to admit that his performance is lacking. He may possibly be overwhelmed by the failure and magnify it out of proportion so that it becomes incapacitating. In either event, this child will have difficulty coping with failure and turning it to his advantage as a learning experience. (67, pp. 342–343)

It might be added that the above problems are not limited to a child whose self-image is already negative; they are perhaps applicable to any child or youth. But the dilemma clearly concerns how to structure feedback so that the child is not led into self-deception and further difficulties in dealing with his environment. As a beginning step toward the resolution of this dilemma the authors recommend, first, that child workers put to use the principle of noncontingent acceptance or response-independent reinforcement (see Chapter 2). Second, research evidence exists to indicate that children generally prefer and make good use of kindly but realistic and honest appraisal of the strengths and limitations of their work (2, 73). Concrete, specific suggestions that help a child improve his performance on meaningful tasks, and praise that is sincere rather than hollow probably best serve a child's interest in the long run (67).

In short, caregivers should provide children with response-independent reinforcement—a benign climate for living and learning—that consists of good humor, fairness, concern, and goodwill or affection without undue sentimentality and a clear set of goals, along with much specific guidance (response-dependent reinforcement) for the skills the child must master to cope successfully with the world in which he lives.

"Teaching" for Self-Development

A final related dilemma concerns the efficacy of "teaching" for self-development. In recent years, a ground swell of concern has occurred about individuality among children and youth. Charges have been made that the schools are becoming progressively more depersonalized, that pressures for intellectual achievement occur at the expense of emotional adjustment, and that school disciplinary practices are unnecessarily severe. The material in Example 11.2 is relevant to the general body of educational criticism.

Perhaps because of such criticism, increasing numbers of educators and psychologists have taken up the banner of emotional education (25). The overriding goal of such education is self-acceptance and positive self-esteem. It is not implied that emotional development has not previously been taken seriously by American school personnel. On the contrary, the value of emotional development has long existed among those who identify with the mental health movement in education. With a few exceptions, however, systematic attempts at fostering self-understanding, self-acceptance, and improved human relations by way of curriculum experiences have not been made. Example 11.5 contains a description of a self-development program that exemplifies recent efforts by psychologists and educators to improve this traditional state of affairs.

11.5 Education for Young Children's Self-Development

Educators who identify broadly with humanistic psychology have found appealing a Human Development Program for very young children created by Howard Bessell and Uvaldo Palomares (5, 6). These authorities have taken the position that remedial means are not the best way to approach the many emotional problems which face adolescents and adults; remediation in their view has simply not been sufficiently effective for the solution of these emotional difficulties. Rather, Bessell and Palomares prefer to apply preventive mental health techniques during childhood, before these problems are developed. The task, as they see it, involves helping children to develop a sound emotional outlook which increases cumulatively their resistance to society's many pestilent features, including aversive human interaction in the schools. A first step in this process is to help the child overcome his fears about such things as his safety, his acceptance by others, his helplessness, and his lack of power. Thus, freedom from fear is seen as a basic prerequisite for sound learning and development.

At least three specific problems contributing to children's fears are taken by Bessell and Palomares to suggest a framework for emotional education: inadequate understanding of the cause–effect relationships in social interaction, insufficient understanding of the motives underlying human behavior, and low self-confidence. These problem areas in combination have provided the stimulus for their human development curriculum, the objectives of which include the achievement of improved (1) *social interaction* skills (understanding and accepting others), (2) *self-awareness* (insight into and acceptance of one's own feelings), and (3) *mastery* (achievement of responsible competence). Also basic to this tripartite framework are the further objectives of self-control and personal authenticity.

The medium for human development education as interpreted by Bessell and Palomares is the Magic Circle. This circular arrangement puts eight to twelve children and the teacher in a smaller (inner) circle with the remaining children seated in a larger, concentric circle. The inner circle of children is the participating body. Members of the outer circle observe. Circle membership varies from day to day as the teacher initiates topics for discussion (twenty-minute periods daily) relevant to the three main process themes. Up to six weeks are devoted in one block to a given theme. The clarification and analysis of children's feelings and perceptions take precedence over a focus on the content of children's verbalizations; consistent attempts are made, however, to help children build a more effective vocabulary for the expression of feeling. Bessell believes that younger children are not yet "at war" with themselves, as are most adults, and therefore they exude a spontaneity that sustains the activity of the Magic Circle. Bessell is also convinced that children (1) will respond favorably to opportunities for sharing in decision-making processes, (2) can assume leadership roles (for Bessell the golden age of leadership development is the period from 6 to 8 years), and (3) will help others, including the teacher, in constructive ways if only they are allowed to do so. Therefore the program is designed to shift leadership responsibility gradually from the teacher to the children. Consequently, leadership tasks may then be shared by the children. However, this shift does not begin until the primary grades. Bessell maintains that the key to successful human relations training is *involvement.* He thus suggests an equation for this purpose—*as responsibility is divided, involvement is multiplied.* In short, Bessell is convinced that to promote self-responsibility, definite opportunities for this must exist in the classroom. The Human Development Program therefore represents a semistructured effort to capitalize on children's social nature and their resources for cooperative personal assistance in order for children to achieve self-responsibility.

In this context, perhaps the most basic dilemma is whether programs such as those described in Example 11.5 should be attempted in the schools. Many questions can be raised. For example, is there a danger that contrived efforts to promote positive self-development through organized curricula will be perceived as artificial by students, and perhaps thus become self defeating? What should be the content of education for self-development? How can the validity of such planned programs be tested? Who will conduct these programs and how extensively must "teaching" personnel be trained?

These are but a few of the questions to be asked about expanding the school curriculum to incorporate self-development education. Of course, such expansion

need not represent a shift of emphasis away from academics to emotional adjustment. It is true, however, that the issue can too easily be translated into a false either–or dichotomy: Either one educates for emotional adjustment or he educates for intellectual excellence. For the authors, experience cannot be this easily compartmentalized. Moreover, intellectual development and emotional development are too intimately related to divorce one from the other. It is both legitimate and desirable, however, to question the validity and value of structured approaches to emotional education.

Although extensive research evidence about this question cannot be marshaled at this time, the few available reports indicate that self-understanding and teacher–student relationships can be improved through relatively systematic human relations training (33, 71). Generally, these programs are addressed broadly toward the study of human motivation. They involve the hypothesis that, as one gains in his understanding of human behavior, he is also likely to gain in self-understanding. Moreover, the idea that gains in self-understanding are related to increased acceptance, both of self and of others, is usually reflected in such programs.

Much additional research is needed to determine such relationships. It seems reasonable to suggest that opportunities for the study of human behavior are desirable on the grounds of general relevance, quite apart from specific and valued mental health outcomes. It is clear to the authors, however, that much opposition exists, some of it extreme, in relation to any sort of "emotional education." For example, some parents known to the authors cry out in fear of thought control, brainwashing, and other indications of subversion in the schools. Others object on philosophical grounds: The schools, they argue, are for academic skill development and the transmission of subject matter knowledge, nothing else. Still others respond with suspended judgment until more "hard" research data about emotional education have accumulated. The authors have also noted extremism to the point of foolishness among parents (and teachers) who believe that the cultivation of mental health is the foremost responsibility of the schools.

The readers are encouraged to discuss these issues among themselves and keep abreast of new developments as they occur. Meanwhile, the authors conclude this section by noting that educational strategies for self-development are appearing with increasing frequency in the professional literature. The full implications of their use remain to be seen.

Summary

The notion of *self* possesses compelling face validity. All of us know that we *are*, we *think*, we *act*, and we consider our thoughts, our actions, and our *being*. However, research about self is often of poor quality, and experts have not agreed about whether, for example, self is object or self is process.

Adolescence, a period when human beings have reached the Piagetian stage of formal operations, is considered by many to be the period when the self must be fully realized, and when the question "Who am I?" must be answered satisfactorily lest later development be handicapped.

Aspects of self-development follow. (1) Self-esteem: How well or how poorly does one regard oneself? (2) Differentiation: How well does one distinguish himself from others, and to what degree is he self-sufficient? (3) Complexity: Is one's notion of the self complex, as in

"girl," "student," "tennis player," "date," "good looking," "short of sense of humor"; or simple, where "I am female" is the only dimension considered. (4) Consistency: Predictability from one time to another. (5) Stability: Does one, for example, vary from day to day in his self-esteem, one day despising himself, the next day esteeming himself highly (this concept is akin to consistency, but is related more to moodiness and temporary fluctuation than to a stable or an unstable personal characteristic)? (6) Accuracy may be another dimension: How well does one's notion of himself or herself fit with the judgments of others to whom one is well known? From research evidence, a reasonably close fit seems desirable.

The self is a learned concept. High self-esteem seems to result when parents are concerned, warm, set clear limits, employ praise as a major control technique, and allow wide latitude to the child as he pursues approval goals. Particularly for males, good physique and early physical maturity seem to be associated with positive self concept and social behavior. In middle age, however, the advantage of early maturers over late maturers may be partially lost.

Until fairly recently, minority group status has been found to be associated with self-debasement, but more recent studies, if anything, suggest the opposite. This may be due to such social changes as racial and ethnic pride, as in "Black is beautiful." However, much careful research is needed to clarify the relationship between self-development and ethnicity.

In general, positive self-esteem is associated with success in school and the peer social group. Advantaged girls (college students) may experience more difficulty in achieving identity—the successful answer to the question "Who am I?"—than advantaged males. This problem is likely a function of the social system, wherein females are not given full recognition for competence and are often forced to choose between career and marriage. Thus, happy identity formation—a sense of personal worth and purpose within today's Western society—may be more difficult for girls than for boys.

The authors believe that investigation of self-development must continue, and urge refinements of research methods. Even with the ambiguities and downright inferiority of much research and writing in the area, they believe that "education in positive development of the self" should be continued in homes, schools, and communities.

REFERENCES

1. Alessi, D. F., and W. A. Anthony. Uniformity of children's attitudes toward physical disabilities. *Exceptional Children*, 1969, *35*, 543–545.
2. Anderson, R. H., and E. R. Steadman. Pupils' reactions to a reporting system. *Elementary School Journal*, 1950, *51*, 136–142.
3. Ausubel, D. P. *Theory and problems of child development*. New York: Grune & Stratton, 1958.
4. Baker, F. Measures of ego identity: A multitrait multimethod validation. *Educational and Psychological Measurement*, 1971, *31*, 165–173.
5. Bessell, H. The content is the medium: The confidence is the message. *Psychology Today*, 1968, *2*, 32–35ff.
6. Bessell, H., and U. H. Palomares. *Methods in human development*. San Diego, Calif.: Human Development Training Institute, 1967.
7. Block, J. Ego identity, role variability, and adjustment. *Journal of Consulting Psychology*, 1961, *25*, 392–397.
8. Bronson, G. W. Identity diffusion in late adolescents. *Journal of Abnormal and Social Psychology*, 1959, *59*, 414–417.
9. Caplin, M. D. The relationship between self concept and academic achievement. *Journal of Experimental Education*, 1969, *37*, 13–16.
10. Carlson, R. Stability and change in the adolescent's self-image. *Child Development*, 1965, *36*, 659–666.
11. Carpenter, T. R., and T. V. Busse. Development of self concept in Negro and White welfare children. *Child Development*, 1969, *40*, 935–939.
12. Coleman, J. S. *Adolescents and the schools*. New York: Basic Books, 1965.
13. Connell, D. M., and J. E. Johnson. Relationship between sex role identification and self esteem in early adolescents. *Developmental Psychology*, 1970, *3*, 268.
14. Constantinople, A. An Eriksonian measure of personality development in college students. *Developmental Psychology*, 1969, *1*, 357–372.
15. Coopersmith, S. *The antecedents of self esteem*. San Francisco: Freeman, 1967.
16. Cross, H. J., and J. G. Allen. Ego identity status, adjustment, and academic achievement. *Journal of Consulting and Clinical Psychology*, 1970, *34*, 288.
17. Dixon, J. C. Development of self-recognition. *Journal of Genetic Psychology*, 1957, *91*, 251–256.
18. Douvan, E., and J. Adelson. *The adolescent experience*. New York: Wiley, 1966.
19. Dreyer, A. S., and D. Haupt. Self-evaluation in young children. *Journal of Genetic Psychology*, 1966, *108*, 185–197.
20. Engel, M., and W. J. Raine. A method for the measurement of the self-concept of children in the third grade. *Journal of Genetic Psychology*, 1963, *102*, 125–137.
21. English, H. B., and A. C. English. *A comprehensive dictionary of psychological and psychoanalytical terms*. New York: McKay, 1958.

22. Epstein, R., and S. S. Komorita. Self esteem, success–failure, and locus of control in Negro children. *Developmental Psychology,* 1971, *4,* 2–8.

23. Erikson, E. H. *Childhood and society* (2nd ed.). New York: Norton, 1963.

24. Erikson, E. H. *Identity: Youth and crisis.* New York: Norton, 1968.

25. Evans, E. D. *Contemporary influences in early childhood education.* New York: Holt, Rinehart and Winston, 1971.

26. Faterson, H. F., and H. A. Witkin. Longitudinal study of development of the body concept. *Developmental Psychology,* 1970, *2,* 429–438.

27. Felker, D. W. Relationship between self-concept, body build, and perception of father's interest in sports in boys. *Research Quarterly,* 1968, *39,* 513–517.

28. Felker, D. W. The relationship between anxiety, self ratings, and ratings by others in fifth-grade children. *Journal of Genetic Psychology,* 1969, *115,* 81–86.

29. Felker, D. W., and R. S. Kay. Self concept, sports interests, sports participation, and body type of seventh- and eighth-grade boys. *Journal of Psychology,* 1971, *78,* 223–228.

30. Garvey, R. Self concept and success in student teaching. *Journal of Teacher Education,* 1970, *21,* 357–361.

31. Gergen, K. J. *The concept of self.* New York: Holt, Rinehart and Winston, 1971.

32. Goldschmid, M. L. The relation of conservation of emotional and environmental aspects of development. *Child Development,* 1968, *39,* 787–802.

33. Griggs, J. W., and M. W. Bonney. Relationship between 'causal' orientation and acceptance of others, 'self-ideal self' congruency, and mental health changes for 4th and 5th grade children. *Journal of Educational Research,* 1970, *63,* 471–477.

34. Guggenheim, F. Self-esteem and achievement expectations for white and Negro children. *Journal of Projective Techniques and Personality Assessment,* 1969, *33,* 63–71.

35. Hall, C. S., and G. Lindzey. *Theories of personality.* New York: Wiley, 1957.

36. Hall, M. M., and W. G. Findley. Ability grouping: Helpful or harmful? *Phi Delta Kappan,* 1971, *52,* 556–557.

37. Harvey, R. C., and R. J. Denby. Life at an early-age: Nourishing self-concept in the classroom. Washington, D. C.: National Clearinghouse on the Teaching of English, 1970.

38. Heath, D. H. *Explorations of maturity.* New York: Appleton, 1965.

39. Hess, R., and D. Croft. *Teachers of young children.* Boston: Houghton Mifflin, 1972

40. Johnson, P. A., and J. R. Staffieri. Stereotypic affective properties of personal names and somatotypes in children. *Developmental Psychology,* 1971, *5,* 176.

41. Jones, J. G., and L. Grieneeks. Measures of self perception as predictors of scholastic achievement. *Journal of Educational Research,* 1970, *63,* 201–203.

42. Jones, J. G., and R. W. Strowig. Adolescent identity and self perception as predictors of scholastic achievement. *Journal of Educational Research,* 1968, *62,* 78–82.

43. Jones, M. C. The later careers of boys who were early- or late-maturing. *Child Development,* 1957, *28,* 113–128.

44. Jones, M. C., and N. Bayley. Physical maturing among boys as related to behavior. *Journal of Educational Psychology,* 1950, *41,* 129–148.

45. Jones, M. C., and P. H. Mussen. Self conceptions, motivations, and interpersonal attitudes of early- and late-maturing girls. *Child Development,* 1958, *29,* 491–501.

46. Jorgensen, E. C., and R. J. Howell. Changes in self, ideal-self correlations for ages 8 through 18. *Journal of Social Psychology,* 1969, *79,* 63–67.

47. Katz, P., and E. Zigler. Self-image disparity: A developmental approach. *Journal of Personality and Social Psychology,* 1967, *5,* 186–195.

48. Kohlberg, L. A cognitive-developmental analysis of children's sex role concepts

and attitudes. In E. E. Maccoby (ed.) *The development of sex differences.* Stanford, Calif.: Stanford University Press, 1966, 82-173.

49. Kubiniec, C. M. The relative efficiency of various dimensions of self concept in predicting academic achievement. *American Educational Research Journal,* 1970, *7,* 321-336.

50. Lipsitt, L. P. A self concept scale for children and its relationship to the Children's form of the Manifest Anxiety Scale. *Child Development,* 1958, *29,* 463–473.

51. Long, B. H., and E. H. Henderson. Self-social concepts of disadvantaged school beginners. *Journal of Genetic Psychology,* 1968, *113,* 41–51.

52. Long, B. H., and E. H. Henderson. Social schemata of school beginners: Some demographic correlates. *Merrill-Palmer Quarterly,* 1970, *16,* 305–324.

53. Long, B. H., E. H. Henderson, and R. C. Ziller. Developmental changes in the self-concept during middle childhood. *Merrill-Palmer Quarterly,* 1967, *13,* 201–214.

54. Long, B. H., F. H. Henderson, and R. C. Ziller. Self-ratings on the semantic differential: content versus response set. *Child Development,* 1968, *39,* 647–656.

55. Lowe, C. The self-concept: Fact or artifact? *Psychological Bulletin,* 1961, *58,* 325–336.

56. Ludwig, D., and M. Maehr. Changes in self concept and stated behavioral preferences. *Child Development,* 1967, *38,* 453–468.

57. Marcia, J. E. Development and validation of ego identity status. *Journal of Personality and Social Psychology,* 1966, *3,* 551–558.

58. Marcia, J. E., and M. L. Friedman. Ego identity status in college women. *Journal of Personality,* 1970, *38,* 249–263.

59. Maw, W. H., and E. W. Maw. Self concepts of high and low curiosity boys. *Child Development,* 1970, *41,* 123–129.

60. McCandless, B. R. *Adolescents: Behavior and development.* Hinsdale, Ill.: Dryden, 1970.

61. McCandless, B. R. *Children: Behavior and development* (2nd ed.). New York: Holt, Rinehart and Winston, 1967.

62. Meadow, K. P. Self image, family climate, and deafness. *Social Forces,* 1969, *47,* 428–438.

63. Meltzer, M. L., and B. Levy. Self esteem in a public school. *Psychology in the Schools,* 1970, *7,* 14–20.

64. Mullener, N., and J. D. Laird. Some developmental changes in the organization of self-evaluation. *Developmental Psychology,* 1971, *5,* 233–236.

65. Mussen, P. H., and M. C. Jones. Self conceptions, motivations, and interpersonal attitudes of late- and early-maturing boys. *Child Development,* 1957, *28,* 243–256.

66. Mussen, P. H., and M. C. Jones. The behavior-inferred motivations of late- and early-maturing boys. *Child Development,* 1958, *29,* 61–67.

67. Nardine, F. E. The development of competence. In G. S. Lesser (ed.) *Psychology and educational practice.* Glenview, Ill.: Scott, Foresman, 1971, 336–356.

68. Newton, E. S. Bibliotherapy in the development of minority group self concept. *Journal of Negro Education,* 1969, *38,* 257–265.

69. Offer, D. *The psychological world of the teenager.* New York: Basic Books, 1969.

70. Ogletree, E. J. Ability grouping: Its effects on attitudes. *Journal of Social Psychology,* 1970, *82,* 137–138.

71. Ojemann, R. Basic approaches to mental health: The human development program at the State University of Iowa. *Personnel and Guidance Journal,* 1958, *36,* 198–206.

72. Oskamp, S. Relationship of self concepts to international attitudes. *Journal of Social Psychology,* 1968, *76,* 31–36.

73. Page, E. B. Teacher comments and student performance. *Journal of Educational Psychology,* 1958, *49,* 173–181.

74. Pederson, D. M., and G. H. Stanford. Personality correlates of children's self

esteem and parental identification. *Psychological Reports,* 1969, *25,* 41–42.

75. Piers, E. V., and D. B. Harris. Age and other correlates of self concept in children. *Journal of Educational Psychology,* 1964, *55,* 91–95.

76. Pringle, M. The emotional and social adjustment of physically handicapped children: A review of the literature published between 1928 and 1962. *Educational Research,* 1964, *6,* 207–215.

77. Purkey, W. W. *Self concept and school achievement.* Englewood Cliffs, N. J.: Prentice-Hall, 1970.

78. Resnick, H. Vocational crystallization and self esteem in college students. *Journal of Counseling Psychology,* 1970, *17,* 465–467.

79. Richardson, S. A., and P. Emerson. Race and physical handicap in children's preference for other children. *Human Relations,* 1970, *23,* 31–36.

80. Richardson, S. A., and J. Royce. Race and physical handicap in children's preference for other children. *Child Development,* 1968, *32,* 467–480.

81. Ringness, T. A. Self concept of children of low, average, and high intelligence. *American Journal of Mental Deficiency,* 1961, *65,* 543–561.

82. Rogers, C. R. *Client-centered therapy.* Boston: Houghton Mifflin, 1951.

83. Rogers, C. R., and R. F. Dymond (eds.). *Psychotherapy and personality change.* Chicago: University of Chicago Press, 1954.

84. Rosenberg, M. *Society and the adolescent self image.* Princeton, N. J.: Princeton University Press, 1965.

85. Sears, R. R. Relation of early socialization experiences to self-concepts and gender role in middle childhood. *Child Development,* 1970, *41,* 267–290.

86. Shaw, M. C. Underachievement: Useful construct or misleading illusion? *Psychology in the Schools,* 1968, *5,* 41–46.

87. Sheldon, W. H. *The varieties of human physique: An introduction to constitutional psychology.* New York: Harper & Row, 1940.

88. Sheperd, C. W., Jr. Childhood chronic illness and visual motor perceptual development. *Exceptional Children,* 1969, *36,* 39–42.

89. Soares, A. T., and L. M. Soares. Self perceptions of culturally disadvantaged children. *American Educational Research Journal,* 1969, *6,* 31–45.

90. Stehbens, J. A., and D. L. Carr. Perceptions of parental attitudes by students varying in intellectual ability and educational efficiency. *Psychology in the Schools,* 1970, *7,* 67–73.

91. Stevenson, H. W. Studies of racial awareness in young children. In W. W. Hartup and N. L. Smothergill (eds.) *The young child.* Washington, D. C.: National Association for the Education of Young Children, 1967, 206–213.

92. Tocco, T. S., and C. M. Bridges, Jr. Mother-child self-concept transmission in Florida Model Follow Through participants. Paper delivered at American Educational Research Association Meeting, New York, February, 1971.

93. Trowbridge, N. T. Effects of socio-economic class on the self-concept of children. *Psychology in the Schools,* 1970, *7,* 304–306.

94. Trowbridge, N. T. Self concept of disadvantaged and advantaged children. Paper read at the American Educational Research Association Meeting, Minneapolis, March, 1971.

95. Waterman, A. S., and C. K. Waterman. The relationship between ego identity status and satisfaction with college. *Journal of Educational Research,* 1970, *64,* 165–168.

96. Waterman, A. S., and C. K. Waterman. A longitudinal study of changes in ego identity status during the freshman year at college. *Developmental Psychology,* 1971, *5,* 167–173.

97. Wattenberg, W. W., and C. Clifford. Relation of self concepts to beginning achievement in reading. *Child Development,* 1964, *35,* 461–467.

98. Weatherley, D. Self-perceived rate of physical maturation and personality in

late adolescence. *Child Development,* 1964, *35,* 1197–1210.

99. White, W. F., and B. O. Richmond. Perception of self and peers by economically deprived black and advantaged white 5th graders. *Perceptual and Motor Skills,* 1970, *30,* 533–534.

100. Williams, R., and S. Cole. Self concept and school adjustment. *Personnel and Guidance Journal,* 1968, *46,* 478–481.

101. Williams, R. L., and H. Byars. Negro self-esteem in a transitional society: Tennessee self concept scale. *Personnel and Guidance Journal,* 1968, *47,* 120–125.

102. Wylie, R. C. The present status of self theory. In E. F. Borgatta and W. W. Lambert (eds.) *Handbook of personality and research.* Chicago: Rand McNally, 1968, 728–787.

103. Wylie, R. C. *The self concept.* Lincoln, Nebr.: University of Nebraska Press, 1961.

104. Zirkel, P. A. Self concept and the "disadvantage" of ethnic group membership and mixture. *Review of Educational Research,* 1971, *41,* 211–225.

105. Zirkel, P. A., and E. G. Moses. Self concept and ethnic group membership among public school students. *American Educational Research Journal,* 1971, *8,* 253–265.

12 Human Development and the Schools: Some Contemporary Problems

America's schools are its most ambitious institutions for the young. The stage for a child's life is set in the home, but for almost all children the play is acted out in school for a crucial formative period of their lives: the years between ages 5 or 6 and 16, usually even older. More importantly than in the family, school is the place where the child and the youth test their formal competencies.

The paramount traditional function of school is to take a youngster with a given level of intellect and cognitive efficiency, who has basic if untrained capacities for inquiry and problem solving, and to cultivate this intellect. Intellectual cultivation includes providing the child's intellect with ample "mental furniture" and a honing of cognitive processes so that, at age 16 or later, a youth can go forth into society capable of economic self-sufficiency, can contribute to the society in which he lives,

and, over all, can enjoy and appreciate the process.

For at least the last forty years, much more than intellectual honing and cognitive storage has been expected of the schools. As American society has grown more and more complex, urban, and technical, schools have been expected to carry more and more of the responsibility for overall social and educational development. The authors know of courses, enterprises, and projects within different schools directed toward all of the following goals; the list is only partial.

1. Transmission of the culture.
2. Skills teaching.
3. Improvement in study habits and problem analysis.
4. Improvement in general self concept and self-esteem.
5. Sex and family life education.
6. Physical fitness and athletic skill.

426

7. Driver education.
8. Home making.
9. Good citizenship.
10. Good race relations.
11. Development of creativity.
12. Vocational training for both males and females.
13. Ethics in human life (related to moral development).
14. Appreciation and improvement of the ecology.
15. Mental health.
16. Social sensitivity.
17. Habit and function improvement (for example, remedial reading and speech).

This is a staggering burden for any social institution, and it is obvious that all such expectations cannot be fulfilled. The schools, even for such traditional functions as (1) and (2) in the list, often fail. There is currently much cynicism and disappointment about schools, much of it well deserved. Particularly under attack is the concept of education as an integral state function, and of education as a commercial commodity rather than "a ticket to a happier life" (65).

In this chapter the authors discuss the structure and function of United States schools, treat some of the pressing contemporary problems in American education, and devote a section to improved human relations in the schools. Except in passing comments, colleges and universities are not included; the concentration is on elementary, middle, junior high, and high schools.

STRUCTURE AND FUNCTION OF AMERICAN SCHOOLS

Structure and function are necessarily linked to each other. For example, if an individual's eye is egg shaped along the horizontal axis, the person functions nearsightedly or myopically; if it is egg shaped along the vertical axis, he is farsighted or presbyopic; if his eyeballs are round, he probably possesses 20–20 vision. In this respect, social institutions are like individuals. To at least a partial degree, both function according to the dictates of their structure.

Structure of Public Schools
Around the world, the schools of all nations are organized somewhere on a continuum between completely centralized and completely decentralized. In many nations, the schools are completely centralized, and a common structure is imposed on all schools. Overall school management, including financing, is done by the federal or national or some other form of central government agency. Curricula are quite uniform; texts are the same across the whole country; qualifications, promotions, and tenure policies for teachers are set at the site of national government; and examinations for students over content (what they have learned and how well) are written, administered, and evaluated by national agencies. In the United States, in line with our democratic tradition (which includes a suspicion of central control), school structure is decentralized. Control rests within the community (we shall see that there are exceptions to this statement in both practice and spirit).

Communities are legally designated as school districts. There may be many districts within a county, an entire county may make up one school district, or a school system may include a given town or city. In some states, there is relatively strong central state control over all the districts and systems within the state; but there is no direct federal control over education.

Hypothetically, the citizens of a school district determine the nature and style of its schools, but in a republican manner through elected representatives (the board of education). The superintendent of schools is the citizen–board agent. The superintendent of schools appoints principals of schools, who are responsible for the operation of the individual units within the total school systems. There is usually a state superintendent of schools. In some states, the state superintendent is elected; in others, he is appointed. Typically, he influences school policy and practice more through moral and fiscal suasion than through direct legal suasion. He has only weak power over individual boards of education or superintendents, although he can advise and administer and interpret statewide dicta; he also typically possesses influence in the sense that he can disburse or withhold state funds for school districts, or Federal funds delegated by the Federal government to the states for distribution to the schools across the state.

At the Federal level, there is a very large bureaucracy, the Department of Health, Education and Welfare, the head of which is a cabinet member and the administrator of which is the commissioner of education, who is a political appointee of the president of the United States. Traditionally, the commissioner of education has had little power; since the mid to late 1950s, however, his power has been rapidly extended as he and his government branch, the United States Office of Education, have been given more monies, and Federal aid to education has become a *fait accompli*. Organizational matters about education within the Federal government are changing so rapidly

at the time this book is being written that the authors will attempt no summary of affairs at the moment, nor will they attempt to predict the future. Suffice it to say that Americans are currently preoccupied, confused, and concerned over the education of their children (including its effectiveness and cost) and that the pressure on educators at all levels, from classroom teachers to the U. S. Commissioner of Education, is indeed intense. The role of the National Institute of Education is developing.

However, the basic principle of United States public education is local control. This fits well with the historic origins of American schools. Historically, in our rural and small town past, school districts were small, communities were quite homogeneous, and each citizen knew what was going on; there was no vast body of professional educators. Today, school districts may be as large as the Los Angeles or the New York City boards of education. Many subcommunities within these vast enterprises believe that their interests are not being served by so centralized a school structure, and there is keen agitation for a return to the community school. When, for example, a poor Puerto Rican or Chicano or Black community (a consumer group) demands control over its local elementary, middle or junior high, or senior high, school, intense social disequilibrium can result. The conflict of forces often involves a relatively liberal teachers' union in direct opposition to the members of a minority group community whose welfare they sincerely believe they should serve. But if the teachers listen to the wishes of the members of the community, they are likely to lose their jobs in favor of people from the same background as the bulk of the members of the community. For example, a WASP or a Jewish teacher or principal is not unlikely to face displacement by a Black, an American-Indian, or a Chicano teacher or principal, sometimes regardless of the merits of either. This issue is discussed in greater detail later in the treatment of race relations. In any event, in many communities there is a power struggle in which almost everyone, currently, seems to be getting hurt, with the children perhaps losing most of all.

To conclude this section on structure of schools, American schools are relatively decentralized, although they become monolithic and huge for some large urban systems. One by-product of community control and decentralization may be a reduction in school quality to the lowest common denominator of community opinion and belief. School boards, administrators, and principals seek to displease no one. Thus they may eschew controversy, innovation, experiment, creativity, and freedom in favor of a bland mediocrity and blanketing authoritarianism that, in the long run, performs a disservice to all (78, 106). We will see some effects of this state of affairs in later sections of the chapter.

The alternative, of course, is centralized school structure. But in such structure, local community interests are likely to be lost; and centralized school organization seems to lead to an elitist school program that is even more disadvantageous to the majority of school children than our current decentralized structure. There is probably an alternative toward the middle, which consists of nationally set standards of excellence and accountability, but standards with sufficient latitude that community interests can be served. Except for private and parochial schools, American students have little choice but

to attend a conventional public school of the nature just described; and their parents have little choice but to send their children to such a school. Some innovative American plans are on their way at the time this book is being written. Other countries provide more latitude. For example, Denmark pays the bill when any set of twenty parents comes up with a reasonable proposal for schooling.

Private and Parochial Schools

Alternatives to public education are available to American parents and their children, usually at a cost. Parochial schools are religious schools, and the largest number of parochial schools is operated by the Roman Catholic Church. The basic organization of parochial schools is not dramatically different from that of public schools, except that control is perhaps more centralized, and is typically religious rather than professional. Money seems currently to be the central problem for both public and parochial schools, and the nature of their interrelations and sharing of community resources is, and for a long time has been, a matter of intense controversy. Since the authors have no answer to how the problems can be settled, they will not even venture a suggestion. The authors state, timidly (because the area is so sensitive and their own expertness in the matter limited), that they favor religious independence in the public schools, because public schools are designed for all; at the same time, they want every American child and youth to get the best possible education across the board.

Private schools fall into profit and nonprofit categories. Among the latter are many interesting "free schools," set up by parents who are discontented with both the quality and the traditionalism of existing public and parochial schools. In time, we may learn much from these free schools. Their proliferation, the authors believe, is an encouraging sign of growth of thought and concern about education in American life. Among these schools, however, are many (most of them in the South) designed to segregate children. Still others are chaotic, mismanaged sites of conflict among zealous parents and teachers (often untrained to provide basic skills instruction), who cannot agree on the goals they desire for children.

In short, the for-profit schools range from well-established, rich, usually very conventional schools, such as some of the prep and day schools, to struggling enterprises set up by someone who has an idea—sometimes a good one, sometimes very far out in a seemingly non-constructive way—about how children and youth should be educated. For one fascinating account of a free private school, see (86).

Private schools are a mixed bag, and no overall judgment can be made about them. Since this is intended as a general book and since the data are not very complete, neither will parochial schools be further discussed. (Interested readers are referred to 87 for a discussion of Catholic education in America.)

Function of Schools

Today, almost everyone agrees on at least two functions of schools for American children. First, we agree that schools should teach the skills necessary to survive in American life, such as clear speech, fluent reading, correct expressive writing, and proficiency with numbers. We also agree that children should emerge from their school years with a knowledge of United States and world history, English literature, and so on. This function the authors call *skills training–cultural trans-*

mission. Its implementation is a basic part of all curricula. About the specifics of the content of the curriculum, there is disagreement. About whether the curriculum should include provision for communication and numbers skills and a degree of cultural sophistication, there is no serious disagreement.

The second function of schools lends itself to more dispute. The authors call it the *actualization* function. No school, it is said by those who support this function, has a right to provide a child with anything less than the very best or better than he can obtain in his own home. For instance, in accordance with the above list, schools should enhance students' self-esteem and social development, should help them find joy in life, should teach them to enjoy playing to the same degree that they know how to read history, and should broaden their horizons of thought, including critical and appreciative abilities. A child or a youth should complete each day, week, or term of school more self fulfilled than when he began it. Critics of this aspect of education often call *actualization* activities frills. Its proponents, notably the humanists, maintain that unless actualization is present, formal skills training is likely not to succeed and, while a degree of cultural transmission may occur, cultural *appreciation* will not.

There is a wave of current dissatisfaction with the structure and function of American public and parochial schools. The structure is denounced as promoting authoritarianism and perpetuating the worst of the lower-middle-class ethic (grubby materialism, absolutist and rigid morality, and so on). School function is denounced as being ineffective in both its skills-training and cultural-transmission function and its actualization function. Many cry, "Our children and youth are neither learning to read *nor* becoming self fulfilled." Others say that the conservative, nurturant, "female" nature of the schools is such that competence is rewarded for neither girls nor boys (and particularly the former), while boys are robbed of their initiative, independence, and autonomy (in short, their manhood) (78, 116). Certainly, the achievement level and pupil morale within inner-city (ghetto) schools is a national disgrace, and our school dropout rate of about one-third of United States children and youth looms as a national disaster. Conventional school emphasis on obedience, orderliness, and tight scheduling has not worked well, and it is clear that we must look for new ideas.

Decentralized control such as that in the United States will permit only slow change in the schools (106), but the authors believe that the current ferment at all levels of society will result in such growth, because, basically, Americans love, believe in, and are very idealistic about their schools. Certainly the dream of universal public education is a magnificent one.

The Role of Psychology

Psychology and psychologists can be useful in schools in that, within the discipline, much information has been gathered about facilitating both traditional (skills training, conventional teaching) and humanistic or actualization goals of education. From behaviorism and cognitive developmental psychology (see Chapter 2) come promising theories about how children learn and about how their cognitive processes (so important in schooling) develop. Research workers and practitioners within behaviorism and humanism (particularly) have developed many methods for providing settings and techniques for more efficient and functional learning. It has been demonstrated again and again that behavior in school settings *is* malleable and that children's behavior and attitudes *can* be altered by applying learning principles and modern teaching–learning strategies.

From humanism and, perhaps, from psychodynamic psychology (as well as from behaviorism) come many guiding principles for promoting the actualization side of schooling, such as improving human relations, enhancing self-esteem, increasing internality of locus of control, and coping with impulsivity. These, too, have been tested with promising results.

Psychologists, the authors believe, have much to offer education. We can start by playing a more effective role in initial teacher training and later in-service training. We can continue by serving as participant observers (for example, as school psychologists) within the schools, and we can, the authors think, be helpful to school people and students for the whole range of educational goals from skills training and engineering through to actualization–humanism.

Implementation

The authors end this section by referring to two general principles of teaching and learning: organized, systematic (yet flexible) presentation strategies and response-dependent positive reinforcement (see Chapter 2). They believe that an application of these principles is desirable for the achievement of most formal aspects of schooling, such as skills training. Teacher skill in reinforcing successful pupil efforts while de-emphasizing less successful or maladaptive responses is, in the authors' opinion, a hallmark of good instruction. So also is skill in the efficient, coherent organization and communication of subject matter content and materials for basic skill development. This organizational–communication ability is especially important for convergent learning outcomes and time and time again appears as a factor in effective teaching (42).

The importance of informal approaches to learning cannot be denied, particularly with pupils capable of much independent learning. It is true that learning experiences can be overly structured and can thus become inflexible for meeting individual differences. Neither is it denied that there is a place for negative reinforcement or "punishments" if they are mild, informational, and occur in the natural context of teacher–pupil exchange, such as negative verbal instruction ("No. That is incorrect. Would you like some suggestions for improvement?" or, "You are nearly right, but this is the way it should have been."). Finally, it is hazardous to use response-dependent reinforcement only to obtain a quiet, orderly classroom at the expense of behavior related to academic competence. It has been shown, however, that such reinforcement *is* effective in securing control of classroom behavior, so that pupils are reasonably orderly, quietly efficient, and cooperative, while at the same time showing signs of happiness and high morale (84).

Human actualization is a more diffuse, unspecifiable matter than skills competence or cultural knowledge. Actualization consists of being happy, creative, or interested and enthusiastic rather than bored and passive or restless. To promote human actualization, the authors believe that significant adults in the child's or the youth's life need to provide a good bit of response-independent reinforcement— rewards to the student simply for being himself, quite aside from anything he may have done at the moment. Attitudes and behavior that convey humor, fair-

ness, concern and interest, and liking for people seemingly are the best of the response-independent reinforcements. In addition, a wealth of varied opportunities for exploration, discussion, and synthesis in a climate relatively free of pressure for achievement and teacher evaluation is recommended.

Concluding Remarks

American schools are decentralized and are hypothetically under community control. In some communities (large cities, for example), a monolithic and authoritarian structure nonetheless results, and the needs of important parts of the community, such as prejudiced-against minorities, may be neglected or even contravened.

Narrowly based community control, on the other hand, often results in reducing the schools to the lowest and (in the short run) safest common denominator of skill and culture. Such control is particularly likely in smaller, homogeneous communities, the authors believe. They think community control is better than central control, but they believe that important perspectives including standards for minima and for accountability may well emerge from a stronger central government role than now exists in the United States.

The two functions of schools about which most citizens agree are the *skills training–cultural transmission* function and the *actualization* function. The latter function, vaguer and more subject to human values, is often open to dispute. On the other hand, education in *living*—in self-fulfillment—is very possibly more important than possession of all the technical and cultural skills in the world.

CONTEMPORARY PROBLEMS

In this section, some of the major problems that are straining both the structure and the functions of the schools are discussed.

School Underachievement and School Dropouts

Few will deny that personal achievement is highly valued in American society. In fact, some observers (for example, 17) report that children's intellectual achievement is the prime concern of American parents. If this is true and if we also consider the value placed on academics by American teachers, it is not surprising that school underachievement among the young is a major source of worry for many adults. Perhaps even more alarming for many adults is the exodus from the schools by large numbers of youth prior to high school graduation. Not all adults, of course, and certainly not all children and youth, are bothered much by these problems. Even some prospective teachers in the authors' classes frequently argue that there is little, if any, relationship between school achievement and post-school success. Certainly some persons have had marked success in life without a background of complete, formal schooling. But, in general, the relationship is strong between amount of education and eventual income, social mobility across generations, political participation, further schooling options, and the like (75). In fact, a recent and elaborate review of studies concerned with these relationships is concluded by this statement: "The evidence is overwhelming in support of the proposition that the post-school opportunity and performance of a pupil are related directly to his educational attainment" (74, p, 14).*

*In contrast, however, the idea that *quality* of schooling is positively related to academic achievement and adult income level is facing serious challenge as this book goes to press. See C. Jencks *et al. Inequality: A reassessment of the effect of family and schooling in America.* New York: Basic Books, 1972.

With this in mind, we examine some factors associated with the school achievement and dropout phenomena, including a reference to efforts that have been made by psychologists and educators to combat the negative effects that frequently accompany poor school performance.

School Underachievement

Most parents and teachers think of underachievement as failure by a pupil to "work up to his potential." Attempts by psychologists to reach an operational definition of underachievement also imply this view. That is, the most widely used definition of underachievement is based on a discrepancy model: the degree of difference between predicted achievement, based on a measure of scholastic aptitude, and actual classroom achievement, as measured by achievement tests or teachers' grades (113). Accordingly, an underachiever is defined as a pupil who performs significantly less well in school than would be predicted from his performance on measures of learning ability or intelligence. On the basis of such a definition, the incidence of underachievement at the high school level has been reported at 26 percent of those students who measure average or above in intelligence (132). This is probably a conservative estimate.

It should be noted that several authorities (for example, 131) are critical of a discrepancy model approach to underachievement. The authors believe, however, that sufficient evidence exists to indicate that underachievement is a *fact*, not simply an *artifact*, of psychological and educational measurement. The evidence is an accumulation of many studies, which include studies designed to examine the onset and the antecedents of underachievement, personality characteristics of underachievers, and ways to assist underachievers toward improved school performance. It should also be pointed out that a predominant number of studies has been made of bright, underachieving males. The reasons are at least fourfold: (1) The discrepancy between high scholastic aptitude and low classroom achievement is more readily apparent among bright students. (2) The low utilization of intellectual resources by individuals whose potential for making contributions to society is high seems especially disturbing to many adults. (3) A failure to utilize one's own potential is often implicated in mental health problems, at least in theories based on the idea of self-actualization. (4) Underachievement is more frequently observed among males than females.

Onset and Antecedents of Underachievement. Longitudinal studies of underachievement are rare. Limited evidence suggests that the pattern can be detected as early as the third grade for boys, and the fifth grade for girls—perhaps even earlier (115). If so, whatever problems underlie underachievement are likely brought to the secondary school, at least in budding form. There, underachievement is often accentuated by certain characteristics of the high school environment: increased academic pressures, peer group values contrary to intellectual and academic striving, necessity for greater independence in learning, and the like.

Generally speaking, data that suggest a fairly early onset of underachievement patterns fit well with data about the stability of school achievement over time. Strong correlations (from .55 to .75, some higher) between elementary and subsequent secondary school achievement exist (15, 29). The idea of a "late bloomer"

—one who starts slowly in school but later suddenly bursts forth with a remarkable improvement in school achievement—also seems to be more myth than reality (123). The implication of these data is that if the problem of pupil underachievement is neglected at the elementary school level, the pattern may stabilize, or worsen, and become increasingly difficult to deal with later. This, of course, is based on the assumption that the school (and home) environment is also stable and reinforces the pattern.

That the roots of underachievement patterns can often be traced to the early school years raises the question of specific *conditions* that early contribute to such patterns. Frequently, the familial relations of underachievers are investigated on the premise that attitudes and values pertinent to achievement striving are formed and nurtured in homes. Of course, it is virtually impossible to determine in a given case whether a certain parent attitude or parent–child relationship precedes the onset of underachievement, much less to determine their direct contribution to the pattern.

Even so, some distinct differences between parents of underachievers and parents of normal achievers have been reported. For example, parents of underachievers are more likely to reject their offspring, de-emphasize independence training, behave inconsistently (for example, alternate between extremes in permissiveness and restrictiveness), provide less powerful models for achievement, foster less masculine sex role identification (for boys), express greater dissatisfaction with themselves as parents, and report higher anxiety, particularly regarding sexuality (51, 57, 112, 114). Again, these data have been derived largely through *post hoc* comparisons of parents whose children are achieving or underachieving. Thus it is not clear whether some of these parental behaviors come before (and therefore possibly contribute to different achievement patterns among their children), or develop as a response to, their children's difficulties. However, as reported throughout this book, there are ample data to document a strong relationship between parental behavior (for example, encouragement and reinforcement for children's achievement and independence) and the development of children's achievement orientation (105).

Some Personality Characteristics of Underachievers. Socialization experiences within the home and the school may also partly account for differences in the personal–social behavior of achievers and underachievers. Among the most consistent differences between these two groups are the greater feeling of hostility toward authority figures and the lesser self-esteem reported by underachievers (90, 113). Other characteristics associated with discrepant achievement, especially among males, include more frequent attentional lapses in school, greater distractibility under stressful conditions, rejection of pressures to participate in structured learning situations, and lessened concern for advance planning and consistency in thought (120). Similar characteristics are reported for females, although in their case, excitability and a greater concern for an interest in social (versus academic) affairs is typical (6, 120). Finally, as noted in Chapter 10, a strong external locus of control is often associated with low achievement.

Characteristics such as these are not apparent in all groups of achievers and pertain more clearly to older students (age 12 and above). But they are useful for describing the general case and may represent the outcome of a socialization experience that is qualitatively different from that of achievers (52).

However, many think about underachievement mostly in terms of a social pathology, a personal deficit model, or a difference in cultural background model (24). Certain school conditions—for example, lack of relevant studies and hostile, incompetent teachers (126, 142)—may contribute to underachievement. In such cases, underachievement may be a normal reaction to an intolerable environment. Where school is seen both as irrelevant and boring, as it is by many severely economically disadvantaged children, particularly those who do not score well on conventional intelligence tests, a pattern of severe underachievement is typical. In such cases, the task of teachers and psychologists is to work toward a transfer of skills and motives from the child's "real life" to his progress in the classroom. In this fashion, the opportunities from middle-class or "advantaged" life that he may wish to take advantage of will be available to him, as they will not be if a pattern of severe underachievement persists (24). Currently many teachers with whom the authors work believe that faulty school environments are more responsible for underachievement than personal or cultural deficiences of students.

Treatment Programs for Underachievers. On the basis of the authors' experience with teachers and parents, it is clear that both groups generally view underachievement as a problem about which something should be done. Ordinarily, some sort of remedial measure is sought. In practice, the chronic underachiever is usually referred by teachers to psychological specialists. Occasionally, however, conscientious teachers modify their instructional tactics in an effort better to meet the needs of the underachiever. Less frequently, an underachiever will himself seek assistance. Many parents are quick to seek help for their underachieving child once they are aware of retarded educational development in the child. The basic dilemma, however, is whether or not to intervene. Students in the authors' own classes, many of whom plan to be teachers, stoutly maintain that any pupil has a right to underachieve, a right that should be respected by teachers and parents. The readers are encouraged to consider this viewpoint and its implications carefully.

Once a decision to do something about underachievement is made, the dilemma becomes which intervention strategy to employ and what criteria should serve as a measure of successful intervention. Strategies in use range from contingency management programs and computer-based instruction (both designed to achieve maximum motivation and learning efficiency) to tutoring and role playing (usually designed to build on interpersonal relationships, develop self-understanding, and in the case of tutoring, provide personalized remedial instruction). However, counseling programs for underachievers, either on an individual basis or on the basis of a group of underachieving peers, represent by far the most commonly reported technique. The criterion dilemma is commonly resolved in favor of some concrete indication of improved achievement—grade point average, for example. Improved attitudes toward self, school, and teachers also are considered as worthy intervention goals.

Analyses of successful treatment programs for underachievers suggest that both therapeutic counseling and academic skill building are important ingredients (8, 56, 96). That is, counseling oriented toward the dynamics of underachievement, together with a specific program of studies for academic areas in which the underachiever experiences difficulty, stands a better chance for success than does either component alone. Warmth, empathy, and sincerity of purpose among personnel in charge of such programs also seem important. Other factors that influence success include the duration of treatment and provision for structured study skills instruction. In short, programs organized to achieve specific goals and to provide extended opportunity for remedial work are preferable to short-term, loosely organized programs (many of which represent nothing more than "rap" sessions). Still other factors are important, including whether or not a program is voluntary. Coercion of the underachiever can often backfire. Finally, even when elaborate provisions for underachievers are made, the net result can be extremely frustrating. Work with alienated junior high school underachievers, for example, has proved to be both difficult and disappointing in terms of long-term scholastic improvement (56). Fortunately, more optimism about the modification of low-achievement patterns among able learners can be generated from programs based on operant conditioning principles (9, 18, 22).

A preventive "therapy," not yet fully tested for effectiveness but with considerable face validity (plausibility), is curricular reform in the guise of introducing relevant curricular content. One prominent example is Black Studies Programs, some of which seem to have been outstandingly effective (from the authors' observations). However, to produce change for children, it is necessary to do more than simply to change books. Interpersonal relations, too, must be altered (106).

School Dropouts

Prolonged underachievement may culminate in the underachiever's prematurely leaving school, although many underachievers continue with their schooling and somehow manage to survive without the rewards accorded school achievers. The dropout, in contrast, is more often the person with an extended history of borderline achievement, if not outright failure. It is true, however, that many school dropouts are intellectually bright and capable of managing their school experience successfully; what they usually lack is motivation for the school experience.

The value of high school graduation for all persons is, of course, a matter for debate. For example, one can argue in favor of the right to leave school. In some cases, it seems also that youth are forced out, as opposed to dropping out, of school. Nevertheless, some basic facts about school dropouts need to be recognized and examined carefully in terms of their implications for both society and the individual (20, 99, 107, 128). The fact that between 1960 and 1971 over seven million youth left school *without* a diploma indicates that overwhelming numbers of persons have found school unsatisfactory for meeting personal needs. By dropping out, they seriously limit any further opportunity for self-development through formal education. Moreover, the fact that roughly 30 percent of the nation's youth annually enters the job market without a high school credential creates for them a dismal

economic outlook, at least on the basis of contemporary labor requirements.

Some Characteristics of School Dropouts

If dropping out of school is symptomatic of something gone wrong with the educational process, educators must study the possible causes carefully. One common approach to such study is based on the old adage about prevention being worth more than cure. For example, school dropouts are often compared with their nondropout peers to identify any characteristics (academic–intellectual, personal–social, or economic factors) that differentiate the two groups. Accordingly, the intent is to pinpoint danger signals among dropouts that can be early detected and acted upon, thereby reducing the probability of eventual school dropout.

Some of the most reliable signals for potential dropout behavior are deficient reading skills, professed noninterest in school, below-grade level of arithmetic achievement, little or no participation in extracurricular activities, chronic absenteeism and tardiness, low socioeconomic background, low degree of emotional support from parents, frequent classroom misbehavior, negative self-esteem, and low educational level of parents (20, 109). In general, the likelihood that a given individual will drop out of school before graduation increases with the number of indicators that apply to him. Again, however, a need for caution—the authors believe that a concept of school dropouts based exclusively on personal "deficiencies" is too simple.

The authors have at least two reasons for their position. First, it is apparent that many academic and personal–social disadvantages can be overcome by a strong, positive parent–child relation-

Even in our advanced society, nearly a third of American youth fail to complete high school education. The dilemma of the school dropout—such as this one in an impoverished mining area of Kentucky—persists as a major social problem. (Wide World Photos)

ship, one that is capable of sustaining motivation for school activities. Second, school dropouts are not all cut from the same cloth. At least three different categories of dropouts can be identified—for example, the involuntary, the retarded, and the capable (38). Each involves different dynamics. Involuntary dropouts are those whose only course of action is to leave school because of some personal crisis beyond their direct control. Retarded students are those whose skills are insufficiently developed to cope with the existing school environment. Capable dropouts are those whose academic skills and personal attributes are adequate for school success; for one reason or another they simply reject the school experience.

School Factors and the Dropout Problem

It is this third category that especially implies a gross incompatibility between the school environment and student needs. This incompatibility is by no means limited to any one socioeconomic stratum. For example, one authority reports that dropouts from lower-social-class backgrounds are more intellectually creative than are stay-ins from similar backgrounds (66). Possibly students who prefer divergency find the outside school environment more stimulating, and thus move away from confines of school. Or, by dropping out, the student may escape the pressures for intellectual conformity in the school. In any case, the implication is that more varied, effective opportunities for creative expression can be a solid step toward a reduction in the dropout rate among talented students.

Still other aspects of school practice warrant consideration in relation to the dropout problem: diversified subject matter and vocational education, the quality of human relations in the classroom, opportunities for student involvement in school policy formation, and supportive psychological services. Such aspects often appear in studies in which school characteristics are related to the dropout rate in particular schools. In one such study, several important services were reported to distinguish schools with low (versus schools with high) dropout rates (107). In order of importance, these services include a planned program for working with the parents of potential dropouts, a grading policy geared to individual progress (versus peer comparison), a full-time counselor load of 350 or fewer students, assigning of potential dropouts to special teachers who themselves desire to work personally with less successful students, reduced class size for potential dropouts (twenty or less), and multitrack occupational–vocational programs (107).

Such services, the authors hope, constitute effective preventive measures. Direct proof of their effectiveness, however, is not easily achieved. Yet it is possible to gain some indication of the relevance of these measures by considering the reasons given by dropouts for leaving school. The single most common reason given, irrespective of sex, race, or social class, is "lack of interest" or "dislike of school."

The authors believe, with others (for example, 99), that these terms usually mask one or more specific concerns dropouts have about school: being discouraged about academic progress, intense dislike for a given teacher or subject, perceived lack of usefulness of the school subjects, and social isolation from peers. Still other reasons for leaving school are perhaps less directly related to the quality of school life—economic situation and the illusion of independence created by certain job prospects.

The authors find much to applaud concerning measures taken by some educators to prevent school dropouts. Unfortunately, however, many attempts are badly timed and become halfhearted, last-ditch efforts either to keep a potential dropout in school or to entice him to return once he has decided to leave. It is clear that a greater variety of preventive programs is now reflected in school practice. Examples include group counseling services, experiments with the nongraded classroom, subsidized work–study programs, broad-scale tutoring, and Dropouts Anonymous (teams of ex-dropouts who provide academic and emotional supports to potential school leavers). Readers interested in more details about these and other programs should consult the references for this chapter, especially 83.

Overachievement

To be completely logical, there is no such thing as overachievement. People never do more than they *can* do. What is meant by the term is not logical, but clinical: The overachieving child or youth is the one who tries too hard and worries too much about his success or failure. When overachievement is defined this way, we see that overachievers are more likely to be motivated by anxiety and fear of failure than by hope of success. They achieve at the expense of their personal relaxation, sense of security, and happiness.

Thus, the kind of overachievement being discussed is related to an individual's personal adjustment. It is only one of a set of tensions the individual should be helped to understand and to reduce in intensity. To avoid redundancy and to keep a long chapter from becoming even longer, the authors believe that all the discussion really required for overachievement has already been given in the section on Anxiety in Chapter 10. On the basis of experience, the authors believe that overachievement is most frequent among children whose parents value them more for extrinsic reasons than for intrinsic reasons; and that overachievement is also more commonly found among children from families that are themselves intensely striving for upward social mobility (the *keep up with the Joneses* syndrome).

Disadvantage and Compensatory Education

During the past fifteen years or so, psychologists and educators have become progressively more aware of and sensitive to the problems of human underdevelopment. In United States culture, these problems are most frequently and obviously associated with poverty and minority group status. In other words, the combined impact of economic hardship and ethnic or racial discrimination has severely limited the self-development opportunities for many Americans. This disadvantage is often further compounded by isolation from the mainstream of American social life, as in the case of mountain white children, descendants of Hispano culture, and reservation-bound American Indians (32).

The problems that culminate in unequal opportunities for self-development in America reflect our total social system. But for the young, it is the American system of public schooling on which much of our attention and ameliorative efforts must be focused. Fortunately, during the 1960s the idea gained support that changes in this system are needed quickly to deal better with the problem of human underdevelopment. One way in which this support materialized was in the form of compensatory education for the disadvantaged. This meant increased Federal and state support for educational program specialization at two principal levels: organized preschool experience (especially for 4-year-olds prior to kindergarten entry) and assistance to school dropouts or potential dropouts (50). Gradually, other directions were taken, including sometimes dramatic curriculum innovation within the K-12 sequence itself, expanded programs for vocational development, and bicultural, bilingual education experiments (41, 83).

Although compensatory education programs vary considerably in their details, they share at least two related goals: "They are *remedial* in that they attempt to fill gaps — social, cultural, or academic — in the child's total education. The are *preventative* in that they try to forestall either initial or contributing failure in school and later life." (50, italics authors') The preventive aspect is perhaps most clearly a characteristic of compensatory education during the early childhood years. As such, several assumptions are present (13). One is that specialized early (versus late) intervention stands a better chance to capitalize on the modifiability and flexibility of the human organism (see Chapter 3). A second assumption is that potential learning disorders that interfere with scholastic development can be identified early and treated preferentially to prevent the cumulative school failure so often characteristic of disadvantaged children. Regardless, both aspects—preventive and remedial—are based on the notion that improved educational opportunity and status will result in a number of gains: progress toward the ideal of true civil rights, enhanced social mobility, more humane race relations, and more equal opportunity to share in this nation's economic resources (50). This is indeed a tall order for any educational system.

In order to explore more fully the matter of compensatory education, with its associated dilemmas, the authors have elected to discuss two basic conceptualizations of such education. They do so at the risk of establishing a false dichotomy, but they believe the differences are basic enough to provide a design for discussion.

Basic Conceptualizations of Compensatory Education

One clear fact must be acknowledged: On most measures of educational achievement, disadvantaged children and youth generally perform less well than their more advantaged peers (40, 143). The reasons offered for this difference, however, are both debatable and significant for shaping one's philosophy of compensatory education. Explanations of this marked difference in school achievement, for example, have taken two basic directions. One involves a consideration of personal "deficiencies" that might be shared by disadvantaged children and youth—deficiencies that somehow impede educational progress in the school. The second direction, in contrast, concerns more an examination of deficient educational practices that may be rooted in social discrimination, incompetence on

"Good morning, pre-head starters..."

A persisting dilemma among educational specialists is how early to begin compensatory education programs. Unfortunately, few authorities are exploring the potential hazards of too-early intervention. (Cartoon from Phi Delta Kappan, *1969, 51 (1), 33. Reproduced by permission of the artist, Henry R. Martin.)*

the part of educators, or school conditions unfavorable to learning that are currently beyond the control of understaffed and ill-equipped school faculties.[1]

These two basic directions for explaining unsatisfactory educational progress among the disadvantaged give rise to two contrasting ameliorative strategies. Both, however, are based on the belief that disadvantaged children and youth can and should perform at higher scholastic levels. These strategies include (1) direct attempts to change (remediate) the per-

[1] A variation on this second theme has involved a search for conflict in cocultural or social class value systems that may affect school behavior. Also involved is the issue of educational and personality measurement, a specification of which is beyond the scope of this book.

sonal characteristics of students or, more specifically, to correct any deficits that seemingly interfere with progress in the educational system as it exists, and (2) efforts to modify or innovate in major ways the educational environments encountered by disadvantaged children and youth. This second approach, of course, is also designed to change behavior (the authors consider education most broadly as behavior change). But this strategy is more clearly attuned than the first to individual differences based on cultural experience and accommodating these differences in the schools.

Changing Personal Characteristics

Two basic problems must be solved by those who attempt to change the personal characteristics of disadvantaged children and youth. One is identifying and explaining what characteristics reliably distinguish the disadvantaged from their more privileged and academically successful peers—characteristics that are clearly related to scholastic progress. A second problem is devising valid and ethical means for the modification of these characteristics. This problem can be thought of as a procedural dilemma as yet unresolved. At the preschool level, for example, the dilemma is summarized by a rift between advocates of the academic preschool (with its sharp focus on cognitive skill development) and the "modern" American nursery school (with its greater emphasis on social development) (88). This rift exists in various guises throughout the entire nation and is not likely to dissipate quickly.

Identifying and Explaining Personal Deficits

As indicated in Chapter 1, individual differences are encountered along a con-

tinuum of genetic and environmental determination, with most behavior being the result of an interaction of genetic and experiential factors. Individual differences, regardless of their cause, can be further classified as cognitive—academic, personal–social, and physical–motor (see also Chapter 1). These classes of behavior —particularly the first two—frequently appear in the research about individual differences as related to social class and ethnicity. For example, disadvantaged children and youth typically demonstrate comparatively lower measured intelligence, self concept of ability, achievement motivation, and sense of personal control over their environment (40). Furthermore, they often manifest higher anxiety, linguistic characteristics that impede achievement in situations geared to standard English, and a level of conceptual activity not conducive to successful abstract problem-solving activity (50, 143). In the context of a deficit-oriented approach to compensatory education, instructional efforts are generally made to increase the level of functioning across these various behavior patterns, notably in the areas of language skills and attitude toward school.

The description of so-called "deficits," of course, does not necessarily reveal anything about the reasons for them. The question of reasons is critical, because if such deficits are strongly determined by heredity, environmental experience may make little difference. Compensatory education would thus be doomed to failure. The nature—nurture issue has been discussed earlier in this book (see Chapter 3) and will not be elaborated on here. It should be noted, however, that with few exceptions (for example, 67) the preferred analysis of development deficits has been based on a concept of environmental (versus genetic) determination. This is especially true of personal–social behaviors, but extends also to the development of learning tactics so critical for academic progress.

To illustrate this point, the authors refer to the analysis of a widely recognized authority on the relationship of race and social class to learning (102). This authority has been specifically concerned with why black children from the lower socioeconomic stratum fail to achieve the same level of school success as their higher socioeconomic class white peers.

Briefly, it is argued, not that inherent racial- or social-class-related deficiencies exist among low-SES (socioeconomic status) black children, but rather that such children initially arrive at school with "less developed learning tactics" than do high-SES whites and that this difference is most marked during the kindergarten year. Moreover, it is believed that while low-SES black children improve their learning skills nearly to the point of equality by first grade, these skills are not as well honed for some modes of receptive and active learning as others. Finally, it is suggested that many impoverished black children are less adequate in their mastery of skills essential for learning under typical classroom conditions (versus the playground or streets of the ghetto, for example).

Accordingly, it is reasoned that such children will require training in elaborative learning techniques, namely: to engage and refine their capacity for imaginative conceptual activity through concrete, explicit, and specific instructional programming.

This recommendation for direct, systematic instruction is, of course, contrary to the desires held for such children by most proponents of free schools and informal education. Most of the early returns on deficit-oriented compensatory education, however, suggest an advantage to structured, task-oriented instruction (34, 41). Ultimately, of course, the issue again concerns what goals are sought by parents and educators for the children in their care and how best to achieve such goals. There is still another, perhaps even deeper issue, which has been chosen for special attention in Example 12.1.

12.1 Cultural Deprivation or Cultural Difference?

Throughout the past decade, a great deal of literature about cultural deprivation has accumulated. The principal theme in this literature is that, because of social–cultural and economic deprivation, vast numbers of children and youth (usually members of minority ethnic groups), fail to develop normally. In short, they manifest certain personal deficits (cognitive and motivational) that progressively interfere with the course of development, especially as such development is affected by formal education. This phenomenon has frequently been discussed in terms of the *cumulative deficit hypothesis* (see Chapter 3).

Recently, however, many authorities have objected to this view of development among poor, minority children and youth. The position taken by Michael Cole and Jerome Bruner exemplifies this difference of viewpoint (24). These authorities argue that cultural deprivation is more accurately a "special case of cultural *difference* that arises when an individual is faced with demands to perform in a manner inconsistent with his past cultural experience" (24, p. 874). This argument is based on their analysis of the cumulative deficit hypothesis, which, it is reasoned, can be contradicted on several grounds. First, and according to the "doctrine of psychic unity" (72), it is argued that one can reach different conclusions about existence depending upon the way one organizes said experience. In the final analysis all ways of organizing experience are arbitrary. Thus, the dominant view of "cultural deprivation" may simply be an artifact of the way the majority culture experience is organized. Second, Cole and Bruner suggest that all peoples are equivalent in their functional linguistic ability. As such, we cannot attribute any less cognitive ability than is necessary for the complex development of language

to any one cultural or ethnic group. Third, Cole and Bruner criticize the "situation bound" nature of psychological experimentation and study. That is, they believe that psychologists (and behavioral scientists generally) too often fail to account for the complex interaction of cultural–social variables that affects human behavior differently in different situations at different points in time. In their words, "Groups ordinarily diagnosed as culturally deprived have the same underlying competence as those in the mainstream of the dominant culture, the differences in performance being accounted for by the situations

Recent analyses of the goals of compensatory education have emphasized the importance of viewing the problem of disadvantaged students as one of cultural difference, not cultural deprivation. (Photo by Hanna W. Schreiber)

and contexts in which the competence is expressed" (24, p. 870).

This third contention can be taken further to illustrate the need for a careful examination of the competence–performance relationship. As Cole and Bruner indicate, psychologists ordinarily strive to maximize children's performance (intellectual or otherwise), after which inferences are made about the children's underlying competence. But, too often, a psychologist's (or an educator's) view of competence is both situation-blind and culture-blind. When this is so, at least two requisite steps are needed: (1) determine whether a given competence in fact is expressed in a given situation; and (2) determine the significance of that situation for a child's "ability to cope with life in his own milieu" (24, p. 874).

Cole and Bruner extend their position to include two important implications for school personnel. First, they call for a recognition and acceptance of the idea that educational difficulties can be analyzed in terms of cultural differences (versus learner pathology). Such a change in outlook among teachers, they claim, should lead to a more positive attitude toward minority group pupils in the schools. If so, the pupils themselves should benefit. Second, Cole and Bruner suggest that the right road to education for minority group pupils is not the one which demands that teachers create new intellectual structures in such pupils. Rather, the task is more skillfully to effect a *transfer* of existing skills to classroom activities.

The Cole and Bruner position summarized here deserves careful attention. If these men are correct, their suggestion regarding *skills transfer* is most relevant. But the authors believe that it is incumbent upon Cole and Bruner and

their followers to develop, and communicate to teachers, sound ways in which this transfer may best be achieved. Otherwise, the suggestion may simply become another unpursued challenge in the arsenal of challenges levied at America's teachers. More basically, it is possible that Cole and Bruner have exaggerated cultural differences unduly. Few would deny that social-class differences in opportunities for social mobility and self-development exist. But, is the present, general cultural experience of low-income Americans, black *and* white, so markedly different from their higher income counterparts that an acceptable common ground for universal education cannot be found?

An Example of Compensatory Education to Change Personal Characteristics

A suitable example of a program of remediation included under compensatory education is Project Upward Bound. Upward Bound is a Federally sponsored pre-college enrichment program created to generate the skills and the motivation thought essential for college success for otherwise ill-prepared disadvantaged youth. Although Upward Bound consists of youth of all races, it is viewed as a particularly significant vehicle for expanding educational opportunities for black youth.

As one of several possible alternatives to increase the number of black youth in American colleges and universities, initial returns concerning the impact of Upward Bound are modestly encouraging. For example, the effects of an Upward Bound experience for 213 black and 90 white (two successive summer programs) high school students (both sexes) have been reported (64). Significantly positive changes for both blacks and whites in self-esteem and internal locus of control (see Chapter 10) were associated with this Upward Bound experience; however, no reliable improvement in academic achievement (as measured by grade point average—G.P.A.) was noted. Noting this disappointing absence of change in achievement, the research workers have admitted the "formidable nature" of such an ameliorative task. They also believe that real progress in compensatory education of the Upward Bound kind will probably depend on basic changes in the educational environments of disadvantaged youth. (We return to this point shortly.)

Follow-up data for Upward Bound participants are also available (35). Specifically, Upward Bound participants who later attended college (versus those participants who did not) reported higher educational aspirations, self-evaluated intelligence, and interpersonal flexibility. These college goers were also characterized by still further differences that possibly reflect the impact of their *total* social environment. Again, as compared to noncollegegoing Upward Bound participants, those who followed their Upward Bound experience by college enrollment had fewer friends whose attitudes were negative or ambivalent toward Upward Bound, came from larger high schools, were likely to come from homes *not* classified at the lowest income level, and had mothers who were present in the home.

Even though it is encouraging that Upward Bound and similar programs have made some contributions to disadvantaged youth, the authors are sobered by its apparent limitations. More comprehensive measures are needed, especially those which provide an educational environment better tailored to the peculiar needs, abilities, and cultural backgrounds of the disadvantaged. At the same time,

the reader must be cautioned about a potential danger of such tailoring, namely: creating a double academic standard that is both demeaning to the youth involved and deplored by parents and educators.

Changing the Characteristics of Educational Environments

A second broad proposal for assisting disadvantaged children and youth concerns a variety of changes in the school environment. These changes are vastly different in their scope (89). For example, the enlistment of more competent teachers with special talents and attitudes may be pursued—teachers who desire (and prefer) to work with the disadvantaged, who can accept and respect cultural differences, and who are sensitive toward and skilled in diagnosing the special needs of less privileged children and youth. Related to this factor is the strategy of providing more teachers who are themselves members of various racial and ethnic groups. Curriculum changes are also advised, particularly in relation to pertinent vocational education and more suitable language arts and social studies experiences.

Even broader in scope, however, are changes (1) that affect social class and ethnic composition of schools and classrooms and (2) that constitute a deliberate effort to promote diversity in educational philosophy and technique in the schools. The first change obviously involves school desegregation. The second concerns a concept of *planned variation* exemplified by Project Follow Through for kindergarten–primary grade children.

School Desegregation

School desegregation can be justified quite apart from any reference to academics. But we can be encouraged by studies that have dealt with the relationship between ethnic integration and academic achievement (125). These studies generally reveal, for example, that blacks who attend integrated schools achieve higher levels of scholastic excellence than do blacks in segregated schools. Of course, school desegregation alone cannot be viewed as a magic means to promote academic development. The critical importance of *classroom* desegregation must be recognized. For instance, increased academic growth (particularly that which involves verbal skills among black youth in large, predominantly white schools) has been observed to occur only for blacks who attend mostly white classes (81).

This evidence does not permit the linking of specific classroom variables with scholastic growth. Several factors are implicated, including increased motivation based on healthy competition with whites, ample numbers of peer models for high achievement, social reinforcement through peer interaction, and higher quality instruction (40). Many blacks make the point, which is well taken, that the inferior position of black students on tests of language and academic achievement comes not as much from segregation as from poor teaching and poor schools. They hold that such results as reported in 40 are due, not to integration, but to the better teaching received by black students when they are in schools with whites. Some black separatists join white separatists in urging separate but *truly equal* educational systems. Some even urge separate but unequal systems, with the educational economic advantage being given, for a change, to schools that are attended by poor blacks (or other prejudiced-against co-cultures).

It must also be noted that school desegregation may create some basic problems of adjustment for minority groups or disadvantaged children and youth. For example, black children oriented toward scholastic achievement may find that the presence of a white teacher and white peers is a "double-edged" situation in the sense that "failure will be more devastating and success more rewarding than similar experiences in the segregated school; moreover, whether the Negro child succeeds or fails will depend to a great extent not only on his actual ability but on his expectations, . . . if he expects to fail, his actual chances of failing will be greater than they would be in an all Negro setting, because his fear of failure will be more intense, . . . on the other hand, if he has a high expectation of success in the integrated school he should be aroused to greater effort than he would be by a similar expectation of success in the segregated school" (69, p. 285).

In short, school desegregation stands to promote many positive humanistic goals, especially over the long term. But it is not all roses. Once integration has begun, careful attention to the quality of teacher–pupil and peer interaction and specific educational activities is imperative. Appropriate psychological services for children and youth during the process of desegregation are also advised. Otherwise, negative side effects of this strategy are likely.

Project Follow Through

Initiated full scale in 1968 as part of the massive Federal design for compensatory education, Project Follow Through provides educational planning guidelines and curricula for kindergarten and primary grade children. This project is based on the assumption that a more sustained pattern of educational growth can be achieved for disadvantaged children who have participated in Project Head Start.

(The reader will recall that Head Start is among the first attempts at compensatory enrichment for 4-year-old children of poverty.) Thus, Project Follow Through may be considered as an extension of Head Start. However, it is significant that Project Follow Through is an attempt to effect change in public school kindergarten–primary education, and it also represents a commitment to educational alternatives for young children.

This commitment to alternatives is indicated by the principle of *planned variation*. That is, Project Follow Through is founded on the idea that a wide range of diverse curricular activities and instructional strategies can be designed that are consistent with alternative philosophies of child growth and education. The net result of this approach has been the conceptualization of some twenty different "models" for early education. For the authors, planned variation reflects a number of implicit beliefs, including the following: (1) that a pluralistic approach to early education is desirable; (2) that sound, judicious experimentation with educational alternatives is good; (3) that there is probably no one "best way" to educate all children; and (4) that community choice in the selection of alternative approaches will increase the probability of successful education.

The curriculum models for Project Follow Through can be analyzed in terms of both similarities and differences (77). For example, there is agreement among Project Follow Through sponsors that any valid approach to early education should reflect certain basic components: provision for meeting different levels of educational readiness among children, individualization of instruction, an attitude among teachers that learning problems are more typically the fault of materials and instructional techniques than a fault

of children, conceptually clear educational objectives, attention to core "school appropriate behaviors" (for example, attentional responses, task orientation, motivation to learn, basic communication skills), provision for learner success and positive self-esteem, and parent involvement.

Differences among Project Follow Through models also exist, however. These differences are largely based on alternative philosophical and theoretical views about learning and the purpose of education (77). For example, one group of programs is based on the principles of behaviorism (see Chapter 2): Education is conceived as a process of establishing precise behavioral objectives, providing systematic presentation strategies, and reinforcing children for desired behavior. Another group of programs is organized primarily to promote broad, general cognitive development, including structures for logical thinking; fewer stringent academic objectives and more child-initiated activities are preferred. Still other programs are pointed toward the more global ideal of self-actualization; informal, educational practices are implemented mainly to provide an atmosphere for children's self-determined learning. Finally, in a smaller number of programs, the concept of client-controlled or community-controlled education with a heavy emphasis on ethnic and co-culture concerns is directly emphasized.

Although comprehensive steps are under way to evaluate Project Follow Through for disadvantaged children, it is premature to generalize about its total impact. The authors see it as an immensely important milestone in the search for more varied and better ways to educate children, disadvantaged or not. The curriculum alternatives provided by Project Follow Through offer a choice of feasible models so that the peculiar needs of children from different community settings may be better met. Regardless of the specific outcomes of Project Follow Through evaluation, we now have a clear precedent for change in public school education.

To conclude this section on compensatory education, the authors believe that more success will be achieved by making substantive changes in the educational environments for disadvantaged children and youth than by attempting crash programs of deficit-oriented instruction. Of course, many complex issues must be faced. For instance, if values that dominate our current educational system generally—industriousness, personal responsibility, self-regulation, skilled communications, punctuality, order, and convergent thinking, for example—are judged inappropriate or irrelevant for certain segments of American society, substitutions will have to be found. The problem is that the formulation of a value base for education that accommodates radically different orientations and functions for large subsegments of society apparently has not yet appeared, much less been agreed upon. Perhaps Cole and Bruner (24) have pinpointed a major part of the problem, at least for psychologists: "When cultures are in competition for resources, as they are today, the psychologist's task is to analyze the source of cultural difference so that those of the minority, the less powerful group, may quickly acquire the intellectual instruments necessary for success of the dominant culture, *should they so choose*" (24, p. 875, italics authors').

Race Relations

America's melting pot has not melted very well. Least blended, as nearly as the authors can tell, are "those of color," although they have the impression that there is a resurgence of social division in all areas—for example, national origin and religion. In this section, the authors wish to make two points.

1. There is plenty of room and reason for racial and ethnic diversity in the United States. While he or she devotes his broadest attention to being a "good American," each boy, girl, youth, or adult has every reason and right to be proud of his own racial and ethnic origins and to understand them in depth through educational experience.
2. While developing such pride and knowledge, each person also needs to accept cultural and racial diversity—not only to accept it, but also to be happy in it and to learn from it.

Much racial, ethnic, and socioeconomic segregation exists in United States schools, yet the schools constitute the arena where, most commonly, children and youth start living and learning with those of different racial and ethnic groups than their own. This section provides some background for understanding and perhaps shaping such living and learning.

To recapitulate, in this book human beings are divided into three races, Caucasoid, Mongoloid, and Negroid. Racially speaking, the United States is made up by about 87 percent Caucasoid people, perhaps 2 percent Mongoloid people (if we include American Indians and predominantly Hawaiian ancestry Hawaiian-Americans), and about 11 percent Negroid people. These percentages are notoriously ambiguous, since race in the United States is almost as much a sociological term as a genetic one.

In this section of the book ethnic relations are also included. An ethnic group is one distinguished by national, linguistic, and customs background from "the majority group." Italian Americans,

Polish Americans, Swedish Americans are all examples of ethnic groups. The Gullahs of the southeastern United States coast are an example of a particular ethnic group within the Negroid race. Puerto Ricans, Cubans, Chicanos, and Jews all have ethnic and frequently religious uniqueness.

By race relations, we essentially mean: How do these groups get along with each other? By *get along*, we further mean such things as are implied in the following questions:

What are the status relations between groups? Do whites typically believe they are better—more elevated in status—than American Indians? Do the latter concur?

What are the economic relations among the groups? Who for the most part has an entrepreneurial, who a wage-earner, relation with whom else?

What are the social relations among the racial and the religious groups? Who most commonly associates and intermarries with whom?

What are the power relations among the groups? Who is most likely to be elected to office, to lobby effectively, to run a political campaign?

Finally, what are the attitudes of one group to another: typically positive and approach oriented, or typically negative and avoidance oriented? Do members of some groups usually fear members of other groups?

The American Ideal

Though we chronically depart from it, the American ideal is that race should be quite irrelevant in judging the worth (including competence) of any human being. Practically speaking (this has been said before, but it is worth repeating), the nation can be divided into at least four categories of people (61).

1. The truly disadvantaged; these are the white, mostly Protestant, chronically poor. Among the Appalachians, their numbers are legion. They are usually referred to as "poor whites," and many think of them as cultural dropouts.

2. Prejudiced-against minority groups whose adjustment is sufficiently different from the core middle-class culture that, on the whole, its members encounter difficulty when they try to achieve positions of power, status, and personal security. Examples of such groups are Blacks, Puerto Ricans, Chicanos, American Indians, Hawaiian Americans, Eskimos, some Cubans, and some Chinese Americans.

3. Prejudiced-against minority groups, most members of which share traditions and have acquired skills that allow them to obtain the "good things" of American life. Examples are Japanese Americans, Jews, many Chinese Americans, and those who have themselves come from Cuba or whose families before them came from Cuba.

4. The white, advantaged culture, 130 million or so white Anglo-Saxon Protestants.[2]

There is much heat but little light concerning the issues that arise from failure to live up to the American ideal. We have amazingly little firm and coherent information about how school integration and segregation affect student relations in a classroom or about how student and teacher relations are affected by race. We do not know for sure whether both black and white students, for example, perform better in integrated classrooms than they do in segregated ones, although there is

[2] Authors' estimate from extrapolations from reports of 1970 U. S. Census data, excluding "poor whites."

some evidence that mixed classrooms benefit those who are low in academic standing, but have little effect on those who are high (78). It is logical to expect that minority group children who are low in school competence will benefit through modeling *if* they come into a situation where they are welcomed and accepted, but that they will be confused, hurt, and made uneasy if they come into a situation where they are rejected. A possible exception may occur when rejection makes them angry and challenges them to extra effort.

Prejudice

From what information the authors have, it seems that prejudice is learned in much the same way other social attitudes are learned (see Chapter 10). A child or a youth is most likely to be prejudiced if he has prejudiced models; if reasons for prejudice have been made explicit (that is, if he has been taught); if he has expressed, rehearsed, and practiced prejudice; and if he has been rewarded for racially prejudiced behavior.

For example, in studies where subjects have ranged from second-graders to senior medical students and noncollege adults from the South and the North, whites living in the South are more prejudiced, or at least admit to being more prejudiced, than those living in the North. However, education affects their prejudice more than it does Northerners': The well-educated Southerner loses prejudice more readily than the well-educated Northerner (79).

Such research findings reflect a learning point of view about race prejudice. Prejudice is normal, in the sense that it is learned; if conditions are correct, it can also be unlearned. But there is another theory of prejudice—the psychodynamic

theory—whose proponents believe that prejudice is simply one of many manifestations of an unhappy and maladaptive personality. Prejudice is "scapegoating" or "projecting"—putting on others the hatred and fears one has for himself and about his own impulses. There are research data to support this point of view, just as there are data to support the learning point of view. For example, one study of boys in an interracial summer camp revealed that living with persons of a different race has no overall effect on people, but that there are differential changes, with some (boys, in this case) staying the same in prejudice, others greatly reducing prejudice, and still others increasing prejudice (85). On the whole, those who lost prejudice during the camp experience had enjoyed camp more and seemed to be more open, well-adjusted boys, whereas those whose prejudice increased had not enjoyed their experience and seemed to have a chip on their shoulders, in that they thought the world was against them. The psychodynamic point of view of prejudice and authoritarianism is that they are closely linked, prejudice being simply one manifestation of an authoritarian and rigid personality. This point of view is best expressed in a classical study to which the interested student should refer (1).

The point of view of the authors is that both theories of prejudice are plausible, at least so far as they know now. The feelings of some prejudiced people they know are so intense that it is difficult to account for them by a straightforward, cognitive learning theory. They seem to be rooted in basic personality structure. On the other hand, in their teaching, the authors have seen so many young people shed prejudice immediately after being exposed to simple anthropological, psychological, and sociological information that they can only believe that, for many, prejudice is no more than a certain form of learning, or a lack of learning.

Development of Racial Awareness and Prejudice

From the rather scanty evidence available (124, for example), prejudice and awareness of one's own race and ethnic group are evidenced by normal children by about age 4. At about this same age children also become aware of their physical attributes (121). There is some historical evidence that black children begin to take a dim view of negritude and that white children begin to exalt whiteness. But one recent study of racial preference and identification indicates a more positive picture of racial identity among black children (62). More such studies should be carried out again in the seventies, because there is much corollary evidence that racial attitudes, focus of pride, and stereotypes are shifting rapidly (see the discussion of self-esteem in the preceding chapter).

The authors' assumption is that racial awareness is a straightforward learning phenomenon, just as is the awareness of one's sex. Certainly, most normal 4- and 5-year-olds are aware that they are Black, or Chicano, or Indian, or white, even as they are aware in a general way of what line of work their mothers and fathers follow and that they are boys or girls. As with all cognitive matters, the concept of race grows more sophisticated, complicated, and value ridden with age.

Finally, among many minority group members, there seems to be prejudice against themselves (79). This phenomenon has been called identification with the aggressor. A minority group that is prejudiced against incorporates the prejudice of the power group to the degree that its members reject themselves and other members of their racial or ethnic group. Indications of the existence of such a phenomenon have been documented among both Blacks and Jews. The authors suspect that this form of maladaptive adjustment is rapidly disappearing, but they have no firm evidence to this effect.

Segregation — Integration

The nation is in flux about segregation–integration. In the seventies, all people from the deepest South to the farthest and most liberal parts of the North accept the fact that schools *must*—and most accept the principle that schools *should*—be integrated. The Supreme Court decision to this effect dating from 1954 has been implemented in at least a token fashion everywhere, and, to the surprise of many, it has been found (as we grow more sophisticated about such matters) that areas of the urban North were operating schools that were as racially segregated as those of the deepest South. The lines between *de jure* segregation (segregation by statute, now outlawed in all 50 of the United States) and *de facto* segregation (mainly sequestered housing put into effect by many ruses, all illegal in the strict sense but very effective nonetheless) have begun to blur. It has been shown that people in the North are as emotional and hostile about Black, American-Indian, or other minority group neighbors as those in the South, and that they raise about as much fuss over busing to achieve integrated schools as their more overtly prejudiced neighbors to the South. No one can afford to be smug about racial relations and race prejudice these days, no matter where he comes from. The matter has even become an issue in calm and tolerant England.

There is no way to predict which way

*Court-ordered desegregated schooling has introduced a facet in the lives of many children —
long rides in buses to distant schools. (Photo by Bruce Roberts)*

United States society will go. Reports vary from the pessimism of the Kerner Commission (we are heading toward a polarized society, one pole black, one pole white, with mutual antagonism between the two) to a naïve optimism that "things are getting better."

The authors see some encouraging signs; in Example 12.2, they review a study on the basis of which it seems as if children, at least, react to competence rather than race as they interact with their teachers.

12.2 Teacher Race and Child Performance (141)

The subjects of this study were second-grade children and their experienced teachers. There were 144 children in all, one-half of whom were black, one-half of whom were white; there were thirty-six boys and thirty-six girls in each racial group; all were considered to be of normal intelligence; and none had repeated a grade. Some of the parents were semiskilled; some, unskilled; and some, unemployed recipients of aid to dependent children. There were six black teachers, six white. Three of each racial group were rated as ineffective by a school psychologist in the large, Midwestern, urban school system from which all subjects came. The school psychologist made the ratings on the basis of personal–professional observation and familiarity with competence ratings from principals.

The black and white, effective and ineffective teachers administered a number of measures of social approach and avoidance tendencies, curiosity, and intelligence to proportional numbers of black and white boys and girls so that, for example, each teacher worked with an equal number of black boys, black girls, white boys, and white girls. The least teacher experience was two years of teaching, the most fifteen years, and the average was six and one-half years. All teachers had volunteered, with their principals' approval.

The most significant revelation resulting from the study was that there was not one single child behavior in any of the three areas (interpersonal distance, curiosity, or behavior and score on a vocabulary intelligence test) that was related to either the race of the teacher or the race of the child. However, the children showed less interpersonal distance from (seemed to "feel closer to") effective black teachers and more interpersonal distance (seemed to "feel further away") from ineffective white teachers. The authors of the article speculate that an effective teaching style for black teachers is imbedded within a warm and supportive approach, whereas for white teachers, it is imbedded within a rather authoritarian, no-nonsense approach.

Other interesting findings emerged from this study. Children from both races obtained better verbal intelligence scores when tested by effective teachers, regardless of the race of the teacher. Black boys were shown to be the least curious of the subgroups of children (see the discussion of intelligence in Chapter 6); but the black boys who were tested by the ineffective black and white teachers showed less curiosity than those tested by effective teachers of both races. White boys were rated as seeking more attention than white girls, but this was not true for black boys and girls. Race of teachers and boys was not related to this finding, although white teachers were more likely than black teachers to rate negative attention seeking high. It is perhaps significant that effective teachers, regardless of race, rated all children higher in positive attention seeking. This possibly betokens a general positive attitude toward children among effective teachers. On the whole, white children were seen as more positive attention seeking than black children.

Results from this study support the authors' conviction that competence constitutes an overriding virtue in American culture and that it transcends matters of race or sex. The results also illustrate that effectiveness of performance is not necessarily linked to emotional attributes. One can be warm or cool, yet still be competent in his tutelage of children, for example.

Even though competence is the overriding variable shown as important in the study reported in Example 12.2, personal characteristics of teachers must certainly play a part in the morale and the learning of a whole integrated class. Seemingly there are three principal components of teacher behavior toward students: (1) child orientation, (2) task orientation, and (3) fairness. This proved to be the case in one large study conducted in the urban Northeast (126).

For black pupils (sixth-graders in this instance), *child orientation* was most closely related to growth in reading skill, while *fairness* was most closely associated with improved conduct. This fits well with other research in which it has been shown that white teachers perceive black inner-city children more negatively than do black teachers; that black pupils are more inclined than white pupils to believe their teachers regard them negatively and more negatively than the teachers maintain they do; and that there are relations between the way children think their teachers regard them and the way children perform (28, 126).

Ethnicity, Race, and Advantage

In the United States, there is often a clear relation between race and ethnicity on the one hand, and between poverty and disadvantage on the other. The proportion (though not the absolute number) of poverty and disadvantage is much higher, for example, among American-Indian, Black, Chicano, and Puerto-Rican families than it is among white families. Thus, children of such families often suffer doubly, once because they are prejudiced against because of skin color, language, dialect, and in some cases religion, and again because many of them are poor. The stereotypes held about the poor are applied to them. Teachers often expect them not to learn well, to be passive and unambitious on the one hand, or perhaps rebellious and otherwise discipline problems on the other. Exaggerated notions of "loose" sex behavior are also held for some minority groups and perhaps for the poor in general, particularly from the time a child reaches adolescence.

All these factors are inclined to set any but the most enlightened and socially oriented teacher against the poor in general, and to some degree particularly against the black, the red, and the brown poor. Fortunately, there are many such enlightened and socially dedicated

teachers, and the authors believe that their number and skill are increasing, although not rapidly enough. Indeed, some depressing findings have emerged from a massive study of the classroom interactions of teachers and their fourth-through seventh-grade pupils in San Francisco and central Texas (142). It is probable that disadvantaged children in these areas included many Black and Chicano children. Teachers' attitudes seemed to affect disadvantaged pupils more than they did advantaged children. Compared with advantaged classes, there was little mutuality between pupils and teachers in disadvantaged classes. Everything went one way (from teacher to child) in a predominantly authoritarian, cold, and negative manner. As a school year wore on, teachers of the disadvantaged became progressively more negative in attitude, and their charges progressively lower in morale. Teachers of advantaged children improved in attitude over the year, although this improved attitude had little effect on morale of students in their classes.

Sadly enough, the more experienced the disadvantaged classroom teacher was, the more negative was her attitude. In fairness to the teachers, of course, two comments must be made. (1) School administrators often punish teachers by assigning them to disadvantaged classes (either because of temperament or because of judged ineffectiveness). (2) Teaching disadvantaged children by traditional classroom methods (characterized by drill, rote learning, lecture, and tight behavior control) usually has very low payoff. Teachers need to be reinforced just as much as children do, and the teacher who never sees success among her or his pupils is likely to become demoralized and bitter.

Finally, there is some indication that

Table 12.1 *Relations between Average Teacher Marks and Standing on Standardized Achievement Test Scores for Black and White Early Seventh-Graders (one-half of each group is black, one-half white).*

Group	Number	Correlation between Standardized Achievement Test Scores and Average Teacher Marks
Advantaged boys	116	.03
Advantaged girls	114	.15
Disadvantaged boys	105	.46
Disadvantaged girls	108	.64

From McCandless, Roberts, and Starnes (80).

teachers grade disadvantaged children more accurately than they do advantaged children (80). It may be that teachers are eager to socialize advantaged children along acceptable lines and that their concern about social development interferes with their judgment about what is actually being learned, whereas teachers have given up on the social development of disadvantaged children and assign grades more in accord with what children are achieving. This practice is not good for either group. The advantaged do not receive accurate feedback; the disadvantaged receive mostly negative feedback. The correlations between teachers' marks and standing on standardized achievement tests revealed in this study are so interesting that a few of them should be reported (see Table 12.1).

Race Relations: Where Are We Now?

It is difficult even to suggest preliminary and tentative answers to the question about where we are with reference to race relations. On the basis of newspaper headlines and news magazine articles and in associating with friends of different races, temperaments, and racial and ethnic makeups, the authors vacillate from depression to hopefulness. That their reac-

tions are mirrored by other students of race relations is indicated by a recent survey reported from the Institute for Social Research at the University of Michigan (133, p. 1).

Those who conducted this study of white attitudes toward black people (on whom race relations are most dramatically focused in this country) posed the following three questions, among others. The first question was: "What is the main cause of the urban riots?" Answers to the one extreme (prejudiced) were such as ". . . agitators. Martin Luther King and Rap Brown and that Black bastard Carmichael." At the other extreme (antiprejudice) was the answer "Dissatisfaction. They are dissatisfied with the way they live, the way they are treated, and their place in the social structure of America."

A second question with representative prejudiced and antiprejudiced answers was: "What should city government do to prevent such disturbances?" Prejudiced answers: "Ship them all back to Africa." "Lock up all the agitators and show them we mean business." An antiprejudiced answer: "Not only promise but actually improve conditions, education, housing, jobs, and social treatment to such a point that something is actually physically there to show them that the city government realizes their problem and is actually doing something concrete about it."

A third question: "Have the disturbances helped or hurt the cause of Blacks?" Prejudiced answer: "Hurt. Whites are starting to wise up what a danger these people can be. They are going to be tough from now on. People are fed up with giving in and giving them everything their little black hearts want." Antiprejudiced answer: "They have helped, because they have forced white people to pay attention and have brought the subject out into the open and you can't ignore it anymore."

In this survey, thousands of American white and black people ranging in age from 16 to 69 were questioned. Fifteen major American cities were represented. The general conclusion is that the white population is not racist in any monolithic way and that whites are inconsistent in their racism. For example, 86 percent of the whites who were questioned said they would not at all mind having a black as supervisor on their job. On the other hand, 51 percent oppose laws to prevent racial discrimination in housing, although 49 percent say they would not at all mind having a black family with about the same income and education move next door. It should be noted here that social-class discrimination is perhaps as important as, and perhaps more important than, race discrimination.

There is widespread agreement among whites that blacks are discriminated against, but they are also impatient that blacks have not done more for themselves. To prevent civil disorder, whites are more likely to think of better policing than they are of urban reform, although few believe that urban reform in and of itself is sufficient. There is almost universal agreement that whites should *not* take the law into their own hands in the case of civil disturbance that is racially related.

The finding also emerges from the study mentioned above that schools below college level (as well as churches) seem to exert no effect on discriminatory attitudes, but rather seem almost to seek to preserve the *status quo* (see the discussion at the beginning of this chapter about actualization functions of schools). The indictment in the study of Protestant and Catholic churches is even more severe. Finally, it is shown that the most effective force toward antiprejudiced attitudes during the past twenty years has been attending college at some point in one's life.

Findings from this massive University of Michigan survey lead to cautious optimism. One conclusion is worth quoting (133, p. 6). During a crucial period in race relations between 1964 and 1970, "on many questions of principle and policy white and black attitudes moved closer together. General measures of feeling toward the other race showed no dramatic change. Reports of cross-racial contacts in various social settings consistently showed increased contact and specifically increased contact as friends." This is true of all social groups, whether suburban or inner city.

Concluding Remarks

From this rather brief treatment of race relations and human development, the conclusion necessarily emerges that we are acutely short of firm, clear, consistent knowledge about the parameters of the issue. We have also seen that matters of race and ethnicity are very much interrelated with social class, politics, and economics and that feelings run high about the issue.

Economic data seem to be clear. In the long run, it is not good for anyone to be poor, regardless of his race, language, or religion; and the presence of the very poor in American society is just as bad for the affluent, but in far less arduous, more subtle, and long-run ways, as it is for the poor themselves.

The authors *do* argue for the American ideal. Race, religion, color, and creed are irrelevant to judgments about one's worth and should thus be irrelevant to his place in society. The authors believe that extensive and intensive racial and social-class interaction is good for everyone, and their reasons for this are not entirely idealistic. From the data they have presented about intellectual, cognitive, social, and personal development, they have concluded that openness to new and varied experience is conducive to constructive human growth along all dimensions. For many, there is no opportunity for any extensive racial and ethnic interaction unless firm legal steps are taken to assure it. The authors firmly believe that the prosperous white suburbanite has as much to learn from extensive multiracial and ethnic interaction as the encapsulated resident of San Francisco's Chinatown or the segregated dweller in Spanish Harlem. Is there any substitute for well-digested breadth of experience?

Finally, the authors commend the efforts of many educators to promote interracial harmony and understanding during the critical and formative early school years. For example, multicultural curricula have been developed for application as early as the nursery school period, an important component of which is parent participation as well (27). Positive interracial attitudes among children have been fostered within preschool programs that are focused, among other things, on organized interracial association and the acquisition by children of knowledge about racial differences (26). The systematic use of multiethnic readers in school has also been associated with positive attitude changes among white children toward their black counterparts (76). Any permanent and progressive positive changes in race relations, however, will probably depend on the degree to which members of all races agree upon, commit themselves to, and work actively to attain, the goal of harmonious racial integration both in and out of the schools. There also remains the continuing dilemma of a balance between social integration on the one hand and a collective national identity (regardless of race or ethnicity) and a clear sense of identity based on one's unique racial or ethnic heritage on the other.

Vocational Development

Introduction

For most American men and for an increasing number of American women, the role of work in their lives is at least as important as their families and leisure time. In American society, we do little more to help people grow into satisfactory vocational adjustment than we do to help them grow into satisfactory family members, fathers, mothers, and consumers of leisure time. Guidance is inadequate in all these areas, although considerable practical information has accrued.

In our society, vocational development is of first-order importance during adolescence. As indicated in Chapter 11, a person's vocational role contributes crucially to his personal identity and status (31). Moreover, judicious vocational choice and appropriate preparation are significant, because there is a clear relation between job satisfaction and mental health during adulthood (5). This section is concerned with an all too brief exploration of career development concepts and the vocational choice process. Most of the data come from white middle-class older children and adolescents; data from college students constitute a disproportionate share of the information. However, there is a body of comparatively recent data about girls and women and minority and less advantaged groups (104). In short, though career development is an extremely critical area for psychological study, the state of our current knowledge is very incomplete (78).

Conceptions of Vocational Development

Vocational development represents several concerns. They range from the influence of socialization practices that culminate in commitment to the work ethic, and determinants of specific vocational choice, to means for predicting occupational success and the ways in which work is related to adult life (129). But conceptual approaches to the psychological study of vocational development and choice can be grouped into four categories (92).

1. A trait-factor system.
2. The sociological model.
3. Self-concept theory.
4. Personality dynamics.

All of these are closely related and oriented to the task of facilitating realistic vocational choice. Each category, however, possesses some distinctive features and implications for vocational guidance and counseling. Taken together, all four approaches contribute to a broadened perspective on the relations of family, community, and school functions to vocational development.

Trait-Factor System. The trait-factor system is the most traditional approach to vocational psychology. Its central premise is that through careful analysis and testing

procedures, an individual's aptitudes and interests can be matched with society's occupational needs and opportunities. Once this match has been made, the individual's vocational problem has been solved. Elaborate vocational testing procedures for measuring personal characteristics have been developed to effect this match, although it has become increasingly clear that the problem is much more complex than the original trait-factor system indicates. Although trait-factor models have been devised (see 59), the trait-factor approach has generally been subsumed by other conceptual approaches to vocational counseling (91).

The Sociological Model. The sociological model is based on the notion that many circumstances beyond an individual's immediate control affect career choice in important ways. The career choice process is complicated, because many events that occur in one's life are not anticipated, and new occupational roles rapidly and unpredictably emerge in a rapidly changing society such as ours, while others disappear or grow scarcer. Because vocational choice (including getting a job and having it continue to exist) may be influenced by such factors, as well as by chance, the task facing adolescents is to develop effective environmental coping techniques. These include a good general education (the *generalist* as opposed to the *specialist* notion of vocational preparation), flexible problem-solving skills, and the ability to analyze opportunity structures.

Self-Concept Theory. The broad dimensions of self-concept development and theory were drawn in Chapter 11. However, little specific reference was made to vocational development. The self-concept approach to vocational development includes specification of stages in vocational development. These range from initial crystallization of vocational *preferences* to eventual plans for advancement within a given vocation. The self-concept approach also provides for the influence of observational learning during childhood and reflects the importance of children's identification with adult work models and concepts of career development (55, 93, 127). The main theme for this approach, however, is how one implements his own self concept through vocational channels. Experiences that result in self-clarification and self-understanding presumably are linked to adequate vocational choice and career development.

Personality Dynamics. Within the personality dynamics theory of vocational development and choice, personality style or type is closely related to career entrance and involvement (92). Socialization practices, which are mediated by parental attitudes, are thought to affect the development of children's motive structures. Ultimately, work comes to be viewed by an individual as a means of satisfying personal motives whose roots go back to early childhood. Three pervasive patterns of parent attitude have been postulated (100): emotional concentration on, acceptance of, and avoidance of, the child. Socialization patterns characterized by one or the other of these will predispose the child to select from occupational clusters that relate to his past experience. For example, a background characterized by warmth, support, and love will orient a child toward occupations that involve close working relations with people. In contrast, cold and rejecting parents are predicted to predispose a child toward impersonal occupations where one works with things, animals, or plants. If one

holds to this school of thought, vocational guidance will be incomplete and will likely be inaccurate unless the early life of the counselee is carefully considered.

The all too frequent accidental and incidental nature of vocational guidance is illustrated in four brief vocational histories given in Example 12.3.

12.3 Four Stories of Vocational Development

Thelma is a young black woman. She dropped out of high school to marry, and had five children by the time she was 24 years old, all of whom are living. Her husband has had difficulties with the law, and has been in and out of jail. They have been recently divorced. Thelma, as a teen-ager, had no vocational plans other, perhaps, than doing household work if the opportunity arose. A little while after her last child was born, a Federally sponsored program for education of young children was established in her neighborhood. It seemed suitable for her younger children; she enrolled them, and agreed to participate in the related parent education program. She did not like the parts of her training that had to do with child care, and offered to act instead as a receptionist. She proved to have a warm and skillful way with people who came to visit the project and who telephoned for appointments or information. As a result, she enrolled in a night secretarial class, in which she was a superior student. As a result of further night study, Thelma has passed high school equivalency examinations and has left the early education project (although her younger children are still enrolled) for a position as a receptionist in an insurance office. She earns an adequate salary, likes the work, and believes she has made it, at least for the time being.

Louis is a boy from a prosperous suburban family. His father is a district manager for a large banking firm. Louis took business courses in high school; majored in business administration in college, graduating with honors; was in the supply branch of the armed services after he was drafted; and emerged from the Southeast Asia war to enter industry in one of the career-ladder spots for a national firm. At 24, he is an efficient junior executive, highly valued by his company. He likes his job.

Before Louis was a teen-ager, with his family's support he was gaining business experience as a paper boy. During high school, he served as secretary-treasurer of both the junior and the senior high school classes of which he was a member, and worked in various businesses all through high school.

Roger, a logger's son, is from the Northwest. He comes from a large family, always on the edge of and sometimes immersed in poverty. At 17, he joined the Merchant Marine as a wiper (the humblest of the functions in the engine room of a merchant vessel). At 18, on shore leave, he got a high school girl friend pregnant, married her, and in the next four years, fathered four children while, at the same time, moving up the career ladder to second engineer.

During a shore-based upgrader course, Roger met a psychologist in charge of diagnostic testing for the class in which he was enrolled, and learned that he was of superior ability. Having been a disadvantaged boy during elementary and high schools, he had always

believed that he was rather stupid academically, although he knew he had mechanical ability. He thought about these things during the next year or so that he was at sea, and decided eventually that he was going to go to college. He worked his way through engineering school and, while he was going to college, fell in love with his female professor after becoming less and less interested in his poorly educated wife. The professor reciprocated; Roger divorced his wife and married the professor. Fifteen years later, he is vice-president of a substantial engineering company, is happy in his second marriage, ministering as best he can to his first wife (who broke down as a result of losing her husband and children, all of whom joined their father and his second wife as soon as they were old enough to make a choice), and is being quite a good father to the four children by his first marriage and the two children by his second.

Nina is the tagalong and by some years the youngest child of a large, comfortably situated family. All her older brothers and sisters are college graduates, and are either successful business and professional people or well-educated housewives who plan to go back to work when their children are a bit older. After a mediocre high school career, Nina entered a liberal arts college, disliked it, and flunked out. She then attended a business school to become a secretary, but was not interested in the curriculum and did not do well. She then asked her family to support her in beauty school, because she has always liked to help her older sisters with their makeup and hairstyles and proved so successful with hair operations that her older brothers repeatedly asked her to cut and style their hair. The parents, with little enthusiasm, agreed to support Nina in this training course. She made it handsomely through beauty school, worked for a time in a style and beauty shop, borrowed money from her family to start her own shop, and now operates it very successfully with the help of five employees.

These illustrations are disguised versions of people the authors know. They are given to illustrate six points: (1) Very little vocational guidance is provided for secondary students in United States schools. (2) Career development is remarkably varied and differs according to one's sex, race, and economic level. (3) Vocational decisions often change. (4) Vocational choice is sometimes a matter of modeling (as in Louis's case); sometimes a matter of accident, as in Thelma's case; and sometimes a matter of incidental learning, as in Nina's and Roger's cases. (5) Delayed vocational choice and change may entail great personal difficulty, as in Roger's case. For him, upward mobility has meant the near destruction of his first wife and has resulted in severe problems for his first family of children. (6) Satisfactory vocational adjustment for an individual may entail what is commonly thought of as downward vocational mobility, as for Nina.

Functions of Work for Older Children and Youth

For a majority of American older children and youth, part-time work begins in their teens and often earlier. They work mainly because they want or need money and/or because they wish to be more independent of their families. Modeling on peers plays a part. Young people work, even when they do not have to or particularly want to, because their friends have part-time jobs. They work because they need to help the family financially. Finally, they often work very early in life because their families believe in the ethic of work. Work broadens their horizons, teaches them to adjust to peers and supervisors, provides leads toward later careers, bores and irritates them, gives them success and failure experiences, and affects them in a multitude of other ways. It is likely (no one has clearly determined this) that early work experience is a beneficial growth experience; on the other hand it is conceivable that it can be a negative growth experience. Working alongside fathers and mothers or modeling on them is a time-honored way of learning an adult role in life. We see that this is as true in modern society (93) as it was historically.

Perhaps the most important function of work for older children and early adolescents is to build a bridge between childhood and adulthood. Work, in a sense, is a "weaning process."

From their early jobs, older children and youth are aided in personal autonomy and independence from their families. Their social lives are usually broadened, not always in a benign, but typically in a constructive, sense; personal flexibility is promoted; and social skills are developed. Adjustment to the remorseless demands of a technological, time-clock-oriented society is made (this may not be good but is usually necessary). Early work and semiwork experiences may be related to later careers (see Nina's incidental experience, Example 12.3, in working with her sisters' hair and makeup, and how this led to a later successful career choice). When an older child or an adolescent succeeds in a work experience, his self-confidence and -esteem are likely to be enhanced. Finally, particularly for advantaged older children and youth, early work experiences are provisional tries or role rehearsals for later life. Thus, they are valuable educational experiences.

Rejection of the Work Ethic

An increasing number of young people seemingly reject the United States work ethic. They want nothing to do with the rat race that has produced ulcers, cardiovascular tension, and overconsumption of alcohol by their elders. Typically, such youth come from advantaged, liberal families. They do not choose to pay the price for economic security, power, status, and prestige that their parents have paid. Thus, some are high school dropouts, and many more (often including gifted and creative people) are college dropouts. Some experts believe that the combined, free, antiestablishment thinking of this group will lead to "the greening of America." Certainly, their liberalizing and sometimes disturbing behavior has produced thoughtfulness and often unease in American society. However, others believe (10) that as this liberal, rebellious, and intelligent segment of society drops out, their logical and "predestined places" in the social order will be taken by conservative and equally intelligent young people from the working class. Thus, instead of the "greening of America," the "blueing of America" will occur.

Occupational Choice and Entry

Immediate occupational choice and entry (very likely to determine one's entire vocational life; see the illustrations in Example 12.3) are likely to depend on the following four personal factors (14).

1. The occupational information possessed.
2. The person's technical qualifications.
3. The person's social role characteristics.
4. The person's reward value hierarchy.

Occupational Information. It is obvious that the more one knows about career possibilities, the wider the range of choices he has. Among disadvantaged youth particularly, vocational drift is the rule. The authors believe it is the responsibility of families and schools (and the latter should ideally be better prepared) to supply all youth with information about the broad range of vocational choice available in a society as technical as ours.

In this context, it is important not only that older children and youth know the range and the kinds of opportunity that may be available for them, but that they have some awareness of the nature of a job as it may relate to job satisfaction. A great deal of such information is now available (for example, 44, 103, 111). For example, eight factors seem essential to the job satisfaction of clerical and craft workers of both sexes (44). (1) The work itself is interesting. (2) The job is not wasteful of time and effort—there is an efficiency factor, in other words. (3) Some freedom in planning the job is made available to the worker, as well as the fourth factor. (4) Some latitude in how the job is actually done. (5) The job provides opportunities. (6) Feedback is given about job performance. (7) Lenient and not too close supervision is provided. (8) The job is worth putting effort into. Remarkably little difference between males and females seems to exist in what makes a job attractive, although there is some difference in satisfaction by level of job. Higher occupational levels assign more value to the intrinsic nature of the job—for example, how interesting is the job and does it provide opportunity for self-expression; lower levels are more likely to value pay, security, and the company of coworkers—extrinsic values (103).

Such differential job values already have been shown to appear as early as the ninth grade as a function of social class and possibly race (111). In this study, inner-city males and females stress the objective qualities (extrinsic) that they would look for when they went to work, while suburban males are more likely to expect self-satisfaction from their work. The highest group in expectation of need satisfaction (from groups of inner-city boys and girls and of suburban boys and girls) are the suburban boys. Over all, regardless of social class and race, males more than females are attracted by jobs that include risk, opportunity for advancement, and prestige, and that have to do with things rather than people. The *personal* satisfaction aspect of work, however, is more likely to be stressed by females than by males. These results, it should be noted, fit well into our discussion of socialization patterns in Chapter 8.

Technical Qualification. The matter of technical qualification requires little discussion. In a technological society, it is obvious that the youth with the best training will best fill a job. He is also most likely to be hired, barring employer bias of some sort (such as bias against females, blacks, or those under age 21).

Social Role Characteristics. We all know that different occupations convey different amounts of social prestige and power. This common knowledge is also well buttressed by research (58). For example, physicians, scientists, and Supreme Court justices have higher prestige than businessmen and those who work with their hands. Thus, it is certain that more youth will *aspire* to (although not necessarily *expect*) prestige occupations; and that lower level jobs will more likely be filled by those who drift into them or take them more or less as a last resort. It is certain that "drift" will lower job morale.

Reward value hierarchies. An individual's reward value hierarchy is also important in determining what sort of job he will take, given the opportunity, and how happy he will be in it once he is settled. A person desiring social prestige may take a low-paying job if it is one that reflects such prestige, rather than a less prestigious job with higher pay. If a person is adventurous, he will choose in one direction; if he values security strongly, his choice will lie in another direction. Many consider reward value hierarchies to be closely related to personality (39, 59), but the research findings are not yet sufficiently clear that really firm vocational guidance can be given on the basis of personality data (39).

Interactions of personal characteristics and other factors. Barring bias factors of one sort or another, it is obvious that high-aptitude, well-informed, well-trained, and personally well-adjusted youth will have more vocational opportunity than those who are less bright, ill trained, and maladjusted; however, other factors affect vocational choice, such as the social structure. A developing nation needs fewer lawyers, for example, than a developed nation, and an agricultural nation does not need many physicists. Social change alters the job picture; for example, even a few years ago it seemed that the demand for secondary and elementary school teachers would never be met. As this book is being written, it is almost impossible for a secondary teacher of English or social studies to find a job; and it has become as much a buyer's market as a seller's for elementary teachers.

Many youth, unfortunately, face non-functional requirements that make vocational choice and placement difficult for them. There is still prejudice (diminishing fairly rapidly, the authors believe and hope) against some minority groups, and women are discriminated against in many cases. A person who is too young or too old is often discriminated against; a fat person has a harder time getting a job than a thin person, and so on.

Guidance and Vocational Development

As is always the case in applying psychology to the lives of actual people, the role of vocational guidance counselor in either the formal sense (for example, the professional guidance counselor) or the informal sense (for example, the parent and the teacher who do not have specific professional guidance training) is part science and part art. The authors suspect that successful vocational guidance and vocational development themselves are also part luck.

For such reasons, this short subsection is avowedly not purely scientific. Candidly, the authors are setting down recommendations for the sort of vocational guidance they would like their own children to have. (These children include both sons and daughters.)

First, the authors firmly believe that competence training in homes and in schools is as important for females as for males; nor do they believe that females should be guided only in the direction of stereotyped "feminine occupations." By the same token, empathy and skill in human relations should be encouraged in boys.

Second, the authors believe that the rewards inherent in the arts, humanities, and social sciences should be made as clear to both female and male children and youth as the rewards in the traditionally "masculine fields," such as science, engineering, and mathematics.

Third, because the American social order and technology change so rapidly and often unpredictably, the authors believe that the best base for vocational development and choice is a solid, wide-ranging general education. They think that such an education can be provided better in the twelve or thirteen years of schooling the modal United States citizen experiences than is currently being provided.

Fourth, the authors believe in modeling and experience as valuable backgrounds for a youth's vocational choice. For this reason, they want their children to know in candid detail the nature, rewards, and vexations of their own occupations and of the occupations of as many of their friends and colleagues as is feasible. They would also like their children to have part-time teen-age (or even earlier) work experience in as many different kinds of job as possible.

Fifth, the authors would like their children to take advantage of professional guidance services in their high schools and their colleges, if they attend. Such guidance should be obtained early, as a majority of youth have made rather firm vocational choices by twelfth grade (60).

The authors have already implied the kinds of information that should be gathered by guidance counselors. First, while the authors recognize the limitations of the trait-factor approach, they believe that it has much to offer if applied flexibly and cautiously. Some encouraging results of this approach have been reported (see the references spotted throughout this section, in addition to, for example, 117, in which information about the usefulness of this approach is reported for working-class boys).

It is also essential that youth be provided with as much accurate and current sociological information about vocational patterns and changes as possible. Such a school function is as legitimate as the teaching of English.

About the last two conceptual approaches to vocational development and choice discussed (self-concept theory and personality dynamics), the authors have reservations. Much of self-concept and personality theory is based on clinical or abnormal psychology; applying it indiscriminantly to normal teen-agers can be hazardous. On the other hand, older children and youth should have access to any available useful information about which types of personality and self concept fit best with which types of vocation. On the surface, it seems that a very gregarious type should steer away from an isolated vocation, for example, and that the insecure, withdrawn person should look to a job where success does not hinge entirely on one's skill in dealing with the public. In this connection, vocational interest tests can provide useful information to youth about themselves and others who share similar clusters of personal preferences, as these clusters may be related to vocational behavior. Such tests are at least indirectly related to personality and self concept. Unfortunately, these tests are often mistaken for indicators of vocational aptitude or for absolute predictors of vocational satisfaction. In short, the authors caution against the potential for misusing and misinterpreting vocational interest inventories.

A Persisting Dilemma about Vocational Guidance

Given the five approaches to vocational development that have been discussed, it is plausible to think that a young person has a good chance of fairly orderly and successful progression toward choice, entry, and, eventually, success and satisfaction in a vocational role. Choices should not be forced prematurely, however, especially in periods where job opportunities and requirements are rapidly changing. The major dilemma for today's youth, as the authors see it, is represented by a conflict during adolescence between two basic developmental tasks (101). The first is identity seeking (see Chapter 11), which, by definition, is an exploratory process. The second is reaching a specific vocational choice, which, by definition, is an entrenching process. All things considered, the authors place the higher priority on identity seeking, especially during early and middle adolescence, whereby the individual tests himself in a wide variety of situations and learns the intricacies of self-evaluation and self-understanding.

It is probably true that the college-bound youth has the advantage over his non-college-bound counterpart in identity seeking; he is in effect buying more time for self-development and self-exploration. Noncollege youth, in contrast, often find themselves forced to make highly specific choices about vocational roles in order simply to survive. It is this group of young people that the authors believe need much

Non-college-bound youth often find little of personal relevance in the school curriculum.
(Wide World Photos)

more attention in the schools than has been given them in the past. Example 12.4 is included to highlight this problem.

12.4 How Do Non-College-Bound High School Graduates Perceive Their Vocational Guidance?

A trio of research workers (11) explored the perceptions of 309 non-college-bound, vocationally oriented high school graduates by conducting in-depth structured interviews. The interviews covered four main topics—educational experiences,

vocational experiences, self concept, and family relationships. Data were gathered two years subsequent to these graduates' high school commencement. The youth involved represented those from both rural and urban environments in four different mid-central states.

Interview data are often difficult to analyze in as objective and technical a fashion as, say, psychological test scores. Nevertheless, a content analysis of the interview responses led the researchers to four major conclusions about these young graduates' impressions of school and family experience. First, non-college-oriented youth generally perceived their school, including teachers and counselors, as favoring the college-bound student. Second, these youth perceived their high school counselors as not very helpful in terms of the details and the realities of assisting employment-bound persons toward satisfactory vocational decisions. Third, these youth were judged generally unable to articulate clearly and realistically a view of self (see also 70). Fourth, and finally, the subjects of this study did not perceive their parents as helping agents in matters of resolving personal, educational, and vocational problems.

It is impossible, of course, to tell from a study such as this whether the perceptions reported by non-college-bound youth accurately reflect their life situations. Nevertheless, perceptions, regardless of their validity, exist and must be dealt with accordingly.

Social Deviancy among Youth

As is true for adults, most youth lead moderately respectable lives, and many of them lead exceptionally constructive lives. Others get into trouble, some quietly, intrapersonally, and sometimes desperately. Others get into trouble more conspicuously. Most pronounced today are troubles involving drug use and abuse, and juvenile delinquency.

Youth and Drugs

Introduction. Although exact figures are not available, youth workers have little reason to doubt that drug use during adolescence has become steadily more widespread during recent years. Of the various substances included in this increased drug-taking behavior, the *hallucinogens* (for example, LSD, mescaline, cannabis), *delirients* (for example, airplane glue,

aerosol sprays), and *depressants* (for example, barbiturates, ethyl alcohol) are most frequently abused by the young. Still other substances, however, have been used by certain segments of the youth population, including the *stimulants* (for example, cocaine, amphetamines) and *opiates* (for example, heroin, morphine).

As the reader may suspect, many factors are associated with patterns of adolescent drug abuse. In the case of delinquency, these factors include age and socioeconomic status. Delirients and depressants, for instance, are used more frequently by younger adolescents (ages 11–14), perhaps because these substances are comparatively easy to secure. Older adolescents (ages 15–19) are increasingly experimenting with the hallucinogens, especially marijuana (140). In addition to age differences, social-class variations in drug abuse are apparent. More frequent use of the opiates and the stimulants occurs among adolescents from the lower social class (for example, 2), although this pattern may be changing.

Finally, it is clear that alcohol is drunk freely by the adolescent, regardless of social class. Possibly because alcohol is such an institutionalized aspect of adult social life (most adults know alcohol from personal use), use of alcohol by youth seems not to create the degree of distress among parents as does the use of other drugs. For this and other reasons, the discussion is focused largely on data concerning youth and hallucinogens, stimulants, and opiates. Judging from mass media reports, adults generally are deeply concerned about youth's experimentation with these drugs *and* the possible consequence of such experimentation: dependence on drugs (25).

A person may depend on drugs for both physical and psychological reasons.

While the use of drugs in former years was a phenomenon more of poverty than of affluence, its spread to the advantaged has generated more public attention, and, it is hoped, a more constructive approach, to the problem. (Photo by Bob Combs)

Thus, adults are clearly concerned about the implications of drug use for a young person's physical and mental health. The following excerpt will clarify the meaning of drug dependence.

Physical dependence refers to the alteration of body functions produced by a drug, such that withdrawal results in the appearance of certain signs and symptoms which vary with the drug of dependence. *Psychological dependence* refers to a person's subjective need for a drug. *Primary psychological dependence* indicates that the need is associated with drug effects which the user considers desirable. *Secondary psychological dependence* indicates that the need is associated with

avoidance of negative effects resulting from the discontinued drug use (25, p. 300).

Adult concern about drug dependence and health is augmented by a fear that drug use leads to delinquent behaviors, such as theft and sexual promiscuity. The relationship between drug abuse and delinquency is poorly documented; but many law enforcement officials known to the authors seem convinced that much of the increase in burglary among youth, for example, is motivated by the need or the desire to support a drug habit. Finally, and especially in the case of the most popular drug—marijuana—drug use is often perceived by adults as symbolizing a life style that runs counter to basic, traditional social values (for example, responsibility, competitiveness, rationality, and deferred gratification). Hence, to many adults the widespread use of drugs by youth represents a threat to the existing social order (68).

Motivation for Drug Abuse. Aside from questions about the consequences of drug taking to health, much of the recent drug research has been designed to explore motivational patterns that underlie drug abuse and the attitudes of youth toward drugs. Most analyses of such research — limited though they may be — reinforce a point made repeatedly throughout this book — human behavior has multiple causes. For example, some investigators (for instance, 122) present data indicating that extensive drug use by many adolescents represents a wish to escape conventional social constraints and pressures. Others (119) emphasize more the idea that certain drugs, especially marijuana, have simply become a symbol for a new social pattern among America's youth in much the same way as did alcohol for previous generations. Still others (54) bring a strong psychoanalytic perspective to drug taking. From this perspective it is argued that immoderate drug use is a pervasive symptom of familiar problems experienced by the young, regardless of their particular generational identity: difficulties with parents (including dependency conflicts), early traumatic experiences, low frustration tolerance, depression, anxiety, and difficulties in establishing mature interpersonal relationships.

A major problem in such analyses, of course, is distinguishing between drug *use* and drug *abuse*. For the authors, it is not plausible to argue that, say, occasional pot smoking at weekend parties can be taken to indicate either personal–social disturbance or intense generational conflict. On the other hand, the persistent and habitual use of drugs to the point where one's life is organized around the acquisition and dispensation of drugs is another matter. Drug abuse, then, refers most specifically to a condition whereby a user's functioning or health — physical and/or psychological — is significantly impaired or results in actions that are harmful to others. It is apparent, however, that even gross comparisons of youth who are and are not "into the drug scene" suggest broad motivational differences between users and nonusers, irrespective of the *abuse* factor. For example, it is reported that marijuana users, as a group, characterize themselves as more alienated from society than do nonusers of the drug (53). Other self-report data illustrate an even broader spectrum of youth motivations for drug taking, many of which can be considered "normal": curiosity seeking, peer group conformity and social acceptance, tension relief, the "thrill" of experiencing a psychotic-like state, and unhappy home life (71, 135).

With the possible exception of curiosity seeking, these professed motives can be phrased in terms of several conceptual themes discussed in previous contexts in this book: (1) drug use as a means of achieving status and recognition within one's peer group; (2) drugs as an illusory promise of identity formulation; and (3) drugs as a means of escaping, if only temporarily, the stresses, anxieties, and increased responsibilities of adolescence. To these may be added the idea of modeling, that is, drug use in imitation of adults who themselves represent a drug-oriented social order (25); but it is difficult to determine the extent to which these themes actually influence the youth drug scene.

Some Personal–Social Characteristics of Adolescent Drug Users. The foregoing themes are useful for a psychological analysis of drug use. However, extensive and well-controlled studies of adolescent drug use are rare; they provide only limited empirical support for generalizations stated thus far in this section. Fortunately, some insight can be gleaned from a handful of studies that concern personality characteristics of adolescent drug users. For example, a predisposition to modify oneself through physical means, such as drugs, has been linked to two aspects of self-perception: general dissatisfaction with self and the absence of any defenses or self-imposed restraints against changing one's behavior with the aid of drugs (16). Both these factors likely contribute to a decision to take drugs. Yet neither necessarily indicates pathology.

On the other hand, excessive drug use — to the point of exclusion from normal school and social activities — can be more clearly associated with personality problems. For example, one authority sees drug excesses as a defense against certain basic feelings (dependency conflicts, sexual desire, hostility) that an adolescent may experience but is unable to deal with satisfactorily (43). The idea is most directly related to escapism mentioned earlier, although this dynamic may involve only a small percentage of adolescent drug users.

Still other research has revealed a relationship between aggression and drug use. Heavy users of the hallucinogenic drugs, for instance, are frequently characterized by high levels of hostility (3, 33).

Such data also indicate that regular drug use may serve a dual purpose: a means for relieving aggressive feelings while simultaneously providing a channel for hostile expression (through law breaking) in a way that is acceptable to both oneself and one's drug-using peers. Perhaps escapism, combined with aggression stirred by frustration, underlies much drug abuse. At least, it seems clear that a plurality of motives or predisposing factors can be explained for drug taking.

The peer involvement suggested above, in addition to the pleasurable physical effects that result from taking many drugs, undoubtedly constitute powerful, immediate, positive reinforcement for drug-taking behavior. In other words, the camaraderie generated by mutual drug taking and the immediate physical sensations provided by many drugs may quickly shape a pattern of preferred social involvement. Given the necessary setting of drug availability, opportunity to experiment, ability to learn the "hows" of drug taking to achieve maximum effects, peer group norms that support drug use — many cases of drug use may simply represent a normally learned set of responses that is maintained by social and other reinforcements (2).

The many facets of adolescent drug use can be summarized by citing three general categories of drug users (30). The largest category consists of individuals who apparently have no serious emotional problems, try drugs primarily out of curiosity, and, once after a brief period of experimentation, decide on their own to stop. Drug dependence is unlikely for these youth; they seldom, if ever, experiment with opiates or stimulants. It is possible, of course, that, after experimentation, many youth find that the moderate and continued use of nonaddicting drugs (as is perhaps the case with marijuana) results in no apparent emotional or physical problems. Such use may even become "socially respectable" within the peer group, despite the legal sanctions involved.

A second category includes youth who may initiate a program of regular drug use only to discover that drug taking interferes with school work and other important activities. They may then abandon the habit, but may need professional assistance to do so. The third category of drug users consists of youth whose adjustment is sufficiently threatened that drugs provide an attempt, however self-defeating in the long run, to escape, avoid, or otherwise cope with their existing problems. Youth so disposed frequently resort to increasingly powerful drugs, and, as their tolerance levels increase, so usually does the probability of genuine dependence. In general, however, it is likely that chronic drug abuse will occur only among those whose preexisting psychological development is tenuous (25). An example of research about drug abuse relevant to this point is described in Example 12.5.

12.5 An Example of Drug Abuse Research

Melvin Cohen and Donald Klein became interested in the relationship of various social and clinical variables (such as intelligence, school adjustment, social class, family relations, and sexual adjustment) to patterns of drug abuse among adolescents and young adults (23). To explore this relationship, Cohen and Klein identified three patient groups from a sample of young (under 25) persons of both sexes—middle class, mostly white, and Jewish—who were admitted

during 1966–1967 for psychiatric help in a New York City hospital. These three groups were delineated on the basis of two characteristics: the number of drugs used prior to hospital admission and the extent of previous drug use. The three groups and their composition are as follows:

1. An "extreme" use group, composed of thirty-nine persons, for whom drug taking was a major activity, that is, daily use of two or more drugs for a period of one month or longer.
2. A "moderate mixed" group, composed of sixteen persons, who used either two or more drugs irregularly or one drug (excluding marijuana) on weekends or at parties.
3. A "moderate marijuana only" group, composed of fifteen persons, who had previously used marijuana not more than twice. These were not considered drug users.

In addition, and for purposes of comparison, a nondrug control group was selected. This group was composed of thirty-five persons matched with the drug sample in terms of admission criteria.

A careful comparison of the various group members resulted in several findings of interest to the student of drug abuse. First, in all drug groups, females were two years younger, on the average, than their male counterparts at time of admission for treatment. Second, those in the "extreme" drug use group generally had higher IQs than their peers in other groups. Third, virtually all drug group subjects had used marijuana at some time; no other drug was reported as having been used exclusively or as frequently. Other drugs used, in order of frequency, included: amphetamines, LSD, barbiturates, and heroin (tried only after previous use of other drugs). In addition, alcohol use was greater among drug users than the controls). Fourth, there were no significant differences between the four groups in family background and school adjustment; however, a trend toward school problems was disclosed for the "extreme" group. Fifth, significantly greater sexual promiscuity was noted for females (versus males) in the drug groups. This promiscuity apparently was not related to economics. Sixth, those in the "extreme" group were found to spend a significantly greater amount of time away from home than were members of other groups. Finally, there was a tendency for "extremes" to be diagnosed as having character disorders, especially emotional instability, rather than any form of psychosis; a greater incidence of psychosis was attributed to the moderate and control groups.

According to Cohen and Klein, these findings are important primarily for two reasons. The first concerns the IQ–drug use relationship. Two possible explanations of this relationship are offered. One is that persons of higher intelligence may be more predisposed to seek out "unusual experiences," such as a psychedelic trip. The other possibility is that, among persons heavily dependent on drugs, only the more intelligent voluntarily request professional help. A third reason (that of the present authors) may be that those with higher IQ seem to be more discontented with themselves (that is, in that they fail to live up to their ideals of what they should be), and are also more clearly able to perceive the difficulties in our complex society (70).

The second finding of importance stressed by Cohen and Klein concerns the drug use–psychiatric disorder relationship. They again offer two possible explanations for the fact that psychotics were not found among the "extremes" but were found in the other groups. First, they state that a psychotic may lack the social skills that are necessary to sustain a pattern of heavy drug use. Second, they argue that heavy drug use may be a method of achieving the "spontaneous euphoria" that periodically occurs among people with disorders characterized by emotional instability. In short, drugs may be used to replicate the best of the world in which an emotionally unstable person lives.

The Dilemma of Drug Education in the Schools. Given the possibility that serious, self-defeating habits may quickly be developed during the vulnerable period of adolescence, the school is increasingly considered a key place in which to concentrate measures that counteract drug use. Moreover, a rationale for the role of the school in this regard can be organized around several issues. One involves the extent to which drug use (including drug pushing) is plainly inconsistent with educational goals, legal sanctions notwithstanding. A second and related issue is the interfering effect that drug abuse may have on academic achievement. A third is the even broader commitment of educators to schooling as a means for more intelligent self-understanding and self-direction among children and youth.

Unfortunately, comprehensive drug education programs have been slow to develop. Many schools were (and still are) ill prepared to establish effective programs when the drug problem became so apparent during the late 1960s (12). Consequently, little is yet known about the impact of drug education on children. On the basis of initial experience in this area, however, useful guidelines for drug education program development have emerged (82, 95, 140). These include the following.

1. Necessity for long-term planning to insure a comprehensive, honest examination of facts and issues concerning drugs and their use.
2. Importance of preventive approaches to the drug problem as opposed to primary or exclusive attention to the rehabilitation of drug-dependent youth.
3. Emphasis on developing among children and youth a respect for the power of drugs, including those used for legitimate medical purposes.
4. Student involvement in planning and executing drug education programs (especially critical at the secondary school level).
5. Attention to the implications of drug taking for the individual adolescent, including the consequences of drug use for personal life style, social relationships, and future orientation.
6. Avoidance of scare tactics and strategies based on moral injunctions.
7. Emphasis on a logical analysis of drug-taking behavior in settings that provide ample opportunity for discussion.

Obviously, teachers must be well informed about drugs and their effects if they wish to be considered credible agents of drug education. Teachers must also be attuned to the social psychology of the drug scene, must be familiar with drug jargon or slang used in the drug culture, and must be prepared to deal sensibly with the pros, as well as the cons, of drug use. Collectively, these skills seem necessary prerequisites for effective communication with the young. Unfortunately, they are sadly lacking in many teachers with whom the authors have recently been associated.

Many readers of this book may find themselves deep in the complexities of developing and implementing drug education programs in the schools. Many of the associated issues are identical with those involved in sex education; that is, decisions about specific program content must be made. The problem of timing is also important, that is, determining when material should be introduced and in what sequence. Instructional methods must be devised, and personnel to effect drug education must be selected. Certainly, the issue of program evaluation cannot be overlooked; this includes a consideration of program objectives *and* the means to measure how well such objectives are achieved.

As this book is being written, many developments that suggest implications for drug education are occurring. For example, there is the continuing dilemma of what effects—physical and psychological, reversible and irreversible, short term and long term—can reliably be attributed to the use of various drugs. Another is what factors actually influence trends in drug use. For example, LSD use reportedly is decreasing, while heroin use is increasing, at the time of this writing. The reason(s) for this situation is not clear. Still other issues prevail, such as the possible legalization of marijuana. These and other issues merit the continued scrutiny of youth workers involved in drug education.

Juvenile Delinquency

Introduction. To establish a context for a discussion of juvenile delinquency and the school, the authors wish to make three basic points. First, perhaps the most central feature of what we call "delinquency" is its antisocial character. As one authority puts it:

"Juvenile delinquency is usually described as norm-violating behavior. Legally a juvenile is delinquent if he commits an act that violates the law and is convicted by the court. Behaviorally, he is delinquent if he expresses aggressive, overt actions contrary to the demands of society. In either case his activity is antisocial" (130, p. 219). This definition of delinquency, while generally satisfactory, needs elaboration to describe more precisely the current status of juvenile delinquency in American society. For example, it is desirable to differentiate between "true delinquency" and "pseudodelinquency" (48). True delinquency can be defined as that which occurs repeatedly, and if the offenses are committed beyond the statutory juvenile court age of 16, they are punishable as either felonies or misdemeanors. Pseudodelinquency, in contrast, refers to occasional deviation from acceptable norms for conduct; it does not indicate a chronic or habitual pattern of criminal acting-out. In the absence of this distinction between true delinquency and pseudodelinquency, practically every juvenile could be classified as delinquent. In other words, authorities generally agree that juvenile delinquency is not an either–or affair. Most children and youth behave in a delinquent manner at some time and in some fashion during the course of their development; but contemporary social concern is stronger in relation to the degree of frequency and the seriousness of delinquent acts.

Second, it is clear that the rate of juvenile delinquency in the United States (and most nations of the world marked by increased economic growth and social complexity) has risen progressively since World War II. This increase, moreover is disproportionate to juvenile population growth over the same time span (139). Whereas in 1960, for instance, approximately twenty delinquency cases per one thousand juveniles (ages 11–17) were reported, roughly twenty-nine per one thousand were recorded in 1968. At the present time, about 3 percent of the juvenile population is referred to juvenile courts during a single year, although over twice this number has been in some kind of trouble with the police (46, 47). Some authorities (for example, 136) estimate that a more accurate rate of true delinquency is about 10 percent of the juvenile population.

Third, it is clear that juvenile delinquency is an extremely complex phenomenon, one that represents multiple (versus single) causation. In fact, much of the research about delinquency has been aimed at dispelling many popular myths concerning the causes of delinquency. Simple explanations based on the singular impact of slum conditions, low intelligence, working mothers, the mass media, and "bad genes" have been abandoned by students of delinquency in favor of more sophisticated hypotheses. Some of these hypotheses are mentioned after a brief description of factors that mediate patterns of delinquency.

Finally, some youth (and these are most often advantaged, intelligent youth high in moral judgment) sometimes commit legally delinquent acts because of sincere, well-thought-out convictions that the social order is wrong. Examples of such official delinquencies by individuals and groups are civil disobedience about such issues and practices as racial discrimination, the draft, napalm, the Southeast Asia war, ecology, and so on.

Some Mediating Factors in Juvenile Delinquency. As with other behavior patterns discussed in this book, patterns of delinquency are mediated by many factors. As examples, three such factors are considered: age, sex, and social class.

Age. At least two basic generalizations about the relationship of age to delinquency patterns have strong factual support. First, a disproportionate number of total criminal offenses occur among the juvenile population, as compared to other age groups. In the home county of one of the authors, for example, over one-half the felonies occurring from 1965–1970 (including murder, rape, auto theft, and assault) were committed by juveniles (110). Second, from preadolescence onward, juvenile delinquency becomes progressively more diverse and serious. According to one report, for instance, the frequency of offenses against *persons* (murder, rape, assault) and *property* (robbery, vandalism, forgery) and *disorderly conduct* increases steadily with age (45). Similarly, other reports (for example, 5) indicate that crimes of aggression increase "precipitously" to about age 19, increase less sharply thereafter, and decline rapidly after age 25.

Reasons most commonly advanced to account for these generalizations include the frustration–aggression hypothesis (see Chapter 10), alienation among youth, delayed maturation (including retarded moral development), differential association by juveniles with delinquent models, and the unadulterated audacity of the young, often manifested in thrill seeking and nose thumbing at the adult establishment (4, 7, 47, 49). Fortunately, there is much evidence to indicate that, for many delinquent youth, antisocial and criminal behavior is a temporary phenomenon. In other words, it has become increasingly clear that juvenile delinquency does not

necessarily lead to adult criminality. This, of course, is no reason for society to take delinquency lightly or to exempt the young from being accountable for their own actions.

Sex. Marked sex differences in delinquency occur throughout adolescence (5, 45, 47, 98). Boys generally begin delinquency earlier and engage in such practice more frequently than girls. This observation has support from juvenile court records, which currently indicate that for every female referral there are from four to five male referrals, with males usually younger at the time of their first referral. Moreover, the basis for court referral is usually different for the two sexes. Boys, for example, are more often referred for theft, assault, vandalism, and other direct, aggressive offenses than are girls. Delinquency among girls, in contrast, more typically consists of sexual promiscuity, petty shoplifting, running away from home, and general incorrigibility.

Sex-related delinquency patterns undoubtedly reflect differences in cultural conditioning, motivation, opportunity, and the degree to which society tolerates deviant behavior among young males and females. It is also apparent, however, that differences exist in the antecedents of delinquency for boys and girls. Family tension and conflict, for example, are often more profound factors in female (versus male) delinquency (47).

Social class. A traditional and popular view of delinquency is that such behavior is primarily a product of low socioeconomic conditions. That delinquency occurs among juveniles of the lower social class cannot be refuted. However, delinquency is by no means limited to this stratum of society. Currently, middle-class delinquency is also commonplace, although it may be more often "hidden" than is lower-class delinquency (that is, it may go undetected or unreported by legal authorities).

Despite the absence of a definitive relationship between social class and delinquency, official records indicate that middle-class delinquency is relatively less serious (47). One extensive analysis of delinquency in terms of the offenders' social-class status illustrates clearly this idea (21). In general, this analysis disclosed that middle-class youths are comparatively "underinvolved" in robbery, truancy, larceny, and vagrancy, while somewhat "overrepresented" in traffic violations, vandalism, joyriding, and violations of liquor and curfew ordinances. Lower-class youth more frequently commit offenses that result in personal gain and in injury (or the threat of injury) to property and people. Finally, there is some indication that *habitual* misconduct is less likely among middle-class juveniles than among lower-class juveniles. This last point may be the clearest of the social-class distinctions.

Not much is known about "upper class" delinquency, perhaps because of its even more hidden nature. Some work in this area has begun, however. For example, one authority reports that upper-class boys in private school settings report more delinquent acts and a more permissive attitude toward deviancy than do their upper- and middle-class counterparts in the public schools (134).

In summary, factors such as age, sex, and social class combine to influence patterns of delinquency in complex ways. Clear age, sex, and social-class differences in both the kind and the frequency of delinquency can be observed. Caution must be exercised, however, in generaliz-

ing about these differences, because of widespread differences in detecting, reporting, and prosecuting juvenile delinquents that occur from one community to another and probably from more advantaged to less advantaged children and youth. The latter are more likely to be caught and prosecuted (78).

Approaches to the Explanation of Juvenile Delinquency. There are many approaches to the explanation of juvenile delinquency in United States culture. Some explanatory concepts have already been mentioned in the section on mediators of delinquency. These and other concepts can be conveniently grouped into one of three broad interpretive frameworks, including the biogenic, psychogenic, and sociogenic perspectives (47). Faulty biology, hereditary defects, or body build and temperament are viewed as principal predisposing factors in delinquency by those who take the *biogenic* perspective. Supporters of the *psychogenic* perspective differ widely on theoretical details, but most stress the notion that delinquency is a symptom of maladjustment or psychic conflict often rooted in faulty parent–child relations. Psychoanalysis, with its emphasis on the impact of early familial experience on emotional development, falls into this category. Those who take the *sociogenic* perspective more typically view delinquency as behavior learned normally within a given social structure, including gangs that evolve into a delinquent subculture. In other words, it is the broader social environment–not psychic disturbance or genetic disorder–that is the generating factor in delinquency according to the sociogenic viewpoint.

As suggested, some authorities lean strongly toward the first two perspectives (for example, 49, 118), while others definitely favor the third (for example, 19, 47). Even within a given approach, however, there is rarely a clear consensus about causal factors. For example, authorities who identify with a sociogenic view of working-class delinquency differ in the extent to which they stress variables such as (1) avenues for status that are denied to lower-class males (opportunity failure), (2) social-class value conflicts, (3) a matriarchal tradition of family relations in lower-class life, and (4) various forms of economic and social deprivation (47). Still other variables also receive attention in sociogenic interpretations of middle-class delinquency. These include the quest for masculinity, a lack of commitment to adult roles and values, status inconsistencies produced by rapid upward social mobility, and various forms of exploitation by the parents of juveniles (for example, excessive pressures for achievement) (36, 94).

The point, again, is that different forms of delinquency probably occur for different reasons. At this time, authorities do not agree that a universal theory of criminal behavior can account for these different forms. To illustrate further the diversity of delinquent behavior and factors that contribute to it, the authors have chosen to describe categories of delinquency in Example 12.6.

12.6 Categories of Delinquent Behavior

The recognition that delinquency has many causes and can take many forms has led to various attempts at categorizing patterns of antisocial behavior. Such categorization is usually done on the basis (1) of clusters of observable behavior, (2) of responses to psychological tests, (3) of analyses of case his-

tory data, and (4) of suspected causal relationships (see, for example, 97). Categorization, in this sense, has at least two potential and interrelated values. First, it assists in an understanding of delinquency among a given group of juveniles. Second, it can be an aid in the differential diagnosis of delinquency in order better to match treatment strategies with causative factors. One such tentative categorization has been proposed by William W. Wattenberg (136), a long-term student of adolescent behavior. This categorization is the result of a synthesis of research about individual differences in delinquent behavior and response to adult intervention. It is important to recognize, however, that no standard terminology has yet been developed to describe these categories and that Wattenberg seems to take a largely psychogenic perspective on delinquency. Moreover, new research may necessitate the modification of such categories. Finally, to the four categories presented here may be added a fifth, namely: the socially and intellectually inept type of delinquent who may respond best to a firm, clearly organized environment based on contingency management.

CATEGORY I. Boys variously designated as explosive, ego-damaged, or unsocialized aggressive, who come out of homes usually described as rejecting and whose offenses are often accompanied by an outpouring of aggression. The tendency is to look to some form of residential treatment as most likely to be effective. This group is generally regarded as one difficult to deal with.

CATEGORY II. Boys and girls whose delinquency seems to have a purposeless, compulsive quality which expresses, if anything, some kind of basic conflict.

These seem to come from homes in which parents are demanding, restrictive, or vacillating. Such young people often react well to probation, counseling, casework, or clinical treatment.

CATEGORY III. Boys and girls who have "weak consciences" but who form many apparently normal, good relationships with their peers. Most often the families live in high-delinquency areas and, typically, do not supervise the young people. Offenses are incubated in groups. The recommended treatment requires placing the young person in a group that exemplifies socially acceptable norms.

CATEGORY IV. Some writers also describe a "cool cat" or "confidence man" personality—boys and girls who are capable of self-control and who deliberately manipulate other people. Neither the description of the causes of this behavior nor the recommended handling of this group is as well documented as the three preceding categories.

Delinquency and the School. Thus far, nothing specific has been said concerning the relationship of juvenile delinquency and schooling. The comments on this point are organized around two themes: (1) delinquency and school achievement, including how the school may contribute to patterns of delinquency, and (2) the role of the school in dealing with the delinquency problem.

Delinquency and school achievement. First, a prominent relationship between school maladaptation and delinquency has long been observed by psychologists and educators (118). Persistent truancy frequently marks the initial step in school maladaptation and delinquency, and, as in the case of school dropouts, a disproportionate number of retarded readers are found among groups of juvenile delinquents, especially boys. Authors (for example, 63) consistently reveal that many chronic delinquents share a relatively low level of conceptual functioning. This includes difficulties in abstract linguistic school tasks, a heavy dependence on concrete thought, impulsivity, low deferred gratification, and low attentiveness. Obviously, such characteristics usually impede rather than facilitate school progress, and may contribute to frustration or failure in academic endeavors.

Second, many authorities (for example, 108), especially those who prefer a sociogenic view of delinquency, believe that negative school experiences act as a powerful propellant of youth into patterns of delinquency. It is often argued that school represents an overwhelming obstacle to goal or status attainment for many youth who are ill equipped or unmotivated for the successful pursuit of school activities. Delinquency, therefore, may be a common response of youth to this developmental hazard. It is perhaps significant that among school dropouts who are also delinquent the incidence of delinquency is greater *before,* as compared to *after,* their leaving school (37).

The school's role in delinquency prevention. The authors again wish to stress that the etiology of delinquency is far more complex than might be indicated by critics who blame the schools for the problem of antisocial behavior. Indeed, one must beware of making the American system of public education a scapegoat for these and other social ills. Yet the authors believe there is sufficient evidence to suggest that the schools contribute, often unwittingly, to patterns of delinquency.

However, positive steps toward a solution to this problem can be taken in at least three related ways.

First, and most obviously, action must be taken to eliminate negative conditions for learning and human interaction that exist within the schools. Such conditions have repeatedly been mentioned throughout this book. Second, the school can be a principal setting for the early identification of potential delinquents. Methods for this purpose, including delinquency prediction scales, have been developed by behavioral scientists (73). In the authors' opinion, these methods merit far more attention by educators than has been given to them in the past.

Third, and finally, the school is in a key position to exercise full cooperation, if not leadership, in implementing community-wide programs for delinquency prevention and treatment. Precedent for this exists (see, for example, 73); however, it is clear that several conditions necessary for success must be met by school personnel. These include a commitment to rehabilitation (versus punitive action), means for involving youth themselves in delinquency prevention and control, provision for highly skilled youth workers, effective channels for communicating the facts about delinquency to the community at large, and procedures for the continual evaluation of ameliorative efforts (73).

TOWARD IMPROVED HUMAN RELATIONS IN THE SCHOOLS

Much of the discussion summarized in this section has been stated in earlier chapters. Some conclusions and recommendations were made explicit, while others were implicit. Because of the importance of the topic, and even at the risk of redundancy, it seems well to include a self-contained section dealing with bettering human relations in schools.

Dimensions of Human Relations in Schools

Schools are complex social and political organizations. At the beginning of this chapter, the structure and function of schools were discussed, most of the attention being devoted to public schools. Human relations are crucial at all school levels. Schools will clearly operate better and with less friction if the following conditions are met.

1. The school board is truly representative of the community, and works conscientiously to realize the needs and wishes of the community. The school board and its precious cargo—the school system itself—stand better to be trusted and supported if such representation occurs.

2. The school board selects the superintendent of schools wisely and then, within the broad outlines of school policy, leaves him free (but accountable) to act as head of the school system.

3. The school superintendent respects the board, recognizes its authority as an arm of the community, and keeps it fully informed, in order to give its members "in-service education" and to keep them knowledgeable, actively participating members of an on-going enterprise.

4. The school superintendent, working in tandem with his faculties, selects principals wisely. Then, in the same manner as mentioned in condition 2, he leaves his individual principals and teachers free to create the best possible school units they can produce. In other words, principals and faculties need substantial freedom to function within a set

of general guidelines for the entire system. All concerned are thus more likely to take pleasure in their work (see the section earlier in this chapter on job characteristics that make for employee morale, page 464). The end result can be beneficial to the students.

5. Principals, the superintendent, and, almost certainly, members of the school faculty should have a hand in the hiring of teachers. Once teachers are retained, the working relationship between teachers and principals should be much like that described above for principals and superintendents and for superintendents and school boards.

6. The authors have known for a long time, and it has been regularly reaffirmed (75, 84, 126, 142), that children and youth are happiest, best behaved, and most efficient in learning when their working–living environment includes an ideal mix of the following characteristics:

a. Much warmth, or child–youth orientation.
b. Task orientation: a businesslike atmosphere with competent leadership

"Open classrooms" and "schools without walls" are just two of the terms applied to new approaches that possess the ambitious intention of transforming American education into a more humane activity for young people, teachers, and the larger society. (Photo by Bruce Roberts)

(this may be more important for advantaged children and youth than for disadvantaged; and warmth or child orientation may be more important for disadvantaged students than for advantaged, although the picture is by no means clear).

c. Fairness.

d. Emphasis on positive (rewarding) methods of individual and class management, rather than negative (punitive or aversive) methods.

e. There is less firm research evidence about the effect of good humor and good manners in a classroom than there is about the first four points listed above, but the authors firmly believe that pleasantness and courtesy are fundamental to good class morale. The authors do not know what role a sense of humor plays in effective teaching. They do know, however, that a sense of humor makes life much easier for the person who has one, probably for the recipient as well.

f. Reciprocal interchanges between teachers and students, as well as among students. Orderly democracy, the authors believe, promotes the best across-the-board school learning of all sorts, whether academic, social, or personal–emotional learning. This belief is supported by reasonably good research evidence. It is also a matter of common sense (after all, we live in a democratic society of a republican form) and personal conviction.

The authors also believe that, when the six classroom characteristics listed above are present, teachers will benefit as much as students. Whether one is a teacher, a student, a principal, a superintendent, or a school board member, it makes for good human relations when he is treated with warmth, task orientation, fairness, emphasis on the positive rather than the negative, good humor, courtesy, a sense of humor, and reciprocality and mutual respect.

7. When schools are well and happily run, most children and youth will be happy with school attendance. Parents, in turn, are pleased and a twofold result is likely: (1) parent-child relations may improve and (2) community support for the school is bound to be enhanced.

Curricular Relevance

Four things can be said about relevance.

1. A thing (including a subject for study) is relevant if one sees it as important for his life and well-being.

2. Something is relevant if one sees that it bears on issues important to him (such as race relations or ecology or employment opportunities for older children and youth).

3. An individual is more likely to see something as relevant when it is discussed or portrayed with conviction, enthusiasm, and competence by a person whose credibility is high.

4. It is clear that when a subject or a skill is seen as relevant, one works very hard to master it and is more likely to do so than if he sees it as irrelevant.

One great value of the reciprocity that exists in a democratic organization is that relevance is easier to develop in such a climate, because free communication increases everyone's chances of learning what everyone else is interested in and regards as relevant.

Even very young children perceive relevance of subject matters and skills. A thrifty friend of the authors', unwilling to buy his 6-year-old son two bicycles—

first, a junior bike suitable for the boy's size; second and depressingly soon thereafter, because of the boy's rapid growth pattern, an adult-sized bicycle — bought only the larger bike and turned his son loose with it on their quiet street. After nearly superhuman efforts and many tumbles, the boy mastered the bicycle. The intensity of his efforts was almost frightening, but his sense of self-esteem was greatly enhanced as a result; and the boy also acquired much prestige from his age mates by being the only one among them who owned and could ride an adult bicycle.

Many 5- and 6-year-olds approach reading with the same zest, but may lose their sense of relevance and enthusiasm as a result of slow progress, poor teaching, or poorly designed curriculum materials, or all three. In the beginning stages of learning for many skills (for example, reading in first grade, a foreign language, early work with numbers, typing) relevance may have to be induced. This can be done when teachers and children are communicating freely and when the teacher is important in the pupil's life. Although many persons deplore extrinsic motivation, it often seems to underlie the first stages of much learning, and the authors see no harm in it, as long as the eventual goal of teaching is to get the student to enjoy the skill or subject for its own sake or to make possible the development of further options for successful learning. The authors have known many persons who came thoroughly to enjoy a skill after they first acquired it only because they had to (as in a core curriculum course) or because they wanted to please someone else. This latter is an important aspect of teacher–pupil relations, and works both ways — pupils usually learn better if they wish to please teachers; teachers usually teach better if they wish to please students.

Relevance is also related to curriculum materials. Healthy portions of the instructional materials of rural youth should be related to the kind of life they know. The 4-H club played an important part in the education of one of the authors, who grew up on a farm. Black studies should certainly be provided for black children and youth in these days and times (for example, 62), as should courses for any of the other prejudiced-against minority groups. Historically, instructional materials for the public schools have been almost exclusively slanted toward the white Anglo-Saxon Protestant middle- and upper-middle class and the Greco–Roman–European–Western culture. The picture is changing rapidly — and high time — but we still have a long way to go in this area.

Programming

Programming — scheduling, sequencing, providing material suitable for the different stages of proficiency development, use of multimedia, selection of textbooks and other curricular material — is a complex matter. The authors do not treat the subject here in any detail; they wish simply to state that the best classroom and school management in the world will not result in learning unless suitable materials and strategies for presenting them are employed. Programming is a matter of materials and engineering. Good education is as dependent on materials and human engineering as is a good interstate highway.

These are matters that must be taken up elsewhere, however, and the authors have neither the room in this chapter nor the expertness to deal with them satisfactorily.

The Role of Rules in
Human Development

The role of rules in child rearing and in teaching differs according to the age of the child. Few rules are relevant for infants, for example, whether they are being reared at home or in a day care center or a kibbutz. The only rules are that the child be kept as happy as possible, clean, dry, and comfortable, and, when awake, that he be given interesting playthings. He must also be given much adult attention and warmth.

As children grow older (2-year-olds, for example), simple rules become necessary: "Don't bite. Don't kick. Don't hit with sticks. Don't run into the street." Later, as the child's experience and language grow, rules must be designed for purposes other than preserving life and limb. They must be applied to social organization and behavior.

A general principle about rules for children 3 or 4 years old or older is that the rules be clear, that they be set in advance of when they are to be enforced, and, whenever possible, that they be set with the mutual consent of the child and the adult. If mutual negotiation is not possible, a clear explanation should be given for the reason for the rule and why it must be enforced. This is the case, for instance, with public school rules about truancy. A child or a youth may not like the rule. He may not obey it. But at least he knows about it, why it exists, and the consequences that follow from its violation.

The authors believe that the basic reason for setting up home or school rules is that each rule benefits the developmental process. This includes rules designed to facilitate school learning. If a rule does not clearly bear on constructive human learning and development, it is both unnecessary and a nuisance. More time and energy will be taken up in enforcing it than it is worth. If a rule clearly has a bearing on development and learning, the children will see it as relevant and reasonable. Mostly, we observe relevant, reasonable rules without much fuss. Doing so makes life easier for both us and the rule enforcers. From this reasoning, we see that there should be as few rules as possible and that each should be very well reasoned indeed.

A few very human exceptions exist to the generalizations given above. The authors know of excellent teachers and parents who cannot abide gum chewing, for example. If they are fair, warm, task oriented—are "relevant" to their students (or their offspring)—they can get away with an occasional idiosyncratic rule. The students (or children) like, respect, and appreciate them enough to be willing to obey as long as the rule is honestly stated: "Don't chew gum in my class (or in the house). It drives me up the wall." The reason for the rule must be honestly given, however. If you tell a gum chewer that he is disturbing another sixth-grader, he knows you are lying. It is *you* he is disturbing, and you had best be honest about it.

The Adversary Relationship

The school system being what it is— rather traditional, rather authoritarian and regimented in most cases, but still very much at the forefront of social action and change—teachers and pupils, administrators and teachers, the school board and the superintendent, or parents and the school board, or any combination of these, may find themselves tensely aligned on opposite sides of the fence.

Such an adversary relationship is discussed by many authors (for example, 78, 137, 138). When it is clear that sides have been chosen and tension either is or may become high, both sides should take a long, hard, evidence-gathering look at their common ground. The authors know a case of a young social science teacher whose class wanted to go to hear a political campaigner who was giving a speech and rally in the town. The instructor at first suspected the motive of his students was frivolous: They simply wanted to get out of school. He resisted his reflex to say "No," however, and said "Maybe, let's talk about it." As he and the students talked, he realized they were quite sincere. He also admitted that he had never himself heard a leading candidate speak and that he too wanted to go. He asked, "What about your classes before and after this class? How can you get yourselves and me squared with these two teachers, whose classes will be disrupted, because you will have to leave one very early and come to the other very late or miss it entirely?" The students agreed to go to the other two teachers to explain, to work something out, and to assure each of the other two teachers that it was not the social science instructor who was egocentrically interrupting the classes before and after his. In turn, the instructor agreed to go to the principal to seek permission if matters could be worked out with the other two teachers. Finally, the instructor and the class agreed to skip the political science topic that had been scheduled for discussion on the day the political candidate was to come to the town.

After all this discussion, a vote was taken. The class voted in a ratio of 5 to 1 to hear the candidate, and the teacher voted with the majority. The other two teachers made arrangements for make-up work, and the principal gave permission. At the end of the whole proceeding, 100 percent of the class and the instructor attended the political speech and rally, and the already good relations between instructor and class were still further improved. The common ground, in other words, was greater than the differences; and all profited from the decision-making process and the experience. This account illustrates that when an analysis of common ground is carefully and calmly made, both sides are typically surprised to find out how much in agreement they are and to learn that the areas of disagreement can be charted and frequently resolved.

One word of caution. Each party to a controversy is likely to overestimate the importance of his position to the other side. In the above case, the instructor almost certainly believed that his students had more interest in his subject than they actually had, had more goodwill toward him than they truly had, and held a keener appreciation of his role as a servant within the system than they truly held. On the other hand, the students probably believed that the instructor trusted them more than he really did, and that he was more open to the extra effort exerted in such a project than he truly was. In short, one should not be naïve about his position vis-à-vis the other side.

Another technique that is useful in cooling the adversary relation (see 138 for details) has been used by social psychologists. Before the two sides on an issue enter into debate (or conflict), side 1 must state clearly, in detail, and to the satisfaction of side 2, all the issues side 2 advocates. The converse is also true. Only when both sides are satisfied with all the terms and premises can debate begin. By this time, issues have been made clear, emotions have usually been reduced, and a mutually acceptable solution has often been reached. Such a procedure also provides good exercise in attention, analysis, and articulation of principles and issues.

Third, we should all be aware of self-fulfilling prophecies. If a teacher expects a classroom of disadvantaged youth to *get him* if they possibly can, he often behaves so as to insure that indeed they try to get him, and they often succeed. On the other hand, if he regards them as a set of individuals who have had hard lives, and if he believes that, somewhere within themselves, they all want to learn and better their lives, he is likely to convey positive expectations. Conversely, if the class believes the teacher is their enemy, they are likely to give him further reason to dislike, punish, and reject them.

Finally, there is an important matter of territoriality. Teachers possess certain prerogatives of experience, training, and knowledge that students do not have. Thus, a teacher has a right to a role of expertness and to some degree of respect because of it. Students, likewise, have territories — their own dignities, their own privacies, their own rights to set their goals so long as the goals do not result in gross and obvious harm to themselves and/or others. Such territorialities should be made explicit, and should be respected.

Although American public schools are locally controlled, today there seems to be need for a central government function that, at the very least, will set minimal standards for education. The schools, broadly speaking, should fulfill the two major functions of cultural transmission and skills teaching and student and teacher actualization, in the sense that, as one result, everyone who experiences schooling should be happier, more secure, and better suited for emotional as well as task-oriented living.

Although there is some disagreement in the matter, it seems well for almost all youth to remain in school until age 16 or so; and for each youth to be able to read, write, handle numbers, and know his culture well. If these goals are granted, underachievement and dropout before high school graduation are serious problems. Nearly a third of American youth fail to finish high school.

Underachievement is defined as a conspicuous failure on a student's part to learn skills and content that, according to his ability, he *can* learn. The pattern of underachievement can be detected by second or third grade. The problem is too complex to summarize, but factors of conflict with parents (perhaps particularly fathers), teachers, lack of adequate models, and low self-esteem are all clearly implicated for large numbers of children and youth. Differences between home and school goals are also major determiners, as are inefficient and sometimes inhumane teaching methods and curricula. Prevention is more efficient than treatment in dealing with underachievement. School dropout is often but not always associated with underachievement.

Some children are "overachievers." Their problem, essentially, is anxiety and excessive fear of failure.

Cultural disadvantage — poverty and/or belonging to prejudiced-against minority groups — is a major correlate of poor school performance, dropping out of school, and experiencing difficulty in coping with life's vocational, economic, legal, and often emotional problems. Compensatory education holds promise, but the earlier it is started, and the more a developmental and preventive approach rather than a remedial or compensatory approach is taken, the better.

An emphasis upon cultural *difference*, not cultural deprivation, seems both correct and promising.

By race relations is meant the way the members of different racial and ethnic groups get along with one another; included are power relations and interpersonal relations. The American ideal, of course, is that race is irrelevant to either a person's position or his activities. Practically speaking, United States society is a long way from the ideal state of affairs.

The authors believe that prejudice can be directly learned and unlearned. They also believe that prejudice is sometimes the result of personal and social maladjustment. Thus, the origins of learning prejudice are obscure, and prejudice smacks of a psychodynamic concept. By the time children reach age 4, they seem to have developed an awareness of their own racial and ethnic group and, all too often, prejudice.

Few firm data are available about the influence of the move toward integrated schools. It may be that there is no simple answer. Because of well-established principles for constructive human development, the authors believe that wide, frequent, and intense association and interaction among individuals from different racial and ethnic groups promote healthy social growth. They also believe that any member of a racial or an ethnic group can profit from knowing members of other groups. The available evidence indicates that the race of a teacher is relatively unimportant to children. The important variables are competence, fairness, and child orientations (by this are meant interest, concern, and liking for children).

Teachers' ways of dealing with children seem to be strongly influenced by the social-class level of the children, with teachers generally reacting less positively to poor children. Since the poor are disproportionately made up of prejudiced-against minority groups, this finding has implications for race relations.

Problems about race relations seem to be most clearly focused on black–white relations. The best conclusions the authors can make are that satisfactory black–white relations are by no means hopeless; that improvement is occurring, particularly among college-educated youth and middle-aged people; and that prejudice cannot be considered a simple, straightforward thing, but is rather as complicated as human nature itself. For instance, most whites seem to be willing to work for black supervisors, but many fewer are willing to have blacks as their neighbors.

Vocational development is a principal growth task for older children and adolescents. It is a major socialization variable, and knowledge about how to help children and adolescents in their vocational development is currently inadequate, although much knowledge is available that can be put to practical use. Four major approaches to vocational development have been made: (1) The *trait-factor* system, in which it is assumed that the individual and the job can be matched by a series of tests and observations. (2) The *sociological model,* under which it is assumed that a person fits himself to the trends of the times: Presence of opportunity allows for wide vocational latitude; absence leads to vocational maladjustment, and perhaps to delinquency. Within this model, it is believed people must be trained for flexibility. (3) In the *self-concept theory*, it is conceived that a person enters a vocation because of certain personal pre-dispositions, and that vocational life helps to clarify and firm up the self concept. (4) Finally, the *personality theory* includes ideas that vocational preferences are shaped by personal predispositions that have their roots in early childhood and that have been shaped by child-rearing practices.

Functions of work for older children and youth include promotion of adjustment to reality, broadening of social horizons, and increases (or decrements) in self-esteem. Work bridges childhood and adulthood. The role in American society of those who reject the work ethic is not yet clear.

Occupational choice and entry are complex functions of occupational information, technical qualifications, and values held by the person. All these interact with occupational prestige and the opportunities available to a particular individual and within the society at a given time.

Finally, the authors believe that a combination of parent and teacher modeling, guidance, and information; experience at different jobs; and professional vocational guidance will lead children and youth successfully through their vocational development and eventually allow them to make a wise and felicitous choice of vocation.

Abuse of drugs is a major problem. It often begins in older childhood, and is a phenomenon with which American society seems ill equipped to cope. While drug abuse in former years was more a phenomenon of poverty than of affluence, the spread of the abuse to the advantaged has resulted in more attention and, the authors hope, a more constructive approach than was formerly given to the problem. Factors of exposure, opportunity, models, fads or current styles,

thrills and kicks, personal–social–emotional difficulties that are often home based, and absence of sound information are all involved in drug use and abuse. The increasing complexity of society, with an attendant desire to escape or ameliorate stress, must also be considered a contributing factor in drug abuse. Because of public attitudes and emotions, at present it is difficult to envision a really effective drug education curriculum within the public schools.

Delinquency among children and youth is a prominent characteristic of the American scene. Old, simplistic ways of regarding juvenile delinquency have been discarded by those who have any extensive knowledge of the field. We know that a broad-based program of law and court reform, changes in social and economic policy, family counseling and parent education, and public and private education are necessary. By and large, when children and youth are provided with *legitimate* opportunities for growth and development, they will choose these opportunities instead of illegitimate opportunities (as in drug abuse and delinquency). It is generally true that males are more likely to be delinquent (and school underachievers) than females.

Six dimensions of human relations within the complex social and political organization of the schools were developed. They include the community, the school board, the superintendent of schools, principals, teachers, and students. Human relations will be improved if people operate with warmth and a child–youth–people orientation, if they keep their minds on the job (which is broad gauge education), if they are fair, if positive or reward styles of interaction and behavior management are emphasized, if people are courteous and good humored and have a sense of humor, and if there is reciprocal interchange among all parties.

Curricular materials should be relevant to the students' own welfare, as well as to issues of pressing community concern. Students will be more highly motivated to master skills and subject matters that they perceive as relevant.

School materials, schedules, and teaching practices should be appropriately age graded and "human engineered." In both families and schools, there should be as few rules as possible, and what rules there are should be clearly and explicitly directed toward constructive goals of human development and learning. Rules should be reasonable, mutually arrived at, and announced before they are enforced.

Within school systems, an adversary relation often develops. People choose sides, and tension and open conflict are likely to result. Ways of cooling the adversary relation are analysis of common ground, full understanding and expression of the premises of each of the two (or more) sides, avoidance of self-fulfilling prophecies (expecting "bad" things of the other side and then behaving so as to make them come true), and respect for "territoriality." By this are meant such things as teachers' rights to be respected as experts, at least to a reasonable degree; and children's and youth's rights to privacy and sensible, nonharmful, personal goal setting.

REFERENCES

1. Adorno, T. W., E. Frenkel-Brunswik, D. J. Levinson, and R. N. Sanford. *The authoritarian personality.* New York: Harper & Row, 1950.

2. Akers, R. Teen-age drinking and drug use. In E. D. Evans (ed.) *Adolescents: Readings in behavior and development.* Hinsdale, Ill.: Dryden, 1970, 267–288.

3. Allen, J. B., and L. J. West. Flight from violence: Hippies and the green rebellion. *American Journal of Psychiatry,* 1968, *125,* 364–370.

4. Ausubel, D. P. Psychological factors in juvenile delinquency. *Catholic Educational Review,* 1966, September, 91–101.

5. Ausubel, D. P. *Theory and problems of adolescent development.* New York: Grune & Stratton, 1954.

6. Bachtold, L. M. Personality differences among high ability underachievers. *Journal of Educational Research,* 1969, *63,* 16–18.

7. Bandura, A., and R. Walters. *Adolescent aggression.* New York: Ronald, 1959.

8. Bednar, R. L., and S. L. Weinberg. Ingredients of successful treatment programs for underachievers. *Journal of Counseling Psychology,* 1970, *17,* 1–7.

9. Bednar, R. L., P. F. Zelhart, L. Greathouse, and S. Weinberg. Operant conditioning principles in the treatment of learning and behavior problems with delinquent boys. *Journal of Counseling Psychology,* 1970, *17,* 492–497.

10. Berger, P. L., and B. Berger. The blueing of America. *The New Republic,* 1971, *164* (No. 14), 20–23.

11. Betz, R. L., K. B. Engle, and G. G. Mallinson. Perceptions of noncollege bound, vocationally-oriented high school graduates. *Personnel and Guidance Journal,* 1969, *47,* 988–994.

12. Bland, H. Problems related to teaching about drugs. *Journal of School Health,* 1969, *39,* 113–115.

13. Blank, M. Implicit assumptions underlying preschool intervention programs. *Journal of Social Issues,* 1970, *26,* 15–34.

14. Blau, P. M., J. W. Gustad, R. Jessor, H. S. Parnes, and R. C. Wilcock. Occupational choice: A conceptual framework. in D. G. Zytowski (ed.) *Vocational behavior: Readings in theory and research.*

New York: Holt, Rinehart and Winston, 1968, 358–370.

15. Bloom, B. S. *Stability and change in human characteristics.* New York: Wiley, 1964.

16. Brehm, M. L., and K. W. Back. Self image and attitude toward drugs. *Journal of Personality,* 1968, *36,* 349–354.

17. Bronfenbrenner, U. The changing American child: A speculative analysis. *Journal of Social Issues,* 1961, *17,* 6–18.

18. Brown, J. C. Effects of token reinforcement administered by peer-tutors on pupil reading achievement and tutor collateral behavior. In *Atlanta Public Schools: End-of-budget period report: Success environment,* 1971, 2. 52 pp.

19. Burgess, R. L., and R. L. Akers. A differential association-reinforcement theory of criminal behavior. *Social Problems,* 1966, *14,* 128–147.

20. Cervantes, L. *The dropout: Causes and cures.* Ann Arbor, Mich.: University of Michigan Press, 1965.

21. Chilton, R. J. Middle-class delinquency and specific offense analysis. In E. W. Vaz (ed.) *Middle-class juvenile delinquency.* New York: Harper & Row, 1967, 91–101.

22. Clark, C. A., and H. J. Walberg. The influence of massive rewards on reading achievement in potential urban dropouts. *American Educational Research Journal,* 1968, *5,* 305–310.

23. Cohen, M., and D. F. Klein. Drug abuse in a young psychiatric population. *American Journal of Orthopsychiatry,* 1970, *40,* 448–455.

24. Cole, M., and J. S. Bruner. Cultural differences and inferences about psychological processes. *American Psychologist,* 1971, *26,* 867–876.

25. Cosgriff, T. M. The problem of drug abuse. *Notre Dame Journal of Education,* 1970, *1,* 289–301.

26. Crooks, R. C. The effects of an interracial preschool program upon racial preference, knowledge of racial differences, and racial identification. *Journal of Social Issues,* 1970, *26,* 137–144.

27. Cross-Cultural Family Center, San Francisco, California: A nursery school providing a multicultural curriculum to promote racial understanding and acceptance. Model programs—childhood education. *ERIC: ED 045 214,* 1971.

28. Davidson, H. H., and G. Lang. Children's perceptions of their teacher's feelings toward them related to self-perception, school achievement, and behavior. *Journal of Experimental Education,* 1960, *29,* 107–118.

29. DeBottari, L. Primary school correlates of secondary school achievement. *Personnel and Guidance Journal,* 1969, *47,* 675–678.

30. Divalina, G. E. Drug use on high school and college campuses. *Journal of School Health,* 1968, *38,* 862–866.

31. Douvan, E., and J. Adelson. *The adolescent experience.* New York: Wiley, 1966.

32. Edington, E. D. Disadvantaged rural youth. *Review of Educational Research,* 1970, *40,* 69–86.

33. Edwards, A. E., M. H. Bloom, and S. Cohen. The psychodelics: Love or hostility potion? *Psychological Reports,* 1969, *24,* 843–846.

34. Edwards, J., and C. Stern. A comparison of three intervention programs with disadvantaged preschool children. *Journal of Special Education,* 1970, *4,* 205–214.

35. Egelund, B., D. E. Hunt, and R. H. Hardt. College enrollment of Upward Bound students as a function of attitude and motivation. *Journal of Educational Psychology,* 1970, *61,* 375–379.

36. Elkind, D. Middle-class delinquency. *Mental Hygiene,* 1967, *51,* 80–84.

37. Elliot, D. S. Delinquency, school attendance and dropout. *Social Problems,* 1966, *8,* 307–314. (a)

38. Elliot, D. S. Dropout and the social milieu of the high school: A preliminary analysis. *American Journal of Orthopsychiatry,* 1966, *36,* 808–817. (b)

39. Elton, C. F., and H. A. Rose. Male occupational constancy and change: Its pre-

diction according to Holland's theory. *Journal of Counseling Psychology,* 1970, *17* (No. 6, Part 2). 19 pp.

40. Epps, E. G. (ed.). Motivation and academic achievement of Negro Americans. *Journal of Social Issues,* 1969, *24.* 164 pp.

41. Evans, E. D. *Contemporary influences in early childhood education.* New York: Holt, Rinehart and Winston, 1971.

42. Evans, E. D. Student activism and teaching effectiveness: Survival of the fittest? *Journal of College Student Personnel,* 1969, *10,* 102–108.

43. Flynn, W. R. The pursuit of purity — a defensive use of drug abuse in adolescence. *Adolescence,* 1970, *5,* 141–150.

44. Ford, R. N., and E. F. Borgatta. Satisfaction with the work itself. *Journal of Applied Psychology,* 1970, *54,* 128–134.

45. Freedman, M. K. Background of deviancy. In W. W. Wattenberg (ed.) *Social deviancy among youth.* Chicago: University of Chicago Press, 1966, 28–56.

46. Gibbons, D. C. *Delinquent behavior.* Fnglewood Cliffs, N. J.: Prentice-Hall, 1970.

47. Gibbons, D. C. *Society, crime, and criminal careers.* Englewood Cliffs, N. J.: Prentice-Hall, 1968.

48. Glueck, E. T. Distinguishing delinquents from pseudodelinquents. *Harvard Educational Review,* 1966, *36,* 119–130.

49. Glueck, S., and E. T. Glueck. *Delinquents and nondelinquents in perspective.* Cambridge, Mass.: Harvard University Press, 1968.

50. Gordon, E. W. Programs of compensatory education. In M. Deutsch, I. Katz, and A. Jensen (eds.) *Social class, race, and psychological development.* New York: Holt, Rinehart and Winston, 1968, 381–410.

51. Gronlund, E., and L. Knowles. Childparent identification and academic underachievement. *Journal of Consulting and Clinical Psychology,* 1969, *33,* 495–496.

52. Gurman, A. S. The role of the family in underachievement. *Journal of School Psychology,* 1970, *8,* 48–53.

53. Harris, E. M. A measurement of alienation in college student marijuana users and non-users. *ERIC: ED 043 059,* 1969.

54. Hartmann, D. A study of drug taking adolescents. *The Psychoanalytic Study of the Child,* 1969, *24,* 384–398.

55. Havighurst, R. J. Youth in exploration and man emergent. In H. Borow (ed.) *Man in a world of work.* Boston: Houghton-Mifflin, 1964, 215–236.

56. Hayden, B. S. The alienated student: An effort to motivate at the junior high level. *Journal of School Psychology,* 1970, *8,* 237–241.

57. Hilliard, T., and R. Roth. Maternal attitudes and the non-achievement syndrome. *Personnel and Guidance Journal,* 1969, *47,* 424–428.

58. Hodge, R. W., P. M. Siegel, and P. H. Rossi. Occupational prestige in the United States, 1925–1963. In D. G. Zytowski (ed.) *Vocational behavior.* New York: Holt, Rinehart and Winston, 1968. 86–95.

59. Holland, J. L. *The psychology of vocational choice: A theory of personality types and model environments.* Waltham, Mass.: Blaisdell, 1966.

60. Hollender, J. W. Development of vocational decisions during adolescence. *Journal of Counseling Psychology,* 1971, *18,* 244–248.

61. Horowitz, F. D., and L. Y. Paden. The effectiveness of environmental intervention programs. In B. M. Caldwell and H. Ricciuti (eds.) *Review of child development research,* Vol. III. New York: Russell Sage. In press.

62. Hraba, J., and G. Grant. Black is beautiful: A reexamination of racial preference and identification. *Journal of Personality and Social Psychology,* 1970, *16,* 398–402.

63. Hunt, D. E., and R. H. Hardt. Developmental stage, delinquency, and differential treatment. *Journal of Research*

in Crime and Delinquency, 1965, 2, 20–31.

64. Hunt, D. E., and R. H. Hardt. The effect of Upward Bound programs on the attitudes, motivation, and academic achievement of Negro Americans. *Journal of Social Issues,* 1969, 25, 117–129.

65. Illich, I. The alternatives to schooling. *Saturday Review,* 1971, 54 (No. 25, June 19), 44–48, 59–60.

66. Janssen, C. Comparative creativity scores of socioeconomic dropouts and non-dropouts. *Psychology in the Schools,* 1968, 5, 183–185.

67. Jensen, A. R. How much can we boost IQ and scholastic achievement? *Harvard Educational Review,* 1969, 39, 1–123.

68. Kaplan, J. *Marijuana: The new prohibition.* New York: World Publishing, 1970.

69. Katz, I. Factors influencing Negro performance in the desegregated school. In M. Deutsch, I. Katz, and A. R. Jensen (eds.) *Social class, race, and psychological development.* New York: Holt, Rinehart, and Winston, 1968, 254–289.

70. Katz, P., and E. Zigler. Self-image disparity: A developmental approach. *Journal of Personality and Social Psychology,* 1967, 5, 186–195.

71. Keeler, M. H. Motivation for marijuana use: A correlate of adverse reaction. *American Journal of Psychiatry,* 1968, 125, 386–390.

72. Kroeber, A. L. *Anthropology.* New York: Harcourt, 1948.

73. Kvaraceus, W. C. Programs of early identification and prevention of delinquency. In W. W. Wattenberg (ed.) *Social deviancy among youth.* Chicago: University of Chicago Press, 1966, 189–220.

74. Levin, H. M., J. W. Guthrie, G. B. Kleindorfer, and R. T. Stout. School achievement and post-school success: A review. *Review of Educational Research,* 1971, 41, 1–16.

75. Lewin, K., R. Lippitt, and R. K. White. Patterns of aggressive behavior in ex-perimentally created "social climates." *Journal of Social Psychology,* 1939, 10, 271–299.

76. Litcher, J. H., and D. W. Johnson. Changes in attitudes toward Negroes of white elementary students after use of multi-ethnic readers. *Journal of Educational Psychology,* 1969, 60, 148–152.

77. Maccoby, E. E., and M. Zellner. *Experiments in primary education: aspects of Project Follow Through.* New York: Harcourt, 1970.

78. McCandless, B. R. *Adolescents: Behavior and development.* Hinsdale, Ill.: Dryden, 1970.

79. McCandless, B. R. *Children: Behavior and development.* New York: Holt, Rinehart and Winston, 1967.

80. McCandless, B. R., A. Roberts, and T. Starnes. Teachers' marks, achievement test scores, and aptitude relations by social class, race, and sex. *Journal of Educational Psychology,* 1972, 63, 153–159.

81. McPartland, J. The relative influence of school and classroom desegregation on the academic achievement of ninth grade Negro students. *Journal of Social Issues,* 1969, 25, 93–102.

82. Merki, D. What we need before drug abuse education. *Journal of School Health,* 1969, 39, 656-657.

83. Mink, O. G., and B. A. Kaplan. *America's problem youth: Education and guidance of the disadvantaged.* Scranton, Pa.: International Textbook, 1970.

84. Moore, T. C., and W. R. Brassell, Jr. *The success environment: An approach to community educational improvement.* Atlanta: Atlanta Public Schools, 1971. End-of-budget period report, grant from Georgia Department of Education, Title III. Project Director: M. Thompson.

85. Mussen, P. H. Some personality and social factors related to changes in children's attitudes toward Negroes. *Journal of Abnormal and Social Psychology,* 1950, 45, 423–441.

86. Neill, A. S. *Summerhill: A radical approach to child rearing.* New York: Hart, 1960.

87. The future of Catholic education in America. *Notre Dame Journal of Education,* 1971, 2, 5–96 (entire issue).

88. Omwake, E. Preschool programs in historical perspective. *Interchange,* 1971, 2, 27–40.

89. Ornstein, A. C., and P. D. Vairo. *How to teach disadvantaged youth.* New York: McKay, 1969.

90. O'Shea, A. J. Low achievement syndrome among bright junior high school boys. *Journal of Educational Research,* 1970, 63, 257–262.

91. Osipow, S. H. Some cognitive aspects of career development. In E. D. Evans (ed.) *Adolescents: Readings in behavior and development.* Hinsdale, Ill.: Dryden, 1970, 224–234.

92. Osipow, S. H. *Theories of career development.* New York: Appleton, 1968.

93. Pallone, N. J., F. S. Richard, and R. B. Hurley. Key influencers of occupational preference among Black youth. *Journal of Counseling Psychology,* 1970, 17, 498–501.

94. Pine, G. J. The affluent delinquent. *Phi Delta Kappan,* 1966, 48, 138–143.

95. Pollock, M. B. Evaluation instrument to appraise knowledge and behavior regarding use of stimulants and depressants. *Research Quarterly,* 1968, 39, 662–667.

96. Quarter, J. J., and R. M. Laxer. A structured program of teaching and counseling for conduct problem students in a junior high school. *Journal of Educational Research,* 1970, 63, 229–231.

97. Quay, H. Dimensions of personality in delinquent boys as inferred from the factor analysis of case history data. *Child Development,* 1964, 35, 479–484.

98. Richards, C. V. Discontinuities in role expectations of girls. In W. W. Wattenberg (ed.) *Social deviancy among youth.* Chicago: University of Chicago Press, 1966, 164–188.

99. Ristow, L. W. Much ado about dropouts.

Phi Delta Kappan, 1965, 46, 461–464.

100. Roe, A. *Psychology of occupations.* New York: Wiley, 1956.

101. Rogers, D. (ed.) *Issues in adolescent psychology.* New York: Appleton, 1969.

102. Rohwer, W. D., Jr. Learning, race, and school success. *Review of Educational Research,* 1971, 41, 191–210.

103. Ronan, W. W. Relative importance of job characteristics. *Journal of Applied Psychology,* 1970, 54, 192–200.

104. Rose, H. A., and C. F. Elton. Sex and occupational choice. *Journal of Counseling Psychology,* 1971, 18, 456–461.

105. Rosen, B. C., and R. D'Andrade. The psychosocial origins of achievement motivation. *Sociometry,* 1959, 22, 185–218.

106. Sarason, S. B. *The culture of the school and the problem of change.* Boston: Allyn and Bacon, 1971.

107. Scales, H. Another look at the dropout problem. *Journal of Educational Research,* 1969, 62, 339–343.

108. Schafer, W. E., and K. Polk. Delinquency and the schools. In *Task force report: Juvenile delinquency and youth crime.* Washington, D. C.: U. S. Government Printing Office, 1967, 222–277.

109. Schreiber, D. (ed.) *Profile of the school dropout.* New York: Random House, 1968.

110. *Seattle Times.* Wednesday, November 10, 1971, Section H, p. 8.

111. Shappell, D. L., and L. G. Hall. Perceptions of the world of work: Inner-city versus suburbia. *Journal of Counseling Psychology,* 1971, 18, 55–59.

112. Shaw, M. C. Note on parent attitudes toward independence training and the academic achievement of their children. *Journal of Educational Psychology,* 1964, 55, 371–374.

113. Shaw, M. C. Underachievement: Useful construct or misleading illusion? *Psychology in the Schools,* 1968, 5, 41–46.

114. Shaw, M. C., and B. E. Dutton. The use of the Parent Attitude Research Inventory with the parents of bright academic

underachievers. *Journal of Educational Psychology,* 1962, *53,* 203–208.

115. Shaw, M. C., and J. T. McCuen. The onset of academic achievement in bright children. *Journal of Educational Psychology,* 1960, *51,* 103–108.

116. Silberman, C. E. Crisis in the classroom; the remaking of American education. New York: Random House, 1970.

117. Silver, H. A., and W. L. Barnette, Jr. Predictive and concurrent validity of the Minnesota Vocational Interest Inventory for vocational high school boys. *Journal of Applied Psychology,* 1970, *54,* 436–440.

118. Silverberg, N. E., and M. C. Silverberg. School achievement and delinquency. *Review of Educational Research,* 1971, *41,* 17–34.

119. Smith, D. E. (ed.). *The new social drug.* Englewood Cliffs, N. J.: Prentice-Hall, 1970.

120. Smith, R. B. A study of personality variables associated with discrepant achievement. *Psychology in the Schools,* 1968, *5,* 75–77.

121. Staffieri, J. R. A study of social stereotype of body image in children. *Journal of Personality and Social Psychology,* 1967, *7,* 101–103.

122. Stearn, J. *The seekers: Drugs and the new generation.* New York: Doubleday, 1969.

123. Stennet, R. G., and H. J. Fienstra. Late bloomers: Fact or fancy? *Journal of Educational Research,* 1970, *63,* 344–346.

124. Stevenson, H. W., and E. C. Stewart. A developmental study of racial awareness in young children. *Child Development,* 1958, *29,* 399–409.

125. St. John, N. H. Desegregation and minority group performance. *Review of Educational Research,* 1970, *40,* 111–134.

126. St. John, N. H. Thirty-six teachers: Their characteristics, and outcomes for black and white pupils. *American Educational Research Journal,* 1971, *8,* 635–648.

127. Super, D. E., R. Starishevsky, N. Matlin, and J. P. Jordaan. *Career development:*

Self-concept theory. New York: College Entrance Examination Board Research Monograph No. 4, 1963.

128. Tannenbaum, A. J. The school dropout today. *IRCD Bulletin,* 1968, *4,* 1–5.

129. Tennyson, W. W. Career development. *Review of Educational Research,* 1968, *38,* 346–366.

130. Thornburg, H. D. *Contemporary adolescence: Readings.* Belmont, Calif.: Brooks-Cole, 1971.

131. Thorndike, R. *The concepts of over- and underachievement.* New York: Columbia University, Teachers College Press, 1963.

132. Tolor, A. Incidence of underachievement at the high school level. *Journal of Educational Research,* 1969, *63,* 63–65.

133. Truax, D. (ed.). Campbell reports on race studies: White attitudes toward Black people. *ISR Newsletter,* 1971, *1* (No. 10, Summer 1971), 4–6.

134. Vaz, E. W. Delinquency and the youth culture: Upper- and middle-class boys. *Journal of Criminal Law, Criminology, and Police Science,* 1969, *60,* 33–46.

135. Vincent, R. J. Investigation of attitudes of eighth, tenth, and twelfth grade students toward smoking marijuana. *Dissertation Abstracts,* 1969, *29,* 3799–3800.

136. Wattenberg, W. W. Review of trends. In W. W. Wattenberg (ed.) *Social deviancy among youth.* Chicago: University of Chicago Press, 1966, 4–27.

137. White, R. K. *Nobody wanted war.* New York: Doubleday, 1968.

138. White, R. K. Three not-so-obvious contributions of psychology to peace. *Journal of Social Issues,* 1969, *25,* 23–39.

139. White House Conference on Children. *Profiles of children.* 1970. Washington, D. C.: U. S. Government Printing Office, 1971.

140. Wolk, D. J. Youth and drugs: Guidelines for teachers. *Social Education,* 1969, *33,* 667–674.

141. Yando, R., E. Zigler, and M. Gates. The influence of Negro and white teachers rated as effective or noneffective on

the performance of Negro and white lower class children. *Developmental Psychology,* 1971, *5,* 290–299.

142. Yee, A. H. Source and direction of causal influence in teacher-pupil relation- ships. *Journal of Educational Psychology,* 1968, *59,* 275–282.

143. Zigler, E. Social class and the socialization process. *Review of Educational Research,* 1970, *40,* 87–110.

Appendix
Statistical and Measurement Considerations

Without some grasp of measurement and statistical concepts and with no appreciation of common research faults, a reader is lost if he ventures into primary sources (original research articles) or tries intelligently to follow the research summarized and discussed in this book.

CORRELATION

A correlation coefficient is an expression of the relation between one thing and another—the degree to which two things vary together. The correlation between height and weight in a sample of fifty young men can be illustrated as follows. First, array the men in order of their height, with the shortest man to the left, the tallest man to the right. Put a card over each man's head indicating his weight. Observation will show a tendency for the shorter men to be lighter, the taller men

heavier. A number of men will be heavier than those taller than they, and vice versa. But, for the group as a whole, greater height will go with greater weight. In other words, height and weight will covary—will be positively correlated with each other.

Correlation coefficients, theoretically, can range from perfect positive (+1.00) to perfect negative (−1.00). The condition of a perfect positive correlation would be met if, in our illustration, the tallest man was the heaviest, the next tallest the next heavy, and so on down the line to the shortest and the lightest man. The more interchange in weight status between men of different height (as, the third from the shortest man is found to be the third from the heaviest), the lower the correlation. If there is no covariance between height and weight, but simply a chance relation, the correlation is zero. If the shortest man were the heaviest, the next shortest man the next heavy, and so on, until the tallest man was revealed to be the lightest, the condition for a perfect negative correlation would be fulfilled.

PREDICTION THROUGH CORRELATION

The principal purpose in calculating a correlation coefficient (r) is to predict one variable from another. Knowledge of a man's height is more useful if it also helps to predict his weight than if it gives no information about him other than how tall he is. Correlations are likely to lead to deceptive inferences about causality: If two things are correlated with each other, it is tempting to say that one "causes" the other. Correctly, we should assume only that they are related, but should also be encouraged to look for the reasons for the relation. In general, tall men are heavier than short men for the rather elementary reason that they have more bones to cover and coordinate with muscle and fat. There is simply more to them. But their height did not cause their weight.

A simple calculation is useful in appraising the predictive value of a correlation coefficient. It is easy (but incorrect) to assume that the rather high correlation of .70 between a test of reading achievement and intelligence for fourth-graders means that all the brighter children read better than those less bright. This correlation indicates a substantial relation between reading and intelligence. Hence, knowledge of the children's intelligence helps to predict their standing in reading ability among other children of their age. But the relation is by no means a perfect one. To determine how much of the total variance of reading (all the factors that influence, or determine, reading skill) is

accounted for by intelligence, one multiplies the correlation between the two by itself: .70 × .70 is equal to .49. Translated, this means that 49 percent of the variance of reading in our sample of fourth-graders is accounted for by the children's intelligence. To put it in other words, the .70 correlation between intelligence and reading accounts for 49 percent of the possible range of factors that enters into making a perfect prediction of where a child stands in his reading group. But 51 percent of the variance remains unaccounted for when we know only the intelligence-test scores of a group of children. Of this unaccounted-for 51 percent of the variance, some are explained by the amount of practice children have had; some are due to parents' intelligence; some can be accounted for by the number of books in the home libraries; some by motivation; some by study efficiency; some by the acuity and coordination of vision, some by testing errors; and so on.

The average correlation of about .50 that has been found between the intelligence of parents and children indicates that only 25 percent of the variance of children's intelligence can be accounted for by the brightness of their parents. A correlation of .20 between children's strength and their speed of response means that only 4 percent of the variance of speed of response is accounted for by strength, leaving 96 percent to be predicted from knowledge of other factors and measurement problems.

Much faulty generalization results from failure to calculate how much of the variance of one variable is due to another with which it is correlated. A correlation of .70 looks reassuringly high, but still leaves us with 51 percent of the variance unaccounted for.

The correlation of about .50, which is

usually found between the intelligence of children and their parents, is often used in ways that are detrimental both to children and to their parents: A teacher assumes that because Daddy is a doctor and Mommy is a lawyer, Junior Number One is bound to be bright. It isn't necessarily so, and the teacher's overexpectations for Junior may do him real harm. On the other hand, the same teacher is equally likely to assume that because Daddy holds down an unskilled job, and both Daddy and Mommy finished only the sixth grade, it follows that Junior Number Two is pretty unlikely to be a profound scholar. The teacher *expects* Junior to do badly. Children tend to behave as influential adults *expect* them to behave. Junior Number Two may do poorly in school, not because he is stupid, but because he is *expected* to do poorly. Of course, poor school achievement is seldom if ever this simply explained, but teacher expectations play an important part in how a child performs. One of the best illustrations of the effects on a child of how the teacher expects him to behave (not only academically but socially is given in Claude Brown's description of his elementary and secondary school days in his autobiography, *Manchild in the Promised Land* (1965). Academically, he performed wretchedly (nor was his social behavior by any means impeccable) in elementary school years. Eventually, teachers, their eyes unclouded by knowledge of or prejudice about relations between intelligence or behavior and family status, perceived that Claude Brown was a bright and (potentially) a good boy (in the sense of his possibly eventually becoming a good citizen). He satisfied both sets of teachers/caretakers. For those who expected him to behave stupidly and undesirably, he behaved stupidly and became a proficient delin-

quent. Later (but gradually and with a good many temporary slips backward) he was equally obliging to those who expected him to behave intelligently in the scholastic sense and constructively as a citizen. At the time he wrote his book, he was a college graduate with further educational ambitions and, even by stringent criteria, a good citizen and a professor.

Our Junior Number One—the son of the doctor–father and lawyer–mother—can also be injured by teacher overexpectations. If he simply *cannot* do advanced work, it is not only pointless to expect him to, but also damaging to him. The fact that he has disappointed a set of teachers, his parents, and his brothers and sisters leaves him, at best, psychologically scarred. A sophisticated search for a nonprofessional career for him, guiding him toward it and helping his family accept it, will, in all likelihood, make both a happier and a more constructive Junior than a simple set of high academic achievement expectations based on the fact that his mother and father are extremely intelligent and well educated.

SOME GENERAL MEASUREMENT CONCEPTS

A *concept* is the general term for the class of behavior you are reading about or which the author of a research paper has studied. Illustrative concepts—expectation—have been discussed in Chapter 6; other examples include cognitive style, creativity, anxiety, and so on.

A *population* is the group an author has studied and on which he reports. A population may consist of 27 hooded rats, 8 babies 4 days old, 10,000 Chicago fifth-grade children, or 100 fathers and mothers of first-graders.

A *normal distribution* is one that lies between the ends of a continuum, and is shaped approximately like a bell. Figure A.1 illustrates a normal distribution.

It can be seen from the figure that there are few (perhaps only one from a large population) at either end A or end B of the continuum. Most people (or cases, or subjects) fall between the ends. To use height as an illustration: Very few ninth-grade boys are only 5 feet tall (end A of the continuum); an equally small number are 7 feet tall (end B of the continuum). The average American ninth-grade boy is about 5 feet 5 or 6 inches tall. This figure is arrived at by hypothetically measuring all ninth-grade American boys, adding their heights together, and dividing by the total number of boys who have been measured. You will, for reasons that have been discussed, arrive at a figure somewhat too great: chronically ill, seriously retarded, some economically disadvantaged boys who have had poor nutrition and hence are not as tall as they may have been with better diets, will not be attending school.

In a normal distribution, as indicated in Figure A.1, the *mean*, or average, and the *median*, or midpoint, are the same. By median is meant that point in the dis-

tribution above and below which exactly one-half the population falls. Means and medians are different from each other when the distribution is *skewed*, or abnormal. If we compute the average annual income of five men picked at random, we may obtain figures as follows: $3000, $4000, $5000, $6000, and $1,000,000. Our mean, in this case, is $203,600. It is ridiculous to assume from the data collected that the average American male earns more than $200,000 a year. By chance, we have secured a *biased* sample.

In such a case, the *median*, or midpoint, probably gives a more accurate, or at least a more meaningful, picture of the true state of affairs in the United States: the median is $5000 and our sample includes two men who earn more than this and two who earn less. Income and education figures for developing countries are often more meaningfully represented by medians than means; in such countries, there are typically few very wealthy men and women and few very highly educated, but a great mass who are desperately poor and/or illiterate. Including those who fall at or near the high-income end of the continuum (the very wealthy, the exceptionally well educated) makes our mean misleadingly high.

Authors frequently speak of relatively *heterogeneous* or *homogeneous* populations. By heterogeneous, they mean that the population includes great differences among its members; in other words, ends A and B of the continuum in Figure A.1 are widely separated. In a homogeneous population, all the members are relatively similar to one another—the ends of the continuum are close together. A population including children from ages 3 to 13, boys and girls, Black, Puerto Rican, and Appalachian, with some of the children coming from very poor homes and others

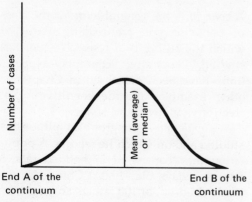

End A of the continuum

End B of the continuum

Figure A.1 *Diagram of a normal distribution.*

from very wealthy homes, would be more heterogeneous for almost any conceivable dimension than a population of fifth-grade boys in a rural Illinois elementary school.

When authors talk of their results having high *variance,* they mean that some children changed not at all or perhaps actually regressed, while others changed a great deal. For low variance, changes tend to be similar in amount and in the same direction. Variance is often expressed as the *standard deviation* (SD). The standard deviation is a statistical term—a figure used to indicate how variable a population or a set of results is. About two-thirds of a population is included in the portion of the curve drawn in Figure A.1 that falls between a score or a measurement one standard deviation below the mean, and a score or a measurement one standard deviation above the mean.

When the reader moves to primary sources, he encounters a number of specific statistical terms, such as Type I analyses of variance, *F*-ratios, *chi*-squares, *taus, W's,* and a host of others. Without having studied statistics, it is impossible for him to make sense of these. He must simply take the author on faith (most editors have checked to see that the authors' statistical procedures are legitimate). But, as has been pointed out, he should—indeed must—know in an elementary sort of way what *levels of statistical significance* or *confidence* mean.

LEVEL OF STATISTICAL CONFIDENCE

The central task of science is to discover lawfulness in its subject matter. Developmental psychologists seek to determine lawfulness in human structure, growth, and function. Statistics are among the tools used to demonstrate lawfulness. Among other tasks assigned to statistics is that of providing an estimate of the confidence that can be placed in our findings. We are particularly interested in whether we can assume that they occurred for reasons other than chance.

Ordinarily, we speak with "confidence" of results that are statistically significant. In this volume, statistical significance refers to any result at or below the .05 (or 5 percent) level of confidence. Such a figure (which may also be referred to as p for probability, $p = .05$) indicates that the results to which it refers are of such magnitude that they would occur by chance only five times in a hundred. The .01 ($p = .01$) level of confidence tells us that results like ours would be expected through chance once in one hundred times; the .001 level of confidence once in a thousand times.

In our earlier example, a correlation of .70 was postulated between intelligence and reading achievement for children in two fourth-grade classrooms. To establish the significance or the level of confidence for this correlation, we can consult a table or go through certain computations. Either of these procedures shows it to be significant at less than the .001 level. That is, a correlation of this magnitude, based on a population of this size, would be expected to occur by chance fewer than once in a thousand times.

For another illustration, suppose that the investigator's purpose is to test the effectiveness of an accelerated reading program. By a process of random selection, one-half the children in four classes of fourth-graders are assigned to an experimental group. The remaining children constitute a control group. The purpose of the study is to see whether the experimental children can be significantly advanced in reading skill over children remaining in the regular reading program by supplying individual instructions and enriched reading materials. Some safeguard must be introduced, however, so that it can be said that any superiority they show is due to the reading program and not to the Hawthorne effect (improvement in performance as a result of taking part in an experiment). This safeguard is introduced by giving the control children an amount of individual attention equal to that given the experimental youngsters, but social rather than instructional in nature; and supplying them with attractive materials that differ in content from those regularly used, but are at the same level of difficulty. Otherwise, the experiences of the two groups are the same.

The children are tested for reading achievement before and after the study. The experimental (accelerated) group does not differ from the control group at the beginning of the study, but has gained a full grade level at its end, while the control group has gained only a half year. Statistical computations relating to this differential gain result in a numerical expression of sufficient size to have occurred by chance only once in one hundred times. In practice, we proceed from this indication of lawfulness to the conclusion that the accelerated reading program was responsible for the difference in experimental and control group gains.

Faulty generalization often results from overconfidence in expressions of statistical significance, such as placing too much faith in a single experiment or study that shows significance at the .05 or .01 level. Less often, insufficient, hence faulty, generalization is made because of skepticism about the level of confidence of a finding.

This can become confusing, even to a rather sophisticated reader. In a study by Dennis and Sayegh[1] the experimental subjects gained significantly in developmental age (at the .03 level). This means that there are but three chances in one hundred that such gains could have come by chance alone. In other words, there are ninety-seven chances in one hundred that the enriched experiences given to five experimental babies were associated with and probably caused by the treatment administered to them by the experimenters. It is difficult to secure a result significant at this level with such a small number of subjects. One's chances of obtaining statistical significance increase the bigger his sample is. But Dennis and Sayegh's control group also increased more rapidly in developmental age than would have been expected during the experiment (the authors are vague about the exact level of significance of the gain). We are told only that "the gains of the control group were smaller. . . . By the sign test, which was used in the case of the experimental group, the change in rate of gain of the control group has a very low level of significance" (p. 88). We are left with the understanding that the experimental group of five babies improved significantly more than the control group of eight babies. But we are not given data sufficient to decide for ourselves (it should be added that the authors are sympathetic to the Dennis and Sayegh point of view) whether or not there was *really* a statistically significant difference between the children given the extra hour of experience each day for fifteen days and those who did not have this experience.

It is for such reasons that the authors

[1] W. Dennis, and T. Sayegh. The effect of supplementary experiences upon the behavioral development of infants in institutions. *Child Development*, 1965, 36, 81–90.

have decided to treat the important question of *how to go about reading a primary source*. A primary source is an article by an author who reports original data, talks about them, analyzes them, formulates results, arrives at conclusions, and sometimes makes recommendations for action based on them. This is a procedure the authors have found useful.

First, read the article either because it interests you or because it is assigned to you in a class. The reading procedure does not differ in either case.

Second, read the summary. What does the author say he has said? In perhaps one-half the summaries of primary source articles, the reader probably cannot tell, either because the author has not bothered to prepare an adequate summary or because he wants to make the summary ambiguous and unrevealing, so the reader must go on reading the entire article to find out what it is about.

Third, read the hypotheses. What is the author investigating? What questions is he trying to answer? Often, the author's hypotheses are backed by much theory. When they are, read backward to see what the theory is, because often the author has repeated his hypotheses one or more times as he discusses the theory that led up to them. If the article has scientific merit, its author has also provided the reader with the logic that led to the hypotheses.

Fourth, move to the method. It has already been mentioned that there are general concepts—for example, dependency or aggression or underachievement. By this stage in reading, you will have discovered what general concept the author has in mind. It has also been previously pointed out that a concept, a general term, must be "brought down to earth." If an author is talking about underachievement

in the sixth grade, exactly how does he bring this general concept down to earth? To him, is an underachiever a child who is in the bottom one-fifth of the class or below the average according to teachers' marks? or according to nationally standardized tests? There can be a great difference here. We know that teachers favor girls over boys when awarding grades, probably because girls are better behaved and the principal frowns on a teacher if she does not maintain good discipline. Thus, because girls give less trouble than boys, the teacher has something of a "halo" effect about girls. They are well behaved, thus they must be bright, thus they should get good marks. Standardized tests are more objective. Few if any important differences in results from such tests are consistently found between boys and girls. The author who uses standardized tests as his measure of underachievement has done a scientifically more acceptable job of anchoring the general concept of underachievement than the research worker who uses teachers' marks. Which is a better definition of underachievement—the bottom one-fifth of the class or all the children who fall below the average of the class? The question cannot be answered so simply. The children's academic aptitude or intelligence must also be taken into consideration, because intelligence is related both to teachers' marks and to performance on achievement tests. The author who chooses a method something like this has behaved soundly. Using the correlation technique to predict what standing in class each child *hypothetically* should have in terms of his intelligence compared with the rest of the class, he chooses as underachievers those who fall markedly below their *ability* as far as their performance is concerned.

Fifth, note what the nature is of the population the author has studied. Is it European, Australian, French, United States? If the last, is it from a lower-class area in New York City or an upper-middle-class suburb of St. Louis, or rural? If the author has not told you this, he has not given enough information for you to make an adequate judgment about his study. Is the population one of boys, girls, or half-and-half? This can make a tremendous difference and, again, if the author has not given you this information, you cannot make your own judgment about the merits of his study or the worth of his conclusions.

Sixth, move on to the author's *results* section. Look first at the tables to see what the author has found out. Only later go on to see what the author says about his tables. The tables and the text sometimes disagree. If they do disagree, the author has not been completely honest.

Seventh, if the author includes a discussion section, read it. Here an author is at liberty to speculate about what his results mean: He is not completely bound by his data; he can ponder about why they do not fit his hypotheses, or why they do. He is free to consider where his results may lead, what relation they bear to other research, where he made his mistakes (if any), what the strong points of his article were, and propose needed new research, either for himself or for someone else.

Eighth, and finally (the ideal way to read an article is with a pen or a pencil in hand, underlining and making marginal notes), go back over the underlinings and comments you have made to formulate your overall impression of the article, make a judgment of its worth, check the author for consistency or inconsistency, and so on.

Glossary*

(Prepared by David M. Schwartz)

ABSOLUTE VERSUS RELATIVE STANDARDS DILEMMA A persistent issue in *socialization* concerning the pros and cons for standards of behavior that are intrinsically right, enduring, and applicable to all particular situations (absolute) or that are flexible and variable from one situation to another, depending on the context (relative).

ACCOMMODATION *Cognitive-developmental* concept underlying the definition of *equilibration* and referring to a child's or an older person's response to *disequilibrium* (resulting from the *assimilation* of new information) by means of transforming, developing, and correcting older, existent notions about experiences and stimuli in accordance with the newly assimilated input, thus alleviating the disequilibrium.

ACHIEVEMENT Record of things that have been accomplished (test scores, relationships, works of art) and conceptualized as being the function of an individual's *competence*. A need for achievement among American youth has been postulated, but it seems doubtful that this need is generalized across all life situations of an individual.

* All italicized terms are defined in this Glossary. In some cases the reader will note a term—for example, cognitive developmental—placed in italics. This usage is meant to refer the reader to the topic area (that is, cognitive-developmental psychology) for which the main term being defined has special importance and significance.

ACTUALIZATION FUNCTION OF SCHOOLS Aspect of schools that should enhance *self-esteem* and social development of students, should help them find joy in life, should teach them to enjoy playing to the same degree that they know how to perform academically, and should broaden their horizons of thought, including critical and appreciative abilities and allowing for healthy growth of the emotional life.

ACTUAL SELF *See* COMPLEXITY.

ADVERSARY RELATIONSHIP Situation that occurs when various parties to controversy find themselves tensely aligned against one another. Such a relationship often develops within school systems. Ways of cooling this situation are analysis of common ground, full understanding of the premises of each side, avoiding expectations about the opposition, and including a respect for the opinion of experts (teachers or students) and the rights of students to control their educational goals.

AFFECT The general term used to deal with emotions, moods, and feelings as opposed to the cognitive or rational processes.

AFFILIATION BEHAVIOR Tendency to depend on another person or other persons, to associate with them, and to form friendships and other attachments. This concept is synonymous with the notion of attachment behavior, as well as the more general construct of *dependence*.

AGE-RELEVANT DEVELOPMENTAL CONCEPT Approach to the description and analysis of developmental change that consists of ordering behaviors at each chosen age level in an *average* or purely *normative-descriptive* approach, with age as the primary developmental index.

AGGRESSION   Concept referring to observable behavior that is verbal (shouting, ridiculing) or physical (hitting, kicking) and whose effects can also be observed, as well as to an intention or a motive, usually inferred from the behavior of the actor, or aggressor; this approach should be used with caution. Other considerations for defining the construct take into account the goal of the aggression—harm for the sake of harm, perhaps provoked by some harsh punishment delivered to the child who responds with aggression to a less threatening person (displaced aggression), or a behavior that is meant to achieve some desired outcome, such as gaining possession of material goods or winning a prize in competition (instrumental aggression). The latter may include harm to others, particularly if the child wishes to obtain quickly or if no constructive alternative exists. The behavior can also be defined in terms of whether it occurs only in certain social settings (situational aggression) or represents a basic tendency for children or youth to show a certain level of behavior across a wide variety of settings (general aggression).

ALLOCENTRIC ORIENTATION   *See* EMPATHY.

ALTRUISM   Kindly, non-self-centered behavior, including sharing, from which no apparent reward is gained other than "feeling good." Empathy and the ability to adopt an *allocentric orientation* (other-centeredness), rather than an *egocentrism,* cognitive or emotional, are necessary for displaying this kind of behavior, though a primitive form of it may be observed from kindergarten onward (expedient altruism) that represents a desire to reap certain rewards for oneself by behaving kindly toward others, reflecting social *conformity* and a possible desire to escape social sanctions or punishments that may result from selfish or antisocial behavior. In contrast, mature altruism (intrinsic altruism) occurs in the absence of external rewards or obvious personal gain.

ANACLITIC IDENTIFICATION   Freudian concept referring to process of identification, beginning in infancy and occurring for both boys and girls (but of major developmental importance to girls), that is characterized as a strong *dependence* and love relation with the mother. With age, the mother's attention is diverted to some degree from her growing child. In response to this, the girl develops her conscience or superego to please her mother so as not to lose her love. Boys are thought to seek to recapture the mother and to have sexual fantasies about her.

ANDROGEN   Male sex hormone affecting the development of biological and, probably, psychological maleness in certain areas—for example, aggressive behavior—as well as factors of growth rate.

ANLAGE BEHAVIORS   Cattell's conceptualization of those preparatory or foundation behaviors which are the basis of both *fluid intelligence* and *crystallized intelligence,* composed of attentional ability (such as short-term memory span for digits) and basic to the ability to attend carefully, concentrate, and resist distraction.

ANTICIPATORY ANXIETY   Emotional response arising in anticipation of dire, but not clearly defined, consequences in situations reflecting possible physical harm, loss of approval or affection from others, inability to cope successfully with the environment, and the like.

ANTICIPATORY GUILT   *See* GUILT ORIENTATION.

ANXIETY   A complex emotional state marked by apprehensiveness and heightened physiological reactions, very similar to what is commonly called fear, but distinguished from that construct by the clarity of reference or cause, inasmuch as fear is set off by objective stimuli whereas the antecedents or stimuli for anxiety are typically vaguer or entirely unknown. Both fear and anxiety share in common attributes of intense personal discomfort, the reduction of which is exceptionally reinforcing, though it may also produce avoidance responses and/or aggressiveness that may be inappropriate. The anxiety construct occupies an important position in *psychodynamic psychology,* particularly in the explanation of anticipatory guilt *(guilt orientation)*. Anxiety responses appear early in child development as *stranger anxiety,* with later forms labeled *separation anxiety, anticipatory anxiety,* and *school anxiety.*

APOLLONIAN NATURE OF MAN   A conceptualization of human nature that emphasizes the thinking, cognizing, symbolic, and appreciative activities of man, along with a stress on planning ahead, motivation to achieve, delay of gratification, and inhibition of impulses.

"APPLIED BEHAVIORISM"   The study of behavior, particularly that of children, in natural environmental settings, such as the school (rather than in the more highly controlled and predictable setting of the laboratory) and represented by the techniques and research methodology of *behavior modification.*

ARRANGED EXPERIENCE   *See* CRYSTALLIZED INTELLIGENCE.

ARTICULATION   Aspect of *language* development dealing with the child's learning of the contrasting speech sounds of his language, the means by which these sounds are produced, and the rules for the usage of the sounds.

ASSIMILATION   *Cognitive-developmental* concept underlying the definition of *equilibration* and referring to the child's or the older person's comprehension of some new experience which must be plugged in, as much as possible, to fit with what has already been experienced and understood at an existing level of comprehension.

ASSOCIATIVE PLAY   *See* PLAY BEHAVIOR.

ASSOCIATIVITY   Piagetian notion of the child's ability to demonstrate that parts of a whole may be combined in different ways without effecting a change in the whole or the end results.

ASYMPTOTE   The highest point of a plotted set of data after which the function or curve levels out, indicating the stable level of a particular variable (such as *intelligence* or some other developmental ability).

ATOMISM   A research strategy, typified by *behaviorist psychology,* of reducing large, global concepts in human development to their simplest component elements and sometimes criticized by opponents of this approach as representing a failure to consider meaningful wholes or important, large segments of behavior, resulting in an ultimately simplistic approach to human development.

ATTACHMENT BEHAVIOR   *See* AFFILIATION BEHAVIOR.

ATTENTION .   A central selective process that is conceptualized as intermediate between the vast stimulus array to which a person is exposed at all times, and the responses he makes to this stimulus array. The process is conceived in two phases:

1. ORIENTATION REACTION   A behavioral alertness or vigilance (perhaps *attention span*) designed to help one identify stimuli and prepare to receive and respond to additional stimulation.
2. SELECTIVE SCANNING (or searching)   A behavioral process by which the individual selects a particular aspect of the environment to "study" or learn about, or by which the individual seeks internal, stored knowledge for some problem-solving or abstract thinking.

ATTENTION SPAN   The range of stimuli that an individual's *orientation reactions* can encompass, in terms of either number or time, and closely related to Cattell's *anlage behaviors,* as well as *short-term memory store.*

AUDITORY DISCRIMINATION   Ability of the child (or an adult) to tell the difference between sounds, particularly *language*-relevant sounds such as vowel and consonant distinctions.

AUTHORITARIAN PARENTAL CONTROL   Baumrind's characterization of parental child-rearing practices that stress control, obedience, absolute standards, use of forceful and punitive disciplinary measures, and emphasis on respect for authority, tradition, and order, with little verbal give-and-take between parent and child.

AUTHORITATIVE PARENTAL CONTROL   Baumrind's characterization of parental child-rearing practices that stress firm rational control with considerable parent-child verbal give-and-take, full recognition and respect for the child's interests, and personal *autonomy* within understood boundaries of disciplined *conformity,* as well as a clear communication of future expectations.

AUTONOMOUS MORALITY   *See* MORAL REALISM VERSUS MORAL RELATIVISM.

AUTONOMY   Concept of self-directedness, closely related to *independence,* and expected to be more evident in males than females in United States culture. The peer group and older siblings, representing somewhat different normative standards than parents, serve to encourage the child to pressure parents into allowing him greater independence of expression. Peer groups also provide a social structure in which the child can rehearse behavioral autonomy (the first alcoholic drink, etc.).

AVERAGE   The statistical term used to indicate a value in a distribution of scores around which all the other values are dispersed. Also, generally used to mean the standard or typical case.

AVERSIVE CONTROL   *Behaviorist* technique for control of behavior by threat or actual delivery of *punishment,* but lacking the overall effectiveness of behavioral control gained by the delivery of *response-dependent* and *response-independent reinforcement.*

"BALANCE THEORY"   *See* HOMEOSTATIC THEORY.

BEHAVIOR MODIFICATION   A set of techniques of *"applied behaviorism"* that utilizes the theoretical research findings from the laboratory to help individuals develop more effective and adaptive behaviors, both social and academic.

BEHAVIORAL CONTROL DILEMMA   A persistent issue in *socialization* concerning the pros and cons of how much freedom and how much restraint should be allowed and/or imposed upon the developing child at home or in school for optimal development.

BEHAVIORAL STABILITY DILEMMA   A persistent issue in developmental psychology, dealing with the relative continuity or discontinuity of various traits and behaviors in individuals over their developmental span, including aspects of personality and *intelligence.*

BEHAVIORIST PSYCHOLOGY (BEHAVIORISM)   A psychological approach to human development primarily concerned with the study of observable behavior that utilizes rigorous scientific experimentation and methodology, involving carefully controlled and executed experiments in which the stimulus variables are appropriately manipulated, exact controls are executed, and the resulting behavior is accurately observed and measured, ultimately leading to a science of behavioral prediction and control.

BIOLINGUISTICS   Scientific discipline, related to *linguistics,* concerned with maturational factors (anatomical and physiological) that set the stage for language development.

BISEXUAL   *See* SEXUAL ORIENTATION.

BODY-TYPE THEORY   *See* SOMATOTYPE THEORY.

BUREAUCRATIC PARENTAL OCCUPATION   A *mediator of developmental change* considered to transcend *social class* lines, characterized by salaried occupations with a high degree of job security, and affecting a wide range of child-rearing practices that stress egalitarian behavior and emphasize social adjustment, or "getting along."

CANALIZATION   Development of a preference for sexual outlets (such as *masturbation*) that are, in reality, merely substitutes for heterosexual intercourse and may come to interfere with the development of a heterosexual relationship involving intercourse.

CATHARSIS   Free expression of *aggression,* either vicariously (in fantasy or by watching others act aggressively), or through play (verbalizing one's feelings, or actual aggressive responses toward some object [doll, toy car, or other object]) that brings about the dissipation or reduction of aggressive tension as well as the lessening of the tendency to perform other aggressive acts.

CENTERING   Phenomenon closely related to *egocentrism* in children, referring to the child's tendency to focus his *attention* on a single aspect of a situation or an event, rendering him unable to take in other aspects of the perceptual field and accounting for his inability to appreciate *invariance despite change* and attain the operation of *conservation.*

CHILD–PEER INTERACTIONS   Conceptualization of experience with peers in terms of influence that this *primary group* exerts on social, academic, and vocational development, and defined in five levels, or strata, of interactions (indicating a trend of ever-widening social interaction):

1. child and near-aged siblings
2. child and neighborhood playmates
3. child and school classmates of same age
4. child and school classmates in other grades and classes and of different ages
5. child and his more abstract, generalized *expectancies* about other children and the ways in which he relates to them

CHOICES SOCIOMETRIC   *See* SOCIOMETRIC TECHNIQUE.

CLASSICAL CONDITIONING (Pavlovian conditioning)   An experimental learning procedure in which a stimulus evoking a given response is presented with a neutral stimulus (one that does not evoke a response) with the result that the previously neutral stimulus comes to evoke the response when presented by itself. According to some theorists, children learn *trust* in an analogous fashion because the infant's cries of distress are repeatedly paired with comfort-giving and other such positive ministrations by his caregivers, thus generalizing *trust* to all significant others.

CLASSICAL, TWO-FACTOR THEORY OF INTELLIGENCE Spearman's conceptualization of cognitive abilities and structure as made up of a *"g", or general, factor* (intelligent, problem-solving, sentient behavior) that is the core of *intelligence,* as well as many *"s," or special, factors* (such as music or motor ability) having little relationship to *"g",* or general, factor.

CLASSIFICATION Piagetian notion of the child's ability to organize an array of objects into hierarchies of classes, including the tasks of multiple classification (simultaneous organization along a number of equivalent dimensions such as color and size) and of superordinate conceptual classification (simultaneous organization along a number of hierarchical dimensions on different conceptual levels).

CLINICAL METHOD A technique for studying human development, involving the use of tests, interviews, and questionnaires, that has been of central importance to the data-gathering and theory construction of *humanistic, psychodynamic,* and *cognitive-developmental psychologies.*

"CLOSED" ATTENTION SET See INTENTIONAL LEARNING.

COGNITION The process by which a person comes to know himself and his world by means of attending to the features of his environment, organizing and codifying his sensations, storing impressions in memory, and manipulating (in thought) the concepts and generalizations that he has formed from these sensations and impressions. This process involves aspects of *language, intelligence, attention, perception, intentional learning, incidental learning, expectancy, cognitive style, curiosity,* and *creativity.*

COGNITIVE STYLE Individual or idiosyncratic variation in modes of perceiving, remembering, and thinking, or distinctive ways of ap-

prehending, storing, transforming, and utilizing information. This aspect of functioning is concerned with the manner and form of *cognition,* rather than a level of skills or abilities.

COGNITIVE-DEVELOPMENTAL PSYCHOLOGY A psychological approach to human development primarily concerned with matters of *intelligence,* thinking, logical processes, *language,* and competence or efficiency, as well as an emphasis on *epistemology,* and best represented by the *developmental stage theory* of J Piaget.

"COLLATIVE STIMULUS PROPERTIES" Berlyne's theoretical construct for explaining that certain stimuli compel or elicit *attention* (produce orientation reactions) more than others, because of intrinsic properties (representing a degree of unexpectedness or uncertainty) that require the individual to study them, comparing and collating information about these properties before they can be fitted into his experience.

COMBINATORY IDENTIFICATION THEORY A theoretical mix of *psychodynamic* and *cognitive-developmental* interpretations of *sex role identification,* making a distinction between *parental identification* and *sex role adoption* in which the child could conceivably identify with a cross-sex parent or not identify at all with a parent, yet still identify with the appropriate sex role. The cognitive-developmental aspects of this view concern sex differences in the actual process and outcome or product of the identification process. Thus, for girls, parental and sex role identification are "lessons to be learned," while, for boys, the two sources of information about role and behavior are "conceptual problems to be understood and solved."

COMMUNICATION STYLE Aspect of language behavior referring to the unique way in which an individual uses his language to express thoughts and feelings, to relate socially to other people, to clarify ideas, and to describe things that have been experienced. *Grammar, articulation, vocabulary,* and *talking rate* combine to produce a language style that has been conceptualized by Bernstein as *elaborative* or *restrictive (communication style),* in reference to differences in the degree of elaboration in *syntax* and *vocabulary,* in focus on clarifying ideas (particularly cause-effect relationships), and in the amount of redundancy or unnecessary repetition, with elaborative style being a more differentiated and precise conceptual tool and restrictive style being a more global, cliché-ridden, informationally barren and imprecise tool.

COMPENSATORY EDUCATION An approach to education programs typically aimed at the disadvantaged population and incorporating remedial goals (attempts to fill social, cultural, or academic gaps in a child's education) and preventive goals (education during the early childhood years when such experiences are hypothesized to stand a better chance of capitalizing on the modifiability and flexibility of the human organism in order to prevent later academic problems from developing).

COMPETENCE A concept used in two different areas and referring to:

1. The characteristic of successfully accomplishing the tasks that one attempts, closely linked to the concepts of *effectance* and *achievement,* and a necessary but not a sufficient condition for good personal-social adjustment.
2. The *linguistics* notion of the child's grasp of the abstract properties of *language* and his means for interpreting and generating linguistic structures, as opposed to *speech* production or *performance (linguistic).*

COMPLEXITY Trend in the development of the *self* in which the young child's view of self, comparatively global and diffuse at first, gradually takes shape in terms of several dimensions, but particularly in the evolved distinction between the *actual self* ("the way I am") and the *ideal self* ("the way I would like to be"). Ever more complex perceptions are built upon the actual self–ideal self distinction, reflecting the individual's increased ability to take a variety of social and personal perspectives in viewing the self.

CONCEPT A general term for the class of behavior one is reading about or which the author of a research paper has studied (for example, *frustration,* regression, *anxiety*).

CONCRETE OPERATIONS PERIOD Piagetian developmental stage, lasting from 7 years to 11 years, during which the child is able to use operations such as *reversibility* (in arithmetic), *classification,* and *seriation* and to achieve increasingly more objective and logical patterns of cognition, but without the ability to perform these operations in logical or abstract terms, needing instead to manipulate actual or concrete quantities.

CONFORMITY Defined as yielding to group pressures and considered to be somewhat negative in United States culture, though a certain degree of yielding is acceptable within the context of maintaining peer group cohesiveness (shared values, activities, goals). Conformity in the peer group context increases in intensity with age to a peak during preadolescence and early adolescence, after which it decreases, reflecting an age-related shift in the locus of children's *dependence* from parents and other adults to peers and peer-oriented recognition and approval. Behavioral yielding is also influenced by group size and composition, extent of unanimity of group consensus, and nature of pressure techniques applied by group members.

CONSERVATION Piagetian notion of child's ability to understand that contextual appearance may change with no effect on other aspects of the substance under observation, an ability to divorce conception from perception that is achieved first with the notion of mass, then with weight, and finally with volume.

CONSISTENCY Trend in the development of the self (containing a large motivational component), involving the evolution of *expectancies* about one's self in the direction of more consistent behavior and self-image, as well as more accurate subjective estimates about what one can or cannot do.

CONTENTIVES Class name for nouns, verbs, and adjectives first used by the child in *telegraphic speech* utterances, an intermediate aspect of grammatical development.

CONTROL GROUP In experimental studies, the group of subjects that receives no experimental treatment, serving as a reference group against which change in the *experimental group* may be measured.

CONVERGENT PRODUCTION OR THINKING Operation referring to *logical induction* (the process of extrapolating general principles from specific instances) or *logical deduction* (the process of extrapolating or deriving specific examples from general principles), usually from possession of a relatively complete set of facts and according to a formal logical procedure. This ability is that which is typically measured in achievement and intelligence tests where a "correct" answer is called for.

COOPERATION   *Prosocial behavior,* including an element of *altruism* and often tinged with enlightened self-interest, developing in infancy as the result of accommodations made between child and parents and maturing through children's games and other peer group interactions. Though essential in a democratic system, cooperation exists within United States culture in an uneasy compromise with competition.

COOPERATIVE PLAY   *See* PLAY BEHAVIOR.

CORRELATION COEFFICIENT (*r*)   A statistical expression of the degree to which two measures vary together, ranging from perfect positive (+1.00) through zero, or no relationship (0.00) to perfect negative (−1.00) relationships. Causal explanations cannot be inferred from correlation, but one may predict the amount of *variance* that one variable or measure contributes to another in a particular relationship by squaring the correlation coefficient (*r²*).

CORRELATIONAL APPROACH   An approach to the study of development that consists of descriptions of behavioral change in relation to *norms* for that behavior as well as to other factors—for example, family background, *socioeconomic status, child-peer interactions, intelligence.*

COUNTERCULTURE   Defined as a group of people that actively rejects the values reflected in the mainstream of American life (intellectual reason over emotion, self-reliance, personal responsibility, delay of gratification, and advance planning). The main progenitors of this movement are said to be white, upper-middle-class youth and intelligent, dissaffected blacks who are reacting to the inauthenticity or hypocrisy of adult-controlled social institutions and are championing a life style that emphasizes the *Dionysian* orientation to life and experience.

COVARIANCE   *See* EQUIVALENCE.

CREATIVITY   Complex cognitive process that requires as yet unknown proportions of knowledge, ability to see new relationships among objects or events, radarlike *attention* to the environment, willingness to engage in fantasy in thought, *hypothesis formulation* and testing, and skill in communicating one's thought to others. With regard to the *process–product distinction, divergent production* is thought to be central to this *process,* while as a *distinction, product,* the concept refers to a novel or an original contribution that is usually satisfying, meaningful, and valuable to the creator and/or his culture.

CRITICAL-PERIODS DILEMMA   A persistent issue for developmental psychology, dealing with the appropriate timing in an individual's growth at which minimum and/or maximum amounts and types of environmental experience are necessary for optimum social–personal, intellectual–academic, and physical–motor development. Within this dilemma are the subissues of *maximum susceptibility* and *cumulative deficits.*

CROSS-CULTURAL STUDY   A type of experimental design in which comparable data are acquired from two or more different cultures for the purpose of testing theories about individual and/or group differences in development and behavior.

CROSS-SECTIONAL STUDY   A type of experimental design in which a number of individuals at different stages of development are studied as a means of drawing general inferences about the progress of development and factors associated with such development.

CRYSTALLIZED INTELLIGENCE   One of Cattell's two factors of *intelligence,* made up of skills that are involved in mastering common elements of the *culture* and developed through experiences that have been arranged, but not necessarily systematically planned, for the child by educational institutions of the society (school, family).

CUE OR DISCRIMINATIVE STIMULUS   *Behaviorist* designation for a stimulus or pattern of stimuli capable of eliciting a particular behavior or class of behaviors because of association of that stimulus or pattern of stimuli with the delivery or nondelivery of *reinforcement.* The concept is central to the notion of *stimulus control* of behavior.

CULTURE   A broadly defined set of customs, roles, and learned behaviors of a particular group of people that is transmitted from one generation to the next as a *formal culture,* being applied in a more particular, flexible, and more loosely defined sense to the individual within some subgroup of the population as the *effective culture.*

"Cultural competence" Notion within the *behaviorist* concept of child development that emphasizes the shaping power of *arranged experience* for the child in order that he achieve maximal skills development and environmental mastery, essentially in keeping with an environmental *determinism* perspective.

Cumulative deficit hypothesis Conceptual subissue within the *critical-periods* literature and meaning that deficiencies or distortions of experiences may pile up or accumulate and progressively interfere more and more with future development, perhaps in a geometric fashion.

Curiosity Form of exploratory behavior for the purpose of changing the stimulus field in which one operates, either by finding out something about a specific object or event or by searching for an interesting environment that enables one to achieve a preferred level of stimulation. The concepts of *epistemic curiosity* and of *diversive exploration* are both aspects of this behavior.

Deduction *See* Convergent production or thinking; Problem-solving process.

Defensive identification (identification with the aggressor) Freudian concept referring to the *process* of *identification* for males. The primary mechanism is the threat of the father as a potential castrator of the son. In response to this threat, the son seeks to act like the aggressor-father, thus gaining some of the power of the father's role as well as some of the intimacy with the mother that the son equates symbolically with the father's role. This latter desire marks the chief feature of *Oedipal dilemma* or *phase*, during which the boy becomes increasingly hostile to his father, as well as fearful of him. The resulting *anxiety* is so painful that the sexual fantasies of possessing the mother and the destruction of the father by *aggression* are both repressed, the *Oedipal dilemma* is resolved, and the boy becomes similar to his father and appropriately masculine in his identification.

Dependence General concept, indicated by a wide variety of seeking and protest behaviors in children and adolescents, that may be interpreted in one of the following ways:

1. Nurturance seeking (seeking affection and protection), which may take the form of clinging or tugging behavior, which in our *culture* is generally approved of, but not encouraged, for children and discouraged in adults, particularly males (emotional dependence).
2. Help-seeking behavior or means-to-end behavior directed toward getting a job done rather than toward gaining social reward, and particularly important and desirable when it involves social interactions that result in the child's mastering difficult problems and learning new skills (instrumental dependence).
3. Behavior defined along the passivity-activity continuum over a wide variety of situations for a child, sometimes contradicting or disproving the stereotyped labeling of the quiet, reticent child as being more dependent than the active child (passive dependence).

Determinism The philosophical position, embodied in *behaviorism*, that man is controlled by the forces of his environment and, hence, is not a free agent to act as he pleases—a position represented by the religious and philosophical doctrine of *free will* and the principles of *humanistic psychology*.

Developmental interaction Conceptual approach used to connote the multiple and varied aspects of physical–motor, personal–social–emotional, and cognitive–intellectual–achievement development that contribute to the child's psychosocial development.

Developmental stage theory Theoretical conceptualization of development used in *psychodynamic psychology* and *cognitive-developmental psychology* in which an individual's growth is characterized as a progression through a sequentially invariant and qualitatively different series of states or stages. Various theories differ about the notion of fixation at some particular point in development, mechanisms underlying rate of individual progress, and implications of various stages for cognitive and emotional growth. Stage theorists include Piaget, Freud, Erikson, and Kohlberg.

Dialect A *language* system, differing to a greater or lesser degree from standard English in terms of a variety of grammatically different additions, deletions, and word combinations as well as the possible incorporation of grammatical rules and vocabulary from non-English linguistic systems. In the schools, use of such nonstandard English becomes particularly problematic (referred to in the *language differences dilemma*).

DIFFERENTIATION (1) Developmental process by which behavior becomes increasingly more precise, complex, and specialized; (2) developmental trend of the *self*, defined by the child's achievement of a less global viewpoint and evaluation of the self, resulting from organization of self-knowledge and self-evaluation that suggests an age-related increase in the capacity to form more specialized, complex impressions and influenced by the steady stream of reactions from others that a child receives during the daily course of events.

DIONYSIAN NATURE OF MAN Conceptualization of human nature that emphasizes the enjoyment and capacity for immediate sensory experiences, a lack of impulse inhibition, motivation to enjoy present experiences on their own terms rather than wait for future gratification, cultivation of deep interpersonal relationships, and a general "back to nature" orientation.

DISCRIMINATION LEARNING SET Acquisition of the ability to perceive differences among stimuli and to respond differentially to these stimuli in terms of a *problem-solving process*, with the most highly developed form of this set being *insight learning*.

DISCRIMINATION SET *See* PERFORMANCE SET.

DISCRIMINATIVE STIMULUS *See* CUE.

DISEQUILIBRIUM *Cognitive-developmental* concept underlying the definition of *equilibration* referring to a child's or an older person's response to newly assimilated information about experiences and stimuli that is not in agreement with past knowledge or *expectancies*, resulting in a mildly unsettling condition that the individual seeks to eliminate by learning about the source of error in his prior knowledge and achieving a more accurate perception of reality and the concurrent removal of the unsettling condition by means of *accommodation*. The concept of "*collative properties of stimuli*" is based on this concept.

DISPLACED AGGRESSION *See* AGGRESSION; PUNISHMENT.

DIVERGENT PRODUCTION OR THINKING Ability to operate on the given elements of the environment in a fluent, flexible, and elaborative fashion to achieve end results that are unexpected and original. This kind of operation is central to the concept of *creativity*, according to some theorists.

DIVERSIVE EXPLORATION Activity occurring when one wishes to combat stimulus deprivation or boredom that occurs when a person is awake and alert and has nothing to do or experience. Such activity in search of novelty may be a contributing factor in classroom discipline problems and delinquency.

DUAL AMBIVALENCE *See* INDEPENDENCE.

DYNAMIC PSYCHOLOGY *See* PSYCHODYNAMIC PSYCHOLOGY.

EARLY CHILDHOOD EXPERIENCES DILEMMA A persistent issue for child-rearing and educational programs concerning practices in early childhood that will result in optimal personality adjustment and cognitive development and including concerns ranging from infant feeding and toilet training (particularly among *psychodynamic* psychologists) to the content of preschool intervention programs.

ECONOMY Age-related trend in perceptual development for children to become more skilled at detecting distinctive characteristics of objects and events that distinguish one thing from another, as well as features of things that remain constant, accompanied by increased ability to perceive the higher order structure or pattern inherent in much of what is perceived.

ECTOMORPH *See* SOMATOTYPE THEORY.

EFFECTANCE Need to do something by oneself with the things in one's environment, probably closely linked to the development of *trust*, as well as the concepts of *competence* and *achievement*, and of particular importance to the development of *self concept*.

EFFECTIVE CULTURE Those particular aspects of shared behavioral uniformity and diversity which actually impinge on and affect individuals and groups within a larger social configuration, operating as *mediators of developmental change* and transmitted to the child by the *primary group* (family, neighbors, close friends, and classmates).

EGO According to Freudian *psychodynamic*

theory, one of the three basic components of personality, comprising the mechanism for association with reality (*reality principle*) and socially appropriate problem-solving behavior that seeks acceptable ways of delaying, substituting, or otherwise handling basic motivations and conflicts between the *id* and the *superego*. Ego strength is considered to be an indicator of *moral development*.

EGOCENTRISM Piagetian concept of the child's inability to understand that others have needs and points of view which differ from his own, resulting in a tendency to evaluate objects and events solely in terms of one's own perspective. With the achievement of *formal operations* and the ability to simultaneously consider multiple points of view, *egocentrism* is dissipated.

EIGHT STAGES OF MAN Erikson's neopsychoanalytic theory postulating a series of eight developmental crises that each person must face in the total span of his development, beginning with *trust versus mistrust*, the foundation stage for all the other psychosocial stages, during which a person learns to be optimistic and trusting, in contrast to cynical and mistrusting, as a function of the accepting treatment given the child by his caregivers. Another important feature of this *developmental stage theory* is the psychosocial moratorium, a prolonged period of adolescence for economically advantaged youth during which they are given more opportunity to work out a resolution to the crisis of identity versus indentity diffusion, provoked by increased differentiation of awareness of others and societal problems, need to choose an occupation and make an ideological commitment in the areas of religion, ethics, and politics, and notable for the active questioning, decision making, and examination of alternatives that goes on during the period.

EJACULATION *See* ORGASM.

ELABORATIVE COMMUNICATION STYLE *See* COMMUNICATION STYLE.

EMOTIONAL DEPENDENCE *See* DEPENDENCE.

EMPATHY Capacity for understanding another individual's thoughts or feelings by being able to take his psychological perspective, and a necessary precursor for the development of *altruism* and *morality*. This concept is similar to the allocentric orientation

notion (a perspective that is "other-centered" rather than cognitively or emotionally *egocentric*).

EMPIRICISM *See* OPERATIONAL DEFINITION.

ENCODING *See* PROBLEM-SOLVING PROCESS.

ENDOMORPH *See* SOMATOTYPE THEORY.

ENTREPRENEURIAL PARENTAL OCCUPATION A *mediator of developmental change*, considered to transcend *socioeconomic class* lines, characterized by occupations involving self-employment or work on a direct-commission basis that often includes risk taking and competition, and affecting a wide range of child-rearing practices that emphasize independence training, mastery of skills, self-reliance, and ample use of psychological techniques of discipline.

EPISTEMIC CURIOSITY Activity directed to gaining, coding, and storing information in the form of symbolic responses that can guide behavior on future occasions, and believed to be motivated by conceptual conflict or conflict due to discrepant thoughts, beliefs, attitudes, or observations. Because of this conflict, the individual seeks information to buttress, support, develop, or refine his prevailing thought, and resolution is considered to be intrinsically reinforcing in this situation.

EPISTEMOLOGY That branch of philosophy concerned with understanding the origin, nature, methods, and limits of knowledge, particularly with reference to human thought and epitomized by the developmental research of J Piaget.

EQUILIBRATION *Cognitive-developmental* concept defined as the achievement by the individual of greater cognitive balance or stability at successively higher levels as he reconciles new experience with past experience, involving the mutual processes of *assimilation* and *accommodation*.

EQUIVALENCE Piagetian notion of a child's ability to understand that objects which differ along one or more dimensions (varying size and texture, for example) may still be similar along some other dimension (such as weight), as well as the concept that some change along one of these dimensions (shape, perhaps) does not necessarily mean that the other dimensions (texture and weight, for example) will also change. This concept is synonymous with the concept of covariance.

ESTROGEN   Female sex hormone affecting the development of biological and, probably, aspects of psychological femaleness—for example—maternal behavior—as well as factors of growth rate.

ETHNIC, or ETHNIC GROUP   *See* ETHNICITY.

ETHNICITY   Concept referring to the *culture,* religion, and *language* traditions of a people or cultural group, such as Italian Americans or Jews, as distinguished from the concept of *race,* or *racial group.*

EVALUATION   *See* PROBLEM-SOLVING PROCESS.

EXPANSION TECHNIQUE   Source of adult influence on the child's grammatical development in which the adult responds to the child's two- or three-word utterance by formulating complete and grammatically correct versions of the child's presumed ideas, using the child's structured utterance as the skeleton of the more complete expression.

EXPECTANCY   Learned disposition of the organism to behave in anticipation of a specific situation as a function of *set (perceptual, performance,* or *learning set),* estimated probability of the occurrence of a particular event in some known setting on the basis of past *reinforcement history,* or the knowledge of behaviors and attitudes that we perceive others to hold us capable of exemplifying, because of subtle and not-so-subtle *cues* that they give us; the self-fulfilling prophecy notion is based on this mechanism. Expectancy can be a useful basis for responding, as well as a harmful one, particularly if such a predisposition serves to block one's perception of a reality that is contrary to the expectation.

EXPEDIENT ALTRUISM   *See* ALTRUISM.

EXPERIMENTAL GROUP   In experimental studies, the group of subjects that is exposed to a particular treatment or independent variable, in contrast to a group of subjects receiving no experimental treatment *(control group).*

EXPERIMENTAL METHOD   A technique for studying development, involving the systematic manipulation of environmental variables in the investigation of the effect of such manipulations on behavior. This approach has been utilized chiefly by *behaviorism* and, to a much lesser extent, by *psychodynamic* and *cognitive-developmental* approaches.

EXPRESSIVE LANGUAGE   *See* LANGUAGE.

EXPRESSIVE ROLE (FEMININE)   *See* SEX ROLE STEREOTYPES.

EXTENDED or KINSHIP FAMILY   A familial constellation or social pattern in which father, mother, children, grandparents, and uncles and aunts all live together or in close proximity, providing many surrogate parents for young children.

EXTENSION TECHNIQUE   Source of adult influence on the child's grammatical development in which the adult responds to the child's two- or three-word utterance by contributing a related idea—carrying the child's idea into a wider range of meaning and experience—representing an *expansion technique* as well as the addition of an idea or ideas to maintain conversational sequence.

EXTERNAL LOCUS OF CONTROL   *See* LOCUS OF CONTROL.

FACTOR ANALYSIS   A statistical method used in test construction and interpretation of scores from batteries of tests. A factor is a commonality among a set of relationships, all expressed in statistical terms and named for the common elements that links a number of components. Guilford's *Structure of Intellect* is derived from use of this technique.

FALLEN ANGEL VIEW OF MAN   View of man's essential nature as basically good. Given the opportunity to grow freely, man will seek to realize himself and will move toward self-fulfillment and a constructive adjustment. *Morality,* in this view, need not (should not) be trained, because it is inherent, although a malign environment could deflect this positive course of development. This attitude is typical of *humanistic psychology* and *cognitive-developmental psychology.*

FEAR   *See* ANXIETY.

FLUID INTELLIGENCE   One of Cattell's two factors of *intelligence,* developing relatively independently of planned or *arranged experiences (crystallized intelligence)* as the result of informal, spontaneous, and necessary interchanges with the environment, as in a baby's visual tracking that becomes the basis for later systematic attentional processes. These unarranged experiences yield skills closely related to Piaget's conceptualization of various cognitive processes, including *object permanence, conservation,* and other processes.

FORMAL CULTURE Broad, shared guidelines held to within a given group of people, involving both uniformity and the organization of diversity in the behavior of its participants, although these formal characteristics may not precisely apply to a particular person or group within that *culture*, as may be seen by the discussion of *effective culture*.

FORMAL OPERATIONS PERIOD (PERSPECTIVISM) Piagetian developmental stage, lasting from the age of 11 years and beyond, during which the child is able to formulate and execute symbolic plans of action based on hypothetical events, considering simultaneously the effects of more than one variable in a problematic situation, otherwise exhibiting the ability to examine logical form independently of an actual situation, as well as a critical facility for detecting logical incongruities in hypothetical contexts. The individual is also able to reflect and evaluate his own cognitive processes.

FREE-WILL DILEMMA *See* DETERMINISM.

FRUSTRATION An emotional state that results when an individual is unable to achieve some desired goal for whatever reason, possibly involving physical pain and threats to one's *self-esteem*, and considered by some theorists to be closely related to the induction of *aggression*.

FUNCTION WORDS Class name for prepositions, conjunctions, and articles (up, to, on, in, but, and, an, the) that are combined with *contentives* to form complete sentences by the young child.

"g" or GENERAL, FACTOR INTELLIGENCE *See* CLASSICAL, TWO-FACTOR THEORY OF INTELLIGENCE.

GENERAL AGGRESSION *See* AGGRESSION.

GENERALIZED IMITATION *See* IMITATION.

GENERATIVE GRAMMAR A construct, hypothesized by Chomsky and of central theoretical importance to *linguistics*, that is said to be an innate and a universal human mechanism by which developing individuals actively structure the *language* spoken in their linguistic community, permitting them to create and understand sentences, some of which they have never heard before.

GENETICS Scientific study of heredity and the means by which hereditary characteristics are transmitted from one generation to an-

other by means of some kind of genetic blueprint.

GENOTYPE Referring to the sum of the individual's genetic endowment and conceptualized in an interactive *nature-nurture* point of view by the following equation:

$$\text{genotype} \times \text{environment} = \textit{phenotype}$$

GRAMMAR Aspect of *language* defined by a complex system of rules for organizing sentence and word forms.

"GUESS WHO" SOCIOMETRIC *See* SOCIOMETRIC TECHNIQUE.

GUILT ORIENTATION Construct common to both *social learning (behaviorist) psychology* and *psychodynamic psychology* that hypothesizes an internalized standard of moral conduct which, if transgressed, gives rise to internal and self-punitive *anxiety* of a neurotic nature. Previous experience with such *anxiety* restrains the individual from committing a similar transgression in the future, avoiding the act due to anticipatory guilt. Psychological child-rearing practices using withdrawal of parental love, rather than physical power-oriented practices, are associated with internalized controls of this nature, and *guilt*, according to Freud, is induced by the *superego*.

HALO EFFECT A tendency of an independent rater or educator to incorrectly rate an individual in a positive or a negative direction on one or more traits, because of prior information with the resultant formation of positive or negative *expectancies* about the individual's total behavioral and/or personality configuration, on the basis of incomplete and possibly inaccurate information.

HAWTHORNE EFFECT A measurable, but transitory, improvement in the performance of subjects in an experiment that is not a function of the experimental treatment, but rather an artifact of participating in some out-of-the-ordinary situation—for example, a novel teaching situation.

HETEROGENEOUS POPULATION A statistical concept referring to a population of subjects that includes a wide variety of differences among its members on some measure or combination of measures.

HETERONOMOUS MORALITY *See* MORAL REALISM VERSUS MORAL RELATIVISM.

HETEROSEXUAL *See* SEXUAL ORIENTATION.

HOLOPHRASTIC UTTERANCE Earliest phase in grammatical development of the child at around the age of 1 year, this one-word expression is related to actions by the child or actions that he desires of other people or objects and requires an awareness of context by the adult for understanding the child's communication.

HOMEOSTATIC THEORY ("BALANCE THEORY") Theoretical notion used to deal with the construct of motivation and stating that organisms, including human beings of all ages, are rewarded by or reinforced for tension that occurs because of some need, since they find it satisfying to have tension reduced. Thus, one can maintain or return to a physical or a psychological "balance" consisting of a relatively low level of *organismic* tension.

HOMOGENEOUS POPULATION A statistical concept referring to a population in which all members are relatively similar to one another on some measure or combination of measures.

HOMOSEXUAL *See* SEXUAL ORIENTATION.

HUMANISTIC PSYCHOLOGY A psychological approach to human development primarily concerned with man's potential, his uniqueness and dignity, behavior that is singularly human, and methods of study based on an affection for and joy in human nature, with stress on the psychology of normality and excellence aspiration, rather than abnormality and pathology. Also emphasized is inquiry into man's higher "needs"—justice, order, and love—and his pursuit of intrinsic and ultimate values of perfection, goodness, beauty, and truth.

HYPOTHESIS FORMULATION *See* PROBLEM-SOLVING PROCESS.

ID According to Freudian *psychodynamic* theory, one of the three basic components of personality comprising the primitive drives, needs, and instinctual impulses that are constantly striving for gratification and are dynamically held in check by the *superego*.

IDEAL SELF *See* COMPLEXITY.

IDENTIFICATION General concept that may be defined and used in three ways:

1. As behavior. When a person behaves like some other person at a high level of generality and abstraction (mannerisms, lan-

guage habits, values, interests, and even thought processes).

2. As motive. Consciously or unconsciously a person is moved toward, or wishes to be and usually then becomes similar to, someone else.

3. As process. The mechanisms through which the child comes to emulate a model.

The general concept, in its various forms, has been applied to the broad topics of *moral development* and *psychosexual development* and occupies a central role in classical *psychodynamic* theory with constructs of *anaclitic identification* and *defensive identification.*

IDENTIFICATION WITH THE AGGRESSOR *See* DEFENSIVE IDENTIFICATION.

IDENTITY FORMULATION A major growth trend of the *self,* implying future development for the individual and involving an awareness of group membership and the expectations, privileges, restraints, and social responsibilities accompanying that membership, this concept can be thought of as a process through which a child gains knowledge of such matters as his name, race, sex role, and social class, and the meanings that these descriptions have for the child's life.

IDENTITY VERSUS IDENTITY DIFFUSION *See* EIGHT STAGES OF MAN.

IDIOGRAPHIC APPROACH An experimental approach to the study of development that focuses on the experience of the individual human being and the unique, single case and emphasizes individual differences among people rather than general patterns and differences among groups of subjects.

IMITATION Important concept in *social learning (behaviorist)* theory and defined as the act of duplicating someone else's behaviors. This class of behaviors (imitative acts) represents to the child a helpful way of learning to solve problems and securing information that is often rewarded or otherwise encouraged by parents and teachers. The concept has been extended to the areas of *identification* and *sex typing* with the construct of generalized imitation, defined as the learned tendency to imitate across a wide variety of situations. Thus the development of "maleness" and "femaleness" can be viewed as the acquisition of large behavioral categories, composed of the social behaviors, attitudes, and interests of one or the other gender. The concept of *modeling* is very similar to that of imitation.

INCIDENTAL LEARNING Behavioral or informational acquisition activity governed by a more "open" attention system, or set, in which the individual is alert to new and meaningful stimuli of either an emergency self-preserving or an enriching-useful kind and flexible enough to change sets appropriately so as to try new strategies and change from one to another activity as needed. Such learning may also be thought of as taking place with no apparent purpose or long-term goal in mind.

INDEPENDENCE Concept touching on the evolution of *dependence behavior* whose form changes with age, in terms both of the objects of one's *dependence* and of the frequency with which such behavior is manifest. As a character trait, this behavioral manifestation is highly regarded in United States culture, particularly for males. Conflict about *independence–dependence* relationships typically intensifies with the onset of adolescence for parents and teachers, as well as for adolescents. Adults may wish to encourage and allow independent behavior, but fear that the adolescent is not ready to handle it; the possible risk of physical harm to him may cause them conflict in ultimately allowing independence. Similarly, the adolescent may wish to exercise his independence, yet continue to seek comfort in the dependence relationship that he has so long experienced within the family. This problematic set of circumstances is termed dual ambivalence, a condition that is sometimes frustrated by absence of communication between adults and adolescents.

INDEPENDENCE VERSUS TRACTABILITY *See* INSTRUMENTAL COMPETENCE.

INDIVIDUATION Trend in the development of the *self,* defined by the extent to which the child distinguishes himself from others. While very young children may represent themselves primarily as similar to or like other children, later, during elementary grade years, self-representation is more likely to be in terms of how one is different from one's peers.

INDUCTION TECHNIQUES Form of reasoning that is considered to be a democratic means of dealing with, and teaching, moral behavior and values to children and, at the same time, encouraging the child to assume a particular orientation to society. Through child-rearing techniques, parents may shape and foster two possible induction orientations:

1. SELF-ORIENTED INDUCTION Similar in content to *shame orientation* in that it seems to encourage the child to conform to a social standard for his own good and to evaluate acts in terms of their ultimate gain for him.
2. OTHER-ORIENTED INDUCTION Consists of pointing out to the child the consequences that his acts may have for others, encouraging him to develop *empathy* for others and to learn to curb his *egocentric* impulses.

"INNER SPEECH" or "INNER LANGUAGE" The self-communicative or intrapersonal aspect of *language,* typified by daydreaming, planning solutions to problems, and giving direction and organization to one's movement, that becomes increasingly more important as cognitive development progresses, particularly in the form of thinking that is characteristic of Piagetian *formal operations period.*

INSIGHT LEARNING (ONE-TRIAL LEARNING) The most advanced form of *discrimination learning set* in which the individual is suddenly able to grasp the nature of the problem and its solution, sometimes after a single trial's exposure to the problem, because of the subject's *learning set.*

INSTRUMENTAL AGGRESSION *See* AGGRESSION.

INSTRUMENTAL COMPETENCE Baumrind's characterization of *socialization* as *product* that is defined along the dimensions of social responsibility (presence or absence of achievement orientation, friendly or hostile behavior, and cooperative or resistive behavior toward peers and adults) and *independence* (dominant and purposive) versus tractability (submissive and aimless in behavior) and is closely associated with an *authoritative parental control* style.

INSTRUMENTAL DEPENDENCE (HELP-SEEKING) *See* DEPENDENCE.

INSTRUMENTAL ROLE (MASCULINE) *See* SEX ROLE STEREOTYPES.

INTEGRATION–COORDINATION Age-related

trend in perceptual development for children to become increasingly more capable of simultaneously processing sensory input from various sensory modalities, enabling them to improve in their understanding of things heard or seen by feeling them and vice versa.

INTELLIGENCE Broadly defined in terms of the ability of an individual to solve problems in ways that help him deal successfully with his environment and determined by a complex interaction of heredity and environmental experience. In terms of the *process–product distinction,* intellectual development as *process* is viewed as the growth of cognitive processes, particularly in areas of increasing ability to conceptualize, understand, and obtain knowledge, while as a *product,* intellectual development is conceptualized as a particular ability or score on an intelligence test as measured at some point in time, such as an *intelligence quotient.*

INTELLIGENCE QUOTIENT (IQ) A standardized index or measurement used in reporting intelligence test scores, representing an individual's performance on an intelligence test (mental age) with chronological age controlled for, and comparable to, general population *norms,* typifying the *psychometric* approach to the concept of *intelligence.*

INTENTIONAL LEARNING Behavioral or informational acquisition activity governed by a "closed" attention system, or set, in which the individual concentrates on one thing at a time and resists distraction until the job is completed, and exemplified by formal classroom learning situations.

INTERDEPENDENCE Behavioral balance between the notion of personal *independence,* particularly in areas of judgment and self-sufficiency for personal survival where it is necessary for achievement of a sense of dignity and *self-esteem,* and some degree of interpersonal dependence.

INTERNAL LOCUS OF CONTROL *See* LOCUS OF CONTROL.

INTERPERSONAL TRUST *See* TRUST.

INTRINSIC ALTRUISM *See* ALTRUISM.

INTUITIVE PHASE *See* PREOPERATIONAL THOUGHT PERIOD.

INVARIANCE DESPITE CHANGE (OBJECT CONSTANCY) Piagetian notion of the child's ability to conceptualize objects and people as maintaining a constant identity, despite certain variations in their appearance because of changes of context and circumstance.

KILLER APE (ORIGINAL SIN) VIEW OF MAN View of man's essential nature as basically evil or, at best, irrational, nonmoral, and antisocial. Moral training is essential "to keep the beast in check" and to civilize him, a view espoused by the major monotheistic religions and by classical *psychodynamic psychology.*

LANGUAGE A complex system for communication, composed of grammatical and semantic properties, as distinguished from *speech* (actual utterances) and functionally conceptualized in terms of *receptive (language)* aspects (the ability to understand and act on the *language* communications that are received) and *expressive (language)* aspects (the ability to spontaneously produce various words, sentences, or constructions in one's language repertoire). Communication through language may be interpersonal or intrapersonal (*inner speech* or self-communication).

LANGUAGE DIFFERENCES DILEMMA A persistent issue, particularly in the schools, when a child (or a group of children), whose principal language form is a *dialect* or a first language different from standard English and whose command of standard English is limited, is required to participate in academic activities that demand facility with the standard form. The issue becomes one of teaching the child to discriminate when and where the use of either native dialect or standard English is appropriate and functional without implying that the non-standard-English user, his culture, or his language is inferior.

LANGUAGE–THOUGHT DILEMMA Persistent issue in *language* development concerned with the question of whether, on the one hand, the pattern and direction of thought is a function of the linguistic structure of a given *language* (*linguistic-relativity hypothesis*) or whether, on the other hand, *language* is structured by logical thought structures, serving only to express thought, as Piaget contends.

LEADERSHIP   Role orientation that exists when a group has a common task as well as the opportunity for some *differentiation* of roles and responsibilities within the group. Popularity is closely related to, but not synonymous with, leadership, which is more likely to fluctuate with the nature of the situation than is popularity. Associated with leadership is a behavioral cluster of qualities (intellectually able, sociable in an active and appropriate way, and reasonably assertive and aggressive, particularly for males). The prime quality that differentiates leadership from friendship or popularity is *competence*. Leadership patterns within a group may be ascertained by use of some variant of the *sociometric technique*.

LEARNING   Term referring to the relatively enduring behavioral changes that come about as a function of experiences, both *arranged* and *unarranged*, resulting from the process of adapting to one's environment.

LEARNING SET   Ability of an individual to perform in a progressively better fashion across a series of problems that have a common basis for solution, but are composed of different stimuli, because of acquisition of some problem-solving strategy.

LEARNING TO LEARN   *See* LEARNING SET.

LIBIDO   Freudian construct that represents psychic (essentially sexual) energy. In the dynamic concept of personality, the libido is in ceaseless struggle with the *ego*, being policed and held in check mainly by the *superego*.

LINGUISTIC COMPETENCE   *See* COMPETENCE.

LINGUISTIC PERFORMANCE   *See* PERFORMANCE (LINGUISTIC).

LINGUISTIC-RELATIVITY HYPOTHESIS   Notion that thought or mental behavior is shaped by the particular *language* through which it is processed, the position being synonymous with the Whorfian hypothesis and representing one extreme in the *language–thought dilemma*.

LINGUISTICS   Scientific discipline investigating the structure and content of *language*, including *grammar*, sound combinations, and meaning, and providing the conceptual basis for *biolinguistics, psycholinguistics,* and *sociolinguistics*.

LOCUS OF CONTROL   Related to Jung's theoretical themes of introversion and extroversion, the concept deals with the way an individual perceives the world he lives in. When a *reinforcement* is perceived by the subject as following some action of his own, but not being entirely contingent upon his action, then, in our *culture*, it is typically perceived as the result of luck, chance, fate, as under the control of powerful others, or as unpredictable because of the great complexity of the forces surrounding him. Such an interpretation by an individual is labeled as belief in external locus of control. If the person perceives that the event is contingent upon his own behavior or his own relative permanent characteristics, this belief is labeled internal locus of control.

LOGICAL DEDUCTION   *See* CONVERGENT PRODUCTION or THINKING.

LOGICAL INDUCTION   *See* CONVERGENT PRODUCTION or THINKING.

LOGICAL POSITIVISM   *See* OPERATIONAL DEFINITION.

LONGITUDINAL STUDY   Type of experimental design in which the same individual is examined at various points during a long period as a means of studying developmental change and factors associated with such change in that particular individual.

LONG-TERM MEMORY STORE   Concept for a particular kind of memory, having a seemingly endless capacity, similar to the notion of a filing system in which information is organized or coded by categories with virtually "permanent" availability.

LOVE WITHDRAWAL TECHNIQUES   Techniques of child rearing in which *punishment* is psychological, in the form of nurturance withdrawal, and may result in a poorer parent–child interaction. There is little consensus as to the effect of these techniques on *moral development*.

MASTURBATION   Achievement of sexual satisfaction by self-stimulation of the genitals. This activity is apparently less prevalent among females than among males in United States culture.

MATURATION   Developmental changes that are extensively if not totally controlled by genetic or hereditary factors, including species-specific behavior, that are less responsive to environmental effects than are social and psychological factors.

MAXIMUM SUSCEPTIBILITY NOTION   A concept

within the *critical-periods* literature, meaning that if a child is too young or too old, a particular set of experiences will have little effect on his development, as well as implying that experience has more effect on an organism the more rapidly that organism is growing and developing.

MEAN, or AVERAGE   A measure of the central tendency of a set of scores, derived by adding all the scores and dividing the sum by the total number of cases.

MEDIAN   A statistical term indicating that point in a distribution of scores above and below which exactly one-half the population falls.

MEDIATORS OF DEVELOPMENTAL CHANGE   Various factors that facilitate, condition, or otherwise modify patterns of developmental change from infancy to young adulthood, including *effective culture, socioeconomic status,* sex, intellectual ability, biological factors, *ethnicity,* schooling, and religion.

MEMORY   *See* PROBLEM-SOLVING PROCESS.

"ME"–"NOT ME" DISTINCTION   Piagetian notion of the child's acquisition of the primitive notion of the *self* as an entity that is independent from the environment, occurring during the *sensorimotor (period) stage.*

"MENTALISM"   A theoretical position involving propositions or assumptions about the mind not subject to open verification through objective observational techniques.

MESOMORPH   *See* SOMATOTYPE THEORY.

MODELING   Important concept in *social learning theory* and defined as a form of learning in which an individual learns to perform an act by observing someone else's performance and receipt of reinforcement for that act. After this observation, the observer may *imitate* (or model) the act he has just observed. The tendency to imitate the model is greatest if that model is perceived as similar, possesses desired characteristics (such as popularity), has rewarded the potential imitator in the past, is accessible for personal association, and is powerful (controls material resources and/or the capacity to punish the *imitator*). This concept has been used to explain the process of *sex typing* and *identification.*

MORAL DEVELOPMENT   Process by which an individual achieves an orientation of *reciprocity,* conforms behaviorally within societal limits of acceptibility, learns to in-

hibit his impulses when necessary or desirable, and to postpone immediate gratification for the sake of later satisfactions, and perceives authority as being rational and essentially well disposed toward all members within the society, thus eliciting similar behavior toward authority.

MORAL   IDENTIFICATION   (INTERNALIZATION)   *Psychodynamic* concept for the *process* by which the child incorporates parental standards and values as one's own in the form of the *superego* or conscience. The strength or quality of one's moral internalization will depend on the degree to which the child's moral models (parents, in most cases) are moral. Once moral identification is achieved, the moral mechanism will cause the child to behave with the same degree of *morality* across all situations demanding moral judgment or action. The strength of moral identification may be inferred by the following (presumed) indicators:

1. Resistance to temptation, such as refusing to cheat even though one knows he cannot be detected.
2. Guilt over deviations.
3. Independence of actions from external sanctions.
4. Confession and assumption of responsibility for one's own actions.

MORAL JUDGMENT   Research area dealing with the evolution of moral values from a *cognitive-developmental* viewpoint and representing Kohlberg's systematization of Piaget's theory of *moral development* (*moral realism versus moral relativism*) in which the child's moral judgment parallels his cognitive development and progresses from an initially premoral orientation (behavior is defined by social sanctions), through a conventional morality (based on role conformity and social law and order), to a postmoral orientation (based on self-defined and self-accepted principles). Kohlberg defines this progression for individuals in terms of scores obtained on the *Moral Judgment Interview,* a series of moral dilemmas to which the subject must supply answers.

MORAL JUDGMENT INTERVIEW   *See* MORAL JUDGMENT.

MORAL REALISM (OR ABSOLUTISM) VERSUS MORAL RELATIVISM   Piaget's *cognitive-developmental* theory of *moral development,* consisting of how one comes to respect the rules of his particular social order and to acquire a sense of justice. At first, the child considers all rules to be sacred and unalterable (moral realism *or* absolutism) and operates in terms of a morality that is determined by others (heteronomous morality). Later, largely because of experience with his peer group, the child grows out of his *egocentrism* through role taking and participation in decisions, as well as parental stress on reasoning or induction, and comes to view laws and social rules as arrangements that come about through reciprocal agreements and function for the good of all those affected by them (moral relativism). Morality comes from within the individual (autonomous morality).

MORALITY Development, formulation, and expression of internal intentions or conscience, focusing a person's outlook on life and involving the direct representation of a person's personal construction of social values and the objective obligations and responsibilities that an individual has to his community and the order of things in his society.

MORPHOLOGY Aspect of language defined by rules for internal structure and form of words, applied spontaneously by the child after the application of sentence form rules (*syntax*) in *expressive language*.

MULTIPLE CLASSIFICATION *See* CLASSIFICATION.

NAMING First phase of the Montessori three-period sequence for vocabulary development in which the adult initiates learning by pointing to and labeling some object that the child is manipulating.

NATIVIST–ENVIRONMENTALIST (RATIONALIST– EMPIRICIST) DILEMMA Persistent issue in *language* development referring to whether language is acquired as a function of universal, innate biological structures that predispose the child to develop language (nativist or rationalist) or whether experiential factors, analyzed in terms of learning principles of environmental *reinforcement* (environmentalist or empiricist) explain language development.

"NATURALISTIC, INDIGENOUS GROWTH" Theory of child development, related to the philosophy of Rousseau, emphasizing freedom in child-rearing and educational practices and the belief that maximum *socializa-* *tion* benefits can be gained by placing children in an enriched, benign, accepting, permissive, informally arranged (low-control) environment, with a high value given to the child's creative self-expression.

NATURE–NURTURE CONTROVERSY A persistent issue for developmental psychology concerning the ways in which heredity (nature) and environment (nurture) combine and interact in behavior and development.

NEONATE A newborn infant.

NOMOTHETIC APPROACH An experimental approach to the study of development that focuses on the study of large groups, and statistical treatment of the data in terms of means, ranges of scores, variances (*heterogeneity* or *homogeniety*) and significant differences between experimental and control groups.

NORM An *average* or typical description of behavior, typically an *age-relevant developmental concept,* that does not explain developmental changes, but can be a convenient, though very general, index for cataloging trends in developmental change.

NORMAL BEHAVIOR DILEMMA A persistent issue in developmental psychology, closely related to the *permanent versus phasic developmental problems dilemma,* and concerned with societal and personal definitions or models of normality.

NORMAL CURVE The plotted form of the *normal distribution,* exemplified by distribution of *intelligence quotients.*

NORMAL DISTRIBUTION A plotting of scores, actual or theoretical, that lies between the ends of a continuum and is shaped like a bell, in which the *mean* and the *median* are the same.

NORMATIVE–DESCRIPTIVE APPROACH An approach to the study of development that consists of charting various behaviors in relation to age changes (age at onset of behavior, age norms describing increases or decreases in behavior).

NUCLEAR FAMILY A familial constellation typical in the United States, in which one or both parents and the children live in their own home, with grandparents and other relatives frequently living some distance away.

OBJECT CONSTANCY *See* INVARIANCE DESPITE CHANGE.

OBJECT PERMANENCE Piagetian notion of the child's ability to conceptualize things (objects, people) as continuing to exist whether or not he can see them.

OCCASIONAL QUESTION TECHNIQUE Source of adult influence on the child's grammatical development in which the adult, by replying to the child's statements with questions, aids the child in clarifying his utterances and in learning the relationship of the declarative and interrogative grammatical forms.

OEDIPAL DILEMMA OR PHASE *See* DEFENSIVE IDENTIFICATION.

ONE-TRIAL LEARNING *See* INSIGHT LEARNING.

ONLOOKER BEHAVIOR *See* PLAY BEHAVIOR.

"OPEN" ATTENTION SET *See* INCIDENTAL LEARNING.

OPERATIONAL DEFINITION A doctrine of scientific investigation, particularly important in *behaviorism,* stating that a *concept* has no meaning unless it can be anchored to some specific operation or set of operations, and necessitating clear specification of both the experimental situation and the behavior to be observed, so that two or more different observers, operating according to these situational and behavioral definitions, can achieve perfect or near-perfect agreement about how many dependent behaviors occurred of each kind and in each situation. This concept of scientific procedure and investigation is synonymous with the tradition of empiricism and the philosophy of science known as logical positivism.

ORGANISMIC VARIABLES *Behaviorist* designation for the state of the organism being investigated, including anatomical and physiological properties.

ORGASM Sexual climax that can be produced in human infants of either sex. After puberty, however, sexual climax in the male is accompanied by ejaculation, the expulsion of semen and seminal fluid from the penis.

ORIENTATION REACTION *See* ATTENTION.

ORIGINAL SIN VIEW OF MAN *See* KILLER APE VIEW OF MAN.

OSSIFICATION The developmental process by which an infant's cartilage is hardened into the sturdy bones of later childhood and adulthood and, finally, the brittle bones of old age.

OTHER-ORIENTED INDUCTION *See* INDUCTION TECHNIQUE.

OVERACHIEVEMENT Clinical concept embodied in the child or the youth who tries too hard and worries too much about his success and failure, more likely to be motivated by anxiety and fear of failure than by hope of success and achieved at the expense of personal relaxation, sense of security, and happiness.

OVERLEARNED-SKILLS THEORY OF INTELLIGENCE Ferguson's learning theory-based explanation of intellectual functioning as a collection of cognitive, problem-solving skills, mastered far beyond the point of initial proficiency (overlearned), that are necessary for a satisfactory and competent adjustment in a particular cultural setting.

PAIRED COMPARISONS SOCIOMETRIC *See* SOCIOMETRIC TECHNIQUE.

PARALLEL PLAY *See* PLAY BEHAVIOR.

PARENTAL BEHAVIOR ADOPTION *See* PARENTAL IDENTIFICATION.

PARENTAL IDENTIFICATION Construct in *combinatory identification theory* defined as internalization of personality characteristics of a given parent, as well as unconscious reactions similar to those of the parent, and dependent, in part, on the child's preference for the parent (parental preference), his understanding of how similar he is to the parent (*perceived parental similarity*), and his adoption of the behavior patterns of one parent or the other (parental behavior adoption).

PARENTAL PREFERENCE *See* PARENTAL IDENTIFICATION.

PASSIVE DEPENDENCE *See* DEPENDENCE.

PAVLOVIAN CONDITIONING *See* CLASSICAL CONDITIONING.

PEERS "VERSUS" PARENTS DILEMMA Cluster of issues related to feelings of parents about their child's choice of the "right" friends (children of whom the parents will approve). Generally, children choose friends whose value orientation is similar to that of their parents, so the case is seldom one of peers against parents, but rather of peers living together and providing one another with learning experiences necessary to consolidate parental values or altering them only slightly, since the peer group, functioning as a social leveler, tends to reduce and moderate any extremes in orientation. Peer influence is at greatest possible variance with parental notions during high school, but the issues of disagreement are relatively superficial (fads in clothing, recreation, and related issues).

PERCEIVED SIMILARITY (PARENTAL SEX ROLE) Construct in *combinatory identification* theory to account for two sources of knowledge that the child uses in the process of achieving his or her *identification:*

1. Perceived parental similarity—the degree to which the child perceives himself (or herself) to be like the mother or the father.
2. Perceived sex role similarity—the degree to which the child perceives himself (or herself) to be like other boys or girls.

PERCEPTION Process of organizing, coding, and interpreting raw sensory input or experience, developed as a complex function of maturation and environmental impact and related to the evolution of cognitive processes. Montessori, in particular, stresses the training of perceptual refinement for the development of more refined and acute thinking, especially for concepts based on meaningful sensory experience.

PERCEPTUAL SET A *readiness,* or a signal, to perceive stimuli in a certain way or to see things that might be lost to others in a competitive array of stimuli as a function of past learning or current state of the organism.

PERFORMANCE (LINGUISTIC) Referring to the spontaneous production or use of grammatical forms of *language,* commonly described as *speech,* as distinguished from some underlying knowledge of language, which is conceptualized as *linguistic competence.*

PERFORMANCE INTELLIGENCE FACTOR A score on the Wechsler intelligence tests, measured by items requiring the construction of geometric designs with the use of small, wooden blocks in conformity with a model and the identification of missing parts from pictures of common objects. This factor is closely related to the quantitative factor found on many paper-and-pencil, group intelligence tests that has to do with number and space concepts.

PERFORMANCE SET Habitual mode of coping with particular kinds of situations requiring an individual to act in some appropriate fashion, of which there are six different types:

1. Warm-up—postural or mental adjustment that facilitates performance.
2. Development of exteroceptive observing processes—orienting sensory receptors to receive stimulus input.
3. Development of internal attentional responses—learning to ignore extraneous stimuli or to attend to stimuli in a way that will optimize future recall.
4. Reduction of emotionality—learning to check strong affective responses that tend to interfere with complex performance.
5. Development of appropriate attending and performance techniques—learning of strategies that will maximize task performance.
6. Discrimination set—learning to detect differences among arrays of stimuli and to respond differentially in an appropriate fashion.

PERMANENT VERSUS PHASIC DEVELOPMENTAL PROBLEMS DILEMMA A persistent issue in developmental psychology, relating to the *behavioral stability dilemma* and referring to various criteria that might be adopted (rigid or flexible, normative, and so on) to determine whether a child's "bad" behavior has negative developmental consequences or is merely temporary and typical of his age group.

PERMISSIVE PARENTAL CONTROL Baumrind's characterization of child-rearing practices that stress nonpunitive parental attitudes toward the child; a positive acceptance of the child's impulses, desires, and actions; low control and emphasis on obedience to externally defined standards; and an attempt on the part of the parent to act as a resource for the child rather than as a directive agent.

PERSPECTIVISM *See* FORMAL OPERATIONS PERIOD.

PHENOTYPE Referring to the class name for the individual's observable qualities, resulting from the interaction of *genotype* with environment and conceptualized by the following equation:

$$\text{genotype} \times \text{environment} = \text{phenotype}$$

PHILOSOPHICAL DILEMMA A matter of unresolved dispute or conflict concerning important questions of value about the goals of human development in society.

PHONEMES   Class name for speech sounds of a *language,* including vowels and consonants.

PLAY BEHAVIOR   Classification of social interactions among young children (ages 2–5) at play in nursery school settings into six categories of social involvement:

1. UNOCCUPIED BEHAVIOR   Smallest extent of social involvement in which the child occupies himself with watching anything that may be of interest.
2. SOLITARY PLAY   Child acts alone, independent of others, making no effort to associate with peers.
3. ONLOOKER BEHAVIOR   Child watches other peers at play with sustained interest and initiation of communication from time to time.
4. PARALLEL PLAY   Child plays with toys similar or identical to those used by children nearby, but according to his own wishes, not playing *with* the others.
5. ASSOCIATIVE PLAY   Social interaction based on play activities of borrowing and lending, with children making no attempt to divide tasks or organize the activity in terms of groups.
6. COOPERATIVE PLAY   Groups are organized for some purpose with leaders and task assignments.

POLITICAL SOCIALIZATION   Process by which children and youth are introduced to political attitudes, behavior, and roles, resulting in development of beliefs concerning political ideals and realities, together with the affective orientation toward the political system(s) of the child's own country (the attitude toward political authority). *Moral development,* at its higher level, shares the same concerns as political socialization in that both are concerned with a pattern of human relationships involving power, authority, and rules and the ways in which these factors affect, and are reflected in, basic value and moral commitments. Developmental trends in political socialization seem to be a function of cognitive growth, representing a shift from comparative political naiveté and ignorance of political realities to a reasonably accurate perception of the implications of government for behavior.

POPULATION   A statistical *concept* referring to the total universe of possible cases in a particular category ("all fifth-graders in the United States") from which a researcher draws a small *sample* ("100 male fifth-graders in Chicago private schools"). The term also refers to the particular group studied by a researcher and on which he reports, in which case the usage is synonymous with the concept of sample. (Compare *sample, homogeneous population, heterogeneous population.*)

POWER ASSERTION TECHNIQUES   Techniques of child rearing in which the parent manages the child by force, physical or emotional, and which may result in a poorer parent–child interaction. Such techniques block the child, frustrate mastery and *competence* needs, and are not successful for instilling *morality,* because the child's attention is focused on the parent and on himself rather than on the more important consequences of his act that elicited the *punishment.* Moreover, the high tension inherent in these control techniques may provoke interfering *anxiety* and fear, which may inhibit or cancel whatever potential learning that does take place in this context.

POWER TESTING   A *psychometric* or measurement principle of test construction in which an individual's score is a function of his ability to solve a series of problems, arranged in order of increasing difficulty, with no time limit imposed.

PREOPERATIONAL THOUGHT PERIOD   Piagetian developmental stage, composed of two phases:

1. PREOPERATIONAL PHASE, ages 2–4, during which the child is unable to take the viewpoint of other people (*egocentrism*) and classifies different environmental stimuli (social and physical) by a single salient feature, often resulting in incorrect instances of categorization.
2. INTUITIVE PHASE, ages 4–7, during which the child is now able to think in terms of classes, to see relationships, to handle numbers, but is at an "intuitive" level because he is unaware of the underlying logic of his *classification.* Gradual development of *conservation* also occurs during this period.

PREPARATORY SET   Predisposition of the organism to act in a particular fashion because of motives or needs (hunger, thirst), instructions, or sense modality preferences (taste, touch, smell, and so on).

PRIMARY GROUP A constellation of people, consisting of family, neighbors, close friends, and classmates, that transmits the customs and values of the *effective culture* to an individual in terms or reward–punishment patterns, behavioral *expectancies,* and so on.

PRIMARY SOURCE A scholarly article by an author who reports original data, talks about them, analyzes them, formulates results, arrives at conclusions, and sometimes makes recommendations for action based on these data.

PROBLEM-SOLVING PROCESS Process of resolving a task difficulty or finding the answer to a question, as broken down into five components:

1. ENCODING   Selective attention to and preferential perceptual analysis of an event.
2. MEMORY Information storage and retrieval.
3. HYPOTHESIS FORMULATION Producing alternative hunches about the problem and its solution.
4. EVALUATION Examining the quality or the validity of one's hunches.
5. DEDUCTION Implementing hypothesis or arriving at conclusions.

PROCEDURAL DILEMMA A matter of unresolved dispute or conflict that occurs in reference to a decision about how to achieve a preferred goal of human development and how best to go about the job of putting a strategy into effect for pursuing stated values.

PROCESS–PRODUCT DISTINCTION Developmentally oriented conceptualization used to distinguish the underlying trend or progress of development (process) from some particular manifestation of that growth trend (product) and exemplified by intelligence which is both a trend in the growth of cognitive abilities (process) and a score on an intelligence test (product).

PRONUNCIATION Final phase of the Montessori three-period sequence for vocabulary development in which the adult caregiver, pointing to the object or quality that was labeled during the *naming* phase and identified in the *recognition* phase, requires the child to describe that object or quality in response to the question "What is this?"

PROSOCIAL BEHAVIORS Behaviors that are socially constructive and which usually result in benefits for both the person who engages in them and for those who receive them. *Trust, altruism,* and *cooperation* are examples of this behavioral category.

PROTESTANT ETHIC Cluster of behavioral characteristics, similar in content to the *entrepreneurial parental occupation* orientation, emphasizing rugged independence, individualism, and the work ethic.

PSYCHOBIOLOGICAL SEXUAL DEVELOPMENT Process by which an individual, regardless of cultural influence, must make certain behavioral adjustments to increased size and strength, to *maturation* of primary and secondary sex characteristics, and to the biological rhythms and pressures that follow *puberty* (menstrual cycle for girls and insistent pressure toward sexual outlet for boys). With sexual maturation, the organism is susceptible to and influenced by sexual reinforcers in a very different way than was possible before pubescence.

PSYCHODYNAMIC PSYCHOLOGY A psychological approach to human development primarily concerned with the early life experiences, notably parent–child and sibling relationships, that are regarded as central in determining the quality of personality development with particular emphasis on emotional experiences and the early *socialization* of human instincts (sex drive, self-preservation, aggression). Concentration is on the individual rather than the *culture,* on traumatic events rather than positive growth experiences, on the way in which personality is structured rather than on how change occurs in human development; and, while the aim is to understand and explain the normal personality, theoretical and practical therapeutic emphasis is almost solely on aberration and disease.

PSYCHOLINGUISTICS Scientific discipline, related to linguistics, concerned with the study of the relationship of *language* to the characteristics of the language user, including a concern for how the individual uses his capacity for language acquisition and his knowledge of the language to understand and produce utterances.

PSYCHOMETRICS The study of psychological

constructs, particularly *intelligence*, by use of various testing and quantifying procedures and instruments. In the study of intelligence, the individual is typically given a standardized series of testing tasks or items, and on the basis of his performance, one or more scores are assigned to him that constitute an index of his intelligence or general problem-solving ability, generally referred to as an *intelligence quotient*, or IQ.

PSYCHOSEXUAL DEVELOPMENT   General concept referring to the psychological ways in which one adjusts to his biologically defined sex role and learns his sexuality, in the broadest sense of that term. As a *process*, the concept refers to only one specific category within the broader domain of human socialization as viewed from a *social learning* perspective. As a *product*, the concept refers to particular social categorizations of people (*homosexual, heterosexual,* manly, feminine, frigid, and so on) that reflect or refer to a set of responses that characterize a person's social and sexual relationships with others. The concept is closely related to *sex typing* and *identification*.

PSYCHOSOCIAL CONFLICT   A condition that results when an individual or a group is faced with things or situations that call for mutually incompatible behavior, either because of their nature or because of the learning history of that individual or group. The more important the possible outcome and the more equal the strength of the competing behavior cues, the more intense the conflict, resulting in a situation that can be comparatively minor and transitory or can persist over time and involve basic aspects of psychological development. Conflict of this nature is often associated with *anxiety, independence–dependence,* and *aggression,* as well as *prosocial behaviors:* trust *versus* mistrust, selfishness *versus* altruism, cooperation *versus* competition. These areas of conflict should be distinguished from cognitive conflict, because of their emotional and social content.

PSYCHOSOCIAL MORATORIUM   *See* EIGHT STAGES OF MAN

PUBERTY   The age at which secondary sex characteristics first appear and sexual organs become functional, marking the onset of adolescence.

PUNISHMENT   Delivery of response-contingent aversive stimulus (capable of producing pain and/or annoyance) used for control of behavior (*aversive control*). When delivered by an authority figure, punishment often inhibits direct expression of children and may lead to greater amounts of aggressive behavior directed toward other objects or persons, especially when the punisher is absent (displaced aggression). Use of this form of behavioral control may stop *all* behaviors, resulting in an inhibited, passive, nonspontaneous child for whom constructive development is difficult, because he so seldom displays behavior that can be rewarded.

QUANTITATIVE INTELLIGENCE FACTOR   *See* PERFORMANCE INTELLIGENCE FACTOR.

RACE, or RACIAL GROUP   Concept referring to a subdivision of the human race characterized by distinguishable physical characteristics transmitted from one generation to another, as distinct from the more general cultural concept of *ethnicity* and consisting of three groups: Caucasian, or Caucasoid; Mongolian, or Mongoloid; and Negro, or Negroid.

RANKING SOCIOMETRIC   *See* SOCIOMETRIC TECHNIQUES.

RATINGS SOCIOMETRIC   *See* SOCIOMETRIC TECHNIQUES.

RATIONALIST–EMPIRICIST DILEMMA   *See* NATIVIST–ENVIRONMENTALIST DILEMMA.

READINESS   Possession of all the prerequisite skills necessary for the mastery of a task at a new level of difficulty by virtue of maturation and/or specific learning experiences.

REALITY PRINCIPLE (EGO FUNCTION)   *Psychodynamic* (Freudian) concept stating that an individual's growth and development are accompanied by an adjustment of his behavior to the contingencies of his environment (physical and social) by delaying, denying, inhibiting, or otherwise altering drive and need satisfaction. The concept is similar to Piaget's notion of *accommodation*.

RECEPTIVE LANGUAGE   *See* LANGUAGE.

RECIPROCITY   A basic component of human *morality* defined as the ability of an individual to see, respect, honor, and facilitate another individual's point of view so long as the integrity of others is not destroyed for the sake of this action. This orientation is ultimately to conscience as a directing agent and to mutual respect and trust. Together with a concern for equality and the welfare of others, reciprocity provides the basis for justice.

RECOGNITION Second phase of the Montessori three-period sequence for vocabulary development in which the adult requires the child to respond to identity statements taking the form of "Give me the _____," the blank being filled by the label that was demonstrated during the first, or *naming,* phase of the sequence.

REFLECTIVITY–IMPULSIVITY Type of *cognitive style,* particularly relevant to the problem-solving process, defined as tendency of children or youth to think carefully about problem solutions or hypotheses before volunteering a specific response (reflectivity) or the alternative tendency to respond quickly and thoughtlessly in new situations without taking sufficient time to think carefully about the nature of the information, the materials, or the alternative responses that they might make (impulsivity).

REINFORCEMENT (RESPONSE-DEPENDENT REINFORCEMENT) The occurrence of some environmental event (positive, such as delivery of food to a hungry subject; or aversive, such as the delivery of painful electric shock) that is contingent on the emission of a given response by the subject and having the effect of increasing or decreasing the probability that the experimental subject will repeat the response in the future under similar environmental conditions.

REINFORCEMENT HISTORY *Behaviorist* conceptualization of an individual's past experience with rewards and *punishments,* including the frequency and consistency with which given behaviors have been rewarded and/or punished (or ignored), giving the scientist a means of explaining individual differences in current behavioral responding among subjects.

RESPONSE VARIABLES *Behaviorist* designation for overt, observable behaviors.

RESPONSE-DEPENDENT REINFORCEMENT *See* REINFORCEMENT.

RESPONSE-INDEPENDENT REINFORCEMENT Similar in concept to the behaviorist concept of *reinforcement* (that is, *response-dependent reinforcement*), but differing from that principle inasmuch as the delivery of a reinforcer is *not* contingent (or dependent upon) the emission of a particular response but is spontaneous or unplanned and may be used, in various applied settings, to favorably influence a child's perceptions of himself and his environment.

RESTRICTIVE COMMUNICATION STYLE *See* COMMUNICATION STYLE.

REVERSIBILITY Piagetian notion of the child's ability to understand that transformational sequences can be traced to their point of origin in order to account for changes in appearance.

"s," or SPECIAL, FACTOR INTELLIGENCE *See* CLASSICAL, TWO-FACTOR THEORY OF INTELLIGENCE.

SAMPLE A small selection of cases drawn from a larger general universe or *population.*

SCHOOL ANXIETY Emotional response, detected in children when they start school, relating to behavior in academic progress (especially reading achievement), but generally decreasing during years of middle childhood and beyond, except among those children with average or below-average intelligence whose academic development is slower than that of their peers.

SCHOOL COMPOSITION DILEMMA Issues relating to the benefits and liabilities of unisexual versus coeducational schools. Arguments revolve around sexual behavior that may or may not be fostered in each setting, as well as more clear-cut issues relating to differences in rate of maturity and activity level for males and females.

SECONDARY GROUP A loosely constituted, peripheral constellation of people, including all the members of an individual's political precinct, his church congregation, members of scouting troops other than his own whom he sees at jamborees but few of whom he knows, and other organizations of people with which he associates infrequently or temporarily that serve to transmit aspects of the effective culture to the individual.

SELECTIVE SCANNING or SEARCHING *See* ATTENTION.

SELECTIVE MODELING (GRAMMATICAL) TECHNIQUE Source of adult influence on the child's grammatical development, in which certain grammatical structures (singular–plural forms, active–passive forms, noun–

verb forms, affirmative–negative forms), and used by the adult who encourages or reinforces the child to produce the utterance.

SELECTIVITY Age-related trend in perceptual development for children to become increasingly more selective in their perceptions as a result of more extensive and systematic perceptual exploration, accompanied by an apparent preference for novel (versus familiar) stimuli.

SELF Central concept in the study of self-development. Controversy revolves around two central concepts of definition:

1. Self as object A person's attitudes, perceptions, feelings, and evaluation of himself as an object—what a person knows and thinks about himself.
2. Self as process Self is considered an amalgam of active processes of thinking, perceiving, and remembering.

SELF-ACTUALIZATION A central concern of *humanistic psychology* dealing with the process by which man realizes and fulfills his own potential, a philosophical position similar to Rousseau's notions of natural man as good, invested with an innate sense of freedom, and capable of self-direction toward some ultimate good.

"SELF COMMUNICATION" *See* "INNER SPEECH"

SELF CONCEPT An individual's awareness of his own characteristics and attributes, and the ways in which he is both like and unlike others. One important dimension of self-concept development is the extent to which an individual can describe himself objectively and accurately.

SELF-ESTEEM Refers to the value a child or a youth puts on himself and his behavior. The concept is intimately related to the *self concept,* because value judgments are so frequently involved in what children learn about themselves from other people.

SELF-FULFILLING PROPHECY *See* EXPECTANCY.

SELF-ORIENTED INDUCTION *See* INDUCTION.

SEMANTIC DEVELOPMENT Development of word meaning, the influence of meaning on *syntax,* and the relationship of meaning to action, all of which are sometimes referred to as vocabulary development.

SENSORIMOTOR PERIOD Piagetian developmental stage, lasting from birth to 18 months or 2 years, during which the infant learns to differentiate himself from objects; seeks stimulation and learns to prolong interesting visual stimuli through mental representation; and discovers, by means of manipulation, that an object retains its identity or meaning despite changes in location and point of view.

SEPARATION ANXIETY Emotional response, occurring between ages 13 and 18 months, manifested over separation from the infant's mother (or caretaker) with whom an *attachment* has usually been well formed.

SEQUENCE-RELEVANT DEVELOPMENTAL CONCEPT Approach to the description and analysis of developmental change based on the idea that changes which ordinarily occur within extended time periods can perhaps be accomplished in a far shorter time through efficient training as long as the individual is physically and/or cognitively in possession of prerequisite skills.

SERIATION Piagetian notion of the child's ability to arrange a series of events or objects in continuum such as "greater than," "less than," "more than," and "fewer than."

SET A condition of *readiness* that predisposes an individual to behave in a particular fashion, as a function either of past experience (*learning*) or some motivational need state of the organism (*preparatory set*). *Perceptual set, performance set,* and *learning set* are subconcepts of this construct.

SEX OBJECT CHOICE *See* SEXUAL ORIENTATION.

SEX ROLE ADOPTION Construct in *combinatory identification theory* to account for the process by which a boy or a girl takes on the behavioral characteristics of a boy, girl, man, or woman with greater likelihood of adopting behaviors that are appropriate to one's own gender, because of mechanism of *perceived similarity.*

SEX ROLE PREFERENCE Construct in *combinatory identification* to account for the process by which a boy or a girl comes to prefer a particular gender role (and greater likelihood of making an identification with the similar sex parent and similar sex gender, because of mechanism of *perceived similarity*).

SEX ROLE STEREOTYPES Patterns of behavior that are considered to be culturally appropriate and valued for males and females, reflecting a complex interaction of biology and learning experiences, and sometimes conceptualized in terms of two role models in United States culture:

1. Instrumental role (masculine) Independence, physical and psychological toughness, self-sufficiency, and initiative, all of which underlie the notion of competence in a competitive, free-enterprise, industrial, and technical society to achieve security, recognition, and material success.
2. Expressive role (feminine) Personal warmth and interest in preventing social and family disruption (strong human relations orientation of nurturance, obedience, sweetness, and so on).

SEX TYPING Acquisition of behavior associated with the male and the female sex roles at various ages during the course of development that can occur consistently or inconsistently with a person's biological gender. The concept also refers to *sexual orientation* (or sex object choice). Particular interest has been focused on two *critical periods* in the child's development:

1. Period from birth to age 2 or 3, during which *identification* is said to take place.
2. Period during early adolescence when the peer group aids in reinforcing and ameliorating sex-appropriate behaviors, providing a social environment for rehearsal of sex-related behaviors, such as courtship activities.

SEXUAL ORIENTATION (SEX OBJECT CHOICE) Referring to preferences of individuals as manifest by sexual interests and behavior that may be directed exclusively toward persons of the opposite sex (*heterosexual*), equally toward persons of both sexes (bisexual), or exclusively toward persons of the same sex (*homosexual*).

SHAME ORIENTATION Construct common to both *social learning (behaviorist)* and *psychodynamic psychologies* that hypothesizes a standard of *moral identification* that is primarily directed toward saving face and not getting caught in the commission of a transgression. Behavioral standards are seen as relative, with a lack of firmly internalized prohibitions of the sort found in *guilt orientation*. Child-rearing practices that emphasize material rewards (for example, an increase in allowance) and punishments (for example, taking away television or automobile privileges) rather than psychological control techniques (withdrawal of love) are associated with this moral perspective.

SHORT-TERM MEMORY STORE Type of memory having a limited capacity (illustrated by ability to hear and recall a string of digits) and short duration for retention of material, related to the concept of *attention span*.

SIGNIFIER–SIGNIFICANT DISTINCTION Piagetian notion of the child's acquisition of the conceptual difference between the word or label (signifier) and the object, event, or characteristic for which the word stands (significant).

SITUATIONAL AGGRESSION *See* AGGRESSION.

SKEWED, or BIASED, DISTRIBUTION A statistical concept referring to a distribution of scores that is not symmetrical or *normal* in which *mean* and *median* are different from each other.

SKILLS TRAINING–CULTURAL TRANSMISSION FUNCTION OF SCHOOLS Teaching of skills necessary to survive in American life, such as clear speech, fluent reading, correct expressive writing, proficiency with numbers, knowledge of history, English literature, and a certain degree of cultural sophistication.

SOCIAL CLASS, or SOCIAL STATUS *See* SOCIOECONOMIC STATUS, or CLASS.

SOCIAL DEVELOPMENT Process closely related to the general topic area of *socialization*, concerned with *child–peer interactions*, as well as interactions with other significant figures who are not parents (aunts, teachers, older siblings), and the effect that interchanges have on the child's personality development. Peers have been found to affect development of *morality, cooperation*, and competition, *sex typing* and courting behavior, *autonomy* and *independence conformity*, and leadership–followership behaviors.

SOCIAL ETHIC Cluster of behavioral characteristics, similar in content to the *bureaucratic parental occupation* orientation, with an emphasis on *cooperation*, cordial compromise, and getting along.

SOCIAL LEARNING THEORY Behaviorally oriented perspective on human development seeking to explain more adequately personality and *social development* by focusing inquiry on man's adaptiveness and capacities for *discrimination learning set*, for self-regulation, and for constructive change as he copes with a changing environment, including changes in his own body as he adapts to the aging process. The concepts of *modeling* and *imitation* are very important explanatory constructs in this theory that account for the ways in which personality and behaviors are influenced by other individuals.

SOCIAL RESPONSIBILITY–IRRESPONSIBILITY *See* INSTRUMENTAL COMPETENCE.

SOCIAL STEREOTYPES *See* SEX ROLE STEREO-TYPES.

SOCIALIZATION In human development, a concept referring to the *process* embodied in child-rearing and educational practices of parents and teachers for the purpose of shaping an individual's personal characteristics and behavior so that the *product* of this socialization experience will conform to cultural–societal expectations and values. The process is interactive (a two-way street) rather than unidirectional, with parents and teachers affecting children, and vice versa.

SOCIOECONOMIC STATUS, or CLASS A stratification or categorization of society that is calculated on the basis of education level of the heads of the family, the father's or mother's occupation, characteristics of the part of town and the house in which one lives, and the source and size of the family income.

SOCIOLINGUISTICS Scientific discipline, related to *linguistics,* concerned with the study of *language* or *dialect* differences associated with ethnic group, geographical, and social class factors, including a focus on the social origins of *communication style,* attitudes toward language, and various social implications of language use.

SOCIOMETRIC TECHNIQUES A general method for mapping of social groups to determine patterns of attraction or popularity, leadership, and rejection among the members. Such social measurement can be made by the following methods:

1. CHOICES The individual is asked to name in order his first three to five best friends (or "rejects").
2. RATINGS The child is asked to rate a list of classmates for leadership and friendship by assigning points according to a scale (1=best friend or best leader through to 5 = not friend, not good leader).
3. PAIRED COMPARISONS Each child judges each other child in class in terms of friendship by pairs.
4. RANKING The entire class is rank ordered.
5. "GUESS WHO" A question, designed to reveal leadership or other sorts of choices,

is given the child, who must supply names of individuals who would fit the question as an answer identification.

SOLITARY PLAY *See* PLAY BEHAVIOR.

SOMATOTYPE THEORY The idea that body build contributes directly to personality characteristics, such as the *self concept,* sociability, and aggressiveness, involving a three-part classification of "pure types":

1. ENDOMORPH Body build is rounded in conformation (pear-shaped), with comparatively wide hips, thick midsection, and a predominance of fatty tissue.
2. MESOMORPH Muscular, narrow hipped, and broad shouldered (the athletic type).
3. ECTOMORPH Leanness (a large external body surface in relation to weight), less muscularity than the mesomorph, and a general gangly appearance.

SPECIFICITY Age-related trend in perceptual development for children to become increasingly specific in perceptual discriminations, accompanied by a reduction in the amount of time required of the child to make a response once something has been perceived, as well as a decreased tendency to overgeneralize stimuli on the basis of *perceived similarity.*

SPEECH *See* LANGUAGE; PERFORMANCE (LINGUISTIC).

SPEED TESTING A *psychometric* or measurement principle of test construction in which an individual's test score is a function of how many items he can successfully complete within a defined time limit.

STABILITY Trend in the development of *self* in which an individual's view of self, including self-regard, becomes better organized and more stable, leading to a greater capacity to resist and recover from environmental disorganization and to ignore appraisals by others of oneself that are incongruent with his own view of himself.

STANDARD DEVIATION (SD) A statistical term used to indicate how variable a population or a set of results is.

STATISTICAL CONFIDENCE, or SIGNIFICANCE A statistical concept referring to the probability at which an obtained result may be assumed to have occurred for reasons other than chance (for example, the experimental treatment). Statistical significance generally refers to any result at or below the .05 (or

5%) level of confidence, indicating that such a result would occur by chance only five times in one hundred.

STATISTICAL NORMALITY Term used to connote a case or a behavioral instance considered to fall within one *standard deviation* above or below the *average* or *mean*. Also, more generally used to denote average, or typical of, the general population.

STATISTICS A group of techniques used to demonstrate or ascertain lawfulness in research and provide an estimate of the confidence that can be placed in empirical findings to see whether they occurred for reasons other than chance.

STIMULUS CONTROL *Behaviorist* concept of behavioral regulation by means of *cues* (or discriminative stimuli) that are present prior to and during the delivery of reinforcement, later coming to signal the potential onset of some reinforcing event (for example, red traffic light signals "stop" to approaching vehicles because traffic is moving in an opposite direction).

STIMULUS VARIABLES *Behaviorist* designation for those events in the social or physical environment of the organism that are contemporaneous with the behavior being observed or that have occurred in the past.

STRANGER ANXIETY Emotional response taking the form of crying and withdrawal from any unfamiliar person, reaching a peak somewhere between the ages of 7 and 9 months and disappearing by the age of 15 months. The response seems to be closer to fear than to *anxiety*.

STRUCTURE OF INTELLECT Guilford's theory of *intelligence*, devised from the technique of factor analysis and composed of 120 factorial cells or combinations of cognitive products, contents, and operations.

SUPEREGO According to Freudian *psychodynamic* theory, one of the three basic components of personality, functioning as the moral "watchdog" mechanism (conscience) to inhibit the primitive impulses of the *id* as well as the monitor of *ego* processes and incorporating parental and social standards of *morality*.

SUPERORDINATE CONCEPTUAL CLASSIFICATION *See* CLASSIFICATION.

SUPERSTITIOUS BEHAVIOR Behavior, irrelevant for reward and thus inefficient, that is maintained for long periods simply because it has

occurred, by chance, in the presence of *reinforcement* (for example, body English used by bowlers and golfers).

SYNTAX Aspect of *language* defined by rules for internal structure and form of sentence or phrase construction, applied spontaneously by the child prior to the application of word form rules *(morphology)* in *expressive (language) speech.*

TABULA RASA VIEW OF MAN View of man's essential nature as neutral (neither good nor evil). *Morality* must be trained by structured or *arranged* (learning) *experiences* so that the end *product* of development is a person who functions usefully in society. This attitude is typical of *behaviorist psychology.*

TALKING RATE *See* WORD FLUENCY.

TELEGRAPHIC SPEECH Intermediate phase in grammatical development of the child, at around age 1½ years, marked by the use of two- and three-word sentences, solely made up of *contentives* (nouns, verbs, and adjectives) for communicating needs and observations.

TRANSSEXUAL An individual who is physiologically of one gender, but who considers himself, or herself, to be psychologically of the opposite gender ("a man trapped in the body of a woman," or vice versa) and whose *sexual orientation (sex object choice)* is toward individuals of the opposite psychological gender (for example, a psychologically female transsexual is sexually attracted to males, even though the transsexual is physically a male).

TRANSITIVITY Piagetian notion of the child's ability to utilize the operation of *seriation* (organize objects in some ordered series) with abstract derivations to solve problems of symbolic logic.

TRANSVESTITE An individual of one gender who dresses in the manner of the opposite gender for the purpose of achieving erotic stimulation, but whose *sexual orientation (sex object choice)* may be *homosexual* or *heterosexual.*

TRUST *Prosocial behavior,* defined as a generalized *expectancy* held by an individual or a group that the word, promise, or verbal or written statement of another individual or group can be relied upon (interpersonal trust), and thought to be learned at the time of infancy as a function of positive interactions between the infant and caretakers.

TRUST VERSUS MISTRUST *See* EIGHT STAGES OF MAN (Erikson).

UNARRANGED EXPERIENCE *See* FLUID INTELLIGENCE.

UNDERACHIEVEMENT Concept based on a discrepancy model, defined as the difference between predicted achievement (based on a measure of scholastic aptitude) and actual classroom achievement (as measured by achievement tests or teacher's grades), and applied to a pupil who performs significantly less well in school than would be predicted from his performance on a measure of learning ability or *intelligence*.

UNOCCUPIED BEHAVIOR *See* PLAY BEHAVIOR.

VARIANCE The square of the *standard deviation*, often used in primary sources to indicate the amount and direction of change in a set of results.

VARIANCE ACCOUNTED FOR (r^2) A statistical method of calculating the predictive value of a *correlation*, obtained by multiplying the *correlation coefficient* between two variables by itself, in order to ascertain the extent of the relationship in question.

VERBAL INTELLIGENCE FACTOR A score on the Wechsler intelligence tests, measured by items requiring word definitions and the ability to give logical answers to reasoning questions.

VOCABULARY DEVELOPMENT *See* SEMANTIC DEVELOPMENT.

WARM-UP SET *See* PERFORMANCE SET.

WHORFIAN HYPOTHESIS *See* LINGUISTIC-RELATIVITY HYPOTHESIS.

WORLD FLUENCY (TALKING RATE) Component of *language* behavior dealing with the rate or frequency with which a child expresses his thoughts and feelings, asks questions, and initiates conversations with others, all of which are subject to the influence of *response-dependent reinforcement* techniques.